Monetary Policy Rules

T0364142

A National Bureau
of Economic Research
Conference Report

Studies in Business Cycles
Volume 31

National Bureau of Economic Research
Conference on Research in Business Cycles

The University of Chicago Press, Chicago 60637
The University of Chicago Press, Ltd., London
© 1999 by the National Bureau of Economic Research
All rights reserved. Published 1999
Paperback edition 2001
10 09 08 07 06 05 04 03 02 01   2 3 4 5 6
ISBN: 0-226-79124-6 (cloth)
ISBN: 0-226-79125-4 (paperback)

Library of Congress Cataloging-in-Publication Data

Monetary policy rules / edited by John B. Taylor.   P bk. ed.
        p.   cm.—(Studies in Business cycles; v. 31)
     Papers based on the National Bureau of Economic Research
     Conference on Research in Business Cycles, held at Standford
     University, 1998.
     Includes bibliographical references and indexes.
     ISBN 0-226-79125-4
     1. Monetary policy—Econometric models—Congresses.
     2. Monetary policy—United States—Econometric models—
     Congresses. I. Taylor, John B. II. National Bureau of Economic
     Research Conference on Research in Business Cycles (1998 : Stanford
     University III. Studies in business cycles ; no. 31.
     HG230.5.M66   2001
     332.4'6—dc21   00-069072
                                                                          CIP

⊚The paper used in this publication meets the minimum requirements of
the American National Standard for Information Sciences—Permanence
of Paper for Printed Library Materials, ANSI Z39.48-1992.

Since this volume is a record of conference proceedings, it has been exempted from the rules governing critical review of manuscripts by the Board of Directors of the National Bureau (resolution adopted 8 June 1948, as revised 21 November 1949 and 20 April 1968).

Contents

Acknowledgments

In addition to all the people who did the economic research, wrote the papers for the volume, commented on papers, participated in the discussion at the conference where the papers were presented, and worked behind the scenes at the National Bureau of Economic Research, I would like to express particular thanks to Martin Feldstein for suggesting that I organize a conference on monetary policy rules and for providing the encouragement and financial support to make sure it happened, to Monika Piazzesi for preparing a very useful summary of the fascinating discussion that took place at the conference, to Kirsten Foss Davis and Rob Shannon for the logistical support that made the conference enjoyable and productive, to Jean Koentop for managing the manuscript here at Stanford as the papers and the discussion summaries were reviewed, to Christina Romer for providing a helpful and timely review of the entire manuscript, and to the students in Economics 234 at Stanford University in the spring quarter of 1998, where many of the papers in the volume were analyzed and discussed in detail.

John B. Taylor

Introduction

John B. Taylor

This book has two broad goals. The first goal is to present econometric evidence on which type of monetary policy rule is likely to be both efficient and robust when used as a guideline for the conduct of monetary policy in the United States. The second goal is to settle several current monetary policy issues—such as the effects of uncertainty about potential GDP growth or the role of the exchange rate in the setting of interest rates—that are most naturally addressed within a framework of monetary policy rules.

To achieve these two goals, a number of economists who are actively engaged in research on monetary policy put their econometric policy evaluation methods to use in order to investigate various monetary policy rules. The economists then came together at a conference in the Florida Keys to discuss their results with policymakers and other economists. This volume—including nine papers, comments on the papers, and discussions from the conference—is the outcome of that effort. Many researchers at universities, central banks, and private financial institutions around the world are now using modern econometric policy evaluation methods to analyze monetary policy rules. We are fortunate that many of them—over 30 individuals are represented in the volume—were able to participate in the project.

A Variety of Models and a Uniform Methodology

The research reported in this volume represents a wide variety of models. The models differ in size: from 3 equations to 98 equations. They differ in degree of openness; some are closed economy models, some are small open econ-

John B. Taylor is the Mary and Robert Raymond Professor of Economics at Stanford University and a research associate of the National Bureau of Economic Research.

The author thanks Arturo Estrella, Robert King, Andrew Levin, Glenn Rudebusch, and Alex Wolman for helpful comments.

omy models, and some are large open economy models. The models also differ in degree of forward looking assumed, in the method of establishing a good microeconomic foundation for the equations, and in the goodness of fit to the data. Some models are estimated with formal econometric methods and fit the historical data tightly. Others are calibrated using rules of thumb or information from other studies, and they give rough approximations to historical data.

To get a feel for the differences between the models, consider some key features of the nine papers. The models developed by Bennett McCallum and Edward Nelson, by Julio Rotemberg and Michael Woodford, and by Robert King and Alex Wolman have a microfoundation built around a *representative agent framework* in which a household maximizes utility over time. The representative agent approach is attractive because it automatically builds in people's responses to policy and because it allows policy to be evaluated using the utility function of the representative agent. These models tend to be smaller than many of the other models in the volume, and they give rough approximations of the quarterly time series in the United States.

Like the models using a representative agent framework, the model used by Nicoletta Batini and Andrew Haldane and the four models used by Andrew Levin, Volker Wieland, and John Williams assume that agents have *rational expectations*. However, the microeconomic foundations for these models are separate decision rules for a household's consumption or for a firm's investment and production, rather than explicit dynamic optimization of a representative agent. These decision rules are motivated by rational behavior and frequently have the same variables as the equations in the explicitly derived models. These rational expectations models are generally more detailed, and they fit the data better than the representative agent models.

The models used by Laurence Ball, by Glenn Rudebusch and Lars Svensson, and by Arturo Estrella and Frederic Mishkin are *non–rational expectations models*. In order to achieve better empirical accuracy (Rudebusch and Svensson) or to focus on other issues such as exchange rates (Ball) or measurement error (Estrella and Mishkin), these models do not build in agents' responses to future policy decisions as the rational expectations models do—whether representative agent models or not. These non–rational expectations models make the simplifying assumption that the parameters will not change when policy changes.

In contrast to these model-based policy evaluation models, my own paper in the volume uses a historical methodology to evaluate policy rules. This approach is similar to that used by Milton Friedman and Anna Schwartz in their monetary history of the United States or to that of Christina Romer and David Romer in their analysis of Federal Open Market Committee decision making. Rather than testing policy rules in a structural model, this paper looks at different historical periods to see if different policy rules result in different macroeconomic outcomes. Moreover, the paper uses a general monetary theory rather than a tightly specified model to interpret the historical data.

Despite these differences, the papers in the volume share an important common methodology that defines the state of the art in monetary policy evaluation research. First, each of the models is a dynamic, stochastic, general equilibrium model. The relevance of expectations of the future and events of the past to current decisions gives the models a dynamic feature. Shocks to preferences, to technology, or simply to decision rules make the models stochastic. The term "general equilibrium" applies because the models pertain to the whole economy, not to an individual sector of the economy.

Second, each of the models incorporates some form of temporary nominal rigidity, usually a variant of staggered wage or price setting, which results in a short-run trade-off between inflation and output or unemployment. With stochastic shocks, the short-run inflation-output relationship can be characterized as a trade-off between the variance of inflation and the variance of output, but none of the models has a long-run trade-off between the level of inflation and unemployment. Several of the papers in the volume break new ground in modeling price rigidities. For example, the paper by King and Wolman derives a firm's pricing rule by analyzing how the firm would maximize its present discounted value in a setting where there are monopolistic competition and infrequent price adjustment opportunities. It is interesting to note that the optimal decision rules resemble the staggered price-setting equations studied by Levin, Wieland, and Williams. King and Wolman show that staggered price setting increases the costs of inflation, an issue that has not been raised in earlier calculations of the welfare costs of inflation. Because of their explicit derivation one can calculate the welfare costs of steady inflation with their model.

Third, for each model the variances can be computed directly or through stochastic simulation, and the measure of economic performance depends on the variance of inflation around the target inflation rate, the variance of real output around a measure of potential or full-employment output, and, in some cases, the variance of unanticipated inflation or the variance of the interest rate. It is possible to feed these variances into an objective function that is a weighted average of the variances, and in some of the papers (Rotemberg-Woodford and King-Wolman), the objective function is the same as the utility function of the representative household.

These common features can be illustrated by noting that all the models can be written in the following general form:

$$(1) \qquad y_t = A(L,g)y_t + B(L,g)i_t + u_t.$$

This equation is the reduced-form solution to the model. The vector y_t contains the endogenous variables. The scalar i_t is the short-term nominal interest rate. The vector u_t is a serially uncorrelated random variable with covariance matrix Σ. The matrices $A(L,g)$ and $B(L,g)$ are polynomials in the lag operator L. These matrix polynomials depend on the parameter vector g, which consists of all the parameters in the policy rule. The policy rule itself can be written as

$$(2) \qquad\qquad i_t = G(L)y_t,$$

where $G(L)$ is a vector polynomial in the lag operator L. Making the parameter vector g explicit in this notation emphasizes that reduced-form parameters in A and B depend on the parameters of the policy rule, an important common feature of these models. For the Ball model, the Rudebusch-Svensson model, and the Estrella-Mishkin model, none of which are rational expectations models, the above equation for y_t is the model itself. For the Rotemberg-Woodford, McCallum-Nelson, and King-Wolman models, there are forward-looking expectations variables that enter through the Euler equations of the representative agent's optimizing problem; these have been solved out using a rational expectations solution method to get the reduced-form equation for y_t. For the Batini-Haldane model and the four models considered by Levin, Wieland, and Williams (Federal Reserve, Fuhrer-Moore, MSR, and linearized Taylor multi-country), there are also forward-looking variables that have been solved out to get the reduced-form equation.

Substitution of the policy rule for i_t into the reduced-form equation for y_t above results in a vector autoregression in y_t. The steady state stochastic distribution of y_t is a function of the parameter vector g of the policy rule. Hence, for any choice of parameters in g one can evaluate an objective function that depends on the steady state distribution of y_t. For example, if the loss function is a weighted average of the variance of inflation and the variance of real output, then the two diagonal elements of the covariance matrix corresponding to inflation and real output are used. Using this approach, the papers in the volume present simulation evidence that helps determine the optimal policy rule.

I believe that there is much to be learned from these simulations, not only from the tables and charts presented in the nine papers, but also from the comments on the papers (many of which also contain new results) and the discussions about the papers. Here I can only summarize some key results. Rather than reviewing each paper and comment separately I will try to organize the summary around the following key issues: (1) robustness of policy rules, (2) usefulness of simple policy rules compared with complex rules, (3) role of the exchange rate, (4) role of inflation forecasts, (5) importance of information lags, (6) uncertainty about potential GDP or the natural rate of unemployment, and (7) implications of the historical evidence.

Robustness of Policy Rules

A number of the papers in this volume propose specific monetary policy rules. Some of these rules are modifications of policy rules that have been proposed in earlier research. Others would involve more substantial changes. Regardless of the specific form, each rule is proposed because, according to the model used in the research, the rule results in good macroeconomic performance. But how robust are the proposed rules? How would the rule proposed by one researcher stand up to scrutiny by other researchers using different models and methods? To answer these questions we asked researchers who participated in the conference to investigate the other researchers' proposals for policy rules using their own models. We did not specify what model (whether large or small, rational or nonrational) should be used. That decision was left up to the researchers. In the end, nine models were used in this robustness exercise. The models, all described in the conference papers published in this volume, are

1. Ball model
2. Batini-Haldane model
3. McCallum-Nelson model
4. Rudebusch-Svensson model
5. Rotemberg-Woodford model
6. Fuhrer-Moore model
7. MSR (small Federal Reserve model)
8. FRB/US (large Federal Reserve model)
9. TMCM (Taylor multicountry model)

The last four of these models (6 through 9) are used in the paper by Levin, Wieland, and Williams, which is a robustness study itself as the title indicates.

Of course, these nine models do not include all possible models that could be used for a robustness study. For example, as part of their comment on the Levin, Wieland, and Williams paper, Lawrence Christiano and Christopher Gust analyze several monetary policy rules using a type of model much different from those used in the other papers. The short-run monetary nonneutralities in the Christiano-Gust model are based on limited participation in financial markets rather than on temporary price and wage rigidities. Christiano and Gust report deterministic simulations and a stability analysis that tend to favor money supply rules over interest rate rules. Note also that the King and Wolman paper was not included in the robustness analysis because the authors believe that their type of model is in an early stage of development, and they are hence not ready to make an empirical identification of business cycle determinants in the way that the robustness analysis requires.

Five different policy rules were selected for the robustness exercise. These rules are of the form

(3) $$i_t = g_\pi \pi_t + g_y y_t + \rho i_{t-1},$$

where i is the nominal interest rate, π is the inflation rate, and y is real GDP measured as a deviation from potential GDP. (The intercept term is ignored here.) The coefficients defining the five policy rules are shown in table 1.

Rules I and II have the interest rate reacting to the lagged interest rate with a response coefficient of one. Rule I has a high weight on inflation compared

Table 1   **Five Conference Rules**

Rule	g_π	g_y	ρ
I	3.0	0.8	1.0
II	1.2	1.0	1.0
III	1.5	0.5	0.0
IV	1.5	1.0	0.0
V	1.2	0.06	1.3

to the weight on output, and rule II has a smaller weight on inflation compared to output. These two rules are referred to as interest-rate-smoothing rules and are the type of rule favored in the simulations in the Levin, Wieland, and Williams paper, though not necessarily with these coefficient values on inflation and output. As I show below these rules sometimes result in more interest rate volatility than rules that do not involve a reaction to the lagged interest rate. Rule III is the simple rule that I proposed in 1992 after considering the policy evaluation results from a number of multicountry models. Rule IV is much like rule III except there is a coefficient of 1.0 rather than 0.5 on real output. The simulation results of several researchers, including Laurence Ball and John Williams, indicate that the interest rate should respond about twice as aggressively to output than the 0.5 response coefficient in the simple rule that I proposed. Rule V is the rule favored in the paper by Rotemberg and Woodford in this volume. This rule is distinctive in that it places a very small weight on real output and a very high weight on the lagged interest rate.

Of course, the policy rules in table 1 do not exhaust all possible policy rules. Table 1 omits rules for the money supply, such as constant growth rate rules. Moreover, two policy rules for the interest rate proposed in this volume—the rule that reacts to exchange rates examined by Ball and the inflation-forecast rules examined by Batini and Haldane and by Rudebusch and Svensson—could also be subjected to robustness analysis. They were not part of this robustness exercise because many of the models do not have exchange rates and because the inflation-forecast rules are themselves model specific, making robustness tests more difficult, as explained in the comment by James Stock in this volume. Although it is quite possible that another policy rule would do better than any of the five policy rules listed in table 1, these rules represent the degree of disagreement that currently exists about the most appropriate form for policy rules.

Assessing the robustness across models is difficult because different models have different absolute measures of performance. One model might show that all the rules work much better—have smaller fluctuations in inflation or real output—than another model shows. In fact, this is the case for the models in this robustness study. For example, the Batini-Haldane model and the Fed's small model (MSR) imply that much better economic performance can be achieved by following an optimal rule than the Fuhrer-Moore model implies.

Moreover, these performance differences across models are fairly arbitrary, because the size of the variances of the shocks in u_t (or more generally the magnitude of each element in the covariance matrix Σ) is assumed in some models. Even in the models where the covariance matrix of the shocks is estimated using formal econometric methods, the estimates depend on arbitrary choices about specification—such as how many lagged endogenous variables or exogenous variables are placed in the model. This lack of uniformity in absolute performance measures means that one must focus on *rankings* of rules across different models. An analogy with expert evaluation in other areas is useful. Consider wine tasting (an analogy pointed out to me by Orley Ashenfelter). A panel of experts is asked to evaluate different wines. But some tasters tend to give high ratings and some tasters tend to give low ratings. Looking at the average rating across tasters will be a mistake because the tasters who give high scores will have greater influence on the average than tasters with low scores. However, by first converting the scores of each taster into a simple ranking of each taster and then adding up ranks, one can eliminate this scale effect. Similarly, one can consider pairwise rankings between two wines that differ in a key characteristic. Of course, in this book we have policy rules rather than wine and models rather than tasters, but the principle is the same.

Consider using this approach to determine the robustness of policy rules that are more responsive to output in comparison to rules that are less responsive. In other words, is the finding that one policy rule is better than another policy rule a robust finding that stands up against the different models in this book? Consider rule III and rule IV, for example. As stated earlier, several researchers have suggested that rule IV is better than rule III in the sense that the variability of inflation and real output is less with rule IV than with rule III. Is this finding robust? Table 2 shows the standard deviations of inflation rate, real output, and interest rate for rule III and rule IV. These standard deviations are obtained from the covariance matrix of the endogenous variables. Several conclusions can be drawn from table 2. First, it is clear that a finding that rule IV dominates rule III is not robust across models. For all models, rule IV gives a lower variance of output than rule III does, which is not surprising with the higher weight on output in rule IV. But for six of the nine models rule IV gives a higher variance of inflation. Raising the coefficient on real output from 0.5 to 1.0 represents a trade-off between inflation variance and output variance. The change in average standard deviations across all the models shown in table 2 indicates such a trade-off, but rule IV's increase in average inflation variability is small compared with the decrease in average output variability. (To be sure, this average change may be influenced by the lack of uniformity in absolute performance levels discussed above.) If we also consider the variability of the interest rate, then the finding that rule IV is better than rule III is even less robust: rule III is higher than rule IV in seven of the eight models that reported interest rate variances. (The average interest rate variance across models is higher with rule IV, though that result is also affected by the arbitrariness of a cardinal

Table 2   Comparative Performance of Two Conference Policy Rules

Model	Standard Deviation		
	Inflation	Output	Interest Rate
Rule III			
Ball	1.85	1.62	–
Batini-Haldane	1.38	1.05	0.55
McCallum-Nelson	1.96	1.12	3.94
Rudebusch-Svensson	3.46	2.25	4.94
Rotemberg-Woodford	2.71	1.97	4.14
Fuhrer-Moore	2.63	2.68	3.57
MSR	0.70	0.99	1.01
FRB	1.86	2.92	2.51
TMCM	2.58	2.89	4.00
Average	2.13	1.94	2.82
Rule IV			
Ball	2.01	1.36	–
Batini-Haldane	1.46	0.92	0.72
McCallum-Nelson	1.93	1.10	3.98
Rudebusch-Svensson	3.52	1.98	4.97
Rotemberg-Woodford	2.60	1.34	4.03
Fuhrer-Moore	2.84	2.32	3.83
MSR	0.73	0.87	1.19
FRB/US	2.02	2.21	3.16
TMCM	2.36	2.55	4.35
Average	2.16	1.63	3.03

scale.) One could formalize these ranking calculations by putting weights on the three standard deviations and then ranking the rules in terms of the values of the objective function in each model. Rule III would rank above rule IV for relatively high weights on inflation and interest rate variability, while rule IV would rank better for high weights on output variability.

Now consider the relative robustness of the three rules that respond to the lagged interest rate (rules I, II, and V) as shown in table 3. Each of these three rules has exactly the same functional form as the others. Hence, this robustness analysis considers the appropriate size of the response coefficients for rules having this functional form. The sum of the ranks of the three rules shows that rule I is most robust if inflation fluctuations are the sole measure of performance; it ranks first in terms of inflation variability for all but one model for which there is a clear ordering. For output, rule II has the lowest (best) sum of the ranks, which reflects its relatively high response to output. However, regardless of the objective function weights, rule V has the highest (worst) sum of the ranks for these three policy rules, ranking first for only one model (the Rotemberg-Woodford model) in the case of output. Comparing these three rules with the rules that do not respond to the lagged interest rate (rules III and

Table 3   **Three Conference Rules That React to Lagged Interest Rates**

| | Standard Deviation | | |
Model	Inflation	Output	Interest Rate
	Rule I		
Ball	2.27	23.06	–
Batini-Haldane	0.94	1.84	1.79
McCallum-Nelson	1.09	1.03	5.14
Rudebusch-Svensson	∞	∞	∞
Rotemberg-Woodford	0.81	2.69	2.50
Fuhrer-Moore	1.60	5.15	15.39
MSR	0.29	1.07	1.40
FRB/US	1.37	2.77	7.11
TMCM	1.68	2.70	6.72
	Rule II		
Ball	2.56	2.10	–
Batini-Haldane	1.56	0.86	0.99
McCallum-Nelson	1.19	1.08	4.41
Rudebusch-Svensson	∞	∞	∞
Rotemberg-Woodford	1.35	1.65	2.53
Fuhrer-Moore	2.17	2.85	8.61
MSR	0.44	0.64	1.35
FRB/US	1.56	1.62	4.84
TMCM	1.79	1.95	5.03
	Rule V		
Ball	∞	∞	∞
Batini-Haldane	∞	∞	∞
McCallum-Nelson	1.31	1.12	2.10
Rudebusch-Svensson	∞	∞	∞
Rotemberg-Woodford	0.62	3.67	1.37
Fuhrer-Moore	7.13	21.2	27.2
MSR	0.41	1.95	1.31
FRB	1.55	6.32	4.67
TMCM	2.06	4.31	4.24

IV, in table 2) shows that the lagged interest rate rules do not dominate rules without a lagged interest rate. Note that the variance of the interest rate is highest for the rules that react to the lagged interest rate according to many of the models. Table 3 also indicates a key reason why rules that react to lagged interest rates work well in some models and poorly in others in comparison with the rules without lagged interest rates. For a number of models the rules with lagged interest rates are unstable or have extraordinarily large variances. Observe that the models that give very poor performance for the lagged interest rate rules are the non–rational expectations models. These rules rely on people's forward-looking behavior: if a small increase in the interest rate does not bring inflation down, then people expect the central bank to raise interest rates by a larger amount in the future. But in a model without forward looking, it is obviously impossible to capture this forward-looking behavior. Because rule V has a lagged interest rate coefficient greater than one, it greatly exploits these expectations effects and is less robust than the other rules when evaluated with non–rational expectations models. These results illustrate the importance of forward-looking behavior. In his comment on the McCallum and Nelson paper, Mark Gertler reports on some preliminary estimation results that may help determine whether models are too forward looking or not forward looking enough.

Many more robustness findings can be found in the individual papers. Although this robustness analysis is very informative, I think it just touches the surface of what can now be done. It would be useful to do this type of robustness analysis for many more policy rules, including rules with the exchange rate, the forecast of inflation, or even more complex rules. There are also important statistical issues, such as measures of significant differences across models arising from the use of rank orders in robustness analysis. In fact, the subject of robustness arose in many of the comments and the discussions at the conference.

For example, in his comment on Ball's paper, Thomas Sargent calculates an alternative policy rule that is robust to changes in the serial correlation structure of the model. In effect, Sargent looks for rules that are robust if the u_t in the notation of equation (1) were serially correlated rather than uncorrelated. Sargent finds that in his robust version of Ball's policy rule, the interest rate responds even more aggressively than the relatively aggressive rule IV above.

Stock's comment on the paper by Rudebusch and Svensson also calculates a robust policy rule. In contrast to Sargent's focus on robustness to different serial correlation assumptions, Stock's policy rule is meant to be robust to different values of the parameters in the IS equation and the price adjustment equation in the Rudebusch-Svensson model. Stock's robust rule is a minimax policy with respect to this parameter uncertainty. Like Sargent, Stock finds that the optimal policy should be more aggressive in responding to inflation and output than the simple rules III and IV. Sargent's and Stock's findings that robust policy rules are more aggressive generated much discussion at the conference.

The Usefulness of Simple Rules Compared with Complex Rules

All five conference rules have a simple functional form, so the results in tables 2 and 3 are not helpful in determining how useful simple rules are compared to complex rules. But several of the papers in the volume address this question. Rudebusch and Svensson find that simple rules perform nearly as well as the optimal rule in their model. Levin, Wieland, and Williams show that simple rules are more robust across models than more complex optimal rules. Their paper reports on a robustness analysis of simple rules versus optimal rules in four models. They find that optimal rules from one model perform much worse than the simple rules when simulated in other models. Evidently, the optimal rule exploits properties of a model that are specific to that model, and when the optimal rule is then simulated in another model those properties are likely to be different and the optimal rule works poorly.

Role of the Exchange Rate

What is the appropriate role for the exchange rate in a monetary policy rule? This question is obviously very important for small open economies that operate under a flexible exchange rate system, but it may be an important issue for larger areas such as the European Central Bank.

The paper by Laurence Ball uses a small open economy model to assess the role of the exchange rate in a monetary policy rule. Ball shows that adding the exchange rate to simple policy rules, such as rule III and rule IV, can improve macroeconomic performance in his model. He adds the exchange rate to the simple policy rules in two places: (1) the monetary conditions index—a weighted average of the interest rate and the exchange rate—replaces the interest rate as the policy instrument, and (2) the lagged exchange rate is added to the right-hand side of the policy rule along with the inflation rate and real output. Alternatively stated, Ball adds both the current and lagged exchange rate to the right-hand side of the policy rule for i_t. Holding inflation variability constant, Ball finds that the standard deviations of output can be reduced by about 17 percentage points by giving the exchange rate a role in the simple policy rule. It would be interesting to see whether this result is robust. Because many of the models in this book are closed economy models, a robustness study will have to be the subject of future research.

Role of Inflation Forecasts

The papers by Batini and Haldane and by Rudebusch and Svensson focus on another key policy issue. They examine whether policy rules in which the interest rate adjusts to forecasts of future inflation perform better than simple rules, such as rule III and rule IV, that respond to current inflation and real output. Rules that respond to the forecast of inflation rather than actual inflation are frequently referred to as "forward-looking" rules, but since forecasts are based on current and lagged data, these rules are no more forward looking than "backward-looking" rules. Inflation-forecast rules implicitly respond to other variables in addition to output and inflation if such variables are useful predictors of future inflation; hence, these rules could in principle work better than rules such as rule III and rule IV.

The papers by Rudebusch and Svensson and by Batini and Haldane examine a number of inflation-forecasting rules with different forecast horizons and parameters. Both papers report that for the appropriate forecast horizon (usually greater than one year) and for the appropriate response coefficient, inflation-forecast rules can improve performance slightly compared with other simple rules. Batini and Haldane report that an inflation-forecast rule with a six-quarter forecast horizon reduces the standard deviation of inflation by 0.1 percentage points (from 1.4 to 1.3 percent) and the standard deviation of output by 0.2 percentage points (from 1.1 to 0.9 percent) compared with rule III.

Importance of Information Lags

Another policy question addressed by the models in this book is the effect of information lags on monetary policy rules. For example, Bennett McCallum has argued that it is not realistic to assume, as in equation (3), that policy can respond to current-quarter values, and that estimated performance would deteriorate if policymakers could only react to the most recently available data. To investigate this problem the researchers were asked to evaluate the performance of the following lagged version of the policy rule in equation (3):

$$(4) \qquad i_t = g_\pi \pi_{t-1} + g_y y_{t-1} + \rho i_{t-1}.$$

To be sure, it is not clear that equation (4) is any more realistic than equation (3) because policymakers have some current-period information available when they make interest rate decisions. In any case, there is virtually unanimous agreement among the models in the book that this one-quarter lag has little effect on economic performance. The variances of inflation and output increase by only a small amount when equation (3) is replaced by equation (4). Hence, it appears that this kind of information lag does not have major implications for policy rules.

Uncertainty about Potential GDP and the Natural Unemployment Rate

In his comments on the Batini and Haldane paper, Donald Kohn emphasizes that economic uncertainty—especially about potential GDP—poses a serious problem for monetary policy rules. Of course, assessing the effects of general model uncertainty, and the robustness of different policy rules to this uncertainty, is a major aim of this book. Two papers in the book specifically address the issue of uncertainty about potential GDP or the natural rate of unemployment. McCallum and Nelson examine the impact of making gross errors in estimating the trend in real GDP. They find that big errors lead to a big deterioration in performance. Similarly, Estrella and Mishkin show that errors in measuring the natural rate of unemployment lead to a worsening of performance. However, Estrella and Mishkin also show that uncertainty about the natural rate of unemployment or potential GDP is additive uncertainty; therefore, the form of the policy rule should not be affected by such uncertainty. Only in the case of multiplicative uncertainty would the policy rule itself be different.

Historical Evidence

Historical analysis of policy rules complements the evidence about the interest rate response to inflation and output found in the simulations. As I show in my paper the estimated response coefficients of monetary policy were much larger in the 1980s and 1990s in the United States than they were during the late 1960s and 1970s. Moreover, the response coefficients appear to have been even lower during the international gold standard period from 1880 to 1914 when inflation and real output were less stable. For example, the estimated inflation response coefficient is about 0.8 for the 1960s and 1970s compared to about 1.5 for the 1980s and 1990s, nearly twice as large. Since the inflation rate and real output were much more stable in the 1980s and 1990s than in the late 1960s and 1970s, or than in the international gold standard period, the result supports the model simulations that predict that such a change would take place. Similar results for the later two periods are reported in recent papers by Judd and Rudebusch (1998) and by Clarida, Galí, and Gertler (1998) as discussed in the comment on my paper by Richard Clarida.

Conclusion

Of the many important findings in this volume several seem particularly important to me. First, the model simulations show that simple policy rules work well; their performance is surprisingly close to that of fully optimal policies. Second, the simulations show that the gains reported in earlier research from using rules with high response coefficients are not robust to the variety of models considered in this volume; however, new approaches to robustness discussed in the volume suggest that rules that are robust to certain kinds of uncertainty may be more aggressive. Third, simulation results show that simple policy rules are more robust than complex rules across a variety of models. Fourth, introducing information lags as long as a quarter does not affect the performance of the policy rules by very much. Fifth, the historical analysis finds a significant correlation between policy rules and economic performance.

The areas of disagreement are also important. First, there is disagreement about whether central banks should react to the exchange rate when setting interest rates, or whether they should use a monetary conditions index. Second, there is disagreement about whether policy should respond to the *lagged* interest rate. Third, there is disagreement about whether the interest rate should respond solely to a measure of *expected future* inflation, rather than actual observed values. In these cases of disagreement, the papers are useful in determining what features of the models lead to the differences. This will be helpful in future research.

These remaining uncertainties and disagreements indicate that there is more work to do in this area. There is much to be learned from studying the many simulations already performed for this volume. The robustness analysis in this book, which is the focus of so many of the papers, comments, and discussions, makes a good start, but it has only scratched the surface. Improving the models, considering additional models, expanding the analysis to other countries, and examining more rules are all essential.

In the meantime, it is wise for policymakers to work with a collection or portfolio of policy rules as mentioned by Martin Feldstein in his comment on the Rotemberg and Woodford paper. Such a portfolio might include the rules of the type examined in table 1. When I proposed a specific simple policy rule in 1992 I suggested that the rule be used as a guideline along with several other policy rules. In his comment on the King and Wolman paper, Benjamin Friedman mentions the distinction between using a monetary policy rule as a guideline and using the rule mechanically. Although all the rules in this book can be written down algebraically—indeed that is one of their main advantages—at least for the near future they will probably be more useful as guidelines than as mechanical formulas for policymakers to follow exactly. By carefully studying the results in this volume, I hope that researchers and policymakers can make monetary policy rules even more useful in the future.

References

Clarida, Richard, Jordi Galí, and Mark Gertler. 1998. Monetary policy rules and macroeconomic stability: Evidence and some theory. NBER Working Paper no. 6442. Cambridge, Mass.: National Bureau of Economic Research.

Judd, John F., and Glenn D. Rudebusch. 1998. Taylor's rule and the Fed: 1970–1997. *Federal Reserve Bank of San Francisco Economic Review*, no. 3:3–16.

1   Performance of Operational Policy Rules in an Estimated Semiclassical Structural Model

Bennett T. McCallum and Edward Nelson

1.1   Introduction

In a series of studies on monetary policy rules, McCallum (1988, 1990, 1993, 1995) has utilized and promoted a research strategy that emphasizes *operationality* and *robustness*. The first of these properties intentionally limits consideration to policy rules (i) that are expressed in terms of instrument variables that could in fact be controlled on a high-frequency basis by actual central banks and (ii) that require only information that could plausibly be possessed by these central banks. Thus, for example, hypothetical rules that treat, say, M2 as an instrument or that feature instrument responses to current-quarter values of real GDP are ruled out as nonoperational. The second property focuses on a candidate rule's tendency to produce at least moderately good performance in a variety of macroeconomic models rather than "optimal" performance in a single model. The idea behind this criterion is that there exists a great deal of professional disagreement over the appropriate specification of crucial features of macroeconomic models, and indeed even over the appropriate objective function to be used by an actual central bank.

Most of the models used in McCallum's own studies have, however, been nonstructural vector autoregression or single-equation atheoretic constructs that are quite unlikely to be policy invariant. Even the so-called structural models in McCallum (1988, 1993) are essentially small illustrative systems that are not based on well-motivated theoretical foundations. Thus these studies have

Bennett T. McCallum is the H. J. Heinz Professor of Economics in the Graduate School of Industrial Administration, Carnegie Mellon University, and a research associate of the National Bureau of Economic Research. Edward Nelson was a Ph.D. student at Carnegie Mellon University at the time of the conference; he is now an analyst in the Monetary Assessment and Strategy Division, Bank of England.

The authors thank Mark Gertler and John Taylor for helpful comments on an earlier draft. The second author acknowledges financial support from the Alfred P. Sloan Foundation.

not contributed any proposed models of their own to be used in a profession-wide exploration of the robustness of candidate rules' properties.

In the present study, accordingly, we formulate, estimate, and simulate two variants of a model of the U.S. economy that is intended to have structural properties. The model is quite small—following in the line of work previously contributed to by Fuhrer and Moore (1995), Yun (1996), Ireland (1997), and Rotemberg and Woodford (1997) among others—but is based on aggregate demand and supply specifications that are designed to reflect rational optimizing behavior on the part of the economy's private actors. Our formulations pertaining to demand are rather orthodox, but in terms of aggregate supply—that is, price adjustment behavior—we consider two alternatives, one of which is not standard. In particular, we begin with the formulation of Roberts (1995), which is based on the well-known models of Calvo (1983), Rotemberg (1982), and Taylor (1980). In addition, however, we develop a modification of the Mussa-McCallum-Barro-Grossman "P-bar model," whose theoretical properties are arguably more attractive. Although we consider only two simple variants of our macroeconomic model, we suggest that its design makes it an attractive starting point for a more extensive robustness study. Our estimation is conducted by instrumental variables and utilizes quarterly U.S. data for 1955–96.

With our estimated model we carry out stochastic and counterfactual historical simulations not only with the class of policy rules promoted in McCallum's previous work but also with rules that are operational versions of the Taylor (1993) type and others with an interest rate instrument. Some of the issues that we explore in these simulations are the following:

Is it true that response coefficients in a rule of the Taylor type should be much larger than recommended by Taylor (1993)?

Is there any tendency for adoption of a nominal GDP target rule to generate instability of real GDP and inflation?

In studying questions such as these, how important is it quantitatively to recognize that actual central banks do not have complete information when setting instrument values for a given period?

How sensitive to measures of "capacity" output are rules that feature responses to output gaps?

Do interest rates exhibit extreme short-run volatility when base money rules are utilized?

Organizationally, we begin in section 1.2 with a discussion of several important background issues. Then sections 1.3 and 1.4 are devoted to specification of the macroeconomic model to be utilized, with the former pertaining to the model's aggregate demand sector and the latter to aggregate supply. Section 1.5 describes data and estimation and reports estimates of the model's basic structural parameters. Simulation exercises with various policy rules are then conducted in sections 1.6 and 1.7 for the two variants of the model, and conclusions are summarized in section 1.8.

1.2   Monetary Policy Rules: Alternatives and Issues

We begin by discussing various forms of possible monetary policy rules and some issues raised by the differences among them. In the previous research by McCallum, quarterly data have been utilized and the principal rule specification has been

$$(1) \qquad \Delta b_t = \Delta x^* - (1/16)(x_{t-1} - b_{t-1} - x_{t-17} + b_{t-17}) + \lambda(x_{t-1}^* - x_{t-1}),$$

with $\lambda \geq 0$. Here b_t and x_t denote logarithms of the (adjusted) monetary base and nominal GNP (or GDP), respectively, for period t. The variable x_t^* is the target value of x_t for quarter t, with these targets being specified so as to grow smoothly at the rate Δx^*. This rate is in turn designed to yield an average inflation rate that equals some desired value—for example, a value such as 0.005, which with quarterly data would represent roughly 2 percent per year.[1] Whereas a growing-level target path $x_t^{*1} = x_{t-1}^{*1} + \Delta x^*$ was used in McCallum's early work (1988), his more recent studies have emphasized growth rate targets of the form $x_t^{*2} = x_{t-1} + \Delta x^*$ or weighted averages such as $x_t^{*3} = 0.8x_t^{*2} + 0.2x_t^{*1}$. In equation (1), the rule's second term provides a velocity growth adjustment intended to reflect long-lasting institutional changes, while the third term features feedback adjustment in Δb_t in response to cyclical departures of x_t from the target path x_t^*, with λ chosen to balance the speed of eliminating $x_t^* - x_t$ gaps against the danger of instrument instability.

More prominent in recent years has been the rule form proposed by Taylor (1993), which we write as

$$(2) \qquad R_t = r^* + \pi_{t-1}^{av} + \mu_1(\pi_{t-1}^{av} - \pi^*) + \mu_2\tilde{y}_t.$$

Here R_t is the quarter t value of an interest rate instrument, π_{t-1}^{av} is the average inflation rate over the four quarters prior to t, π^* is the target inflation rate, and $\tilde{y}_t = y_t - \bar{y}_t$ is the difference between the (logs of) real GDP y_t and its capacity or natural rate value $\bar{y}_t$. The policy feedback parameters μ_1 and μ_2 are positive—each of them equals 0.5 in Taylor's (1993) example[2]—so that the interest rate instrument is raised in response to values of inflation and output that are high relative to their targets.

There are two major reasons for the greater prominence of Taylor's rule (2) as compared with rule (1). First, it is specified in terms of an interest rate instrument variable, which is much more realistic.[3] Second, from several studies including Taylor (1993), Stuart (1996), Clarida, Galí, and Gertler (1998), among others, it appears to be the case that actual policy in recent years, say after

---

1. Whatever the desired quarterly inflation rate, Δx^* is set equal to that value plus an estimated long-run average rate of growth of real output, a number assumed to be independent of the policy rule adopted.

2. When annualized values of inflation and the interest rate are used.

3. Virtually all central banks of industrialized countries use some short-term (nominal) interest rate as their instrument or "operating target" variable. For an extensive recent discussion, see Bank for International Settlements (1997).

1986, has been rather well described by a formula such as Taylor's with coefficients quite close to his for some major countries.

As specified by Taylor (1993), however, rule (2) is not fully operational since it assumes unrealistically that the central bank knows the value of real GDP for quarter t when setting the instrument value R_t for that quarter. In fact, there is considerable uncertainty regarding the realized value of real GDP even at the end of the quarter in actual economies.[4] In addition, it is far from obvious how $\bar{y}_t$ should be measured—even in principle—as is emphasized in McCallum (1997), and different measures can imply significantly different instrument settings.[5] The first of these objections can be easily overcome by using the value of y_t expected to prevail at the start of period t. Also, in the same spirit, some more rational representation of expected future inflation could be used in place of π_{t-1}^{av}. Overcoming the second objection, regarding the measurement of $\bar{y}_t$, could be more difficult.

Alterations in rule (1) could also be considered, such as using the expectation of x_t^* (or of x_{t+1}^*) rather than actual x_{t-1}^* as the basis for feedback adjustments. More generally, the target values in rules (1) and (2) could be exchanged, to provide rules with (i) a base instrument and π^* and $\bar{y}$ targets and (ii) an interest instrument plus a Δx_t target. In the work that follows, we shall explore several such variants of policy rules.

In this regard, some analysts might suggest that the monetary base instrument be discarded since actual central banks are not inclined even to consider the use of a b_t instrument.[6] Several academics have hypothesized that policy could be made more effective if a base instrument were utilized, however,[7] and there are clearly some disadvantages of the interest rate scheme. In particular, there is an observable tendency for an interest instrument to become something of a target variable that is thus adjusted too infrequently and too timidly (see Goodhart 1997). In any event, the question of the comparative merits of b_t and R_t instruments is one that seems to warrant scientific study—indeed, more than is provided below.

The foregoing paragraphs have been concerned with policy rules from a normative perspective. In estimating and evaluating a macroeconomic model, however, it is useful to consider what policy rule or rules have in fact been utilized during the sample studied. In that regard, it might be argued that no

---

4. In the United States, e.g., the recent study of Ingenito and Trehan (1997) indicates that the "forecast" error for real GDP at the end of the quarter is about 1.4 percent, implying that annualized growth rates for the quarter would have a 95 percent confidence interval of about ±2.8 percent, thereby possibly ranging from boom to deep recession values. This result is based on revised data, so it abstracts from the problem of data revision.

5. These two objections to rule (2) should not be understood as criticisms of Taylor's (1993) paper, which was written mainly to encourage interest in monetary rules on the part of practical policymakers—and was in that regard extremely successful.

6. Goodhart (1994) has claimed that tight monetary base control is essentially infeasible.

7. Among these academics are Brunner and Meltzer (1983), Friedman (1982), McCallum (1988), and Poole (1982).

rule has been in place, that the Federal Reserve has instead behaved in a discretionary manner. But we believe that there has clearly been a major component of Fed behavior that is *systematic,* as opposed to random, and this component can be expressed in terms of a feedback formula.[8] Of course, there can be little doubt but that there have been changes during our 1955–96 sample in the systematic component's specification, with prominent dates for possible changes including October 1979, late summer 1982, August 1987, and a few others.[9] Thus we have experimented with both slope and constant-term dummy variables. After considerable empirical investigation we have ended with an estimated rule of the form

(3) $R_t = \mu_0 + \mu_1 R_{t-1} + \mu_2 E_{t-1}\Delta x_t + \mu_3 E_{t-1}\tilde{y}_t + \mu_4 d_{1t} + \mu_5 d_{2t} E_{t-1}\Delta x_t + e_{Rt},$

where $\tilde{y}_t$ is the output gap (the log deviation of output from its flexible-price level), d_{1t} and d_{2t} are dummy variables that take on the value 1.0 in 1979:4–82:2 and 1979:4–96:4 respectively, and e_{Rt} is a serially independent disturbance. Thus our estimated rule for 1955:1–96:4 is one that combines the interest rate instrument from rule (2) with a nominal GDP target as in rule (1), as well as an extra countercyclical term. The rule is operational because the monetary authority responds to period $t - 1$ forecasts of Δx_t and $\tilde{y}_t$, not their realized values. The inclusion of dummies in equation (3) allows for shifts in the policy rule occurring in late 1979, presumably due to the change in operating procedures and anti-inflationary emphasis that was announced on 6 October. Of these, the dummy d_{1t} captures a possible intercept shift occurring during the period of nonborrowed reserves targeting, and the interactive dummy $d_{2t} E_{t-1}\Delta x_t$ reflects a permanent shift in the Federal Reserve's objectives after 1979. The empirical results of our investigation are reported below in section 1.5.[10]

Returning to the normative topic of effective rule design, several prominent issues concerning target variables will be studied in sections 1.6 and 1.7. One of these involves the claim, expressed by Ball (1997) and Svensson (1997), that targeting of nominal GDP growth rates (or growing levels) will tend to induce undesirable behavior of inflation and output gap variables. It is not difficult to show that Ball's drastic result of dynamic instability of π_t and $\tilde{y}_t$ holds only under some highly special model specifications, but it is possible that much greater volatility would obtain than with alternative target variables, so a quantitative examination of the issue is needed.

8. On this topic, see Taylor (1993), McCallum (1997), and Clarida et al. (1998).
9. The study by Clarida et al. (1998) considers one possible break, in October 1979, and finds significant differences in estimated policy rule coefficients before and after that date.
10. As the experiments in this paper are concerned with counterfactual policy rules, we do not use rule (3) in our simulations in sections 1.6 and 1.7. Our reason for nevertheless estimating and reporting eq. (3) is to demonstrate that rulelike behavior is a reasonable characterization of postwar data and to indicate the importance of the regime dummies d_{1t} and d_{2t}, which we include in our instrument set when estimating our structural model in section 1.5.

1.3   Aggregate Demand Specification

This section describes the aggregate demand side of our model; what follows is essentially a condensed presentation of the derivations in McCallum and Nelson (forthcoming). We assume that there is a large number of infinitely lived households, each of which maximizes

(4)
$$E_t \sum_{j=0}^{\infty} \beta^j U(C_{t+j}, M_{t+j}/P_{t+j}^A),$$

where C_t denotes the household's consumption in period t and M_t/P_t^A denotes its end-of-period real money holdings, M_t being the nominal level of these money balances and P_t^A the general price level. Real money balances generate utility by facilitating household transactions in period t. The instantaneous utility function $U(C_t, M_t/P_t^A)$ is of the additively separable form:

(5)
$$U(C_t, M_t/P_t^A) = \sigma(\sigma - 1)^{-1} C_t^{(\sigma-1)/\sigma} \exp \omega_t$$
$$+ (1 - \gamma)^{-1} (M_t/P_t^A)^{1-\gamma} \exp \chi_t,$$

with $\sigma > 0$ and $\gamma > 0$. Here ω_t and χ_t are both preference shocks, whose properties we specify below.

Each household also acts as a producer of a good, over which it has market power. To this end, it hires N_t^d in labor from the labor market, paying real wage W_t/P_t^A for each unit of labor. With this labor and its own capital stock K_t (which depreciates at rate δ) it produces its output Y_t via the technology $Y_t = A_t K_t^\alpha (N_t^d)^{1-\alpha}$, where A_t is an exogenous shock that affects all households' production. The household sells its output at price P_t. Each household consumes many goods, consisting of some of the output produced by other households; the C_t that appears in the household's utility function is an index of this consumption, and P_t^A indexes the average price of households' output.

As is standard in the literature, we assume that the demand function for good i is of the Dixit-Stiglitz form, and that also the producer is obliged to set production equal to this demand:

(6)
$$A_t K_t^\alpha (N_t^\alpha)^{1-\alpha} = (P_t/P_t^A)^{-\theta} Y_t^A,$$

with $\theta > 1$ and Y_t^A denoting aggregate output.

The household is also endowed with one unit of labor each period, and supplies N_t^s of this to the labor market. The household's budget constraint each period is then

(7)
$$(P_t/P_t^A)^{1-\theta} Y_t^A - C_t - K_{t+1} + (1 - \delta)K_t + (W_t/P_t^A)N_t^s$$
$$- (W_t/P_t^A)N_t^d + TR_t - M_t/P_t^A + M_{t-1}/P_t^A$$
$$- B_{t+1}(1 + r_t)^{-1} + B_t = 0.$$

In equation (7), B_{t+1} is the quantity of government bonds bought by the household in period t; each of these is purchased for $(1 + r_t)^{-1}$ units of output and redeemed for one unit of output in period $t + 1$. TR_t denotes lump-sum government transfers paid to the household in period t. Letting ξ_t denote the Lagrange multiplier on constraint (6) and λ_t the multiplier on (7), the household's first-order conditions with respect to C_t, M_t/P_t^A, K_{t+1}, and B_{t+1} are

$$(8) \qquad C_t^{-1/\sigma} \exp \omega_t = \lambda_t,$$

$$(9) \qquad (M_t/P_t^A)^{-\gamma} \exp \chi_t = \lambda_t - \beta E_t \lambda_{t+1}(P_t^A/P_{t+1}^A),$$

$$(10) \qquad \lambda_t = \beta(1 - \delta)E_t\lambda_{t+1} + \alpha\beta E_t\xi_{t+1}A_{t+1}K_{t+1}^{\alpha-1}(N_{t+1}^d)^{1-\alpha},$$

$$(11) \qquad \lambda_t = \beta E_t\lambda_{t+1}(1 + r_t).$$

Because leisure does not enter its utility function, the household's optimal labor supply is $N_t^S = 1$ each period, although, since we assume below that the labor market does not clear, this desired labor supply will not be the realized value of labor utilized.

As an employer of labor, the household's first-order condition with respect to N_t^d is

$$(12) \qquad \lambda_t(W_t/P_t^A) = (1 - \alpha)\xi_t A_t K_t^\alpha (N_t^d)^{-\alpha}.$$

Equation (12) indicates that, as in Ireland (1997), the markup of price over marginal cost is equal to λ_t/ξ_t. The household has one more first-order condition, pertaining to its optimal choice for P_t. We defer the analysis of this decision until section 1.4.

We now construct a log-linear model of aggregate demand from the above conditions. While we use equation (10) in our calculations of the implied steady state level of investment, $\bar{I}$, we do not use an approximation of equation (10) to describe quarter-to-quarter fluctuations in capital or investment. Instead, we treat capital as exogenous and, for tractability, let the movements of log investment around its steady state value be a random walk. Thus we have

$$(13) \qquad i_t = g_k + i_{t-1} + e_{it},$$

where $g_k \geq 0$ is the average growth rate of capital, $E_{t-1}e_{it} = 0$, and $E(e_{it}^2) = \sigma_{ei}^2$. In equation (13) and below, lowercase letters denote logarithms of variables.

It would be standard practice to complete our specification of technology with the usual log-linear law for capital accumulation,

$$(13a) \qquad k_{t+1} = \frac{1 - \delta}{1 + g_k}k_t + \frac{\delta + g_k}{1 + g_k}i_t,$$

along with a law of motion for the (log) technology shock a_t. But since we are treating capital movements as exogenous, and since leisure does not appear in the household's utility function, the "flexible-price" or "capacity" level of log output, $\bar{y}_t = a_t + \alpha k_t$, is exogenous in our setup. It makes sense therefore to make assumptions directly about the $\bar{y}_t$ process, instead of its two components. By doing so we lose the connection between investment and capacity output implied by equation (13a), but this does not seem a serious omission for purposes of business cycle analysis because of the minor contribution that investment makes to the existing capital stock during a typical business cycle. We assume that $\bar{y}_t$ follows an AR(1) process:

$$(14) \qquad \bar{y}_t = \varsigma + \rho_{\bar{y}}\bar{y}_{t-1} + e_{yt},$$

where $|\rho_{\bar{y}}| \leq 1$ and $e_{yt} \sim N(0,\sigma_{ey}^2)$, $E_{t-1}e_{yt} = 0$.[11]

Define the nominal interest rate as $R_t = r_t + E_t\Delta p_{t+1}$, where $\Delta p_{t+1} \equiv \log$ (P_{t+1}^A/P_t^A). Then equations (8), (11), and (14) and the economy's resource constraint imply (after log-linearization)

$$(15) \quad y_t = E_t y_{t+1} - \sigma(C^{ss}/Y^{ss})(R_t - E_t\Delta p_{t+1} - \bar{r}) + \sigma(C^{ss}/Y^{ss})(\omega_t - E_t\omega_{t+1}),$$

where the superscript ss denotes steady state value. We assume that the preference shock ω_t is an AR(1) process with AR parameter $|\rho_v| < 1$. Then if we define $v_t \equiv \sigma(1 - \rho_v)\omega_t$, it is the case that

$$(16) \qquad v_t = \rho_v v_{t-1} + e_{vt},$$

and so equation (15) becomes

$$(17) \quad y_t = E_t y_{t+1} - \sigma(C^{ss}/Y^{ss})(R_t - E_t\Delta p_{t+1} - \bar{r}) + (C^{ss}/Y^{ss})v_t,$$

which is like the optimizing IS functions of Kerr and King (1996), Woodford (1996), and McCallum and Nelson (forthcoming).

Let $m_t - p_t$ denote the logarithm of M_t/P_t^A. Then log-linearizing equation (9), we have (up to a constant)

$$(18) \quad \begin{aligned} m_t - p_t &= (\sigma\gamma)^{-1}(Y^{ss}/C^{ss})y_t - (\sigma\gamma)^{-1}(I^{ss}/C^{ss})i_t \\ &\quad - (\gamma R^{ss})^{-1}(R_t - R^{ss}) + \gamma^{-1}(\chi_t - \omega_t), \end{aligned}$$

where $R^{ss} = r^{ss} + (\Delta p)^{ss}$. This money demand function has scale (consumption) elasticity $(\sigma\gamma)^{-1}$ and (annualized) interest semielasticity $-0.25(\gamma R^{ss})^{-1}$. We permit the shocks ω_t and χ_t to be arbitrarily correlated; hence, it is simpler to define the composite disturbance $\eta_t = \gamma^{-1}(\chi_t - \omega_t)$ and make assumptions directly about η_t. Then equation (18) may be written

$$(19) \quad \begin{aligned} m_t - p_t &= (\sigma\gamma)^{-1}(Y^{ss}/C^{ss})y_t - (\sigma\gamma)^{-1}(I^{ss}/C^{ss})i_t \\ &\quad - (\gamma R^{ss})^{-1}(R_t - R^{ss}) + \eta_t, \end{aligned}$$

---

11. In our empirical work we use a measure of $\bar{y}_t$ (described in section 1.4) that grows over time, but in stochastic simulations we adopt the standard practice of abstracting from this growth.

and we assume η_t is AR(1):

$$(20) \qquad\qquad \eta_t = \rho_\eta \eta_{t-1} + u_t,$$

where $|\rho_\eta| < 1$ and $u_t \sim N(0,\sigma_u^2)$, $E_{t-1}u_t = 0$. Since we have allowed u_t and e_{vt} to be correlated, we may write the latter as

$$(21) \qquad\qquad e_{vt} = \psi_u u_t + \varepsilon_{vt},$$

where $\varepsilon_{vt} \sim N(0,\sigma_{\varepsilon v}^2)$, $E_{t-1}\varepsilon_{vt} = 0$, and $E_t(u_t\varepsilon_{vt}) = 0$. Thus the aggregate demand block of our model consists of the behavioral equations (17) and (19), together with (13) and the laws of motion (14), (16), (20), and (21).

1.4   Price Level Adjustment

In this section we develop the particular model of individual and aggregate price adjustments that will be utilized below. For a typical producer, let $\bar{p}_t$ represent the value of p_t—its output price in log terms—that would be optimal in period t if there were no nominal frictions, and let $\bar{y}_t$ be the corresponding level of (log) output y_t, which we will for shorthand refer to as "capacity" output. The producer faces a demand curve of the form

$$(22) \qquad\qquad y_t = y_t^A - \theta(p_t - p_t^A),$$

where y_t^A and p_t^A are indexes of aggregate values of y_t and p_t, these being appropriate averages of the values relevant for the individual producers.[12] From equation (22) we note that

$$(23) \qquad\qquad y_t - \bar{y}_t = \theta(\bar{p}_t - p_t).$$

Perhaps the most widely used model of gradual price adjustment at present is the Calvo-Rotemberg model, which is justified by Rotemberg (1987) as follows. Although $\bar{p}_t$ would be charged in t by the typical firm if there were no adjustment costs, in the presence of such costs (assumed quadratic) the producer will instead choose p_t to minimize

$$(24) \qquad\qquad E_t\sum_{j=0}^{\infty} \beta^j[(p_{t+j} - \bar{p}_{t+j})^2 + c_1(p_{t+j} - p_{t+j-1})^2],$$

where $c_1 > 0$ reflects the cost of price changes in relation to the opportunity cost of setting a price different from $\bar{p}_t$. From expression (24) one can find the first-order optimality condition and rearrange to obtain the relation

$$(25) \qquad\qquad \Delta p_t = \beta E_t\Delta p_{t+1} + (1/c_1)(p_t - \bar{p}_t).$$

---

12. Thus $p_t^A = [\int_0^1 p_t(i)^{1-\theta} di]^{1/(1-\theta)}$ and $y_t^A = [\int_0^1 y_t(i)^{(\theta-1)/\theta} di]^{\theta/(\theta-1)}$ with $\theta > 1$, where $p_t(i)$ and $y_t(i)$ pertain to producer i, as in Dixit and Stiglitz (1977). In the text, the indices are suppressed for the sake of notational simplicity.

Then using equation (23), we have for the typical producer

(26) $$\Delta p_t = \beta E_t \Delta p_{t+1} + (\theta/c_1)(y_t - \bar{y}_t).$$

Assuming symmetry across firms, equation (26) can be used for aggregative analysis. Both Rotemberg (1987) and Roberts (1995) show that an indistinguishable relation is implied by Calvo's (1983) model that emphasizes staggered setting of "contract" prices to prevail until a new price-change opportunity arrives, with probabilities of these arrivals being constant and exogenous. Also, Roberts (1995) shows that the two-period version of Taylor's (1980) well-known model of staggered wage contracts gives a relation that is basically similar.

In what follows, consequently, we shall utilize a quarterly version of Roberts's formulation of the Calvo-Rotemberg model in one variant of our macroeconomic system. There are, however, two theoretical drawbacks to this model. First, the assumed quadratic cost of changing prices is rather unattractive theoretically. One reason is that one might expect the magnitude of price-change costs to be independent of the size of the change, especially if these are to be interpreted as literal resource costs of preparing new price lists, and so forth. More basically, however, it seems somewhat undesirable to emphasize costs of changing prices, which are rather nebulous, while neglecting the costs of changes in output rates, which are more concrete and arguably quite substantial.[13] Second, as is shown below, the Calvo-Rotemberg model does not satisfy the natural rate hypothesis.[14]

Accordingly, let us consider a reformulated setup in which the producer chooses p_t to minimize expression (27) rather than (24):

(27) $$E_{t-1} \sum_{j=0}^{\infty} \beta^j [(p_{t+j} - \bar{p}_{t+j})^2 + c_2(\tilde{y}_{t+j} - \tilde{y}_{t+j-1})^2].$$

Here $\tilde{y}_t = y_t - \bar{y}_t$, so we are assuming that it is costly for a producer to alter his output rate, relative to capacity, from its previous value. The reason for using $(\tilde{y}_{t+j} - \tilde{y}_{t+j-1})^2$ rather than $(y_{t+j} - y_{t+j-1})^2$ is that changes in capacity stem primarily from technological improvements or capital installations,[15] neither of which give rise to changes in the labor force needed to produce $\bar{y}_t$—but it is labor force changes that provide the primary rationale for the presumption that output changes are costly.[16] Neither $(\tilde{y}_{t+j} - \tilde{y}_{t+j-1})^2$ nor $(y_{t+j} - y_{t+j-1})^2$ is entirely appropriate, perhaps, but the former seems somewhat preferable theoretically; and it gives rise to a tidy, tractable model, as will be seen shortly. Another feature of expression (27) to be noted is that the presence of E_{t-1} before

13. On this topic see Gordon (1990, 1146).
14. Empirically, it has been suggested that the model does not imply as much persistence of inflation rates as exists in the U.S. data. On this, see Ball (1994), Fuhrer and Moore (1995), and Nelson (1998).
15. There may in actuality be installation costs for new capital goods, but if so, this can in principle be taken account of in the IS portion of the model, not the price-setting portion.
16. Models with quadratic costs of changing employment appear frequently in Sargent (1979).

the summation sign implies that p_t is chosen before the producer knows about demand conditions during t; that is, p_t is predetermined in each period.[17] Then on the basis of the prevailing p_t, output in t is taken to be demand determined. Labor-leisure trade-offs are assumed relevant for the determination of $\bar{y}_t$, but not for temporary departures of y_t from $\bar{y}_t$. This is in accordance with the "installment payment" nature of current wages, as emphasized by Hall (1980).

Next we can define $\tilde{p}_t = p_t - \bar{p}_t$ and, in light of relation (23), can rewrite expression (27) as

$$(28) \qquad E_{t-1} \sum_{j=0}^{\infty} \beta^j [\tilde{p}_{t+j}^2 + c(\tilde{p}_{t+j} - \tilde{p}_{t+j-1})^2],$$

where now $c > 0$ is the cost of output "gap" changes in relation to departures of p_t from $\bar{p}_t$. It might appear that $c\theta^2$ should appear in expression (28) where c does, but θ^2 can be absorbed into c (and indeed this is entirely consistent with a symmetric treatment of the two terms). To minimize expression (28), the relevant first-order condition is

$$(29) \qquad E_{t-1}[\tilde{p}_t + c(\tilde{p}_t - \tilde{p}_{t-1}) - \beta c(\tilde{p}_{t+1} - \tilde{p}_t)] = 0$$

or

$$(30) \qquad E_{t-1}\tilde{p}_t = \alpha\tilde{p}_{t-1} + \alpha\beta E_{t-1}\tilde{p}_{t+1},$$

where $\alpha = c/(1 + c + c\beta)$. Then since this relation in effect involves only the single variable $\tilde{p}_t$, we can see that its MSV solution will be of the simple form $E_{t-1}\tilde{p}_t = \phi\tilde{p}_{t-1}$, with $E_{t-1}\tilde{p}_{t+1} = E_{t-1}\phi\tilde{p}_t = \phi^2\tilde{p}_{t-1}$.[18] Substitution into equation (30) gives $\phi\tilde{p}_{t-1} = \alpha\tilde{p}_{t-1} + \alpha\beta\phi^2\tilde{p}_{t-1}$, so ϕ must satisfy

$$(31) \qquad \alpha\beta\phi^2 - \phi + \alpha = 0.$$

Thus the MSV solution for ϕ is

$$(32) \qquad \phi = \left(1 - \sqrt{1 - 4\alpha^2\beta}\right)/2\alpha\beta.$$

From the definition of α, we know that $4\alpha^2\beta < 1$, so ϕ in equation (32) is real. With $0 < \beta < 1$, we have $\phi > \alpha$, so the forward-looking objective increases the inertia of $\tilde{p}_t$. Also, it is the case that ϕ lies in the interval $(0, 1)$.[19]

In any event, we have developed a price adjustment rule of the form $p_t - E_{t-1}\bar{p}_t = \phi(p_{t-1} - \bar{p}_{t-1})$. Thus by simple rearrangement we can write

17. This is our assumption regarding price stickiness per se. Implicitly, it embodies the assumption that sellers' costs of changing prices are prohibitive within periods but negligible between periods.

18. MSV stands for "minimal state variable." Thus we are adopting the bubble-free solution, in the manner outlined by McCallum (1983).

19. To show that $4\alpha^2\beta < 1$, it suffices to show that $(1 + \beta)^2 > 4\beta$. But that is equivalent to $1 + 2\beta + \beta^2 > 4\beta$. Then subtracting 4β from each side, we have $1 - 2\beta + \beta^2 > 0$, which is certainly true since the left-hand side is $(1 - \beta)^2$. Next, that $\phi > 0$ is clear from inspection of eq. (32), given that $0 < 4\alpha^2\beta < 1$. To see that $\phi < 1$, note that this is the same as $1 - \sqrt{1 - 4\alpha^2\beta} < 2\alpha\beta$, which reduces to $\alpha(1 + \beta) < 1$. Since $1/\alpha = 1/c + 1 + \beta$, the last inequality holds.

(33) $\qquad p_t - p_{t-1} = (1 - \phi)(\bar{p}_{t-1} - p_{t-1}) + E_{t-1}(\bar{p}_t - \bar{p}_{t-1}),$

which can be seen to be equivalent to the price adjustment formula that was termed the "P-bar model" by McCallum (1994). This model was developed and utilized by Herschel Grossman, Robert Barro, Michael Mussa, and McCallum in the 1970s and early 1980s; for references, see McCallum (1994, 251–52).

An important feature of the model, not noted in previous work, is that equation (23) permits the MSV solution $E_{t-1}\tilde{p}_t = \phi\tilde{p}_{t-1}$ to be alternatively expressible as

(34) $\qquad E_{t-1}\tilde{y}_t = \phi\tilde{y}_{t-1}.$

Thus in analytical or numerical solutions of a macromodel that includes the P-bar price adjustment theory, equation (34) can be included as the relation that governs price adjustment behavior. From the perspective of an undetermined-coefficients solution procedure, equation (34) fails to provide conditions relating to the coefficients on current shocks in the solution expression for $\tilde{y}_t$ (or for y_t given $\bar{y}_t$). But these are compensated by the restriction that p_t is predetermined and thus the shock coefficients in its solution equation are zeros. Thus, with this approach, the variable $\bar{p}_t$ need not be included in the analysis at all!

To illustrate the solution approach, suppose only for this paragraph that monetary policy was conducted in a manner that leads nominal income, x_t in log terms, to behave as follows:

(35) $\qquad \Delta x_t = \psi \Delta x_{t-1} + \xi_t,$

where $0 < \psi < 1$ and ξ_t is white noise. Then one could consider the system consisting of equations (34) and (35) and the identity $\Delta x_t = \Delta p_t + y_t - y_{t-1}$, where we temporarily adopt the assumption that $\Delta \bar{y}_t = 0$. How does inflation Δp_t behave in this system? By construction, the MSV solution will be of the form

(36) $\qquad \Delta p_t = \phi_{11} \Delta x_{t-1} + \phi_{12} y_{t-1} + \phi_{13} \xi_t,$

(37) $\qquad y_t = \phi_{21} \Delta x_{t-1} + \phi_{22} y_{t-1} + \phi_{23} \xi_t,$

in which we know a priori that $\phi_{13} = \phi_{21} = 0$ and $\phi_{22} = \phi$. Substitution into equation (35) gives

(38) $\qquad \phi_{11} \Delta x_{t-1} + \phi y_{t-1} + \phi_{23} \xi_t - y_{t-1} = \psi \Delta x_{t-1} + \xi_t.$

Thus $\phi_{11} = \psi$, $\phi_{12} + \phi - 1 = 0$, and $\phi_{23} = 1$ are implied by undetermined-coefficients reasoning, which completes the solution.

It may also be noted that equation (34) provides the basis for an extremely simple proof that the P-bar model satisfies the strict version of the natural rate hypothesis. This version states that $E\tilde{y}_t \equiv 0$, for *any* monetary policy, even one with accelerating inflation. But the application of the unconditional expecta-

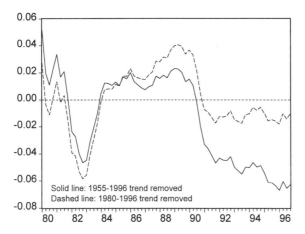

Fig. 1.1   Measures of detrended output, 1980–96

tions operator to each side of equation (34) yields $E\tilde{y}_t = \phi E\tilde{y}_t$, which with $\phi > 0$ implies that $E\tilde{y}_t \equiv 0$. With the Calvo-Rotemberg model (26), by contrast, we have $E(y_t - \bar{y}_t) = (c_1/\theta)E(\Delta p_t - \beta E_t\Delta p_{t+1})$. Using Roberts's (1995) approximation of $\beta \approx 1$, we have $E(y_t - \bar{y}_t) = (c_1/\theta)E(\Delta p_t - E_t\Delta p_{t+1})$, so any policy that yields on average an increasing or decreasing inflation rate will keep $E\tilde{y}_t \neq 0$.[20] Indeed, if $\beta < 1$ is retained, then even a constant $E\Delta p_t \neq 0$ will keep $E\tilde{y}_t \neq 0$.

In implementing our model—indeed, any model with gradual price adjustment—a very important issue is how to measure $\bar{y}_t$ and therefore $\tilde{y}_t$. Much of the policy rule literature, including Taylor (1993) and Rotemberg and Woodford (1997), simply uses deviations from a fitted linear time trend for $\tilde{y}_t$, thereby implicitly estimating $\bar{y}_t$ as the fitted trend. This seems unsatisfactory both practically and in principle. Practically, one major difficulty is that the resulting measure can be excessively sensitive to the sample period used in fitting the trend. To illustrate this sensitivity, figure 1.1 plots $\tilde{y}_t$-values for the United States over 1980–96 based on trends fitted (i) to a 1980–96 sample period and (ii) to the 1955–96 period that we use below. Clearly, they give markedly different pictures of the behavior of $\tilde{y}_t$ over the period 1990–96. And neither of them reflects the widely held belief that output has been unusually high relative to capacity in 1995 and 1996.

In principle, the fitted trend method—even if the detrending is done by a polynomial trend or the Hodrick-Prescott filter—seems inappropriate because it does not properly reflect the influence of technology shocks. Suppose that the production function is

20. It is interesting to note that the Calvo-Rotemberg-Taylor model implies that an increasing inflation rate will reduce $\tilde{y}_t$ whereas a typical NAIRU model implies that an increasing inflation rate will raise $\tilde{y}_t$—permanently. Both implications seem theoretically unattractive, although the former is perhaps less implausible (and certainly less dangerous from a policy perspective).

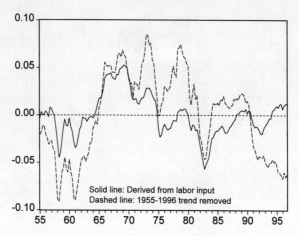

Fig. 1.2   Output gap measures

(39) $$y_t = \alpha_0 + \alpha_1 t + \alpha k_t + (1 - \alpha)n_t + a_t,$$

where k_t and n_t are logs of capital and labor input, while a_t is a technology shock. Then if $\bar{n}_t$ is the value of n_t under flexible prices, $\bar{y}_t$ equals $\alpha_0 + \alpha_1 t + \alpha k_t + (1 - \alpha)\bar{n}_t + a_t$ and so reflects the realization of a_t. But the fitted trend methods do so either not at all or inadequately.

The approach that we use below relies on the observation that equation (39) implies

(40) $$\tilde{y}_t = y_t - \bar{y}_t = (1 - \alpha)(n_t - \bar{n}_t).$$

Of course, this requires that we have some measure of $\bar{n}_t$. In general, it will depend on households' labor supply behavior as well as producers' demand, but for the present study we are adopting the simplifying assumption that labor supply is inelastic, that is, that $\bar{n}_t$ is a constant. Then variations in $\tilde{y}_t$ will be proportional to variations in n_t, the hours worked per household under sticky prices. We assume that this actual employment level is demand determined in each period.[21] The measure that we use for n_t is total man-hours employed in nonagricultural private industry divided by the civilian labor force. A plot of the implied $\tilde{y}_t$, using $\alpha = 0.3$, is shown in figure 1.2, together with the fitted trend value based on the 1955–96 sample period.

1.5   Model Estimation

We estimate our model by instrumental variables. Some of the system's equations are estimated on a single-equation basis, but the two aggregate demand relations are estimated jointly:

---

21. Thus, as stated above, we are assuming that current-period wages are irrelevant for determination of current-period employment.

$$(41) \quad y_t = b_0 + E_t y_{t+1} - \sigma(C^{ss}/Y^{ss})(R_t - E_t \Delta p_{t+1}) + (C^{ss}/Y^{ss})v_t,$$

$$
\begin{aligned}
(42) \quad m_t - p_t &= c_0 + (\sigma\gamma)^{-1}(Y^{ss}/C^{ss})y_t - (\sigma\gamma)^{-1}(I^{ss}/C^{ss})i_t \\
&\quad - (\gamma R^{ss})^{-1}R_t + \eta_t.
\end{aligned}
$$

Here equations (41) and (42) are the IS and LM equations (17) and (19), allowing for constant terms. We estimate these equations jointly to take into account the cross-equation restriction (the appearance of the parameter σ in both equations), as well as possible cross-correlation between v_t and η_t via equation (21).

One advantage of the instrumental variables procedure is that if the orthogonality conditions involving the instruments and the model errors are valid, parameter estimation is consistent under quite general assumptions about the serial correlation of the disturbances, and the precise form of the serial correlation does not have to be specified in estimation. To benefit from this advantage, we do not impose, in our estimation of equations (41) and (42), the AR(1) assumptions about the v_t and η_t processes that we make in our general equilibrium model (in eqs. [16] and [20]).

Equations (41) and (42) contain the expectational variables $E_t y_{t+1}$ and $E_t \Delta p_{t+1}$. We proceed with estimation of the system by replacing these expected values with their corresponding realized values, thereby introducing expectational errors such as $y_{t+1} - E_t y_{t+1}$ into the equations' composite disturbances. To obtain consistent estimates, we instrument for all the variables in equations (41) and (42). Because of the likely serial correlation in the error terms of the first two equations, lagged endogenous variables are not admissible instruments; only strictly exogenous variables are legitimate candidates. We therefore use as instruments a constant, a time trend, lags one and two of Δg_t^{def} (i.e., the log change in quarterly defense spending), plus the dummy variables d_{1t} and d_{2t}, which take the value unity in 1979:4–82:2 and 1979:4–96:4, respectively.

Money is measured by the St. Louis monetary base, new definition, R_t is the Treasury bill rate (measured in quarterly fractional units), and p_t is the log GDP deflator, defined as $x_t - y_t$. The income variables x_t and y_t are logs of nominal and real GDP, with values of GNP spliced on for observations prior to 1959:1. Also, i_t is gross private fixed investment. All data except interest rates are seasonally adjusted. We fix C^{ss}/Y^{ss} at 0.81, I^{ss}/Y^{ss} at 0.19, and R^{ss} at 0.014. The estimates of equations (41) and (42) are then

$$
\begin{aligned}
(43) \quad \hat{y}_t &= -0.973 + E_t y_{t+1} - \underset{(0.017)}{0.203}(C^{ss}/Y^{ss})(R_t - E_t \Delta_t p_{t+1}), \\
&\quad\;\; {\scriptstyle(0.129)} \\
&\quad \bar{R}^2 = 0.999,\ \text{SEE} = 0.0098,\ \text{DW} = 1.35
\end{aligned}
$$

$$
\begin{aligned}
(44) \quad \widehat{(m - p_t)} &= -0.007 + \underset{(0.001)}{0.753}(Y^{ss}/C^{ss})[y_t - (I^{ss}/Y^{ss})i_t] - \underset{(0.015)}{0.152}(R^{ss})^{-1}R_t, \\
&\quad \bar{R}^2 = 0.942,\ \text{SEE} = 0.0617,\ \text{DW} = 0.14.
\end{aligned}
$$

The estimates imply an intertemporal elasticity of substitution of $\sigma = 0.20$ (standard error 0.018) and an interest elasticity of money demand of $-\gamma^{-1} = -0.15$ (standard error 0.015). In turn, these estimates imply a consumption elasticity of money demand of $(\sigma\gamma)^{-1} = 0.75$. The reported standard errors need to be interpreted with caution both because of the residual autocorrelation and because of the trending behavior of the y_t and $m_t - p_t$ series.[22]

For the variant of our model that uses the P-bar price-setting specification, aggregate supply behavior is represented compactly by equation (34). As in section 1.4, we measure $\tilde{y}_t$ by $1 - \alpha$ times $n_t - \bar{n}$, where $\bar{n}$ is the mean of log hours and $\alpha = 0.3$. Equation (34) implies that the expectational error $\tilde{y}_t - \phi\tilde{y}_{t-1}$ should be white noise, but in preliminary estimation of ϕ we found substantial serial correlation in the estimated residuals. We therefore decided to correct for first-order serial correlation in our estimation of ϕ, although such serial correlation is ignored both in our theoretical model and in the stochastic simulations of that model in section 1.7 below.[23] Estimation by instrumental variables, with the instruments being those used for equations (41) and (42) plus lags two to four of $\tilde{y}_t$, produces

$$(\widehat{E_{t-1}\tilde{y}_t}) = 0.891\tilde{y}_{t-1},$$
(45)
$$(0.063)$$

$$\bar{R}^2 = 0.956, \text{ SEE} = 0.0047, \text{ DW} = 1.95,$$
$$\text{estimated AR(1) correction parameter} = 0.59.[24]$$

Our measure of (log) potential output $\bar{y}_t$ is obtained by adding our estimated $\tilde{y}_t$ measure to y_t. We found that a random walk (with drift) process ($\rho_{\bar{y}} = 1.0$ in eq. [14]) describes the $\bar{y}_t$ series well.[25] Subject to that restriction, the constant (or "drift") term in equation (14) becomes interpretable as the long-run growth rate of capacity output.[26] For the investment-output ratio to be a mean-reverting

---

22. We assume that $m_t - p_t - (\sigma\gamma)^{-1}(Y^{ss}/C^{ss})[y_t - (I^{ss}/Y^{ss})i_t]$ is a stationary process. It is common in the empirical literature instead to estimate money demand functions such as (19) using cointegration methods, with $m_t - p_t$, y_t, and R_t modeled as I(1) series. We do not do so because treating R_t as I(1) is incompatible with our theoretical model unless Δp_t is I(1). It is also inconsistent with most estimated policy rules, including our own specification (50) below, which model nominal interest rates as stationary within each policy regime.

We also experimented with a first-differenced money demand function, finding it produced a poorer fit and less plausible parameter estimates than eq. (44).

23. Our need to correct for serial correlation indicates that the first-order dynamics of the output gap implied by eq. (34) are rejected by the data. In future work we hope to generalize the P-bar specification to allow for more realistic dynamics.

24. Eq. (45) is based on the assumption that $\tilde{y}_t = \phi\tilde{y}_{t-1} + \tilde{e}_{yt}$, with $\tilde{e}_{yt}$ following $\tilde{e}_{yt} = \rho_e\tilde{e}_{yt-1} + \varepsilon_t$, with ε_t white noise. By substitution, $\tilde{y}_t = (\phi + \rho_e)\tilde{y}_{t-1} - \phi\rho_e\tilde{y}_{t-2} + \varepsilon_t$. The parameters ϕ and ρ_e appear symmetrically in this expression and thus cannot be individually identified without further information; to identify them, we assume that ϕ is the larger of the two parameters.

25. The behavior of our empirical measure of capacity output therefore supports the analytical model of Clarida, Galí, and Gertler (forthcoming), in which it is assumed that $\bar{y}_t$ follows a random walk.

26. And also as the long-run growth rate of actual output, since the output gap is assumed to average zero over our sample period.

series, the drift terms in equations (13) and (14) must be identical, and we therefore estimate those equations jointly subject to that restriction:

$$(46) \qquad \widehat{(\Delta i_t)} = 0.0073, \qquad \text{SEE} = 0.0250, \text{DW} = 0.99,$$
$$ (0.0052)$$

$$(47) \qquad \widehat{(\Delta \bar{y}_t)} = 0.0073, \qquad \text{SEE} = 0.0070, \text{DW} = 2.00,$$
$$ (0.0052)$$

implying $g_k = \varsigma = 0.0073$, $\sigma_{ei}^2 = (0.0250)^2$, and $\sigma_{ey}^2 = (0.0070)^2$. The Durbin-Watson statistic for equation (46) indicates strong serial correlation in the estimated residuals, contrary to the assumptions of our model, and suggests some deficiencies in the dynamic specification of the latter.

To simulate our model, we need to have values for the AR parameters and innovation variances in equations (16) and (20). Fitting an AR(1) model by least squares to the estimated residuals, $\hat{\eta}_t$, of equations (43) and (44) produces

$$(48) \qquad \hat{v}_t = 0.3233\hat{v}_{t-1}, \qquad \text{SEE} = 0.0114,$$
$$ (0.073)$$

$$(49) \qquad \hat{\eta}_t = 0.9346\hat{\eta}_{t-1}, \qquad \text{SEE} = 0.0225,$$
$$ (0.028)$$

so that $\rho_v = 0.3233$, $\rho_\eta = 0.9346$, $\sigma_{ev}^2 = (0.0114)^2$, and $\sigma_u^2 = (0.0225)^2$. The residuals of equation (49) are virtually uncorrelated with those of equation (50), leading us to set $\psi_u = 0$ and $\sigma_{ev}^2 = (0.0114)^2$ in equation (21).

Finally, we turn to the policy rule. To describe actual policy behavior, we use equation (3), although our simulations in the next section will consider alternative, counterfactual policy rules. Since we specify the error term in equation (3) as an innovation, lagged endogenous variables are legitimate instruments in the estimation of the equation. Our instrument list for this equation consists of a constant, a time trend, d_{1t}, d_{2t}, Δx_{t-1}, Δx_{t-2}, $d_{2t-1} \cdot \Delta x_{t-1}$, $d_{2t-2} \cdot \Delta x_{t-2}$, Δp_{t-1}, Δp_{t-2}, and n_{t-1}.[27] The resulting estimated rule is

$$\hat{R}_t = 0.103 + 0.866R_{t-1} + 0.023E_{t-1}\tilde{y}_t + 0.117E_{t-1}\Delta x_t$$
$$\phantom{\hat{R}_t =} (0.035) \quad (0.049) \qquad (0.005) \qquad\quad (0.034)$$

$$(50) \qquad + 0.002d_{1t} + 0.064d_{2t} \cdot E_{t-1}\Delta x_t,$$
$$ (0.001) \qquad (0.031)$$

$$\bar{R}^2 = 0.939, \text{ SEE} = 0.0017, \text{ DW} = 1.99.$$

The large coefficient on the lagged dependent variable suggests a high degree of interest rate smoothing. The coefficient on the interactive dummy $d_{2t} \cdot E_{t-1}\Delta x_t$ indicates a substantial permanent increase in the restrictiveness of

27. As before, we use $0.7n_t$ to measure (up to a constant) the output gap $\tilde{y}_t$.

monetary policy from 1979. After 1979, a 1 percent increase in expected nominal income growth leads to a steady state increase in the nominal interest rate of 1.35 percentage points, compared to only 0.87 points prior to 1979. This result is similar to the post-1979 increase in the coefficient on expected inflation in Clarida et al.'s (1998) estimates of the Taylor rule. The estimated intercept shift in the 1979–82 period is statistically significant and amounts to an upward shift of 0.8 percentage points when the interest rate is measured in annualized percentage units.

In the variant of our model that includes the Calvo-Rotemberg price-setting specification, the aggregate supply equation (26) appears. As is conventional, we set $\beta = 0.99$. The remaining coefficient in the equation is the ratio θ/c_1. Using annual data, Roberts (1995) estimates this coefficient to be about 0.08. His version of equation (26), however, contained an additive disturbance term. Our equation (26), by contrast, has no explicit shock term; the randomness in inflation comes only from the stochastic behavior of the right-hand-side variables $E_t \Delta p_{t+1}$ and $\tilde{y}_t$. As a result, a much higher value of θ/c_1 than Roberts's estimate, such as 0.30, is required to produce plausible inflation variability, for any of the policy rules that we consider. Thus 0.30 is the value of θ/c_1 that we employ. With θ, which is interpretable as the inverse of the aggregate markup under the aggregation scheme that we have used, set to 6, a value of $\theta/c_1 = 0.30$ implies $c_1 = 20$.

1.6 Simulation Results I

In this section we report simulation results for the variant of our macroeconomic model that uses the Calvo-Rotemberg specification of price adjustment behavior. In calculating these results, as well as those in the next section, we have made one change in the aggregate demand portion of our model, replacing $E_t y_{t+1}$ with $E_{t-1} y_{t+1}$ on the right-hand side of the expectational IS function (43). This change, which represents a modification of the same basic type as those employed by Rotemberg and Woodford (1997), but less severe, produces more plausible values for the variability of inflation in all our simulations (for both the specifications of aggregate supply that we contemplate).[28]

We begin with simulations involving versions of the Taylor rule, some of them suggested by the conference organizer to facilitate comparison across papers by different researchers. In particular, table 1.1 includes results for various values of the policy parameters μ_1, μ_2, and μ_3 in a rule of the form

$$(51) \qquad R_t = \mu_0 + \mu_1 \Delta p_t + \mu_2 \tilde{y}_t + \mu_3 R_{t-1},$$

where μ_0 is in principle set so as to deliver the chosen average inflation rate and where policy responses are unrealistically assumed to reflect contemporaneous

---

28. This is particularly important in the context of the P-bar variant, where the two forward-looking components of the model interact in an overly sensitive way. In subsequent work, we plan to explore different modifications of our IS function, as suggested by the results of Campbell and Mankiw (1989) and Fuhrer (1997).

responses to the state of the economy. In the original Taylor rule $\mu_3 = 0$, but we have also considered cases with $\mu_3 = 1$ (to reflect interest rate smoothing by the Fed) and $\mu_3 = 1.2$ (to investigate a case recommended by Rotemberg and Woodford, chap. 2 of this volume). The simulation results reported are standard deviations (in annualized percentage units) of inflation Δp_t, the output gap $\tilde{y}_t$, and the interest rate R_t.[29] In these simulations constant terms are not included, so the standard deviation of Δp_t is interpretable as the root-mean-square deviation from the inflation target value π^*, as is also the case for $\tilde{y}_t$. The values reported are mean values over 100 replications, with each simulation being for a sample period of 200 quarters.[30] In solving the model, we use the algorithm of Paul Klein (1997), which builds on that in King and Watson (forthcoming).

Examination of the results in table 1.1 shows that they suggest that for a given value of the smoothing parameter μ_3, stronger responses to Δp_t or $\tilde{y}_t$—that is, higher values of μ_1 or μ_2—lead invariably to lower standard deviations of that variable. Indeed, higher values of μ_1 or μ_2 lead in most cases to lower standard deviations of both Δp_t and $\tilde{y}_t$ (basically because of the nature of the price adjustment equation). This suggests that if there were no concern for variability of the interest rate, the central bank could achieve extremely good macroeconomic performance merely by responding very strongly to current departures of inflation and output from their target values. In our opinion, however, that would be a highly unrealistic conclusion to draw; the conduct of monetary policy by actual central banks is much more difficult than that. But such a conclusion tends to be obtained from exercises in which the central bank is assumed to possess knowledge of Δp_t and $\tilde{y}_t$ when setting its instrument value (R_t in this case) for period t. In other words, the policy rule (51) does not represent an operational specification.

Because of this type of concern, the conference organizer suggested that results also be obtained for a specification like equation (51) but with inflation and the output gap lagged one quarter. Thus we next conduct simulations with

$$(52) \qquad R_t = \mu_0 + \mu_1 \Delta p_{t-1} + \mu_2 \tilde{y}_{t-1} + \mu_3 R_{t-1}$$

as the policy rule and report the results in table 1.2.

For the cases where $\mu_1 = 1.5$ and there is no interest rate smoothing ($\mu_3 = 0$), the standard deviation of inflation is virtually identical in table 1.2 to the corresponding rules in table 1.1. As in table 1.1, rules with smoothing ($\mu_3 = 1.0$) deliver better results with respect to both inflation and output gap variability than the corresponding rules without smoothing. However, while table 1.1 indicated that with smoothing the standard deviation of inflation could be reduced to values as low as 0.65, the lowest standard deviation of inflation in

---

29. For the purpose of comparison, the actual historical values over 1955–96 are 2.41, 2.23, and 2.80.

30. We ran simulations of 253 periods and ignored the initial 53, so as to abstract from start-up departures from stochastic steady state conditions.

Table 1.1   Simulation Results with Calvo-Rotemberg Variant: Taylor Rule, Contemporaneous Response

Values of μ_1, μ_3	Value of μ_2				
	0.0	0.5	1.0	3.0	10.0
1.5, 0.0	2.01	1.96	1.93	1.78	1.40
	1.15	1.12	1.10	1.03	0.82
	3.02	3.94	3.98	5.72	10.31
3.0, 0.0	1.78	1.78	1.72	1.60	1.29
	1.03	1.03	1.00	0.94	0.77
	5.34	5.84	6.13	7.59	11.53
10.0, 0.0	1.24	1.20	1.19	1.14	0.98
	0.75	0.73	0.72	0.69	0.60
	12.35	12.33	12.63	13.49	15.74
1.2, 1.0	1.32	1.25	1.19	1.10	0.97
	1.13	1.11	1.08	1.02	0.85
	2.38	2.94	3.41	5.42	10.63
3.0, 1.0	1.14	1.11	1.09[a]	0.98	0.82
	1.04	1.03	1.03[a]	0.97	0.81
	4.51	4.95	5.14[a]	6.80	10.00
10.0, 1.0	0.85	0.83	0.83	0.78	0.65
	0.86	0.85	0.85	0.82	0.71
	9.32	9.51	9.90	10.71	13.40
1.2, 1.3	1.31[b]	1.32	1.36	1.54	1.64
	1.12[b]	1.11	1.11	1.05	0.94
	2.10[b]	1.64	2.03	5.01	10.51

Note: Table reports standard deviations of Δp_t, $\bar{y}_t$, and R_t, respectively (percent per annum).
[a]$\mu_2 = 0.8$, not 1.0.
[b]$\mu_2 = 0.06$, not 0.0.

table 1.2 is 1.00. It is also clear from table 1.2 that responding to lagged instead of contemporaneous data reduces policymakers' ability to stabilize output: the output gap standard deviation ranges from 0.60 to 1.15 in table 1.1, while in table 1.2 it ranges from 1.16 to 1.34.

Table 1.1 suggested that there were benefits in terms of both inflation and output gap variability from high values of μ_1 or μ_2, such as 10.0. In table 1.2, on the other hand, these benefits are less clear. Whereas in table 1.1, changing the output gap response coefficient μ_2 from 3.0 to 10.0 unambiguously improved performance with respect to both inflation and the output gap, in table 1.2 this increase in μ_2 delivers poorer performance on output gap variability and, in most cases with interest rate smoothing, on inflation variability too. Raising μ_1 from 3.0 to 10.0 does improve inflation performance, just as it did in table 1.1, but in contrast to table 1.1, it fails to improve output gap performance appreciably.

While the results in table 1.2 indicate that there is some deterioration in policy performance with rule (52) instead of (51), the deterioration is not particularly drastic, and the rules still deliver dynamically stable results with large

Table 1.2   **Simulation Results with Calvo-Rotemberg Variant: Taylor Rule, Lagged Response**

Values of μ_1, μ_3	Value of μ_2				
	0.0	0.5	1.0	3.0	10.0
1.5, 0.0	1.91	1.88	1.84	1.68	1.37
	1.21	1.22	1.21	1.19	1.19
	2.87	3.43	3.94	6.06	13.86
3.0, 0.0	1.71	1.68	1.66	1.54	1.31
	1.19	1.19	1.19	1.17	1.19
	5.14	5.62	6.17	8.12	15.79
10.0, 0.0	1.33	1.31	1.29	1.26	1.18
	1.19	1.18	1.18	1.20	1.26
	13.26	13.66	14.10	16.20	24.28
1.2, 1.0	1.33	1.27	1.23	1.20	1.25
	1.18	1.18	1.17	1.18	1.26
	2.27	2.78	3.29	5.51	12.76
3.0, 1.0	1.19	1.17	1.15[a]	1.10	1.11
	1.16	1.17	1.17[a]	1.17	1.25
	4.24	4.65	4.96[a]	6.95	13.50
10.0, 1.0	1.03	1.04	1.03	1.01	1.00
	1.17	1.18	1.19	1.20	1.27
	9.50	9.98	10.23	11.78	17.53
1.2, 1.3	1.34[b]	1.34	1.40	1.62	1.88
	1.18[b]	1.16	1.18	1.19	1.34
	2.03[b]	2.49	3.04	5.19	12.61

Note: Table reports standard deviations of Δp_t, $\bar{y}_t$, and R_t, respectively (percent per annum).
[a]$\mu_2 = 0.8$, not 1.0.
[b]$\mu_2 = 0.06$, not 0.0.

values of μ_1 or μ_2. That finding comes as a surprise to us, but having obtained it we believe that it can be understood as follows. There are two properties of the model at hand that defuse the tendency, mentioned in McCallum (1997, sec. 6), for explosive instrument instability to arise when strong feedback responses are based on lagged variables. First, the values of two parameters crucial for the transmission of policy actions to Δp_t are quite small; these are the slope of the "IS function" with respect to the real interest rate ($\sigma \cdot C^{ss}/Y^{ss}$ in eq. [15])[31] and the slope of the price adjustment relation (θ/c_1 in eq. [26]). The smallness of the former implies that aggregate demand responses to changes in R_t are small, and the latter makes aggregate demand changes have small effects on inflation. Second, the Calvo-Rotemberg version of our model is one in which there is no autoregressive structure apart from what is contained in the disturbance terms and the policy rule. The model, that is, is entirely forward looking. We conjecture that models with backward looking IS and price adjust-

---

31. Our estimated value is less than 1/20 of the value used by, e.g., Rotemberg and Woodford (1997; chap. 2 of this volume).

ment specifications would possess much more of a tendency to generate dynamic instability for large values of μ_1 and μ_2.[32]

Another operationality concern expressed by McCallum (1997) involves a lack of knowledge about $\bar{y}_t$, the market-clearing value of y_t. Suppose, then, that the central bank believes that a fitted linear trend line represents $\bar{y}_t$, while in fact our measure is correct. Then the central bank would use detrended y_t instead of $\bar{y}_t$ in its policy rule and would measure output gap fluctuations in relation to this fitted trend. To get an idea of the implications, we redo the table 1.1 case with $\mu_1 = 1.2$, $\mu_2 = 1.0$, and $\mu_3 = 1.0$ under this assumption. Then the standard deviation of Δp_t turns out to be 3.41 instead of 1.19, according to our model, and the central bank would believe that the standard deviation of $\bar{y}_t$ was 3.91 (although it would actually be 1.09—almost the same as in table 1.1). Also, the standard deviation of R_t would rise from 3.41 to 4.77.[33]

One issue mentioned in our introduction is the stability and desirability of nominal income targeting. To determine whether effects on Δp_t and $\bar{y}_t$ would be much different if targets were set for $\Delta x_t = \Delta p_t + \Delta y_t$, we have conducted simulations using the rule

(53) $$R_t = \mu_0 + \mu_1 \Delta x_t + \mu_3 R_{t-1},$$

and also with Δx_{t-1} replacing Δx_t, for $\mu_3 = 0$ and $\mu_3 = 1.0$. These results are reported in table 1.3. There we see that nominal income targeting with an interest instrument performs reasonably well. It permits considerably more variability of inflation than does the Taylor rule but tends to stabilize output (in relation to $\bar{y}_t$) almost as well. It should be noted that the good performance in terms of $\bar{y}_t$ occurs despite the absence of that variable or $\bar{y}_t$ in the policy rule. An advantage of nominal income (growth rate) targeting is that it does not require the central bank to measure capacity output. More interest rate variability occurs for most parameter values, but such variability is quite low (and the Δp_t and $\bar{y}_t$ standard deviations are reasonably small) when μ_1 is assigned the small value of 0.1 with $\mu_3 = 1.0$.

As in table 1.2, for moderate values of the feedback coefficient there is a deterioration in performance with respect to $\bar{y}_t$ variability, but little deterioration in Δp_t variability, when feedback is applied with a one-period lag, that is, to the value of Δx_{t-1} rather than Δx_t. Another similarity with tables 1.1 and 1.2 is that making the feedback coefficient large (in this case, increasing μ_1 in eq. [53] from 3.0 to 10.0) delivers an improvement in performance with respect to $\bar{y}_t$, Δp_t, and Δx_t variability (at the cost of increased R_t volatility) when policy responds to contemporaneous data, but not when policy responds to lagged information. In the latter case, raising μ_1 from 3.0 to 10.0 actually delivers

32. Even in the present model we found instability to prevail if μ_1 was raised to 1,000 (!) and to prevail at lower values of μ_1 if σ was increased sharply. With contemporaneous feedback, there is no instability even in these cases.

33. These results are generated by replacing $\bar{y}_t$ with y_t in eq. (51), re-solving the model, and then looking at simulation results for Δp_t, y_t, and R_t.

Table 1.3   **Simulation Results with Calvo-Rotemberg Variant: Nominal Income Target, Interest Rate Instrument**

Value of μ_1	Contemporaneous Response Value of μ_3		Lagged Response Value of μ_3	
	0.0	1.0	0.0	1.0
0.10		1.96		1.96
		1.22		1.23
		6.18		6.29
		0.65		0.63
0.50		1.85		1.84
		1.13		1.19
		5.60		6.22
		2.80		2.78
1.00		1.76		1.79
		1.05		1.18
		5.11		6.35
		5.11		5.17
1.50	2.44	1.71	2.48	1.75
	1.11	0.99	1.25	1.18
	5.14	4.70	5.23	6.60
	7.71	7.06	10.13	7.55
3.00	2.50	1.63	2.53	1.70
	1.00	0.87	1.31	1.19
	4.17	3.82	7.69	7.17
	12.52	10.18	23.07	14.33
10.00	1.92	1.49	All variables	2.00
	0.69	0.65	explosive	2.25
	2.00	2.05		18.16
	19.96	17.33		93.84

Note: Table reports standard deviations of Δp_t, $\tilde{y}_t$, Δx_t, and R_t, respectively (percent per annum).

instrument instability when there is no interest rate smoothing. With smoothing, dynamic stability prevails for all variables, but the standard deviations of $\tilde{y}_t$, Δp_t, Δx_t, and R_t are all decidedly increased. Thus tables 1.2 and 1.3 are both supportive of the notion that assigning very high values to response coefficients is counterproductive when policy can only respond to lagged information.

Next we retain nominal income as the target variable but consider the use of Δb_t—the growth rate of the monetary base—as the instrument. In particular, we consider two versions of McCallum's rule (1), one with a "levels" target path $x_t^{*1} = x_{t-1}^{*1} + \Delta x^*$ and the other with a "growth rate" target $x_t^{*2} = x_{t-1} + \Delta x^*$. Stochastic simulation results analogous to those discussed above are presented in table 1.4. There it will be seen that performance is quite close to that in table 1.3, where nominal income targeting is attempted with R_t as the instrument variable. Throughout table 1.4, the variability of nominal income growth is about the same as it is with the best of the lagged response rules in table 1.3; moreover, the variability of inflation is lower than it is table 1.3 and

Table 1.4   Simulation Results with Calvo-Rotemberg Variant: Nominal Income
Target, Monetary Base Instrument

Value of λ in Rule (1)	Levels Target, x^{*1}	Growth Rate Target, x^{*2}
0.25	1.05	1.05
	1.29	1.30
	5.25	5.27
	1.88	1.80
0.50	1.07	1.00
	1.29	1.27
	5.25	5.19
	1.96	1.72
1.00	1.03	1.01
	1.27	1.28
	5.25	5.20
	1.02	1.78
3.00	1.04	1.01
	1.28	1.26
	5.39	5.16
	3.06	2.11
10.00	1.04	0.99
	1.28	1.25
	5.89	5.31
	3.73	4.30

Note: Table reports standard deviations of Δp_t, $\tilde{y}_t$, Δx_t, and R_t, respectively (percent per annum).

is comparable to the values obtained in table 1.2 with the operational Taylor rule (52). In addition, there is no apparent tendency for interest rate variability to increase sharply when the base is used.

A comparison of the levels target and growth rate target rule performances in table 1.4 shows, somewhat surprisingly, that the results are little different and, in particular, that $\tilde{y}_t$ variability is not lower with the growth rate specification. For both rule types, another striking feature is how insensitive the variability of the nominal income growth rate is to changes in the value of the response coefficient λ.[34] Presumably this is the case because the parameter values estimated in section 1.5 imply an extremely small response of aggregate demand to real money balances $(b_t - p_t)$.

It should be emphasized that the stochastic simulation exercises underlying tables 1.1 through 1.4 do not serve to bring out one aspect of operationality claimed by McCallum (1988) for rule (1), namely, its nondependence on the long-run average growth rate of base velocity. That nondependence, which is

34. The levels target results suggest that nominal income growth Δx_t variability is *increasing* in λ; this reflects the fact that in the simulations, the levels target is a constant, so successful nominal income targeting implies that x_t is $I(0)$. Δx_t is therefore $I(-1)$, and hence will tend to be highly variable, the more so when nominal income targeting is pursued vigorously (i.e., with high values of λ). The standard deviation of the *level* of nominal income in the simulations underlying the first column of table 1.1 *is* decreasing in λ, taking the values 1.44, 1.35, 1.26, 1.15, and 1.10 for $\lambda = $ 0.25, 0.50, 1.00, 3.00, and 10.00, respectively.

not possessed by most rules with base or reserve aggregate instruments, is basically irrelevant for the stochastic simulations in which constant terms are omitted. Thus the velocity correction term in rule (1) could be omitted without any appreciable effect on the results of table 1.4, which is most definitely not the case for the counterfactual historical simulations reported in, for example, McCallum (1988, 1993). Accordingly, we plan to include some simulations of this latter type in subsequent work.

1.7 Simulation Results II

In this section we report stochastic simulation results analogous to those of tables 1.1 through 1.4 but now using the P-bar price adjustment relation. Table 1.5 gives standard deviations of Δp_t, $\bar{y}_t$, and R_t for the same values of μ_1, μ_2, and μ_3 as those considered in table 1.1, under the assumption of contemporaneous feedback responses to Δp_t and $\bar{y}_t$. Again it is the case that an increase in μ_1 (μ_2) reduces the variability of Δp_t ($\bar{y}_t$), but it is not now the case that increasing either μ_1 or μ_2 tends to reduce the variability of both Δp_t and $\bar{y}_t$. Instead, there

Table 1.5   **Simulation Results with P-Bar Variant: Taylor Rule, Contemporaneous Response**

			Value of μ_2		
Values of μ_1, μ_3	0.0	0.5	1.0	3.0	10.0
1.5, 0.0	8.53	9.67	10.68	14.20	31.38
	2.48	2.39	2.31	1.98	0.55
	12.80	13.70	14.42	16.93	30.24
3.0, 0.0	2.88	3.13	3.37	4.51	12.74
	2.51	2.43	2.34	2.15	0.78
	8.64	8.83	9.01	10.01	19.75
10.0, 0.0	0.76	0.81	1.18	2.00	3.39
	2.49	2.43	2.04	1.57	0.89
	7.63	7.63	8.34	11.78	18.46
1.2, 1.0	3.61	3.71	4.14	6.72	19.00
	2.51	2.42	2.24	1.88	0.44
	5.32	5.68	5.86	7.17	13.86
3.0, 1.0	1.95	1.96	1.98[a]	2.97	6.11
	2.53	2.42	2.36[a]	2.06	1.49
	6.26	6.33	6.27[a]	7.14	10.10
10.0, 1.0	0.70	0.69	0.71	0.95	1.99
	2.42	2.32	2.34	2.12	1.66
	6.88	6.83	6.95	7.52	10.44
1.2, 1.3	3.76[b]	3.74	4.10	6.51	12.61
	2.51[b]	2.35	2.27	1.82	1.15
	4.49[b]	4.65	4.98	6.02	8.72

Note: Table reports standard deviations of Δp_t, $\bar{y}_t$, and R_t, respectively (percent per annum).
[a] $\mu_2 = 0.8$, not 1.0.
[b] $\mu_2 = 0.06$, not 0.0.

Table 1.6   **Simulation Results with P-Bar Variant: Taylor Rule, Lagged Response to $\bar{y}$, Contemporaneous to Δp**

Values of μ_1, μ_3	Value of μ_2				
	0.0	0.5	1.0	3.0	10.0
1.5, 0.0	8.53	9.92	11.23	16.15	29.51
	2.48	2.42	2.35	2.09	1.59
	12.80	13.92	14.88	18.52	28.78
3.0, 0.0	2.88	3.25	3.54	5.23	11.08
	2.51	2.53	2.44	2.35	2.08
	8.64	9.04	9.13	10.18	13.78
10.0, 0.0	0.76	0.80	0.88	1.24	2.86
	2.49	2.42	2.45	2.39	2.32
	7.63	7.57	7.55	7.67	8.33
1.2, 1.0	3.60	3.79	4.19	7.00	15.30
	2.56	2.43	2.39	2.19	1.62
	5.32	5.74	6.12	7.99	12.75
3.0, 1.0	1.95	1.95	2.07[a]	3.17	7.50
	2.47	2.48	2.47[a]	2.39	2.09
	6.16	6.31	6.43[a]	7.17	9.51
10.0, 1.0	0.69	0.69	0.75	1.01	2.45
	2.44	2.44	2.51	2.39	2.30
	6.83	6.80	7.01	6.95	7.50
1.2, 1.3	All variables	3.75	All variables	All variables	13.68
	explosive[b]	2.50	explosive	explosive	1.68
		4.81			10.79

Note: Table reports standard deviations of Δp_t, $\bar{y}_t$, and R_t, respectively (percent per annum).
[a] $\mu_2 = 0.8$, not 1.0.
[b] $\mu_2 = 0.06$, not 0.0.

is a variability trade-off at work, with increases in μ_2 often increasing the variability of Δp_t. The existence of interest rate smoothing, with $\mu_3 = 1$, is helpful in most cases and is so to a greater extent than in table 1.1. Overall, the variability of Δp_t, $\bar{y}_t$, and R_t is considerably greater than in table 1.1. For $\bar{y}_t$, its magnitude is much more realistic, but for Δp_t or R_t it is somewhat excessive.

Table 1.6 is partly but not entirely analogous to table 1.2, in which lagged values of Δp_t and $\bar{y}_t$ are used in rule (52). When such values are utilized, dynamically explosive results are obtained for most parameter configurations. Consequently, table 1.6 reports values for feedback responses to the lagged value of $\bar{y}_t$ but to the current value of Δp_t. This modification seems justifiable from an operationality perspective because Δp_t is a predetermined variable in the P-bar variant of our model, so Δp_t is in principle observable at the end of period $t - 1$. The resulting standard deviations are quite close to those of table 1.5 for small and moderate values of μ_1 and μ_2 but are larger for high values of these feedback parameters. There is no evident tendency toward dynamic instability, however, except in the "Rotemberg-Woodford" cases with $\mu_3 = 1.3$.

Table 1.7   **Simulation Results with P-Bar Variant: Nominal Income Target, Interest Rate Instrument**

	Contemporaneous Response Value of μ_3		Lagged Response Value of μ_3	
Value of μ_1	0.0	1.0	0.0	1.0
0.10		7.46		7.51
		2.07		2.10
		8.50		8.56
		1.77		1.72
0.50		4.36		4.67
		2.27		2.19
		5.85		6.13
		4.07		3.72
1.00	27.65	2.97	38.87	3.56
	1.77	2.24	1.73	2.21
	28.62	4.58	39.42	5.16
	28.62	5.67	39.28	5.12
1.50	6.82	2.25		3.41
	2.31	2.09	All variables	2.17
	8.22	3.90	explosive	4.96
	12.33	6.78		6.26
3.00	2.70	1.47		
	2.06	1.97	All variables	All variables
	3.91	2.95	explosive	explosive
	11.75	9.54		
10.00	0.98	0.96		
	1.67	1.64	All variables	All variables
	1.67	1.67	explosive	explosive
	16.71	15.77		

Note: Table reports standard deviations of Δp_t, $\tilde{y}_t$, Δx_t, and R_t, respectively (percent per annum).

Next we consider the effect of an incorrect belief by the central bank that a fitted trend line represents $\bar{y}_t$ when in fact our measure is correct. With the P-bar price adjustment relation included, rather than the Calvo-Rotemberg version, this effect is considerably smaller. Thus, in the particular case mentioned in section 1.6—that is, with $\mu_1 = 1.2$, $\mu_2 = 1.0$, and $\mu_3 = 1.0$—the Δp_t and $\tilde{y}_t$ standard deviations increase only from 4.14 and 2.24 (respectively) to 4.80 and 2.35. The reduction in this effect obtains, clearly, because the P-bar specification makes $\tilde{y}_t$ very strongly related to $\tilde{y}_{t-1}$. If the central bank responds more vigorously to its (incorrect) beliefs about $\tilde{y}_t$, however, the deleterious effect will be somewhat larger. With $\mu_2 = 3.0$, for example,[35] the standard deviations increase from 6.72 and 1.88 to 10.50 and 2.15.

With nominal income targeting and an interest instrument, the results with the P-bar variant of our model are given in table 1.7. There the results are

35. With μ_1 and μ_3 as before.

Table 1.8   Simulation Results with P-Bar Variant: Nominal Income Target,
                   Monetary Base Instrument

Value of λ in Rule (1)	Levels Target, x^{*1}	Growth Rate Target, x^{*2}
0.25	6.67	7.17
	2.24	2.20
	7.70	8.26
	2.47	2.29
0.50	6.38	6.88
	2.27	2.27
	7.51	7.95
	2.61	2.40
1.00	6.08	6.38
	2.28	2.27
	7.20	7.49
	2.83	2.56
3.00	5.48	5.28
	2.18	2.30
	6.61	6.62
	3.55	3.23
10.00	5.00	3.62
	2.19	2.26
	6.09	5.14
	5.50	5.02

Note: Table reports standard deviations of Δp_t, $\bar{y}_t$, Δx_t, and R_t, respectively (percent per annum).

much more favorable with μ_3 equal to 1.0 rather than zero, that is, with interest smoothing. The ability of rule (53) to keep Δx_t close to its target value is about the same as with the Calvo-Rotemberg variant, but results in terms of the variability of Δp_t (and to a lesser extent $\bar{y}_t$) are much less desirable. Clearly, the dynamic relationship between Δp_t and $\bar{y}_t$ is very different with these two price adjustment specifications.

Finally, in the table 1.8 case with rule (1), in which Δb_t is the instrument variable (and x_t or Δx_t the target variable), the performance is about the same as in table 1.7. For a given level of R_t variability, that is, the standard deviations of Δx_t, Δp_t, and $\bar{y}_t$ are about the same. Furthermore, the figures indicate a low degree of responsiveness of nominal income variability to the feedback parameter λ, although the responsiveness is considerably greater than it was with the Calvo-Rotemberg variant of our model (in table 1.4). Again, this low responsiveness is largely a result of the optimizing IS specification that we employ, which implies that aggregate demand is quite insensitive to the quantity of real money balances.

1.8   Conclusions

Some conclusions from the simulation results hold for both variants of our model—that is, with both price adjustment relations. The first of these is that the inclusion of the R_{t-1} interest-smoothing term in the Taylor rule is helpful in reducing the variability of Δp_t and $\bar{y}_t$ for given values of the policy response parameters μ_1 and μ_2, while also reducing R_t variability. Second, for moderate values of response coefficients, the use of lagged rather than contemporaneous values of $\bar{y}_t$ does not bring about any major deterioration in results and does not generate any severe danger of instrument instability.[36] Third, nominal income targeting with an R_t instrument is only mildly effective but shows no noticeable tendency to generate dynamic instability, provided that interest rate smoothing is employed.[37] Fourth, nominal income targeting with a monetary base instrument does not imply drastically greater R_t variability than with an interest instrument. It is, however, only weakly effective—the standard deviation of Δx_t is not very responsive to the feedback parameter λ.[38]

Other conclusions are more sensitive to the model variant. For example, pure inflation targeting ($\mu_1 > 0$, $\mu_2 = 0$) is quite effective in the Calvo-Rotemberg specification but significantly less so with the P-bar relation. More generally, increasing μ_1 or μ_2 tends (for moderate ranges of those parameters) to reduce *both* inflation and output gap variability with the Calvo-Rotemberg variant; by contrast, the P-bar specification generates a trade-off between inflation and output gap variability, so that raising μ_2 for a given μ_1 yields improved output gap performance at the expense of more variable inflation. Furthermore, performance deteriorates sharply if the central bank responds to an incorrect measure of capacity output ($\bar{y}_t$) when the Calvo-Rotemberg relation is used but does so only moderately with the P-bar specification. And nominal income targeting holds down inflation variability much better with the Calvo-Rotemberg version of the model. Finally, when policy responds to lagged rather than contemporaneous output gap data, increasing the value of the Taylor rule response coefficient on the output gap to a very high level (say 10) tends to be counterproductive—in the sense of increasing rather than decreasing output gap variability—when the Calvo-Rotemberg specification of aggregate supply is used. This result does not carry over when the P-bar specification is employed.

These last-mentioned conclusions illustrate the importance, mentioned in our introduction, of the robustness of proposed rules to model specification. In future work, we hope to conduct a small robustness study of our own while also investigating several issues that we have not yet been able to explore.

---

36. This is not true, as mentioned, for lagged Δp_t-values in the P-bar variant, in which case Δp_t is itself a predetermined variable.

37. With strong feedback or with $\mu_3 = 0$ in the lagged response cases, dynamic instability obtains. It is not, however, of the type mentioned by Ball (1997), which involves instability of Δp_t and $\bar{y}_t$ even though Δx_t is stabilized.

38. This conclusion might be changed by alternative specifications of relations analogous to our eqs. (17) and (19).

References

Ball, Laurence. 1994. Credible disinflation with staggered price setting. *American Economic Review* 84:282–89.

———. 1997. Efficient rules for monetary policy. NBER Working Paper no. 5952. Cambridge, Mass.: National Bureau of Economic Research.

Bank for International Settlements. 1997. Implementation and tactics of monetary policy. Conference Paper no. 3. Basel: Bank for International Settlements.

Brunner, Karl, and Allan H. Meltzer. 1983. Strategy and tactics for monetary control. *Carnegie-Rochester Conference Series on Public Policy* 18:59–103.

Calvo, Guillermo A. 1983. Staggered prices in a utility-maximizing framework. *Journal of Monetary Economics* 12:383–98.

Campbell, John Y., and N. Gregory Mankiw. 1989. Consumption, income and interest rates: Reinterpreting the time series evidence. In *NBER macroeconomics annual 1989*, ed. O. J. Blanchard and S. Fischer, 185–216. Cambridge, Mass.: MIT Press.

Clarida, Richard, Jordi Galí, and Mark Gertler. 1998. Monetary policy rules and macroeconomic stability: Evidence and some theory. NBER Working Paper no. 6442. Cambridge, Mass.: National Bureau of Economic Research.

———. Forthcoming. The science of monetary policy. *Journal of Economic Literature.*

Dixit, A. K., and Joseph E. Stiglitz. 1977. Monopolistic competition and optimum product diversity. *American Economic Review* 67:297–308.

Friedman, Milton. 1982. Monetary policy: Theory and practice. *Journal of Money, Credit and Banking* 14:98–118.

Fuhrer, Jeffrey C. 1997. Towards a compact, empirically-verified rational expectations model for monetary policy analysis. *Carnegie-Rochester Conference Series on Public Policy* 47:197–230.

Fuhrer, Jeffrey C., and George R. Moore. 1995. Inflation persistence. *Quarterly Journal of Economics* 109:127–59.

Goodhart, Charles A. E. 1994. What should central banks do? What should be their macroeconomic objectives and operations? *Economic Journal* 104:1424–36.

———. 1997. Why do the monetary authorities smooth interest rates? In *European monetary policy*, ed. S. Collignon, 119–74. London: Pinter.

Gordon, Robert J. 1990. What is new Keynesian economics? *Journal of Economic Literature* 28:1115–71.

Hall, Robert E. 1980. Labor supply and aggregate fluctuations. *Carnegie-Rochester Conference Series on Public Policy* 12:7–33.

Ingenito, Robert, and Bharat Trehan. 1997. Using monthly data to predict quarterly output. *Federal Reserve Bank of San Francisco Economic Review,* no. 3:3–11.

Ireland, Peter N. 1997. A small, structural, quarterly model for monetary policy evaluation. *Carnegie-Rochester Conference Series on Public Policy* 47:83–108.

Kerr, William, and Robert G. King. 1996. Limits on interest rate rules in the *IS* model. *Federal Reserve Bank of Richmond Economic Quarterly* 82:47–75.

King, Robert G., and Mark W. Watson. Forthcoming. System reduction and solution algorithms for singular linear difference systems under rational expectations. *International Economic Review.*

Klein, Paul. 1997. Using the generalized Schur form to solve a system of linear expectational difference equations. Stockholm: Institute for International Economic Studies. Working paper.

McCallum, Bennett T. 1983. On non-uniqueness in rational expectations models: An attempt at perspective. *Journal of Monetary Economics* 11:139–68.

———. 1988. Robustness properties of a rule for monetary policy. *Carnegie-Rochester Conference Series on Public Policy* 29:173–203.

————. 1990. Targets, indicators, and instruments of monetary policy. In *Monetary policy for a changing financial environment,* ed. W. S. Haraf and P. Cagan, 44–70. Washington, D.C.: AEI Press.

————. 1993. Specification and analysis of a monetary policy rule for Japan. *Bank of Japan Monetary and Economic Studies* 11:1–45.

————. 1994. A semi-classical model of price adjustment. *Carnegie-Rochester Conference Series on Public Policy* 41:251–84.

————. 1995. Monetary policy rules and financial stability. In *Financial stability in a changing financial environment,* ed. K. Sawamoto, Z. Nakajima, and H. Taguchi, 389–421. London: Macmillan.

————. 1997. Issues in the design of monetary policy rules. NBER Working Paper no. 6016. Cambridge, Mass.: National Bureau of Economic Research. (In *Handbook of macroeconomics,* ed. John B. Taylor and Michael Woodford. Amsterdam: North Holland, forthcoming.)

McCallum, Bennett T., and Edward Nelson. Forthcoming. An optimizing *IS-LM* specification for monetary policy and business cycle analysis. *Journal of Money, Credit and Banking* 31.

Nelson, Edward. 1998. Sluggish inflation and optimizing models of the business cycle. *Journal of Monetary Economics* 42:303–22.

Poole, William. 1982. Federal Reserve operating procedures: A survey and evaluation of the historical record since October 1979. *Journal of Money, Credit and Banking* 14:575–96.

Roberts, John M. 1995. New Keynesian economics and the Phillips curve. *Journal of Money, Credit, and Banking* 27:975–84.

Rotemberg, Julio J. 1982. Sticky prices in the United States. *Journal of Political Economy* 90:1187–1211.

————. 1987. The new Keynesian microfoundations. In *NBER macroeconomics annual 1987,* ed. Stanley Fischer, 69–104. Cambridge, Mass.: MIT Press.

Rotemberg, Julio J., and Michael Woodford. 1997. An optimization-based econometric framework for the evaluation of monetary policy. In *NBER macroeconomics annual 1997,* ed. Ben S. Bernanke and Julio J. Rotemberg, 297–346. Cambridge, Mass.: MIT Press.

Sargent, Thomas J. 1979. *Macroeconomic theory.* San Diego: Academic Press.

Stuart, Alison. 1996. Simple monetary policy rules. *Bank of England Quarterly Bulletin* 36:281–87.

Svensson, Lars E. O. 1997. Inflation targeting: Some extensions. NBER Working Paper no. 5962. Cambridge, Mass.: National Bureau of Economic Research.

Taylor, John B. 1980. Aggregate dynamics and staggered contracts. *Journal of Political Economy* 88:1–23.

————. 1993. Discretion versus policy rules in practice. *Carnegie-Rochester Conference Series on Public Policy* 39:195–214.

Woodford, Michael. 1996. Control of the public debt: A requirement for price stability? NBER Working Paper no. 5684. Cambridge, Mass.: National Bureau of Economic Research.

Yun, Tack. 1996. Nominal price rigidity, money supply endogeneity, and business cycles. *Journal of Monetary Economics* 37:345–70.

Comment   Mark Gertler

Introduction

Ben McCallum has written many papers on the topic of monetary policy rules. His work has heavily influenced my own thinking on the subject. The current paper, coauthored with Ed Nelson, is yet another stimulating effort in this area.

Overview

The objective here is to study the performance of simple monetary policy rules within a small model of the U.S. economy. Two aspects of the analysis distinguish the approach: First, the authors derive the model from first principles and estimate (most) of the key parameters. The motive is to take the Lucas critique seriously by working with a structural model but at the same take the model seriously enough to make use of its identifying restrictions in the estimation of parameters.

Second, the authors investigate robustness. In particular, they explore the sensitivity of the results to two alternative specifications of price adjustment and several alternative informational scenarios. Here the goal is to address what might appropriately be called "McCallum critique," namely, that the primary obstacle facing policymakers is uncertainty about the exact structure of the economy. For this reason, as McCallum has repeatedly emphasized, it is important when doing policy evaluation to explore how a given rule works across different plausible economic environments.

Much of the analysis proceeds as follows: Let r_t be the net nominal short-term interest rate at time t, Δp_t the percentage change in the price level from $t - 1$ to t, y_t the log of output at t, and $\bar{y}_t$ the log of the natural rate of output at t (defined as the level that would arise under perfectly flexible prices). Each variable, further, is expressed as a deviation from its deterministic long-run trend. The authors then consider the family of three-parameter interest rate feedback policy rules given by

$$(1) \qquad r_t = \mu_1 \Delta p_t + \mu_2(y_t - \bar{y}_t) + \mu_3 r_{t-1},$$

with $\mu_1 > 1$, $\mu_2 > 0$, and $\mu_3 > 0$.

As is consistent with the evidence, the short-term nominal rate is treated as the policy instrument. The target inflation rate defines the steady inflation rate. The target level of output is the natural rate. The rule then has the central bank raise the short rate above trend if either inflation or output is above target. The feedback policy thus has the form of a Taylor rule, but with the addition of the

Mark Gertler is professor of economics at New York University and a research associate of the National Bureau of Economic Research.

The author thanks Sangeeta Prataap for helpful research assistance.

lagged interest rate that serves to introduce serial dependence in r_t. The authors proceed to explore how different numerical choices for the parameter vector $\{\mu_1, \mu_2, \mu_3\}$ affect the unconditional variance of inflation, the output gap, and the short-term interest rate.

Punchlines: Hypothetical versus Historical Policy Rules

Importantly, the kind of three-parameter policy rule characterized by equation (1) does a reasonably good job of capturing actual policy for the United States over the Volcker and Greenspan eras. It is thus possible to measure the hypothetical policy rule against historical policy in a reasonably direct manner. With this observation in mind, the authors' main punchlines are as follows: Rules that perform well across a broad range of scenarios have (i) μ_1 and μ_3 large relative to actual policy and (ii) μ_2 small relative to actual policy.

Thus policies that seem to work well are, relative to actual practice, more aggressive in responding to inflation and less aggressive in responding to the output gap. They also allow for more serial dependence in the interest rate. These types of policies work well in the sense that they produce relatively lower volatility in inflation, the output gap, and the interest rate. Further, they perform well not only within the class of policy rules given by equation (1) but also as compared to other types of feedback policies, such as adjusting rates in response to a nominal GDP target or using a narrow money aggregate as the policy instrument.

Where I'm Headed

In order to understand how these results come about, I will review briefly each of the models that the authors employ. To foreshadow, I conclude that the qualitative conclusions are sensible but that the quantitative conclusions the authors derive appear highly sensitive to model structure. In this vein, neither of the models that the authors consider appears to provide an adequate characterization of the data.

I focus particular attention on the price adjustment equations. The first model the authors study employs the widely used Calvo-Rotemberg formulation of gradual price adjustment. Here I show, based on a very simple and direct test, that this formulation does not capture the apparent inertia in inflation. The second model employs what the authors call "the P-bar formulation" of price adjustment. It is based (in part) on partial adjustment of output. I show in this case, again based on a very simple and direct test, that this version of the model fails to capture the hump-shaped dynamics in output.

On the other hand, it is a great virtue of the authors' approach that the structural equations they derive have directly testable implications. As I show, even though both models are rejected, each is so in a way that provides some guidance for how the respective framework needs to be modified. I conclude with some observations about the problem of model uncertainty.

Model 1: Calvo-Rotemberg Price Adjustment

The baseline framework is what McCallum and Nelson have referred to in previous work as an "optimizing IS-LM model." It is essentially a dynamic general equilibrium framework modified to allow for money (which enters individual utility functions separately), monopolistic competition, and price stickiness. The authors motivate price stickiness by assuming quadratic costs of changing nominal prices, following Rotemberg (1982). It is also possible, however, to derive the same kind of aggregate supply curve using Calvo's (1983) formulation of Taylor's (1980) time-dependent staggered price-setting model. In addition, the authors assume that investment is exogenous and obeys a random walk about trend.

The Formal Model

Given this environment, the model may be reduced to three equations: an IS curve, an aggregate supply (AS) curve, and an interest rate feedback policy. The latter is given by equation (1). The IS and AS curves are given by equations (2) and (3), respectively, as follows:

$$(2) \qquad y_t = -\sigma(r_t - E_t \Delta p_{t+1}) + E_t y_{t+1} + v_t,$$

$$(3) \qquad \Delta p_t = \lambda(y_t - \bar{y}_t) + \beta E_t \Delta p_{t+1},$$

where v_t is an aggregate demand shock (specifically a preference shock). Given that investment is exogenous, the IS curve is essentially a consumption Euler equation, where the coefficient σ is the intertemporal elasticity of substitution. The AS curve has the general form of a standard Phillips curve, except that the cost push term depends on expected future inflation, rather than current inflation.

The authors then proceed to explore how varying the parameters of the policy rule affects the unconditional variances of Δp_t, $y_t - \bar{y}_t$, and r_t. To understand the logic behind the results they obtain it is first useful to iterate forward both the IS and AS curves:

$$(4) \qquad y_t = -\sigma \sum_{k=0}^{\infty} E_t(r_{t+k} - \Delta p_{t+k+1}) + u_t,$$

$$(5) \qquad \Delta p_t = \sum_{k=0}^{\infty} \beta^k \lambda(y_{t+k} - \bar{y}_{t+k}),$$

where $u_t = \sum_{k=0}^{\infty} E_t v_{t+k}$. Importantly, forward-looking expectations drive the behavior of both output and inflation. The IS curve (4) relates output inversely to the long-term real rate (i.e., the expected sum of short-term real rates). The AS curve (5) relates inflation to the discounted sum of the current and expected future output gaps.

Intuition for the Main Results

An important implication of the AS curve is that despite the presence of price inertia, there is no trade-off between stabilization of inflation and stabilization of the output gap. Adjusting the interest rate to stabilize $y_t - \bar{y}_t$ also stabilizes Δp_t and vice versa. It is thus apparent why an aggressive interest rate response to inflation (a high value of μ_1) works well, in the sense of producing low volatility of both inflation and output.

If there are no informational frictions, responding aggressively to the output gap (a high value of μ_2) also works well. However, if potential output, $\bar{y}_t$, is not directly observable, it pays to make the interest rate less responsive to output movements and more responsive to inflation (i.e., a high value of μ_1 along with a low value of μ_2). This is particularly true if supply shocks are an important source of variation in output (i.e., if movements in $\bar{y}_t$ are important in the overall movement in y_t). In this instance, adjusting rates to stabilize y_t will increase the volatility of both the output gap and inflation, as equation (5) suggests.

Finally, interest rate smoothing (a high value of μ_3) is desirable because it permits the central bank to dampen the volatility of inflation and output with less adjustment in the short-term rate than otherwise. As Rotemberg and Woodford emphasize (chap. 2 in this volume), raising the serial dependence parameter μ_3 increases the sensitivity of long-term rates to movements in current short-term rates (since it implies a larger adjustment of expected future short rates than otherwise). Smoothing thus increases the potency of a given change in the short rate, since it is ultimately the long-term rate that affects the output gap and (indirectly) inflation. The importance of future expectations to current behavior in this framework tends to enhance the gains from smoothing. The gains would be diminished, for example, if some of the interest rate sensitivity of output was due to the short-term rate, independent of the long-term rate.

Brief Assessment

Overall, I find the analysis appealing and think that the qualitative results I discussed above may survive in richer frameworks. The quantitative results (i.e., what values of the policy rule parameter vector $\{\mu_1, \mu_2, \mu_3\}$ produce the most desirable outcomes) do, however, depend on the model structure. Here I have some concerns. To be fair to the authors, so do they. Neither the IS nor the AS curve appears to offer an adequate characterization of the data.

Three issues arise with the IS curve. First, there are no endogenous dynamics: output depends only the long-term rate and an exogenous forcing process. While admittedly it is difficult to say anything with certainty in macroeconomics, my sense is that the hypothesis of no endogenous output dynamics is unlikely to survive careful empirical scrutiny. Nor is it compelling from a theoretical viewpoint (given the likelihood of adjustment costs and so on). Second, the real interest rate affects the economy only by inducing intertemporal sub-stitution in consumption. The evidence (including many recent identified vec-tor autoregression studies) suggests that durable goods, including housing, autos, and producer durable equipment, bear the main brunt of monetary pol-icy.[1] Thus it is problematic as to whether the authors' model really pins down the correct interest sensitivity of output. Finally, the vector autoregression ev-idence suggests a lag of at least six to nine months in the impact of interest rates on the economy (though some sectors such as housing respond more quickly). In the authors' model, the response is immediate.

I raise these issues not to be picky. Rather, if we are to take seriously the quantitative policy rule that the analysis recommends, it is imperative that we have a (reasonably) correct structural empirical link between short-term rates and the real sector.

The absence of a short-run output-inflation trade-off is a striking implica-tion of the AS curve. It is thus particularly important to assess the reasonable-ness of this relationship. At issue is whether this pure forward-looking formu-lation of price dynamics captures the degree of inflation persistence that is present in the data. Others have raised this concern. There is, however, a rela-tively simple test of this proposition. I turn to this next.

Inflation Persistence in the Calvo-Rotemberg Model: A Simple Test

The aggregate supply curve may be expressed as[2]

$$(6) \qquad \Delta p_t = \lambda(y_t - \bar{y}_t) + \beta \Delta p_{t+1} + \varepsilon_{t+1},$$

where $\varepsilon_{t+1} = -\beta(\Delta p_{t+1} - E_t \Delta p_{t+1})$. Since $E_t \varepsilon_{t+1} = 0$, after controlling for its predictive content for $y_t - \bar{y}_t$ and Δp_{t+1}, no variable dated t or earlier should help predict Δp_t. This implication leads to a simple test that is much in the spirit of Hall's (1978) and Campbell and Mankiw's (1989) test of the consump-tion Euler equation. In particular, consider the instrumental variables estima-tion of the following equation:

$$(7) \qquad \Delta p_t = \pi_1(y_t - \bar{y}_t) + \pi_2 \Delta p_{t+1} + \pi_3 \Delta p_{t-1} + \varepsilon_t$$

under the null of equation (6): $\pi_2 = \beta$ (a number close to one) and $\pi_3 = 0$.

To test the null I proceed as follows: I measure output and inflation using the same data as Rudebusch and Svensson (chap. 5 in this volume). The per-centage change in the GDP deflator is the measure of inflation. The output gap is the percentage deviation of output from a quadratic trend. Each variable is expressed as a deviation from a constant mean. The data is quarterly, over the period 1960:1–97:3. Finally, I use as instruments the lagged output gap and

---

1. For evidence on the responsiveness of the different components of output to monetary policy, see Bernanke and Gertler (1995).
2. The analysis in this section is based on some work in progress with Jordi Galí.

two lags of inflation, all of which are legitimate instruments under the null hypothesis. Instrumental variables estimation of equation (7) then yields

$$(8) \qquad \Delta p_t = 0.030(y_t - \bar{y}_t) + 0.375 \Delta p_{t+1} + 0.585 \Delta p_{t-1},$$
$$\qquad\qquad (0.039) \qquad\qquad (0.148) \qquad (0.125)$$

where the numbers in parentheses are standard errors.

Several results stand out. First, the null is clearly rejected.[3] Lagged inflation has a significant and quantitatively important impact on inflation. A 1 percent rise in the lagged inflation rate lifts current inflation 0.585 percent, everything else equal. The effect is significantly different from zero. This evidence is, at least on the surface, inconsistent with the premise of no short-run output-inflation trade-off. The possible implication is that the authors' analysis may overstate the desirability of rules that react to inflation in a very aggressive manner.

On the other hand, expected future inflation also enters significantly: A 1 percent rise in expected future inflation raises current inflation by 0.319 percent; and the effect differs significantly from zero. Thus the forward-looking aspect of inflation that the model emphasizes is clearly present in the data. Thus I believe that the direction one should take is to build on this framework and not to abandon it. Modifying this model to account for the persistence in inflation should be a priority for future research in this area.[4]

Model 2: "P-Bar" Price Adjustment

The P-bar model begins with the premise that there are quadratic costs of adjusting output relative to capacity. Strictly speaking, however, these costs are in expectation since producers lock in a nominal price ex ante and not output. In response to shocks ex post, the nominal price stays fixed, but output is free to adjust.

---

3. Some qualification of the test is in order. If the excess demand variable, $y_t - \bar{y}_t$, in eq. (7) is measured with error, then it is possible that rejection could occur even if the null is true. Whether measurement error could explain the degree of rejection I find is problematic, however. I note that the results are robust to using the Congressional Budget Office's measure of potential output to construct the output gap. Note also that, in general, the proper measure of excess demand in these models is (detrended) real marginal cost (see, e.g., Goodfriend and King 1997). In the McCallum-Nelson framework the output gap varies proportionally with real marginal cost, so in this instance it is legitimate to use the output gap as the excess demand measure. In work in progress with Jordi Galí, I am exploring how direct use of marginal cost as the excess demand variable affects the results. Preliminary results suggest that (i) marginal cost works better than output as a gap variable (in the sense that the slope coefficient is statistically significant) and (ii) the forward-looking term becomes more important relative to the backward-looking one, though the null model is still rejected.

4. Larry Ball suggested that in analogy to Campbell and Mankiw, the evidence could be explained by inflation being the product of a convex combination of rational forward-looking setters and rule-of-thumb price setters (the latter perhaps being the same individuals who are rule-of-thumb consumers in the Campbell-Mankiw setup).

The Formal Model

In any event, let $\bar{p}_t$ be the nominal price that would arise if prices were perfectly flexible. Then the P-bar model leads to an AS curve of the following form (the IS curve remains the same):

$$(9) \qquad p_t - E_{t-1}\bar{p}_t = \phi(p_{t-1} - \bar{p}_{t-1}),$$

with $0 < \phi < 1$. The gap between the price level and the market-clearing price level closes monotonically.

I am skeptical of this model of price behavior since the market-clearing price level is likely to drive much of the dynamics of the actual price level. Put differently, the behavior of the price level is likely to closely resemble what would be generated by a real business cycle augmented with money. Since this latter type of framework has difficulty accounting for price dynamics, it is my conjecture that the same is likely to be true of the P-bar model.

A Simple Test

As with the Calvo-Rotemberg framework, a simple test of the P-bar specification is available. As the authors show, the model implies that, in expectation, the output gap closes monotonically. That is, equation (9) implies

$$(10) \qquad E_{t-1}(y_t - \bar{y}_t) = \phi(y_{t-1} - \bar{y}_{t-1}).$$

We can then rewrite equation (10) in terms of observables, as follows:

$$(11) \qquad y_t - \bar{y}_t = \phi(y_{t-1} - \bar{y}_{t-1}) + \eta_t,$$

where $\eta_t = (y_t - \bar{y}_t) - E_{t-1}(y_t - \bar{y}_t)$ and, accordingly, $E_{t-1}\eta_t = 0$. Then consider the following regression equation:

$$(12) \qquad y_t - \bar{y}_t = \psi_1(y_{t-1} - \bar{y}_{t-1}) + \psi_2(y_{t-2} - \bar{y}_{t-2}) + \omega_t$$

under the null $0 < \psi_1 < 1$ and $\psi_2 = 0$.

Since under the null the error term is orthogonal to variables dated time t and earlier, it is possible to estimate equation (12) using least squares. Doing so yields

$$(13) \qquad \begin{array}{c} y_t - \bar{y}_t = 1.233(y_{t-1} - \bar{y}_{t-1}) + 0.320(y_{t-2} - \bar{y}_{t-2}), \\ (0.078) \qquad\qquad\qquad (0.078) \end{array}$$

where the standard errors are in parentheses. The model is clearly rejected since ψ_1 is significantly above unity and ψ_2 is significantly above zero. Intuitively, the P-bar model implies that the output gap always converges monotonically to trend in expectation. This is inconsistent with the familiar hump-shaped output dynamics that appear to be present in the data.

Again, I stress that it is a great virtue of the authors' approach that the model is testable in a simple but highly informative way.

Hypothetical versus Historical Policy

I conclude with some remarks about how the hypothetical policy rules that perform best compare with actual historical policy. Least squares estimation of the policy rule (1) over the Volcker-Greenspan regimes (1979:4–97:3) yields

$$
(14) \qquad r_t = \underset{(0.085)}{0.245}\,\Delta p_t + \underset{(0.061)}{0.097}(y_t - \bar{y}_t) + \underset{(0.48)}{(0.860)}r_{t-1},
$$

where r_t is the deviation of the federal funds rate from its mean and, as before, Δp_t is the percentage change in the GDP deflator expressed as a deviation from its sample mean. Also, as before, the numbers in parentheses are standard errors. Note that if we let r_t^* denote the long-run response of the funds rate, then equation (14) implies

$$
(15) \qquad r_t^* = 1.75\,\Delta p_t + 0.68(y_t - \bar{y}_t).
$$

The two gap coefficients are thus in the same ballpark as those used in the simple Taylor rule (1.75 vs. 1.50 on Δp_t and 0.68 vs. 0.50 on $y_t - \bar{y}_t$).

The rules that perform well in the simulations call for a much more aggressive adjustment of rates to inflation than occurs in practice (e.g., 3.000 vs. 0.245) and greater lagged dependence (1.00 vs. 0.86). This conclusion is rather puzzling given that both Volcker and Greenspan have the reputation of being hardnosed about controlling inflation.

The question then arises whether something may be missing from the analysis. As I argued earlier, one possibility is that model misspecification is a factor. For example, given that the aggregate supply curve does not seem to capture the persistence in inflation, the model may understate the output volatility costs of aggressive inflation policies.

Another possibility is that the experiment undertaken does not adequately capture the environment in which policy decisions are made. In particular, in the simulations the model is treated as if it characterizes the way the economy works with certainty, even though it is estimated with error and has a structure that is open to debate. In practice, however, Alan Greenspan does not know how the economy operates with nearly as great confidence as is presumed in the hypothetical experiments. Directly accounting for this uncertainty about the way the world works would seem to be the logical next step in this research agenda.

References

Bernanke, Ben, and Mark Gertler. 1995. Inside the black box: The credit channel of monetary policy transmission. *Journal of Economic Perspectives* 9:27–48.
Calvo, Guillermo. 1983. Staggered prices in a utility maximizing framework. *Journal of Monetary Economics* 12:383–98.

Campbell, John, and N. Gregory Mankiw. 1989. Consumption, income and interest rates: Reinterpreting the time-series evidence. In *NBER macroeconomics Annual 1989*, ed. O. J. Blanchard and S. Fischer, 185–216. Cambridge, Mass.: MIT Press.

Goodfriend, Marvin, and Robert King. 1997. The new neoclassical synthesis. In *NBER macroeconomics annual 1997*, ed. Ben S. Bernanke and Julio J. Rotemberg, 221–82. Cambridge, Mass.: MIT Press.

Hall, Robert. 1978. Stochastic implications of the life-cycle/permanent income hypothesis: Theory and evidence. *Journal of Political Economy* 86 (December): 971–87.

Rotemberg, Julio. 1982. Sticky prices in the United States. *Journal of Political Economy* 90:1187–1211.

Taylor, John. 1980. Aggregate dynamics and staggered contracts. *Journal of Political Economy* 88:195–214.

Discussion Summary

Bob Hall pointed out the fact that potential output is measured by hours per worker, a concept used in the cyclical productivity literature, especially by Susanto Basu. Basu interprets hours per worker as the firm's current position on its upward-sloping marginal cost schedule, which is defined, as in this paper, by adjustment costs. Since hours per worker, however, are much less persistent than unemployment, Hall suggested a more traditional measure of the output gap based on inverting and smoothing Okun's law used in Hall and Taylor (1991). In this case, the output gap is inferred from the unemployment gap. *McCallum* replied that the estimated coefficients of a second-order autoregression of the output gap measure used in the paper are similar to those of unemployment indicating that the two series are equally persistent.

James Stock emphasized the importance of a stable relationship between inflation and whatever measure of potential output is used. In this sense, unemployment or the Federal Reserve's capacity utilization rate may constitute good measures of potential GDP. Stock also suggested estimating the trend in output with more flexible specifications along the lines of Kuttner (1994) and Stock and Watson (1998).

As to the instrumental variables used in the estimations, Stock noted that identification is mostly achieved by the constant, the dummy variables, and the time trend, with the quarterly growth rate of government spending being only a weak instrument. He also suggested that an approach with nonstochastic instruments might be justified with integrated time series, but this would raise a new set of issues not addressed in the paper. Some estimations show Durbin-Watson statistics of below 0.2, which, in combination with the previous argument, indicate the presence of serious econometric problems that may lead to distributional questions and even biased estimates.

Laurence Ball pointed out that Roberts (1997) empirically rejects the model proposed in Roberts (1995) referred to in the paper and constructs a model in which some of the agents have backward-looking expectations. This assumption on expectation formation may be problematic, especially in situations of future policy changes. He then asked whether the coefficients on past and future inflation in the regressions performed in Gertler's discussion could be interpreted as a test of the Roberts (1997) model. *Gertler* cautioned that the coefficients are only consistently estimated under the null, but he agreed with the general intuition.

Ben Friedman remarked that the typical policy rules recommended in these papers seem to be more aggressive than the rules actually employed by central banks. This is to be expected when taking into account the central banks' uncertainty about the true model of the economy. The methodological approach in the literature is to ignore such parameter uncertainty in the derivation of policy implications. However, this uncertainty matters for the Fed's decision making. *Donald Kohn* explained that data observations that are at variance with what the central bank expects may be interpreted both as new shocks to the economy and as misspecifications of the economic model. While prudent behavior by central banks may partially be explained by Brainard uncertainty, what decisions are appropriate in such a situation is mostly still an open question.

Friedman then wondered about the robustness of the results derived in the paper with respect to mismeasurement in inflation. *Nelson* replied that as long as the measurement error in inflation was constant over time, the error would be absorbed into the constant terms in the model's equations. However, Nelson expressed doubts regarding robustness when measurement errors are time varying.

Lars Svensson liked the microfoundations of the paper but criticized its abuse of the notion of targeting. For example, the paper talks about "inflation targeting" and "nominal GDP targeting" when denoting cases in which the respective variables appear as arguments in the central bank's reaction function. Svensson clarified that the arguments of the reaction function are more appropriately called indicator variables, while the arguments of the loss function are more appropriately called targets.

Michael Woodford questioned the microfoundations of the "P-bar" model. Persistence in the effects of a monetary policy shock on output is all explained by the adjustment costs in output. Despite these adjustment costs, output is able to move away from trend because prices are fixed one period in advance. If the adjustment costs are assumed to be high in order to generate a significant persistence in the output response, then it is no longer clear why suppliers match whatever demand is realized without changing prices. Thus large costs in changing prices have to be assumed as well. *McCallum* replied that the P-bar model is the only model presented at the conference that conforms to Lucas's definition of the natural rate hypothesis, which is that monetary policy does not have long-run effects on output relative to capacity.

References

Hall, Robert, and John Taylor. 1991. *Macroeconomics: Theory, performance, and policy.* New York: Norton.

Kuttner, Kenneth N. 1994. Estimating potential output as a latent variable. *Journal of Business and Economic Statistics* 12 (3): 361–68.

Roberts, John M. 1995. New Keynesian economics and the Phillips curve. *Journal of Money, Credit and Banking* 27:975–84.

———. 1997. Is inflation sticky? *Journal of Monetary Economics* 39 (2): 173–96.

Stock, James, and Mark W. Watson. 1998. Median unbiased estimation of coefficient variance in a time varying parameter model. *Journal of the American Statistical Association* 93:349–58.

2 Interest Rate Rules in an Estimated Sticky Price Model

Julio J. Rotemberg and Michael Woodford

This paper seeks to evaluate monetary policy rules that generalize the rule proposed by Taylor (1993). In particular, we consider rules in which the Fed sets the federal funds rate as a function of the history of inflation, output, and the federal funds rate itself. Even though this is not part of Taylor's original formulation, we introduce the possibility that the federal funds rate depends on the history of the funds rate itself in order to allow for interest rate smoothing of the kind that appears to be an important feature of current Fed policy. We also consider the character of optimal policy, that is, the policy that maximizes the utility of the representative agent, assuming unlimited information about the exogenous disturbances to the economy. We then compare optimal policy in this unrestricted sense with the best rule of the generalized Taylor family.

We evaluate these rules under the assumption that interest rate, inflation, and output determination in the U.S. economy can be compactly represented by the small structural model whose parameters we estimate in Rotemberg and Woodford (1997). This is a rational expectations model derived from explicit intertemporal optimization, in which firms are unable to change their prices every period, and in which purchases are determined somewhat in advance of when they actually take place. In evaluating different monetary rules we use two approaches. The first approach is simply to compute the welfare of the

Julio J. Rotemberg is the MBA Class of 1942 Professor of Business Administration at the Harvard Business School and a research associate of the National Bureau of Economic Research. Michael Woodford is the Harold Helm '20 Professor of Economics and Banking at Princeton University and a research associate of the National Bureau of Economic Research.

The authors thank Marc Giannoni for excellent research assistance and Larry Christiano, Martin Feldstein, Hans Genberg, Mark Gertler, Marvin Goodfriend, Huw Pill, Argia Sbordone, Lars Svensson, and John Taylor for comments. They also thank the Harvard Business School Division of Research and the National Science Foundation, through a grant to the NBER, for research support.

representative household according to our model of the U.S. economy. Because this places great strain on the assumptions that the model contains accurate descriptions of the preferences of American residents, and that we have correctly identified the nature of the real disturbances to which monetary stabilization policy must respond, we also study separately the variability of output, inflation, and interest rates induced by different policy rules. This latter way of characterizing economic performance under alternative rules is less dependent on the "deep structural" interpretation of the residuals in our structural equations, although it is, of course, still dependent on the specification of those structural equations and on the statistical properties of their disturbance terms.

We proceed as follows. In section 2.1, we describe the structure of the model, which is discussed more thoroughly in Rotemberg and Woodford (1997, 1998). Section 2.2 is devoted to the analysis of simple policy rules that represent variations on the rule proposed by Taylor (1993), while section 2.3 considers optimal policy. Section 2.4 concludes.

2.1 A Framework for Analysis

We begin by reviewing the structure of the estimated sticky price model developed in Rotemberg and Woodford (1997). This also allows us to derive the utility-based measure of deadweight loss due to price level instability that is the basis for our subsequent discussion of optimal policy.

2.1.1 A Small, Structural Model of the U.S. Economy

We suppose that there is a continuum of households indexed by i, where i runs between 0 and 1. Each of these households produces a single good while it consumes the composite good. The utility of household i at t is given by

$$(1) \qquad E_t \sum_{T=t}^{\infty} \beta^{T-t}[u(C_T^i;\xi_T) - v(y_T^i;\xi_T)],$$

where β is a discount rate, y_t^i is the household's production of its own good, and ξ_t is a vector of preference (or technological) disturbances. The argument C_t^i represents an index of the household's purchases of the continuum of differentiated goods produced in the economy. Following Dixit and Stiglitz (1977), this index is given by

$$(2) \qquad C_T^i \equiv \left[\int_0^1 c_T^i(z)^{(\theta-1)/\theta} dz \right]^{\theta/(\theta-1)},$$

where $c_t^i(z)$ is the quantity purchased of good z and the constant elasticity of substitution θ is assumed to be greater than one. We assume that all purchasers, including the government, care only about an aggregate of the form (2). As usual, this implies that the total demand $y_t(z)$ for differentiated good z is given by a constant-elasticity demand function

$$(3) \qquad\qquad y_t^z = Y_t \left(\frac{p_t(z)}{P_t} \right)^{-\theta} ,$$

where $p_t(z)$ is the period t price of good z, P_t is the price index defined by

$$(4) \qquad\qquad P_t \equiv \left[\int_0^1 p_t(z)^{1-\theta} dz \right]^{1/(1-\theta)} ,$$

and Y_t measures aggregate demand for the composite good defined by equation (2).

One of the delays we assume is that households must choose their index of purchases C_t^i at date $t - 2$. As we show in Rotemberg and Woodford (1997) this, or an assumption like it, seems necessary if one wishes to explain the response of U.S. GDP to monetary disturbances, because this response is itself delayed by about two quarters. This delay implies that the standard Euler equation for optimal intertemporal allocation of consumption spending need not hold, except (approximately) conditional on information available two periods in advance. Because C_t^i is chosen in advance, household optimization requires only

$$(5) \qquad\qquad E_t[u_C(C_{t+2}^i; \xi_{t+2})] = E_t(\lambda_{t+2}^i P_{t+2}),$$

where λ_t^i is a Lagrange multiplier indicating the marginal utility for household i of additional nominal income in period t. Assuming borrowing limits that never bind in equilibrium, these marginal utilities of income must satisfy

$$(6) \qquad\qquad \lambda_t^i = \beta R_t E_t \lambda_{t+1}^i ,$$

where R_t is the gross return on a riskless nominal one-period asset in which the household invests at t. We assume the existence of complete insurance markets, so that all households consume the same amount at any time and have the same marginal utility of income. Then equations (5) and (6) also hold when we drop the i superscripts and interpret them as equations relating aggregate consumption C_t to the marginal utility of income λ_t of the representative household. However, because of the conditional expectations in equation (5), these two equations still do not imply the standard Euler equation relating aggregate consumption spending in two consecutive periods to the real rate of return between those two periods. Finally, substituting into equation (5) the equilibrium requirement that $C_t = Y_t - G_t$, where G_t represents exogenous variation in government purchases of the composite good, we obtain an equilibrium relation between the index of aggregate demand Y_t and variations in the marginal utility of income, which provides the crucial link in our model between interest rate variations and aggregate demand.

For our numerical work, we rely on log-linear approximations to the model's structural equations. We assume an equilibrium in which the economy always stays near a steady state path, which represents a stationary, deterministic equilibrium in the case of no exogenous disturbances ($\xi_t = 0$ and $G_t = \overline{G}$ at all times) and a monetary policy consistent with stable prices. In this steady state, output is constant at a level $\overline{Y}$ (defined below), and consumption is constant at the level $\overline{C} \equiv \overline{Y} - \overline{G}$.[1] It follows that the marginal utility of *real* income, $\lambda_t P_t$, is also constant, at the value $\overline{\lambda} \equiv u_C(\overline{C};0)$. We log-linearize the structural equations of the model around these steady state values. Percentage deviations in the marginal utility of consumption $u_C(C_t;\xi_t)$ around the steady state value u_C $(\overline{C};0)$ can be written as $-\tilde{\sigma}(\hat{C}_t - \overline{C}_t)$, where $\hat{C}_t \equiv \log(C_t/\overline{C})$, $\overline{C}_t$ is an exogenous shift variable (a certain linear combination of the elements of ξ_t),[2] and $\tilde{\sigma} \equiv -u_{CC}\overline{C}/u_C$, where the partial derivatives are evaluated at the steady state level of consumption. With this substitution, the log-linear approximations to equations (5) and (6) are given by

(7)
$$-\tilde{\sigma}E_{t-2}(\hat{C}_t - \overline{C}_t) = E_{t-2}\hat{\lambda}_t,$$

(8)
$$\hat{\lambda}_t = \hat{R}_t - \pi_{t+1} + E_t\hat{\lambda}_{t+1},$$

where $\hat{R}_t \equiv \log(R_t/R^*) = \log(\beta R_t)$ is the percentage deviation of the short-run nominal interest rate from its steady state value, $\pi_t \equiv \log(P_t/P_{t-1})$ is the inflation rate, and $\hat{\lambda}_t \equiv \log(\lambda_t P_t/\overline{\lambda})$ measures the percentage deviation of the marginal utility of real income from its steady state value. (Eq. [8] refers to actual rather than expected inflation because inflation π_{t+1} is known with certainty at date t in our model.)

A similar log-linear approximation to the market-clearing condition allows us to replace $\hat{C}_t - E_{t-2}\overline{C}_t$ with $s_C^{-1}(\hat{Y}_t - \hat{G}_t)$, where $s_C \equiv \overline{C}/\overline{Y}$, $\hat{Y}_t \equiv \log(Y_t/\overline{Y})$, and $\hat{G}_t$ collects the exogenous disturbance terms that shift the relation between aggregate demand and the marginal utility of consumption. Substituting this into equation (7) yields

(9)
$$E_{t-2}\hat{\lambda}_t = -\sigma E_{t-2}(\hat{Y}_t - \hat{G}_t),$$

where $\sigma \equiv s_C^{-1}\tilde{\sigma}$. Then taking the conditional expectation of equation (8) two periods earlier and substituting equation (9), we obtain

(10) $$E_{t-2}(\hat{Y}_t - \hat{G}_t) = -\sigma^{-1}E_{t-2}(\hat{R}_t - \pi_{t+1}) + E_{t-2}(\hat{Y}_{t+1} - \hat{G}_{t+1}).$$

(Thus, in our log-linear approximation, the standard Euler equation does hold, but only conditional on lagged information.) Solving forward, we may equivalently write

1. Throughout these derivations, we assume an economy with zero growth for simplicity. More properly, we assume a deterministic trend for real activity, and variables such as Y_t refer to detrended values, which take constant values in the steady state. In our estimation of the model, we use a series for $\hat{Y}_t$ obtained by removing a linear trend from the log of real GDP.

2. Details of this and other aspects of our Taylor series expansions are presented more fully in the appendix.

(11) $\hat{Y}_t = \hat{G}_t - \sigma^{-1} E_{t-2} \sum_{T=t}^{\infty} (\hat{R}_T - \pi_{T+1})$.

Equation (11) plays a role analogous to the "IS equation" of traditional Keynesian models but is consistent with intertemporal optimization.[3] It relates output to the long-run real interest rate (with a negative sign) and to autonomous spending disturbances. The latter include disturbances both to private impatience to consume resources and to government spending, summarized in the composite disturbance term $\hat{G}_t$. We assume that $\hat{G}_t$ is determined at $t - 1$, so that it is determined after C_t has already been chosen, but in time for the central bank to adjust the period t interest rate R_t in response to it. Letting $\hat{G}_t$ be determined after $\hat{C}_t$ ensures that output is not predetermined as of $t - 2$ (i.e., it allows us an interpretation for the output innovations in our vector autoregression—VAR—model of the U.S. data), even though output responds with a two-period delay to exogenous disturbances to monetary policy.

The source of the real effects of monetary policy in our model is that prices do not adjust immediately to shocks. Following Calvo (1983), we assume that prices are changed at exogenous random intervals.[4] Specifically, a fraction $1 - \alpha$ of sellers get to choose new prices at the end of any given period, whereas the others must continue using their old prices. Of those who get to choose new prices, a fraction γ start charging the new price at the beginning of the next period. The remaining fraction $1 - \gamma$ must wait until the following period to charge the new price, or put differently, they must post their prices one quarter in advance. These assumed delays explain why no prices respond in the quarter of the monetary disturbance and why the largest response of inflation to a monetary shock takes place only two quarters after the shock.

Let p_t^1 denote the price set by sellers that decide at date $t - 1$ on a new price to take effect at date t, and p_t^2 the price set by sellers that decide at date $t - 2$ on a new price to take effect only two periods later. These prices are chosen to maximize the contributions to expected utility resulting from sales revenues on the one hand, and the disutility of output supply on the other, at each of the future dates and in each of the future states in which the price commitment still applies. This means that p_t^1 is chosen to maximize

(12) $\Phi_{t-1}(p) \equiv E_{t-1} \sum_{T=t}^{\infty} (\alpha\beta)^{T-t} [\lambda_T (1 - \tau) p Y_T (p/P_T)^{-\theta} - v(Y_T(p/P_T)^{-\theta}; \xi_T)]$

over p. Here we have substituted the demand function (3) into the household's objective function, written λ_T for the marginal utility (in units of period T util-

---

3. Except for our introduction of the two-period delay in the determination of interest-sensitive purchases, our derivation of this "expectational IS equation" follows the earlier work of authors such as Koenig (1987), Kerr and King (1996), McCallum and Nelson (forthcoming), and Woodford (1996).
4. This general approach to modeling the dynamics of price adjustment is adopted in a large number of recent quantitative equilibrium business cycle studies, beginning with Yun (1996) and King and Watson (1996).

ity flow) of additional nominal income during period T, and assumed that revenues each period are taxed at the constant rate τ.[5] The factor α^{T-t} appears as the probability that the price that is charged beginning in period t is still in effect in period $T \geq t$ (where we assume that this contingency is independent of all aggregate disturbances). Note that our assumption of complete contingent claims markets (including full opportunities for households to insure one another against idiosyncratic risk associated with different timing of their price changes) implies that the marginal utility of income process $\{\lambda_T\}$ is the same for all households and can be treated as an exogenous stochastic process by an individual household (whose pricing decisions will have only a negligible effect on aggregate prices, aggregate incomes, and aggregate spending decisions). Similarly, an individual household treats the processes $\{P_T, Y_T\}$ as exogenous in choosing its desired price. The optimizing choice of p_t^1 then must satisfy the first-order condition

(13)
$$\Phi'_{t-1}(p_t^1) = 0,$$

where the prime denotes the derivative with respect to p in the explicit expression given in equation (12).

As before, we wish to log-linearize this equilibrium condition around a steady state in which $Y_t = \overline{Y}$, $P_t/P_{t-1} = 1$, $p_t^1/P_t = 1$, and $\lambda_t P_t = \overline{\lambda}$ at all times. (The requirement that these constant values satisfy equation [13] when $\xi_t = 0$ at all times determines the steady state value $\overline{Y}$.)[6] Percentage deviations of $v_y(y_t^j; \xi_t)$ from its steady state value can be written as $\omega(\hat{y}_t^j - \overline{Y}_t)$, where $\omega \equiv v_{yy}\overline{Y}/v_y$, with partial derivatives evaluated at the steady state, $\hat{y}_t^j \equiv \log(y_t^j/\overline{Y})$, and $\overline{Y}_t$ is a certain linear function of ξ_t. Using this notation, the log-linear approximation to equation (13) takes the form

(14)
$$E_{t-1}\sum_{T=t}^{\infty} (\alpha\beta)^{T-t}[(\hat{\lambda}_T + \hat{Y}_T - (\theta - 1)\hat{p}_{t,T}^1)$$
$$- \omega(\hat{Y}_T - \theta\hat{p}_{t,T}^1 - \overline{Y}_T) - (\hat{Y}_T - \theta\hat{p}_{t,T}^1)] = 0,$$

where in addition $\hat{p}_{t,T}^1 \equiv \log(p_t^1/P_T)$. Introducing the notation[7]

$$\hat{X}_t \equiv \frac{1 - \alpha}{\alpha}\log\left(\frac{p_t^1}{P_t}\right),$$

so that

---

5. The allowance for nonzero τ is primarily so that we can linearize around a steady state in which the constant level of output is efficient. The convenience of this for our purposes is discussed in the appendix.

6. Under the assumption that $\tau = -(\theta - 1)^{-1}$, this requires that $\overline{Y}$ satisfy the equation $u_c(\overline{Y} - \overline{G}; 0) = v_y(\overline{Y}; 0)$, which also defines the efficient level of output.

7. The factor $(1 - \alpha)/\alpha$ turns out to be convenient in giving a simpler form to equations such as eq. (20) below.

$$\hat{p}^1_{t,T} = \frac{\alpha}{1 - \alpha}\hat{X}_t - \sum_{s=t+1}^{T} \pi_s \, ,$$

we can solve equation (14) to obtain

(15)
$$\hat{X}_t = \frac{1 - \alpha}{\alpha}\frac{1 - \alpha\beta}{1 + \omega\theta} E_{t-1}\sum_{T=t}^{\infty} (\alpha\beta)^{T-t}[-\hat{\lambda}_T + \omega(\hat{Y}_T - \bar{Y}_T)$$
$$+ (1 + \omega\theta)\sum_{s=t+1}^{T} \pi_s]$$

as the optimizing choice of the relative price in period t of goods with new prices chosen just the period before.

We can use equation (9) to eliminate the $E_{t-1}\hat{\lambda}_T$ terms in equation (15), for all $T > t$. Taking the conditional expectation of equation (8) at $t - 1$ and using equation (9), we see that we can also write

(16)
$$E_{t-1}\hat{\lambda}_t = \phi_{t-1} - \sigma E_{t-1}(\hat{Y}_t - \hat{G}_t),$$

where

(17)
$$\phi_t \equiv E_t[\hat{R}_{t+1} - \pi_{t+2} - \sigma(\hat{Y}_{t+2} - \hat{G}_{t+2} - \hat{Y}_{t+1} + \hat{G}_{t+1})]$$
$$= E_t\sum_{T=t+1}^{\infty} (\hat{R}_T - \pi_{T+1}) - E_{t-1}\sum_{T=t+1}^{\infty} (\hat{R}_T - \pi_{T+1}).$$

Note that the final equality in expression (17) follows from substitution of (11). Then, substituting equations (9) and (16) into (15), we obtain

(18)
$$\hat{X}_t = \frac{1 - \alpha}{\alpha}\frac{1 - \alpha\beta}{1 + \omega\theta}\left\{E_{t-1}\sum_{T=t}^{\infty} (\alpha\beta)^{T-t}[(\sigma + \omega)(\hat{Y}_T - \hat{Y}_T^S)\right.$$
$$+ (1 + \omega\theta)\sum_{s=t+1}^{T} \pi_s] - \phi_{t-1}\bigg\}$$
$$= \frac{1 - \alpha}{\alpha}\frac{1 - \alpha\beta}{1 + \omega\theta}\left\{E_{t-1}\sum_{T=t}^{\infty} (\alpha\beta)^{T-t}[(\sigma + \omega)(\hat{Y}_T - \hat{Y}_T^S)\right.$$
$$+ (1 + \omega\theta)\frac{\alpha\beta}{1 - \alpha\beta}\pi_{T+1}] - \phi_{t-1}\bigg\},$$

where

$$\hat{Y}_t^S \equiv \frac{\omega}{\omega + \sigma}E_{t-1}\bar{Y}_t + \frac{\sigma}{\omega + \sigma}\hat{G}_t$$

is a composite exogenous disturbance. We can think of $\hat{Y}_t^S$ as representing variation in the "natural" or "potential" level of output, since it is expected deviations $\hat{Y} - \hat{Y}^S$, rather than deviations in the level of output relative to trend, that results in a desire by price setters to increase the *relative* price of their goods, which in equilibrium requires inflation of the average level of prices. (An equilibrium in which no prices are ever changed is consistent with eq. [18] as long as $\hat{Y}_t = \hat{Y}_t^s$ at all times and interest rates vary so as to ensure that $\phi_t = 0$ at all times. Note that the latter condition ensures that eq. [10] and hence [11] is also satisfied at all times.)

We turn next to the price-setting decision of sellers that choose a new price p_t^2 at $t - 2$ to apply beginning in period t. Because such a price is expected to apply in periods $t + j$ with exactly the same probabilities as for the price p_t^1, the objective of these sellers is simply $E_{t-2}\Phi_{t-1}(p)$, and the first-order condition that determines p_t^2 is given by $E_{t-2}\Phi_{t-1}(p_t^2) = 0$. Comparison with equation (13) implies that, in our log-linear approximation,

$$(19) \qquad \log p_t^2 = E_{t-2} \log p_t^1.$$

Finally, our definition of the price index (4) implies that this index evolves according to

$$P_t = [\alpha P_{t-1}^{1-\theta} + (1 - \alpha)\gamma(p_t^1)^{1-\theta} + (1 - \alpha)(1 - \gamma)(p_t^2)^{1-\theta}]^{1/(1-\theta)}.$$

Dividing both sides by P_t, log-linearizing, and substituting equation (19), we obtain

$$\pi_t = \gamma \hat{X}_t + (1 - \gamma)\left[E_{t-2}\hat{X}_t - \frac{1 - \alpha}{\alpha}(\pi_t - E_{t-2}\pi_t)\right].$$

Taking the conditional expectation of both sides at $t - 2$, one observes that $E_{t-2}\pi_t = E_{t-2}\hat{X}_t$. Substitution of this then allows the equation to be written in the form

$$(20) \qquad \pi_t = \psi \hat{X}_t + (1 - \psi)E_{t-2}\hat{X}_t,$$

where $\psi \equiv \gamma\alpha/[1 - \gamma(1 - \alpha)]$. This indicates how aggregate inflation results from the incentives of individual price setters to choose a higher relative price.

These results may be collected in the form of an implied aggregate supply relation between inflation variation and deviations of output from potential. Equation (18) may be expressed in quasi-differenced form as

$$
\begin{aligned}
\hat{X}_t &= \kappa(\hat{Y}_t - \hat{Y}_t^s) + (1 - \alpha)\beta E_{t-1}\pi_{t+1} + \alpha\beta E_{t-1}\hat{X}_{t+1} - \frac{\kappa}{\sigma + \omega}\phi_{t-1} \\
&= \kappa(\hat{Y}_t - \hat{Y}_t^s) + \beta E_{t-1}\hat{X}_{t+1} - \frac{\kappa}{\sigma + \omega}\phi_{t-1},
\end{aligned}
$$
(21)

where $\kappa \equiv (1 - \alpha)(1 - \alpha\beta)(\omega + \sigma)/\alpha(1 + \omega\theta)$, and the second line follows from the fact that equation (20) implies that $E_{t-2}\pi_t = E_{t-2}\hat{X}_t$. Solving this forward, we obtain

$$\hat{X}_t = \kappa E_{t-1}\left[\sum_{T=t}^{\infty} \beta^{T-t}(\hat{Y}_T - \hat{Y}_T^s)\right] - \frac{\kappa}{\sigma + \omega}\phi_{t-1},$$

where we have used the fact that equation (17) implies that $E_{t-1}\phi_t = 0$. Substitution of this into equation (20) then yields

$$
\begin{aligned}
\pi_t = (1 - \psi)E_{t-2}\pi_t &+ \psi\Big\{\kappa E_{t-1}\sum_{T=t}^{\infty}\beta^{T-t}(\hat{Y}_T - \hat{Y}_T^S) \\
&- \frac{\kappa}{\omega + \sigma}\Big[E_{t-1}\sum_{T=t}^{\infty}(\hat{R}_T - \pi_{T+1}) - E_{t-2}\sum_{T=t}^{\infty}(\hat{R}_T - \pi_{T+1})\Big]\Big\}.
\end{aligned}
$$
(22)

This is our aggregate supply (AS) equation, relating inflation variation to deviations of output from potential. Because prices are set in advance, expectations of future increases in output relative to Y^S also raise prices. In addition, inflation declines when the long-term real interest rate at t is higher than had been expected at $t - 1$. The reason for this is that such upward revisions raise the returns households can expect to earn from their revenues at t. As a result, they are inclined to raise these revenues by cutting their prices. Only surprise variations in the long rate contribute to this term because only those variations result in changes in the current marginal utility of income that are not reflected in the current level of aggregate consumption demand, and hence in the output gap.

To complete our model specification, we posit that interest rates are set according to a feedback rule of the form

$$
(23) \quad r_t - r^* = \sum_{j=0}^{m_\pi} a_j(\pi_{t-j} - \pi^*) + \sum_{j=0}^{m_Y} b_j\hat{Y}_{t-j} + \sum_{j=1}^{m_R} c_j(r_{t-j} - r^*).
$$

Here r_t is the continuously compounded nominal interest rate (identified with log R_t in terms of our theoretical model, and with the federal funds rate in our empirical implementation of the model), r^* is the steady state value of r implied by the policy rule, and π^* is the steady state inflation rate implied by the rule. In equilibrium, the steady state nominal interest rate r^* must equal the sum of the equilibrium steady state real interest rate ρ and the steady state inflation rate π^*. Thus, if ρ is independent of the monetary policy rule (as our model implies),[8] the monetary authority's choice of π^* implies a value for r^*. Thus the pair of values π^* and r^* represent only a single free parameter in the specification of the policy rule, which we shall treat in the subsequent discussion as the choice of π^*.[9]

The aim of our paper is to discuss the effects of alternative rules of the form

8. Up to the log-linear approximation used in all of our computations of the equilibria associated with alternative policy rules, the steady state real interest rate is given by $\rho = -\log\beta$, as a consequence of eq. (6).

9. We need not assume that the monetary authority actually knows the true value of ρ. The rule (23) involves a single constant term $K = (1 - \sum_j c_j)r^* - \sum_j a_j\pi^*$, and it is this that the authority must know in order to implement the rule. However, according to our model, a given value of K implies (generically) a unique value of π^* (which may or may not be correctly estimated by the authority). We choose to parameterize alternative policy rules in terms of π^* rather than in terms of K because of the simpler interpretation of the latter parameter.

(23). In our discussion, we will generally treat separately the effects of the parameters a_j, b_j, and c_j, which indicate how the interest rate reacts to the history of the economy, and the effects of the choice of π^*. This is because, in our log-linear approximation to the model's equilibrium conditions, the parameter π^* has no effect on the implied responses to shocks (and hence on the equilibrium variability of the various state variables), while the parameters a_j, b_j, and c_j have no effect on the implied steady state (and hence on the average equilibrium values of the state variables). We may thus study separately the determination of the steady state and the determination of fluctuations around the steady state, and different parameters of the policy rule matter for each of these investigations. Our overall welfare criterion (discussed in the next subsection) depends, however, on both aspects of equilibrium, and so on both sets of policy parameters.

Our complete model of the economy consists of the IS and AS equations (11) and (22) together with the monetary policy rule (23). To evaluate the effect of changing the monetary rule we need to know both the parameters of the model as well as the stochastic process for the two structural disturbances $\hat{G}_t$ and $\hat{Y}_t^s$, the first of which affects only our IS equation while the second affects only our AS equation. In Rotemberg and Woodford (1997, 1998) we describe both our method for estimating and calibrating the behavioral parameters and our approach to reconstructing the structural disturbances and their stochastic process. Here we give an outline of this approach.

We start with a recursive VAR model of the state vector[10]

$$(24) \qquad Z_t = [\hat{r}_t, \hat{\pi}_{t+1}, \hat{Y}_{t+1}]',$$

where $\hat{r}_t \equiv r_t - r^*$ and $\hat{\pi}_t \equiv \pi_t - \pi^*$.[11] We estimate a system of the form

$$(25) \qquad \overline{Z}_t = B\overline{Z}_{t-1} + U\overline{e}_t,$$

where the vector $\overline{Z}_t$ is the transpose of $[Z_t', Z_{t-1}', Z_{t-2}']$ and U is a lower triangular matrix with ones on the diagonal and nonzero off-diagonal elements only in the first three rows, the off-diagonal elements of which are estimated so as to make the residuals in $\overline{e}_t$ orthogonal to one another. The first three rows of the vectors $\overline{e}_t$ contain the VAR residuals $e_{1,t}$, $e_{2,t}$, and $e_{3,t}$, while the other elements are zero. The number of lags included in our VAR is sufficient to eliminate nearly all evidence of serial correlation in the disturbances.

The first equation in this VAR is our estimate of the monetary policy rule.

---

10. In fact, we estimate a VAR model of r_t and π_t that includes constant terms in the equations and use these constant terms to obtain our econometric estimates of r^* and π^*. The latter estimates then imply our estimated value for the model parameter ρ (and hence β). In the exposition here, we drop the constant terms for simplicity.

11. Note that, with these definitions, $\hat{r}_t = \hat{R}_t - \pi^*$. The difference in the definitions follows from the difference in the rate of inflation in the steady state with respect to which deviations are calculated under the two definitions. It is also worth noting that $\hat{r}_t$ bears the same relation to $\hat{R}_t$ as $\hat{\pi}_t$ bears to π_t.

This estimated rule has the same structure as rule (23), except that it also includes a white noise residual $e_{1,t}$. Note that while the interest rate comes first in the casual ordering, the timing of the variables ensures that the interest rate in period t responds to inflation and output in period t, while these variables only react to lagged interest rates. We suppose that $e_{1,t}$ is independent of the two "real" disturbances $\hat{Y}_t^s$ and $\hat{G}_t$, so that it is exclusively a monetary policy disturbance. (Note that these identifying assumptions are ones that are implied by the decision lags assumed in our theoretical model.) Under these assumptions, we can estimate not only the coefficients of the historical monetary policy rule but also the impulse responses of output, inflation, and the interest rate to a monetary policy disturbance. We can then recover most of the structural parameters of our model by minimizing the discrepancy between the estimated responses of these variables to the monetary disturbance $e_{1,t}$ and the responses predicted by our theoretical model when the systematic part of the monetary policy rule is given by the estimated coefficients in equation (23).[12] By calibrating the remaining parameters on the basis of other evidence, we obtain numerical values for the model parameters α, β, γ, σ, θ, and ω. These are, respectively, 0.66, 0.99, 0.63, 0.16, 7.88, and 0.47, so that κ equals 0.024 and ψ equals 0.53.

Armed with our parameter values and the VAR, we can reconstruct the stochastic processes for the structural disturbances as follows.[13] Equation (11) gives $\hat{G}_t$ as the sum of $\hat{Y}_t$ and σ times the expected long-term real rate. Given that the VAR allows us to forecast both inflation and interest rates, this expected long-term real rate is a function of $\overline{Z}_t$. Similarly, solving equation (20) for $\hat{X}_t$ as a function of inflation and expected inflation, and substituting this into (21), we find that $\hat{Y}_t^s$ must be given by

$$\hat{Y}_t^s = \hat{Y}_t - \frac{1}{\kappa\psi}\pi_t + \frac{1-\psi}{\kappa\psi}E_{t-2}\pi_t + \frac{\beta}{\kappa}E_{t-1}\pi_{t+1} - \frac{1}{\omega+\sigma}\phi_{t-1}.$$

Furthermore, using equation (17), the last term in this equation can be written as a function of expectations of future interest rates and inflation rates, as of periods $t-1$ and $t-2$. Using the VAR to forecast future variables, the right-hand side of the equation then depends just on $\overline{Z}_{t-1}$, on $\overline{Z}_{t-2}$, and on the model parameters. It is thus straightforward to use the structural parameters as well as the matrices B and U to compute matrices C and D such that

(26) $s_t \equiv [\hat{G}_{t+1}, \hat{Y}_{t+1}^s]' = C\overline{Z}_{t-1} + D\overline{e}_t.$

The resulting historical time series for the two disturbances s_t could then be identified with the residuals of the model's structural equations.

If the model fit the properties of the U.S. time series perfectly, the vector s_t

12. Our estimation strategy is discussed in more detail in appendix 1 of Rotemberg and Woodford (1998).

13. Rotemberg and Woodford (1998) provides more details about both this method of construction and the properties of the constructed series.

constructed in this way would be orthogonal to the identified monetary policy disturbance $e_{1,t}$. In practice, the right-hand side of equation (26) does depend on the first element of the vector of VAR residuals $\bar{e}_t$, which we identify as the monetary policy disturbance. Perhaps more troubling is the observation that if the real disturbances s_t are generated by a law of motion of the kind implied by conjoining equation (26) with equation (25) for the evolution of $\bar{Z}_t$, then we should not expect all three of the independent structural disturbances $\bar{e}_t$ that matter for the evolution of s_t to be revealed by data on the three variables in Z_t alone. (This is because one of the VAR innovations corresponds to the monetary policy shock, so that only the other two orthogonal innovations can reveal information about the real disturbances.) But this would mean that forecasts of the future values of the variables in Z_t using the VAR should not correspond, in principle, to the expectations of these variables conditional on the public's information set (assuming that the public has complete information about the structural disturbances); and thus our method for identifying the historical series for our structural equation residuals would not be internally consistent.

We prefer instead to work with a theoretical model not subject to this last problem, that is, one in which the evolution of the real disturbances s_t depends only on two orthogonal disturbances each period, which then should in principle correspond to the two VAR residuals $\bar{e}_{2t}$ and $\bar{e}_{3t}$. The structural disturbances s_t of our theoretical model then have moments that do not correspond precisely to those of the residuals of our model equations; but this discrepancy will exist only insofar as our model (quite apart from the law of motion chosen for the structural disturbances) is in fact inconsistent with the estimated VAR (and in particular, with the estimated impulse responses to a monetary policy shock). We accordingly consider a law of motion

$$(27) \qquad s_t = CZ^{\dagger}_{t-1} + D^{\dagger}e^{\dagger}_t$$

for the structural disturbances, where the matrix C is the one referred to in equation (26), $D\dagger$ corresponds to D with the first column deleted, and $e^{\dagger}_t$ is a vector of two orthogonal white noise disturbances (which correspond to $\bar{e}_{2t}$ and $\bar{e}_{3t}$). Here $Z^{\dagger}_t$ is a vector of exogenous state variables that evolve according to

$$(28) \qquad Z^{\dagger}_t = BZ^{\dagger}_{t-1} + U^{\dagger}e^{\dagger}_t,$$

where B is the same as in equation (25) and $U^{\dagger}$ corresponds to U with the first column deleted.

Note that because the elements of $Z^{\dagger}_t$ refer to exogenous states (underlying states for the dynamics of the real disturbances s_t), unlike the elements of Z_t (which correspond to endogenous variables of our model), this specification does *not* imply the existence of any feedback from the evolution of the endogenous variables to the exogenous disturbance processes s_t. What this construction *does* guarantee is that the empirical impulse response functions of infla-tion, output, and interest rates to the two VAR disturbances orthogonal to the monetary policy shock are identical to the impulse responses predicted by our theoretical model. This property of the predicted impulse responses is inde-pendent of the structural parameters assumed in the model. Thus, given this method for constructing the laws of motion for the real disturbances, only the estimated responses to the monetary policy shock contain any information that can be used to help identify the structural parameters. This is our justification for the strategy that we use for parameter estimation, mentioned above.

It is worth noting that the stochastic processes for the real disturbances that we obtain with this method imply a great deal of variability for both $\hat{G}_t$ and $\hat{Y}_t^s$. For example, the standard deviations of these two series are 29.5 and 13.7 percent, respectively.[14] This extreme volatility is consistent with the fact that the literature reports many "failures" in fitting equations very similar to our IS and AS curves by either ordinary least squares or by using lags as instruments. Our interpretation of these "failures" is that they say simply that these equa-tions are subject to disturbances whose variance is large and whose serial cor-relation pattern is rich (so that they are correlated with the lags that are used as instruments).

In this paper, we evaluate monetary rules by evaluating how well they per-form when the economy is buffeted by these shocks to $\hat{G}$ and $\hat{Y}^s$. In other words, we are asking how the U.S. economy would perform if it were subject to structural disturbances whose properties are the same as those that have affected it in the past while, at the same time, the way interest rates are set by the central bank is different. Because the structural equations (11) and (22) follow simply from the Euler equations for optimal intertemporal behavior on the part of households, and so can be derived without reference to any particu-lar specification of the monetary policy rule, they should remain invariant un-der contemplated changes in that rule. Thus our stochastic simulation method-ology responds to the Lucas (1976) critique of more traditional methods of econometric policy evaluation.[15]

---

14. This compares, e.g., with a standard deviation of only 2.1 percent for our detrended output process $\hat{Y}_t$. The high volatility of the constructed $\hat{G}_t$ process is mainly due to its high serial correla-tion (serial correlation coefficient of .92), rather than to extraordinary volatility of the $\hat{G}_t$ innova-tions, which correspond in fact to the $\hat{Y}_t$ innovations in our VAR model. It is possible that the data would be better described by a model in which C_t, $\overline{C}_t$, and G_t are not required to have a common deterministic trend. The volatility of the constructed $\hat{Y}_t^s$ process, instead, is largely due to the presence of a very volatile transitory component. E.g., the standard deviation of $E_{t-2}\hat{Y}_t^s$ is only 4.3 percent.

15. It should go without saying that this does not imply that the model is necessarily correct. If our model is incorrectly specified, changes in the monetary policy rule will have effects other than those implied by our analysis. What makes the model preferable to purely backward-looking mod-els is that, as stressed by Lucas (1976), it is highly implausible that purely backward-looking specifications of IS and AS curves will remain invariant with respect to changes in the monetary rule.

2.1.2   The Welfare Loss from Price Level Instability

One of the primary advantages of our derivation of our structural equations from explicit optimizing foundations is that we are able to evaluate alternative monetary policy rules in terms of their welfare effects. Specifically, we consider the effects on the average level of welfare

$$(29) \qquad W = E\left(u(C_t;\xi_t) - \int_0^1 v(y_t(z);\xi_t)dz\right)$$

in the stationary equilibrium associated with one or another policy rule within the class that we consider.

Here the expectation is over alternative possible histories of the preference shocks ξ_t (which include the effects of technology shocks, since technological possibilities are implicit in our assumed disutility of supplying output). We only consider the welfare associated with alternative stationary rational expectations equilibria, in which all relative quantities are stationary and all quantities are trend stationary. Thus we can evaluate an unconditional expectation in expression (29) for each of the equilibria that we consider. We also restrict our attention to monetary policy rules that result in unique stationary rational expectations equilibria (in terms of inflation, all relative prices, detrended output, and all relative quantities); we thus obtain a unique welfare measure for each policy rule in the admissible set. Given that we evaluate the unconditional expectation, rather than conditioning on the current state of the economy at some particular date at which the policy choice is to be made, the criterion (29) is equivalent to comparing equilibria on the basis of the average level of expected utility of the households in our model (for the unconditional expectation of the latter quantity is simply $(1 - \beta)^{-1}W$). We evaluate the unconditional expectation in order to obtain a policy evaluation criterion that is not subject to any problem of time consistency.[16]

Following Rotemberg and Woodford (1998), we take a second-order Taylor series approximation of this welfare measure around the steady state values of the stationary variables that affect utility. The "steady state values" represent the constant equilibrium values of these variables in the absence of real disturbances, and in the case of a deterministic monetary policy consistent with zero inflation.[17] The steady state considered for this purpose also involves a tax rate τ that is set so that the steady state level of output is efficient. (This involves a small output *subsidy,* in order to counteract the distortion caused by monopoly power.) Consideration of a Taylor series expansion around these values means that our approximate welfare measure will accurately rank alternative policy rules insofar as they result in only a small degree of variability of the relevant

16. For an alternative approach, cf. King and Wolman (1998).
17. The rate of inflation matters for the evaluation of eq. (29) in such a steady state because it determines the dispersion of relative prices and hence the dispersion of the relative quantities produced of the various goods z.

state variables *and* they result in average values of the state variables that are close to the assumed steady state values. Thus our analysis should be most reliable in the case of rules that imply an average rate of inflation not too different from zero and an average level of output near the optimal steady state level $\bar{Y}$, and in which the fluctuations in both inflation and output are small. In fact, the policies that we characterize as optimal within various families of possible policy rules all imply low inflation rates, and also low variability of inflation and output, in the case that the variability of the real disturbances (represented by ξ_t) is small enough.

Linearization around this particular (optimal) steady state is extremely convenient since our approximate measure of W takes an especially simple form in that case. In particular, in this case our second-order approximation for W depends only on a first-order approximation to the equilibrium responses of inflation and output to the exogenous shocks. This means that we can solve a log-linear approximation to the model's equilibrium conditions using standard linear methods, as sketched in the previous subsection, and obtain an approximation to W that neglects only terms of third order and higher in the deviations from the steady state. This result depends on the absence of any first-order contribution to our welfare measure from changes in the average level of output under alternative rules (as a result of the optimality of the level $\bar{Y}$ relative to which we consider deviations); for if W contained a term of first order in the average level of output, then *second-order* terms in the equations determining output would matter for a second-order approximation to W.

In fact, in the calculations reported here, we furthermore assume that the tax rate τ actually varies depending on the monetary policy rule, so as to ensure that $E \log Y_t = \log \bar{Y}$ in any event. This allows us to obtain a measure of the deadweight loss associated with price level instability that abstracts from any effects of alternative monetary policies on the long-run average level of output. While many analyses of the welfare effects of monetary policy have emphasized exactly such effects,[18] we think there is good reason to abstract from them. Our primary reason is that there exist other policy instruments, such as the general level of and structure of taxation, which allow the government to influence the average level of output while, at the same time, being much less well suited for the achievement of stabilization objectives since they cannot be adjusted quickly and precisely in response to shocks. It thus makes sense to assume that, in an optimal policy regime, the other instruments are chosen to achieve the desired average level of output for a given monetary policy, while the monetary policy rule is chosen to minimize those contributions to deadweight loss that are independent of the economy's average level of output. We do this by choosing the monetary policy rule that maximizes W under the assumption that the other instruments are adjusted in the manner stated in response to any change in the monetary policy rule.

18. See, e.g., Bénabou and Koniezcny (1994), King and Wolman (1996), and Feldstein (1997).

Abstracting from these effects also has the advantage of making our results independent of a feature of our model about which we are especially uncomfortable, namely, its predictions about the effects of sustained inflation on the long-run level of output.[19] One might think that sustained inflation should result in adaptations that eliminate any effects of the average inflation rate on average output. One such adaptation would be price commitments that specify a constant rate of price increase of π^* between the occasions on which the commitments are modified, as assumed in Yun (1996). With this modification, our model would come to satisfy the "natural rate hypothesis." In the modified model, the correct second-order approximation to W would be exactly the one that we report here, but then it would apply to small fluctuations in the rate of inflation around *any* average value π^*.[20]

We show in the appendix that, under these assumptions, a second-order approximation for W is given by

$$W = -\frac{1}{2}u_c\bar{Y}(\sigma + \omega)\,\text{var}\{E_{t-2}(\hat{Y}_t - \hat{Y}_t^s)\}$$

$$(30) \qquad -\frac{1}{2}u_c\bar{Y}(\theta^{-1} + \omega)E\,\text{var}_z\{\log y_t(z)\}$$

$$+ \text{ terms independent of policy} + \mathcal{O}(\|\xi\|^3),$$

where the suppressed final terms are either independent of the evolution of the endogenous variables or of third order or smaller in the size of the exogenous disturbances. Note that this welfare measure depends solely on the allocation of real resources, summarized by the pattern of levels of production $\{y_t(z)\}$ at each point in time. However, equation (30) indicates that welfare depends not only on the degree to which aggregate output deviates from the natural level of output Y^s but also on the degree of (inefficient) dispersion of output levels across the different varieties of goods being produced at each point in time.

The dispersion of output levels directly corresponds, in equilibrium, to the degree of dispersion of output prices. Prices differ across goods, in turn, only because of variation in the overall price level (together with the fact that different suppliers adjust their prices at different times). The $E\,\text{var}_z\{\log y_t(z)\}$ term in equation (30) can accordingly be expressed as a function of the aggregate inflation process, as shown in the appendix. With this substitution, we obtain

19. E.g., McCallum and Nelson (chap. 1 of this volume) criticize the Calvo model of price setting on the ground that its failure to conform to the natural rate hypothesis is unrealistic. Our closely related model has exactly the feature that they criticize.

20. King and Wolman (1998) also argue, on alternative grounds, that optimal policy should involve a steady state inflation rate of $\pi^* = 0$, despite the fact that a small positive inflation rate can raise steady state output by lowering average markups, and that (if one assumes $\tau = 0$, as they do) this would raise the steady state value of the period utility flow $u(C) - v(y)$. Their argument involves calculation of the optimal time-dependent policy (under commitment) to maximize the average level of discounted utility over the infinite horizon. They show that this optimal time-dependent (and time-inconsistent) policy involves a commitment to an inflation rate that converges to zero asymptotically, even though the optimal *stationary* rate of inflation would be positive.

$$W = -\frac{1}{2}u_c\bar{Y}\left\{(\omega + \sigma)\,\text{var}\{E_{t-2}(\hat{Y}_t - \hat{Y}_t^s)\}\right.$$

(31)
$$+ \frac{\theta(1 + \theta\omega)}{(1 - \alpha)^2}\left[\alpha\,\text{var}\{E_{t-2}\pi_t\} + \alpha\pi^{*2}\right.$$

$$\left.\left.+ \left(\alpha + \frac{1 - \gamma}{\gamma}\right)\text{var}\{\pi_t - E_{t-2}\pi_t\}\right]\right\} + \text{t.i.p.} + \mathcal{O}(\|\xi\|^3).$$

Here π^* again denotes the steady state rate of inflation associated with a given policy rule (the rate of inflation when the shocks $\xi_t = 0$ for all time); it corresponds, neglecting terms of second order or higher, to the average rate of inflation (or to the unconditional mean of π) in the stationary equilibrium. The notation "t.i.p." refers to the terms that are independent of policy.

Expression (31) can be written more compactly as

(32) $$W = -\Omega(L + \pi^{*2}) + \text{t.i.p.} + \mathcal{O}(\|\xi\|^3),$$

where

(33) $$L = \text{var}\{\pi_t\} + (\psi^{-1} - 1)\,\text{var}\{\pi_t - E_{t-2}\pi_t\} + \Lambda\,\text{var}\{E_{t-2}(\hat{Y}_t - \hat{Y}_t^s)\}$$

and $\Omega, \Lambda > 0$. The quantity $L + \pi^{*2}$ represents the measure of deadweight loss due to price level instability that we shall use to evaluate alternative monetary policies. Here the loss measure L collects the terms that depend solely on the degree of variability of inflation and the output gap, while π^{*2} is proportional to the deadweight loss due to nonzero inflation, even when it is perfectly steady.[21]

Note that our loss measure L is similar in form to a type of ad hoc loss function,

$$\text{var}\{\pi_t\} + \lambda\,\text{var}\{\hat{Y}_t - \hat{Y}_t^s\},$$

for some $\lambda > 0$, assumed in many analyses of optimal monetary policy (e.g., Taylor 1979; Bean 1983). Our utility-based derivation, however, allows us to assign a specific numerical weight to the relative importance of stabilization of output around Y^s, as opposed to inflation stabilization. It also clarifies the kinds of stabilization that are important. Because of the lags involved in pric-

21. Note that the latter measure considers only the welfare costs of steady inflation that result from the relative price distortions that follow from the lack of continuous price adjustment. As noted earlier, we abstract from any effects of steady inflation on the steady state level of aggregate output. We also abstract from other welfare costs of inflation, such as the costs of economizing on real money balances, that are emphasized in many discussions of this issue. It seems likely that the effects that we neglect should, if anything, make it even more desirable that average inflation be low. Since many of our results consider the trade-off between stabilization objectives and the objective of a low average rate of inflation, and since our results, when we consider the overall minimization of $L + \pi^{*2}$, recommend a low average rate of inflation in any event, we do not feel that an attempt to quantify such additional considerations is likely to change our conclusions dramatically.

ing, it turns out to be desirable to reduce the variability of both expected inflation and unexpected inflation. Moreover, the variability of unexpected inflation
deserves somewhat greater weight, unlike what the ad hoc loss function above
would imply. The analysis also makes it clear that it is the variability of quarter-
to-quarter inflation, rather than some longer horizon average rate of inflation,
or the deviation of the price level from some deterministic or stochastic trend
path, that is most closely related to the welfare losses due to price level instability. Finally, it makes it clear that it is the variability of $\hat{Y} - \hat{Y}^s$, rather than
the variability of deviations of output from trend or the variability of output
growth, that matters for welfare. Specifically, it is the variability of the part of
$\hat{Y} - \hat{Y}^s$ that is forecastable two quarters earlier that policy should seek to minimize.

It is worth noting that all three of the terms in equation (33) are directly
related, in different ways, to inflation variability. For the analysis of optimal
policy below, it is helpful to rewrite L so that it depends only on the stochastic
process for the relative price variable $\hat{X}$. We show in the appendix that the
model's structural equations imply that equation (33) may be rewritten in the
form

$$(34) \qquad L = \mathrm{var}\{E_{t-2}\hat{X}_t\} + \psi\,\mathrm{var}\{\hat{X}_t - E_{t-2}\hat{X}_t\} + \frac{\Lambda}{\kappa^2}\,\mathrm{var}\{E_{t-2}(\hat{X}_t - \beta\hat{X}_{t+1})\}.$$

This shows that the deadweight losses measured by L are zero if variations in
$\hat{X}$ are eliminated (as we show below to be possible in principle). Thus a constant rate of inflation is both necessary and sufficient for achievement of the
minimum value of $L = 0$. This means that, even though our proposed welfare
criterion (30) assigns ultimate importance *only* to the efficiency of the level of
real activity in each sector of the economy, it in fact justifies giving complete
priority to inflation stabilization as opposed to output stabilization.

Given the model, one can compute the value of L as well as that of its components for any rule that sets the interest rate as a function of the history of
inflation and output in such a way that there is a unique stationary equilibrium.
But this still leaves open the question of whether there is a trade-off between
stabilizing the economy by reducing L and keeping a low steady state level of
inflation. As suggested by Summers (1991), the requirement that nominal interest rates must always be positive implies that a low average rate of inflation
is inconsistent with a great deal of stabilization. The reason is that a low average rate of inflation implies that the average interest rate is low, and this means
that the interest rate cannot be too variable. At the same time, keeping the
variability of interest rates low weakens the government's ability to reduce L
by having the interest rate respond to shocks. To see this, it is worth displaying
the relation between interest rates and $\hat{X}$ implied by our model.

This relationship can easily be derived from the equilibrium conditions (17),
(20), and (21), together with the requirement that

(35)
$$E_t(\hat{Y}_{t+2} - \hat{G}_{t+2}) = \hat{Y}_{t+2} - \hat{G}_{t+2},$$

which is implied by the fact that interest-sensitive purchases in period $t + 2$ are determined at t. We first take the difference between equation (21) and the expectation of this equation at $t - 2$, and use equations (17) and (35) to obtain

$$(\hat{X}_t - \beta E_{t-1}\hat{X}_{t+1}) - E_{t-2}(\hat{X}_t - \beta\hat{X}_{t+1})$$

$$= \kappa[(\hat{G}_t - \hat{Y}_t^s) - E_{t-2}(\hat{G}_t - \hat{Y}_t^s)] - \frac{\kappa}{\omega + \sigma}\phi_{t-1}.$$

Using this expression to substitute for ϕ_{t-1} in equation (21), we obtain

(36) $$\hat{Y}_t = \hat{Y}_t^s + \kappa^{-1}E_{t-2}(\hat{X}_t - \beta\hat{X}_{t+1}) + [(\hat{G}_t - \hat{Y}_t^s) - E_{t-2}(\hat{G}_t - \hat{Y}_t^s)].$$

We now rewrite equation (17) using (36) to substitute for $\hat{Y}_t$ and the expression just above to substitute for ϕ_{t-1}. This yields

(37)
$$E_t\hat{R}_{t+1} = E_t\hat{X}_{t+2} + \hat{\rho}_t + \frac{\sigma}{\kappa}E_t[(\hat{X}_{t+2} - \beta\hat{X}_{t+3}) - (\hat{X}_{t+1} - \beta\hat{X}_{t+2})]$$

$$- \frac{\omega}{\kappa}[E_t(\hat{X}_{t+1} - \beta\hat{X}_{t+2}) - E_{t-1}(\hat{X}_{t+1} - \beta\hat{X}_{t+2})],$$

where we have used the fact that equation (20) implies that $E_{t-2}\pi_t = E_{t-2}\hat{X}_t$, and where

(38)
$$\hat{\rho}_t \equiv \omega[(\hat{G}_{t+1} - \hat{Y}_{t+1}^s) - E_{t-1}(\hat{G}_{t+1} - \hat{Y}_{t+1}^s)]$$

$$- \sigma[E_t(\hat{G}_{t+2} - \hat{Y}_{t+2}^s) - (\hat{G}_{t+1} - \hat{Y}_{t+1}^s)].$$

Note that $\hat{\rho}_t$ is an exogenous stochastic process that can be expressed as a function of the history of the shocks $\bar{e}_{it}$.

Equation (37) represents the only restriction implied by our model on the behavior of $\hat{R}_t$ given the evolution of $\hat{X}_t$. For any given process for $\hat{X}_t$, the variance of $\hat{R}_t$ is obviously minimized by setting $\hat{R}_{t+1}$ equal to the right-hand side of equation (37). In the case where one wishes to stabilize prices completely, this means that $\hat{R}_{t+1}$ is given by $\hat{\rho}_t$, as discussed in Rotemberg and Woodford (1997). This means that the interest rate at $t + 1$ must rise whenever $\hat{G}_{t+1} - \hat{Y}_{t+1}^s$ increases unexpectedly at t. If, instead, upward revisions in $\hat{G}_{t+1} - \hat{Y}_{t+1}^s$ are matched by upward revisions in $\hat{X}_{t+1}$, $\hat{R}_{t+1}$ need not rise as much. In other words, if inflation is allowed to respond to these shocks, the interest rate does not have to respond as much to them.

We propose a simple representation of the quantitative connection between average inflation and the variability of interest rates as in Rotemberg and Woodford (1997). In particular, we suppose that, along any equilibrium path, the lowest possible value of r^* (and π^*) consistent with a given degree of interest rate variability is given by

(39) $r^* = \rho + \pi^* = k\sigma(\hat{R})$,

where $\sigma(\hat{R})$ refers to the standard deviation of the unconditional distribution for $\hat{R}_t$ in the stationary equilibrium associated with a given policy rule. We let the factor k equal 2.26, which is the ratio of the mean funds rate to its standard deviation under the historical regime, so that, in effect, we are assuming that this is the minimum possible value for this ratio.[22] For any monetary policy rule we consider, we thus compute the variance of the nominal funds rate, and then use equation (39) to determine the associated value of π^*. We then compare policy rules according to how low a value they imply for the overall deadweight loss measure $L + \pi^{*2}$.[23]

While minimizing the welfare losses of the agents in the economy is a rather obvious objective for policy, it is worth looking more generally at the effect of different monetary policy rules on the variances of output, inflation, and interest rates. This analysis has several benefits. First, it provides intuition for our results concerning the effects of different rules on $L + \pi^{*2}$. Second, because this analysis is not as dependent on the subset of parameters that we calibrate, it remains valid even if some our calibrations are inappropriate.

Finally, the model may be incorrect in ways that maintain the validity of our estimates of the structural parameters but vitiate our welfare analysis. We do not know the precise range of variations on the model for which this would be true. One simple example would be if there are changes over time in the elasticity of substitution of different goods for each other. This would imply that the Dixit-Stiglitz aggregator varies over time. The resulting changes in the elasticity of demand faced by each firm would lead firms to desire changes in the ratio of price to marginal cost. As far as the algebra of the model is concerned, such changes in the desired markup have the same effect as changes in Y_t^s. The difference is that, under this alternative interpretation, it is no longer socially desirable for output to track the time variation in Y_t^s. In particular, variation in desired markups would justify an objective of reducing the variance of output relative to trend more than is implied by our minimization of $L + \pi^{*2}$ below. For this reason, as well as for comparability of our results with those of other studies, we look at a relatively wide range of consequences of the monetary rules we study.

22. Note that our definitions imply that $\hat{R}_t = r_t - \rho$, so that $\sigma(\hat{R}) = \sigma(r)$. We refer to $\sigma(\hat{R})$ in eq. (39) because the structural equations of our model are written in terms of the variable $\hat{R}_t$, and so we solve for the equilibrium fluctuations in that variable.

23. The advantage of this substitute for the more rigorous approach of imposing the requirement that $R_t \geq 0$ at all times, given estimated shock distributions with bounded supports, is a considerable saving in computational effort. First, imposing a constraint of the form (39), our optimization problem continues to be a linear-quadratic one (if we use approximation [32] to the objective and a log-linear approximation to the model structural equations), and as a result the optimal policy is described by a linear rule, which we can obtain using linear methods. Second, under this form of constraint, the optimal policy does not depend on any more detailed description of the distribution of the exogenous shocks e_t^j than their means and variances. This means that we do not need to estimate more detailed properties of these distributions and that our conclusions do not depend on properties of such distributions that are likely to be very poorly estimated in a sample of our size.

2.2   Consequences of Simple Policy Rules

As noted earlier, we wish to compare a variety of types of monetary policy rules that make the interest rate r_t depend on the history of output, inflation, and the interest rate itself. In this section, we explore the effects of varying the parameter in some very simple rules of this kind. These simple rules, which are variants of the rule proposed by Taylor (1993), have some practical advantages. Their simplicity makes them easy to understand so that a central bank that adopted them ought to find it easy to explain what it is doing. As a result, the public ought to find it easy to monitor the central bank's compliance with its rule. Finally, the use of similar rules in the other papers in this volume makes our results concerning the desirability of these rules directly comparable to theirs.

When we study rules that can be described by only a small number of parameters, we study the consequences of parameter variation for two sorts of issues. First we analyze the range of parameter values that ensures that a determinate rational expectations equilibrium exists; as an extensive prior literature has stressed, determinacy of equilibrium cannot be taken for granted in rational expectations models, especially in the case of a monetary policy defined by an interest rate rule. (See, e.g., Bernanke and Woodford 1997 for general discussion of this issue, and illustrations in the context of a model similar to the one that we use here.) Next we study the effect of parameter variation within the range of parameter values for which equilibrium is determinate.

2.2.1   Performance Measures for Alternative Rules

For each of the rules we consider, we compute a number of statistics relating to the variability of inflation, output, and interest rates in the unique stationary rational expectations equilibrium associated with that rule. These statistics are reported in table 2.1 for a number of rules of particular interest. The significance of the parameters a, b, and c that define these rules is explained below.[24]

Among the specific rules included in the table are several that are also considered in other papers in this volume. These are labeled A_i through D_i, with i equal to 0 in the case of rules where the interest rate responds to contemporaneous output and inflation, and i equal to 1 in the case where it responds with a lag. The table also reports the effects of setting the parameters at the values that represent the best rule (in the sense of minimization of our utility-based loss measure $L + \pi^{*2}$) within each of several families of simple rules discussed below (these are labeled E_0, F_0, and G_0, and E_1 and G_1). Finally, we also report the statistics associated with our estimate of actual U.S. policy during the period 1979–95 (rule H), and for the unconstrained optimal policy according to our model, discussed in section 2.3 (rule I).

---

24. Briefly, in each case, a measures the extent to which the funds rate responds to deviations of inflation or the price level from its target value, b measures the extent to which the funds rate responds to deviations of output from trend, and c measures the extent to which the funds rate responds to deviations in its own lagged value.

Table 2.1   Statistics for Several Policy Rules

	a	b	c	var$\{R\}$	var$\{Y\}$	var$\{\pi\}$	var$\{\Delta p^\infty\}$	β^∞	var$\{\pi - E\pi\}$	var$\{E(Y - Y^s)\}$	L	π^*	$L + \pi^{*2}$
Contemporaneous-data Taylor rules													
A_0	3.00	0.80	1.00	6.24	7.24	0.66	4.00	3.82	0.27	8.77	1.32	2.66	8.38
B_0	1.20	1.00	1.00	6.41	2.73	1.82	16.05	5.44	0.48	11.69	2.80	2.74	10.29
C_0	1.50	0.50	0.00	17.14	3.87	7.34	121.14	11.14	0.81	13.86	8.72	6.37	49.29
D_0	1.50	1.00	0.00	16.26	1.79	6.76	100.77	9.80	0.83	14.63	8.18	6.13	45.73
E_0	1.22	0.06	1.28	1.88	13.47	0.38	1.47	−1.86	0.19	11.37	1.09	0.11	1.10
F_0	2.88	0.02	0.00	8.65	15.42	1.04	16.77	6.38	0.37	10.35	1.86	3.66	15.26
Lagged-data Taylor rules													
A_1	3.00	0.80	1.00	5.89	10.32	0.66	4.20	3.84	0.28	6.56	1.23	2.50	7.47
B_1	1.20	1.00	1.00	5.99	3.30	1.83	16.30	5.43	0.49	9.58	2.71	2.54	9.18
C_1	1.50	0.50	0.00	13.83	4.63	5.97	94.12	10.04	0.78	11.17	7.19	5.42	36.55
D_1	1.50	1.00	0.00	14.86	3.32	5.85	83.99	9.08	0.81	11.69	7.12	5.73	39.91
E_1	1.27	0.08	1.28	1.87	13.92	0.37	1.12	−1.35	0.19	12.18	1.12	0.10	1.13
Price level targeting rules													
G_0	0.26	0.07	1.03	2.00	11.14	0.34	0.00	0.00	0.23	11.93	1.11	0.21	1.16
G_1	0.38	0.10	0.85	2.04	11.35	0.34	0.00	0.00	0.25	12.57	1.15	0.24	1.21
Estimated historical U.S. policy													
H	–	–	–	7.64	4.79	2.28	26.19	5.60	0.66	12.14	3.43	3.26	14.06
Optimal policy													
I	–	–	–	1.93	11.30	0.39	1.77	−2.19	0.20	7.57	0.93	0.15	0.95

The statistics reported in table 2.1 include the variance of output around trend, the variance of inflation, and the variance of the federal funds rate. In addition to these conventional statistics, we also report the variance of quarterly innovations in the rational forecast of the long-run price level. This is the variance of changes in the variable

$$\rho_t^{\infty} \equiv E_t \lim_{T \to \infty}(\log P_T - T\pi^*),$$

which is just the stochastic trend in the price level in the sense of Beveridge and Nelson (1981). (Note that it follows from this definition that the first difference of p^{∞} is also the innovation in this variable.) We include this statistic as an alternative index of the degree of price stability associated with different equilibria. The advantage of this statistic is that it reflects the extent to which agents make capital gains and losses on long-term nominal contracts and some analysts have expressed concern over these (e.g., Hall and Mankiw 1994). Finally, we also report the coefficient β^{∞} of a regression of the innovation at t in the forecast of the long-run price level p^{∞} on the quarter t innovation in the (log) price level at $t + 1$. (Recall that, according to our model, the price level P_{t+1} is determined at date t.) This coefficient tells us whether inflation innovations in quarter t eventually lead to a higher price level or whether instantaneous increases in the price level are later offset by subsequent expected reductions in prices. In the case of a random walk in the log price level, we should find $\beta^{\infty} = 1$, while if temporary price level increases are eventually completely offset, we should find $\beta^{\infty} = 0$.

The first column of table 2.1 serves as a key for figures 2.1, 2.2, and 2.3, where the consequences of these rules for the variability of output, inflation, interest rates, and long-run price-level forecasts are plotted. Figure 2.1 has a certain similarity to the policy frontier shown in Taylor (1979), in that rules that have smaller standard deviations of inflation tend to involve larger standard deviations of output and vice versa. The only rules that appear to be "dominated" in this plot are the rules with labels in the series C_i and D_i. These are simple "Taylor rules" that make the funds rate a function only of current inflation and output, and they respond much more strongly to output fluctuations than does our optimal rule in that family (labeled F_0). The rules in families C_i and D_i are worse than the B_i rules because they induce a higher standard deviation of inflation without reducing the standard deviation of output. Interestingly, the rule F_0, which is the best rule of this type in terms of minimizing our utility-based loss measure, is something of an outlier as well in that it involves more variability of both inflation and output relative to other rules in the set. From the point of view solely of the criteria plotted in this figure, historical policy seems to be slightly worse than the rules described by B_i, but not significantly so.

Figure 2.2 paints a different picture, one that involves pure dominance relations and no trade-offs. Once again, the rules C_i and D_i are particularly bad in

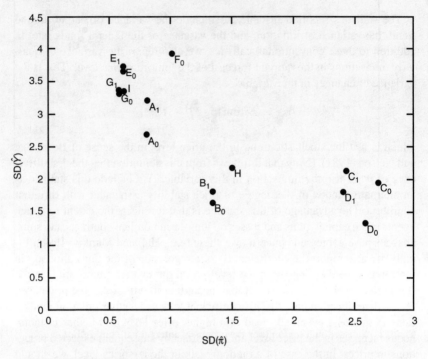

Fig. 2.1   Selected rules: standard deviations of output and inflation

that they now also involve a high standard deviation of the funds rate. Among the remaining rules, those with a lower standard deviation of inflation tend to have a lower standard deviation of the funds rate so they allow average inflation to be lower as well. Thus the best rules in this plot are the rules E_i, which, as we shall see below, also minimize $L + \pi^{*2}$ among rules that are as simple as these. These involve low standard deviations of both inflation and interest rates, while the other rules perform worse on both dimensions. When coupled with the results of figure 2.1, we see that—leaving aside C_i and D_i—the rules we consider here have the property that those that reduce the standard deviation of output tend to raise the standard deviations of inflation and interest rates simultaneously.

Figure 2.3 shows the implications of these rules for the variance of inflation and the variance in the innovation of the forecast of the long-run price level. We see in this figure that the specific rules we consider rank equally along these two dimensions. The price level rules G_i and the E_i rules have both the lowest variance of inflation and the smallest innovations in the long-run price level. That the price level rules have low variances in the long-run price level is not surprising, since they ensure the price level is stationary. What is perhaps more surprising is that the best of the rules that respond to deviations of the inflation rate from target have this property as well.

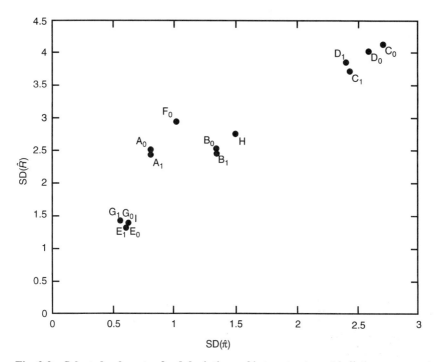

Fig. 2.2   Selected rules: standard deviations of interest rate and inflation

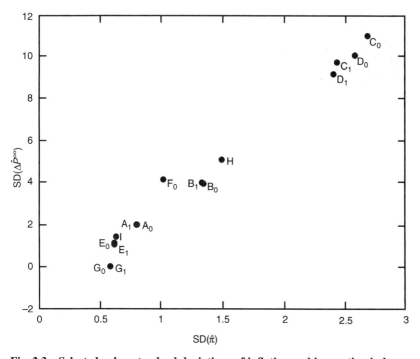

Fig. 2.3   Selected rules: standard deviations of inflation and innovation in long-run price level

The regression coefficients β^∞ of the innovation in the long-run price level on the current price level innovation reported in table 2.1 help to explain this finding. This coefficient is obviously zero for the price level rules, since these equilibria involve no change in the forecast of the long-run price level at any time. For the E_i rules as well as for the rule marked I, which is the rule that minimizes $L + \pi^{*2}$ among all possible rules, this coefficient is actually smaller than -1. This means that increases in the contemporaneous price level eventually lead to a lower price level, and, indeed, to a lower price level by an amount that is even greater than the size of the initial price level innovation (but with an opposite sign). Thus, while the long-run price level is not being stabilized, expected reductions in future inflation more than offset the initial increase in the price level. This stands in sharp contrast to the other rules reported in the table. For these rules, this coefficient exceeds one so that increases in the current price level lead to even larger increases in the long-run price level. This means that, on average, increases in inflation are followed by further inflation. This clearly destabilizes the long-run price level. In addition, because expected future inflation leads price setters who can change their prices at t to raise their prices by more, it also means that inflation at t is increased by policies that follow inflation at t with further inflation. For this reason, policies with high values of β^∞ have both variable inflation and large variances in the innovation of the long-run price level.

The remaining columns of table 2.1 report statistics that measure various components of the utility-based measure of deadweight loss derived in the previous section. The columns labeled var$\{\pi\}$, var$\{\pi - E\pi\}$, and var$\{E(Y - Y^s)\}$ report the values of the three unconditional variances that receive positive weights in expression (33) for the loss measure L. The third column from the right then reports the implied value for L. This is our summary measure of the deadweight losses due to variability of inflation and output, in units of the variance of inflation. We scale inflation so that $\pi = 1$ corresponds to a 1 percent inflation per year. Hence, $L = 1$ indicates the same degree of deadweight loss as results from this inflation rate. The next to last column reports the minimum value of π^* consistent with the degree of funds rate variability required by the policy rule, using equation (39) to derive this. Finally, the last column reports the implied value of $L + \pi^{*2}$, our total measure of deadweight loss.

One interesting fact about the table is that the ranking of alternative rules according to their implications for the variability of $\hat{Y} - \hat{Y}^s$ is quite different from their ranking according to their implications for the variability of output relative to its deterministic trend path. The rule D_0, which minimizes var$\{\hat{Y}\}$ among those considered in the table, implies the *highest* degree of variability of output relative to the natural level $\hat{Y}^s$. This indicates that responding to deviations of output from a deterministic trend, while perhaps successful as a way of stabilizing output around that trend, may well be counterproductive if one is interested in keeping output close to its natural level. (Cf. figs. 2.6 and 2.8 below, for further illustration of this point.)

Another fact that is apparent from the table is that the ranking of different rules according the value achieved for L is essentially the same as their ranking in terms of the variability of inflation. Thus our utility-based welfare criterion $L + \pi^{*2}$ leads to conclusions that are similar to those that would be reached by giving some weight to the reduction of both the variability of inflation and the variability of the funds rate. In both these respects, the rules labeled E_i, G_i, and I are better than the others. We turn now to a more systematic exploration of the consequences of parameter variations, in order to clarify why this is so.

2.2.2   Simple "Taylor Rules"

We first consider the consequences of varying a and b in simple "Taylor rules" of the form

$$(40) \qquad \hat{r}_t = a\hat{\pi}_t + b\hat{Y}_t,$$

where once again $\hat{r}_t \equiv r_t - r^*$ and $\hat{\pi}_t \equiv \pi_t - \pi^*$. Note that both the rule C_0 proposed by Taylor (1993) and the related rule considered by Henderson and McKibbin (1993) belong to this family. Our aim here is to highlight the trade-offs involved in the choice between having interest rates respond to output and having interest rates respond to inflation.

In the case of simple Taylor rules of the form (40) with a constrained to be positive, our loss criterion $L + \pi^{*2}$ reaches a minimum when a equals 2.88 and b equals 0.02. The consequences of this rule for our loss measures is displayed in table 2.1, where the rule is designated F_0. As one might guess, this rule (which places essentially all of the weight on inflation variations rather than output variations) allows much greater variations in output relative to trend than do rules C_0 and D_0. However, according to our model, it leads to *less* variability of output relative to its natural level, which is what matters for our loss measure. It also results in significantly less variability of inflation, and noticeably less variability of the funds rate. (It is actually the latter difference that is most significant for our loss measure, because of the reduction in the average inflation rate π^* that it allows.) The ultimate result is a reduction in deadweight loss by a factor of three, relative to the other proposals. However, our model and our loss measure imply that this rule would not represent an improvement on historical U.S. policy in the Volcker-Greenspan period. To do better we must not simply vary the weights on inflation and output but must consider at least slightly more sophisticated rules.

Before turning to other families of rules, it is worth noting that the welfare criterion $L + \pi^{*2}$ reaches an even lower value, according to our model, if we allow a and b to be negative in equation (40). The optimum then involves a equal to -1 and b equal to -1.3. The idea that negative values of a and b are acceptable may be surprising. For this reason, figure 2.4 displays both the region where equilibrium is determinate as well as a contour plot of $L + \pi^{*2}$ as we vary a and b. The equilibrium is not unstable for any of these parameter

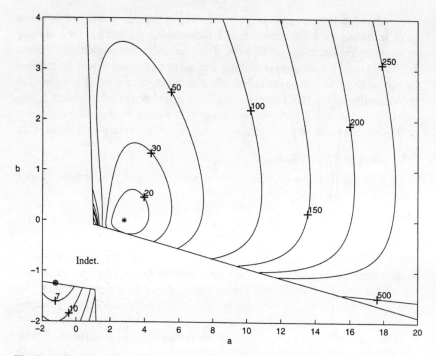

Fig. 2.4 Simple Taylor rules: $L + \pi^{*2}$ as a function of a and b

values (i.e., a stationary equilibrium always exists), but equilibrium is indeterminate in the region labelled "Indet." Indeterminacy arises, for example, when b is zero and a is small and positive. This indeterminacy implies, among other things, that inflation can vary simply as a result of changes in expectations. A "sunspot" can lead inflation at t to rise, for example. The real interest rate would then fall (because the nominal interest rate responds little) and the resulting increase in output means that expected future inflation is lower than current inflation. Thus the change in the expected future path of inflation that is required to justify the initial change in inflation is consistent with expected future inflation converging back to the target inflation rate π^*. In this case, a stationary rational expectations equilibrium is possible in which such fluctuations occur simply because they are expected to.

If, instead, a is large and positive, no such equilibrium is possible. Any increase in inflation above its unique saddle-path value is matched by increases in real interest rates that imply that output must fall. This, in turn, implies that expected future inflation rates must be higher than current inflation, given the nature of our AS curve. Thus inflation must be expected to explode, and since this is not consistent with stationarity, inflation must equal its saddle-path value in the unique stationary equilibrium. Similarly, as mentioned above, the equilibrium is determinate when a and b are both negative.

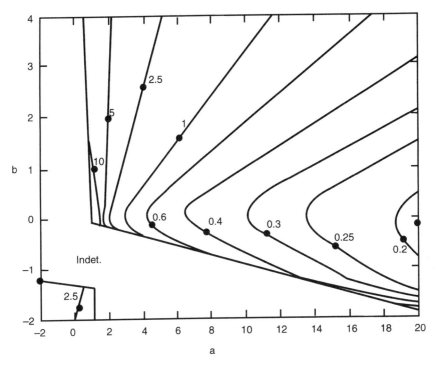

Fig. 2.5   Simple Taylor rules: var $\{\hat{\pi}\}$ as a function of a and b

Figure 2.4 presents contour lines for the value of our loss measure $L + \pi^{*2}$ in the regions where equilibrium is determinate. Policy F_0 appears as a star on this figure, at the point of a local minimum of the loss measure. However, the region of determinate equilibria with negative a and b also contains a local minimum. This point, which is shown with a star inside a circle, is actually the global minimum value. Nonetheless, we have chosen to present the local minimum F_0 in table 2.1, on the ground that restricting attention to values $a >$ 0 corresponds to rules that are more similar to the Taylor and Henderson-McKibbin proposals. In addition, once we consider more general families of rules, we do find that the best rules involve tightening monetary policy (i.e., raising the funds rate) in response to inflation increases, as conventional wisdom (at least since the work of Wicksell [1907]) would indicate.

Similar contour plots for other statistics reported in table 2.1 provide further insight into why our loss measure varies with a and b as it does. Figure 2.5 shows the contour plots of the variance of inflation, while figure 2.6 shows the contour plots for the variance of $\hat{Y} - \hat{Y}^s$. These figures are essentially identical to each other, and they are both similar to the contour plot for L itself. There is thus no trade-off between stabilizing inflation and stabilizing $\hat{Y} - \hat{Y}^s$; the same parameters stabilize both. This follows immediately from our AS curve, which

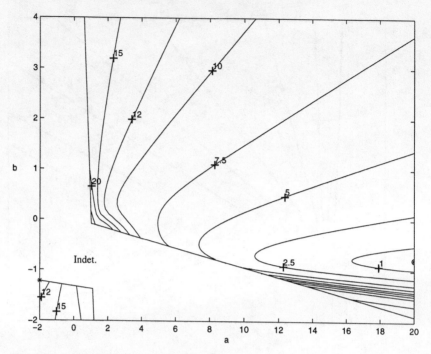

Fig. 2.6   Simple Taylor rules: var $\{\hat{Y} - \hat{Y}^s\}$ as a function of a and b

relates inflation to departures of $\hat{Y}$ from $\hat{Y}^s$. For the ranges considered in our figures, a wheel marks the global optimum for the performance criterion being considered. Thus the figures show that these variances become as small as possible when a is at its maximum possible value of 20 while b is set to a small negative number. Making a big contributes to stabilization because it ensures that interest rates rise a lot when either $\hat{G}$ rises or $\hat{Y}^s$ falls. This ensures that inflation does not rise much in either case and that, at least after the demand for output adjusts to changes in real rates, output does not rise in the former case while it declines substantially in the latter.

As figure 2.7 indicates, the rule that minimizes L by setting a equal to 20 leads to very variable interest rates. This is in part due to the delays in the response of output to interest rates. These delays imply that changes in $\hat{G}_t$ that become known at $t - 1$ inevitably change output at t since C_t is predetermined. This leads firms to raise their prices at t unless long-term real interest rates rise unexpectedly. With c equal to zero, this means that prices can only be stabilized if the nominal interest rate at t rises a great deal. The resulting variability of interest rates then requires a high average inflation rate for interest rates never to be negative. This high inflation is so costly, at least relative to the benefits of the additional stabilization that is possible with a high value of a, that the contour plots for the variance of the interest rate are essentially identical to the contour plots for $L + \pi^{*2}$. The point that minimizes the variance of

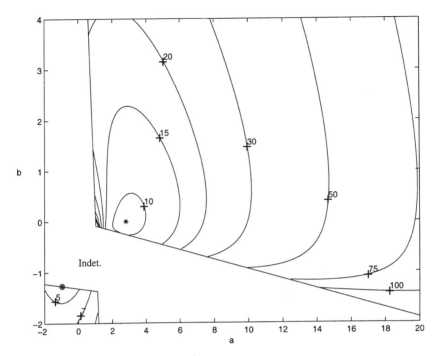

Fig. 2.7 Simple Taylor rules: var$\{\hat{R}\}$ as a function of a and b

interest rates has a sufficiently stable inflation to be quite desirable as far as total welfare is concerned.

It is interesting to note that the stabilization of output requires a quite different set of parameters. This is demonstrated in figure 2.8, which gives the contour plots for the variance of output. This variance is reduced by keeping a small and positive while making b very large. Not surprisingly, output is stabilized if the real interest rate is raised significantly by the central bank whenever output rises, while it is lowered when output declines. What is interesting here is that the effects of the policy parameters on the variance of $\hat{Y} - \hat{Y}^s$, which are essentially the same as the effects on L, are very different from the effects on the variance of Y. The reason is that the VAR of Rotemberg and Woodford (1997) identifies large short-run fluctuations in $\hat{Y}^s$. As long as these are treated as variations in the welfare-maximizing level of output, setting b large is not desirable, and indeed, stabilization of $\hat{Y} - \hat{Y}^s$ requires that b be negative at least when a is 20. Even higher values of a reduce the variance of $\hat{Y} - \hat{Y}^s$ still further. Obviously, the result that the stabilization of $\hat{Y}$ relative to $\hat{Y}^s$ requires very different policies from those that stabilize output relative to trend is very sensitive to the assumption that our estimate of $\hat{Y}^s$ is indeed the welfare-maximizing level of output. This conclusion would presumably change dramatically if movements in $\hat{Y}^s$ were viewed as resulting from changes in distortions such as changes in desired markups. From an empirical point of view

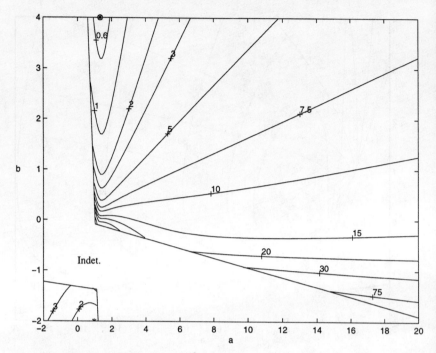

Fig. 2.8   Simple Taylor rules: var$\{\hat{Y}\}$ as a function of a and b

these two interpretations may be difficult to disentangle because we identify $\hat{Y}^s$ by measuring shifts in the empirically estimated AS equation given by (22). Unfortunately, changes in desired markups will shift this equation just as much as changes in technology or other changes in the welfare-maximizing level of output.

2.2.3   Rules That Involve a Lagged Interest Rate

We achieve improvements in household welfare if we generalize the family of simple Taylor rules to allow the funds rate to respond also to lagged values of itself. We thus consider generalized Taylor rules of the form

$$(41) \qquad \hat{r}_t = a\hat{\pi}_t + b\hat{Y}_t + c\hat{r}_{t-1},$$

where we now allow c to be greater than zero. This allows for interest rate smoothing, so that sustained changes in output and inflation lead to only gradual changes in interest rates. Actual policy in the United States and elsewhere seems to involve some degree of interest rate smoothing, though academic commentators have often questioned why this should be so.[25] Nor is there any reason to restrict attention to the case $0 \leq c < 1$, though only in that case can

25. See, e.g., Goodfriend (1991), Rudebusch (1995), Goodhart (1997), and Sack (1998).

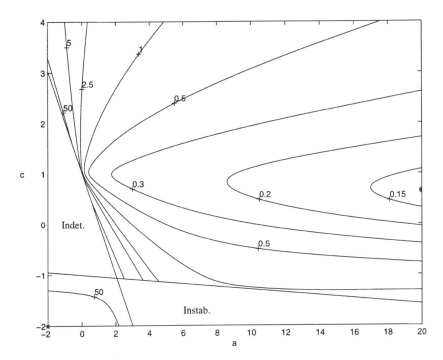

Fig. 2.9   Generalized Taylor rules: var{$\hat{\pi}$} as a function of a and c

the policy rule be described as involving partial adjustment toward a "target" funds rate that depends on current output and inflation, as assumed in Clarida, Galí, and Gertler (1998), for example. An alternative is to follow Fuhrer and Moore (1995) and model U.S. interest rates by supposing that c is equal to one, so that it is *changes* in the funds rate, rather than the level of the funds rate, that respond to deviations of inflation and output from their typical levels. Policy proposals of this kind are considered elsewhere in this volume with rules A_0 and B_0 in table 2.1 being examples of such rules. We find that policies that involve values of c even greater than one often result in determinate rational expectations equilibria in our model, and so we consider arbitrary positive values of c. In fact, rules with $c > 1$ turn out to possess an important advantage, and this is one of our most important findings.

To gain some insight into the consequences of varying c, we set b equal to zero and discuss contour plots in the $\{a, c\}$-plane for various measures of economic performance. Our motivation for starting with plots that set b equal to zero is that, as we show below, the welfare optimum obtains near this point. Moreover, the resulting family of rules has a very simple interpretation as the family in which interest rates depend only on inflation and lagged interest rates. Figure 2.9 displays the resulting contour plots for var{$\hat{\pi}$}, which, once again, are essentially identical to those for both the variance of $\hat{Y} - \hat{Y}^s$ and for

L itself. One interesting aspect of this figure is that it shows that determinacy obtains with c greater than one even if a is negative so that the Fed reacts perversely to inflation by cutting rates when inflation rises. The reason is that, as in the earlier case with negative values of a, these rules also induce explosions in response to deviations of inflation and output from saddle-point paths.

One surprising aspect of the figure is that it shows that "explosive" monetary rules in which c exceeds one do not produce explosive equilibria. In a way, this potential explosiveness of interest rates is effective at keeping the economy on track in this model. It means that, unless the price level reacts properly, the real interest rate falls or increases exponentially. An exponential increase in real rates represents a rather substantial reduction in expected future aggregate demand and thus leads firms to cut prices. The result is that the economy stays on a nonexplosive path in which increases in inflation are matched by subsequent reductions in inflation that ensure that the interest rate does not explode. In fact, higher values of c actually increase the range of values of a for which a determinate equilibrium exists, by helping to solve the problem of indeterminacy discussed above.

The figure also shows that, within the range being considered, the goal of inflation stabilization is furthered by setting a as large as possible. The variance of inflation reaches its minimum value (over the range of rules shown in the figure) when a equals 20 and c takes a positive value less than one. If the range of the figure were extended, the optimum would involve even higher values of a. Thus the key to inflation stabilization remains making sure that the interest rate reacts vigorously to inflation.

Interestingly, a higher value of c turns out to be better if one seeks to stabilize the long-run price level. This can be seen in figure 2.10, which shows that, for any given value of a, the variance of Δp^∞ reaches a minimum of zero for c equal to one. Further insight into this behavior of the variance of Δp^∞ can be obtained from figure 2.11, which shows β^∞ as a function of a and c. This figure shows that, when c is zero, β^∞ is greater than one so that initial increases in inflation are followed by further inflation. The reason for this is that an increase in $\hat{G}_t$ raises the price level at t somewhat in spite of the increase in interest rates that takes place at t. But unless the price level continues rising, interest rates would immediately return to their steady state level. The result is that, in equilibrium, prices do keep rising because the initial increase in prices means that marginal cost has gone up for the firms that did not raise their prices at t. Consequently, increases in the price level at t are followed by further increases in prices, which, admittedly, are kept somewhat in check by the fact that the interest rate remains somewhat above the steady state for some time.

If, instead, c is made higher, the interest rate tends to stay high after an increase in $\hat{G}$ even if the price level ceases to rise. This means that firms can be induced not to change their prices in the aftermath of an increase in $\hat{G}$. The result is that initial increases in prices are followed by smaller increases so that β^∞ is smaller and the variance of Δp^∞ falls. Setting c equal to one as suggested

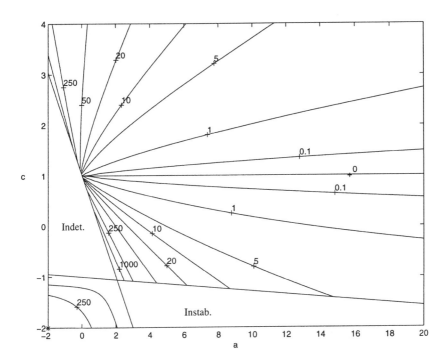

Fig. 2.10 Generalized Taylor rules: $\mathrm{var}\{\Delta p^{\infty}\}$ as a function of a and c

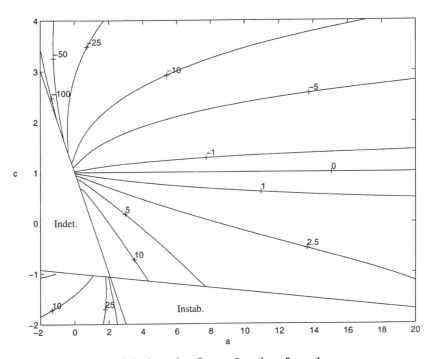

Fig. 2.11 Generalized Taylor rules: β^{∞} as a function of a and c

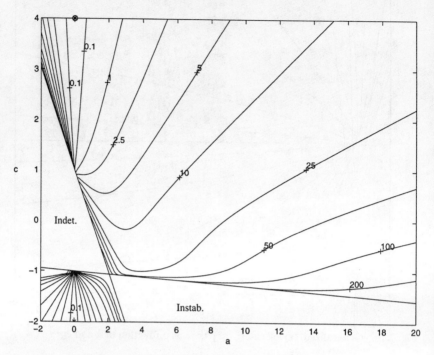

Fig. 2.12   Generalized Taylor rules: var$\{\hat{R}\}$ as a function of a and c

by Fuhrer and Moore (1995) makes β^∞ equal to zero so that the shocks have no effect on the long-run price level. Even higher values of c imply that initial increases in inflation are followed by such high real rates that the expected long-run price level is lower than the initial price level so that β^∞ is negative.

For a given initial increase in inflation and interest rates, higher values of c imply that the long-run real rate rises more both because future short rates are expected to be higher and because future inflation is expected to be lower. Since unexpected increases in the long-term real rate prevent prices from rising this means that, for given a, increases in $\hat{G}$ (and reductions in $\hat{Y}^s$) lead to smaller immediate price and interest rate increases the higher is c. This is reflected in figure 2.12, which shows that, for each a, the interest rate is less variable the higher is c. It also shows that, not surprisingly, the variance of interest rates increases with a.

While we have focused on stabilizing the variability of interest rates because of their implication for average inflation, the Fed also seems to be concerned with stabilizing the *change* in the funds rate from one week or month to the next. This would explain Rudebusch's (1995) finding that changes in the target rate are followed by further changes in the same direction. Figure 2.13 thus displays the variance of the change in interest rates in the $\{a, c\}$-plane. Interestingly, this figure is nearly identical to the figure for the variance of the interest

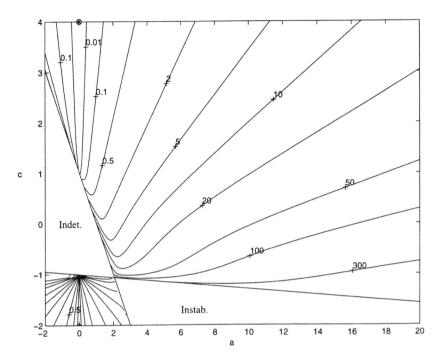

Fig. 2.13   Generalized Taylor rules: var$\{\hat{R}_t - \hat{R}_{t-1}\}$ as a function of a and c

rate itself. Thus, in our model, stabilization of the short-term nominal rate is achieved in the same way as stabilization of the quarterly change in this rate.

As we saw in figure 2.9, setting c to a very high value destabilizes the inflation rate. In part this is because sufficiently high values of c imply that increases in inflation at t must be matched by reductions in inflation in the future. These predictable movements in inflation both raise the variance of $\hat{\pi}$ and increase the loss L. For that reason, figure 2.14 shows that $L + \pi^{*2}$ reaches its lowest value for a low value of a and a moderate value of c. This minimum is very close to the point that minimizes $L + \pi^{*2}$ within the family (41) since this minimum obtains when a, b, and c equal 1.22, 0.06, and 1.28, respectively. This is the rule labeled E_0 in table 2.1.

2.2.4   Rules Using Only Lagged Data

One criticism sometimes leveled (see, e.g., McCallum 1997) against all rules of the kind considered thus far is that they require the Fed to make use of data about current output and inflation that it does not actually have when it sets the current interest rate. There are two reasons why such variables may simply be unobservable by the central bank. These are that some important economic data are collected retrospectively and that even the data that are collected concurrently need to be processed before their message about the econ-

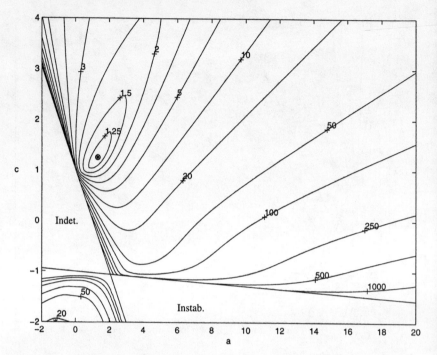

Fig. 2.14   Generalized Taylor rules: $L + \pi^{*2}$ as a function of a and c

omy as a whole can be distilled. A further difficulty with responding to contemporaneous variables may be that, even if these are observable immediately, the political process of responding to them takes time.

None of this denies that the central bank continually updates its estimate of the current state of the economy. And it should be recalled that our model of the delays in the response of output and inflation implies that the relevant data exist in principle in the quarter *prior* to the one in which the data must be used under rules (40) and (41). However, it is reasonable to suppose that the central bank's estimate of the state of the economy generally differs from the economy's actual state. In this case, responding to the current estimate of the current state differs from rules (40) and (41). If rules of the form (40) and (41) are applied to the error-ridden current estimates, the interest rate is affected by the measurement error, and a thorough evaluation of these rules would require an analysis of these effects.

Thus we now suppose instead that the Federal Reserve does not respond to output and inflation variations except with a one-quarter lag. In this class of rules,

$$(42) \qquad \hat{r}_t = a\hat{\pi}_{t-1} + b\hat{Y}_{t-1} + c\hat{r}_{t-1}.$$

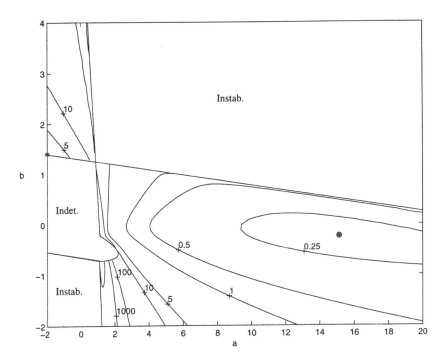

Fig. 2.15   Lagged response rules: var{$\hat{\pi}$} as a function of a and b

Considering the effect of such a lag also allows us to compare our results with other papers in this volume since some of these also include the rules we label A_1 through D_1 in table 2.1.

Even if the Fed had a reasonably accurate estimate of the current state of the economy, there would be good reasons to be interested in lagged-data rules of this form. In particular, the use of such rules would make Fed operations more transparent to the public at large if the public only had this lagged information. By avoiding the use of information that the public does not have, it becomes both easier to describe Fed operations and easier for people to detect when the Fed has departed from the rule. An alternative, of course, might be to respond to internal estimates and publish these estimates of the state of the economy as they become available. The study of this alternative, and its effects on transparency given that this estimate will at least sometimes be wrong, is clearly beyond the scope of this paper.

We start in figure 2.15 by displaying how the variance of inflation varies with a and b when c is set equal to zero. This figure is quite different from figure 2.5, which involves the same parameters and performance criterion in the case of contemporaneous Taylor rules. Unlike what occurs with rules where the interest rate responds contemporaneously, large values of a and b lead to

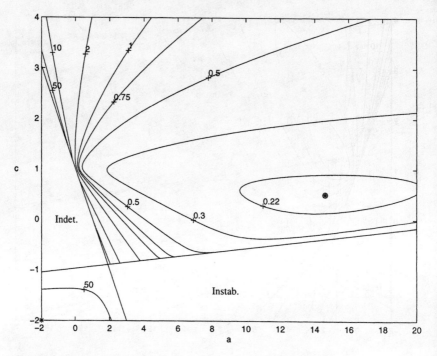

Fig. 2.16   Lagged response rules: var$\{\hat{\pi}\}$ as a function of a and c

unstable equilibria in the case where the interest rate responds only to lagged output and inflation. Ignoring b, this can be understood as follows. Inflationary shocks now lead to delayed increases in interest rates, which imply delayed reductions in inflation. The rule then requires that subsequent interest rates fall so that inflation rises once again. For a sufficiently strong reaction of interest rates to lagged inflation, that is, a high value of a, the resulting oscillations are explosive. Thus the parameters that minimize the variance of $\hat{\pi}$ in the case of a contemporaneous rule no longer do so when the government can only react with a delay. In particular, this minimization now requires that a be equal to about 15.

Figure 2.16, which gives the contour plot for the variance of $\hat{\pi}$ when b is set to zero while a and c are allowed to vary, tells a similar story. Again, high values of a lead to explosive equilibria. By contrast, high values of c with low values of a do not. Note that high values of c coupled with moderate values of a mean that the eventual reaction of interest rates to increased inflation is extremely large. Nonetheless, these rules are less destabilizing than having the interest rate respond strongly to inflation after a delay of one quarter.

Even in the case of rules that react with a lag, the stabilization of interest rates continues to require high values of c together with small values of a. The result is that figure 2.17 shows that $L + \pi^{*2}$ achieves a minimum for a combi-

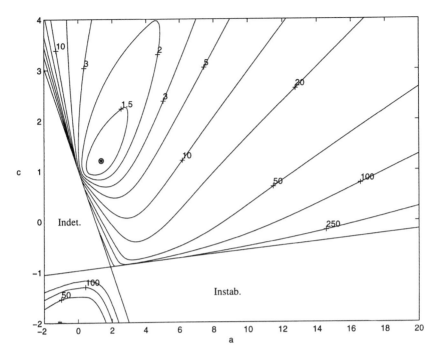

Fig. 2.17   Lagged response rules: $L + \pi^{*2}$ as a function of a and c

nation of a and c that is quite similar to the combination that was optimal in the case where the interest rate reacted contemporaneously. Moreover, the minimum value of $L + \pi^{*2}$ within the family (42) is obtained for very similar parameters. In particular, it requires that a, b, and c be equal to 1.27, 0.08, and 1.28, respectively.

This is the rule called E_1 in table 2.1. Clearly, these parameters are very similar to those (the rule E_0) that minimize $L + \pi^{*2}$ when contemporaneous data are used. What is more surprising, however, is that table 2.1 indicates that the minimized value of $L + \pi^{*2}$ is very similar in the two cases. In other words, this welfare criterion equals 1.10 when the best contemporaneous rule is used, while it equals 1.13 when the best of the rules that respond to lagged values is used. Recall that the units of this welfare criterion are squares of percentage *yearly* inflation rates. Thus the difference in loss is equivalent to the difference between having a completely stable annual inflation rate of 1.06 percent per year and having a completely stable annual inflation rate of 1.05 percent per year. The difference is trivial.

This similarity is not surprising once one recognizes that the optimal contemporaneous rule involves a high value of c. This fact means that, even in the case of contemporaneous rules, most of the reaction of interest rates to an inflationary shock such as an increase in $\hat{G}$ or a reduction in $\hat{Y}^s$ takes place with a delay. Given this, it is not surprising that the further delay that comes about from responding to inflation and output with a lag has trivial welfare consequences. From an economic perspective, what is important is that delayed responses still allow for substantial revisions in long-term real interest rates, and it is these that help stabilize inflation.

2.2.5 Price Level Targeting Rules

In this subsection we consider the possibility of making the funds rate respond to deviations of the price *level* from some target path (assumed to be a deterministic trend with growth rate π^*), rather than responding to inflation. In particular, we consider rules of the form

$$(43) \qquad \hat{r}_t = a\hat{P}_t + b\hat{Y}_t + c\hat{r}_{t-1}.$$

The rule given by (43) has the advantage that (if $a \neq 0$) it makes the price level stationary around the target (deterministic trend) path. Such rules thus reduce $\text{var}\{\Delta p^\infty\}$ to the maximum possible extent by ensuring this variance is zero. This may be considered a desirable goal of policy; for example, Hall and Mankiw (1994) discuss the advantages of a price level targeting rule in this regard.[26] Such rules also address the desire expressed by the 90 percent of the respondents to Shiller's (1997) survey, that any change in the price level be subsequently reversed. We wish to consider whether rules of this kind are also desirable in terms of the other measures of performance that we treat here, or to what degree one might have to sacrifice other goals for the sake of stability of the long-run price level forecast.

Figure 2.18 displays the contour plots of $L + \pi^{*2}$, once again setting b equal to zero. As the figure shows, price level rules tend to be unstable when a is negative and c is large; lower values of c with negative values of a lead to indeterminate equilibria instead. Within the positive orthant, these rules do lead to determinate equilibria, however. In particular, points with positive a and c equal to zero lead to unique determinate equilibria. Since the same is true for rules in the family (41) with b equal to zero, c equal to one, and a positive, the corresponding equilibria must be the same. To see this, note that, when b is zero, c is one, and a is positive, rules in family (41) take the form

$$(44) \qquad \Delta\hat{r}_t = a\Delta\hat{P}_t.$$

Price level rules in the family (43) must also satisfy this equation when b and c are zero since, in this case, (44) is just the first difference of (43). Thus, if the equilibrium with the first-differenced rule (44) is unique, it must be the same as that of the corresponding price level rule. This explains why we found that rules in the family (41) with b equal to zero and c equal to one had the

---

26. But for a contrary view of the relative desirability of inflation stabilization and price level stabilization, see, e.g., Gertler (1996).

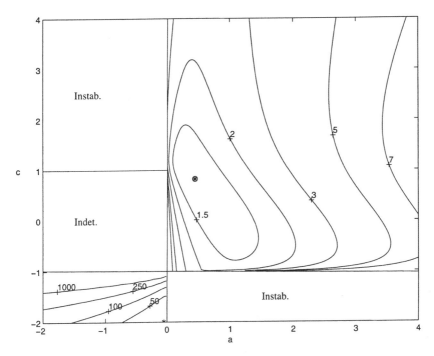

Fig. 2.18   Price level rules: $L + \pi^{*2}$ as a function of a and c

dual property that the long-run price level was stable and that β^∞ was equal to zero. These rules were in fact equivalent to price level rules.

However, the optimal price level rule is not a member of the family (41) because the optimal b and c within the class (43) are not equal to zero. In particular, the lowest value for $L + \pi^{*2}$ within the family of price level rules (43) obtains when a, b, and c equal 0.26, 0.07, and 1.03, respectively. Because the optimal b is zero, this point is close to the optimum depicted in figure 2.18. Once again, the desire to stabilize interest rates leads to a high value of c, though this parameter has a somewhat different meaning in the context of price level rules than it does in the context of the family (41).

Perhaps the most interesting aspect of these price level rules is that even the best such rule is somewhat worse from the perspective of $L + \pi^{*2}$ than the best rule that responds to contemporaneous inflation. Indeed, household welfare is slightly lower than it would be if the central bank followed the best rule that responds only to the lagged levels of inflation and output. The best among the rules that respond to lagged output and the lagged price *level* is even worse. Admittedly, the resulting differences in our welfare criterion are small, but it is worth knowing that price level rules are not particularly attractive in this context.

One could argue that these results do not really say whether it is worth stabilizing the price level, because we are only looking at a very narrow class of rules. To see whether one can obtain some incremental improvement in our criterion function by responding to *both* the price level and the rate of inflation, we analyze hybrid rules of the form

$$(45) \qquad \hat{r}_t = a_0 \hat{P}_t + a_1 \hat{P}_{t-1} + b\hat{Y}_t + c\hat{r}_{t-1}.$$

When we choose parameters a_0, a_1, b, and c to minimize $L + \pi^{*2}$, we obtain the values $a_0 = 1.22$, $a_1 = -1.22$, $b = 0.06$, and $c = 1.28$. Since $a_1 = -a_0$, the optimal member of this family is a member of the more restricted family (41) and, in fact, it is once again the rule labeled E_0 in table 2.1. There is thus nothing to be gained, from the point of view of our utility-based welfare criterion, by generalizing this family to add a term that ensures that the interest rate reacts to the price level, even though adding even a small term of that kind would serve to stabilize the long-run price level.

The reason is that the best rule within the class (41) involves some base drift, and this base drift is optimal. Interestingly, this base drift is very different from, and in some ways exactly opposite to, the base drift that people usually worry about. In particular, it is *not* optimal to respond to shocks that temporarily raise inflation by allowing the price level to be higher forever—that is, to choose a rule that implies $\beta^\infty > 0$. On the contrary, as discussed earlier, what is optimal is to have such shocks be followed by price declines that are sufficiently large that, eventually, the price level ends up *below* its initial value (when corrected for the average rate of inflation π^*). This is advantageous because the expectation of future price declines, by itself, dampens the initial inflationary effect of increases in $\hat{G}$ and reductions in $\hat{Y}^s$. It is then possible to obtain the same degree of current price stabilization without having to raise interest rates so much. For this reason, the variability of interest rates is lower in the E_i rules than in the best price-level-targeting rules. This additional stability of interest rates is what makes the E_i rules more attractive from the point of view of the loss criterion $L + \pi^{*2}$ as well.

2.3 Optimal Policy

In this section we consider the best policy rule, from the point of view of minimization of our deadweight loss measure $L + \pi^{*2}$. We start by analyzing not monetary rules per se but allocations. In particular, we ask what (conditional) paths of output, inflation, and interest rates achieve the lowest value of $L + \pi^{*2}$ while being consistent with our IS and AS curves as well as with the stochastic process for $\hat{G}_t$ and $\hat{Y}_t^s$ given in equations (27) and (28). In other words, we compute the optimal response of the whole economy to these structural disturbances.

We then show that this optimal response of the economy is the unique equilibrium that emerges when the interest rate is set according to a rule belonging to the general class (23). This means that one cannot do better from the point of view of minimizing $L + \pi^{*2}$ than using a rule within this class. Moreover, it should be obvious that the member of this class that induces the optimal allocation is also the optimal rule within the class (23).

2.3.1   Optimal Responses of the Economy to Real Disturbances

In this subsection we compute the optimal allocation and characterize it as a response of the economy to the innovations in $\hat{G}_t$ and $\hat{Y}_t^s$. For this purpose we start by constructing a moving average representation of the stochastic process for the real disturbances $\hat{G}$ and $\hat{Y}^s$. From equations (28) and (27) it follows that these variables can be written as functions of the history of the two independent identically distributed (i.i.d.) shocks in $e_t^\dagger$. Since these two shocks consist of $e_{2,t}$ and $e_{3,t}$, we can rewrite the stochastic process of the structural disturbances as

$$(46) \qquad \hat{G}_{t+1} = \sum_{i=2}^{3} \sum_{j=0}^{\infty} \Phi^i_{Gj} e_{i,t-j}, \qquad \hat{Y}^s_{t+1} = \sum_{i=2}^{3} \sum_{j=0}^{\infty} \Phi^i_{Sj} e_{i,t-j}.$$

The exact decomposition of the two shocks in (46) is irrelevant for present purposes; each is allowed to affect the evolution of both structural disturbances.

We now consider how the endogenous variables ought to evolve. Because we can write our loss measure in the form (34), it suffices to consider the evolution of $\hat{X}$. It should be obvious from equation (34) that there is no advantage to any random movements in $\hat{X}$ apart from those needed for $\hat{X}_t$ to respond to the shocks that contain information about the evolution of the real disturbances. Thus we may restrict attention to processes $\hat{X}$ that may be written in the form

$$(47) \qquad \hat{X}_{t+1} = \sum_{i=2}^{3} \sum_{j=0}^{\infty} \Phi^i_{Xj} e_{i,t-j}.$$

Substituting this into equation (34), we find that L equals

$$(48) \quad L = \sum_{i=2}^{3} \sigma^2_i \left[\sum_{j=1}^{\infty} (\Phi^i_{Xj})^2 + \psi(\Phi^i_{X0})^2 + \frac{\Lambda}{\kappa^2} \sum_{j=1}^{\infty} (\Phi^i_{Xj} - \beta\Phi^i_{Xj+1})^2 \right],$$

where σ^2_i is the variance of $e_{i,j}$. We seek to obtain parameters Φ_{Xj} that make L as low as possible for a given variance of the funds rate, subject also to any constraints on the joint evolution of $\hat{X}$ and $\hat{R}$ implied by our structural model.

Using equations (38) and (46) we can write $\hat{\rho}_t$ as a function of the lagged es. This means that using equation (47) in (37) we obtain an expression for the funds rate as a function of the history of the shocks,

(49)
$$\hat{R}_{t+1} = \sum_{i=2}^{3} \sum_{j=0}^{\infty} \Phi^i_{Rj} e_{i,t-j},$$

where the coefficients Φ^i_{Rj} can be written as functions of the coefficients Φ^i_{Gj}, Φ^i_{Sj}, and Φ^i_{Xj}. This in turn allows us to write

(50)
$$\text{var}\{\hat{R}\} = \sum_{i=2}^{3} \sum_{j=0}^{\infty} (\Phi^i_{Rj})^2 \sigma_i^2.$$

The characterization of the optimal process $\hat{X}$ then reduces to the choice of coefficients Φ^i_{Xj} to minimize the Lagrangian $L + \lambda \, \text{var}\{\hat{R}\}$, where we substitute expression (48) for L and (50) for var$\{\hat{R}\}$. Here $\lambda \geq 0$ is a multiplier indicating the weight placed on the variance of the funds rate. By minimizing the Lagrangian for different choices of $\lambda \geq 0$, we obtain the family of constrained optimal equilibria. This family corresponds to the frontier of minimum possible values of L for any given level of var$\{\hat{R}\}$ (and hence of π^*) that we report in Rotemberg and Woodford (1997).

There exists a particular value of λ such that the marginal reduction in π^{*2} from raising λ further (using eq. [39] to determine the lowest value of π^* consistent with any given value of var$\{\hat{R}\}$) is of the same size as the resulting increase in L.[27] The constrained optimal equilibrium associated with this particular value of λ achieves the minimum value of $L + \pi^{*2}$ among all allocations consistent with the structural equations of our model. The variability of inflation, output, the funds rate, and long-run price level growth in this allocation are indicated by point I in figures 2.1, 2.2, and 2.3 above, and the row labeled I in table 2.1.

Observe that the optimal allocation does not involve complete stabilization of inflation or of the long-run price level. This is not because complete stabilization is impossible in principle, but because complete stabilization would require too great a degree of volatility of the funds rate, and consequently too high an average inflation rate.[28] Thus the concern expressed by Summers (1991)—that the desire to maintain a very low average rate of inflation conflicts with the desire to use interest rates as an instrument of stabilization, given the existence of a zero nominal interest rate floor—matters quantitatively in the context of our model. On the other hand, our results imply that it is possible, at least in principle, to stabilize both inflation and the funds rate—and thus both the average rate of inflation and the variance of inflation—to a greater extent than has been achieved by historical policy. This can be seen

27. As reported in Rotemberg and Woodford (1997), the value of λ is approximately 0.2249.
28. As explained in subsection 2.1.2 above, complete stabilization of the path of the price level would require that $\hat{R}_t = \hat{\rho}_{t-1}$ each period. Given our estimated shock processes, this would imply a standard deviation of funds rate variations of 27 percentage points—10 times the funds rate volatility associated with historical policy. (See table 2 in Rotemberg and Woodford 1997.) Using eq. (39) to determine the minimum required value for π^*, we conclude that the average inflation rate would have to equal 58 percent per year.

from the relative locations of points H and I in figure 2.2. Similarly, table 2.1 shows that both L and π^* are lower with the optimal policy than with historical policy.

2.3.2   Implementing the Optimal Allocation

While the optimal allocation is consistent with equation (49), it is important to stress that equation (49) does not represent a viable policy proposal, even if the Fed could directly observe the structural disturbances and infer the history of the shocks e_{it}. Such a way of setting interest rates would, instead, result in price level indeterminacy because the path of the funds rate would be exogenously specified, with no feedback from the evolution of prices or real activity.[29] Thus the construction of a feedback rule for the funds rate that implements the optimal allocation—that is not only consistent with it but also renders it the unique stationary equilibrium consistent with the proposed policy rule—remains a nontrivial problem. Furthermore, it is of considerable interest to ask how policy should make use of the information revealed by the evolution of inflation and output, as in the various variants of the Taylor rule discussed in section 2.2. Thus we are especially interested in finding a rule of the form

$$(51) \qquad C(L)\hat{r}_t \;=\; A(L)\hat{\pi}_t \;+\; B(L)\hat{Y}_t,$$

where $A(L)$, $B(L)$, and $C(L)$ are finite-order lag polynomials, that implements the optimal allocation.

To do this, we first consider whether any rule of this form is consistent with the stochastic processes for interest rates, inflation, and output that characterize this allocation. Substituting expression (47) into (20) and (36), we can write $\hat{\pi}_t$ and $\hat{Y}_t$ as moving averages of $e_{2,t}$ and $e_{3,t}$. These moving average representations for the optimal evolution of inflation and output can be written compactly as

$$(52) \qquad \hat{Z}_t \;\equiv\; \begin{bmatrix} \hat{\pi}_t \\ \hat{Y}_t \end{bmatrix} \;=\; \Phi_Z(L)e_{t-1},$$

where

$$e_t \;\equiv\; \begin{bmatrix} e_{2,t} \\ e_{3,t} \end{bmatrix}.$$

Similarly writing equation (49) as $\hat{R}_t = \Phi_R(L)e_{t-1}$, it would then seem natural to attempt to obtain a representation of the form

$$(53) \qquad \hat{R}_t \;=\; \theta(L)\hat{Z}_t.$$

---

29. The result that equilibrium is indeterminate in this case can be observed from the fact that the point $a = 0, b = 0$ is in the zone of indeterminacy in figs. 2.4 through 2.8, or similarly that the point $a = 0, c = 0$ is in the zone of indeterminacy in figs. 2.9 through 2.12.

by writing $\theta(L) \equiv \Phi_R(L)\Phi_Z^{-1}(L)$. Unfortunately, $\Phi_Z(L)$ does not prove to be invertible, since the polynomial $|\Phi_Z(z)|$ has a root inside the unit circle.[30] This root is $1/c$, where c is approximately 1.3267. We can, however, write $\Phi_Z(L) = (1 - cL)D(L)$, where $D(L)$ is invertible so that $(1 - cL)e_{t-1}$ is equal to $D(L)^{-1}\hat{Z}_t$. This means that

(54) $$(1 - cL)\hat{R}_t = (1 - cL)\Phi_R(L)e_{t-1} = \tilde{\theta}(L)\hat{Z}_t,$$

where $\tilde{\theta}(L) \equiv \Phi_R(L)D(L)^{-1}$.

This gives us a relation of the form (51) between the funds rate, its own past values, and current and past values of inflation and output. The two elements $(i = 1, 2)$ of the matrix lag polynomial $\tilde{\theta}(L)$ can be written as

$$\tilde{\theta}_i(L) \equiv \sum_{j=0}^{\infty} \tilde{\theta}_{ij} L^j,$$

where the coefficients $\tilde{\theta}_{ij}$ are square-summable, so that long lags j contribute only a small amount to the overall variation in the right-hand side of equation (54). However, the coefficients $\tilde{\theta}_{ij}$ die out for large j only relatively slowly; they evolve asymptotically according to the difference equation

$$\tilde{\theta}_{ij} = -\tilde{a}\tilde{\theta}_{i,j-1} - \tilde{b}\tilde{\theta}_{i,j-2},$$

where the coefficients $\tilde{a}$ and $\tilde{b}$ are approximately equal to 1.0404 and 0.9643, respectively.[31] These values imply that the characteristic equation $z^2 + \tilde{a}z + \tilde{b} = 0$ has a pair of complex roots with modulus approximately equal to 0.9820. Thus the coefficients $\tilde{\theta}_{ij}$ decline in magnitude only at an average rate of less than 2 percent per quarter; a very long distributed lag is required for an accurate approximation to the exactly optimal rule of the form (54). The length of the distributed lag that is needed can be reduced significantly by further quasi differencing of $\hat{R}_t$, yielding a rule of the form (51), where $A(L) \equiv a_0 + a_1L + a_2L^2 \cdots \equiv (1 + \tilde{a}L + \tilde{b}L^2)\tilde{\theta}_1(L)$, $B(L) \equiv b_0 + b_1L + b_2L^2 \cdots \equiv (1 + \tilde{a}L + \tilde{b}L^2)\tilde{\theta}_2(L)$, and $C(L) \equiv 1 - c_1L - c_2L^2 \cdots \equiv (1 + \tilde{a}L + \tilde{b}L^2)(1 - cL)$. The coefficients in the matrix lag polynomials $A(L)$ and $B(L)$ then become negligible much sooner.

Ignoring the constant, the policy rule that we derive in this fashion can then be written as

---

30. We demonstrate this numerically by truncating the infinite lag polynomial $\Phi_Z(L)$ at a finite number of lags and solving for the roots of $|\Phi_Z(z)|$. In our numerical work, we use the terms for $j = 0$ through 130 in eq. (47). We stop at lag 130 because both $\Phi_Z(1)$ and our estimate of the root of $|\Phi_Z(z)|$, which lies inside the unit circle, are little affected by the addition of further terms.

31. We determined this by inspection of the coefficients $\tilde{\theta}_{ij}$, which can be computed recursively. The coefficients that we compute obey the stated recursion, up to four decimal places of accuracy, for both $i = 1$ and 2, for all values of j between 61 and 92. After this, the recursion breaks down, presumably because a small numerical error in our estimate of c introduces a nontrivial error into our computation of $\tilde{\theta}_{ij}$ for larger values of j.

$$\hat{r}_t = .29\hat{r}_{t-1} + .42\hat{r}_{t-2} + 1.28\hat{r}_{t-3}$$

$$+ .22\hat{Y}_{t-1} - .25\hat{Y}_{t-2} + \cdots$$

(55)
$$+ .16\hat{\pi}_t + 1.00\hat{\pi}_{t-1} + 2.45\hat{\pi}_{t-2} - 1.45\hat{\pi}_{t-3} + .74\pi_{t-4}$$

$$- .08\hat{\pi}_{t-5} + .25\hat{\pi}_{t-6} + .33\hat{\pi}_{t-7} + .23\hat{\pi}_{t-8} + .25\hat{\pi}_{t-9}$$

$$+ .19\hat{\pi}_{t-10} + .17\hat{\pi}_{t-11} + .13\hat{\pi}_{t-12} + .09\hat{\pi}_{t-13} + .06\hat{\pi}_{t-14} + \cdots,$$

where the omitted terms in $\hat{Y}_{t-j}$ are all of size 0.01 or smaller (to two decimal places) and the omitted terms in $\hat{\pi}_{t-j}$ are all of size 0.03 or smaller (to two decimal places).[32] Supposing that the monetary policy rule is given by expression (55), we find that our model has a unique stationary rational expectations equilibrium. Furthermore, this unique equilibrium involves responses of output, inflation, and interest rates to the real shocks that closely approximate the optimal responses derived in the previous subsection. Thus we conclude that rule (55) does belong to the admissible class of interest rate feedback rules resulting in a determinate equilibrium; that it represents a good approximation to the optimal rule within the general class of rules of the form (51); and that the optimal rule within this class implements the optimal allocation as defined above. Rule (55) is accordingly the optimal policy rule, labeled I in table 2.1 and in figures 2.1, 2.2, and 2.3.

Several features of this optimal interest rate feedback rule are worth noting. First, the coefficient on $\hat{\pi}_t$ is a small positive number, which means that the optimal rule calls for some immediate tightening in response to an observation of inflation above the target level. However, most of the tightening prescribed by the rule in response to an inflation rate above target occurs later. This subsequent tightening is reflected both in the series of positive coefficients on lagged inflation deviations $\hat{\pi}_{t-j}$ in rule (55), and in the series of positive coefficients on lagged deviations of the funds rate itself. Even putting aside the consequences of the lagged funds rate terms, the $\hat{\pi}_{t-j}$ terms in (55) prescribe a much larger response to lagged inflation than to current inflation; for example, these terms place an average weight of 0.7 on the rate of inflation over quarters 1 through 4 prior to the quarter in which the funds rate is being set, or four times the weight that is placed on inflation in the current quarter.

Second, the coefficient on $\hat{Y}_t$ is exactly zero. This means that the optimal response to an innovation in $\hat{G}_t$ that increases output relative to what it would have been forecast to be a quarter earlier is to keep the interest rate at t unchanged. This does not mean that there is no optimal response to observed

32. For $j = 50$ and above, the terms in $\hat{\pi}_{t-j}$ are all .0001 or smaller, while the same is true of the $\hat{Y}_{t-j}$ terms for $j = 19$ and above. Whether the small nonzero values that we still obtain for large j indicate that further quasi differencing is needed in order to obtain a rule of the form (51). with finite lag polynomials, or are simply due to numerical error, we have not been able to determine.

variations in output relative to trend, but that the optimal response is a delayed one. Moreover, the interest rate ought to respond more to the *growth rate* of output a quarter earlier than to the *level* of output.[33]

Finally, the lag polynomial $C(L)$ has a root inside the unit circle, equal to the reciprocal of $c = 1.33$. Thus, just as in our optimal generalized Taylor rules, the optimal rule calls not simply for interest rate smoothing but for an explosively growing response of the funds rate to deviations of inflation from target. These explosions are avoided only if subsequent deviations with the opposite sign eventually counteract the effects of an initial deviation. If the inflation rate were permanently above its target, interest rates would grow asymptotically as $(1.33)^t$, just as if we chose $c = 1.33$ in the case of the family of simple rules (41). This explosive behavior is of course exactly what we concluded was desirable in our previous discussion of simple rules, and indeed the value $c = 1.33$ is not too different from the most desirable value of c in the case of simple rules.

One way of comparing the implications of rule (55) with those of other candidate interest rate rules is to plot its implications for the cumulative response of the funds rate to a sustained deviation of either inflation from target or output from its trend level. This particular way of describing the various feedback rules has the advantage of being independent of the degree of quasi differentiation that may have been used in the way that the rule is stated; for example, it treats expressions (54) and (55) as equivalent. The prescribed cumulative responses of the funds rate to sustained 1 percent deviations in the two variables are displayed in the two panels of figure 2.19. Each panel compares the prescribed response of the funds rate under four different rules: our estimate of historical U.S. policy over the period 1979–95, the rule proposed by Taylor (1993) as a rough description of recent U.S. policy, the optimal rule E_0 within the family (41), and our unrestricted optimal rule (55). We see in the top panel that, after two quarters of inflation being above target, the first two rules (which are quite similar to each other in this respect) involve much smaller responses of the interest rate to the inflation deviation than the latter two. Our unrestricted optimal rule is actually less aggressive than the optimal rule of the form (41) over the horizon displayed in this panel. Indeed, the initial reaction to inflation is actually smaller in this unrestricted optimum than it is in the case of the simple Taylor rule. This serves to highlight once again the fact that our model recommends postponing the reaction of interest rates while simultaneously increasing the absolute magnitude of these delayed reactions.

The bottom panel shows the responses to a sustained output deviation. Here the Taylor rule and our estimate of actual policy involve much stronger reactions of the interest rate over the first three quarters than are implied by either

---

33. Interestingly, our estimated historical policy rule for the United States, reported in Rotemberg and Woodford (1997), also implies more response to the growth rate than to the detrended level of real GDP; but the historical rule can be more accurately described as making the funds rate respond to $\hat{Y}_t - \hat{Y}_{t-2}$ rather than to $\hat{Y}_{t-1} - \hat{Y}_{t-2}$.

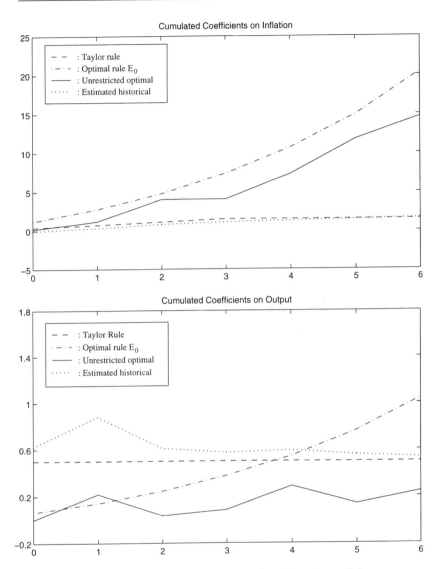

Fig. 2.19   Cumulative interest rate response under alternative policies

of the optimal rules. For the unrestricted optimal rule, the reaction remains more muted for the entire six-quarter horizon displayed here. This indicates an important difference between actual policy, at least as either Taylor or we have characterized it, and optimal policy according to our model: our model suggests that interest rate responses to output above trend should be much weaker, at least in the first few quarters, than they actually are. On the other hand, this does not mean that optimal policy would not involve interest rates eventually being raised. For the optimal policy in the class (41), interest rates are actually higher after five quarters of high output than they would be under actual policy or the simple Taylor rule. If one extends the plot a few more quarters, this is also true of the unrestricted optimal policy, and both optimal rules (unlike the two characterizations of actual policy) imply that the funds rate eventually explodes.

A final feature of the optimal rule that is worth pointing out is its implication for long-run price level stability. We observe that the optimal rule has the form of an inflation-targeting rule, rather than a price-level-targeting rule, and indeed it does not imply trend stationarity of the price level. On the other hand, it *does* imply a tendency for unexpected increases in the price level to be subsequently offset by (forecastable) price level declines. This is indicated by a coefficient β^∞ that is negative, indicating that unexpected price level increases are eventually more than completely offset by subsequent price level declines, as in the case of the optimal simple rules E_0 and E_1. As a result, optimal policy involves a significant degree of stabilization of the rate of change of long-run price level forecasts—the standard deviation of Δp^∞ is reduced by a factor of four, relative to our estimate of historical policy.

Finally, it is worth asking to what extent our analysis implies that a simple rule such as E_0 or E_1 can be improved upon by using additional information. We have already observed that, according to our structural model, the history of inflation and output variations alone, if observed with sufficient accuracy and timeliness, provide all of the information needed to implement the optimal equilibrium. Thus a sufficiently flexible rule of the form (51) suffices. But as a practical matter, it is probably even more interesting to observe that our results imply that the unrestricted optimal rule is not too different from, and not too much better than, the optimal rule within a simple family such as (41). Ninety-nine percent of the nearly 15-fold reduction in the size of the deadweight loss $L + \pi^{*2}$ that is achievable by going from actual policy to optimal policy can be obtained by adopting the simple rule E_0. Furthermore, if E_0 is not considered operational due to its reliance on measures of the current quarter's inflation and output, the simple rule E_1, which requires only the previous quarter's data, results in performance that is nearly as good. Thus our analysis supports the view that simple policy rules, variations on the sort of rule proposed by Taylor (1993), have highly desirable properties both from the point of view of stabilizing inflation, interest rates, and the long-run price level, as well as from the point of view of economic welfare.

2.4 Conclusions

Our results offer a number of conclusions of importance for the design of a monetary policy rule. All of our conclusions are subject, of course, to the caveat that the seriousness with which they should be taken depends on one's confidence in the extent to which the specification of our structural model is not grossly incorrect.

Probably our most important conclusion is that a simple interest rate feedback rule of the kind proposed by Taylor (1993) can achieve outcomes nearly as good as are achievable in principle by *any* policy, assuming that the commitment of the monetary authority to the rule can be made sufficiently credible. At least in the context of the simple structural model that we consider, an interest rate feedback rule that uses only information about the recent behavior of inflation and output does quite well (and only the response to the recent level of inflation matters much for this). Furthermore, performance under the best rule of this kind is not significantly reduced if *lagged* inflation data are used. Thus lags in the availability of accurate measurements of inflation are not necessarily a serious problem for the implementation of such a rule.

It is worth noting in particular that a "backward-looking" rule, in which interest rates respond to measures of inflation that has already occurred, rather than to forecasts (of one sort or another) of future inflation (as in the rules considered by Rudebusch and Svensson, in chap. 5 of this volume, and Batini and Haldane, in chap. 4), do quite well. We show that, at least in our simple model, the theoretically optimal policy has a backward-looking representation, given by expression (55). Perhaps more to the point, even very simple backward-looking rules, such as rules E_0 and E_1 in table 2.1, are quite good approximations to optimal policy.

It is interesting to note that we obtain this result despite using a structural model that implies that monetary policy has no effects on inflation until the following quarter (and the largest effect only after two quarters), and no effects on real activity until after two quarters. Lags in the effects of a monetary policy change do *not* imply that an effective policy must be "forward looking." The crucial insight is that there is no need for *policy* to be forward looking as long as the *private sector* is. A commitment to raise interest rates later, after inflation increases, is sufficient to cause an immediate contraction of aggregate demand in response to a shock that is expected to give rise to inflationary pressures. This channel should be effective as long as aggregate demand depends on expected *future* interest rates (or, equivalently, on *long* rates) and not simply on current short rates; as long as the monetary authority is understood to be committed to adhering to the contemplated policy rule in the future, and not only at the present time; and as long as private agents have model-consistent (or "rational") expectations. Indeed, if, as our model implies, aggregate demand is affected *only* by expectations of future interest rates, and not by unexpected interest rate variations (either immediately or with a lag), then a credible commitment to systematically respond in the future is the only way in which monetary policy can be effective. But when one conceives policy in these terms, there is no need for that commitment about future action to involve a commitment to be forward looking at that future date.

Despite our general support for the type of policy rule proposed by Taylor, our analysis suggests that the best rules differ from the specific rule that he proposes in important respects. Probably the most important difference is our conclusion that short-term interest rates should depend not only on deviations of inflation from target but also on their *own* past values—ideally with a coefficient even greater than one. A less radical-sounding version of our proposal would be to make the *change* in the funds rate, rather than the *level* of the funds rate, a function of deviations of inflation from its target value, as is also found to be desirable in the forward-looking models studied by Levin, Wieland, and Williams (chap. 6 of this volume). It is interesting to note that in forward-looking models of these kinds, such dependence, even with a coefficient greater than one on the lagged value, does not lead to instrument instability. This result contrasts sharply with the conclusion that one would obtain using a traditional, purely backward-looking macroeconometric model, such as the one considered by Rudebusch and Svensson (chap. 5 of this volume).

In our analysis, the desirability of such dependence on the lagged funds rate does not rest on any assumption that variability in the change in the funds rate from one period to the next is a bad thing in itself. Rather, it represents a way of allowing the central bank to commit itself to raise interest rates later, in response to an increase in inflation that is not offset by a subsequent (and sufficiently prompt) inflation decline, without having to have much of the *eventual* interest rate response occur immediately. Assuming that the private sector understands this commitment and is forward looking in its behavior, this allows the central bank to have a large effect on aggregate demand without having (in equilibrium) to move interest rates very much. This in turn is desirable if one wishes to maintain a low volatility of interest rates. We argue that a low volatility of the funds rate is in fact desirable as it allows a given degree of inflation stabilization to be consistent with a lower *average* rate of inflation, due to the zero floor for the nominal funds rate.

Our results here plainly depend on the assumption not only that the private sector is forward looking but that private agents fully understand and believe in the central bank's policy rule. One might wonder whether such an analysis gives a correct account of the consequences of adopting such a rule, especially in the short run, given that it would represent a significant departure from present policy (according to our estimates). Nonetheless, our analysis shows that the possibility of achieving a significant degree of stabilization without a great deal of interest rate volatility through this channel is an important advantage of a high degree of credibility for the central bank's commitment to a monetary policy rule. This helps to clarify why the design of arrangements under which such a rule could be credible could have significant benefits.

Another respect in which our conclusions differ from Taylor's proposal is that we find little gain from making interest rates depend on the current level of economic activity. We find that optimal rules within our simple families involve a small positive response to the level of detrended output, but it is much more modest than the sort of response suggested by Taylor, or indicated by our estimate of actual U.S. policy. The reason it is undesirable to respond to output deviations, in our model, is that deviations of output from trend have so little to do with deviations of output from *potential* (which, according to our estimates, is quite volatile). It is possible that an alternative interpretation of the residuals in our aggregate supply equation, under which they would not all represent variations in the *efficient* level of output, would increase the role for responses to output variations in an optimal rule. Alternatively, it is possible that if we considered other real variables (such as employment) along with variations in detrended output, we would be able to construct a better proxy for deviations of output from potential (as proposed, e.g., by McCallum and Nelson in chap. 1 of this volume), to which it would be desirable for interest rates to respond.

Finally, our results shed light on the debate about the relative advantages of price level targeting and inflation targeting. We find that under a desirable policy, the central bank should consistently act to subsequently reverse any movements of inflation above its target level, rather than simply preventing further price increases without undoing the ones that have already occurred. Nonetheless, according to our analysis, there is no special significance to the goal of returning the price level to a deterministic target path. Our optimal policy rules actually imply that an unexpected increase in inflation should *decrease* the expected long-run price level. Such an outcome is obtained by a policy that involves no reference to a target price level path. It follows simply from the dependence of the funds rate on the lagged funds rate, mentioned above, which has the consequence that, in equilibrium, inflation increases must be followed by subsequent, and even greater, inflation declines in order to avoid causing the funds rate to grow explosively.

Appendix
Derivation of the Utility-Based Loss Function

Here we present further details of the derivation of equations (30), (31), (33), and (34), which describe our utility-based loss function $L + \pi^{*2}$. We begin with the derivation of equation (30) as a second-order Taylor series approximation to (29). Note that our objective function is of the form $W \equiv Ew_t$, where w_t is the average utility flow (integrating over the continuum of households) each period. This utility flow may be written as a function solely of the pattern of real activity $\{y_t(z)\}$ within a period, and the exogenous shocks:

$$(A1) \qquad w_t = u(Y_t - G_t; \xi_t) - \int_0^1 v(y_t(z); \xi_t)dz.$$

We begin by considering a Taylor series expansion for each of the two terms in this expression, expanding around the levels of output $y_t(z) = \bar{Y}$ for each z and the values $G_t = \bar{G}$ and $\xi_t = 0$ for the exogenous shocks. Here $\bar{Y}$ represents the level of output in an *optimal* steady state; it represents the constant equilibrium level of output in an equilibrium with no variation in the values of G_t and

ξ_t around their steady state values, a constant price level, and a tax rate $\tau = \tau^*$ $\equiv -(\theta - 1)^{-1}$ that perfectly offsets the distortion resulting from firms' monopoly power. (As we shall see, our loss function takes an especially simple form in this case, and we wish to direct attention to the terms in it that survive even under these ideal circumstances. We leave for further work the analysis of how the welfare effects of monetary policy change when one considers possible interactions between monetary policy and distortions other than the one resulting from sluggish nominal price adjustment.) The steady state value $\overline{G}$ is chosen to equal $E(G_t)$, and the shocks ξ_t are normalized so that $E(\xi_t) = 0$; thus the steady state values of the exogenous variables equal their unconditional means.

A second-order Taylor series expansion for the first term on the right-hand side of equation (A1) is given by

$$
\begin{aligned}
\text{(A2)} \quad u &= u(\overline{C};0) + u_C(C_t - \overline{C}) + u_\xi \xi_t \\
&\quad + \frac{1}{2}u_{CC}(C_t - \overline{C})^2 + u_{C\xi}(C_t - \overline{C})\xi_t + \frac{1}{2}u_{\xi\xi}\xi_t^2 + \mathcal{O}(\|\xi\|^3)
\end{aligned}
$$

$$
\begin{aligned}
\text{(A3)} \quad &= u(\overline{C};0) + u_C\overline{Y}(\hat{Y}_t + \frac{1}{2}\hat{Y}_t^2 - \tilde{G}_t) + u_\xi \xi_t \\
&\quad + \frac{1}{2}u_{CC}\overline{Y}^2(\hat{Y}_t - \tilde{G}_t)^2 + u_{C\xi}\overline{Y}(\hat{Y}_t - \tilde{G}_t)\xi_t + \frac{1}{2}u_{\xi\xi}\xi_t^2 + \mathcal{O}(\|\xi\|^3)
\end{aligned}
$$

$$
\begin{aligned}
\text{(A4)} \quad &= u_C\overline{Y} \cdot \hat{Y}_t + \frac{1}{2}(u_C\overline{Y} + u_{CC}\overline{Y}^2)\hat{Y}^2 \\
&\quad - u_{CC}\hat{Y}^2(\tilde{G}_t + s_C\overline{C}_t)\hat{Y}_t + \text{t.i.p.} + \mathcal{O}(\|\xi\|^3)
\end{aligned}
$$

$$
\begin{aligned}
\text{(A5)} \quad &= u_C\overline{Y} \cdot \hat{Y}_t + \frac{1}{2}(u_C\overline{Y} + u_{CC}\overline{Y}^2)\hat{Y}^2 \\
&\quad - u_{CC}\hat{Y}^2 \cdot \hat{G}_t\hat{Y}_t + \text{t.i.p.} + \text{unf.} + \mathcal{O}(\|\xi\|^3).
\end{aligned}
$$

In (A2) we simply expand in terms of the index of aggregate consumption C_t, where $\overline{C} \equiv \overline{Y} - \overline{G}$, and each of the partial derivatives is evaluated at the steady state values $(\overline{C};0)$. Here the term $\mathcal{O}(\|\xi\|^3)$ indicates that we neglect terms that are of third or higher order in the deviations of the various variables from their steady state values. In the case of a monetary policy rule that implies $\pi^* = 0$ and a tax rate $\tau = \tau^*$, the variables will deviate from these values in an equilibrium only because of fluctuations in the shocks G_t and ξ_t around their steady state values. In this case, the omitted terms are all of third or higher order in the size of the exogenous shocks (and we use $\|\xi\|$ to indicate the a measure of the size of these shocks, where the size of fluctuations in G_t is intended to be included). More generally, the omitted terms also include terms that are of third or higher order in deviations of π^* from the value zero and of

τ from the value τ^*; but we shall (for now) retain terms that are of first or second order in perturbations of those assumptions about long-run aspects of policy. In equation (A3) we rewrite the expressions in terms of $\hat{Y}_t \equiv \log(Y_t/\bar{Y})$ and $\tilde{G}_t \equiv (G_t - \bar{G})/\bar{Y}$, using the Taylor expansion

$$Y_t = \bar{Y}(1 + \hat{Y}_t + \frac{1}{2}\hat{Y}_t^2) + \mathcal{O}(\|\xi\|^3).$$

In equation (A4) we suppress the terms that are independent of policy (because they involve only constants and exogenous disturbances), denoted "t.i.p." as in the text, and make use of the definition $u_{c\xi}\xi_t = -u_{cc}\bar{C}C_t$ to obtain a scalar representation of the disturbance to the marginal utility of consumption. Finally, in equation (A5) we recall the notation

$$\hat{G}_t \equiv \tilde{G}_t + s_C E_{t-2}\bar{C}_t = \tilde{G}_t + s_C\bar{C}_t + \text{unf.},$$

where "unf." stands for an unforecastable term (i.e., a term x_t with the property that $E_{t-2}x_t = 0$). Unforecastable terms may be neglected because we are ultimately interested only in the unconditional expectation of each of the terms in equation (A5).

Similarly, a second-order Taylor series expansion of household z's disutility of working is given by

$$v = v(\bar{Y};0) + v_y(y_t(z) - \bar{Y}) + v_\xi\xi_t$$

$$+ \frac{1}{2}v_{yy}(y_t(z) - \bar{Y})^2 + v_{y\xi}(y_t(z) - \bar{Y})\xi_t + \frac{1}{2}v_{\xi\xi}\xi_t^2 + \mathcal{O}(\|\xi\|^3)$$

(A6)

$$= v_y\bar{Y} \cdot \hat{y}_t(z) + \frac{1}{2}(v_y\bar{Y} + v_{yy}\bar{Y}^2)\hat{y}_t(z)^2 - v_{yy}\bar{Y}^2 \cdot \hat{y}_t(z)\bar{Y}_t$$

$$+ \text{t.i.p.} + \mathcal{O}(\|\xi\|^3),$$

where now $\hat{y}_t(z) \equiv \log(y_t(z)/\bar{Y})$ and $\bar{Y}_t$, defined by the relation $v_{y\xi}\xi_t = -v_{yy}\bar{Y}\bar{Y}_t$, provides a scalar measure of disturbances to the marginal disutility of supply. Integrating equation (A6) over z we obtain

$$\int_0^1 v(y_t(z);\xi_t)dz = v_y\bar{Y} \cdot E_z\hat{y}_t(z) + \frac{1}{2}(v_y\bar{Y} + v_{yy}\bar{Y}^2) \cdot [E_z\hat{y}_t(z)]^2$$

(A7)

$$+ \frac{1}{2}(v_y\bar{Y} + v_{yy}\bar{Y}^2)\,\text{var}_z\hat{y}_t(z) - v_{yy}\bar{Y}^2 \cdot E_z\hat{y}_t(z)$$

$$+ \text{t.i.p.} + \mathcal{O}(\|\xi\|^3).$$

Next we wish to express the terms in equation (A7) involving the population average $E_z\hat{y}_t(z)$ in terms of the Dixit-Stiglitz output aggregate $\hat{Y}_t$ instead. To do so, we first compute a Taylor series expansion for the right-hand side of the aggregator equation (2), obtaining

$$\hat{Y}_t = E_z \hat{y}_t(z) + \frac{1}{2} \frac{\theta - 1}{\theta} \text{var}_z \hat{y}_t(z) + \mathcal{O}(\|\xi\|^3).$$

Solving this equation for $E_z \hat{y}_t(z)$ and substituting into equation (A7) yields

$$\int_0^1 v(y_t(z); \xi_t) dz = v_y \overline{Y} \cdot \hat{Y}_t + \frac{1}{2}(v_y \overline{Y} + v_{yy} \overline{Y}^2) \hat{Y}_t^2$$

(A8)
$$+ \frac{1}{2}(\theta^{-1} v_y \overline{Y} + v_{yy} \overline{Y}^2) \text{var}_z \hat{y}_t(z) - v_{yy} \overline{Y}^2 \cdot \hat{Y}_t \overline{Y}_t$$

$$+ \text{t.i.p.} + \mathcal{O}(\|\xi\|^3).$$

Substituting equations (A5) and (A8) into (A1), we obtain

$$w_t = u_C \overline{Y} \left[\hat{Y}_t + \frac{1}{2}(1 - \sigma) \hat{Y}_t^2 + \sigma \hat{G}_t \hat{Y}_t \right]$$

$$- v_y \overline{Y} \left[\hat{Y}_t + \frac{1}{2}(1 + \omega) \hat{Y}_t^2 + \frac{1}{2}(\theta^{-1} + \omega) \text{var}_z \hat{y}_t(z) - \omega \overline{Y}_t \hat{Y}_t \right]$$

(A9)
$$+ \text{t.i.p.} + \text{unf.} + \mathcal{O}(\|\xi\|^3)$$

$$= -\frac{1}{2} u_C \overline{Y}[(\sigma + \omega) \hat{Y}_t^2 - 2(\sigma + \omega) \hat{Y}_t^s \hat{Y}_t + (\theta^{-1} + \omega) \text{var}_z \hat{y}_t(z)]$$

$$+ \text{t.i.p.} + \text{unf.} + \mathcal{O}(\|\xi\|^3).$$

Note that in deriving (A9) from the line above we have (at last) used the assumption that $\overline{Y}$ is the efficient level of output, so that $u_C = v_y$, and the definition

$$\hat{Y}_t^s \equiv (\sigma + \omega)^{-1} (\sigma \hat{G}_t + \omega E_{t-1} \overline{Y}_t) = (\sigma + \omega)^{-1} [\sigma \hat{G}_t + \omega \hat{Y}_t] + \text{unf.}$$

Then taking the unconditional expectation of equation (A9), we obtain

(A10)
$$W = -\frac{1}{2} u_C \overline{Y}[(\sigma + \omega) \text{var}\{\hat{Y}_t - \hat{Y}_t^s\} + (\sigma + \omega)[E(\hat{Y}_t)]^2$$

$$+ (\theta^{-1} + \omega) E \text{var}_z \hat{y}_t(z)] + \text{t.i.p.} + \mathcal{O}(\|\xi\|^3).$$

As promised, we have obtained a welfare measure that allows us to compute all second-order or lower terms in W using only a first-order (log-linear) approximation to the equilibrium solution for the pattern of activity $\{y_t(z)\}$, since no terms of order $\mathcal{O}(\|\xi\|^2)$ in the solution for $y_t(z)$ have any effect on terms of order lower than $\mathcal{O}(\|\xi\|^3)$ in equation (A10).[34] If we furthermore assume that the

---

34. This result depends on our having linearized around the efficient $\overline{Y}$, since otherwise our expression for W would contain a term that is linear in $E(\hat{Y}_t)$. However, even without this choice, we could have obtained the same result by assuming that tax policy adjusts in response to any change in the monetary policy rule in order to preserve a particular value for $E(\hat{Y}_t)$, where this quantity then becomes one of the terms independent of the monetary policy rule. In fact, we assume that taxes respond to keep output fixed in the work reported here in any event.

tax rate τ (or some other aspect of "long-run" policy) is adjusted so as to guarantee that $E(\hat{Y}_t) = 0$ (i.e., log Y_t equals log $\bar{Y}$ on average) *regardless* of the monetary policy rule, then the $[E(\hat{Y}_t)]^2$ term in equation (A10) can also be suppressed, as this term is also independent of the monetary policy rule. Our decision to assume this results from a belief, as discussed in the text, that monetary policy is not an appropriate instrument with which to seek to affect the long-run average level of economic activity, given the existence of other instruments with which policymakers may more directly seek to offset the distortion resulting from suppliers' market power. Finally, noting that $\hat{Y}_t$ equals $E_{t-2}\hat{Y}_t$ plus a forecast error term that is both unforecastable and independent of monetary policy, one can show that

$$\mathrm{var}\{\hat{Y}_t - \hat{Y}_t^s\} = \mathrm{var}\{E_{t-2}(\hat{Y}_t - \hat{Y}_t^s)\} + \text{t.i.p.}$$

Substitution of this into equation (A10), along with the stipulation that $E(\hat{Y}_t) = 0$ regardless of monetary policy, then yields equation (30).

Some might prefer instead an analysis that would assume a tax rate τ that remained invariant under alternative monetary policy rules. In this case, we would not be able to drop the $[E(\hat{Y}_t)]^2$ term in equation (A10). However, our model implies that

$$E(\hat{Y}_t) = \frac{1 - \beta}{\kappa} E(\hat{X}_t) + \mathcal{O}(\|\xi\|^2) = \frac{1 - \beta}{\kappa} E(\pi_t) + \mathcal{O}(\|\xi\|^2),$$

where the first equality follows from taking the unconditional expectation of all terms in equation (21), and the second from taking the unconditional expectation of all terms in (20). (Note that in the log-linear approximations to the model equations reported in the paper, we routinely suppress terms of order $\mathcal{O}(\|\xi\|^2)$.) Thus the only difference in the alternative case would be the presence of an additional negative term in π^{*2} in equation (31). This would have no effect on the definition of the loss from incomplete stabilization L in equation (33), but it would mean that in (32) we would have $L + \mu\pi^{*2}$ instead of $L + \pi^{*2}$, for a certain $\mu > 1$, as our overall deadweight loss measure. This would imply that the optimal point on the $L - \pi^*$ frontier (discussed and graphed in Rotemberg and Woodford 1997) would be slightly different from the one that we assume here, involving a slightly smaller, though still slightly positive, value of π^*. Such a change makes no qualitative difference, however, in the conclusions announced here about the nature of optimal policy.

Next we turn to the derivation of equation (31) from (30). As noted in the text, we need to show that the dispersion of levels of production across differentiated goods is a function of the degree of variability of the aggregate price level. We begin by noting that output dispersion follows from price dispersion, since equation (3) implies that

(A11) $$E\,\mathrm{var}_z\{\log y_t(z)\} = \theta^2\,E\,\mathrm{var}_z\{\log p_t(z)\}.$$

To relate the cross-sectional variance of prices to the variability over time of the price index P_t, we begin by recalling that in any period t, a fraction α of suppliers charge the same price as at $t - 1$ (and the distribution of their prices is the same as the distribution of period $t - 1$ prices); a fraction $(1 - \alpha)\gamma$ charge a common new price p_t^1 chosen at $t - 1$, and a fraction $(1 - \alpha)(1 - \gamma)$ charge a common new price p_t^2 chosen at $t - 2$. Then, introducing the notation $\bar{p}_t \equiv E_z \log p_t(z)$, we obtain

$$
\begin{aligned}
\operatorname{var}_z\{\log p_t(z)\} &= \operatorname{var}_z\{\log p_t(z) - \bar{p}_{t-1}\} = E_z\{[\log p_t(z) - \bar{p}_{t-1}]^2\} + (\Delta\bar{p}_t)^2 \\
&= \alpha E_z\{[\log p_{t-1}(z) - \bar{p}_{t-1}]^2\} + (1 - \alpha)\gamma(\log p_t^1 - \bar{p}_{t-1})^2 \\
&\quad + (1 - \alpha)(1 - \gamma)(\log p_t^2 - \bar{p}_{t-1})^2 + (\Delta\bar{p}_t)^2 \\
&= \alpha \operatorname{var}_z\{\log p_{t-1}(z)\} + (1 - \alpha)\gamma(\log p_t^1 - \bar{p}_{t-1})^2 \\
&\quad + (1 - \alpha)(1 - \gamma)(\log p_t^2 - \bar{p}_{t-1})^2 + (\Delta\bar{p}_t)^2 .
\end{aligned}
$$

(A12)

Taking the unconditional expectation of both sides of (A12) then yields

$$
\begin{aligned}
E \operatorname{var}_z\{\log p_t(z)\} &= \gamma E[(\log p_t^1 - \bar{p}_{t-1})^2] + (1 - \gamma)E[(\log p_t^2 - \bar{p}_{t-1})^2] \\
&\quad - (1 - \alpha)^{-1}E[(\Delta\bar{p}_t)^2].
\end{aligned}
$$

(A13)

Similar reasoning as is used in deriving equation (A12) also yields

$$
\begin{aligned}
\bar{p}_t - \bar{p}_{t-1} &= E_z[\log p_t(z) - \bar{p}_{t-1}] \\
&= \alpha E_z[\log p_{t-1}(z) - \bar{p}_{t-1}] + (1 - \alpha)\gamma(\log p_t^1 - \bar{p}_{t-1}) \\
&\quad + (1 - \alpha)(1 - \gamma)(\log p_t^2 - \bar{p}_{t-1}) \\
&= (1 - \alpha)\gamma(\log p_t^1 - \bar{p}_{t-1}) + (1 - \alpha)(1 - \gamma)(\log p_t^2 - \bar{p}_{t-1}).
\end{aligned}
$$

(A14)

Taking the expectation of (A14) conditional on date $t - 2$ information, one obtains

(A15) $$E_{t-2}(\bar{p}_t - \bar{p}_{t-1}) = (1 - \alpha)(\log p_t^2 - \bar{p}_{t-1}) + \mathcal{O}(\|\xi\|^2),$$

using the facts that $\log p_t^2 = E_{t-2} \log p_t^1 + \mathcal{O}(\|\xi\|^2)$ and that all date $t - 1$ prices are known at $t - 2$. This combined with (A14) implies that

(A16) $$
\begin{aligned}
(\bar{p}_t - \bar{p}_{t-1}) - (1 - \gamma)E_{t-2}(\bar{p}_t - \bar{p}_{t-1}) &= (1 - \alpha)\gamma(\log p_t^1 - \bar{p}_{t-1}) \\
&\quad + \mathcal{O}(\|\xi\|^2).
\end{aligned}
$$

Furthermore, given that we are expanding around a steady state with zero inflation, the right-hand sides of both equations (A15) and (A16) consist solely of terms of order $\mathcal{O}(\|\xi\|)$. Thus by squaring (A15) and taking the unconditional expectation, we obtain

$$E[(\log p_t^2 - \bar{p}_{t-1})^2] = (1 - \alpha)^{-2} E[(E_{t-2}\Delta \bar{p}_t)^2] + \mathcal{O}(\|\xi\|^3)$$

$$= (1 - \alpha)^{-2} \text{var}\{E_{t-2}\Delta \bar{p}_t\} + (1 - \alpha)^{-2}(E\Delta \bar{p}_t)^2 + \mathcal{O}(\|\xi\|^3).$$

A similar expression for $E[(\log p_t^1 - \bar{p}_{t-1})^2]$ is implied by (A16). Substituting these expressions into (A13) then yields

$$\text{(A17)} \quad E \text{ var}_z\{\log p_t(z)\} = \frac{\alpha}{(1 - \alpha)^2}[\text{var}\{E_{t-2}\Delta \bar{p}_t\} + (E\Delta \bar{p}_t)^2]$$

$$+ \frac{1 - \gamma(1 - \alpha)}{\gamma(1 - \alpha)^2} \text{var}\{\Delta \bar{p}_t - E_{t-2}\Delta \bar{p}_t\} + \mathcal{O}(\|\xi\|^3).$$

Finally, the definition of the price index (4) implies that

$$\bar{p}_t = \log P_t + \mathcal{O}(\|\xi\|^2).$$

Making this substitution in equation (A17), we obtain

$$\text{(A18)} \quad E \text{ var}_z\{\log p_t(z)\} = \frac{\alpha}{(1 - \alpha)^2}[\text{var}\{E_{t-2}\pi_t\} + (E\pi_t)^2]$$

$$+ \frac{1 - \gamma(1 - \alpha)}{\gamma(1 - \alpha)^2} \text{var}\{\pi_t - E_{t-2}\pi_t\} + \mathcal{O}(\|\xi\|^3).$$

Substitution of equations (A11) and (A18) into (30), and the fact that (as a consequence of our definition of π^*) $E\pi_t = \pi^* + \mathcal{O}(\|\xi\|^2)$, then yields equation (31). This last expression can in turn obviously be written in the form (32), where L is defined by (33), and

$$\Omega \equiv \frac{1}{2}u_c\bar{Y}\theta(1 + \theta\omega)\frac{\alpha}{(1 - \alpha)^2}, \qquad \Lambda \equiv \frac{(1 - \alpha)\kappa}{(1 - \alpha\beta)\theta}.$$

Finally, we can rewrite L so that it depends only on the stochastic process for the relative price variable $\hat{X}$. To do this, note first that equation (21) implies that

$$\text{(A19)} \qquad E_{t-2}(\hat{Y}_t - \hat{Y}_t^s) = (1/\kappa)E_{t-2}(\hat{X}_t - \beta\hat{X}_{t+1}).$$

At the same time, equation (20) implies that

$$\text{(A20)} \qquad \pi_t - E_{t-2}\pi_t = \psi(\hat{X}_t - E_{t-2}\hat{X}_t),$$

so that

$$\text{(A21)} \qquad \text{var}\{\pi_t\} = \text{var}\{E_{t-2}\hat{X}_t\} + \psi^2 \text{var}\{\hat{X}_t - E_{t-2}\hat{X}_t\}.$$

Substituting the expressions in (A19), (A20), and (A21) into equation (33), we obtain (34).

References

Bean, Charles R. 1983. Targeting nominal income: An appraisal. *Economic Journal* 93 (December): 806–19.

Bénabou, Roland, and Jerzy D. Konieczny. 1994. On inflation and output with costly price changes: A simple unifying result. *American Economic Review* 84 (March): 290–97.

Bernanke, Ben S., and Michael Woodford. 1997. Inflation forecasts and monetary policy. *Journal of Money, Credit and Banking* 24 (November): 653–84.

Beveridge, Stephen, and Charles R. Nelson. 1981. A new approach to the decomposition of economic time series into permanent and transitory components with particular attention to measurement of the "business cycle." *Journal of Monetary Economics* 7, no. 2 (March): 151–74.

Calvo, Guillermo. 1983. Staggered prices in a utility-maximizing framework. *Journal of Monetary Economics* 12 (3): 383–98.

Clarida, Richard, Jordi Galí, and Mark Gertler. 1998. Monetary policy rules in practice: Some international evidence. *European Economic Review* 42:1033–67.

Dixit, Avinash K., and Joseph E. Stiglitz. 1977. Monopolistic competition and optimum product diversity. *American Economic Review* 67 (3): 297–308.

Feldstein, Martin. 1997. Capital income taxes and the benefit of price stability. NBER Working Paper no. 6200. Cambridge, Mass.: National Bureau of Economic Research, September.

Fuhrer, Jeffrey C., and Geoffrey Moore. 1995. Monetary policy trade-offs and the correlation between nominal interest rates and real output. *American Economic Review* 85 (March): 219–39.

Gertler, Mark. 1996. Discussion of Friedman and Kuttner, "A price target for U.S. monetary policy?" *Brookings Papers on Economic Activity,* no. 1:126–34.

Goodfriend, Marvin. 1991. Interest rate smoothing in the conduct of monetary policy. *Carnegie-Rochester Conference Series on Public Policy* 34:7–30.

Goodhart, Charles A. E. 1997. Why do monetary authorities smooth interest rates? In *European monetary policy,* ed. S. Collignon. London: Pinter.

Hall, Robert E., and N. Gregory Mankiw. 1994. Nominal income targeting. In *Monetary policy,* ed. N. Gregory Mankiw. Chicago: University of Chicago Press.

Henderson, Dale, and Warren McKibbin. 1993. An assessment of some basic monetary policy regime pairs. In *Evaluating policy regimes: New research in macroeconomics,* ed. R. Bryant. Washington, D.C.: Brookings Institution.

Kerr, William, and Robert G. King. 1996. Limits on interest rate rules in the *IS* model. *Federal Reserve Bank of Richmond Economic Quarterly* 82 (spring): 47–76.

King, Robert G., and Mark W. Watson. 1996. Money, prices, interest rates and the business cycle. *Review of Economics and Statistics* 78 (February): 35–53.

King, Robert G., and Alexander L. Wolman. 1996. Inflation targeting in a St. Louis model of the 21st century. *Federal Reserve Bank of St. Louis Review* 78 (3): 83–107.

Koenig, Evan F. 1987. A dynamic optimizing alternative to traditional *IS-LM* analysis. Discussion Paper no. 87-07. Seattle: University of Washington, Department of Economics, May.

Lucas, Robert E., Jr. 1976. Econometric policy evaluation: A critique. *Carnegie-Rochester Conference Series on Public Policy* 1:19–46.

McCallum, Bennett T. 1997. Comment on Rotemberg and Woodford, "An optimization-based econometric framework for the analysis of monetary policy." In *NBER macroeconomics annual 1997,* ed. Ben S. Bernanke and Julio J. Rotemberg, 355–59. Cambridge, Mass.: MIT Press.

McCallum, Bennett T., and Edward Nelson. Forthcoming. An optimizing *IS-LM* specification for monetary policy and business cycle analysis. *Journal of Money, Credit and Banking* 31.

Rotemberg, Julio J., and Michael Woodford. 1995. Dynamic general equilibrium models with imperfectly competitive product markets. In *Frontiers of business cycle research*, ed. Thomas Cooley. Princeton, N.J.: Princeton University Press.

———. 1997. An optimization-based econometric framework for the evaluation of monetary policy. In *NBER macroeconomics annual 1997*, ed. Ben S. Bernanke and Julio J. Rotemberg, 297–346. Cambridge, Mass.: MIT Press.

———. 1998. An optimization-based econometric framework for the evaluation of monetary policy: Expanded version. NBER Technical Working Paper no. 233. Cambridge, Mass.: National Bureau of Economic Research, May.

Rudebusch, Glenn D. 1995. Federal Reserve interest rate targeting, rational expectations and the term structure. *Journal of Monetary Economics* 35:245–74.

Sack, Brian. 1998. Does the Fed act gradually? A VAR analysis. Finance and Economics Discussion Paper no. 98-17. Washington, D.C.: Board of Governors of the Federal Reserve System, April.

Shiller, Robert. 1997. Why do people dislike inflation? In *Reducing inflation: Motivation and Strategy*, ed. Christina D. Romer and David H. Romer. Chicago: University of Chicago Press.

Summers, Lawrence. 1991. How should long term monetary policy be determined? *Journal of Money, Credit and Banking* 23 (August): 625–31.

Taylor, John B. 1979. Estimation and control of an econometric model with rational expectations. *Econometrica* 47:1267–86.

———. 1993. Discretion versus policy rules in practice. *Carnegie-Rochester Conference Series on Public Policy* 39:195–214.

Wicksell, Knut. 1907. The influence of the rate of interest on prices. *Economic Journal* 17:213–20.

Woodford, Michael. 1996. Control of the public debt: A requirement for price stability? NBER Working Paper no. 5684. Cambridge, Mass.: National Bureau of Economic Research, July.

Yun, Tack. 1996. Nominal price rigidity, money supply endogeneity, and business cycles. *Journal of Monetary Economics* 37 (2): 345–70.

Comment   Martin Feldstein

The paper by Julio Rotemberg and Michael Woodford is a complex and rich virtuoso performance. It is worth careful reading not only because of the difficult technical problem that they solve but also because of the extension that they propose to the basic Taylor rule, making the optimal interest rate a function of the past interest rate with a coefficient greater than one. Although I have reservations about specific aspects of the paper, I think it is an important contribution to the analysis of model-based monetary rules that will serve as a base for further useful developments.

Martin Feldstein is the George F. Baker Professor of Economics at Harvard University and president of the National Bureau of Economic Research.

Collections of Rules

Before commenting on the Rotemberg and Woodford paper itself, I will discuss the broader issue of the appropriate role of formal monetary policy rules. I think that such rules should not be viewed as substitutes for judgment by the monetary authorities but rather as inputs into that judgmental process. A good rule is therefore one that provides a useful starting point for central bank deliberations.

More specifically, I believe that a central bank can benefit from having a *collection* of alternative good rules, that is, rules that have optimal properties in a variety of models. I envisage central bank officials or staff using such a collection of rules each time a federal funds rate decision must be made. Before the decision is taken, the staff would calculate what the optimal federal funds rate would be according to each of the several different rules.[1] If the different rules all point to the same decision, the central bank's choice should be relatively easy. If they do not, the officials and staff have to dig deeper into the reasons for the differences and the authorities have to consider more carefully the decision that seems best in the current circumstances.

I emphasize the idea of using a collection of rules in this way because of the uncertainty inherent in the monetary policy process. There are two types of uncertainty for which this approach can be helpful: model uncertainty and situation uncertainty.

Ben McCallum has emphasized *model uncertainty* in his important writing on the choice of a monetary policy rule. McCallum's research imagines trying alternative rules in a variety of models and picking the single rule that does well under a variety of model assumptions. That approach may be too optimistic. There may be no rule that does uniformly better in a broad class of plausible economic models. Moreover, the rule that is optimal for the true structure of the economy may not do very well at all over a wide range of other possible models of the economy. McCallum's procedure may nevertheless help monetary authorities to develop and use a collection of rules by excluding some rules completely and by suggesting that certain rules deserve more weight in the central bank's thinking than others because of their robustness to different plausible models of the economy.

The second type of uncertainty, *situation uncertainty*, is the uncertainty about the current state of the economy and about where the economy would be going with no change in the federal funds rate. The expected values of uncertain estimates and of uncertain forecasts can be used in the decision rules only in very special circumstances. A prudent decision maker would therefore consider the optimal policy under different assumptions about the unobserv-

---

1. In the spirit of the Rotemberg and Woodford paper, I will discuss rules in terms of the federal funds rate rather than in terms of an optimal monetary aggregate, but the logic of what I say can obviously be transposed to models that indicate optimal monetary aggregates.

able state of the economy and about its future path. This would be done with a collection of rules since a single rule may not reflect the sensitivity of the optimal policy to the situation uncertainty.

All of this sounds like a lot of information for central bank decision makers to absorb. But it basically comes down to a list of the optimal federal funds value implied by each model in the collection, cross-classified by each set of alternative forecast scenarios (where forecasts include the current as well as future values of key economic magnitudes).

The Lagged Interest Rate and the Weakness of Monetary Policy

This brings me back to the Rotemberg and Woodford paper. An important feature of their work is that it extends the traditional Taylor rule by making the current optimal interest rate depend on the lagged interest rate as well as on inflation and output. In their analysis, the optimal response of the current optimal interest rate to the lagged value of the interest rate may have a coefficient greater than one because doing so significantly reduces the resulting average rate of inflation.

Although I find the analysis that leads Rotemberg and Woodford to this conclusion quite interesting, in the end I am not persuaded. Let me therefore review the logic behind their rule specification and then explain why I am not convinced. The starting point of the Rotemberg-Woodford analysis is the fact that the nominal interest rate that the central bank sets must be greater than or equal to zero. If the inflation rate is high, the mean value of this nominal interest rate will be high and the standard deviation of the fluctuations in that nominal rate can also be large. But if the inflation rate is low, the mean nominal interest rate will also be relatively low and the standard deviation of the interest rate must be small so that the actual nominal interest rate that the central bank sets is never required to be less than zero.

The Rotemberg-Woodford analysis shows that a monetary policy rule with a lagged value of the interest rate with a coefficient greater than one permits a low rate of inflation. This occurs because (in their rational expectations analysis) the public understands the rule and knows that when the Fed raises the interest rate it will go on raising the rate until the effect of this autoregressive process is dominated by a decline in actual inflation. This is sufficient to cause the actual inflation rate to decline before the rate is raised very much. They note that this low-inflation outcome comes with a high price in terms of increased variance of output.

I believe that their analysis overstates the extent to which low inflation requires volatile output. I think that a richer class of rules would also show that the autoregressive interest rate with the coefficient greater than one is also not necessary for low inflation.

A key limitation of the Rotemberg-Woodford analysis that they impose in order to carry out the complex rational expectations calculations is that the policy rule is linear. Thus the response of the interest rate must be the same to low and high rates of inflation. This means that if a large interest rate decrease is not possible (because of the nonnegativity constraint), there cannot be a large interest rate increase to dampen inflation. The substitute for large interest rate increases is the lagged interest rate with a coefficient greater than one because, as I noted above, individuals understand the autoregressive rule and respond to small interest rate increases in a way that damps economic activity.

In actual practice (although not in their model) it would of course be possible to have an asymmetric (i.e., nonlinear) rule. The magnitude of the interest rate increase when inflation is regarded as too high could be much greater than the magnitude of the decrease when inflation is low and output is regarded as too low. This would make it unnecessary to have the lagged interest rate to signal the expected future tightening of interest rates when inflation is deemed to be too high.

The nonlinear rule means that high interest rates can be used to damp strong demand. But what about situations of weak demand? Rotemberg and Woodford are certainly correct that when inflation is low, the real interest rate cannot be reduced much because the nominal interest rate cannot be negative. But that need not mean that monetary policy is ineffective in dealing with weak demand. A central bank that cannot reduce the real interest rate can still increase demand through open market sales of the domestic currency for foreign currencies. Reducing the currency's value through such unsterilized intervention increases exports and reduces imports. The closed economy character of the Rotemberg-Woodford model precludes that, but it is a feature of the real world that needs to be taken into account.

Similarly, a sustained weakness of demand may be a reason for a fiscal stimulus—as in Japan today—which can be effective if the monetary authority keeps the real interest rate and the exchange rate from rising in response to the fiscal expansion. This too can prevent output declines even though interest rates cannot move down.

For these reasons, I remain to be convinced of the desirability of the lagged interest rate with a greater-than-one coefficient that Rotemberg and Woodford find in their optimal policy rule. I hasten to add that a lagged interest rate in the optimal response function may be a good idea for other reasons—uncertainty about economic conditions, the need to appear consistent, and the potential adverse effects of interest rate volatility on financial institutions—but that is a separate matter.

In a richer analysis, it may also be desirable to have asymmetric policy responses and unsterilized foreign exchange intervention. But those are matters that require further analysis.

Sticky Prices

The Rotemberg-Woodford analysis is both sparse and sophisticated. It is sparse in the sense that it boils down to two equations describing the behavior of households and price-setting sellers. It is sophisticated in that it presents dynamic optimizing behavior of those agents with respect to a continuum of commodities in a rational expectations framework. But to make monetary policy effective in this framework and to create the observed stylized fact of a two-quarter lag in the impact of monetary policy, Rotemberg and Woodford introduce arbitrary lags into the behavior of both the households and the sellers.

I find this mixture of brilliant rational expectations optimizing behavior on the one hand and arbitrary lags on the other very disconcerting. Moreover, to the extent that the optimal policy rules are sensitive to the resulting lag pattern, as presumably they are since that is where the impact of monetary policy originates, how much weight should be put on rules that reflect arbitrarily imposed lag structures? What would happen if different assumptions were made about the lags in household and firm behavior?

Since the strength of the Rotemberg-Woodford model is its optimizing rational expectations framework, it would be interesting to drop the arbitrary lags and derive lags from the assumption that individuals and firms are following some kind of optimal Bayesian learning strategy. The resulting lags might produce a model that is too difficult for policy optimization of the type developed in section 2.3 of the paper, but such a change would give a more logically consistent basis for simulating alternative rules.

Since this paper already represents an enormous amount of complex work, it seems greedy of me to ask for more. The extension to Bayesian learning of the rational expectations model is certainly work for another paper.

Final Thoughts

But there is one exercise that could easily be done and that I think would be quite interesting. That would be to pick a few historical dates and calculate what the different rules described in this paper would mean for the optimal interest rate at those dates. At a minimum, it would be interesting to see how much the optimal interest rates differ across the different rules.

There is a final question that I would like to raise about the role of public confidence. I believe one of the reasons monetary policy has been effective in reducing inflation in the United States and in many other countries in recent years is that the Federal Reserve and other monetary authorities have stated the goal of reducing inflation and have, to a greater or lesser extent, specified numerical targets for future inflation.

To what extent would the effectiveness of monetary policy be enhanced in practice by using a rule or a collection of rules that emphasizes price stability? And to what extent is that effectiveness weakened by using an explicit monetary rule that attempts to optimize multiple criteria? Shifting from the existing informal emphasis on price stability to anything like a Taylor rule surely requires consideration of that issue.

Discussion Summary

In response to Martin Feldstein's point about the Lucas critique, *Michael Woodford* clarified that the assumption in the paper is not that agents do not act on the basis of knowledge of the monetary policy rule. The reason why the Lucas critique does not apply to the model is that optimal behavior is described by Euler equations that do not depend on the coefficients of the policy rule. These Euler equations are the first two equations in the model. This means that when changing the coefficients of the monetary policy rule, two of the three equations that characterize the equilibrium remain unchanged. *Glenn Rudebusch* noted that the Lucas critique still affects the results of the paper since the parameter estimates for the first two equations were obtained using a historical VAR reaction function. A different assumption about the historical reaction function would lead to different parameter estimates.

Lars Svensson asked whether the rules derived in the paper are only constrained optimal. *Woodford* responded that the rules are actually globally optimal assuming complete information about the underlying state variables, the real disturbances. The best rule in the family of rules that only respond to inflation and output observations is equivalent to the optimal rule. The intuition behind this result is that there are two real disturbances in the model and observing two endogenous variables gives enough information about these real disturbances.

Svensson also suggested an intuition for the response coefficient c on the lagged federal funds rate being above unity. Ideally, the central bank would like to affect long interest rates and thereby aggregate demand. The optimal way to do this is to have a large positive response coefficient on the lagged short rate. This will make future short rates react to the current short rate, which in turn will affect the long rate. Thus the rule works like a threat to do something in the future.

Donald Kohn remarked that the high coefficient on the lagged funds rate was interesting since central banks do not have a series of yield raises in mind when they reverse policy. They know they are too easy or too tight, but they have no idea by how much. Since they tend to think they are off by a fairly small amount initially, central banks often perceive bond markets as overreacting to their initial move. Looking at federal funds futures and forward rates, bond markets rarely call correctly the amount by which the Federal Reserve changes rates and almost always anticipate that the tightening or easing will persist beyond the point it actually stops and begins to be reversed.

Lawrence Christiano noted that a policymaker faced with a recommended rule might not follow the rule exactly but just a rule nearby. The graphs in the paper seem to suggest that if a rule with slightly different parameter values than the optimal rule of the model is picked, the result may be catastrophic. The problem arises in particular at the boundaries of indeterminacy and explosiveness regions. Also, the results may change dramatically when parameter uncertainty is accounted for. *Woodford* responded that these features would have to be built into the model to provide answers to these questions.

Ben Friedman emphasized the importance of distinguishing between two kinds of rules: rules and rules of thumb. First, when evaluating *rules of thumb*—that is, some indicative guide used as input into the judgmental process—the whole class of arguments stemming from time inconsistency in support of the rule is unavailable. Second, if a model is solved on the presumption that the rule is a *rule*—that is, the dynamic equilibrium is solved based on the assumption that agents form expectations based on commitment—then the results cannot be used to justify a rule of thumb. *Ralph Bryant* noted that the evaluation of committed rules is still useful when thinking about rules of thumb. For example, the inference drawn about what variables to consider in a setting with committed rules can be carried over to rules of thumb. *Frederic Mishkin* remarked that the distinction is also important for the communication of policy advice to central banks. Central bankers often get upset when they hear the word "rules" because, given that the true model of the economy is not known, they want to have some discretion available to them.

Nicoletta Batini wondered how the rules in the paper compared to forward-looking rules. With the output predetermined at $t - 2$ and a coefficient on the lagged interest rate bigger than one, a feedback on current-dated variables may be de facto equivalent to a forward-looking rule. *Woodford* replied that in equilibrium the federal funds rate depends on expected future inflation. In this sense, the rule is similar to a forward-looking rule that depends directly on expected inflation.

Volker Wieland noted that, according to the paper, rules that are very effective in stabilizing inflation would require a fairly high degree of interest rate variability and thus frequently violate the zero-bound constraint on nominal interest rates—especially in a low-inflation environment. In recent work Fuhrer and Madigan (1997) incorporate the zero bound explicitly in a small macroeconomic model of the U.S. economy and use deterministic simulations to evaluate the effect of the zero bound in the event of a negative demand shock. They find only modest effects on output adjustment with a zero inflation target. However, Orphanides and Wieland (1998) find that in a stochastic framework with shocks similar to those in the 1980s and 1990s, the zero bound significantly increases the variability of output and inflation and introduces a long-run trade-off between inflation and output at inflation targets below 2 percent.

Bob Hall expressed three criticisms of the behavioral assumptions made by the paper. First, it is not clear why the public is devoted to a monetary unit. In fact, most intermediate product transactions are set in real terms, not in nominal terms. Second, firms change prices as frequently as they change quantities. Third, firms do not grant their customers call options. In wholesale, these options are not granted at all. In retail, while many call options are granted, these are with respect to limited quantities, and when firms run out, they reconsider their prices.

References

Fuhrer, Jeffrey, and Brian Madigan. 1997. Monetary policy when interest rates are bounded at zero. *Review of Economics and Statistics* 79:573–85.
Orphanides, Athanasios, and Volker Wieland. 1998. Price stability and monetary policy effectiveness when nominal interest rates are bounded at zero. Finance and Economics Discussion Paper no. 98-35. Washington, D.C.: Board of Governors of the Federal Reserve System.

3 Policy Rules for Open Economies

Laurence Ball

3.1 Introduction

What policy rules should central banks follow? A growing number of economists and policymakers advocate targets for the level of inflation. Many also argue that inflation targeting should be implemented through a "Taylor rule" in which interest rates are adjusted in response to output and inflation. These views are supported by the theoretical models of Svensson (1997) and Ball (1997), in which the optimal policies are versions of inflation targets and Taylor rules.

Many analyses of policy rules assume a closed economy. This paper extends the Svensson-Ball model to an open economy and asks how the optimal policies change. The short answer is they change quite a bit. In open economies, inflation targets and Taylor rules are suboptimal unless they are modified in important ways. Different rules are required because monetary policy affects the economy through exchange rate as well as interest rate channels.[1]

Section 3.2 presents the model, which consists of three equations. The first is a dynamic, open economy IS equation: output depends on lags of itself, the real interest rate, and the real exchange rate. The second is an open economy Phillips curve: the change in inflation depends on lagged output and the lagged change in the exchange rate, which affects inflation through import prices. The

Laurence Ball is professor of economics at Johns Hopkins University and a research associate of the National Bureau of Economic Research.

The author is grateful for research assistance from Qiming Chen, Nada Choueiri, and Heiko Ebens, and for comments and advice from Bob Buckle, Pedro deLima, Eric Hansen, David Gruen, David Longworth, Tiff Macklem, Scott Roger, Thomas Sargent, John Taylor, and seminar participants at the Federal Reserve Bank of Kansas City and the Reserve Banks of Australia and Canada.

1. Svensson (forthcoming) also examines alternative policy rules in an open economy model. That paper differs from this one and from Svensson (1997) in stressing microfoundations and forward-looking behavior, at the cost of greater complexity.

final equation is a relation between interest rates and exchange rates that captures the behavior of asset markets.

Section 3.3 derives the optimal instrument rule in the model. This rule differs in two ways from the Taylor rule that is optimal in a closed economy. First, the policy instrument is a weighted sum of the interest rate and the exchange rate—a "monetary conditions index" like the ones used in several countries. Second, on the right-hand side of the policy rule, inflation is replaced by "long-run" inflation. This variable is a measure of inflation adjusted for the temporary effects of exchange rate fluctuations.

Section 3.4 considers several instrument rules proposed in other papers at this conference. I find that most of these rules perform poorly in my model.

Section 3.5 turns to inflation targeting. In the closed economy models of Svensson and Ball, a simple version of this policy is equivalent to the optimal Taylor rule. In an open economy, however, inflation targeting can be dangerous. The reason concerns the effects of exchange rates on inflation through import prices. This is the fastest channel from monetary policy to inflation, and so inflation targeting implies that it is used aggressively. Large shifts in the exchange rate produce large fluctuations in output.

Section 3.6 presents a more positive result. While pure inflation targeting has undesirable effects, a modification produces much better outcomes. The modification is to target "long-run" inflation—the inflation variable that appears in the optimal instrument rule. This variable is not influenced by the exchange-rate-to-import-price channel, and so targeting it does not induce large exchange rate movements. Targeting long-run inflation is not exactly equivalent to the optimal instrument rule, but it is a close approximation for plausible parameter values.

Section 3.7 concludes the paper.

3.2   The Model

3.2.1   Assumptions

The model is an extension of Svensson (1997) and Ball (1997) to an open economy. The goal is to capture conventional wisdom about the major effects of monetary policy in a simple way. The model is similar in spirit to the more complicated macroeconometric models of many central banks.

The model consists of three equations:

(1)
$$y = -\beta r_{-1} - \delta e_{-1} + \lambda y_{-1} + \varepsilon,$$

(2)
$$\pi = \pi_{-1} + \alpha y_{-1} - \gamma(e_{-1} - e_{-2}) + \eta,$$

(3)
$$e = \theta r + v,$$

where y is the log of real output, r is the real interest rate, e is the log of the real exchange rate (a higher e means appreciation), π is inflation, and ε, η, and

ν are white noise shocks. All parameters are positive, and all variables are measured as deviations from average levels.

Equation (1) is an open economy IS curve. Output depends on lags of the real interest rate and the real exchange rate, its own lag, and a demand shock.

Equation (2) is an open economy Phillips curve. The change in inflation depends on the lag of output, the lagged change in the exchange rate, and a shock. The change in the exchange rate affects inflation because it is passed directly into import prices. This interpretation is formalized in the appendix, which derives equation (2) from separate equations for domestic goods and import inflation.

Finally, equation (3) posits a link between the interest rate and the exchange rate. It captures the idea that a rise in the interest rate makes domestic assets more attractive, leading to an appreciation. The shock ν captures other influences on the exchange rate, such as expectations, investor confidence, and foreign interest rates. Equation (3) is similar to reduced-form equations for the exchange rate in many textbooks.

The central bank chooses the real interest rate r. One can interpret any policy rule as a rule for setting r. Using equation (3), one can also rewrite any rule as a rule for setting e, or for setting some combination of e and r.[2]

A key feature of the model is that policy affects inflation through two channels. A monetary contraction reduces output and thus inflation through the Phillips curve, and it also causes an appreciation that reduces inflation directly. The lags in equations (1), (2), and (3) imply that the first channel takes two periods to work: a tightening raises r and e contemporaneously, but it takes a period for these variables to affect output and another period for output to affect inflation. In contrast, the direct effect of an exchange rate change on inflation takes only one period. These assumptions capture the common view that the direct exchange rate effect is the quickest channel from policy to inflation.

3.2.2   Calibration

In analyzing the model, I will interpret a period as a year. With this interpretation, the time lags in the model are roughly realistic. Empirical evidence suggests that policy affects inflation through the direct exchange rate channel in about a year, and through the output channel in about two years (e.g., Reserve Bank of New Zealand 1996; Lafleche 1996).

The analysis will use a set of base parameter values. Several of these values are borrowed from the closed economy model in Ball (1997). Based on evidence discussed there, I assume that λ, the output persistence coefficient, is 0.8; that α, the slope of the Phillips curve, is 0.4; and that the total output loss from a 1-point rise in the interest rate is 1.0. In the current model, this total

---

2. Note I assume that policymakers set the *real* interest rate. In practice, the interest rates controlled directly by policymakers are nominal rates. However, policymakers can move the real interest rate to their desired level by setting the nominal rate equal to the desired real rate plus inflation.

effect is $\beta + \delta\theta$: β is the direct effect of the interest rate and $\delta\theta$ is the effect through the exchange rate. I therefore assume $\beta + \delta\theta = 1.0$.

The other parameters depend on the economy's degree of openness. My base values are meant to apply to medium to small open economies such as Canada, Australia, and New Zealand. My main sources for the parameters are studies by these countries' central banks. I assume $\gamma = 0.2$ (a 1 percent appreciation reduces inflation by two-tenths of a point) and $\theta = 2.0$ (a 1 point rise in the interest rate causes a 2 percent appreciation). I also assume $\beta/\delta = 3.0$, capturing a common rule of thumb about IS coefficients. Along with my other assumptions, this implies $\beta = 0.6$ and $\delta = 0.2$.[3]

3.3 Efficient Instrument Rules

Following Taylor (1994), the optimal policy rule is defined as the one that minimizes a weighted sum of output variance and inflation variance. The weights are determined by policymakers' tastes. As in Ball (1997), an "efficient" rule is one that is optimal for some weights, or equivalently a rule that puts the economy on the output-inflation variance frontier. This section derives the set of efficient rules in the model.

3.3.1 Variables in the Rule

As discussed earlier, we can interpret any policy rule as a rule for r, a rule for e, or a rule for a combination of the two. Initially, it is convenient to consider rules for e. To derive the efficient rules, I first substitute equation (3) into equation (1) to eliminate r from the model. I shift the time subscripts forward to show the effects of the current exchange rate on future output and inflation. This yields

(4) $$y_{+1} = -(\beta/\theta + \delta)e + \lambda y + \varepsilon_{+1} + (\beta/\theta)v,$$

(5) $$\pi_{+1} = \pi + \alpha y - \gamma(e - e_{-1}) + \eta_{+1}.$$

Consider a policymaker choosing the current e. One can define the state variables of the model by two expressions corresponding to terms on the right-hand sides of equations (4) and (5): $\lambda y + (\beta/\theta)v$ and $\pi + \alpha y + \gamma e_{-1}$. The future paths of output and inflation are determined by these two expressions, the rule for choosing e, and future shocks. Since the model is linear-quadratic, one can show the optimal rule is linear in the two state variables:

(6) $$e = m[\lambda y + (\beta/\theta)v] + n(\pi + \alpha y + \gamma e_{-1}),$$

where m and n are constants to be determined.

In equation (6), the choice of e depends on the exchange rate shock v as

---

3. Examples of my sources for base parameter values are the Canadian studies of Longworth and Poloz (1986) and Duguay (1994) and the Australian study of Gruen and Shuetrim (1994).

well as observable variables. By equation (3), v can be replaced by $e - \theta r$. Making this substitution and rearranging terms yields

$$(7) \qquad wr + (1 - w)e = ay + b(\pi + \gamma e_{-1}),$$

where

$$w = m\beta\theta/(\theta - m\beta + m\beta\theta), \qquad a = \theta(m\lambda + n\alpha)/(\theta - m\beta + m\beta\theta),$$

$$b = n\theta/(\theta - m\beta + m\beta\theta).$$

This expresses the optimal policy as a rule for an average of r and e.

3.3.2 Interpretation

In the closed economy model of Svensson and Ball, the optimal policy is a Taylor rule: the interest rate depends on output and inflation. Equation (7) modifies the Taylor rule in two ways. First, the policy variable is a combination of r and e. And second, inflation is replaced by $\pi + \gamma e_{-1}$, a combination of inflation and the lagged exchange rate. Each of these modifications has a simple interpretation.

The first result supports the practice of using an average of r and e—a "monetary conditions index" (MCI)—as the policy instrument. Several countries follow this approach, including Canada, New Zealand, and Sweden (see Gerlach and Smets 1996). The rationale for using an MCI is that it measures the overall stance of policy, including the stimulus through both r and e. Policymakers shift the MCI when they want to ease or tighten. When there are shifts in the e/r relation—shocks to equation (3)—r is adjusted to keep the MCI at the desired level.

The second modification of the Taylor rule is more novel. The term $\pi + \gamma e_{-1}$ can be interpreted as a long-run forecast of inflation under the assumption that output is kept at its natural level. With a closed economy Phillips curve, this forecast would simply be current inflation. In an open economy, however, inflation will change because the exchange rate will eventually return to its long-run level, which is normalized to zero. For example, if e was positive in the previous period, there will be a depreciation of e_{-1} at some point starting in the current period. By equation (2), this will raise inflation by γe_{-1} at some point after the current period. I will use the term "long-run inflation" and the symbol π^* to stand for $\pi + \gamma e_{-1}$.

More broadly, one can interpret $\pi + \gamma e_{-1}$ as a measure of inflation that filters out direct but temporary effects of the exchange rate. For a given output path, an appreciation causes inflation to fall, but it will rise again by γe_{-1} when the appreciation is reversed. The adjustment from π to π^* is similar in spirit to calculations of "core" or "underlying" inflation by central banks. These variables are measures of inflation adjusted for transitory influences such as changes in indirect taxes or commodity prices. Many economists argue that policy should respond to underlying inflation and ignore transitory fluctuations. My model supports this idea for the case of fluctuations caused by exchange rates.

3.3.3 Efficient Coefficients for the Rule

The coefficients in the policy rule (7) depend on the constants m and n, which are not yet determined. The next step is to derive the efficient combinations of m and n—the combinations that put the economy on the output-inflation variance frontier. As discussed in the appendix, the set of efficient policies depends on the coefficients in equations (1), (2), and (3) but not on the variances of the three shocks (although these variances determine the absolute position of the frontier). For base parameter values, I compute the variances of output and inflation for given m and n and then search for combinations that define the frontier.

Figure 3.1 presents the results in a graph. The figure shows the output-inflation variance frontier when the variance of each shock is one. For selected points on the frontier, the graph shows the policy rule coefficients that put the economy at that point. It also shows the weights on output variance and inflation variance that make each policy optimal.

Two results are noteworthy. The first concerns the weights on r and e in the MCI. There is currently a debate among economists about the appropriate weights. Some argue that the weights should be proportional to the coefficients on e and r in the IS equation (e.g., Freedman 1994). For my base parameters, this implies $w = 0.75$, that is, weights of 0.75 on r and 0.25 on e. Others suggest a larger weight on e to reflect the direct effect of the exchange rate on inflation (see Gerlach and Smets 1996). In my model, the optimal weight on e is larger than 0.25, but by a small amount. For example, if the policymaker's objective function has equal weights on output and inflation variances, the MCI weight on e is 0.30. The weight on e is much smaller than its relative short-run effect on inflation. The only exceptions occur when policymakers' objectives have very little weight on output variance.[4]

The second result concerns the coefficients on y and π^*, and how they compare to the optimal coefficients on y and π in a closed economy. Note that a 1 point rise in the interest rate, which also raises the exchange rate, raises the MCI by a total of $w + \theta(1 - w)$. Dividing the coefficients on y and π^* by this expression yields the responses of r to movements in y and π^* (holding constant the exchange rate shock v). These responses are the analogues of Taylor rule coefficients in a closed economy. For equal weights in policymakers' objective functions, the interest rate response to output is 1.04 and the response to π^* is 0.82. Assuming the same objective function, the corresponding re-

---

4. One measure of the overall effect of e on inflation is the effect through appreciation in one period plus the effect through the Phillips curve in two periods. This sum is $\gamma + \delta\alpha = 0.28$. The corresponding effect of r on inflation is $\beta\alpha = 0.24$. The MCI would put more weight on e than on r if it were based on these inflation effects.

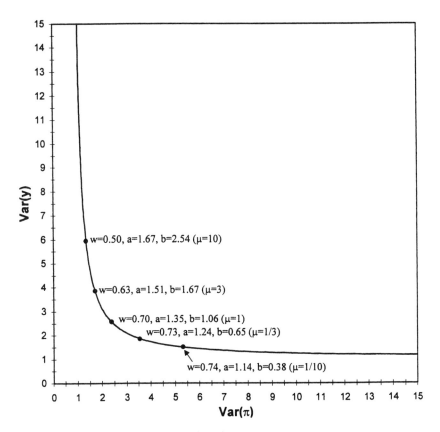

Fig. 3.1   Output-inflation variance frontier
Note: Objective function = var(y) + μ var(π).

sponses in a closed economy are 1.13 for output and 0.82 for inflation (Ball 1997). Thus the sizes of interest rate movements are similar in the two cases.

3.4   Other Instrument Rules

This paper is part of a project to evaluate policy rules in alternative macro-economic models. As part of the project, all authors are evaluating a list of six rules to see whether any performs well across a variety of models. Each of the rules has the general form

(8) $r = ay + b\pi + cr_{-1}$,

where a, b, and c are constants. Table 3.1 gives the values of the constants in the six rules.

All of these rules are inefficient in the current model. There are two separate

Table 3.1   **Alternative Policy Rules**

	Rule					
	1	2	3	4	5	6
a	0.8	1	0.5	1	0.06	0.08
b	2	0.2	0.5	0.5	0.2	0.3
c	1	1	0	0	2.86	2.86
Base case						
var(y)	531.59	4.42	2.62	1.86	∞	∞
var(π)	5.18	6.55	3.43	4.05	∞	∞
Closed economy						
var(y)	∞	6.53	2.77	1.81	∞	∞
var(π)	∞	7.59	3.91	4.22	∞	∞

problems. First, the rules are designed for closed economies and therefore do not make the adjustments for exchange rate effects discussed in the last section. Second, even if the economy were closed, the coefficients in most of the rules would be inefficient. To distinguish between these problems, I evaluate the rules in two versions of my model: the open economy case considered above and a closed economy case obtained by setting δ and γ to zero. The latter is identical to the model in Ball (1997).[5]

Table 3.1 presents the variances of output and inflation for the six rules. The rules fall into two categories. The first are those with c, the coefficient on lagged r, equal to or greater than one (rules 1, 2, 5, and 6). For these rules, the output and inflation variances range from large to infinite, both in closed and open economies. This result reflects the fact that efficient rules in either case do not include the lagged interest rate. Including this variable leads to inefficient oscillations in output and inflation.

The other rules, numbers 3 and 4, omit the lagged interest rate ($c = 0$). These rules perform well in a closed economy. Indeed, rule 4 is fully efficient in that case; rule 3 is not quite efficient, but it puts the economy close to the frontier (see Ball 1997). In an open economy, however, rules 3 and 4 are inefficient because they ignore the exchange rate. Rule 4, for example, produces an output variance of 1.86 and an inflation variance of 4.05. Using an efficient rule, policy can achieve the same output variance with an inflation variance of 3.54.

Recall that the set of efficient rules does not depend on the variances of the model's three shocks. In contrast, the losses from using an inefficient rule generally do depend on these variances. For rules 3 and 4, the losses are moderate when demand and inflation shocks are most important, but larger when the exchange rate shock is most important. That is, using r as the policy instrument

5. In the closed economy case, I continue to assume β + δθ = 1. Therefore, since δ is zero, β is raised to one.

is most inefficient if there are large shocks to the r/e relation. In this case, r is an unreliable measure of the overall policy stance.

3.5   The Perils of Inflation Targeting

This section turns from instrument rules to target rules, specifically inflation targets. In the closed economy Svensson-Ball model, inflation targeting has good properties. In particular, the set of efficient Taylor rules is equivalent to the set of inflation target policies with different speeds of adjustment. In an open economy, however, inflation targeting can be dangerous.

3.5.1   Strict Inflation Targets

As in Ball (1997), strict inflation targeting is defined as the policy that minimizes the variance of inflation. When inflation deviates from its target, strict targeting eliminates the deviation as quickly as possible. I first evaluate this policy and then consider variations that allow slower adjustment.

Trivially, strict inflation targeting is an efficient policy: it minimizes the weighted sum of output and inflation variances when the output weight is zero. Strict targeting puts the economy at the northwest end of the variance frontier. In figure 3.1, the frontier is cut off when the output variance reaches 15; when the frontier is extended, the end is found at an output variance of 25.8 and inflation variance of 1.0. Choosing this point implies a huge sacrifice in output stability for a small gain in inflation stability. Moving down the frontier, the output variance could be reduced to 9.7 if the inflation variance were raised to 1.1, or to 4.1 if the inflation variance were raised to 1.6. Strict inflation targeting is highly suboptimal if policymakers put a nonnegligible weight on output.

The output variance of 25.8 compares to a variance of 8.3 under strict inflation targeting in the closed economy case. This difference arises from the different channels from policy to inflation. In a closed economy, the only channel is the one through output, which takes two periods (it takes a period for r to affect y and another period for y to affect π). With these lags, strict inflation targeting implies that policy sets expected inflation in two periods to zero. In an open economy, by contrast, policy can affect inflation in one period through the direct exchange rate channel. When policymakers minimize the variance of inflation, they set next period's expected inflation to zero:

(9) $$E\pi_{+1} = 0.$$

Equation (9) implies large fluctuations in the exchange rate because next period's inflation can be controlled only by this variable. Intuitively, inflation in domestic goods prices cannot be influenced in one period, so large shifts in import prices are needed to move the average price level. (The appendix formalizes this interpretation.) The large shifts in exchange rates cause large output fluctuations through the IS curve.

This point can be illustrated with impulse response functions. Substituting equation (5) into equation (9) yields the instrument rule implied by strict inflation targeting:

$$(10) \qquad e = (\alpha/\gamma)y + (1/\gamma)(\pi + \gamma e_{-1}).$$

(Note this is a limiting case of eq. [7] in which the MCI equals the exchange rate.) Using equations (4), (5), and (10), I derive the dynamic effects of a unit shock to the Phillips curve. Figure 3.2 presents the results. Inflation returns to target after one period, but the shock triggers oscillations in the exchange rate and output. The oscillations arise because the exchange rate must be shifted each period to offset the inflationary or deflationary effects of previous shifts. These results contrast to strict inflation targeting in a closed economy, where an inflationary shock produces only a one-time output loss.[6]

3.5.2 The Case of New Zealand

These results appear to capture real-world experiences with inflation targeting, particularly New Zealand's pioneering policy in the early 1990s. During that period, observers criticized the Reserve Bank for moving the exchange rate too aggressively to control inflation. For example, Dickens (1996) argues that "whiplashing" of the exchange rate produced instability in output. He shows that aggregate inflation was steady because movements in import inflation offset movements in domestic goods inflation. These outcomes are similar to the effects of inflation targeting in my model.

Recently, the Reserve Bank has acknowledged problems with strict inflation targeting:

> If the focus of policy is limited to a fairly short horizon of around six to twelve months, the setting of the policy stance will tend to be dominated by the relatively rapid-acting direct effects of exchange rate and interest rate changes on inflation. In the early years of inflation targeting, this was, in fact, more or less the way in which policy was run. . . . Basing the stance of policy solely on its direct impact on inflation, however, is hazardous. . . . It is possible that in some situations actions aimed at maintaining price stability in the short term could prove destabilizing to activity and inflation in the medium term. (Reserve Bank of New Zealand 1996, 28–29)

The Reserve Bank's story is similar to mine: moving inflation to target quickly requires strong reliance on the direct exchange rate channel, which has adverse side effects on output.[7]

---

6. Black, Macklem, and Rose (1997) find that strict inflation targeting produces a large output variance in simulations of the Bank of Canada's model. Their interpretation of this result is similar to mine.

7. The Reserve Bank discusses direct inflation effects of interest rates as well as exchange rates because mortgage payments enter New Zealand's consumer price index.

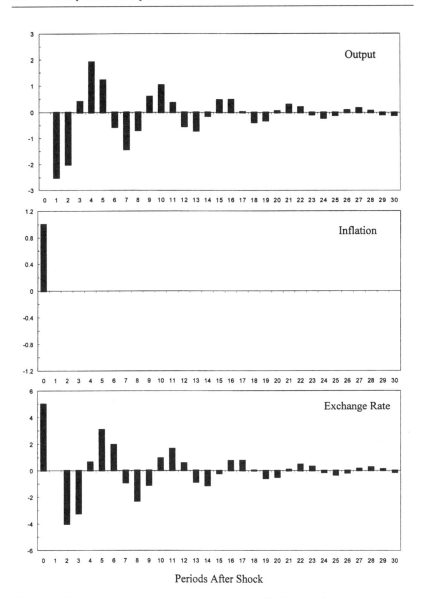

Fig. 3.2   **Strict inflation targets: responses to an inflation shock**

3.5.3   Gradual Adjustment?

The problems with strict inflation targeting have led observers to suggest a modification: policy should move inflation to its target more slowly. The Reserve Bank of New Zealand has accepted this idea; it reports that "in recent years the Bank's policy horizon has lengthened further into the future" and that this means it relies more heavily on the output channel to control inflation (1996, 29).

In the current model, however, it is not obvious what policy rule captures the goal of "lengthening the policy horizon." One natural idea (suggested by several readers) is to target inflation two periods ahead rather than one period:

$$(11) \qquad E\pi_{+2} = 0.$$

This condition is the one implied by strict inflation targeting in the closed economy model. In that model, the condition does not produce oscillations in output.

In the current model, however, equation (11) does not determine a unique policy rule. Since policy can control inflation period by period, there are multiple paths to zero inflation in two periods. By the law of iterated expectations, $E\pi_{+1} = 0$ in all periods implies $E\pi_{+2} = 0$ in all periods. Thus a strict inflation target is one policy that satisfies equation (11). But there are other policies that return inflation to zero in two periods but not one period.[8]

The same point applies to various modifications of equation (11). For example, in the closed economy model, any efficient policy can be written as an inflation target with slow adjustment: $E\pi_{+2} = qE\pi_{+1}, 0 \leq q \leq 1$. This condition is also consistent with multiple policies in the current model. There does not appear to be any simple restriction on inflation that implies a unique policy with desirable properties. Policymakers who wish to return inflation to target over the "medium term" need some additional criterion to define their rule.[9]

3.6   Long-Run Inflation Targets

This section presents the good news about inflation targets. The problems described in the previous section can be overcome by modifying the target variable. In light of earlier results, a natural modification is to target long-run inflation, π^*.

3.6.1   The Policies

Strict long-run inflation targeting is defined as the policy that minimizes the variance of $\pi^* = \pi + \gamma e_{-1}$. To see its implications, note that equation (2) can be rewritten as

$$(12) \qquad \pi^* = \pi^*_{-1} + \alpha y_{-1} + \eta.$$

---

8. An example is a rule in which policy makes no contemporaneous response to shocks, but the exchange rate is adjusted after one period to return inflation to target in two periods.

9. Another possible rule is partial adjustment in one period: $E\pi_{+1} = q\pi$. This condition defines a unique policy, but the variance of output is large. The condition implies the same responses to demand and exchange rate shocks as does strict inflation targeting. These shocks have no contemporaneous effects on inflation, so policy must fully eliminate their effects in the next period, even for $q > 0$.

This equation is the same as a closed economy Phillips curve, except that π^* replaces π. The exchange rate is eliminated, so policy affects π^* only through the output channel. Thus policy affects π^* with a two-period lag, and strict targeting implies

$$(13) \qquad E\pi^*_{+2} = 0.$$

In contrast to a two-period-ahead target for total inflation, equation (13) defines a unique policy.

There are two related motivations for targeting π^* rather than π. First, since π^* is not influenced by the exchange rate, policy uses only the output channel to control inflation. This avoids the exchange rate "whiplashing" discussed in the previous section. Second, as discussed in section 3.3, π^* gives the level of inflation with transitory exchange rate effects removed. Targeting π^* keeps underlying inflation on track.

In addition to strict π^* targeting, I consider gradual adjustment of π^*:

$$(14) \qquad E\pi^*_{+2} = qE\pi^*_{+1}, \qquad 0 \le q \le 1.$$

This rule is similar to the gradual adjustment rule that is optimal in a closed economy. Policy adjusts $E\pi^*_{+2}$ part of the way to the target from $E\pi^*_{+1}$, which it takes as given. The motivation for adjusting slowly is to smooth the path of output.

In practice, countries with inflation targets do not formally adjust for exchange rates in the way suggested here. However, adjustments may occur implicitly. For example, a central bank economist once told me that inflation was below his country's target but that this was desirable because the currency was temporarily strong and policy needed to "leave room" for the effects of depreciation. Keeping inflation below its official target when the exchange rate is strong is similar to targeting π^*.

3.6.2   Results

To examine π^* targets formally, I substitute equations (12) and (1) into condition (14). This leads to the instrument rule implied by π^* targets:

$$(15) \qquad w'r + (1 - w')e = a'y + b'\pi^*,$$

where

$$w' = \beta/(\beta + \delta), \quad a' = (1 - q + \lambda)/(\beta + \delta), \quad b' = (1 - q)/[\alpha(\beta + \delta)].$$

This equation includes the same variables as the optimal rule in section 3.3, but the coefficients are different. The MCI weights are given exactly by the relative sizes of β and δ; for base parameters, $w' = 0.75$. The coefficients on y and π^* depend on the adjustment speed q.

The appendix calculates the variances of output and inflation under π^* targeting. Figure 3.3 plots the results for q between zero and one. The case of

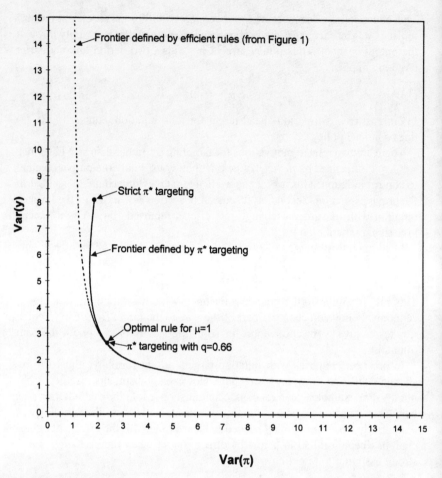

Fig. 3.3 π* Targeting

strict π* targeting corresponds to the northwest corner of the curve. For comparison, figure 3.3 also plots the set of efficient policies from figure 3.1.

The figure shows that targeting π* produces more stable output than targeting π. This is true even for strict π* targets, which produce an output variance of 8.3, compared to 25.8 for π targets. Figure 3.4 shows the dynamic effects of an inflation shock under π* targets and confirms that this policy avoids oscillations in output. Strict π* targeting is, however, moderately inefficient. There is an efficient instrument rule that produces an output variance of 8.3 and an inflation variance of 1.2. Strict π* targets produce the same output variance with an inflation variance of 1.9.

As the parameter q is raised, so adjustment becomes slower, we move southeast on the frontier defined by π* targeting. This frontier quickly moves close

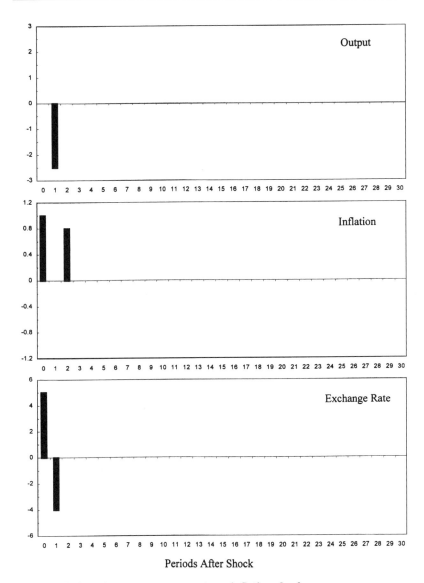

Periods After Shock

Fig. 3.4   Strict π* targets: responses to an inflation shock

to the efficient frontier. Thus, as long as policymakers put a nonnegligible weight on output variance, there is a version of π* targeting that closely approximates the optimal policy. For example, for equal weights on inflation and output variances, the optimal policy has an MCI weight w of 0.70 and output and π* coefficients of 1.35 and 1.06. For a π* target with $q = 0.66$, the corresponding numbers are 0.75, 1.43, and 1.08. The variances of output and inflation are 2.50 and 2.44 under the optimal policy and 2.48 and 2.48 under π^* targeting.

3.7 Conclusion

In a closed economy, inflation targeting and Taylor rules perform well in stabilizing both output and inflation. In an open economy, however, these policies perform poorly unless they are modified. Specifically, if policymakers minimize a weighted sum of output and inflation variances, their policy instrument should be an MCI based on both the interest rate and the exchange rate. The weight on the exchange rate is equal to or slightly greater than this variable's relative effect on spending. As a target variable, policymakers with this paper's objective function should choose "long-run inflation"—an inflation variable purged of the transitory effects of exchange rate fluctuations. This variable should also replace inflation on the right-hand side of the instrument rule.

Several countries currently use an MCI as their policy instrument. In addition, some appear to have moved informally toward targeting long-run inflation, for example by keeping inflation below target when a depreciation is expected. A possible strengthening of this policy is to make long-run inflation the formal target variable. In practice, this could be done by adding an adjustment to calculations of "underlying" inflation: the effects of the exchange rate could be removed along with other transitory influences on inflation. At least one private firm in New Zealand already produces an underlying inflation series along these lines (Dickens 1996).

Appendix

Domestic Goods and Imports

Here I derive the Phillips curve, equation (2), from assumptions about inflation in the prices of domestic goods and imports. Domestic goods inflation is given by

$$(A1) \qquad \pi^d = \pi_{-1} + \alpha' y_{-1} + \eta'.$$

This equation is similar to a closed economy Phillips curve: π^d is determined by lagged inflation and lagged output.

To determine import price inflation, I assume that foreign firms desire constant real prices in their home currencies. This implies that their desired real prices in local currency are $-e$. However, they adjust their prices to changes in e with a one-period lag. Like domestic firms, they also adjust their prices based on lagged inflation. Thus import inflation is

(A2) $$\pi^m = \pi_{-1} - (e_{-1} - e_{-2}).$$

Finally, aggregate inflation is the average of (A1) and (A2) weighted by the shares of imports and domestic goods in the price index. If the import share is γ, this yields equation (2) with $\alpha = (1 - \gamma)\alpha'$ and $\eta = (1 - \gamma)\eta'$.

The Variances of Output and Inflation

Here I describe the computation of the variances of output and inflation under alternative policies. Consider first the rule given by equations (6) and (7). Substituting equations (4) and (5) into equation (6) yields an expression for the exchange rate in terms of lagged e, π, and y

(A3) $e = (\lambda z + \alpha n)y_{-1} + n\pi_{-1} - (\beta/\theta + \delta)ze_{-1} + \gamma ne_{-2} + z\varepsilon$

$$+ \; n\eta + \beta mv + \beta zv_{-1}, \quad z = \lambda m + \alpha n.$$

This equation and equations (4) and (5) define a vector process for e, π, and y:

(A4) $$X = \Phi_1 X_{-1} + \Phi_2 X_{-2} + E,$$

where $X = [y\;\pi\;e]'$.

The elements of E depend on the current and once-lagged values of white noise shocks. Thus E follows a vector MA(1) process with parameters determined by the underlying parameters of the model. X follows an ARMA(2, 1) process. For given parameter values and given values of the constants m and n, one can numerically derive the variance of X using standard formulas (see Hendry 1995, sec. 11.3). To determine the set of efficient policies, I search over m and n to find combinations that minimize a weighted sum of the output and inflation variances.

To determine the variances of output and inflation under a π^* target, note that equation (15) is equivalent to equation (7) with m set to $\theta/(\theta\delta + \beta)$ and n set to $\theta(1 - q)/[\alpha(\theta\delta + \beta)]$. For a given q, the variances of output and inflation under equation (15) are given by the variances for the equivalent version of equation (7).

References

Ball, Laurence. 1997. Efficient rules for monetary policy. NBER Working Paper no. 5952. Cambridge, Mass.: National Bureau of Economic Research, March.

Black, Richard, Tiff Macklem, and David Rose. 1997. On policy rules for price stability. In *Price stability, inflation targets and monetary policy,* ed. Bank of Canada. Ottawa: Bank of Canada.

Dickens, Rodney. 1996. Proposed modifications to monetary policy. Wellington: Ord Minnett New Zealand Research, May.

Duguay, Pierre. 1994. Empirical evidence on the strength of the monetary transmission mechanism in Canada: An aggregate approach. *Journal of Monetary Economics* 33 (February): 39–61.
Freedman, Charles. 1994. The use of indicators and of the monetary conditions index in Canada. In *Frameworks for monetary stability,* ed. Tomas J. T. Balino and Carlo Cottarelli. Washington, D.C.: International Monetary Fund.
Gerlach, Stefan, and Franks Smets. 1996. MCIs and monetary policy in small open economies under floating exchange rates. Basel: Bank for International Settlements, November.
Gruen, David, and Geoffrey Shuetrim. 1994. Internationalisation and the macroeconomy. In *International integration of the Australian economy,* ed. Philip Lowe and Jacqueline Dwyer. Sydney: Reserve Bank of Australia.
Hendry, David F. 1995. *Dynamic econometrics.* Oxford: Oxford University Press.
Lafleche, Therese. 1996. The impact of exchange rate movements on consumer prices. *Bank of Canada Review,* winter 1996–97, 21–32.
Longworth, David J., and Stephen S. Poloz. 1986. A comparison of alternative monetary policy regimes in a small dynamic open-economy simulation model. Bank of Canada Technical Report no. 42. Ottawa: Bank of Canada, April.
Reserve Bank of New Zealand. 1996. *Briefing on the Reserve Bank of New Zealand.* Wellington: Reserve Bank of New Zealand, October.
Svensson, Lars E. O. 1997. Inflation forecast targeting: Implementing and monitoring inflation targets. *European Economic Review* 41:1111–46.
———. Forthcoming. Open-economy inflation targeting. *Journal of International Economics.*
Taylor, John B. 1994. The inflation/output variability trade-off revisited. In *Goals, guidelines, and constraints facing monetary policymakers,* ed. Jeffrey C. Fuhrer. Boston: Federal Reserve Bank of Boston.

Comment   Thomas J. Sargent

Summary

I offer two related, apparently but not necessarily contradictory, criticisms of Laurence Ball's model. First, the model incorporates too little rational expectations; second, it assumes too much rational expectations. The private sector uses too little rational expectations (at least compared to the government); and the government uses too much (in view of how little rational expectations Ball has built into the private sector's model—and in view of Ball's empirical approach to his model as an approximation). Let me explain from the beginning.

Ball ascribes a return function to the government (a weighted sum of unconditional variances of inflation and output) then solves a "modern" single-agent control problem to deduce an optimal rule for monetary policy. He models the economy as being like *nature,* a time-invariant system of stochastic difference

Thomas J. Sargent is senior fellow at the Hoover Institution, the Donald Lucas Professor of Economics at Stanford University, and a research associate of the National Bureau of Economic Research.

equations, driven by serially uncorrelated shocks, presenting state and control vectors to the policymaker.[1] The policymaker views the model economy as "known" and "fixed" (with respect to the policymaker's choices). Though Ball's model is estimable using modern methods (the "duals" of the control theoretic methods he uses), Ball abstains from estimation and instead resorts to "calibration." In calibrating, Ball implicitly treats his model somehow as an approximation, not to be taken literally empirically. This empirical approach is compatible with Ball's motivation of his work as a sensitivity exercise designed to explore how augmenting the government's model to incorporate aspects of a foreign sector will affect the character of optimal rules that he had deduced earlier from a related closed economy model (Ball 1997). Ball does a good job of explaining the alterations he has made to the baseline closed economy model, of interpreting how they make the optimal rule change, and of informally explaining how the optimal rule corresponds to practices observed in some small open economies. The optimal rule contains the "advice" Ball coaxes from his formal model.[2]

Ball also evaluates six arbitrary rules. Within the confines of this single paper, comparing the operation of these rules is of less interest than just looking at the optimal rule. These comparisons acquire interest as ingredients of a robustness calculation only when they are put together with the workings of these six rules within the *different* models represented in the other papers in the conference.

To supplement Ball's acknowledgment in the text that the government's model is "pre–Lucas critique" (although cleverly constructed to embody one version of the natural rate hypothesis), I recommend Robert King and Mark Watson's (1994) "revisionist history" of the Phillips curve. King and Watson use theory and empirical evidence to document how the type of "unit root" specification of the Phillips curve used by Ball reflects the serial correlation structure of inflation detected only over the last 25 years or so, which emerged hand in hand with our current fiat monetary policy regime. Our earlier monetary regime was associated with much lower serial correlation of inflation, and a different apparent intertemporal Phillips curve.[3] I recommend Ball's (1995) *Journal of Monetary Economics* paper (where the government sets a repeated economy strategy and the private economy makes predictions that reflect the government's strategy) as an example of an analysis with optimizing behavior on all sides, a setup not subject to my first criticism (though possibly to my second one).

1. Ball thus adheres to Einstein's dictum that while nature might be complicated, it is not cruel. Contrast this modern view with the malevolent view of nature embraced by the "robust" monetary authority to be described shortly.
2. He computes an optimal rule for each value of a relative weight parameterizing the government's objective function.
3. Robert Hall makes related and more extensive observations in his comment on chap. 9 of this volume.

Ball can argue somewhat convincingly that despite imperfect "microfoundations," and despite vulnerability to the Lucas critique, a model of his type can somehow be a good approximation to a "truer" (bigger? general equilibrium?) model. Accepting this defense against the charge of too little rational expectations in the model strengthens my second criticism and prompts retreat from the rational expectations that Ball ascribes to the government in formulating its control problem. If the model is an approximation, the optimal policy rule ought to incorporate this attitude. This attitude recommends "postmodern" or "robust" rather than "modern" control theory. A quest for robustness overshadows this conference, so I want to explore how a preference for robustness would affect Ball's analysis.

Modern and Robust Government Problems

Ball's control problem is a member of the following class. Where x_t and u_t are the state and control vectors and z_t is a vector representing the decision maker's rewards, the government's model is

(1a) $$x_{t+1} = Ax_t + Bu_t + Cw_{t+1},$$

(1b) $$u_t = -Fx_t,$$

(1c) $$z_t = Hx_t,$$

where $\{w_{t+1}\}$ is a martingale difference sequence with unity contemporaneous covariance matrix, adapted to its own history.[4] The government chooses a feedback rule of the form (1b) to achieve an objective that Ball formulates as the unconditional variance of z_t. For the purpose of formalizing the control problem, it is useful to express the model in the form

(2) $$z_t = G(L)w_t \equiv H[I - (A - BF)L]^{-1}Cw_t,$$

Equation (2) shows how the white noise shocks w_t affect the variables the government cares about. For Ball, the problem is to maximize minus the unconditional variance of z, by choice of F. This can be expressed in the frequency domain as choosing an F to maximize

4. For Ball's model, we can take

$$x_t = \begin{bmatrix} y_t & \pi_t & e_{t-1} & v_t \end{bmatrix}', \quad u_t = e_t, \quad A = \begin{bmatrix} \lambda & 0 & 0 & \beta/\theta \\ \alpha & 1 & \gamma & 0 \\ 0 & 0 & 0 & 0 \\ 0 & 0 & 0 & 0 \end{bmatrix},$$

$$B' = \begin{bmatrix} -(\beta/\theta + \delta) & -\gamma & 1 & 0 \end{bmatrix}, \quad C = \begin{bmatrix} 1 & 0 & 0 \\ 0 & 1 & 0 \\ 0 & 0 & 0 \\ 0 & 0 & \sqrt{2} \end{bmatrix}.$$

(3) $$H^2 = -Ez_t z_t' = -\int_\Gamma [G(\zeta)G(\zeta)']\,d\zeta,$$

where ζ is a complex variable, Γ is the unit circle, and the prime denotes matrix transposition and complex conjugation. This problem is "modern" in the sense that the government is assumed to know enough about the model to have rational expectations. It treats the model as known and true. This means that the government knows: (1) $G(L)$ and how it depends on F and (2) that the shock process w_t is serially uncorrelated.

Robust control theory would back away from the rational expectations assumption and endow the government with the view that while "good," its model is not "true," only an approximation. Suspicion that the model is an approximation imparts a preference for "robustness," that is, acceptable performance of a rule across a range of models "in the vicinity" of the government's—"in the vicinity" because the model is viewed as a useful approximation. To formalize this approach, robust decision theory treats the model not as true but as a base or reference model around which the government suspects approximation errors.[5] The key is to describe the form that the approximation errors can take, and how "big" they can be. Approximation errors have fruitfully been formulated as showing up as a shock process $\{w_t\}$ that is arbitrarily serially correlated, not serially uncorrelated as specified. If the shocks have spectral density $S_w(\zeta)$ rather than I, then the variance of z_t is not given by the second equality in equation (3) but by

(4) $$\tilde{H}_2 = -\int_\Gamma G(\zeta)S_w(\zeta)G(\zeta)'\,d\zeta.$$

The robust decision maker seeks a rule that delivers an "acceptable" $\tilde{H}_2$ over a domain of somewhat arbitrary $S_w(\zeta)$. To construct the domain of approximation errors, some sort of "constant variance" restraint $\int_\Gamma S_w(\zeta)\,d\zeta = I$ is imposed on the potentially perturbed error processes.

To design a robust rule, the decision maker performs a worst case analysis. He solves a problem of the form

(5) $$\max_F \min_{S_w(\zeta)} \tilde{H}_2 \quad \text{such that} \quad \int_\Gamma S_w(\zeta)\,d\zeta = I.$$

The F that solves this max-min problem works better than the modern rule across much of the domain of unknown error serial correlation specifications. The associated minimizing $S_w(\zeta)$ is the "most pessimistic" view of the shock serial correlation process, an artifact of computing a rule designed to work well over a variety of $S_w(\zeta)$.[6]

---

5. For general background on robust control, see Zhou (1996), Başar and Bernhard (1995), and Mustafa and Glover (1990). See Whittle (1990) for an account of risk-sensitive control, and Hansen and Sargent (1995) for a recursive reformulation of risk sensitivity designed to accommodate discounting.

6. Max-min problems of this type occur widely in analyses of robustness. For a related problem in quite a different context, see Fudenberg and Levine (1995).

Notice how this formulation makes the specification error show up as a perturbed shock process that nevertheless feeds through the system in the way the model specifies. This is a restrictive way of modeling "misspecification," though as Hatanaka's (1975) work emphasized, arbitrarily serially correlated errors provide specifications so flexible that they often undermine econometric identifiability. A restrictive aspect of the present way of modeling specification errors is that the misspecified errors are supposed to feed through the system just as those in the reference model.

Remarkably, but maybe not surprisingly, because this *is* a form of Knightian uncertainty, there is a sense in which the robust decision maker turns back from the Lucas critique. Thus, for a *given* reference model, variations in the shock serial correlation process within the domain satisfying the constraint in problem (5) are presumed to leave the robust decision rule intact. Here I am interpreting the Lucas critique as but an application of the principle, already well reflected in "Keynesian" contributions like Kareken, Muench, and Wallace (1973),[7] stating that optimal decision rules depend on laws of motion or transition laws expressing the "constraints," which in the modern setting always include descriptions of the serial correlation patterns of the shocks. The robust controller's behavior partly belies that principle.[8]

Problem (5) embodies a game, not real, but a mental one, played in the mind of a monetary authority, who as an instrument for attaining a robust rule contemplates the reactions of a diabolical nature that is not "fixed" and that in response to *its* choice of F, responds by "choosing" a shock process serial correlation structure to harm the monetary authority. The point is not that the policymaker expects the worst but that by planning against it he assures acceptable performance under a range of specification errors.

Problem (5) leads to what is called the H^∞ formulation of robust decision theory.[9] A less extreme and more convenient formulation is the "minimum entropy" criterion, according to which the government just maximizes

$$(6) \qquad H_{\text{entropy}} = -\log \det \int_\Gamma [\kappa I - G(\zeta)G(\zeta)'] \, d\zeta.$$

This criterion is defined only for $\kappa \geq \kappa_b$, where κ_b is the minimum positive scalar for which the integrand is positive semidefinite.[10] The decision rule F that maximizes criterion (6) approximates the decision rule F that solves prob-

7. Their monetary authority has rational expectations and recommends "look at everything" rules, just like Ball's.
8. The robust decision maker's behavior *does* vary systematically with respect to variations in his reference model, the version of the Lucas critique that survives under robust decision theory.
9. See Mustafa and Glover (1990); see Hansen and Sargent (1998) for the formulations of H^∞ control modified to incorporate discounting. Hansen and Sargent also describe the "minimum entropy" formulation below and how it relates to the H^∞ criterion. In an interesting example, Kasa (1998) studies how a robust controller would behave in ways that an outsider might interpret as responding to adjustment costs.
10. Hansen and Sargent (1998) derive this criterion for discounted problems relate it to the H^∞ and risk-sensitivity formulations.

Table 3C.1   **Robust Policy Rules**

σ	$\bar{a}$	$\bar{b}$
0	1.04	.82
$-.1$	1.17	1.13
$-.2$	1.55	2.08

lem (5) as $\kappa \searrow \kappa_b$. Further, the parameter $\kappa > 0$ is interpretable in terms of the risk-sensitive formulation of Whittle (1990) and Hansen and Sargent (1995). In particular, κ equals minus the reciprocal of the risk-sensitivity parameter, σ.[11] Formulation (6) provides a "smooth" one-parameter family of approximators of (5). For $\sigma = 0$, we have the modern case, while for σ approaching $-\kappa_b^{-1}$, we attain the case envisaged in (5).

Examples

Using criterion (6), I have computed decision rules for three values of $-\kappa^{-1}$ $\equiv \sigma$, namely, $\sigma = 0$, $-.1$, and $-.2$. I prefer to parameterize in terms of σ because of its link to risk sensitivity, but this is just a matter of taste. The value $\sigma = 0$ corresponds to Ball's calculations and checks my calculations against his.[12] For Ball's parameter values and the case of equal weights on inflation and output variances in the government's objective, I calculated the responses of the interest rate, r to output y and the monetary conditions index π^* given in table 3C.1. Here $r = \bar{a}y + \bar{b}\pi^*$, where $\bar{a}$ and $\bar{b}$ are calculated just as in the $\sigma = 0$ case as explained by Ball. These numbers agree with Ball's in the $\sigma = 0$ case. Note how the interest rate becomes *more* sensitive to both y and π^* as the absolute value of σ rises (i.e., as the preference for robustness increases). This aspect of the rules illustrates that the "caution" induced by activating the preference for robustness does not translate into "doing less." Caution is relative to a worst case pattern of the shock process, which depends on the specification of the reference model. In particular, the specification of the model affects the magnitude and the serial correlation properties of the worst case shocks, and thus influences how the policymaker responds to actual shocks.[13]

To shed light on how a preference for robustness surfaces, it is useful to display the optimized $G(\zeta)$ functions in the frequency domain. Figure 3C.1 displays the maximum singular value of $G(\zeta)G(\zeta)'$ by frequency for $\sigma = 0$, $-.1$, and $-.2$. As σ rises in absolute value, the maximum singular value across

11. See Anderson, Hansen, and Sargent (1997) and Hansen and Sargent (1998). These papers also relate the risk-sensitive formulation to measures of model misspecification like those used by White (1982) and Sims (1972).

12. They agree where they should.

13. That robust control can be "more active" comes through in results reported by Zhou (1996, 438–39).

While the optimal rules remain linear, their dependence on innovation variances reflects a breakdown of "certainty equivalence."

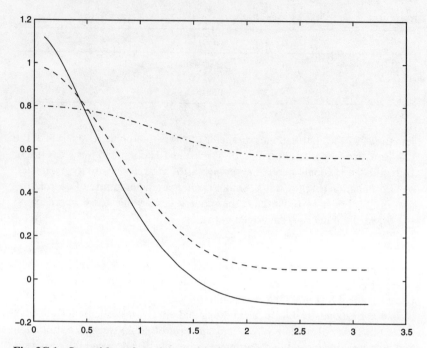

Fig. 3C.1   Logarithm of maximum singular values of $G(\zeta)$ for three values of σ

Note: $\sigma = 0$, $-.1$, and $-.2$ are indicated by solid, dashed, and dash-dotted lines, respectively. Angular frequency (from 0 to π) is the ordinate, the logarithm of the maximum singular value the coordinate.

frequencies falls, but the area under the curve rises.[14] This pattern captures how worst case performance improves as σ rises in absolute value, at the cost of worse performance at the reference model. In particular, think about how the "great deceiver" feared in problem (5) would respond to a $G(\zeta)$ having the pattern of maximum singular values associated with the $\sigma = 0$ case in figure 3C.1. The deceiver could lower the utility of the monetary authority (raise the weighted average of variances) by concentrating the spectral power of the shock process near the frequencies at which the maximum singular value is highest. To protect itself against such a malevolent nature, the monetary authority can design a rule to lower the maximum singular value, although this causes the average level of the maximum singular values across frequencies to drift upward (which lowers the value of the monetary authority's objective under the assumption that the reference model is *true*). In Ball's model, flattening the maximum singular values across frequencies can be achieved by making the interest rate respond more to both y and π^*.

14. The L^{∞} norms for $\sigma = 0$, $-.1$, and $-.2$ are 3.13, 2.68, and 2.22; the L^2 norms are 1.57, 1.61, and 1.97.

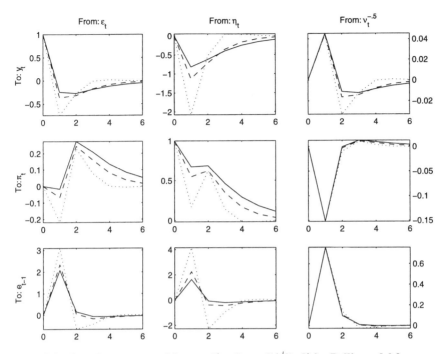

Fig. 3C.2   Impulse response of $[y \ \pi \ e_{-1}]'$ to $[\varepsilon_t \ \eta_t \ (1/\sqrt{2})v_t]'$ for Ball's model for three values of σ

Note: $\sigma = 0, -.1$, and $-.2$ are indicated by solid, dashed, and dotted lines. The shocks correspond to columns, the variables to rows.

Figure 3C.2 depicts the impulse response functions with respect to the w_ts (i.e., the $G(L)$s) for the three values of $\sigma = 0, -.1$, and $-.2$. Close inspection of these figures confirms how making σ more negative leads to "whiter" impulse responses. The "less colorful" impulse responses reflect the "flattening" across frequencies of the maximum singular values as σ (which is nonpositive) is raised in absolute value. Thus the "more active" responses in the rules for more negative σs, depicted in table 3C.1, deliver whiter spectral outcomes (assuming the reference model to be true).

Thus this particular way of framing the class of misspecifications to be protected against causes "more caution" to translate into "more activity." How can this happen? One way to approach this question is to study how the "worst case" conditional means of the shocks, call them $\hat{w}_{t+j}$, respond to the true shocks w_t. Hansen, Sargent, and Tallarini (forthcoming) report a formula for such worse case conditional means. The formula shows how the worst case conditional means are linear functions of the state of the system x_t. This makes it possible to compute impulse responses of the worst case shocks with respect to the w_ts. Figure 3C.3 depicts the impulse responses of these worst case conditional means in the shocks with respect to the w_ts for $\sigma = -.1$ and $-.2$; for

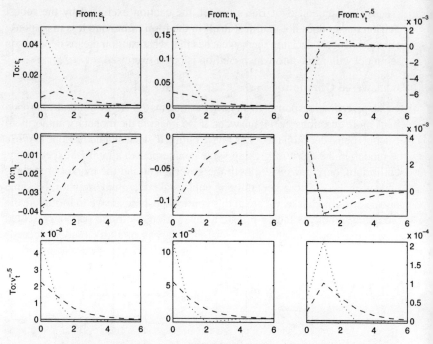

Fig. 3C.3   Impulse response of the worst case $[\varepsilon_t\ \eta_t\ (1/\sqrt{2})v_t]'$ with respect to $[\varepsilon_t\ \eta_t\ (1/\sqrt{2})v_t]'$ for Ball's model for two values of σ

Note: $\sigma = -.1$ and $-.2$ are indicated by dashed and dotted lines. The shocks correspond to columns, the worst case shocks to rows.

$\sigma = 0$, these worst case means are identically zero. The impulse responses in figure 3C.3 show how for Ball's model, the worst case conditional means in the shocks change both in size and in their serial correlation properties as σ becomes more negative. Figure 3C.3 shows how the worst case conditional means of shocks become larger as σ grows in absolute value, and that they respond as though the worst case shocks are serially correlated.[15] This makes the robust decision maker respond to what the reference model asserts are white noise shocks as though they were positively serially correlated. To guard against the worst case, the robust decision maker exercises caution by "pressing the brakes" or "pushing on the accelerator" more than would the modern decision maker. This is reasonable because a shock is interpreted as being larger and more persistent than it is supposed to be by the reference model. This helps to explain the pattern of the table 3C.1 responses.

---

15. The figures also show that the worst case shocks are less serially correlated for the σ that is larger in absolute value. In interpreting this diminished serial correlation, it has to be remembered that these objects are the outcome of the "game" associated with a minimax problem, and that the great deceiver picking these worst case errors faces a different feedback rule F for each σ.

Thus, in the context of Ball's model, the caution exercised by the robust decision maker does not manifest itself in the form of moving less in response to shocks. Robust decision theory teaches that what caution means depends on the model with respect to which caution is being exercised.

Unanswered Questions

The preceding response to my two criticisms of Ball's general approach opens more questions than it answers. If we imagine the monetary authority to be using robust decision theory as I have outlined, what should be done to close the model, in the spirit of seeking some counterpart to a rational expectations equilibrium, only now where both the government and the market are robust decision makers? More generally, if policymakers are entertaining the same doubts across models as we are at this conference, how are we to formulate the forecasting problems facing private agents? Along with the papers presented in this conference, my "robust decision" analysis of Ball's model proceeds without any sort of "robust equilibrium" concept.[16] Maybe such an equilibrium concept could help us.[17]

References

Anderson, Evan. 1998. Uncertainty and the dynamics of Pareto optimal allocations. Chicago: University of Chicago. Manuscript.
Anderson, Evan, L. P. Hansen, and T. J. Sargent. 1997. Robustness and risk-sensitivity in general equilibrium. Chicago and Palo Alto: University of Chicago and Hoover Institution. Manuscript.
Ball, Laurence. 1995. Time-consistent policy and persistent changes in inflation. *Journal of Monetary Economics* 36 (2): 329–50.
———. 1997. Efficient rules for monetary policy. NBER Working Paper no. 5952. Cambridge, Mass.: National Bureau of Economic Research.
Başar, Tamar, and Pierre Bernhard. 1995. *H∞-optimal control and related minimax design problems: A dynamic game approach.* Boston: Birkhäuser.
Fudenberg, Drew, and David Levine. 1995. Universal consistency and cautious fictious play. *Journal of Economic Dynamics and Control* 19 (July): 1065–89.
Hansen, L. P., and T. J. Sargent. 1995. Discounted linear exponential quadratic Gaussian control. *IEEE Transactions on Automatic Control* 40 (May): 968–71.
———. 1998. Alternative representations of discounted robust linear quadratic control. Chicago and Palo Alto: University of Chicago and Hoover Institution. Manuscript.

---

16. E.g., the agents inside the four models compared in chap. 6 of this volume, by Levin, Wieland, and Williams, all live in secure rational expectations environments and have no need to trouble themselves with the doubts over models that preoccupy Levin, Wieland, and Williams. I believe that the three authors' comforting finding of robustness across models might mainly reflect the proximity of the four models. Note that the four models compared are all rational expectations models with "forward-looking" private sectors, and all have been thoughtfully designed to fit recent U.S. data and to incorporate similar monetary control channels. It would be more challenging for rules also to be robust against the non-forward-looking models illustrated by those of Ball and, in chap. 5, of Rudebusch and Svensson.

17. Evan Anderson (1998) studies a multiple-agent environment with robust decision makers whose preferences for robustness diverge.

Hansen, L. P., T. J. Sargent, and T. D. Tallarini Jr. Forthcoming. Robust permanent income and pricing. *Review of Economic Studies.*

Hatanaka, Michio. 1975. On the global identification of the dynamic simultaneous equations model with stationary disturbances. *International Economic Review* 16 (3): 545–54.

Kareken, J. A., T. Muench, and N. Wallace. 1973. Optimal open market strategy: The use of information variables. *American Economic Review* 68 (1): 156–72.

Kasa, Kenneth. 1998. Observational equivalence of H^∞ control problems. San Francisco: Federal Reserve Bank of San Francisco. Manuscript.

King, Robert G., and Mark W. Watson. 1994. The post-war U.S. Phillips curve: A revisionist econometric history. *Carnegie-Rochester Conference Series on Public Policy* 41:157–219.

Mustafa, Denis, and Keith Glover. 1990. *Minimum entropy H^∞ control.* Berlin: Springer.

Sims, C. A. 1972. Approximate prior restrictions on distributed lag estimation. *Journal of the American Statistical Association* 67 (1): 169–75.

White, Halbert. 1982. Maximum likelihood estimation of misspecified models. *Econometrica* 50 (1): 1–25.

Whittle, Peter. 1990. *Risk-sensitive optimal control.* New York: Wiley.

Zhou, Kemin, with John C. Doyle and Keith Glover. 1996. *Robust and optimal control.* London: Prentice-Hall.

Discussion Summary

Regarding Sargent's discussion of the paper, *Bob Hall* conjectured that since a Bayesian does not respect the Knightian distinction between risk and uncertainty, all knowledge could be properly summarized in a Bayesian framework. *Sargent* replied that with an infinite-dimensional parameter space as given here, the Bayes consistency theorem breaks down. As an early reference on this issue, Sargent cited Christopher Sims's thesis.

David Longworth noted that the model's policy recommendation was very similar to what the Bank of Canada has been doing in the past, for example, deriving the MCI weights from the IS curve and carefully considering the exchange rate effect on inflation. A simple extension of the model would be to allow for cross-correlation between the error in the IS curve and the error in the exchange rate equation. The reason this is interesting is that this correlation, that is, the degree to which exchange rates are driven by nonfinancial fundamentals, determines the desirability of the MCI as a target variable in the short run. For example, the Reserve Bank of Australia and the Bank of England both tend to think that there is a high correlation between these error terms for their respective home countries. Under those circumstances, it is not desirable to leave the MCI unchanged over one period. On the contrary, the Bank of Canada believes this correlation to be very small in Canada (especially when one abstracts from shocks to commodity prices and from readily observable shocks to the IS curve).

Laurence Meyer remarked that this is a timely paper for two reasons. First, exchange rates have been very important through import prices in the recent U.S. inflation experience. Second, globalization leads to increased openness that affects the way monetary policy should respond. Meyer then expressed reluctance to use the MCI as a policy instrument. He argued that the optimal response of interest rates to changes in the exchange rate depends on the source and the persistence of the change. Also, the MCI is an incomplete measure of overall financial conditions. It leaves out such variables as long interest rates and equity prices, which might be equally or more important. Meyer proposed interpreting the paper as having an interest rate instrument that reacts to the exchange rate.

Frederic Mishkin mentioned the New Zealand experience, where exchange rate effects are much faster than interest rate effects. That creates an instrument instability and controllability problem as described in the paper, in particular with rigid bands and a short horizon.

Andrew Levin noted that the appendix of his paper with Wieland and Williams presented at the conference summarized some analysis of the importance of openness for U.S. policy rules. Stochastic simulations of the Taylor multicountry model and deterministic simulations of the Federal Reserve Board global model show that the optimal policy rules are essentially identical for different assumptions on foreign policy. This can be interpreted as evidence for the size of the external sector in the U.S. economy being small and the passthrough of exchange rates into prices being slow. In the context of Ball's model, this means that the δ and γ coefficients seem to be very small for the United States. *Ball* responded that the applicability of the model to the case of the United States is still an open question. He also expressed surprise over the ongoing discussion about the importance of recent events in Asia for the United States.

Lars Svensson noted that the Bank of Sweden is not using the MCI but a repurchase rate as a policy instrument. The MCI is used as a measure of the impact of monetary policy on aggregate demand.

Svensson also remarked that the exchange rate equation, equation (3) in the paper, is not consistent with the exchange rate being an asset price, that is, with interest rate parity. Furthermore, Svensson had recently addressed this problem in a forward-looking framework where he obtained an MCI that depended on the real exchange rate and a long real interest rate, as opposed to the short rate. Thus the resulting MCI in such a framework is very different from the measure being used by actual central banks. *Richard Clarida* suggested interpreting equation (3) as a link between the log real exchange rate and an interest differential. Such an equation can be derived from underlying principles as in Campbell and Clarida (1987), but a necessary condition for that proportionality to hold is that the real interest rate follow an AR(1) process. Without this assumption, the entire term structure of interest rates enters the equation. Moreover, when the policymaker chooses the exchange rate e, he only chooses the current interest rate r in the paper. In a more general model, this amounts to choosing the entire time path of r, so that the resulting MCI would not have as nice a representation in terms of current variables as in the paper.

Ben McCallum wondered about the paper's use of real variables to measure the MCI. First, the MCI used by actual central banks like New Zealand and Canada is measured in terms of nominal variables. How should such an MCI measure be deflated? This is not clear since subtracting the expected inflation rate would be appropriate to calculate real interest rates and dividing by the price level would be appropriate to obtain the real exchange rate. Second, policy indicators should ideally be nominal variables instead of real ones.

John Taylor noted that small economies have a desire to prevent exchange rate fluctuations and many papers at the conference discuss interest rate smoothing. What about exchange rate smoothing? *Lars Svensson* answered that with a short horizon for inflation targeting, there is a tendency to move the exchange rate too much. With a longer horizon, the exchange rate is smoothed to stabilize the consumer price index. *David Longworth* added that it would be important to include tables in the paper showing the variance of interest and exchange rates across different policy rules. This is particularly important for the comparison of rules targeting π (actual inflation) and π^* (long-run inflation).

Nicoletta Batini remarked that it would be interesting to see how rules with different target specifications, for example domestic inflation, compare to the "long-run" inflation target in the paper. Use of targets that—in an economy that imports only final goods—are not influenced by the exchange-rate-to-import-price channel may remove the need for an ad hoc target à la Ball. Also, the use of an MCI as an instrument is not desirable because it requires measuring the equilibrium exchange rate in addition to the equilibrium interest rate and the output gap as in more conventional, Taylor-type simple rules.

Reference

Campbell, John, and Richard Clarida. 1987. The dollar and real interest rates: An empirical investigation. *Carnegie-Rochester Conference Series on Public Policy* 27: 103–39.

4 Forward-Looking Rules for Monetary Policy

Nicoletta Batini and Andrew G. Haldane

4.1 Introduction

It has long been recognized that economic policy in general, and monetary policy in particular, needs a forward-looking dimension. "If we wait until a price movement is actually afoot before applying remedial measures, we may be too late," as Keynes (1923) observes in *A Tract on Monetary Reform.* That same constraint still faces the current generation of monetary policymakers. Alan Greenspan's Humphrey-Hawkins testimony in 1994 summarizes the monetary policy problem thus: "The challenge of monetary policy is to interpret current data on the economy and financial markets with an eye to anticipating future inflationary forces and to countering them by taking action in advance." Or in the words of Donald Kohn (1995) at the Board of Governors of the Federal Reserve System: "Policymakers cannot avoid looking into the future." Empirically estimated reaction functions suggest that policymakers' actions match these words. Monetary policy in the G-7 countries appears in recent years to have been driven more by anticipated future than by lagged actual outcomes (Clarida and Gertler 1997; Clarida, Galí, and Gertler 1998; Orphanides 1998).

But how best is this forward-looking approach made operational? Friedman's (1959) *Program for Monetary Stability* cast doubt on whether it could

Nicoletta Batini is analyst in the Monetary Assessment and Strategy Division, Monetary Analysis, Bank of England. Andrew G. Haldane is senior manager of the International Finance Division, Bank of England.

The authors have benefited greatly from the comments and suggestions of Bill Allen, Andy Blake, Willem Buiter, Paul Fisher, Charles Goodhart, Mervyn King, Paul Levine, Tiff Macklem, David Miles, Stephen Millard, Alessandro Missale, Paul Mizen, Darren Pain, Joe Pearlman, Richard Pierse, John Taylor, Paul Tucker, Ken Wallis, Peter Westaway, John Whitley, Stephen Wright, and especially discussant Don Kohn and other seminar participants. The views expressed within are not necessarily those of the Bank of England.

be. Likening economic forecasting to weather forecasting, he observes: "Leaning today against next year's wind is hardly an easy task in the present state of meteorology." Yet this is just the task present-day monetary policymakers have set themselves: in effect, long-range weather forecasting in a stochastic world of time-varying lags and coefficients. That is a tough nut to crack even for meteorologists. It is not altogether surprising, then, that solving the equivalent problem in a monetary policy context has met with different solutions among central banks.

The more innovative among these solutions have recently been adopted by countries targeting inflation directly. These countries now include New Zealand, Canada, the United Kingdom, Sweden, Finland, Australia, and Spain (see Haldane 1995; Leiderman and Svensson 1995). In the first three of these countries, monetary policy is based on explicit (and in some cases published) inflation forecasts.[1] These forecasts are the de facto intermediate or feedback variable for monetary policy (Svensson 1997a, 1997b; Haldane 1997). The aim of this paper is to evaluate that particular approach to the general problem of the need for forward-lookingness in monetary policy.

This is done by evaluating a class of simple policy rules that feed back from expected values of future inflation—inflation-forecast-based rules. These rules are simple, and so are analogous to the Taylor rule specifications that have recently been extensively discussed in an academic and policy-making context. Because they are forecast based, the rules mimic (albeit imperfectly) monetary policy behavior among inflation-targeting central banks in practice.[2] And despite their simplicity, these forecast-based rules have a number of desirable features, which mean they may approximate the optimal feedback rule.

The class of forecast-based rules that we consider take the following generic form:

$$(1) \qquad r_t = \gamma r_{t-1} + (1 - \gamma)r_t^* + \theta(E_t \pi_{t+j} - \pi^*),$$

where r_t denotes the short-term ex ante real rate of interest, $r_t \equiv i_t - E_t \pi_{t+1}$, where i_t are nominal interest rates; r_t^* denotes the equilibrium value of real interest rates; $E_t(\cdot) = E(\cdot \mid \Phi_t)$, where Φ_t is the information set available at time t and E is the mathematical expectations operator; π_t is inflation ($\pi_t \equiv p_t^c - p_{t-1}^c$, where p_t^c is the log of the consumer price index); and π^* is the inflation target.[3]

According to the rule, the monetary authorities control deterministically nominal interest rates (i_t) so as to hit a path for the short-term real interest rate

---

1. In the other inflation-targeting countries, inflation forecasts are sometimes less explicit but nevertheless a fundamental part of the monetary policy process.
2. We discuss below the places in which the forecast-based rules we consider deviate from real-world inflation targeting.
3. The rule could be augmented with other—e.g., explicit output—terms. We do so below. This then takes us close to the reaction function specification found by Clarida et al. (1998) to match recent monetary policy behavior in the G-7 countries.

(r_t). Short real rates are in turn set relative to some steady state value, determined by a weighted combination of lagged and equilibrium real interest rates. The novel feature of the rule, however, is the feedback term. Deviations of *expected* inflation (the feedback variable) from the inflation target (the policy goal) elicit remedial policy actions.

The policy choice variables for the authorities are the parameter triplet $\{j, \theta, \gamma\}$. The parameter γ dictates the degree of interest rate smoothing (see Williams 1997). So, for example, with $\gamma = 0$ there is no instrument smoothing. The parameter θ is a policy feedback parameter. Higher values of θ imply a more aggressive policy response for a given deviation of the inflation forecast from its target. Finally, j is the targeting horizon of the central bank when forming its forecast. For example, in the United Kingdom the Bank of England feeds back from an inflation forecast around two years ahead (King 1997).[4] The horizon of the inflation forecast (j) and the size of the feedback coefficient (θ), as well as the degree of instrument smoothing (γ), dictate the speed at which inflation is brought back to target following inflationary disturbances. Because they influence the inflationary transition path, these policy parameters clearly also have a bearing on output dynamics.

As defined in equation (1), inflation targeting amounts to a well-defined monetary policy rule. That view is not at odds with Bernanke and Mishkin's (1997) characterization of inflation targeting as "constrained discretion." There is ample scope for discretionary input into any rule—equation (1) particularly so. These discretionary choices include the formation of the inflation expectation itself and the choice of the parameter set $\{j, \theta, \pi^*\}$. They mean that equation (1) does not fall foul of the critique of inflation targeting made by Friedman and Kuttner (1996): that it is rigid as a monetary strategy and hence destined to the same failures as, for example, strict monetary targeting.

This is fine as an intuitive description of a forecast-based policy rule such as rule (1). But what, if any, theoretical justification do these rules have? And, in particular, why might they be preferred to, for example, Taylor rules? Several authors have recently argued that, in certain settings, expected-inflation-targeting rules have desirable properties (inter alia, King 1997; Svensson 1997a, 1997b; Haldane 1998). For example, in Svensson's model (1997a), the optimal rule when the authorities care only about inflation is one that sets interest rates so as to bring expected inflation into line with the inflation target at some horizon ("strict" inflation-forecast targeting). When the authorities care also about output the optimal rule is to less than fully close any gap between expected inflation and the inflation target ("flexible" inflation-forecast targeting).[5]

The rules we consider here differ from those in Svensson (1997a) in that

---

4. This comparison is not exact because j defines the *feedback* horizon under the rule, whereas in practice in the United Kingdom two years refers to the *policy* horizon (the point at which expected inflation and the inflation target are in line).

5. Rudebusch and Svensson consider empirically rules of this sort in chap. 5 of this volume.

they are simple feedback rules for the policy instrument, rather than complicated optimal targeting rules. Simple feedback rules have some clear advantages. First, they are directly analogous to, and so comparable with, the other policy rule specifications discussed in the papers in this volume, including Taylor rules. Second, simple rules are arguably more robust when there is uncertainty about the true structure of the economy. And third, simple rules may be advantageous on credibility and monitorability grounds (Taylor 1993). The last of these considerations is perhaps the most important in a policy context, for one way to interpret the output from these rules is as a cross-check on actual policy in real time. For that to be practical, any rule needs to be simple and monitorable by outside agents.

At the same time, the simple forecast-based rules we consider do have some clear similarities with Svensson's optimal inflation-forecast-targeting rules. Monetary policy under both rules seeks to offset deviations between expected inflation and the inflation target at some horizon.[6] More concretely, even simple forecast-based specifications can be considered "encompassing" rules, in the following respects:

Lag Encompassing. The lag between the enactment of monetary policy and its first effects on inflation and output are well known and widely documented. The monetary authorities need to be conscious of these lags when framing policy; they need to be able to calibrate them reasonably accurately; and they then need to embody them in the design of their policy rules. Without this, monetary policy will always be acting after the point at which it can hope to head off incipient inflationary pressures. Such myopic policy may itself then become a source of cyclical (in particular, inflation) instability, for the very reasons outlined by Friedman (1959).[7]

By judicious choice of j, the lead term on expected inflation in equation (1), simple forecast-based rules can be designed so as to embody automatically these transmission lags. In particular, the feedback variable in the rule can be chosen so that it is directly under the control of the monetary authorities— inflation j periods hence. The policymakers' feedback and control variables are then explicitly aligned. Transmission lags are the most obvious (but not the only) reason why monetary policy needs a forward-looking, preemptive dimension. Embedding these lags in a formal forecast-based rule is simple recognition of that fact.[8] Reflecting this, lag encompassing was precisely the motiva-

6. In particular, since the rules we consider allow flexibility over both the forecast horizon (j) and the feedback parameter (θ)—both of which affect output stabilization—their closest analogue is Svensson's flexible inflation-forecast-targeting rule.

7. Former vice-chairman of the Federal Reserve Alan Blinder observes: "Failure to take proper account of lags is, I believe, one of the main sources of central bank error" (1997).

8. Svensson (1997a) shows, in the context of his model, that rules with this lag-encompassing feature secure the minimum variance of inflation precisely because they guard against monetary policy acting too late.

tion behind targeting expected inflation in those countries where this was first adopted: New Zealand, Canada, and the United Kingdom.

Information Encompassing. Under inflation-forecast-based rules, the inflation expectation in rule (1) can be thought of as the intermediate variable for monetary policy. It is well suited to this task when judged against the three classical requirements of any intermediate variable: it is controllable, predictable, and a leading indicator. Expected inflation is, almost by definition, the indicator most closely correlated with the future value of the variable of interest. In particular, expected inflation ought to embody all information contained within the myriad indicators that affect the future path of inflation. Forecast-based rules are, in this sense, information encompassing. That is not a feature necessarily shared by backward-looking policy rules—for example, those considered in the volume by Bryant, Hooper, and Mann (1993).

Of course, any forward-looking rule can be given a backward-looking representation and respecified in terms of current and previously dated variables. For example, in the aggregate-demand/aggregate-supply model of Svensson (1997a), the optimal forward-looking rule can be rewritten as a Taylor rule—albeit with weights on the output gap and inflation that are likely to be very different from one-half. But that will not necessarily be the case in more general settings where shocks come not just from output and prices. Taylor-type rules will tend then to feed back from a restrictive subset of information variables and so will not in general be optimal.[9] By contrast, inflation-forecast-based rules will naturally embody all information contained in the inflation reduced-form of the model: extra lags of existing predetermined variables and additional predetermined variables, both of which would typically also enter the optimal feedback rule. For that reason even simple forecast-based rules are likely to take us close to the optimal state-contingent rule—or at least closer than Taylor-type rule specifications.

Output Encompassing. As specified in equation (1), inflation-forecast-based rules appear to take no explicit account of output objectives. The inflation target, π^*, defines the nominal anchor, and there is no explicit regard for output stabilization. But π^* is not the only policy choice parameter in equation (1). The targeting horizon (j) and feedback parameter (θ)—the two remaining policy choice variables—can in principle also help to secure a degree of output smoothing. These parameters can be chosen to ensure that an inflation-forecast-based rule better reflects the authorities' preferences in situations where they care about output as well as inflation variability. To see how these policy parameters affect output stabilization, consider separately shocks to demand and supply.

---

9. Black, Macklem, and Rose (1997) illustrate this in a simulation setting.

In the case of demand shocks, inflation and output stabilization will in most instances be mutually compatible. Demand shocks shift output and inflation in the same direction relative to their baseline values. So there need not then be any inherent trade-off between output and inflation stabilization in the setting of monetary policy following these shocks. A rule such as equation (1) will automatically secure a degree of output stabilization in a world of just demand shocks. Or, put differently, because it is useful for predicting future inflation, the output gap already appears implicitly in an inflation-forecast-based rule such as equation (1).

For supply shocks, trade-offs between output and inflation stability are more likely because they will tend then to be shifted in opposite directions. But inflation targeting does not imply that the authorities are opting for a corner solution on the output-inflation variability trade-off curve in these situations. For example, different inflation forecast horizons—different values of j—will imply different points on the output-inflation variability frontier. Longer forecast horizons smooth the transition of inflation back to target following inflation shocks, in part because policy then accommodates (rather than offsets) the first-round effects of any supply shocks.[10] The feedback coefficient (θ) also has a bearing on output dynamics, for much the same reason. So a central bank following an inflation-forecast-based rule can, in principle, simply choose its policy parameters $\{j, \theta, \gamma\}$ so as to achieve a preferred point on the output-inflation variability spectrum. Certainly, the simple forecast-based policy rule (1) ought not to be the sole preserve of monomaniacal inflation fighters.

This paper aims to put some quantitative flesh onto this conceptual skeleton. It evaluates simple forecast-based rules against the three encompassing criteria outlined above.[11] The type of policy questions this then enables us to address include: What is the optimal degree of policy forward-lookingness? And what does this depend on? Can inflation-only rules secure sufficient output smoothing? How do simple forecast-based rules compare with the fully optimal rule? And with simple Taylor rules?

To summarize our conclusions up front, we find quantitative support for all

10. This is broadly the practice followed in the United Kingdom. The Bank of England is required to write an open letter to the Chancellor in the event of inflation deviating by more than 1 percentage point from its target, stating the horizon over which inflation is to be brought back to heel. Longer horizons might be chosen following large or persistent supply shocks, so that policy does not disturb output too much en route back to the inflation target. That is important because the United Kingdom's inflation target, while giving primacy to price stability, also requires that the Bank of England take account of output and employment objectives when setting monetary policy. Other design features of inflation targets can ensure a sufficient degree of output stabilization. E.g., in New Zealand there are inflation target exemptions for "significant" supply shocks (see Mayes and Chapple 1995); while in Canada there is a larger inflation fluctuation margin to help insulate against shocks (see Freedman 1996).

11. Previous empirical simulation studies that have considered the performance of forward-looking rules include Black et al. (1997), Clark, Laxton, and Rose (1995), and Brouwer and O'Regan (1997).

three of the encompassing propositions. Because inflation-forecast-based policy rules embody transmission lags, they generally help improve inflation control (lag encompassing). These rules can be designed to smooth the path of output as well as inflation, despite not feeding back from the former explicitly (output encompassing). And inflation-forecast-based rules deliver clear welfare improvements over Taylor-type rules, which respond to a restrictive subset of information variables (information encompassing).

The paper is planned as follows. Section 4.2 outlines our model. Section 4.3 calibrates this model and conducts some deterministic experiments with it. Section 4.4 uses stochastic analysis to evaluate the three conceptual properties of forecast-based rules—lag encompassing, information encompassing, and output encompassing—outlined above. Section 4.5 briefly summarizes.

4.2   The Model

To evaluate equation (1), and variants of it, we use a small open economy, log-linear calibrated rational expectations macromodel. It has similarities with the optimizing IS-LM framework recently developed by McCallum and Nelson (forthcoming) and Svensson (forthcoming), and hence indirectly with the stochastic general equilibrium models of Rotemberg and Woodford (1997) and Goodfriend and King (1997). The open economy dimension is important when characterizing the behavior of inflation-targeting countries, which tend to be just such small open economies (see Blake and Westaway 1996; Svensson, forthcoming). The exchange rate also has an important bearing on output-inflation dynamics in our model, in keeping with the results of Ball (chap. 3 of this volume). Having a pseudostructural model is important too, given the susceptibility of counterfactual policy simulations to Lucas critique problems.

The model is kept deliberately small to ease the computational burden. But a compact model is also useful in helping clarify the transmission mechanism channels at work and the trade-offs that naturally arise among them. And despite its size, the model embodies the key features of the small forecasting model used by the Bank of England for its inflation projections. The model is calibrated to match the dynamic path of output and inflation generated by structural and reduced-form models of the United Kingdom economy in the face of various shocks.

The model comprises six behavioral relationships, listed as equations (2) through (7) below:

(2)
$$y_t - y_t^* = \alpha_1 y_{t-1} + \alpha_2 E_t(y_{t+1}) + \alpha_3(i_t - E_t \pi_{t+1})$$
$$+ \alpha_4(e_t + p_t^c - p_t^{cf}) + \varepsilon_{1t},$$

(3)
$$m_t - p_t^c = \beta_1 y_t + \beta_2 i_t + \varepsilon_{2t},$$

(4)
$$e_t = E_t e_{t+1} + i_t - i_t^f + \varepsilon_{3t},$$

$$(5) \qquad\qquad p_t^d = \tfrac{1}{2}(w_t + w_{t-1}),$$

$$(6) \qquad w_t - p_t^c = \chi_0(E_t w_{t+1} - E_t p_{t+1}^c) + (1 - \chi_0)(w_{t-1} - p_{t-1}^c)$$
$$+ \chi_1(y_t - y_t^*) + \varepsilon_{4t},$$

$$(7) \qquad\qquad p_t^c = \phi p_t^d + (1 - \phi)e_t.$$

All variables, except interest rates, are in logarithms. Importantly, in the simulations all behavioral relationships are also expressed as deviations from equilibrium. So, for example, we set the (log) natural rate of output, y_t^*, equal to zero. We also normalize to zero the (log) foreign price level and foreign interest rate, $p_t^{cf} = i_t^f = 0$, and the (implicit) markup in equation (5) and foreign exchange risk premium in equation (4).

Equation (2) is a standard IS curve, with real output, y_t, depending negatively on the ex ante real interest rate and the real exchange rate (where e_t is the foreign currency price of domestic currency), $\{\alpha_3, \alpha_4\} < 0$. The former channel is defined over short rather than long real interest rates. We could have included a long-term interest rate in our model, linking long and short rates through an arbitrage condition, as in Fuhrer and Moore's (1995a) model of the United States. But in the United Kingdom, unlike in the United States, expenditure is more sensitive to short than to long interest rates, owing to the prevalence of floating-rate debt instruments.

Output also depends on lags of itself, reflecting adjustment costs and, more interestingly, a lead term. The latter of these is motivated by McCallum and Nelson's (forthcoming) work on the form of the reduced-form IS curve that arises from a fully optimizing general equilibrium macromodel. We experiment with this lead term below, even though we do not use it in our baseline simulations. The term ε_{1t} is a vector of demand shocks, for example, shocks to foreign output and fiscal policy.

Equation (3) is an LM curve.[12] Its arguments are conventional: a nominal interest rate, capturing portfolio balance, and real output, capturing transactions demand.[13] The term ε_{2t} is a vector of velocity shocks. Equation (4) is an uncovered interest parity condition. We do not include any explicit foreign exchange risk premium. The shock vector ε_{3t} comprises foreign interest rate shocks and other noise in the foreign exchange market, including shocks to the exchange risk premium.

Equations (5) and (6) define the model's supply side. They take a similar form to that of other staggered contract models.[14] Equation (5) is a markup equation. Domestic output prices (in logs, p_t^d) are a constant markup over weighted average contract wages (in logs, w_t) in the current and preceding peri-

---

12. This is largely redundant in our analysis since we are focusing on interest rate rules that assume that the demand for money is always fully accommodated at unchanged interest rates.

13. McCallum and Nelson (forthcoming) show that this form of the LM curve can also be derived as the reduced form of an optimizing stochastic general equilibrium model.

14. In particular, they are similar to those recently developed by Fuhrer and Moore (1995a) for the United States. For an early formulation of such model, see Buiter and Jewitt (1981).

ods. Equation (6) is the wage-contracting equation. Under this specification, wage contracts last two periods.[15] Agents in today's wage cohort bargain over *relative* real consumption wages. Today's real contract wage is some weighted average of the real contract wage of the "other" cohort of workers: that is, wages already agreed upon in the previous period and those expected to be agreed upon in the next period. We do not impose symmetry on the lag and lead terms in the contracting equation, as in the standard Fuhrer and Moore (1995b) model. Instead we allow a flexible mixed lag-lead specification, which nests more restrictive alternatives as a special case (see Blake 1996; Blake and Westaway 1996). This flexible mixed specification is found in Fuhrer (1997) to be preferred empirically. It also allows us to experiment with the degree of forward-lookingness in the wage-bargaining process. The lag-lead weights are restricted to sum to unity, however, to preserve price homogeneity in the wage-price system (a vertical long-run Phillips curve). Also in the wage-contracting equation is a conventional output gap term, capturing tightness in the labor market. The shock vector, ε_{4t}, can be thought to capture disturbances to the natural rate of output and similar such supply shocks.

This relative wage-price specification has both theoretical and empirical attractions. Its theoretical appeal comes from work as early as Duesenberry (1949), which argued that wage relativities were a key consideration when entering the wage bargain. The empirical appeal of the relative real wage formulation is that it generates inflation persistence. This is absent from a conventional two-period Taylor (1980) contracting specification (Fuhrer and Moore 1995a; Fuhrer 1997), which instead produces price level persistence.[16] Equation (7) defines the consumption price index, comprising domestic goods (with weight ϕ) and imported foreign goods (with weight $1 - \phi$).[17] Note that equation (7) implies full and immediate passthrough of import prices (and hence exchange rate changes) into consumption prices—an assumption we discuss further below.

Some manipulation of equations (5), (6), and (7) gives the reduced-form Phillips curve of the model:

$$
(8) \qquad
\begin{aligned}
\pi_t &= \chi_0 E_t \pi_{t+1} + (1 - \chi_0)\pi_{t-1} + \chi_1(y_t + y_{t-1}) \\
&\quad + \mu[(1 - \chi_0)\Delta c_t - \chi_0 E_t \Delta c_{t+1}] + \varepsilon_{5t},
\end{aligned}
$$

where $c_t \equiv e_t - p_t^c$ (the real exchange rate), $\mu \equiv 2(1 - \phi)$, Δ is the backward difference operator, and $\varepsilon_{5t} \equiv \varepsilon_{4t} + \chi_0[(p_t^c - E_{t-1}p_t^c) - (w_t - E_{t-1}w_t)]$, where the composite error now includes expectational errors by wage bargainers.

15. We could have lengthened the contracting lag—e.g., to four periods, which in our calibration is one year—to better match real-world behavior. But two lags appeared to be sufficient to generate the inflation persistence evident in the data, when taken together with the degree of backward-lookingness embodied in the Phillips curve.

16. As Roberts (1995) discusses, Taylor contracting can deliver inflation persistence if, e.g., expectations are made "not quite rational." Certainly, a variety of mechanisms other than the one adopted here would have allowed us to introduce inflation persistence into the model.

17. With the foreign price level normalized to zero in logs.

Equation (8) is the open economy analogue of Fuhrer and Moore's (1995a) Phillips curve specification (see Blake and Westaway 1996). The inflation terms—a weighted backward- and forward-looking average—are the same as in the closed economy case. There is inflation persistence. The specification differs because of additional (real) exchange rate terms, reflecting the price effects of exchange rate changes on imported goods in the consumption basket.[18]

The transmission of monetary impulses in this model is very different from the closed economy case, in terms of size and timing of the effects: we illustrate these effects below. There is a conventional real interest rate channel, working through the output gap and thence onto inflation. But in addition there is a real exchange rate effect, operating through two distinct channels. First, there is an indirect output gap route running through net exports and thence onto inflation. And second, there are direct price effects via the cost of imported consumption goods and via wages and hence output prices. The latter channel means that disinflation policies have a speedy effect on consumer prices (p_t^c), if not on domestically generated prices (p_t^d)—see Svensson (forthcoming). This direct exchange rate channel thus has an important bearing on consumer price inflation and output dynamics, which we illustrate below. Because these direct exchange rate effects derive from the (potentially restrictive) assumption of full and immediate passthrough of exchange rate changes to consumption prices, however, we also experiment below with a model where passthrough is sluggish or incomplete. This specification might be more realistic if, for example, we believe that foreign exporters "price to market," holding the foreign currency prices of their exported goods relatively constant in the face of exchange rate changes, or if home-country retail importers absorb the effects of exchange rate changes in their margins.

The model (2)–(7) is clearly not structural in the sense that we can back out directly from its taste and technology parameters. Nevertheless, as McCallum and Nelson (forthcoming) have recently shown, a system such as (2)–(7) can be derived as the linear reduced-form of a fully optimizing general equilibrium model, under certain specifications of tastes and technology. That ought to confer some degree of policy invariance on model parameters—and hence some immunity from the Lucas critique.

4.3   Deterministic Policy Analysis

4.3.1   Calibrating the Model

To assess the properties of the model described above, we begin with some deterministic simulations. For this we need to calibrate the behavioral parameters in equations (2) through (7). As far as possible, we set our baseline cali-

---

18. Plus the effects of the composite error term.

brated values in line with prior empirical estimates on quarterly data. Where this is not possible—for example, in the wage-contracting equation—we calibrate parameters to ensure a plausible dynamic profile from impulse responses. We also experiment below, however, with some deviations from the baseline parameterization, in particular the degree of forward-lookingness in the model. For the IS curve (2), we set $\alpha_1 = 0.8$, which is empirically plausible on quarterly data. For the moment we set $\alpha_2 = 0$, ignoring until later any direct forward-lookingness in the IS curve. We set the real interest rate (α_3) and real exchange rate (α_4) elasticities to -0.5 and -0.2, respectively. Both are in line with empirical estimates from the Bank of England's forecasting model. For the LM curve we set $\beta_1 = 1$ and $\beta_2 = 0.5$, so that money is unit income elastic and has an interest semielasticity of one-half. Both of these restrictions are broadly satisfied on U.K. data (Thomas 1996).

On the contracting equation (6), our baseline model sets $\chi_0 = 0.2$, so that contracting is predominantly backward looking. This specification matches the pattern of the data much better than an equally weighted formulation, both in the United States (Fuhrer 1997) and in the United Kingdom (Blake and Westaway 1996).[19] The output sensitivity of real wages is set at 0.2 ($\chi_1 = 0.2$), in line with previous studies.[20] We set ϕ, the share of domestically produced goods in the consumption basket, equal to 0.8, in line with existing shares.

Turning to the policy rule (1), for consistency with the model this is also simulated as a deviation from equilibrium. That is, we set π^* (the inflation target) and r_t^* (the equilibrium real rate) to zero. Because of this, our simulations do not address questions regarding the optimal level of π^*. For example, our model does not broach issues such as the stabilization difficulties caused by the nonnegativity of nominal interest rates. We are implicitly assuming that the level of π^* has been set such that this constraint binds with only a negligibly small probability. Nor do we address issues such as time variation in r_t^*.

In terms of the parameter triplet $\{j, \theta, \gamma\}$, in our baseline rule we set $\gamma = 0.5$—a halfway house between the two extreme values of interest rate smoothing we consider; $\theta = 0.5$—around the middle of the range of feedback parameters used in previous simulation studies (Taylor 1993a; McCallum 1988; Black et al. 1997); and $j = 8$ periods. Because the model is calibrated to match quarterly profiles for the endogenous variables, this final assumption is equivalent to targeting the quarterly inflation rate two years ahead. This is around the horizon from which central banks feed back in practice. For example, the Bank of England's "policy rule" has been characterized as targeting the inflation rate two years or so ahead (King 1996).[21]

---

19. The lag-lead weights chosen here are very similar to those found empirically in the United States by Fuhrer (1997).

20. The elasticity of real wages is close to that found by Fuhrer (1997) in the United States of 0.12.

21. Though the United Kingdom's inflation target is defined as an annual percentage change in price levels, which means that this comparison is not exact: see below.

Because the model (2)–(7) and the baseline policy rule (1) are log-linear, we can solve the system using the method of Blanchard and Kahn (1980). Denote the vector of endogenous variables z_t.[22] The model (1)–(7) has a convenient state-space representation,

$$
(9) \qquad \begin{bmatrix} q_{t+1} \\ E_t x_{t+1} \end{bmatrix} = A \begin{bmatrix} q_t \\ x_t \end{bmatrix} + B\varepsilon_t,
$$

where q_t is a vector containing z_{t-1} and its lags, x_t is a vector containing z_t, $E_t z_{t+1}$, $E_t z_{t+2}$, and so forth, and, as usual, E_t is the expectations operator using information up to time t. The solution to equation (9) is obtained by implementing the Blanchard and Kahn (1980) method with a standard computer program that solves linear rational expectations models.[23] This program imposes the condition that there are no explosive solutions, implying a relationship $E_t x_{t+1} + N q_{t+1} = 0$, where $[N \; I]$ is the set of eigenvectors of the stable eigenvalues of A.

We then evaluate the various rules by conducting stochastic policy simulations and calculating in each case unconditional moments of the endogenous variables. To conduct the simulations we need a covariance matrix of the shocks for the exogenous variables.

There are a variety of ways of generating these shocks. The theoretical model (2)–(7) does not have enough dynamic structure to believe that its empirically estimated residuals are legitimate measures of primitive shocks. Alternatively, and at the other end of the spectrum, we could use atheoretic time series or vector autoregression (VAR) models to construct structural shocks. But that approach is not without problems either. Identification restrictions are still required to unravel the structural shocks from the reduced-form VAR residuals. Because these restrictions are just-identifying, they are nontestable. Further, in the VAR literature these restrictions usually include orthogonality of the primitive disturbances, $E_t(\varepsilon_{it}e_{jt}') = 0$ for all $i \neq j$. That is not a restriction we would want necessarily to impose a priori.[24]

We steer a middle course between these alternatives, using a covariance matrix of structural shocks derived from the Bank of England's forecasting model.[25] This confers some advantages. First, and importantly, our analytical model can be considered a simplified version of this forecasting model, only without its dynamic structure. This lends some coherence to the deterministic and stochastic parts of the analysis. Second, the structural shocks from the forecasting model permit nonzero covariances.

For IS, LM, and Phillips curve shocks, we simply take the moments of the

22. Boldface denotes vectors and matrices.
23. This was conducted within the ACES/PRISM solution software (Gaines, Al'Nowaihi, and Levine 1989).
24. Though see Leeper, Sims, and Zha (1996). Black et al. (1997) generate identified VAR residuals without imposing this restriction.
25. This matrix is available from the authors on request.

residuals from the Bank's forecasting model over the sample period 1989:1–97:3. Our sample period excludes most of the 1970s and 1980s, during which time the variance of shocks for all of the variables was (sometimes considerably) higher. Using a longer sample period would rescale upward the variances we report. The exchange rate is trickier. For that, we use quarterly Money Market Services Inc. survey data to capture exchange rate expectations over our sample, using the dollar-pound exchange rate as our benchmark.[26] The exchange rate residuals were then constructed from the arbitrage condition (4), plugging in the survey expectations and using quarterly data for the other variables. Not surprisingly, the resulting exchange rate shock vector has a large variance, around 10 times that of the IS, LM, and Phillips curve shocks. Given its size, we conducted some sensitivity checks on the exchange rate variance. Rescaling the variance does not alter the conclusions we draw about the relative performance of the rules.

4.3.2   A Disinflation Experiment

To assess the plausibility of the system's properties, we displaced deterministically the intercept of each equation in the model (the IS equation, the money demand equation, the aggregate supply equation, and the exchange rate equation) by 1 percent and traced out in each case the resulting impulse response. Each of these impulse responses gave dynamic profiles that were theoretically plausible. For example, a permanent negative supply shock—a rise in the NAIRU, say—shifted inflation and output in opposite directions on impact and lowered output below baseline in steady state; whereas a permanent positive demand shock—a rise in overseas demand, say—shifted output and inflation in the same direction initially but was output neutral in steady state.

To illustrate the calibrated model's dynamic properties, consider the effects of a shock to the reaction function (1). Consider in particular a disinflation—a lowering of the inflation target, π^*—of 1 percentage point. The solid lines in figure 4.1 plot the responses of output and inflation to this inflation target shock. Impulse response profiles are shown as percentage point deviations from baseline values.

The economy has returned to steady state after around 16 quarters (four years). At that point, inflation is 1 percentage point lower at its new target and output is back to potential. But the transmission process in arriving at this endpoint is protracted. Output is below potential for the whole of the period, with a maximum marginal effect of around 0.2 percentage points after around 5 quarters. Output falls partly as a result of a policy-induced rise in real interest rates (of around 0.14 percentage points) and partly as a result of the accompanying real exchange rate appreciation (of around 0.57 percentage points). The

---

26. A preferred exchange rate measure would have been the United Kingdom's trade-weighted effective index. But there are no survey data on exchange rate expectations of this index. We also looked at the behavior of the deutsche mark–pound and yen-pound exchange rates. The variance of the dollar-pound residuals was somewhere between that of mark-pound and yen-pound.

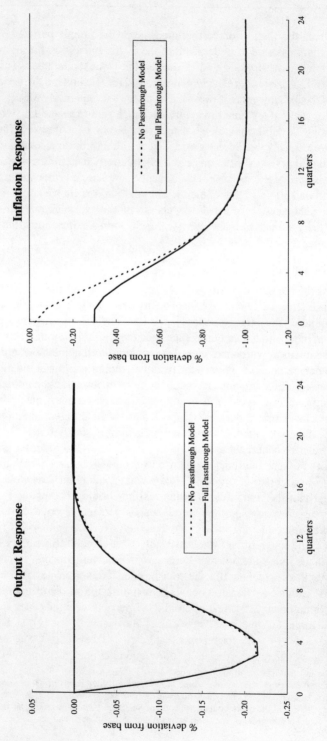

Fig. 4.1 Output and inflation responses to inflation target shock

path of output and its maximum response are broadly in line with simulation responses from VAR-based studies of the effects of monetary policy shocks in the United Kingdom (Dale and Haldane 1995).[27] The cumulative loss of output—the sacrifice ratio—is around 1.5 percent. This sacrifice ratio estimate is not greatly out of line with previous U.K. estimates (Bakhshi, Haldane, and Hatch 1999) but is if anything on the low side (see below).

Inflation undergoes an initial downward step owing to the impact effect of the exchange rate appreciation on import prices. Although the effect of the exchange rate shock is initially to alter the price *level*, this effect gets embedded in wage-bargaining behavior and so has a durable impact on measured inflation. Thereafter, inflation follows a gradual downward path toward its new target, under the impetus of the negative output gap. The inflation profile and in particular the immediate step jump in inflation following the shock are not in line with prior reduced-form empirical evidence on the monetary transmission mechanism.

The simulated inflation path is clearly sensitive to the assumptions we have made about exchange rate passthrough—namely, that it is immediate and complete. In particular, it is the full-passthrough assumption that lies behind the initial jump in inflation following a monetary disturbance. So one implication of this assumption is that monetary policy in an open economy can affect consumer price inflation with almost no lag (Svensson, forthcoming). There may well of course be adverse side effects from an attempt to control inflation in this way, such as real exchange rate and hence output destabilization. We illustrate these side effects below. But more fundamentally, the monetary transmission lag, and hence the implied degree of inflation control, is clearly acutely sensitive to the exchange rate passthrough assumption we have made.

As a sensitivity check, the dotted lines in figure 4.1 show the responses of output and inflation if we assume no direct exchange rate passthrough into consumer prices.[28] Monetary policy impulses are then all channeled through output, either via the real interest rate or via the real exchange rate. The resulting output path is little altered. But as we might expect, the downward path of inflation is more sluggish, mimicking the output gap. It is in fact now rather closer to that found from VAR-based studies of the effects of monetary policy in the United Kingdom. Given the clear sensitivity of the inflation profile to the passthrough assumption, we use both passthrough models below when considering the effects of transmission lags on the optimal degree of policy forward-lookingness.

27. Though the shocks are not exactly the same.
28. Which we reproduce by assuming the import content of the consumption basket is zero. This would be justified if, e.g., all imported goods were intermediate rather than final goods or, more generally, if the effects of exchange rate changes were absorbed in foreign exporters' or domestic retailers' margins rather than in domestic currency consumption prices. See Svensson (forthcoming) for a comparison of inflation-targeting rules based on consumer and producer prices.

4.3.3   Some Limitations of the Simulations

The impulse responses suggest that our model is a reasonable dynamic representation of the effects of monetary policy in a small open economy such as the United Kingdom, Canada, or New Zealand—the three longest-serving inflation targeters. Nevertheless, the simulated model responses are clearly a simplified and stylized characterization of inflation targeting as exercised in practice. Two limitations in particular are worth highlighting.

First, we impose model consistency on all expectations, including the inflation expectations formed by the central bank that serve as its policy feedback variable. This is coherent as a simulation strategy, as otherwise we would have to posit some expectational mechanism that was potentially different from the model in which the policy rule was being embedded. But the assumption of model-consistent expectations has drawbacks too. For example, it underplays the role of model uncertainties. These uncertainties are important, but a consideration of them is beyond the scope of the present paper. Further, the simulations assume that the inflation target is perfectly credible. So the shock to the target shown in figure 4.1 is, in effect, believed fully and immediately. This helps explain why the sacrifice ratio implied by figure 4.1 is lower than historical estimates; it is the full-credibility case. While the assumption of full credibility is limiting, it is not obvious that it should affect greatly our inferences about the relative performance of various rules, which is the focus of the paper.

Second, and relatedly, under model-consistent expectations monetary policy is assumed to be driven by the specified policy rule. In particular, the inflation forecast of the central bank—the policy feedback variable—is conditioned on the inflation-targeting policy rule (1). This differs somewhat from actual central bank practice in some countries. For example, in the United Kingdom the Bank of England's published inflation forecasts are usually conditioned on an assumption of unchanged interest rates.[29] This means that there is not a direct read-across from our forecast-based rules to inflation targeting in practice in some countries.

Even among those countries that use it, however, the constant interest rate assumption is seen largely as a short-term expedient. It is not appropriate, for example, when simulating a forward-looking model—as here—because it deprives the system of a nominal anchor and thus leaves the price level indeterminate. So in our simulations we instead condition monetary policy (actual and in expectation) on the reaction function (1). This delivers a determinate price level. Simulations conducted in this way come close to mimicking current monetary policy practice in New Zealand (Reserve Bank of New Zealand 1997). There, the Reserve Bank of New Zealand's policy projections are based on an explicit policy reaction function, which is very similar to the baseline

---

29. This is also often the case with forecasts produced for the Federal Reserve Board's "Green Book" (see Reifschneider, Stockton, and Wilcox 1996).

rule (1). The Bank of England also recently began publishing inflation projections based on market expectations of future interest rates, rather than constant interest rates. This means that differences between the forecast-based rule (1) and inflation targeting in practice may not be so sharp.

4.4 Stochastic Policy Analysis

We now turn to consider the performance of the baseline rule (1) and compare it with alternative rules. This is done by embedding the various rules in the model outlined above and evaluating the resulting (unconditional) moments of output, inflation, and the policy instrument—the arguments typically thought to enter the central bank's loss function. Specifically, following Taylor (1993), we consider where each of the rules places the economy on the output-inflation variability frontier.

4.4.1 Lag Encompassing: The Optimal Degree
of Policy Forward-Lookingness

The most obvious rationale for a forward-looking monetary policy rule is that it can embody explicitly the lags in monetary transmission. But how forward looking? Is there some optimal forecasting horizon from which to feed back? And, if so, what does this optimal targeting horizon depend on?

Answers to these questions are clearly sensitive to the assumed length of the lag itself. So we experiment below with both our earlier models: one assuming full and immediate import price passthrough (a shorter transmission lag), and the other no immediate passthrough (a longer transmission lag). Figure 4.2 plots the locus of output-inflation variability points delivered by the rule (1) as the horizon of the inflation forecast (j) is varied. Two lines are plotted in figure 4.2, representing the two passthrough cases. Along these loci, we vary j between zero (current-period inflation targeting) and 16 (four-year-ahead inflation-forecast targeting) periods.[30] Our baseline rule ($j = 8$) lies between these extremes. The two remaining policy choice parameters in rule (1), $\{\gamma, \theta\}$, are for the moment set at their baseline values of 0.5.[31] Points to the south and west in figure 4.2 are clearly welfare superior, and points to the north and east inferior.

Several points are clear from figure 4.2. First, irrespective of the assumed degree of passthrough, the optimal forecast horizon is always positive and lies somewhere between three and six quarters ahead. This forecast horizon secures as good inflation performance as any other, while at the same time delivering lowest output variability. The latter result arises because three to six quarters is around the horizon at which monetary policy has its largest marginal

---

30. Some of the longer horizon feedback rules were unstable, which we discuss further below. In fig. 4.2 we show the maximum permissible feedback horizon: 14 periods for the full-passthrough case and 12 periods for the no-passthrough case.
31. We vary them both in turn below.

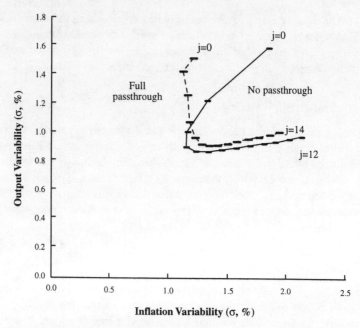

Fig. 4.2 *j*-Loci: full- and no-passthrough cases

impact. The (integrals of) real interest and exchange rate changes necessary to hit the inflation target are minimized at this horizon. So too, therefore, is the degree of output destabilization (the integral of output losses). At shorter horizons than this, the adjustment in monetary policy necessary to return inflation to target is that much greater—the upshot of which is a destabilization of output. Once we allow for the fact that central banks in practice feed back from annual inflation rates, whereas our model-based feedback variable is a quarterly inflation rate, the optimal forecast horizon implied by our simulations (of three to six quarters) is rather similar to that used by inflation-targeting central banks in practice (of six to eight quarters).[32]

Second, taking either passthrough assumption, feeding back from a forecast horizon much beyond six quarters leads to worse outcomes for *both* inflation and output variability. This is the flip side of the arguments used above. Just as short-horizon targeting implies "too much" of a policy response to counteract shocks, long-horizon targeting can equally imply that policy does "too little," thereby setting in train a destabilizing expectational feedback. This works as follows.

Beyond a certain forecast horizon, the effects of any inflation shock have

32. This comparison is also not exact because the two definitions of horizon are different: the *feedback* horizon in the rule and the *policy* horizon in practice (the point at which expected inflation is in line with the inflation target) are distinct concepts.

been damped out of the system by the actions of the central bank: expected inflation is back to target. This implies that, beyond that horizon, our forward-looking monetary policy rule says "do nothing"; it is entirely hands-off. In expectation, policy has already done its job. But an entirely "hands-off" policy will be destabilizing for inflation expectations—and hence for inflation to-day—if it is the policy path actually followed in practice. This is because of the circular relationship between forward-looking policy behavior and forward-looking inflation expectations. The one generates oscillations in the other, which in turn give rise to further feedback on the first. Beyond a certain thresh-old horizon—when policy is very forward looking—this circularity leads to explosiveness. So this is one general instance in which forward-looking rules generate instabilities: namely, when the forecast horizon extends well beyond the transmission lag.[33] The possibility of instabilities and indeterminacies aris-ing in forecast-based rules is discussed in Woodford (1994) and Bernanke and Woodford (1997). The mechanism here is very similar.

Third, the main differences between the two passthrough loci show up at horizons less than four quarters. Over these horizons, the full-passthrough lo-cus heads due south, while the no-passthrough locus heads southwest. With incomplete passthrough, policy forward-lookingness reduces both inflation and output variability. This is because inflation transmission lags are lengthier in this particular case. Embodying these (lengthier) lags explicitly in the policy reaction function thus improves inflation control; it guards against monetary policy acting too late. Preemptive policy helps stabilize inflation in the face of transmission lags. At the same time it also helps smooth output, for the reasons outlined above.

The same is generally true in the full-passthrough case, except that most of the benefits then accrue to output stabilization. The gains in inflation stabili-zation from looking forward are small because inflation control can now be secured relatively quickly through the exchange rate effect on consumption prices. But the gains in output stabilization are still considerable because shorter forecast-horizon targeting induces larger real interest rate and in partic-ular real exchange rate gyrations, with attendant output costs.

All in all, figure 4.2 illustrates fairly persuasively the case for policy forward-lookingness. Using a forecast horizon of three to six quarters delivers far superior outcomes for output and inflation stabilization than, say, current-period inflation targeting. Largely, this is the result of transmission lags. Forecast-based rules are, in this sense, lag encompassing. This also provides some empirical justification for the operational practice among inflation-targeting central banks of feeding back from inflation forecasts at horizons beyond one year.

Plainly, the optimal degree of policy forward-lookingness is sensitive to the model (and in particular the lag) specification. In the baseline model, this lag

---

33. We highlight some other cases below.

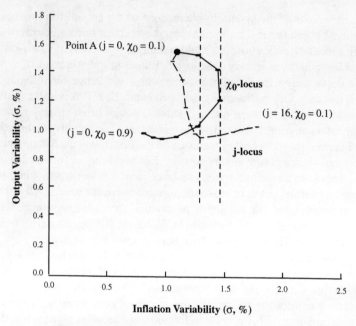

Fig. 4.3 *j*-Locus and χ_0-locus

structure hinges on the assumed degree of stickiness in wage setting. This stickiness in turn depends on the nature of wage-price contracting and on the degree of forward-lookingness in wage bargaining. Given this, one way to interpret the need for forward-lookingness in policy is that it is serving to compensate for the backward-lookingness in wage bargaining—whether directly through wage-bargaining behavior or indirectly due to the effect of contracting. In a sense, forward-looking monetary policy is acting, in a second-best fashion, to counter a backward-looking externality elsewhere in the economy. It is interesting to explore this notion further by considering the trade-off between the degree of backward-lookingness on the part of the private sector in the course of their wage bargaining and the degree of forward-lookingness on the part of the central bank in the course of its interest rate setting.[34]

Figure 4.3 illustrates this trade-off. Point A in figure 4.3 plots the most backward-looking aggregate (wage setting plus policy setting) outcome. The central bank feeds back from current inflation when setting policy ($j = 0$) and wage bargainers assign a weight of only 0.1 to next period's inflation rate when entering the wage bargain ($\chi_0 = 0.1$). This results in a very poor macroeconomic outcome, in particular for output variability. In hitting its inflation target, the central bank acts myopically. And the myopia of private sector agents then

---

34. Equivalently, we could have looked at the effects of altering the length of wage contracting.

aggravates the effects of bad policy on the real economy through inflation stickiness.

The solid line emanating from point A traces out the locus of output-inflation variabilities as χ_0 rises from 0.1 to 0.9, so that wage bargaining becomes progressively more forward looking. Policy, for now, remains myopic ($j = 0$). In general, the upshot is a welfare improvement. With wages becoming a jump(ier) variable, even myopic policy can bootstrap inflation back to target following shocks. Moreover, wage flexibility means that these inflation adjustments can be brought about at lower output cost. So both inflation and output variability are damped. Fully flexible wages take us closer to a first best. There is little need for policy to then have a forward-looking dimension.

The same is not true, of course, when wages embody a high degree of backward-lookingness. The dashed line in figure 4.3 plots a j-locus with $\chi_0 = 0.1$. Though the resulting equilibria are clearly second best in comparison with the forward-looking private sector equilibria, forward-looking monetary policy does now secure a significant improvement over the bad backward-looking equilibrium at point A. In this instance, policy forward-lookingness is serving as a surrogate for forward-looking behavior on the part of the private sector.

Finally, the two vertical lines in figure 4.3, drawn at $j = 6$ and $\chi_0 = 0.3$, indicate degrees of *economy-wide* forward-lookingness beyond which the economy is unstable. For example, neither of the combinations $\{j = 6, \chi_0 = 0.4\}$ and $\{j = 7, \chi_0 = 0.3\}$ yields stable macroeconomic outcomes. This suggests that, just as a very backward-looking behavioral combination yields a bad equilibrium (point A), so too does a very forward-looking combination. It also serves notice of the potential instability problems of forecast-based rules. In general, policy forward-lookingness is only desirable as a second-best counterweight to the lags in monetary transmission. The first best is for the lags themselves to shrink—for example, because private sector agents become more forward looking. When this is the case, there is positive merit in the central bank itself not being too forward looking because that risks engendering instabilities.

Figure 4.4 illustrates the above points rather differently. It generalizes the baseline model to accommodate forward-lookingness in the IS curve, following McCallum and Nelson (forthcoming). Specifically, we set (somewhat arbitrarily) $\alpha_1 = \alpha_2 = 0.5$, so that the backward- and forward-looking output terms in the IS curve are equally weighted.[35] The solid line in figure 4.4 plots the j-locus in this modified model, with the dashed line showing the same for the baseline model.

The modified model j-locus generally lies in a welfare-superior location to that under the baseline model, at least at short targeting horizons. For small j,

---

35. McCallum and Nelson's (forthcoming) baseline model has $\{\alpha_1 = 0, \alpha_2 = 1\}$. That formulation is unstable in our model.

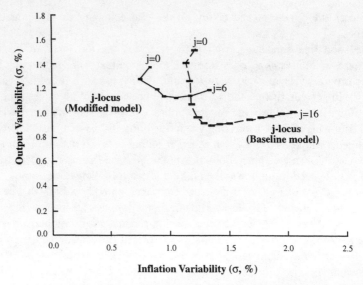

Fig. 4.4   *j*-Loci: baseline and modified models

both inflation and output variability are lower in the modified model. Increasing private sector forward-lookingness takes us nearer the first best. Policy forward-lookingness clearly still confers some benefits, since the modified model *j*-locus moves initially to the southwest. But these benefits cease much beyond *j* = 3; and beyond *j* = 6 the system is explosive. So, again, policy forward-lookingness is only desirable when used as a counterweight to the lags in monetary transmission, here reflected in the backward-looking behavior of the private sector; it is not, of itself, desirable. The less of this intrinsic sluggishness in the economy, the less the need for compensating forward-lookingness through monetary policy.

4.4.2   Output Encompassing: Output Stabilization through Inflation Targeting

Although the policy rule (1) contains no explicit output terms, it is already clear that inflation-forecast-based rules are far from output invariant. Figure 4.2 suggests that lengthening the targeting horizon up to and beyond one year ahead can secure clear and significant improvements in output stabilization. Judicious choice of the forecast horizon should allow the authorities, operating according to rule (1), to select their preferred degree of output stabilization.

That is not to say, however, that the output stabilization embodied in policy rules such as rule (1) cannot be improved upon. For example, might not output stabilization be further improved by adding explicit output gap terms to equation (1)? Figure 4.5 shows the effect of this addition. The dashed line simply redraws the full-passthrough *j*-locus from figure 4.2. The ray emerging from

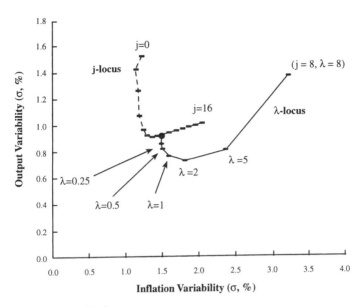

Fig. 4.5 *j*-**Locus and λ-locus**

this line, starting from the base-case horizon ($j = 8$) and moving initially to the south, plots outcomes from a rule that adds output gap terms to rule (1) with successively higher weights.[36] These weights, denoted λ, run from 0.1 to 8.[37]

Two main points are evident from figure 4.5. First, adding explicit output terms to a forward-looking policy rule does appear to improve output stabilization, with no costs in terms of inflation control—provided the weights attached to output are sufficiently small. The ray moves due south for $0 < λ < 1$. Second, when $λ > 1$ some output-inflation variability trade-off does start to emerge, with improvements in output stabilization coming at the cost of greater inflation variability. Indeed, for $λ > 2$ we begin to move in a northeasterly direction, with both output and inflation variability worsening. At $λ = 10$, the system is explosive. In general, though, figure 4.5 seems to indicate that the addition of output gap terms to a forward-looking rule does yield clear welfare improvements for small enough λ. Put somewhat differently, it appears to suggest that an inflation-forecast-based rule cannot synthetically recreate the degree of output stabilization possible by targeting the output gap explicitly.

However, this conclusion ignores the fact that the feedback coefficient on expected inflation, θ, can also be altered and that this parameter itself influences output stabilization. Figure 4.6 plots a set of *j*-loci varying the value of

36. The corresponding ray in the no-passthrough case is very similar. So we stick here with the full-passthrough base case.
37. Weights much above 8 were found to generate instability; see below.

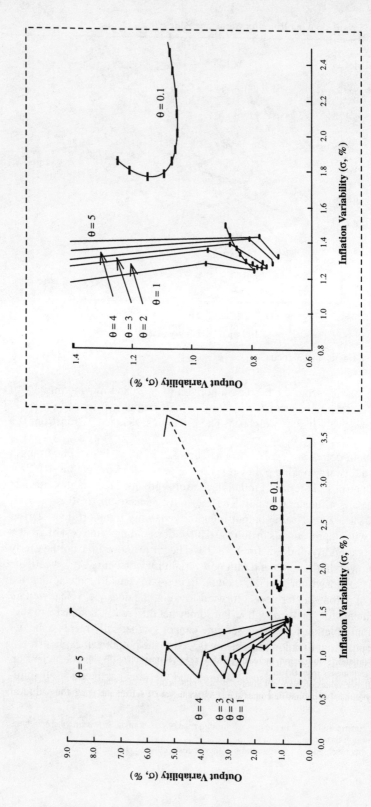

Fig. 4.6 *j*-Loci: θ varying

θ between 0.1 and 5.[38] Increasing θ tends to take us in a southwesterly direction; that is, it lowers both output and inflation variability.[39] Aggressive feedback responses are welfare improving and, in particular, are output stabilizing. This reason is that agents factor this aggressiveness in policy response into their expectations when setting wages. Inflation expectations are thus less disturbed following inflation shocks. Inflation control, via this expectational mechanism, is thereby improved. And with inflation expectations damped following shocks, there is then less need for an offsetting response from monetary policy. As a consequence, output variability is also reduced by the greater aggressiveness in policy responses.[40]

The gains in inflation stabilization are initially pronounced as θ rises above its 0.5 baseline value. These inflation gains cease—indeed, go into reverse—beyond $\theta \approx 1$. Thereafter, most of the gains from increasing θ show up in improved output stabilization, usually at the expense of some destabilization of inflation. The inflation-forecast-based rule delivering lowest output variability is $\{j = 5, \theta = 5\}$. This gives a standard deviation of output $\sigma_y = 0.71$ percent and of inflation $\sigma_\pi = 1.32$ percent.[41] So can *this* rule be improved upon by the addition of explicit output terms?

The answer, roughly speaking, is no. Adding an explicit output weight to the rule $\{j = 5, \theta = 5\}$ yields unstable outcomes. The trajectories that result from adding output terms to other j-loci with smaller θ are shown in figure 4.7. The gain in output stabilization from adding explicit output terms seems to be very marginal. Moreover, it comes at the expense of a significant destabilization of inflation. For example, the parameter triplet $\{j, \theta, \lambda\}$ delivering the lowest output variability is $\{j = 5, \theta = 4, \lambda = 1\}$. This yields $\sigma_y = 0.69$ percent and $\sigma_\pi = 1.37$ percent—an output gain of only 0.02 percentage points and an inflation loss of 0.05 percentage points in comparison with the rule that gives no weight to output whatsoever, $\{j = 5, \theta = 5, \lambda = 0\}$.[42] It is clear that the optimal λ is now smaller even than in the earlier ($\theta = 0.5$) case. Any $\lambda > 1$ now takes us into unambiguously welfare-inferior territory. In forward-looking rules there would seem to be benefits from placing a *higher* relative weight on expected inflation than on output. Indeed, to a first approximation, a weight of zero on output ($\lambda = 0$) comes close to being optimal.

Figure 4.7 suggests that there is, in effect, an output variability threshold at around $\sigma_y = 0.70$ percent. None of the rules, with or without output gap terms,

38. At values of $\theta > 5$, the system was again explosive.
39. This is less clear for high values of θ ($\theta > 1$). The benefits then tend to be greater for output than for inflation stabilization. Increasing θ also increases instrument variability, from 0.27 to 1.35 percent as θ moves from 0.1 to 5.
40. Higher values of θ are not always welfare enhancing. Larger values of θ also increase the diversity of macroeconomic outcomes at extreme values of j. For example, current-period inflation targeting ($j = 0$) leads to a very high output variance when θ is large. And when j is large, high values of θ increase the chances of explosive outcomes. For example, when $j = 5$ simulations are explosive beyond a five-quarter forecasting horizon.
41. Output variability is then considerably lower than in the $\{j = 8, \theta = 0.5\}$ base case ($\sigma_y = 0.93$ percent).
42. It also raises instrument variability from 1.8 to 1.92 percent.

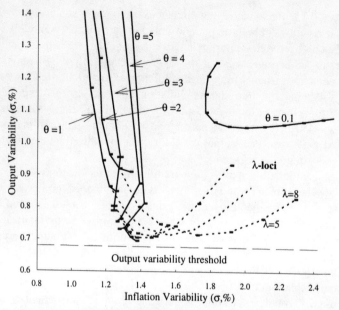

Fig. 4.7   Output variability threshold

can squeeze output variability much beyond that threshold. By appropriate choice of $\{j, \theta\}$, inflation-forecast-based rules appear capable of taking us to that threshold, give or take a very small number. Almost any amount of output smoothing can be synthetically recreated with an inflation-only rule. Forecast-based rules are, in this sense, output encompassing. Inflation nutters and output junkies may disagree over the parameters in rule (1)—that is a question of policy tastes. But they need not differ over the arguments entering this rule—that is a question of policy technology.

4.4.3   Information Encompassing: A Comparison with Alternative Rules

Another of the supposed merits of an inflation-forecast-based rule is that it embodies—and thus implicitly feeds back from—all information that is relevant for predicting the future dynamics of inflation. For this reason, it may approximate the optimal state-contingent rule. Certainly, by this reasoning, forward-looking rules should deliver outcomes at least as good as rules that feed back from a restrictive subset of information variables, such as output and inflation under the Taylor rule. These are empirically testable propositions.

To assess how close our forecast-based rule takes us to macroeconomic nirvana, we solve for the time-inconsistent *optimal* state-contingent rule in our system. This is the rule that solves the control problem

$$(10) \quad \min_{r_t} \mathcal{L} = E_t \sum_{i=0}^{\infty} \beta^i [\omega(\pi_{t+i} - \pi^*)^2 + (1 - \omega)(y_{t+i} - y^*)^2 + \xi r_{t+1}^2],$$

Table 4.1   Comparing Optimal (OPT) and Inflation Forecast-Based (IFB{j, θ}) Rules (standard deviation σ in percent)

Rule	σ_y	σ_π	σ_r	$\mathscr{L}$
OPT	0.782	1.103	1.033	41.83
IFB{$j = 0$, θ = 0.5}	1.52	1.199	0.925	76.37
IFB{$j = 3$, θ = 0.5}	1.07	1.17	0.61	52.61
IFB{$j = 6$, θ = 0.5}	0.91	1.34	0.51	54.18
IFB{$j = 9$, θ = 0.5}	0.94	1.57	0.40	68.04
IFB{$j = 0$, θ = 5.0}	8.86	1.49	10.33	755.8
IFB{$j = 5$, θ = 5.0}	0.716	1.32	1.34	53.91

Note: The value of the smoothing parameter is γ = 0.5.

where ω denotes the relative weight assigned to inflation deviations from target vis-à-vis output deviations from trend and ξ is the weight assigned to instrument variability.

Because there are three arguments in the loss function, the easiest way to summarize the performance of the various rules relative to the optimal rule is by evaluating stochastic welfare losses ($\mathscr{L}$), having set common values for the preference parameters {β, ω, ξ}. We (somewhat arbitrarily) set β = 0.998, ω = 0.5, and ξ = 0.1. So inflation and output variability are equally weighted, and both are given higher weight than instrument variability. Table 4.1 then compares welfare losses from the optimal rule (OPT) with those from two specifications of the inflation-forecast-based (IFB) rule (θ = 0.5 and θ = 5) for various values of j.[43] Table 4.1 also shows the standard deviations of output, inflation, and (real) interest rates that result from each of these policy rule specifications.

Current-period inflation targeting ($j = 0$) clearly does badly by comparison with the optimal rule. For example, the rule {$j = 0$, θ = 0.5} delivers welfare losses that are 85 percent larger than the first best. Inflation-*forecast*-based rules clearly take us much closer—if not all the way—to that welfare optimum.[44] For example, {$j = 6$, θ = 0.5} delivers a welfare loss only 30 percent worse than the optimum. The optimal values of {j, θ} cannot be derived uniquely from table 4.1, since they clearly depend on the (arbitrary) values we have assigned to the preference parameters {ω, ξ} in the objective function. But for our chosen preference parameters, the best forecast horizon appears to lie between three and six periods, irrespective of the value of θ.

We can also compare these forward-looking rules with a variety of simple, backward-looking Taylor-type formulations, which feed back from contempo-

---

43. Where the optimal rule, the associated moments of output, inflation, and the interest rate, and the value of the stochastic welfare loss are calculated using the OPT routine of the ACES/ PRISM solution package. See n. 23.

44. As we discuss below, altering the smoothing parameter, γ, takes us nearer still to the first best.

Table 4.2   **Comparison of Optimal (OPT), Inflation Forecast-Based (IFB{j, θ}), and Taylor (T1/T2{a, b, c}) Rules (standard deviation σ in percent)**

Rule	σ_y	σ_π	σ_r	$\mathcal{L}$
OPT	0.78	1.10	1.03	41.83
IFB{$j = 6, \theta = 0.5$}	0.91	1.34	0.51	54.18
IFB{$j = 5, \theta = 5.0$}	0.72	1.32	1.34	53.91
T1{$a = 2, b = 0.8, c = 1$}	1.84	0.94	1.79	92.69
T1{$a = 0.2, b = 1, c = 1$}	0.86	1.56	0.99	68.22
T1{$a = 0.5, b = 0.5, c = 0$}	1.05	1.38	0.55	61.96
T1{$a = 0.5, b = 1, c = 0$}	0.92	1.46	0.72	61.97
T1{$a = 0.2, b = 0.06, c = 1.3$}		Unstable		
T2{$a = 2, b = 0.8, c = 1$}	2.24	1.02	2.44	130.9
T2{$a = 0.2, b = 1, c = 1$}	1.11	1.58	1.40	82.44
T2{$a = 0.5, b = 0.5, c = 0$}	1.11	1.38	0.56	64.48
T2{$a = 0.5, b = 1, c = 0$}	0.99	1.44	0.76	64.21
T2{$a = 0.3, b = 0.08, c = 1.3$}		Unstable		

Note: The value of the smoothing parameter is $\gamma = 0.5$.

raneous or lagged values of output and inflation. In particular, for comparability with the other studies in this volume, we consider two types of rule:

$$(11) \qquad r_t = a\pi_t + b(y_t - y_t^*) + cr_{t-1},$$

$$(12) \qquad r_t = a\pi_{t-1} + b(y_{t-1} - y_{t-1}^*) + cr_{t-1},$$

for a variety of values of {a, b, c} listed below.[45] We classify the first T1{a, b, c} rule and the second T2{a, b, c} rules. The rule T1{$a = 0.5, b = 0.5, c = 0$} is of course the well-known Taylor rule. A comparison of these rules with the OPT and IFB rules is given in table 4.2.

We draw several general conclusions from table 4.2. First, looking just at the performance of the backward-looking rules, it appears that placing a higher weight on output than on inflation yields welfare improvements. This is different than was found to be the case with forward-looking rules. Second, because they are based on an inferior (time $t - 1$) information set, the T2 rules do worse than the T1 rules. The difference in welfare losses is not, however, that great. This suggests that, at least over the course of one quarter, information lags do not impose that much of a welfare cost. Third, both of the rules placing a small weight on output ($b < 0.1$) and a large weight on smoothing ($c > 1$) yield unstable outcomes in our model. Higher weights on output ($b > 0.5$) or lower weights on smoothing ($c < 1$) are necessary to deliver a stable equilibrium. Fourth, even the best performing backward-looking rule—interestingly,

45. One difference from the other exercises is that here the policy instrument is the short-term real (rather than nominal) interest rate. This should not affect the relative performance of the rules. But we have subtracted one from the inflation parameter, a, when simulating the backward-looking policy rules to ensure comparability with the other studies.

the Taylor rule—delivers a welfare outcome almost 50 percent worse than the optimum. By comparison, the best forward-looking rule delivers a welfare loss that is around 30 percent worse than the optimum.

The final conclusion is evidence of the information-encompassing nature of inflation-forecast-based rules. A forward-looking rule conditions on all variables that affect future inflation and output dynamics, not just output and inflation themselves. In the context of our simple open economy model, an important set of additional state variables are (lagged values of) the exchange rate, as well as additional lags of wages and prices. Just as the optimal feedback rule conditions on these state variables, so too will inflation-forecast-based rules. That is not a feature shared by Taylor rules. In larger models than the one presented here, these extra conditioning variables would include those other information variables affecting future inflation dynamics, such as (lagged) asset and commodity prices. These variables will be captured in forward-looking rules, but not in Taylor-type specifications. In general, the larger the model, the more diffuse will be the information sets of Taylor-type and forward-looking rules.[46] The welfare differences between forward- and backward-looking rules are thus also likely to be larger in these bigger models. So while inflation-forecast-based rules cannot take us all the way to the first best, in general they seem likely to take us further in that direction than Taylor-type specifications, at the same time as they retain the simplicity and transparency of the Taylor-type rules.

4.4.4   Other Policy Parameters

Finally, we explore two further design features of inflation-forecast-based rules. First, what is the preferred degree of interest rate smoothing, γ, in such a rule? And second, how does a regime of price *level* targeting compare with the inflation-targeting specifications considered so far?

On *interest rate smoothing,* the solid line in figure 4.8 replots the j-locus from the baseline rule. The rays (*dotted lines*) emanating from this at $j = \{3, 6, 9\}$ periods illustrate how output-inflation variabilities are affected as γ varies between zero (no smoothing) and one. These rays are almost horizontal. Instrument smoothing delivers greater inflation stability, with relatively few countervailing output costs. For example, inflation variability is lowered by 33 percent when moving from $\gamma = 0$ to $\gamma = 1$, for $\{j = 6, \theta = 0.5\}$. This arises because rules with higher degrees of smoothing deliver more persistent interest rate responses. These policy responses in turn have a larger impact effect on the exchange rate—and hence on inflation itself.[47] This sharper inflation control comes at some output cost, though our simulations suggest that this cost is fairly small. The benefits of instrument smoothing are smaller (and potentially

---

46. This is, e.g., what Black et al. (1997) find when simulating the larger scale Bank of Canada Quarterly Projection Model.

47. This is even true—though to a lesser extent—in the no-passthrough case.

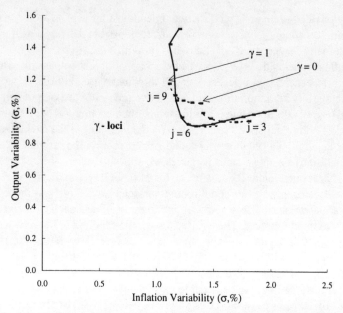

Fig. 4.8   *j*-Locus and γ-locus

trivial) at higher values of θ, however, because policy aggressiveness does the same job as instrument persistence in improving inflation control.

If we evaluate welfare losses using the earlier parameterization of the loss function, then the no-smoothing rule $\{\gamma = 0, j = 6, \theta = 0.5\}$ delivers a welfare loss that is 14 percent higher than that from the high-smoothing rule $\{\gamma = 1, j = 6, \theta = 0.5\}$. Indeed, the latter rule now takes us within 25 percent of the optimal rule. So it seems in general that relatively high degrees of interest rate smoothing are welfare enhancing, but that the extent of this welfare improvement may be small if policy is already aggressive.

On *price level targeting,* our baseline rule now takes the modified form:

$$(13) \qquad r_t = \gamma r_{t-1} + (1 - \gamma)r_t^* + \theta(E_t p_{t+j}^c - p^{c*}).$$

Monetary policy now shoots for a deterministic price level path, p^{c*}, which we again normalize to zero (in logs). Using the baseline model and the parameter settings $\{\gamma = 0, \theta = 0.5\}$,[48] figure 4.9 plots the *j*-locus that results from the price level rule (13). The baseline inflation-forecast-based rule (1) is also shown for comparison (*dashed line*). For most values of *j*, the price level-targeting rule delivers welfare-inferior outcomes to the inflation-targeting rule: both output and inflation variability are higher. This is particularly true of short-horizon (e.g., current period) price level targeting. Other studies have

---

48. Higher values than this tended to be unstable.

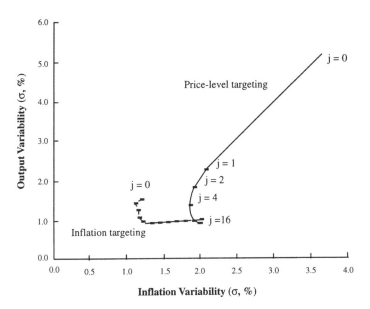

Fig. 4.9   Inflation and price level targeting

also found this to be the case (Duguay 1994; Fillion and Tetlow 1993; Lebow, Roberts, and Stockton 1992; Haldane and Salmon 1995). Nevertheless, for large enough *j*, price-level-targeting rules still perform little worse (and in some cases perhaps better) than inflation-targeting rules.

Moreover, this comparison may unfairly disadvantage price level targeting. The baseline model still embodies a relatively high degree of *inflation* persistence. It is questionable whether such persistence would survive the move to a monetary regime that delivered price level stationarity. In that situation, *price level* persistence might be a more realistic specification of price dynamics. In the context of our model, wage contracting might then be better characterized by a conventional Taylor staggered contract wage specification, rather than the Fuhrer-Moore formulation we have used so far.[49] That is, the contracting equation (6) would be replaced by

$$(14) \qquad w_t = \chi_0 E_t w_{t+1} + (1 - \chi_0) w_{t-1} + \chi_1 (y_t - y_t^*) + \varepsilon_4,$$

and the Phillips curve equivalent of equation (8) would now be

$$(15) \qquad \pi_t = E_t \pi_{t+1} + \chi_1 (y_t + y_{t-1}) - \rho(E_t \Delta c_{t+1}) + \varepsilon_5,$$

where $\rho \equiv (1 - \phi)/\phi$. Inflation no longer depends on lagged values; it is a jump variable.

49. Though, in principle, the relative wage formulation of Fuhrer and Moore (1995a) is meant to be a structural relationship, and thus immune to the Lucas critique.

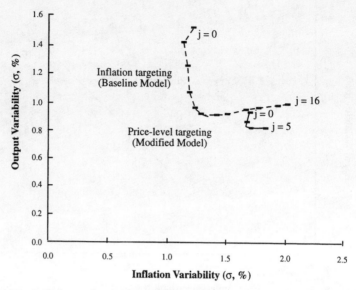

Fig. 4.10   Inflation and price level targeting

The solid line in figure 4.10 plots the *j*-locus for the price level policy rule (13), with equation (15) now replacing equation (8) in the model. This locus clearly lies to the south of the *j*-locus under inflation targeting using the baseline model (*dashed line*). Price level targeting now does as good (or better) a job of stabilizing output as inflation targeting. This is the result of the increased flexibility in prices. Inflation variability remains higher than under some specifications of inflation targeting, but never excessively so. In sum, even the *short-term* output-inflation variability costs of price level targeting appear to be much less pernicious than may have typically been thought likely, under certain parameterizations of the underlying model and policy rule and assuming perfect credibility of such a regime.[50] For a comprehensive welfare theoretic comparison, the longer term benefits of a price level standard would need to be set against these (potential) short-term costs.

4.5   Conclusions

It is widely recognized that monetary policy needs a forward-looking dimension. Inflation-targeting countries have explicitly embodied that notion in the design of their forecast-based policy rules. In principle, these rules confer some real benefits: they embody explicitly transmission lags (*lag encom-*

---

50. Williams (1997) and Black et al. (1997) reach similar conclusions in their studies of the United States and Canada, respectively. In a theoretical context, Svensson (1996) also argues that price level targeting need not raise output-inflation variabilities.

passing); they potentially embody all information useful for predicting future inflation (*information encompassing*); and, suitably designed, they can achieve a degree of output smoothing (*output encompassing*). This paper has evaluated quantitatively these features of an inflation-forecast-based rule using simulation techniques. Our main conclusions follow:

1. On lag encompassing, an inflation forecast horizon of three to six quarters appears to deliver the best performance, in the context of our inflation-forecast-based policy rules. Shorter horizons than this risk raising both output and inflation variability—the result of policy lags—while longer horizons risk macroeconomic instability. In general, the greater the degree of forward-lookingness on the part of the private sector, the less the compensating need for forward-lookingness by the central bank. These results support the forecast-based approach to monetary policy making pursued by inflation-targeting central banks in practice.

2. An inflation-forecast-based rule, with an appropriately chosen targeting horizon, naturally embodies a degree of output stabilization. Moreover, any degree of output smoothing can be synthetically recreated by judicious choice of the parameters entering an inflation-forecast-based rule. There is no need for any *explicit* output terms to enter this rule. That is evidence of the output-encompassing nature of inflation targeting based around inflation forecasts.

3. While not taking us all the way to the welfare optimum, forecast-based rules do seem capable of securing welfare-superior outcomes to backward-looking specifications, the type of which have been the mainstay in the literature to date. That is evidence of the information-encompassing nature of forecast-based policy rules.

We have also evaluated forecast-based price level rules for monetary policy. Under certain parameterizations, they perform creditably even as a short-run macroestabilizer. Perhaps, so soon after having secured low inflation, there is understandable caution about pursuing something as new as a price level standard. Perhaps. Inflation targeting is indeed an embryonic monetary framework, whose performance has yet to be properly tested. But price level targeting, indubitably, is not.

References

Bakhshi, H., A. G. Haldane, and N. Hatch. 1999. Some costs and benefits of price stability in the United Kingdom. In *The costs and benefits of price stability,* ed. M. Feldstein. Chicago: University of Chicago Press.

Bernanke, B. S., and F. S. Mishkin. 1997. Inflation targeting: A new rule for monetary policy? *Journal of Economic Perspectives* 11:97–116.

Bernanke, B. S., and M. Woodford. 1997. Inflation forecasts and monetary policy. *Journal of Money, Credit and Banking* 29:653–84.

Black, R., T. Macklem, and D. Rose. 1997. On policy rules for price stability. In *Price stability, inflation targets and monetary policy*, ed. Bank of Canada. Ottawa: Bank of Canada.

Blake, A. 1996. Forecast error bounds by stochastic simulation. *National Institute Economic Review* 64 (May): 72–78.

Blake, A. P., and P. F. Westaway. 1996. Credibility and the effectiveness of inflation targeting regimes. *Manchester School* 64:28–50.

Blanchard, O. J., and C. M. Kahn. 1980. The solution of linear difference models under rational expectations. *Econometrica* 48:1305–11.

Blinder, A. S. 1997. What central bankers could learn from academics—and vice versa. *Journal of Economic Perspectives* 11:3–19.

Brouwer, G. de, and J. O'Regan. 1997. Evaluating simple monetary-policy rules for Australia. In *Monetary policy and inflation targeting*, ed. P. Lowe. Sidney: Reserve Bank of Australia.

Bryant, R. C., P. Hooper, and C. Mann. 1993. *Evaluating policy regimes.* Washington, D.C.: Brookings Institution .

Buiter, W. H., and I. Jewitt. 1981. Staggered wage setting with real wage relativities: Variations on a theme of Taylor. *Manchester School* 49:211–28.

Clarida, R., J. Galí, and M. Gertler. 1998. Monetary policy rules in practice: Some international evidence. *European Economic Review* 42:1033–67.

Clarida, R., and M. Gertler. 1997. How the Bundesbank conducts monetary policy. In *Reducing inflation: Motivation and strategy*, ed. C. Romer and D. Romer. Chicago: University of Chicago Press.

Clark, P., D. Laxton, and D. Rose. 1995. Capacity constraints, inflation and the transmission mechanism: Forward-looking versus myopic policy rules. IMF Working Paper no. 75. Washington, D.C.: International Monetary Fund.

Dale, S., and A. G. Haldane. 1995. Interest rates and the channels of monetary transmission: Some sectoral estimates. *European Economic Review* 39:1611–26.

Duesenberry, J. S. 1949. *Income, savings, and the theory of consumer behaviour.* Cambridge, Mass.: Harvard University Press.

Duguay, P. 1994. Some thoughts on price stability versus zero inflation. Ottawa: Bank of Canada. Mimeograph.

Fillion, J.-F., and R. Tetlow. 1993. Zero-inflation or price-level targeting? Some answers from stochastic simulation on a small open-economy macro model. In *Economic behaviour and policy choice under price stability*, ed. Bank of Canada. Ottawa: Bank of Canada.

Freedman, C. 1996. What operating procedures should be adopted to maintain price stability? In *Achieving price stability*. Kansas City: Federal Reserve Bank of Kansas City.

Friedman, B. M., and K. N. Kuttner. 1996. A price target for U.S. monetary policy? Lessons from the experience with money growth targets. *Brookings Papers on Economic Activity*, no. 1:77–146.

Friedman, M. 1959. *A program for monetary stability.* New York: Macmillan.

Fuhrer, J. C. 1997. The (un)importance of forward-looking behaviour in price specifications. *Journal of Money, Credit and Banking* 29 (3): 338–50.

Fuhrer, J. C., and G. R. Moore. 1995a. Forward-looking behaviour and the stability of a conventional monetary policy rule. *Journal of Money, Credit and Banking* 27: 1060–70.

———. 1995b. Inflation persistence. *Quarterly Journal of Economics* 110:127–59.

Gaines, J., A. Al'Nowaihi, and P. Levine. 1989. ACES package for the solution of one-country linear rational expectations models. London: London Business School. Mimeograph.

Goodfriend, M., and R. G. King. 1997. The new neoclassical synthesis and the role of monetary policy. In *NBER macroeconomics annual 1997,* ed. B. S. Bernanke and J. J. Rotemberg. Cambridge, Mass.: MIT Press.

Haldane, A. G., ed. 1995. *Targeting inflation.* London: Bank of England.

———. 1997. Designing inflation targets. In *Monetary policy and inflation targeting,* ed. P. Lowe. Sidney: Reserve Bank of Australia.

———. 1998. On inflation-targeting in the United Kingdom. *Scottish Journal of Political Economy* 45 (1): 1–32.

Haldane, A. G., and C. K. Salmon. 1995. Three issues on inflation targets. In *Targeting inflation,* ed. A. G. Haldane. London: Bank of England.

Keynes, J. M. 1923. *A tract on monetary reform.* London: Macmillan.

King, M. A. 1996. Direct inflation targets. Paper presented at the symposium on Geldpolitische in Europe, Frankfurt, April.

———. 1997. The inflation target five years on. *Bank of England Quarterly Bulletin* 37:434–42.

Kohn, D. 1995. Comment. In *NBER macroeconomics annual 1995,* ed. B. S. Bernanke and J. J. Rotemberg, 227–33. Cambridge, Mass.: MIT Press.

Lebow, D. E., J. M. Roberts, and D. J. Stockton. 1992. Economic performance under price stability. Working Paper no. 125. Washington, D.C.: Board of Governors of the Federal Reserve System.

Leeper, E. M., C. A. Sims, and T. Zha. 1996. What does monetary policy do? *Brookings Papers on Economic Activity,* no. 2:1–63.

Leiderman, L., and L. E. O. Svensson, eds. 1995. *Inflation targets.* London: Centre for Economic Policy Research.

Mayes, D., and B. Chapple. 1995. Defining an inflation target. In *Targeting inflation,* ed. A. G. Haldane. London: Bank of England.

McCallum, B. T. 1988. Robustness properties of a rule for monetary policy. *Carnegie-Rochester Conference Series on Public Policy* 29:172–203.

McCallum, B. T., and E. Nelson. Forthcoming. An optimizing *IS-LM* specification for monetary policy and business cycle analysis. *Journal of Money, Credit, and Banking* 31.

Orphanides, A. 1998. Monetary policy rules based on real-time data. Finance and Economics Discussion Paper no. 98-03. Washington, D.C.: Board of Governors of the Federal Reserve System.

Reifschneider, D. L., D. J. Stockton, and D. W. Wilcox. 1996. Econometric models and the monetary policy process. Washington, D.C.: Board of Governors of the Federal Reserve System. Manuscript.

Reserve Bank of New Zealand. 1997. *Monetary policy statement 1997.* Wellington: Reserve Bank of New Zealand.

Roberts, J. M. 1995. New Keynesian economics and the Phillips curve. *Journal of Money, Credit and Banking* 27:975–84.

Rotemberg, J. J., and M. Woodford. 1997. An optimisation-based econometric framework for the evaluation of monetary policy. In *NBER macroeconomics annual 1997,* ed. B. S. Bernanke and J. J. Rotemberg. Cambridge, Mass.: MIT Press.

Svensson, L. E. O. 1996. Price level targeting versus inflation targeting: A free lunch? NBER Working Paper no. 5719. Cambridge, Mass.: National Bureau of Economic Research.

———. 1997a. Inflation-forecast targeting: Implementing and monitoring inflation targets. *European Economic Review* 41:1111–46.

———. 1997b. Inflation targeting: Some extensions. NBER Working Paper no. 5962. Cambridge, Mass.: National Bureau of Economic Research.

———. Forthcoming. Open-economy inflation targeting. *Journal of International Economics.*

Taylor, J. B. 1980. Aggregate dynamics and staggered contracts. *Journal of Political Economy* 88:1–24.

———. 1993. Discretion versus policy rules in practice. *Carnegie-Rochester Conference Series on Public Policy* 39:195–214.

Thomas, R. S. 1996. Understanding broad money. *Bank of England Quarterly Bulletin* 36:163–79.

Williams, J. 1997. Simple rules for monetary policy. Washington, D.C.: Board of Governors of the Federal Reserve System. Manuscript.

Woodford, M. 1994. Nonstandard indicators for monetary policy: Can their usefulness be judged from forecasting regressions? In *Monetary policy,* ed. N. Gregory Mankiw. Chicago: University of Chicago Press.

Comment   Donald L. Kohn

I appreciate this opportunity to discuss the paper by Batini and Haldane. I have a few comments on the paper, and I also want to take this opportunity to talk a bit about the use—or nonuse—of policy rules by policymakers at the Federal Reserve. In both cases, my intent is to raise questions that Batini and Haldane, and other authors working in this area, might consider addressing to better meet the needs of those policymakers.

With regard to the paper, my questions relate to three conclusions of the paper for policymakers—one implicit and the other two explicit: First, central banks should consider the exchange rate channel for policy: open economy effects are important. Second, central banks should be forward looking, but not too forward looking. Third, central banks do not need to include output smoothing explicitly in their reaction functions.

On the first point, I found the open economy aspect of the model useful and appropriate. I thought the authors structured the transmission sensibly— probably because we tend to view it quite similarly in analysis at the Federal Reserve. The exchange rate has two channels through which to affect inflation—indirectly through net exports and the output gap, and directly through effects on prices—and their interactions influence the dynamics of the response of inflation to monetary policy or to an exchange rate shock. The demand channel will have potentially lasting effects on the inflation rate, while the supply-side price level effect has a mostly temporary impact. Monetary policymakers need to be aware of these differences as they assess incoming data and form new forecasts after an exchange rate change. Moreover, the policy instrument in the model appropriately remains the short-term interest rate, which responds to changes in the exchange rate indirectly through their effect

Donald L. Kohn is director of the Division of Monetary Affairs, Board of Governors of the Federal Reserve System.

The views expressed are the author's and not necessarily those of other Federal Reserve staff or the Board of Governors.

on the inflation forecast, not in an automatic, predetermined way, as would result if the central bank targeted a monetary conditions index (MCI). The policy response to variations in the exchange rate ought to depend on the reasons for those variations and their consequences. And the MCI arbitrarily elevates exchange rates relative to many other important aspects of financial conditions—for example, credit conditions, bond rates, or equity prices—in the policy process.

Even though the United States is not as open as the United Kingdom, exchange rates have proved to be an important channel of policy influence and a source of shocks—in some cases persisting for some time, as in the 1980s. Exchange rates and the foreign sector play a substantial role in the large-scale models we have at the Federal Reserve Board, but they do not always get the attention they deserve in smaller scale models sometimes used to examine policy strategies.

In this light, I would have benefited from a fuller treatment of the exchange rate channel. The authors begin with some sensitivity analysis of alternative specifications of this channel but do not follow through in the rest of the paper. In addition, as the authors note, the exchange rate shocks are not derived by using a model of exchange rate movements as a baseline, but rather by comparing actual rates to the forecasts of market participants responding to a survey, and the misses are an order of magnitude larger than the other shocks. I wondered whether the market forecasts from which these shocks were drawn were consistent with the underlying model of covered interest arbitrage. Spot exchange rate movements themselves have deviated from the implications of this arbitrage condition over extended periods, presenting challenges to forward-looking central banks. It would be interesting to know how sensitive the paper's conclusions—for example, about the appropriate forecast horizon for policy-making or the losses from omitting explicit output targets—were to the size and nature of the exchange rate shocks. Among other things, it might help those of us in not quite so open economies judge the generality of the results.

The analysis that produced the second conclusion—that central banks need to be forward looking, but not too much—also was informative and raised questions. When a shock hits the system, something else must change to damp the resulting fluctuations in output and prices. It can be the private sector directly altering its spending and price and wage setting, or it can be the central bank adjusting to its interest rate target, which in turn induces stabilizing private sector behavior. The authors usefully discuss trade-offs in terms of forward-looking behavior to stabilize economies. If the private sector looks ahead, the central bank need not be so forward looking, presumably because private parties anticipating the central bank's eventual response will make decisions that have the effect of offsetting the shock. All the private sector needs to know is how the central bank will react, and it can adapt to a wide range of strengths of reactions, without seriously affecting the volatility of output and inflation. Even central banks that react weakly to inflation forecasts can make up for that by persisting in their policy moves. That persistence will get built into asset markets—in this model, the exchange rate—to influence private spending. Central banks need to look well into the future primarily when private spenders are not looking ahead but instead are responding gradually to incoming information. Adaptive expectations tend to produce long lags in the effects of policy changes, and under these circumstances, anticipatory policy can pay important dividends in stabilizing the economy and the inflation rate.

One aspect of the model results was the relatively narrow time frame for forward-looking behavior that produced favorable results. This knife-edge quality raised questions about the characteristics of the model. Obviously, if both the private sector and central bank are mostly backward looking, it will take a while to damp the effects of shocks, which have to get built into actual prices and output to elicit responses. But in this model, the deterioration in performance for backward-looking policies seemed especially marked and stood in contrast to other results at this conference. Moreover, the central bank and the private sector can be too forward looking as well in the model. In effect, stabilizing actions do not occur because all actors are looking beyond the shock to the return of stability. I suspect that excessively forward-looking private and public sectors have not been a cause of economic problems over the years. Perhaps private agents really do rely mostly on recent information to form expectations. And certainly central banks would modify reaction functions if they sensed destabilizing behavior. It would be interesting to see how sensitive the model's results in this regard were to its specifications—in particular, to its version of the central bank reaction function—and how the model would have to be modified to produce more believable outcomes.

The third conclusion I want to comment on concerns the use of a central bank reaction function that includes only the deviation of inflation from its objective. This and other papers show that by altering its response to inflation deviations, the degree of interest rate smoothing, and the length of the targeting horizon, a central bank using only an inflation forecast can come fairly close to replicating the results it would obtain by explicitly including output smoothing among its objectives. Still, it does not follow that excluding the output gap is appropriate. If output smoothing is a legitimate goal of central banks—if the public expects it in the context of pursuing price stability—deviations of output from potential ought to be among the variables the central bank responds to. Welfare losses are likely to be reduced, even if only by a little, and we cannot be certain that larger reductions would not be forthcoming under different model specifications. More fundamentally, I presume these reaction functions represent what the central bank talks about in its reports and testimonies. It is important for the public and financial markets to understand the central bank's motives. Being explicit about output-smoothing goals and the role they play in policy adjustment should promote better policy making, more reenforcing market reactions, and greater public understanding and support.

Several of my questions involved how robust the results in the Batini and

Haldane paper would be to different parameters and model structures, and uncertainties about the answers to such questions are the principal reasons why in practice monetary policymakers do not, at least consciously, commit to following rules.

Federal Open Market Committee (FOMC) members are regularly given some information on the predictions from monetary policy rules. Among the material they receive before each committee meeting is a chart that shows historic and projected federal funds rates under the staff forecast relative to the results of two conventional backward-looking rules. One is the Taylor rule, the other an estimated version of that rule fitted over the 1987–96 period, including a gradual adjustment of the federal funds rate to its equilibrium level. Each rule is examined under a variety of output and inflation gap measures; alternative measures can make a significant difference in the readings for the federal funds rate.[1] For the estimated rule, members see a one-standard-deviation band related to parameter uncertainty around the national target. Some individual members with a particular interest in rules receive other simulations or rule outcomes done both at the Board and the Reserve Banks.

Members have used this information in two ways. One is as a benchmark for the stance of policy—how is it positioned relative to past committee responses to similar combinations of output and inflation gaps. It has also been used not so much as a guide to the precise numerical target for policy but to structure thinking about the implications of incoming information for the direction of policy action. But, in truth, only a few members look at this or similar information regularly, and the number does not seem to be growing. I would like to take a few minutes to speculate on why this might be, and what general avenues research might take to make these exercises more useful.

Members seem to regard the use of rules to guide policy as questionable in part because they are quite uncertain about the quantitative specifications of the most basic inputs required by most rules and model exercises. They have little confidence in estimates of the size of the output gap, the level of the natural or equilibrium real interest rate, or even the level of the actual real interest rate, since inflation expectations are at best only imperfectly observable. They see enough evidence of changes in the world around them to distrust the estimates of these variables that they get from history, whether that history is embodied in simple means, single-equation reaction functions, or complex empirical models.[2] And as a consequence of these changes, they do not see their past actions as a very firm guide to current or future policy.

---

1. Deriving the results from alternative output and inflation gap measures raised some complex issues having to do with the consistency of the natural real interest rate across inflation indexes and over time as relative trends in inflation measures shifted.

2. To be sure, policymakers need to have judgments (at least implicitly) on these variables when they make discretionary policy decisions. But they are freer to allow the full range of recent information to affect these estimates, and they can calibrate their responses to these variables depending on the particular circumstances.

Let's look at the difficulties with estimating some of these key variables, bearing in mind that what seem like small deviations in a historical context can loom very large to a policymaker considering a 25 or 50 basis point rate adjustment. One important source of uncertainty about output gaps, and to a lesser extent inflation gaps, is data revisions. One of my colleagues finds substantial differences, ranging up to 200 basis points in some quarters, between Taylor rules calculated with data available at the time the decision was made and those calculated with the series that exist several years later (Orphanides 1998). Among other things, such differences raise questions about the efficacy of rules derived from revised data. The output gap is vulnerable to revisions and to uncertainties about the level of potential output. Some revisions after the fact are based partly on the observation that actual inflation did not turn out close to projections based on previous estimates of the gap. These sorts of revisions can make policy that seemed at the time about in line with past experience or a sensible response to the existing situation look very different when viewed in retrospect. Right now, the level and rate of growth of potential output is a major issue and cause of uncertainty in policy deliberations.

Estimates of the equilibrium real short-term rate of interest in effect embody all the information about the economy and economic relationships. They depend on the levels of supply and demand in the economy, their interactions, the behavior of other financial variables, and the responses of spending and prices to these variables. Judging equilibrium real interest rates from simple historical averages is surely wrong, given shifts over time in key supply and demand factors, such as fiscal policy and the behavior of labor markets. Even inferences from more complex models that try to take account of many of these influences are suspect, in light of the necessarily limited amount of information they can incorporate and the evolution of underlying structures and relationships; for example, the decline of availability constraints in credit markets from the lifting of Regulation Q and the growth of credit securitization has probably raised equilibrium real interest rates over the last 20 years.

The conference organizer is to be commended for placing some emphasis on dealing with uncertainty. But it is just a start. We tend to treat each type of uncertainty separately. An investigator may carefully address the risks of structural change and parameter uncertainty in one specific model. Yet another may consider the implications of not knowing which, among several different models, is a better representation of reality. But in fact different sources of uncertainty may interact in complex ways, and policymakers must face them and form judgments all at once. In addition, policymakers often face skewed notions of uncertainty—if a parameter has changed, it is more likely to be in a particular direction suggested by incoming data. Finally, the specification of the loss function itself may be uncertain. How can we be sure in a democracy that the utility of the public can be represented by a quadratic function—so important to our certainty-equivalent results—or that the public would be equally averse to misses on both sides of targets under all circumstances. As I observe FOMC discussions, and worry about the source of potential policy errors, I sense that additional research into the conduct of policy under uncertainty would be especially fruitful and welcome.

So policymakers shy away from rule-based decisions because the rules assume they know too much. But rules can also be perceived as assuming policymakers know too little. Policymakers use incoming information to assess the source and persistence of specific shocks. Deviations from expectations are examined for clues as to whether they arise from the supply or demand sides of the economy and whether they are a consequence of a temporary disturbance to an unchanged underlying structure or represent a lasting alteration to parameter values or model structure. In this examination, policymakers use all available information, including much that is outside the structure of typical models. To the extent that they can reach a judgment on the most likely nature of the shock, they can modify the policy response to improve on the outcome of the rule.

Of course, the authors of this paper and others would point out that all this information should be encompassed by forecasts of inflation or output gaps, and that policymakers should just make their best guess about the future and act on it, perhaps modifying the trajectory of action to take account of parameter uncertainty. One reason policymakers might seem hesitant to take this advice can be seen in figure 4C.1. It shows the central tendency of the range of projections by FOMC members and Blue Chip panelists of inflation and unemployment for each of the last few years. These forecasts were made at the middle of the previous year, which comes fairly close to matching the four- to six-quarter-ahead forecasting horizon that falls out of the Batini-Haldane simulations as close to optimal.

As is readily apparent, both policymakers and private forecasters have persistently underestimated the strength of aggregate demand and hence overpredicted the level of the unemployment rate, in the bottom panel. Nonetheless, they have also consistently overpredicted inflation by substantial amounts. (Data that have become available since the conference confirm that these trends continued in 1998.) Apparently, the world has changed in some significant way—or there has been an astounding series of temporary supply shocks—and more quickly or persistently than policymakers or professional forecasters could anticipate.

Naturally, as policymakers receive evidence that their knowledge of the structure of the economy is deficient, they have tended to reduce the weight they place on forecasts in making their decisions. In light of the many simulations, not including those of Batini and Haldane, that show that backward-looking policy is almost as effective as forecast-based policy, perhaps this is not a problem. But I still harbor the suspicion that policymakers trying to look even a bit inaccurately into the future can produce superior outcomes. The private sector in this situation is likely to be at least as confused as the central bank, and hence its actions based on its expectations and forecasts also may not be stabilizing. And even backward-looking policy is hampered by questions about what the output gap actually is or was. This circumstance suggests

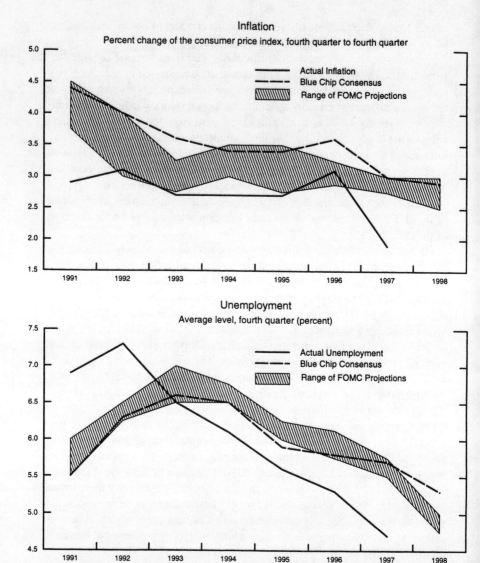

Fig. 4C.1 Inflation and unemployment forecasts from previous July

Note: The FOMC projections are the central tendency of the projections of the governors and reserve bank presidents from the Monetary Policy Report to the Congress on July of the year prior to the year shown. The Blue Chip consensus is from the Blue Chip Economic Indicators published in the same month as the report.

to me another possible avenue of research, which would examine the interactions between uncertainty and the appropriate weight to be put on forecasts and incoming data.

Finally, I would note that the behavior of asset markets—especially financial asset markets—has contributed substantially to uncertainty about the natural real rate of interest and to central bank decisions to deviate from past patterns of behavior. In these models and reaction functions, the natural rate of interest is an index for a broader array of financial conditions. Batini and Haldane add the exchange rate, which is essential, and others have included long-term interest rates in their models. But over the last 10 years, changes in credit availability and equity prices have played key roles in determining the stance of monetary policy in the United States and elsewhere, for example, Japan. Incorporating richer financial sectors in empirical models and thinking about interactions between asset prices and aggregate demand, inflation, and monetary policy would be another helpful direction to take. And fuller treatment of asset markets would open up another important issue—the implications of divergent views between the central bank and private savers and investors, in contrast to the usual assumption of consistent views held by both the private sector and the central bank. Such divergences are not unusual, and they find expression in actual asset prices that the central bank occasionally finds difficult to justify or understand, and that the central bank anticipates might be corrected at some point, with implications for output and prices.

By noting the impediments to greater rule-based decision making in the central bank, and by suggesting a daunting research agenda, I do not want to leave the impression that the research in the Batini and Haldane paper and more generally at the conference isn't quite productive for monetary policy making. Such research helps to establish theoretical and empirical structures for considering the stance of policy. It pinpoints key variables that should be taken into account when policy is made, and it has something to say about how the size of individual parameters might influence stabilizing monetary policy. It has already provoked some potentially useful debates concerning, for example, the role of forecasts in policy, the strength of policy responses, the place of output gaps in provoking policy actions, the rationale for strings of policy moves, and the effects of uncertainty. Systematic consideration of these issues and others will continue to be useful to policymakers. The Batini and Haldane paper is an interesting addition to this important literature.

Reference

Orphanides, Athanasios. 1998. Monetary policy rules based on real-time data. Finance and Economics Discussion Paper no. 98-03. Washington, D.C.: Board of Governors of the Federal Reserve System.

Discussion Summary

Andrew Levin noted that the results in both his paper with Wieland and Williams and the Rotemberg and Woodford paper presented at the conference show that for closed economies, there does not seem to be much evidence that model-based inflation forecasts work better than current inflation, the current output gap, and the lagged interest rate. The different results obtained for closed and open economies can in part be explained by the high variance of exchange rate shocks in open economy models. The fundamental mechanism seems to be that forward-looking rules perform better than rules based on current variables in an environment with temporary shocks to inflation. This issue is also related to the length of the horizon considered. The simulation results of all four models in the Levin, Wieland, and Williams paper show that a longer measure of inflation generally works better since temporary shocks are smoothed out automatically. The Batini and Haldane paper only considers one-quarter changes in the consumer price index which are very volatile. When four-, eight-, or twelve-quarter changes in prices are used, the advantages of using forecast-based rules disappear.

Michael Woodford remarked that his paper with Rotemberg shows that pure forward-looking rules are far from being optimal. As already mentioned in the comment by Donald Kohn, the familiar intuition that important lags in the effects of monetary policy require rules based on inflation and output forecasts does not work in models with a forward-looking private sector. The first reason for this, common to many models with forward-looking elements (e.g., Mc-Callum-Nelson and Rotemberg-Woodford), is that aggregate demand depends on the long rate of interest, that is, expectations of future short rates, rather than just the current short rate. Therefore, monetary policy has to change people's expectations about future short rates, which is why backward-looking rules for the short rate are not necessarily bad. A second reason, specific to the Rotemberg-Woodford model, is that there are lags in the aggregate demand equation that arise because agents have to use old information in deciding on their spending. For this reason, spending decisions do not depend on past interest rates but on past expectations of current interest rates leading to a lag in the effect of monetary policy. These lags do not have the same implication of wanting the short rate to respond to forecasts, since future aggregate demand does not depend on the current funds rate but on current expectations of future funds rates. According to this setup, only the commitment to changing the federal funds rate in the future has an effect on aggregate demand.

David Longworth noted that there is an underlying tension between the uncertainty of policymakers about the true model of the economy and their desire to include more variables like exchange rates and asset prices in the monetary policy reaction rule. Longworth also stressed that the Bank of England obtains a low variance in inflation without an exchange rate in the policy rule.

Frederic Mishkin wondered about the intuition for the very short horizon of the forward-looking rules used in the paper. This might be related to the fact that the paper looks at the United Kingdom, whereas for the United States about two years seem appropriate. Mishkin also asked about the reasons why the Rudebusch and Svensson paper did not find these forward-looking rules as successful as in the present paper. *John Taylor* asked why the Rotemberg-Woodford rule, or any rule of interest rate smoothing, does not perform well in the paper, even though it uses a forward-looking model. *Mark Gertler* suggested that a possible answer to these questions consisted in the exchange rate channel, which makes lagged inflation a better forecast of future inflation in a closed economy than in an open economy.

5 Policy Rules for Inflation Targeting

Glenn D. Rudebusch and Lars E. O. Svensson

5.1 Introduction

In this paper, we use a small empirical model of the U.S. economy to examine the performance of policy rules that are consistent with a monetary policy regime of inflation targeting. In the real world, explicit inflation targeting is currently pursued in New Zealand, Canada, the United Kingdom, Sweden, Australia, and the Czech Republic. Inflation targeting in these countries is characterized by (1) a publicly announced numerical inflation target (either in the form of a target range, a point target, or a point target with a tolerance interval), (2) a framework for policy decisions that involves comparing an inflation forecast to the announced target, thus providing an "inflation-forecast targeting" regime for policy, where the forecast serves as an intermediate target (cf. Haldane 1998; King 1994; Svensson 1997a), and (3) a higher than average degree of transparency and accountability.[1]

Glenn D. Rudebusch is research officer at the Federal Reserve Bank of San Francisco. Lars E. O. Svensson is professor of international economics at the Institute for International Economic Studies, Stockholm University, and a research associate of the National Bureau of Economic Research.

The authors thank James Stock, Frederic Mishkin, and other conference participants for comments. The paper was also presented at the Federal Reserve Bank of San Francisco–Center for Economic Policy Research, Stanford University, conference on Central Bank Inflation Targeting, 6–7 March 1998. The authors thank Ben Bernanke, Carl Walsh, and other conference participants for comments. Part of the paper was written when Lars Svensson visited the Reserve Bank of New Zealand and Victoria University of Wellington. He thanks these institutions for their hospitality. The views expressed in the paper do not necessarily reflect the views of the Federal Reserve Bank of San Francisco, the Federal Reserve System, or the Reserve Bank of New Zealand. The authors thank Charlotta Groth and Heather Royer for research assistance, and Christina Lönnblad for secretarial assistance.

1. The rapidly growing literature on inflation targeting includes the conference volumes Leiderman and Svensson (1995), Haldane (1995), Federal Reserve Bank of Kansas City (1996), and Lowe (1997). See also the survey by Bernanke and Mishkin (1997).

We model an inflation-targeting policy regime using loss functions over policy goals. In our loss functions, inflation targeting always involves an attempt to minimize deviations of inflation from the explicit inflation target. In addition, however, our inflation-targeting loss functions also allow concerns about real output (or more precisely about the variability of output because the natural rate hypothesis is assumed). That is, we would argue there is no necessary connection between the specification of the loss function (other than that inflation variability must enter with a nonnegligible weight) and the specification of an inflation-targeting policy regime.[2] For support of this view, see, for example, the recent discussion by Fischer (1996), King (1996), Taylor (1996), and Svensson (1996) in Federal Reserve Bank of Kansas City (1996).[3] Thus we interpret inflation targeting as consistent with a conventional quadratic loss function, where in addition to the variability of inflation around the inflation target there is some weight on the variability of the output gap.[4]

In examining policy rules that are consistent with inflation targeting, we consider two broad classes of rules: instrument rules and targeting rules. An explicit instrument rule expresses the monetary policy instrument as an explicit function of available information. We examine both optimal unrestricted instrument rules (a tradition that goes back at least to Taylor 1979; recent contributions include Blake and Westaway 1996) as well as optimal simple or restricted instrument rules, which involve only a few parameters or arguments (e.g., current inflation and output as in Taylor's 1993 rule). However, no central bank, whether inflation targeting or not, follows an explicit instrument rule (unrestricted or simple). Every central bank uses more information than the simple rules are based on, and no central bank would voluntarily restrict itself to react mechanically in a predescribed way to new information. The role of unrestricted or simple explicit instrument rules is at best to provide a baseline and comparison to the policy actually followed.

A targeting rule may be closer to the actual decision framework under inflation targeting. It is represented by the assignment of a loss function over devia-

---

2. One may argue, though, that the high degree of transparency and accountability serves to increase the commitment to minimizing the loss function, and to ensure that any concern about the real economy is consistent with the natural rate hypotheses and therefore reduces, or eliminates, any inflation bias.

3. As discussed in Svensson (forthcoming b), concerns about the stability of the real economy, model uncertainty, and interest rate smoothing all have similar effects under inflation targeting, namely, a more gradualist policy. Thus, if inflation is away from the inflation target, it is brought back to target more gradually (under "flexible" rather than "strict" inflation targeting, the inflation forecast hits the target at a horizon that is longer than the shortest possible). Svensson (1997b) argues that all inflation-targeting central banks in practice behave in this way, possibly with differing weights on the different reasons for doing so.

4. Because inflation-targeting central banks, like other central banks, also seem to smooth interest rates, our loss function also includes some weight on the variability of interest rate changes.

tions of a goal variable from a target level, or deviations of an intermediate target variable from an intermediate target level (cf. Rogoff 1985; Walsh 1998; Svensson 1997a, forthcoming b). A targeting rule, combined with a particular model, is only an *implicit* instrument rule; typically, the equivalent of a first-order condition has to be solved in order to find the corresponding *explicit* instrument rule. (For an intermediate target variable that the central bank has complete control over, the first-order condition is trivial: equality between the intermediate target variable and the target level.) As an example, note that one interpretation of "inflation-forecast targeting" is that the policy instrument is adjusted such that a conditional inflation forecast (the intermediate target variable) hits the inflation target at an appropriate horizon. Combined with a particular model, the instrument then becomes an implicit function of current information; when the corresponding system of equations is solved for the instrument, the explicit instrument rule results. We shall examine several such targeting rules below.

Our analysis proceeds as follows. Section 5.2 presents the empirical model we use, which is a simple two-equation model of U.S. output and inflation, somewhat similar to the theoretical model in Svensson (1997a). The model captures some realistic dynamics (e.g., monetary policy actions affect output before inflation) in a very simple but tractable form. Section 5.3 first attempts to reduce the confusion caused by the literature's use of two different meanings of "targeting" and then presents the different instrument and targeting rules we examine. Section 5.4 reports our results, with focus on output and inflation variability under a large set of various policy rules. We find that some simple instrument and targeting rules involving inflation forecasts do remarkably well in minimizing the loss function (relative to the optimal rule). Other policy rules, some of which are frequently used in the literature as representing inflation targeting, do less well. Finally, section 5.5 concludes.

5.2 An Empirical Model of U.S. Output and Inflation

5.2.1 Motivation

Our choice of an empirical model of output and inflation is motivated by three considerations. First, we choose a simple linear model (as well as quadratic preferences below), so our analysis will be tractable and our results transparent. Our model consists of an aggregate supply equation (or "Phillips curve") that relates inflation to an output gap and an aggregate demand equation (or "IS curve") that relates output to a short-term interest rate. Obviously, our model glosses over many important and contentious features of the monetary transmission mechanism. Still, we feel that the model has enough richness—for example, in dynamics—to be of interest, especially when judged relative to some of the models used in previous theoretical discussions.

Second, our model captures the spirit of many practical policy-oriented macroeconometric models. Some (e.g., McCallum 1988) have argued that because there is no academic consensus on the structure of the economy, any proposed monetary policy rule should perform well in a variety of models. We are completely sympathetic to this argument. We believe that robustness to plausible model variation is a crucial issue and one that this conference volume, taken as a whole, should provide some insight into. However, we also believe that monetary policy analysis will be most convincing to central bankers (who are, of course, among the most important ultimate consumers of this research) if it is conducted using models that are similar in structure to the ones actually employed by central bankers. Thus, for example, at this stage of analysis, we focus our attention on a model that (1) uses a short-term interest rate as the policy instrument with no direct role for monetary aggregates, (2) is specified in terms of output gaps from trend instead of output growth rates, and (3) includes a Phillips curve with adaptive or autoregressive expectations that is consistent with the natural rate hypothesis. Such a structure is typical of many central bank policy models (including, e.g., the 11 models described in the central bank model comparison project for the Bank for International Settlements 1995), and because our empirical analysis uses U.S. data, we will be keen to match the properties of the Federal Reserve's venerable MPS macroeconometric model.[5] Of course, the appropriate way to model expectations for policy analysis remains particularly contentious (see, e.g., the early discussion by Lucas 1976 and Sims 1982). We are persuaded that the importance of the Lucas critique is in large measure an empirical issue as in, for example, Oliner, Rudebusch, and Sichel (1996). In this regard, Fuhrer (1997) tests an autoregressive Phillips curve like ours against a forward-looking version and cannot reject it. Moreover, many policymakers appear more comfortable with the backward-looking version, including Federal Reserve Governor Meyer (1997) and former vice-chairman Alan Blinder (1998). Finally, in this regard, it should be noted that our backward-looking expectations may be particularly appropriate during the introduction of a new rule for inflation targeting. As stressed by Taylor (1993) and Bomfim and Rudebusch (1997), rational expectations may be unrealistic during the transition period when learning about the new policy rule is taking place.

Our third consideration in model selection is empirical fit to the data. To judge whether our model is able to reproduce the salient features of the data, we compare its fit and dynamics to an unrestricted vector autoregression

---

5. In 1996, the FRB/US model replaced the MPS model as the Federal Reserve Board's main quarterly macroeconometric model. The major innovation of this model is its ability to explicitly model various types of expectations including model-consistent ones (see Brayton and Tinsley 1996). Still, across a range of expectations processes, the properties of the new model are broadly similar to those of our model. E.g., the FRB/US model exhibits an output sacrifice ratio of between 2 and 5, which, as noted below, brackets our model's sacrifice ratio of about 3.

(VAR). VARs have become a very popular tool recently for describing the dynamics of monetary transmission, and they are a natural benchmark for model evaluation. Indeed, if one dislikes the structural interpretation that we attach to our model, one can simply consider it a reduced-form VAR and so our analysis is similar in spirit to Feldstein and Stock (1994) or Cecchetti (1995).

5.2.2   Model Estimates

The two equations of our model are

$$(1) \quad \pi_{t+1} = \alpha_{\pi 1}\pi_t + \alpha_{\pi 2}\pi_{t-1} + \alpha_{\pi 3}\pi_{t-2} + \alpha_{\pi 4}\pi_{t-3} + \alpha_y y_t + \varepsilon_{t+1},$$

$$(2) \quad y_{t+1} = \beta_{y1}y_t + \beta_{y2}y_{t-1} - \beta_r(\bar{i}_t - \bar{\pi}_t) + \eta_{t+1},$$

where π_t is quarterly inflation in the GDP chain-weighted price index (p_t) in percent at an annual rate, that is, $400(\ln p_t - \ln p_{t-1})$; $\bar{\pi}_t$ is four-quarter inflation in the GDP chain-weighted price index, that is, $(1/4)\sum_{j=0}^{3}\pi_{t-j}$; i_t is the quarterly average federal funds rate in percent at an annual rate; $\bar{i}_t$ is the four-quarter average federal funds rate, that is, $(1/4)\sum_{j=0}^{3}i_{t-j}$; y_t is the percentage gap between actual real GDP (q_t) and potential GDP (q_t^*), that is, $100(q_t - q_t^*)/q_t^*$. These five variables were de-meaned prior to estimation, so no constants appear in the equations.

The first equation relates inflation to a lagged output gap and to lags of inflation.[6] The lags of inflation are an autoregressive or adaptive representation of inflation expectations, which is consistent with the form of the Phillips curve in the MPS model described in Brayton and Mauskopf (1987). In our empirical analysis below, we will not reject the hypothesis that the coefficients of the four inflation lags sum to one; thus we will use an accelerationist form of the Phillips curve, which implies a long-run vertical Phillips curve. The second equation relates the output gap to its own lags and to the difference between the average funds rate and average inflation over the previous four quarters— an approximate ex post real rate. The third term is a simple representation of the monetary transmission mechanism, which, in the view of many central banks, likely involves nominal interest rates (e.g., mortgage rates), ex ante real short and long rates, exchange rates, and possibly direct credit quantities as well. Equation (2) appears to be a workable approximation of these various intermediate transmission mechanisms.

The estimated equations, using the sample period 1961:1–96:2, are shown below. (Coefficient standard errors are given in parentheses, and the standard error of the residuals and Durbin-Watson statistics also are reported.)

---

6. Our series on the output gap is essentially identical to those that have been used in a variety of Federal Reserve and other government studies including, e.g., Congressional Budget Office (1995) and Hallman, Porter, and Small (1991). Our estimation results were little changed by using a flexible trend for potential output such as a quadratic trend.

$$\pi_{t+1} = .70\pi_t - .10\pi_{t-1} + .28\pi_{t-2} + .12\pi_{t-3} + .14y_t + \varepsilon_{t+1},$$
$$\quad\quad (.08)\quad (.10)\quad\quad (.10)\quad\quad (.08)\quad\quad (.03)$$

$$SE = 1.009, \quad DW = 1.99,$$

$$y_{t+1} = 1.16y_t - .25y_{t-1} - .10(\bar{i}_t - \bar{\pi}_t) + \eta_{t+1},$$
$$\quad\quad (.08)\quad\quad (.08)\quad\quad (.03)$$

$$SE = 0.819, \quad DW = 2.05.$$

The equations were estimated individually by ordinary least squares.[7] The hypothesis that the sum of the lag coefficients of inflation equals one had a p-value of .42, so this restriction was imposed in estimation.[8]

The subsample stability of our estimated equations is an important condition for drawing inferences from our model—whether it is given a structural or reduced-form (VAR) interpretation. In particular, because ours is a backward-looking model, the Lucas critique may apply with particular force. The historical empirical importance of this critique can be gauged by econometric stability tests (again, see Oliner et al. 1996). Our estimated equations appear to easily pass these tests. For example, consider a stability test from Andrews (1993): the *maximum* value of the likelihood ratio test statistic for structural stability over all possible breakpoints in the middle 70 percent of the sample. For our estimated inflation equation, the maximum likelihood ratio test statistic is 9.77 (in 1972:3), while the 10 percent critical value is 14.31 (from table 1 in Andrews 1993). Similarly, for the output equation, the maximum statistic is 7.87 (in 1982:4), while the 10 percent critical value is 12.27.

5.2.3 Comparison to Other Empirical Estimates

It is useful to compare our model with other empirical estimates in order to gauge its plausibility and its conformity to central bank models. From the perspective of monetary policy, two features are of particular interest: (1) the sensitivity of real activity to movements in the policy instrument and (2) the responsiveness of inflation to slack in the economy. Table 5.1 provides some evidence on both of these issues with a comparison of simulations from our model (1)–(2) and the MPS model, which was used regularly in the Federal Reserve's forecasting process for over 25 years. The experiment considered (as outlined in Smets 1995 and Mauskopf 1995) assumes that the Federal Reserve raises the federal funds rate by 1 percentage point for two years and then returns the funds rate to its original level thereafter. Table 5.1 reports for output and inflation the average difference between this simulation and a constant

---

7. Almost identical parameter estimates were obtained by the seemingly unrelated regressions and by system maximum likelihood methods because the cross-correlation of the errors is essentially zero.

8. This p-value is obtained from the usual F-statistic. Of course, nonstandard near-unit distributions may apply (see Rudebusch 1992), but these are likely to push the p-value even higher.

Table 5.1   **Model Responses to a Funds Rate Increase (annual average difference from baseline in percentage points)**

	Years after Funds Rate Increase		
	1	2	3
Output gap			
MPS[a]	−.07	−.45	−.99
Our model	−.07	−.41	−.66
Inflation			
MPS[a]	−.00	−.03	−.26
Our model	−.00	−.08	−.25

[a]From table II.1 in Mauskopf (1995).

funds rate alternative in each of the first three years after the funds rate increase. The responses of the MPS model and our model to this temporary tightening of monetary policy are quite similar. In both models, output averages almost 0.5 percentage points lower in year 2 and between two-thirds and 1 percentage point lower in year 3, while inflation falls by about a quarter of a percentage point by year 3. Both models require about 3.3 years of a 1 percentage point output gap in order to induce a 1 percentage point change in the inflation rate—that is, they exhibit an output sacrifice ratio of just over 3.[9] Most important, the magnitude of the link between the funds rate and inflation, which will be crucial for our inflation-targeting analysis, is essentially the same across the two models.[10]

Finally, it is also useful to compare the fit and impulse responses of our model to those of a VAR. While one may be deeply skeptical of the use of VARs for certain structural investigations (see Rudebusch 1998a), they can provide simple atheoretical summaries of the general dynamics of the data and thus can provide a useful benchmark for the overall fit of a model. Our model can be viewed as two restricted equations from a trivariate VAR with four lags. The VAR output equation regresses the gap on four lags of π, y, and i. The VAR inflation equation regresses inflation on the same lags as well as the contemporaneous value of the gap.[11] Table 5.2 compares the Schwarz and Akaike information criteria (SIC and AIC, respectively) for each VAR equation with those of our structural model. These two model selection criteria, which are functions of the residual sum of squares, are differentiated by their degrees-of-

9. For comparison, with a rough back-of-the-envelope calculation Ball (1994) reports an output sacrifice ratio for the United States of 2.4.

10. Our model estimates appear comparable to other recent small empirical structural models of the United States, including Fuhrer and Moore (1995), Clark, Laxton, and Rose (1996), and Fair and Howrey (1996). This is true even though the models use different interest rates in the IS curve: Fuhrer and Moore use an ex ante real long rate, Clark et al. use an ex ante real short rate, and Fair and Howrey use a nominal short rate. In fact, over the postwar historical sample, the four measured rates used appear to have moved together fairly closely.

11. Thus our VAR has a Cholesky factorization with a causal order of output, inflation, and, finally, the funds rate.

Table 5.2   Model Selection Criteria

	SIC	AIC
Inflation equation		
VAR	736.8	698.8
Our model	705.0	690.3
Output equation		
VAR	652.2	617.1
Our model	639.7	630.9

Note: SIC = Schwarz information criterion; AIC = Akaike information criterion.

freedom penalty for the number of parameters estimated. As shown in table 5.2, the structural model's inflation equation is favored over the VAR's inflation equation by both the SIC and the AIC. For the output equation, there is a split decision. The SIC, which more heavily penalizes extra parameters, favors the structural model, while the AIC favors the VAR. Overall, the information criteria do not appear to view our structural model restrictions unfavorably.

As a final comparison of our structural model to the VAR, figure 5.1 shows their responses to various shocks. This exercise completes the VAR with the usual VAR funds rate equation that regresses the funds rate on four lags of the three variables as well as contemporaneous values of the output gap and inflation. This VAR funds rate equation—with its interpretation as a Federal Reserve reaction function—is also added as a third equation to our model. The impulse responses of this structural system are shown as solid lines in figure 5.1, while the usual VAR impulse responses are shown as long-dashed lines along with their 95 percent confidence intervals as short-dashed lines. Because the funds rate reaction function equation is identical across the two systems, any differences in dynamics are attributable to the structural model restrictions on the output and inflation equations.

Figure 5.1 suggests that these restrictions do not greatly alter the dynamics of the model relative to an unrestricted VAR. In response to a positive funds rate shock, output and inflation decline in a similar manner in each system.[12] Also, a positive output shock persists over time and boosts inflation in a like fashion in both models. Only for an inflation shock (the left-hand column of fig. 5.1) do our model's responses edge outside the VAR's confidence intervals. This discrepancy reflects our model's output sensitivity to the real interest rate, which falls after an inflation shock because the VAR funds rate reaction function has such an extremely weak interest rate response to inflation. The implausibility of such VAR reaction functions, which mix several decades of very different Federal Reserve behavior, is highlighted in Rudebusch (1998a) and Judd and Rudebusch (1998). As shown below, with more plausible reaction

---

12. There is a modest, insignificant "price puzzle" exhibited by the VAR but not the structural model.

functions where the Fed raises the funds rate by more than inflation shock (so the real rate rises, as in the Taylor rule), output will fall following an inflation shock in the structural model.

5.3   Monetary Policy Rules

5.3.1   Instrument Rules and Targeting Rules

As noted in our introduction, by an (explicit) *instrument rule,* we mean that the monetary policy instrument is expressed as an explicit function of available information. Classic examples of instrument rules are the McCallum (1988) rule for the monetary base and the Taylor (1993) rule for the federal funds rate. By a *targeting rule,* we mean that the central bank is assigned to minimize a loss function that is increasing in the deviation between a target variable and the target level for this variable. The targeting rule will, as we shall see, imply an *implicit* instrument rule.

In the literature, the expression "targeting variable x_t," or "having a target level x^* for variable x_t," has two meanings. According to the first meaning, the expression above is used in the sense of "*setting a target* for variable x."[13] Thus "having a target" means "*using all relevant available information* to bring the target variable in line with the target," or more precisely to minimize some loss function over expected future deviations of the target variable from the target level, for instance, the quadratic loss function

$$\min_{i_t} E_t \sum_{\tau=0}^{\infty} \delta^{\tau}(x_{t+\tau} - x^*)^2,$$

where δ, $0 < \delta < 1$, is a discount factor and E_t denotes the expectations operator conditional on information available in period t. We will use "targeting" according to this first meaning, following, for instance, Rogoff (1985), Walsh (1998), and Svensson (1997a, forthcoming b).

According to the second meaning, "targeting" and "targets" imply a particular *information restriction* for the instrument rule, namely, that the instrument must only depend on the gap between the target variable and the target level (and lags of this gap or lags of itself, or both).[14] Thus the instrument rule is typically restricted to be

$$A(L)i_t = B(L)(x_t - x^*),$$

---

13. This is in line with *Webster's Ninth New Collegiate Dictionary:* **target** *vt* (1837)   **1:** to make a target of; *esp:* to set as a goal   **2:** to direct or use toward a target.

14. See, e.g., Judd and Motley (1992), McCallum (1997), and Bernanke and Woodford (1997). Bernanke and Woodford's criticism of Svensson's (1997a) use of the term "inflation-forecast targeting" seems to take the second meaning of "targeting" for granted and disregard the first meaning (which indeed is the one used in Svensson 1997a).

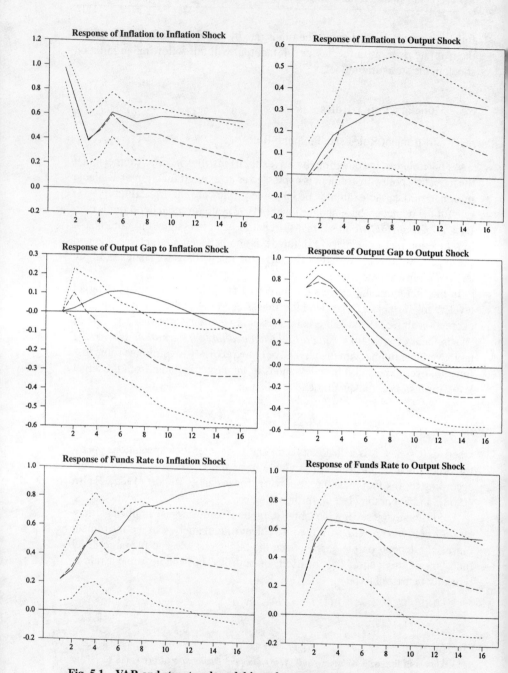

Fig. 5.1   VAR and structural model impulse responses

Note: Solid, impulse responses of the structural model (amended with the VAR interest rate equation). *Long dashes,* impulse responses of the VAR, with 95 percent confidence intervals (*short dashes*).

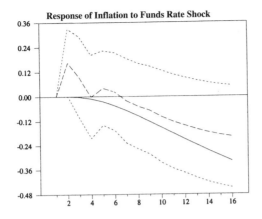

Response of Inflation to Funds Rate Shock

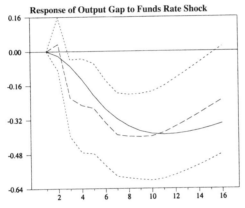

Response of Output Gap to Funds Rate Shock

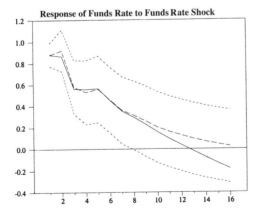

Response of Funds Rate to Funds Rate Shock

where $A(L)$ and $B(L)$ are polynomials in the lag operator L. To convey the second meaning, "responding only to $x_t - x^*$" seems more precise. Note that "inflation targeting" according to this second meaning, but *not* according to the first meaning, might correspond to an instrument rule like

$$i_t = hi_{t-1} + \phi(\pi_t - \pi^*).$$

This instrument rule turns out to perform much worse than other instrument rules. Note also that "inflation-forecast targeting" according to the second meaning (as in, e.g., Haldane 1997), but generally *not* according to the first meaning, might be an instrument rule like

$$i_t = hi_{t-1} + \phi(\pi_{t+T|t} - \pi^*),$$

where $\pi_{t+T|t}$ denotes some conditional inflation forecast of inflation T quarters ahead (more on this below).

A targeting rule for a *goal* variable is hence equivalent to having an objective for this variable. Examples of such rules are "annual inflation shall fall within the interval 1–3 percent per year on average at least three years out of four" and "minimize the expected value of a discounted sum of future weighted squared deviations of annual inflation from 2 percent per year and squared output gaps." We shall assume an objective of the latter kind.

Similarly, a targeting rule for an *intermediate target* variable is equivalent to having a loss function for this intermediate target variable (an intermediate loss function), where the target level sometimes is not constant but depends on current information. The targeting rule can also be expressed as an equation that the target variable shall fulfill, for instance that the target level for the intermediate target is an explicit function of available information. The equation for the intermediate target variable may be interpreted as a first-order condition of an explicit or implicit loss function for the goal variable (see Svensson 1997a, forthcoming b, for examples). Thus a targeting rule in the end expresses the intermediate target level as a function of current information. Examples of intermediate target rules are "minimize the expected future deviation of M3 growth from the sum of a given inflation target, a forecast of potential output growth, and a velocity trend," "keep the exchange rate within a ± 2.25 percent band around a given central parity," and "adjust the instrument such that the forecast for inflation four to eight quarters ahead, conditional on the current state of the economy and on holding the instrument at constant level for the next eight quarters, is 2 percent per year." We shall consider some targeting rules of this last kind.

A targeting rule in a given model implies a particular instrument rule, but this instrument rule is *implicit* rather than explicit. That is, the targeting rule has to be solved for the instrument rule in order to express it as a function of current information.

5.3.2 The Model

Let the model be given by equations (1) and (2), and let ε_t and η_t be i.i.d. zero-mean disturbances with variances σ_ε^2 and σ_η^2 and covariance $\sigma_{\varepsilon\eta}$. The coefficients of the lagged inflation terms in equation (1) are restricted to sum to one,

$$\sum_{j=1}^{4} \alpha_{\pi j} = 1.$$

In our analysis, we will interpret "inflation targeting" as having a loss function for monetary policy where deviations of inflation from an explicit inflation target are always given some weight, but not necessarily all the weight. In particular, for a discount factor δ, $0 < \delta < 1$, we consider the intertemporal loss function in quarter t,

$$(3) \qquad\qquad E_t \sum_{\tau=0}^{\infty} \delta^\tau L_{t+\tau},$$

where the period loss function is

$$(4) \qquad\qquad L_t = \overline{\pi}_t^2 + \lambda y_t^2 + v(i_t - i_{t-1})^2$$

(π_t and $\overline{\pi}_t$ are now interpreted as the deviation from a constant given inflation target) and $\lambda \geq 0$ and $v \geq 0$ are the weights on output stabilization and interest rate smoothing, respectively.[15] We will refer to the variables $\overline{\pi}_t$, y_t, and $i_t - i_{t-1}$ as the goal variables. As defined in Svensson (forthcoming b), "strict" inflation targeting refers to the situation where only inflation enters the loss function ($\lambda = v = 0$), while "flexible" inflation targeting allows other goal variables (nonzero λ or v).

When $\delta \to 1$, the sum in equation (3) becomes unbounded. It consists of two components, however: one corresponding to the deterministic optimization problem when all shocks are zero and one proportional to the variances of the shocks. The former component converges for $\delta = 1$ (because the terms approach zero quickly enough), and the decision problem is actually well defined also for that case. For $\delta \to 1$, the value of the intertemporal loss function approaches the infinite sum of unconditional means of the period loss function, $E[L_t]$. Then the scaled loss function $(1 - \delta)E_t\sum_{\tau=0}^{\infty}\delta^\tau L_{t+\tau}$ approaches the unconditional mean $E[L_t]$. It follows that we can also define the optimization problem for $\delta = 1$ and then interpret the intertemporal loss function as the unconditional mean of the period loss function, which equals the weighted sum of the unconditional variances of the goal variables,

$$(5) \qquad\qquad E[L_t] = \text{var}[\overline{\pi}_t] + \lambda \, \text{var}[y_t] + v \, \text{var}[i_t - i_{t-1}].$$

---

15. Then i_t can be interpreted as the deviation of the federal funds rate from the sum of the inflation target and the natural real interest rate (the unconditional mean of the real interest rate).

We shall use equation (5) as our standard loss function, hence assuming the limiting case $\delta = 1$.

5.3.3   State-Space Representation

The model (1)–(2) has a convenient state-space representation,

$$(6) \qquad X_{t+1} = AX_t + Bi_t + v_{t+1}.$$

The 9×1 vector X_t of state variables, the 9×9 matrix A, the 9×1 column vector B, and the 9×1 column disturbance vector v_t are given by

$$X_t = \begin{bmatrix} \pi_t \\ \pi_{t-1} \\ \pi_{t-2} \\ \pi_{t-3} \\ y_t \\ y_{t-1} \\ i_{t-1} \\ i_{t-2} \\ i_{t-3} \end{bmatrix}, \quad A = \begin{bmatrix} \sum_{j=1}^{4} \alpha_{\pi j} e_j + \alpha_y e_5 \\ e_1 \\ e_2 \\ e_3 \\ \beta_r e_{1:4} + \beta_{y1} e_5 + \beta_{y2} e_6 - \beta_r e_{7:9} \\ e_5 \\ e_0 \\ e_7 \\ e_8 \end{bmatrix}, \quad B = \begin{bmatrix} 0 \\ 0 \\ 0 \\ 0 \\ -\beta_r/4 \\ 0 \\ 1 \\ 0 \\ 0 \end{bmatrix}, \quad v_t = \begin{bmatrix} \varepsilon_t \\ 0 \\ 0 \\ 0 \\ \eta_t \\ 0 \\ 0 \\ 0 \\ 0 \end{bmatrix},$$

where e_j $(j = 0, 1, \ldots, 9)$ denotes a 1×9 row vector, for $j = 0$ with all elements equal to zero, for $j = 1, \ldots, 9$ with element j equal to unity and all other elements equal to zero, and where $e_{j:k}$ $(j < k)$ denotes a 1×9 row vector with elements $j, j + 1, \ldots, k$ equal to 1/4 and all other elements equal to zero.

Furthermore, it is convenient to define the 3×1 vector Y_t of goal variables. It fulfills

$$(7) \qquad Y_t = C_X X_t + C_i i_t,$$

where the vector Y_t, the 3×9 matrix C_X, and the 3×1 column vector C_i are given by

$$Y_t = \begin{bmatrix} \overline{\pi}_t \\ y_t \\ i_t - i_{t-1} \end{bmatrix}, \quad C_X = \begin{bmatrix} e_{1:4} \\ e_5 \\ -e_7 \end{bmatrix}, \quad C_i = \begin{bmatrix} 0 \\ 0 \\ 1 \end{bmatrix}.$$

Then the period loss function can be written

$$(8) \qquad L_t = Y_t' K Y_t,$$

where the 3×3 matrix K has the diagonal $(1, \lambda, \nu)$ and all its off-diagonal elements are equal to zero.

5.3.4   Linear Feedback Instrument Rules

We will consider the class of linear feedback instruments rules, that is, rules of the form

$$(9) \qquad\qquad i_t = fX_t,$$

where f is a 1×9 row vector. This class of rules includes the optimal instrument rule (see below).

For any given instrument rule of the form (9), the dynamics of the model follows

$$X_{t+1} = MX_t + v_{t+1},$$

$$Y_t = CX_t,$$

where the matrices M and C are given by

$$(10) \qquad\qquad M = A + Bf,$$

$$(11) \qquad\qquad C = C_X + C_i f.$$

For any given rule f that results in finite unconditional variances of the goal variables, the unconditional loss (5) fulfills[16]

$$(12) \qquad\qquad E[L_t] = E[Y_t'KY_t] = \text{trace}(K\Sigma_{YY}),$$

where Σ_{YY} is the unconditional covariance matrix of the goal variables (see the appendix).

5.3.5   The Optimal Instrument Rule

With equations (6) and (8), the problem is written in a form convenient for the standard stochastic linear regulator problem (cf. Chow 1970, Sargent 1987). Minimizing expression (3) in each quarter, subject to equation (6) and the current state of the economy, X_t, results in a linear feedback rule for the instrument of the form (9). In the limit when $\delta = 1$, the optimal rule converges to the one minimizing expression (5). The expression for the optimal instrument rule is given in the appendix.[17]

5.3.6   Inflation Forecasts

Given the lags in the monetary transmission mechanism, inflation-targeting central banks focus on inflation forecasts. Indeed, several of these banks have started to publish inflation reports that are completely devoted to describing the recent history and future prospects for inflation. The actual inflation forecasts that have been reported have fallen into two broad categories depending

---

16. The trace of a matrix A, trace(A), is the sum of the diagonal elements of A.

17. Since there are no forward-looking variables, we need not distinguish between the commitment and discretion solutions because they are the same.

on how monetary policy is projected forward: constant-interest-rate inflation forecasts and rule-consistent inflation forecasts.

Constant-Interest-Rate Inflation Forecasts

Inflation-targeting central banks often refer to, and report, inflation forecasts conditional on a given constant interest rate. We will call such forecasts "constant-interest-rate inflation forecasts." Such inflation forecasts are frequently used in the following way. If a constant-interest-rate inflation forecast for the current interest rate is above (below) target for a given horizon, monetary policy has to be tightened (eased) and the interest rate increased (decreased). If the inflation forecast is on target, the current interest rate setting is deemed appropriate (see, e.g., Mayes and Riches 1996; Svensson 1997a). Such forecasts, based on a fixed nominal rate, may seem overly simplistic,[18] but they have been widely used at central banks, perhaps most notably at the Bank of England, where (before operational independence in 1997) the Bank produced such forecasts because it could not presuppose policy changes by the government.[19]

In an attempt to represent this, it is convenient to define the "T-quarter-ahead constant-interest-rate inflation forecast." By this we mean a forecast of four-quarter inflation $T \geq 2$ quarters ahead, conditional on a given constant current and future interest rate (and on the current state variables X_t). Denote this conditional forecast by $\bar{\pi}_{t+T|t}(i)$, for the given constant current and future interest rate i. It is given by

(13) $$\bar{\pi}_{t+T|t}(i) \equiv e_{1:4}\tilde{M}^{T-1}(AX_t + Bi),$$

where $\tilde{M}$ is a 9×9 matrix given by

(14) $$\tilde{M} = A + Be_7$$

(we note that $e_7 X_{t+1} = i_t$).

Consider also the T-quarter-ahead constant-interest-rate inflation forecast in quarter t, when the interest rate is held constant at a level equal to that of the previous quarter, i_{t-1}. This conditional inflation forecast, the "T-quarter-ahead unchanged-interest-rate inflation forecast," $\bar{\pi}_{t+T|t}(i_{t-1})$, fulfills

$$\bar{\pi}_{t+T|t}(i_{t-1}) \equiv e_{1:4}\tilde{M}^{T-1}(AX_t + Bi_{t-1})$$
(15) $$= e_{1:4}\tilde{M}^{T-1}(AX_t + Be_7 X_t)$$
$$= e_{1:4}\tilde{M}^T X_t.$$

18. Indeed, given a long enough forecast horizon, the forecasted inflation path will normally be explosive.

19. However, even after operational independence, the Bank's forecasts have assumed unchanged short-term interest rates (see Britton, Fisher, and Whitley 1998). Similarly, it is our

Rule-Consistent Inflation Forecasts

There are of course many other assumptions that one could make about monetary policy in order to produce inflation forecasts. For example, one could condition on a constant *real* interest rate, or one could set the rate in each future period according to a given reaction function for policy. Recently, the Reserve Bank of New Zealand (1997) has moved beyond constant-interest-rate forecasts and started to report official inflation forecasts conditional on a particular reaction function. (This results in inflation forecasts always returning to the target.) Below, we shall also consider a rule that employs such forecasts.

5.3.7 Simple Instrument Rules

By a simple instrument rule we mean an instrument rule of the form (9), where the vector f is restricted in some way. We will distinguish no fewer than nine types of simple instrument rules by characterizing them in terms of three forms and three arguments.[20]

Three Forms

We consider three forms: smoothing, level, and difference; the latter two are special cases of the first form. The *smoothing* form, denoted S, is given by

$$i_t = hi_{t-1} + gX_t,$$

(16)

$$f = he_7 + g,$$

where h is a coefficient and g is a 1×9 row vector of response coefficients. When the coefficient h fulfills $0 < h \leq 1$, this form of instrument rule is characterized by "partial adjustment," or "smoothing," of the instrument. The larger the coefficient h, the more smoothing (the more partial the adjustment).

Recall that i_t is the deviation from the average nominal interest rate, which in our model equals the sum of the inflation target (the average inflation rate) and the natural real interest rate (the average real interest rate). If we, temporarily in this paragraph, let all variables denote absolute levels and denote the average level of variable x_t by x^0, we can write form (16) as

$$i_t = hi_{t-1} + (1 - h)i^0 + g(X_t - X^0)$$

(17)

$$= hi_{t-1} + (1 - h)(r^0 + \pi^*) + g(X_t - X^0)$$

$$= hi_{t-1} + (1 - h)(r^0 + \bar{\pi}_t) + \tilde{g}(X_t - X^0),$$

---

impression that internal staff forecasts at the Federal Reserve Board are often conditioned on a constant federal funds path. Thus constant-interest-rate forecasts may have some general advantages—perhaps, in ease of communication, as noted by Rudebusch (1995).

20. The theory and practice of simple policy rules is examined in Currie and Levine (1984).

where $\tilde{g} \equiv g - (1 - h)e_{1:4}$ and we have used $i^0 = r^0 + \pi^*$. Thus form (16) is equivalent to (17), which is a frequent way of writing instrument rules.[21]

The *level* form, denoted L, is the special case of the autoregressive form when $h = 0$, whereas the *difference* form, denoted D, is the special case when $h = 1$.[22]

Three Arguments (Restrictions on g)

We consider three combinations of arguments (variables that the instrument responds to). That is, we consider three different restrictions on the vector g of response coefficients. First, we consider a response to $\overline{\pi}_t$ and y_t, denoted $(\overline{\pi}_t, y_t)$, which implies[23]

$$gX_t = g_\pi \overline{\pi}_t + g_y y_t,$$

$$g = g_\pi e_{1:4} + g_y e_5,$$

where g_π and g_y are the two response coefficients. Second, we consider a response to the T-quarter-ahead unchanged-interest-rate inflation forecast only, denoted $\overline{\pi}_{t+T|t}(i_{t-1})$. This implies

$$gX_t = g_\pi \overline{\pi}_{t+T|t}(i_{t-1}),$$

$$g = g_\pi e_{1:4} \tilde{M}^T,$$

where we have used equation (15). Finally, we consider a response to both the T-quarter-ahead unchanged-interest-rate inflation forecast and the output gap, denoted $(\overline{\pi}_{t+T|t}(i_{t-1}), y_t)$, which implies

$$gX_t = g_\pi \overline{\pi}_{t+T|t}(i_{t-1}) + g_y y_t,$$

$$g = g_\pi e_{1:4} \tilde{M}^T + g_y e_5.$$

A particular instrument rule is denoted Ta, with the type T = S, L, or D, and the argument $a = (\overline{\pi}_t, y_t)$, $\overline{\pi}_{t+T|t}(i_{t-1})$, or $(\overline{\pi}_{t+T|t}(i_{t-1}), y_t)$. By a *Taylor-type rule* we mean a simple instrument rule of the form L$(\overline{\pi}_t, y_t)$,

$$i_t = g_\pi \overline{\pi}_t + g_y y_t.$$

21. Clarida, Galí, and Gertler (1997, 1998) model interest rate smoothing as

$$i_t = hi_{t-1} + (1 - h)(\overline{\pi}_t + \tilde{g}X_t),$$

which is obviously consistent with eq. (17) (as long as $h \neq 1$) since we can identify $(1 - h)\tilde{g}$ above with $\tilde{g}$ in eq. (17).

22. Note that since $i_{t-1} = X_{t-1} = e_7 X_t$, we can always write $i_t = fX_t$ as $i_t = i_{t-1} + (f - e_7)X_t$. Thus, unless g_7 is restricted to fulfill $g_7 = 0$, the difference form does not imply any restriction.

23. Note that responding to $\overline{\pi}_t$ means responding to the discrepancy between inflation and the inflation target, since $\overline{\pi}_t$ is the deviation from the mean, and the mean coincides with the inflation target, since there is no inflation bias in our model.

The classic *Taylor rule* (Taylor 1993) is a Taylor-type rule with $g_\pi = 1.5$ and $g_y = 0.5$.[24]

We do not include the case of a response to only $\overline{\pi}_t$, $gX_t = g_\pi \overline{\pi}_t$, since it consistently performed very badly.

An Information Lag

McCallum has in several papers, for instance McCallum (1997), argued that it is more realistic from an information point of view to restrict the instrument in quarter t to depend on the state variables in quarter $t - 1$,

$$i_t = fX_{t-1}.$$

On the other hand, it can be argued that the central bank has much more information about the current state in the economy than captured by the few state variables in the model. Then, assuming that the state variables in quarter t are known in quarter t is an implicit way of acknowledging this extra information.[25] This is the main reason why our baseline case has the instrument depending on the state variables in the same quarter.

For comparability with results of other authors, we nevertheless would like to be able to restrict the instrument to depend on state variables one quarter earlier. Thus we consider the case when there is response to $\overline{\pi}_{t-1}$ and y_{t-1}, denoted $(\overline{\pi}_{t-1}, y_{t-1})$, with and without interest rate smoothing,

$$(18) \qquad i_t = hi_{t-1} + g_\pi \overline{\pi}_{t-1} + g_y y_{t-1}.$$

This requires some technical modifications in our state-space setup, which are detailed in the appendix.

An Instrument Rule with Response to a Rule-Consistent Inflation Forecast

Consider the following rule:

$$(19) \qquad i_t = hi_{t-1} + \phi \pi_{t+T|t},$$

where $\phi > 0$ and $\pi_{t+T|t}$ ($T \geq 2$) is the rational expectation of π_{t+T}, conditional on X_t, equation (6), and equation (19). Thus $\pi_{t+T|t}$ is a rule-consistent inflation forecast as described above, although in this case the rule being conditioned on includes the forecast. This rule, where the instrument responds to a rule-consistent inflation forecast, is not an explicit instrument rule because it does not express the instrument as an explicit function of current information (or, in the context of our model, of predetermined variables). It is not a targeting rule,

24. See McCallum (1988), Bryant, Hooper, and Mann (1993), Judd and Motley (1992), and Henderson and McKibbin (1993) for other examples of explicit instrument rules.

25. In fact, obtaining a good description of the real-time information set of policymakers is a complicated assignment (see Rudebusch 1998a). E.g., simply lagging variables ignores data revisions (see Diebold and Rudebusch 1991).

in the sense we have used the term, since it is not explicitly related to some loss function. Nor does it express an intermediate target level as a function of current information. The rule is an *equilibrium condition* because the right-hand side of equation (19) is endogenous and depends on the rule itself. Hence, it is an *implicit* instrument rule. The self-referential, rational expectations nature of the rule complicates its analytical derivation in terms of an explicit instrument rule.[26] However, the rule remains a simple instrument rule similar in form to the $S(\overline{\pi}_{t+T|t}(i_{t-1}))$ rule described above, only the instrument responds to an endogenous variable rather than a predetermined one. We consequently denote the rule in equation (19) by $S(\pi_{t+T|t})$.

Like the $S(\overline{\pi}_{t+T|t}(i_{t-1}))$ rule, the $S(\pi_{t+T|t})$ rule has considerable intuitive appeal, inasmuch as it implies that if new information makes the inflation forecast at the horizon T increase, the interest rate should be increased, and vice versa. Even better, however, the $S(\pi_{t+T|t})$ rule uses an inflation forecast that can be conditional on a nonconstant interest rate path. The $S(\pi_{t+T|t})$ rule is similar to the reaction function used in the Bank of Canada's Quarterly Projection Model (see, e.g., Colletti et al. 1996) and the Reserve Bank of New Zealand's Forecasting and Policy System (see Black et al. 1997), and identical to the rule considered by Batini and Haldane in chapter 4 of this volume.[27] Indeed, this rule appears to be a frequent reference rule among inflation-targeting central banks. It is (when $h = 1$) what Haldane (1997) calls "the generic form of the feedback rule under an inflation target," which "encapsulates quite neatly the operational practice of most inflation targeters."

Nevertheless, the $S(\pi_{t+T|t})$ rule is not derived as a first-order condition of some loss function corresponding to inflation targeting.[28] The question then arises: How efficient is this rule in achieving an inflation target? This question is particularly relevant because of its use in the inflation projections by two prominent inflation-targeting central banks, and because of its intuitive appeal to many as representing generic inflation targeting. Consequently, we examine the performance of this rule within the framework of our model.

---

26. In equilibrium, the rational expectations inflation forecast becomes an endogenous linear function of the state variables (where the coefficients depend on the parameters T, ϕ, and h), which by eq. (19) results in eq. (9). For $T = 2$, the explicit instrument rule is easy to derive. For $T \geq 3$, the derivation is more complex. The details are provided in the appendix.

27. It is also used in Black, Macklem, and Rose (1997).

28. Because the rule is not derived as a first-order condition, its precise form is not obvious. As alternatives to eq. (19) one can consider

$$i_t = hi_{t-1} + (1 - h)\overline{\pi}_t + \phi\pi_{t+T|t},$$

or even

$$i_t = hi_{t-1} + g_\pi \overline{\pi}_t + \phi\pi_{t+T|t},$$

where g_π is unrestricted.

Optimal Simple Instrument Rules

In order to find the optimal simple instrument rule for a given type of rule and with a given combination of arguments, we optimize equation (5) over g, h, and ϕ taking the corresponding restrictions into account.

5.3.8   Targeting Rules

The Optimal Targeting Rule

Above we have noted the existence of an optimal instrument rule. Of course, the corresponding minimization problem defines an optimal targeting rule as well. Here, however, we show that the first-order condition for an optimum can be interpreted as an optimal intermediate targeting rule.

Consider the first-order condition for minimizing expressions (3) and (8) subject to (6) and (7),

$$
\begin{aligned}
0 &= \sum_{\tau=0}^{\infty} \frac{\partial Y'_{t+\tau|t}}{\partial i_t} KY_{t+\tau|t} \\
&= C'_i KY_t + \sum_{\tau=1}^{\infty} B'(A^{\tau-1})'C'_X KY_{t+\tau|t},
\end{aligned}
$$

(20)

where we have used that

$$
\frac{\partial Y_t}{\partial i_t} = C_i, \quad \frac{\partial Y_{t+\tau|t}}{\partial i_t} = C_X \frac{\partial X_{t+\tau|t}}{\partial i_t} = C_X A^{\tau-1} B, \quad \tau = 1, 2, \ldots,
$$

and let the discount factor fulfill $\delta = 1$. This is a linear relation between the current and conditionally forecasted future goal variables, $Y_{t+\tau|t}$, $\tau = 0, 1, 2, \ldots$, conditional on the current instrument and the future policy. The task of the monetary authority can be described as setting an instrument in the current quarter so as to achieve the relation (20). This relation can then be interpreted as an intermediate target path for the forecast of future goal variables. That is, the forecasts of future goal variables are considered intermediate target variables. Then the task of the monetary authority is to choose, conditional on the current state variable X_t, a current instrument i_t and a plan $i_{t+\tau|t}$ ($\tau = 1, 2, \ldots$) for future instruments, such that the resulting conditional forecasts of future goal variables $Y_{t+\tau|t}$ fulfill the intermediate target (20), where

$$
Y_t = C_X X_t + C_i i_t,
$$

$$
\begin{aligned}
Y_{t+\tau|t} &= C_X X_{t+\tau|t} + C_i i_{t+\tau|t} \\
&= C_X A^{\tau} X_t + \sum_{j=0}^{\tau-1} C_X A^{\tau-1-j} B i_{t+j|t} + C_i i_{t+\tau|t},
\end{aligned}
$$

where $\tau = 1, 2, \ldots$ and we have used that

$$X_{t+\tau+1|t} = AX_{t+\tau|t} + Bi_{t+\tau|t}$$

$$= A^{\tau+1}X_t + \sum_{j=0}^{\tau} A^{\tau-j}Bi_{t+j|t}.$$

We note that the $Y_{t+\tau|t}$ ($\tau = 0, 1, 2, \ldots$) that fulfill equation (20) can be seen as impulse responses of the goal variables for the optimal solution, for impulses that put the economy at its initial state. We can now imagine a governor or a board of governors pondering over a set of alternative current and future instrument settings and alternative forecasts for the goal variables that have been provided for consideration by the central bank staff, in order to decide on the current instrument setting. When the governor or board of governors ends up selecting one instrument path and corresponding goal variable forecasts that they believe are best, their behavior (if rational) can be seen as implicitly selecting forecasts that fulfill equation (20) for some implicit weight matrix K in their loss function.

In general, equation (20) involves a relation between all the goal variables. The case when inflation and the output gap are the only goal variables is examined in Svensson (1997a, forthcoming b). Since, by the Phillips curve (1), the forecast of output can be written as a linear function of the forecast of inflation, this linear function can then be substituted for the output forecast in equation (20), which results in a relation for the forecast of future inflation only. That relation can be interpreted as an intermediate target for the inflation forecast. In the special case examined in Svensson (1997a, forthcoming b), these relations for the inflation forecast are both simple and optimal. In the general case these relations need not be optimal. Here we will examine them as potential simple targeting rules, called inflation-forecast-targeting rules.

Simple Targeting Rules

Consider targeting rules for the T-quarter-ahead constant-interest-rate inflation forecast. These rules imply implicit instrument rules that are normally not "simple," since they normally depend on most state variables. We will consider four kinds of simple targeting rules, namely, strict and flexible inflation-forecast targeting, with and without smoothing.

In Svensson (1997a), the following first-order condition for the inflation forecast is derived, for the case of flexible inflation targeting with some nonnegative weight on output stabilization, $\lambda \geq 0$, but zero weight on interest rate smoothing, $\nu = 0$,

$$\pi_{t+2|t}(i_t) - \pi^* = c(\lambda)(\pi_{t+1|t} - \pi^*).$$

In the model in Svensson (1997a), $\pi_{t+1|t}$ is predetermined, $\pi_{t+2|t}(i_t)$ is the inflation forecast for the earliest horizon that can be affected, and $c(\lambda)$ is an increasing function of λ, fulfilling $0 \leq c(\lambda) < 1$, $c(0) = 0$, and $c(\lambda) \to 1$ for $\lambda \to \infty$.

In the present model, we can consider a generalization of this framework,

(21) $\overline{\pi}_{t+T|t}(i_t) \; = \; c\,\overline{\pi}_{t+1|t}\,,$

where c and T fulfill $0 \leq c < 1$ and $T \geq 2$. This we refer to as *flexible T-quarter-ahead inflation-forecast targeting*, denoted FIFT(T).

The expression (21) denotes a targeting rule, where the corresponding instrument rule is *implicit*. In order to solve for the instrument rule, we use equation (13) to write equation (21) as

$$e_{1:4}\tilde{M}^{T-1}(AX_t + Bi_t) \; = \; ce_{1:4}AX_t\,.$$

Then the implicit instrument rule can be written

$$i_t \; = \; g(c, T)X_t\,,$$

where the row vector $g(c, T)$ is a function of c and T given by

(22) $g(c, T) \equiv \dfrac{e_{1:4}(cI - \tilde{M}^{T-1})A}{e_{1:4}\tilde{M}^{T-1}B}\,,$

where I is the 9×9 identity matrix (note that $e_{1:4}\tilde{M}^{T-1}B$ is a scalar and $e_{1:4}(cI - \tilde{M}^{T-1})A$ is a 1×9 row vector).

Strict T-quarter-ahead inflation-forecast targeting, denoted SIFT(T), is the special case of equation (21) when $c = 0$,

(23) $\overline{\pi}_{t+T|t}(i_t) \; = \; 0\,.$

The corresponding implicit instrument rule is

(24) $i_t \; = \; g(0, T)X_t\,,$

where

(25) $g(0, T) \equiv -\dfrac{e_{1:4}\tilde{M}^{T-1}A}{e_{1:4}\tilde{M}^{T-1}B}$

Note that the numerator in equation (25) equals the constant-interest-rate inflation forecast corresponding to a zero interest rate, $\overline{\pi}_{t+T|t}(0)$. The denominator, $e_{1:4}\tilde{M}^{T-1}B$, is the constant-interest-rate policy multiplier for the four-quarter inflation T quarters ahead, since by equation (13)

(26) $\dfrac{\partial\,\overline{\pi}_{t+T|t}(i)}{\partial i} \; = \; e_{1:4}\tilde{M}^{T-1}B\,.$

Hence, very intuitively the instrument rule corresponding to strict inflation-forecast targeting can be written as

$$i_t \; = \; -\dfrac{\overline{\pi}_{t+T|t}(0)}{\partial\,\overline{\pi}_{t+T|t}(i)/\partial i_t}\,,$$

the negative of the *zero-interest-rate* inflation forecast divided by the constant-interest-rate policy multiplier.

We can equivalently write this instrument rule in terms of *changes* in the interest rate. By equation (13) we have

$$\overline{\pi}_{t+T|t}(i_t) - \overline{\pi}_{t+T|t}(i_{t-1}) = e_{1:4} \tilde{M}^{T-1} B(i_t - i_{t-1}).$$

By equation (23) we can write

$$i_t - i_{t-1} = -\frac{\overline{\pi}_{t+T|t}(i_{t-1})}{e_{1:4} \tilde{M}^{T-1} B} = -\frac{e_{1:4} \tilde{M}^{T} X_t}{e_{1:4} \tilde{M}^{T-1} B} = (f(0, T) - e_7) X_t.$$

Very intuitively, the interest rate adjustment equals the negative of the *unchanged-interest-rate* inflation forecast for the unchanged interest rate divided by the constant-interest-rate policy multiplier.

Note that strict inflation-forecast targeting implies that the inflation forecast conditional on the future instrument rule (24), rather than conditional on a constant interest rate, deviates from zero,

$$E_t \overline{\pi}_{t+T} \neq 0,$$

and in practice reaches zero later than T quarters ahead. This is apparent from the impulse responses for $\overline{\pi}_{t+T|t}$ under strict inflation-forecast targeting.

Note that strict T_1-quarter inflation-forecast targeting may be approximately equal to flexible T_2-quarter flexible inflation-forecast targeting, when the horizon for strict inflation targeting exceeds that of flexible inflation targeting, $T_1 > T_2$.

The above targeting rules can be considered under *smoothing* (partial adjustment) of the interest rate,

$$i_t = h i_{t-1} + (1 - h) g(c, T) X_t,$$

$$f = h e_7 + (1 - h) g(c, T),$$

where it may be reasonable to restrict the smoothing coefficient h to fulfill $0 \leq h < 1$. Note that under smoothing, h is not generally the "net" coefficient on i_{t-1}, since $g_7(c, T)$ is generally not zero. These targeting rules under smoothing are denoted FIFTS(T) and SIFTS(T), respectively.

The *optimal* inflation-forecast-targeting rules are found by minimizing the loss function (5) over the parameters c, h, and T, taking into account the restrictions on these and that $T \geq 2$ is an integer. For instance, under strict inflation targeting without smoothing, we have $c = h = 0$, and the only free parameter is T.

Table 5.3 **Results on Volatility and Loss with Various Rules ($\lambda = 1$, $\nu = 0.5$)**

Rule	Std[$\bar{\pi}_t$]	Std[y_t]	Std[$i_t - i_{t-1}$]	Loss	Rank
Optimal	2.15	2.24	1.68	11.08	1
L($\bar{\pi}_t, y_t$)					
$\quad g_\pi = 2.72, g_y = 1.57$	2.18	2.24	1.74	11.27	5
L($\bar{\pi}_{t+Tt}(i_{t-1})$)					
$\quad T = 8; g_\pi = 2.55$	2.42	2.27	2.07	13.15	18
L($\bar{\pi}_{t+Tt}(i_{t-1}), y_t$)					
$\quad T = 8; g_\pi = 2.53, g_y = 0.29$	2.44	2.15	2.20	13.01	17
S($\bar{\pi}_t, y_t$)					
$\quad g_\pi = 2.37, g_y = 1.44, h = 0.14$	2.18	2.25	1.68	11.23	4
S($\bar{\pi}_{t+Tt}(i_{t-1})$)					
$\quad T = 8; g_\pi = 1.89, h = 0.46$	2.15	2.47	1.53	11.89	12
S($\bar{\pi}_{t+Tt}(i_{t-1}), y_t$)					
$\quad T = 8; g_\pi = 1.54, g_y = 0.45, h = 0.60$	2.15	2.25	1.68	11.09	2
S(π_{t+Tt})					
$\quad T = 8; \phi = 2.62, h = 0.32$	2.15	2.45	1.53	11.77	11
$\quad T = 12; \phi = 3.65, h = 0.38$	2.13	2.41	1.55	11.58	10
$\quad T = 16; \phi = 5.52, h = 0.41$	2.13	2.40	1.57	11.51	7
SIFT(T)					
$\quad T = 8$	1.40	2.84	7.44	37.65	22
$\quad T = 12$	1.81	2.44	3.15	14.17	19
$\quad T = 16$	2.21	2.27	2.03	12.05	13
FIFT(T)					
$\quad T = 8; c = 0.72$	2.24	1.82	5.31	22.41	21
$\quad T = 12; c = 0.39$	2.17	2.11	2.72	12.86	16
$\quad T = 16; c = 0.01$	2.22	2.26	2.02	12.05	13
SIFTS(T)					
$\quad T = 8; h = 0.59$	1.51	3.39	3.88	21.29	20
$\quad T = 12; h = 0.45$	1.87	2.60	1.94	12.16	15
$\quad T = 16; h = 0.31$	2.24	2.34	1.47	11.57	8
FIFTS(T)					
$\quad T = 8; c = 0.66, h = 0.71$	2.15	2.26	1.86	11.42	6
$\quad T = 12; c = 0.35, h = 0.47$	2.18	2.28	1.59	11.17	3
$\quad T = 16; c = 0.00, h = 0.31$	2.24	2.34	1.47	11.57	8

5.4   Results

5.4.1   Optimized Rules

In this subsection, we consider the performance of various rules for several illustrative cases of different preferences over goal variables. The rules we consider have been optimized in terms of their parameter settings for the given preferences and the given form of the rule assumed.

Tables 5.3 through 5.7 provide results for five different sets of preferences over goals. In each table, the volatility of the goal variables (measured as the unconditional standard deviations), the minimized loss, and the relative ranking in terms of loss are shown for 22 different rules. Loss is calculated under

Table 5.4　　　　　Results on Volatility and Loss with Various Rules ($\lambda = 0.2$, $\nu = 0.5$)

Rule	Std[$\bar{\pi}_t$]	Std[y_t]	Std[$i_t - i_{t-1}$]	Loss	Rank
Optimal	1.97	2.64	1.55	6.47	1
$L(\bar{\pi}_t, y_t)$					
$\quad g_\pi = 3.17, g_y = 1.22$	2.00	2.61	1.65	6.71	10
$L(\bar{\pi}_{t+Tt}(i_{t-1}))$					
$\quad T = 8; g_\pi = 2.65$	2.37	2.28	2.17	9.00	17
$L(\bar{\pi}_{t+Tt}(i_{t-1}), y_t)$					
$\quad T = 8; g_\pi = 2.69, g_y = -0.25$	2.36	2.41	2.10	8.92	16
$S(\bar{\pi}_t, y_t)$					
$\quad g_\pi = 2.34, g_y = 1.03, h = 0.30$	2.00	2.64	1.56	6.60	9
$S(\bar{\pi}_{t+Tt}(i_{t-1}))$					
$\quad T = 8; g_\pi = 1.63, h = 0.69$	1.97	2.75	1.53	6.58	8
$S(\bar{\pi}_{t+Tt}(i_{t-1}), y_t)$					
$\quad T = 8; g_\pi = 1.42, g_y = 0.16, h = 0.74$	1.97	2.64	1.55	6.48	2
$S(\pi_{t+Tt})$					
$\quad T = 8; \phi = 2.35, h = 0.62$	1.97	2.73	1.53	6.55	7
$\quad T = 12; \phi = 3.86, h = 0.71$	1.97	2.69	1.54	6.50	5
$\quad T = 16; \phi = 8.33, h = 0.47$	1.97	2.68	1.54	6.49	4
SIFT(T)					
$\quad T = 8$	1.40	2.84	7.44	31.21	22
$\quad T = 12$	1.81	2.44	3.15	9.42	19
$\quad T = 16$	2.21	2.27	2.03	7.95	14
FIFT(T)					
$\quad T = 8; c = 0.69$	2.13	1.87	5.38	19.68	21
$\quad T = 12; c = 0.24$	1.99	2.24	2.88	9.10	18
$\quad T = 16; c = 0.00$	2.21	2.27	2.03	7.95	14
SIFTS(T)					
$\quad T = 8; h = 0.71$	1.62	3.84	3.34	11.16	20
$\quad T = 12; h = 0.60$	1.93	2.74	1.60	6.51	6
$\quad T = 16; h = 0.45$	2.28	2.39	1.25	7.11	12
FIFTS(T)					
$\quad T = 8; c = 0.53, h = 0.79$	1.98	2.67	1.67	6.74	11
$\quad T = 12; c = 0.08, h = 0.60$	1.98	2.65	1.52	6.48	2
$\quad T = 16; c = 0.00, h = 0.45$	2.28	2.39	1.25	7.11	12

the assumption that output and inflation variability are equally distasteful ($\lambda = 1$) in table 5.3 and that output variability is much less costly ($\lambda = 0.2$) in table 5.4 and much more costly ($\lambda = 5$) in table 5.5. Variability of nominal interest rate changes are also costly in these three tables ($\nu = 0.5$).[29] Variation in the costs of variability of interest rate changes are considered in tables 5.6 ($\nu = 0.1$) and 5.7 ($\nu = 1.0$) (both assuming $\lambda = 1$). The preferences in table 5.3 imply a concern not only about inflation stabilization but also about output stabilization and interest rate smoothing, which we believe is realistic for many central banks, also inflation-targeting ones. Comparison with tables 5.4

29. Such costs are suggested, in part, by the concern central banks display for financial market fragility (see, e.g., Rudebusch 1995).

Table 5.5   **Results on Volatility and Loss with Various Rules ($\lambda = 5$, $\nu = 0.5$)**

Rule	Std[$\bar{\pi}_t$]	Std[y_t]	Std[$i_t - i_{t-1}$]	Loss	Rank
Optimal	2.65	1.86	2.36	26.99	1
$L(\bar{\pi}_t, y_t)$					
$\quad g_\pi = 2.15$, $g_y = 2.17$	2.69	1.89	2.16	27.46	4
$L(\bar{\pi}_{t+T|t}(i_{t-1}))$					
$\quad T = 8$; $g_\pi = 2.13$	2.69	2.22	1.70	33.32	17
$L(\bar{\pi}_{t+T|t}(i_{t-1}), y_t)$					
$\quad T = 8$; $g_\pi = 2.24$, $g_y = 1.40$	2.80	1.83	2.69	28.17	7
$S(\bar{\pi}_t, y_t)$					
$\quad g_\pi = 1.26$, $g_y = 2.35$, $h = -0.11$	2.68	1.88	2.27	27.39	3
$S(\bar{\pi}_{t+T|t}(i_{t-1}))$					
$\quad T = 8$; $g_\pi = 2.03$, $h = 0.06$	2.67	2.23	1.59	33.29	16
$S(\bar{\pi}_{t+T|t}(i_{t-1}), y_t)$					
$\quad T = 8$; $g_\pi = 1.78$, $g_y = 1.27$, $h = 0.31$	2.65	1.87	2.31	27.15	2
$S(\bar{\pi}_{t+T|t})$					
$\quad T = 8$; $\phi = 2.62$, $h = -0.15$	2.65	2.21	1.62	32.81	15
$\quad T = 12$; $\phi = 3.16$, $h = -0.11$	2.61	2.19	1.65	32.06	12
$\quad T = 16$; $\phi = 3.91$, $h = -0.09$	2.59	2.18	1.67	31.78	11
SIFT(T)					
$\quad T = 8$	1.40	2.84	7.44	69.88	22
$\quad T = 12$	1.81	2.44	3.15	37.89	20
$\quad T = 16$	2.21	2.27	2.03	32.59	13
FIFT(T)					
$\quad T = 8$; $c = 0.81$	2.64	1.70	5.15	34.71	18
$\quad T = 12$; $c = 0.64$	2.70	1.91	2.49	28.61	8
$\quad T = 16$; $c = 0.44$	2.79	2.02	1.78	29.86	10
SIFTS(T)					
$\quad T = 8$; $h = 0.35$	1.44	3.04	5.07	61.07	21
$\quad T = 12$; $h = 0.15$	1.82	2.47	2.69	37.50	19
$\quad T = 16$; $h = 0.02$	2.21	2.27	1.99	32.59	13
FIFTS(T)					
$\quad T = 8$; $c = 0.80$, $h = 0.52$	2.63	1.87	2.52	27.48	5
$\quad T = 12$; $c = 0.64$, $h = 0.22$	2.71	1.95	1.94	28.15	6
$\quad T = 16$; $c = 0.44$, $h = 0.03$	2.79	2.03	1.71	29.85	9

through 5.7 allows us to note the consequences of relatively more or less emphasis on output stabilization and interest rate smoothing.

The first rule at the top of each table is the unrestricted optimal control rule—the obvious benchmark. The optimal rule in table 5.3 produces volatility results not too far from our historical sample results, which are Std[$\bar{\pi}_t$] = 2.33, Std[y_t] = 2.80, and Std[$i_t - i_{t-1}$] = 1.09. The next four rows consider level rules with current inflation and output, $L(\bar{\pi}_t, y_t)$, future inflation $L(\bar{\pi}_{t+8|t}(i_{t-1}))$, and future inflation and current output $L(\bar{\pi}_{t+8|t}(i_{t-1}), y_t)$ as arguments (where the forecasts are the 8-quarter-ahead "unchanged-interest-rate" four-quarter inflation forecast). The next three rows consider smoothing instrument rules with the same arguments. The following three rows are for the interest-

Table 5.6   Results on Volatility and Loss with Various Rules ($\lambda = 1, \nu = 0.1$)

Rule	Std$[\overline{\pi}_t]$	Std$[y_t]$	Std$[i_t - i_{t-1}]$	Loss	Rank
Optimal	1.96	2.12	3.02	9.25	1
$L(\overline{\pi}_t, y_t)$					
$\quad g_\pi = 3.43, g_y = 2.50$	2.01	2.18	2.71	9.51	5
$L(\overline{\pi}_{t+T|t}(i_{t-1}))$					
$\quad T = 8; g_\pi = 3.46$	2.11	2.35	2.99	10.86	20
$L(\overline{\pi}_{t+T|t}(i_{t-1}), y_t)$					
$\quad T = 8; g_\pi = 3.41, g_y = 1.00$	2.18	2.05	3.53	10.18	11
$S(\overline{\pi}_t, y_t)$					
$\quad g_\pi = 2.80, g_y = 2.80, h = -0.16$	2.00	2.15	2.90	9.46	4
$S(\overline{\pi}_{t+T|t}(i_{t-1}))$					
$\quad T = 8; g_\pi = 3.15, h = 0.31$	1.94	2.47	2.47	10.51	18
$S(\overline{\pi}_{t+T|t}(i_{t-1}), y_t)$					
$\quad T = 8; g_\pi = 2.79, g_y = 1.06, h = 0.47$	1.96	2.14	2.98	9.29	2
$S(\overline{\pi}_{t+T|t})$					
$\quad T = 8; \phi = 5.01, h = -0.01$	1.94	2.45	2.49	10.37	13
$\quad T = 12; \phi = 7.99, h = 0.06$	1.92	2.41	2.55	10.13	9
$\quad T = 16; \phi = 13.66, h = 0.09$	1.91	2.39	2.58	10.04	8
$SIFT(T)$					
$\quad T = 8$	1.40	2.84	7.44	15.54	22
$\quad T = 12$	1.81	2.44	3.15	10.19	12
$\quad T = 16$	2.21	2.27	2.03	10.41	14
$FIFT(T)$					
$\quad T = 8; c = 0.61$	1.95	1.97	5.54	10.75	19
$\quad T = 12; c = 0.27$	2.02	2.21	2.84	9.78	7
$\quad T = 16; c = 0.00$	2.21	2.27	2.03	10.41	14
$SIFTS(T)$					
$\quad T = 8; h = 0.34$	1.43	3.03	5.14	13.86	21
$\quad T = 12; h = 0.11$	1.82	2.46	2.80	10.15	10
$\quad T = 16; h = 0.06$	2.20	2.26	2.15	10.41	14
$FIFTS(T)$					
$\quad T = 8; c = 0.60, h = 0.45$	1.95	2.13	3.08	9.30	3
$\quad T = 12; c = 0.27, h = 0.13$	2.03	2.23	2.46	9.73	6
$\quad T = 16; c = 0.00, h = -0.06$	2.20	2.26	2.15	10.41	14

rate-smoothing rule $S(\pi_{t+T|t})$, using the 8-, 12-, and 16-quarter-ahead rule-consistent quarterly inflation forecasts. The final twelve rows of each table present various implicit inflation-forecast-targeting rules at horizons of 8, 12, and 16 quarters. For all of the rules (except the optimal one), the relevant optimal rule parameters are given in the tables as well.

These tables suggest several conclusions: First, simple instrument rules appear to be able to perform quite well in our model. Consistently across the tables, the top-performing rule is the $S(\overline{\pi}_{t+8|t}(i_{t-1}), y_t)$ one, which reacts to the constant-interest-rate inflation forecast and the current output gap. Indeed, these simple "forward-looking" Taylor-type rules are always extremely close to matching the optimal rule in terms of overall loss. This result is somewhat

Table 5.7 **Results on Volatility and Loss with Various Rules ($\lambda = 1$, $\nu = 1$)**

Rule	Std[$\bar{\pi}_t$]	Std[y_t]	Std[$i_t - i_{t-1}$]	Loss	Rank
Optimal	2.27	2.29	1.33	12.17	1
L($\bar{\pi}_t, y_t$)					
$\quad g_\pi = 2.44$, $g_y = 1.23$	2.29	2.28	1.42	12.49	8
L($\bar{\pi}_{t+T|t}(i_{t-1})$)					
$\quad T = 8$; $g_\pi = 2.24$	2.60	2.24	1.79	14.99	17
L($\bar{\pi}_{t+T|t}(i_{t-1}), y_t$)					
$\quad T = 8$; $g_\pi = 2.23$, $g_y = 0.07$	2.61	2.20	1.82	14.97	16
S($\bar{\pi}_t, y_t$)					
$\quad g_\pi = 1.12$, $g_y = 1.04$, $h = 0.27$	2.29	2.30	1.34	12.33	4
S($\bar{\pi}_{t+T|t}(i_{t-1})$)					
$\quad T = 8$; $g_\pi = 1.47$, $h = 0.54$	2.27	2.47	1.24	12.82	12
S($\bar{\pi}_{t+T|t}(i_{t-1}), y_t$)					
$\quad T = 8$; $g_\pi = 1.18$, $g_y = 0.30$, $h = 0.65$	2.27	2.30	1.34	12.18	2
S($\bar{\pi}_{t+T|t}$)					
$\quad T = 8$; $\phi = 1.92$, $h = 0.45$	2.26	2.45	1.25	12.71	10
$\quad T = 12$; $\phi = 2.52$, $h = 0.50$	2.25	2.42	1.26	12.54	9
$\quad T = 16$; $\phi = 3.63$, $h = 0.53$	2.25	2.41	1.27	12.48	7
SIFT(T)					
$\quad T = 8$	1.40	2.84	7.44	65.29	22
$\quad T = 12$	1.81	2.44	3.15	19.13	19
$\quad T = 16$	2.21	2.27	2.03	14.11	15
FIFT(T)					
$\quad T = 8$; $c = 0.77$	2.45	1.75	5.21	36.19	21
$\quad T = 12$; $c = 0.47$	2.30	2.04	2.64	16.43	18
$\quad T = 16$; $c = 0.12$	2.32	2.20	1.95	14.02	14
SIFTS(T)					
$\quad T = 8$; $h = 0.66$	1.56	3.62	3.54	28.08	20
$\quad T = 12$; $h = 0.56$	1.91	2.70	1.68	13.77	13
$\quad T = 16$; $h = 0.45$	2.28	2.39	1.25	12.47	6
FIFTS(T)					
$\quad T = 8$; $c = 0.69$, $h = 0.79$	2.28	2.33	1.47	12.77	11
$\quad T = 12$; $c = 0.40$, $h = 0.59$	2.27	2.31	1.31	12.19	3
$\quad T = 16$; $c = 0.05$, $h = 0.45$	2.32	2.36	1.23	12.46	5

surprising given that the inflation forecast incorporated into these rules is simply a single 8-quarter-ahead inflation projection conditioned on an unchanged interest rate path.

Perhaps even more surprising, the current inflation and output Taylor-type rules—L($\bar{\pi}_t, y_t$) and S($\bar{\pi}_t, y_t$)—are nearly as good. Particularly, in table 5.3 (with $\lambda = 1$), these rules perform with output and inflation gap variances that are similar to those of the optimal rule. In order to understand the exceptional performance of these rules, it is instructive to compare the coefficients of these simple rules to those of the optimal rule. The optimal rule in table 5.3 (the optimal rules from the other tables have broadly similar parameterizations) has the form

$$i_t = .88\pi_t + .30\pi_{t-1} + .38\pi_{t-2} + .13\pi_{t-3} + 1.30y_t - .33y_{t-1} + .47i_{t-1}$$
$$- .06i_{t-2} - .03i_{t-3}.$$

The $L(\overline{\pi}_t, y_t)$ rule, for example, comes close to matching this by setting the first four parameters all equal to 0.68 (i.e., $g_\pi/4$), the y_t parameter equal to 1.57, and the other parameters equal to zero. Because the Taylor rule has received so much attention, it is also interesting to note that across all of the tables the parameters for our $L(\overline{\pi}_t, y_t)$ Taylor-type rules are fairly high. Instead of the original Taylor rule parameters of 1.5 on inflation (g_π) and 0.5 on output (g_y), our optimal $L(\overline{\pi}_t, y_t)$ rules sets these parameters above 2 and 1, respectively, in all of the tables.[30]

Second, in distinct contrast to the simple rules that include contemporaneous output gaps, the simple instrument rules that respond only to inflation forecasts do quite poorly—even when the weight on output stabilization is small, as in table 5.4. Of course, the optimal rule does include large coefficients on output, but presumably these reflect in large part the inflation-forecasting properties of output (especially for low λ). However, the simple instrument rules $L(\overline{\pi}_{t+8|t}(i_{t-1}))$ and $S(\overline{\pi}_{t+8|t}(i_{t-1}))$ that incorporate only future inflation do not fare very well. One might conjecture that these rules do poorly because of the mechanical nature of the forecasts used, which are simple projections assuming a constant nominal funds rate. However, the $S(\pi_{t+8|t})$ rule, which conditions the inflation forecast on a time-varying, rule-consistent interest rate path, does little better than the $S(\overline{\pi}_{t+8|t}(i_{t-1}))$ rule. More likely, the restricted fashion in which the inflation forecasts enter the rule—the instrument responds only to the deviation between the forecast and the inflation target—is to blame. This illustrates what was emphasized in subsection 5.3.7, namely, that these rules are not first-order conditions to our loss function. However, note that these rules do better for a smaller λ (table 5.4) and worse for a larger λ (table 5.5). This indicates that they are closer to a first-order condition of a loss function that only involves inflation stabilization and interest rate smoothing.[31]

Third, the inflation-forecast-targeting rules perform quite well given enough flexibility and interest-rate-smoothing ability. The FIFTS rule (flexible inflation-forecast targeting with smoothing) is essentially able to match the performance of the $S(\overline{\pi}_{t+8|t}(i_{t-1}), y_t)$ rule—and hence the optimal rule—in all cases except when there is a very high weight on output stabilization (table 5.5). Across all of the tables, the best inflation-forecast horizon to use with this rule is usually 12 quarters but sometimes 8 quarters. The IFT rules without

---

30. Ball (1997), in a simple, calibrated theoretical model similar to our own, argues that the optimal Taylor-type rule should have higher coefficients than the original Taylor rule. However, Ball also argues that in the optimal rule the output parameter should be larger than the inflation parameter, which is generally contrary to our results.

31. The length of the forecast horizon (T) in the $S(\pi_{t+T|t})$ rule makes only a modest contribution. I.e., the targeting horizon trade-off discussed in Haldane (1997) is relatively modest in our model with this rule.

interest rate smoothing are heavily penalized by the cost of large changes in the nominal interest rate instrument. Note that this is true even in table 5.6 when the cost of variability of interest rate change is quite low.

To augment the tables, figure 5.2 shows the trade-offs between inflation variability and output gap variability that result for varying the weight on output stabilization (λ) from 0 to 10 and assuming $\nu = 0.5$.[32] The trade-off resulting from the optimal rule is shown as a solid line. For increasing λ, the optimal rule corresponds to points further southeast on the curve. The dashed lines correspond to the smoothing rules $S(\overline{\pi}_t, y_t)$, $S(\overline{\pi}_{t+8|t}(i_{t-1}))$, $S(\overline{\pi}_{t+8|t})$, and $S(\overline{\pi}_{t+8|t}(i_{t-1}), y_t)$. Only the last of these is consistently close to the optimal rule. Note that $S(\overline{\pi}_{t+8|t})$ is close to the optimal rule for small λ.

Also, the triangle shows the sample (1960:1–96:2) standard deviations of inflation and the output gap. The circle shows the standard deviations that result from an estimated Taylor-type rule for the sample 1985:1–96:2 (with $g_\pi = 1.76$ and $g_y = 0.74$). The square shows the standard deviations that result from the Taylor rule (with $g_\pi = 1.5$ and $g_y = 0.5$).

The trade-offs from flexible inflation-forecast targeting with smoothing (FIFTS) at 8-, 12-, and 16-quarter horizons are shown as the dashed-dotted lines. For $T = 8$ quarters, the trade-off is consistently close to that of the optimal rule.

The trade-offs from flexible inflation-forecast targeting without smoothing (FIFT) are shown as the dotted lines. A shorter horizon T is associated more with less output variability than with less inflation variability (cf. table 5.3).

Finally, figures 5.3 and 5.4 give the dynamic impulse responses of the model under various optimal simple smoothing rules and targeting rules, respectively. All of the rules have broadly similar features, especially a large, quick interest rate rise in response to a positive inflation or output shock.[33] There are, however, some subtle but telling differences among the rules. In figure 5.3, the $S(\overline{\pi}_{t+8|t})$ rule, which considers only the inflation forecast, has the mildest response to an output shock, which allows inflation (through the Phillips curve) to get a bit more out of control and requires a slightly longer slowdown in output to compensate. In figure 5.4, the inflation-targeting rules without smoothing show large initial interest rate spikes in response to the shocks. With smoothing, however, the FIFTS rule is able to mimic the hump-shaped pattern of interest rates of the smoothing instrument rules.

5.4.2 Common Conference Rules

In this subsection, we consider the five rules that are to be common across all of the investigations at this conference. These rules and our results on volatility and loss (assuming $\lambda = 1$ and $\nu = 0.5$) are summarized in table 5.8. The

---

32. Although plots of such trade-offs are common in the literature, they sweep interest-rate-smoothing considerations under the rug, so we have some preference for the tabular results.

33. Note the great contrast between figs. 5.3 and 5.4 and the left two columns of fig. 5.1. Again, the poor results in fig. 5.1 can be traced to the misspecification of the VAR interest rate equation.

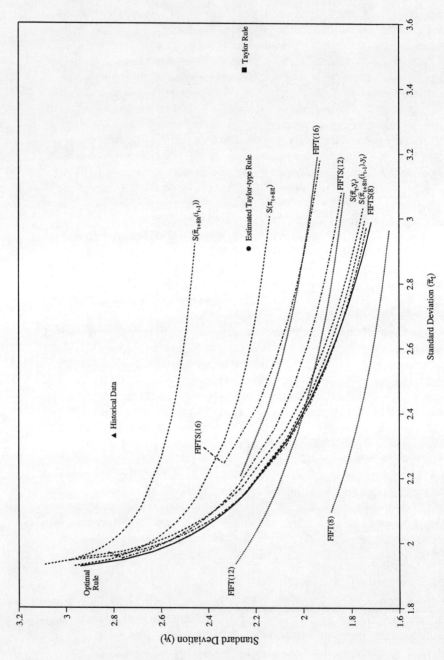

Fig. 5.2 Policy rule frontiers

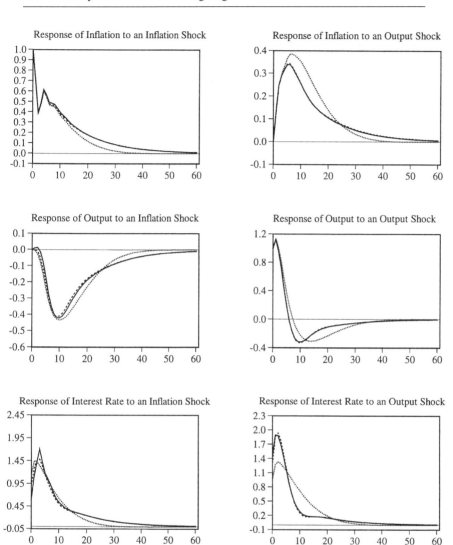

Fig. 5.3   **Impulse responses for smoothing rules ($\lambda = 1$, $\nu = 0.5$)**
Note: Solid, $S(\overline{\pi}_t, y_t)$; dashes, $S(\overline{\pi}_{t+8|t}(i_{t-1}), y_t)$; dots, $S(\pi_{t+8|t})$.

results with lagged information, which are shown in the lower half of table 5.8, are qualitatively the same as those with contemporaneous information, so we concentrate on the latter.

First, consider the two level rules (in our terminology) that are common. Rules III(1) and IV(1) have much weaker inflation and output response coefficients than our optimal $L(\overline{\pi}_t, y_t)$ rule (in table 5.3), and inflation variability under the common rules is much larger than with the optimal ones, while out-

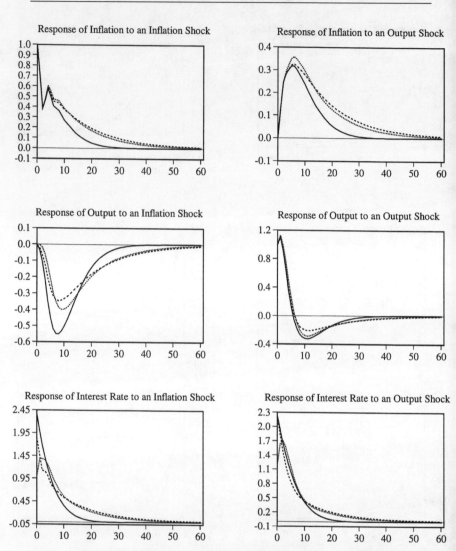

Fig. 5.4   Impulse responses for inflation-targeting rules ($\lambda = 1$, $\nu = 0.5$)
Note: Solid, SIFT (12); *dashes,* FIFT (12); *dots,* FIFTS (12).

put variability is slightly lower and variability of interest rate changes is about the same. The parameters of the common conference rules could only be optimal for a very large λ (much greater than 10).

Second, the set of common conference rules included two difference rules and one smoothing rule with $h = 1.3$. None of these rules provided dynamically stable solutions in our model. Note that the optimal value of h for rule $S(\overline{\pi}_t, y_t)$ equals 0.14 in table 5.3 and is hence not close to one. The optimal

Table 5.8   **Results for Conference Rules ($\lambda = 1$, $\nu = 0.5$)**

Rule	Std[$\bar{\pi}_t$]	Std[y_t]	Std[$i_t - i_{t-1}$]	Std[i_t]	Loss
With contemporaneous information; $i_t = hi_{t-1} + g_\pi\bar{\pi}_t + g_y y_t$					
Rule I(1); D($\bar{\pi}_t, y_t$)					
$g_\pi = 3.00$, $g_y = 0.80$, $h = 1.00$		Dynamically unstable			
Rule II(1); D($\bar{\pi}_t, y_t$)					
$g_\pi = 1.20$, $g_y = 1.00$, $h = 1.00$		Dynamically unstable			
Rule III(1); L($\bar{\pi}_t, y_t$)					
$g_\pi = 1.50$, $g_y = 0.50$, $h = 0.00$	3.46	2.25	0.71	4.94	17.25
Rule IV(1); L($\bar{\pi}_t, y_t$)					
$g_\pi = 1.50$, $g_y = 1.00$, $h = 0.00$	3.52	1.98	1.03	4.97	16.86
Rule V(1); S($\bar{\pi}_t, y_t$)					
$g_\pi = 1.20$, $g_y = 0.06$, $h = 1.30$		Dynamically unstable			
Optimal L($\bar{\pi}_t, y_t$)					
$g_\pi = 2.72$, $g_y = 1.57$, $h = 0.00$	2.18	2.24	1.74	5.11	11.27
Optimal D($\bar{\pi}_t, y_t$)					
$g_\pi = 0.07$, $g_y = 0.27$, $h = 1.00$	3.85	3.80	1.07	7.80	30.42
With lagged information; $i_t = hi_{t-1} + g_\pi\bar{\pi}_{t-1} + g_y y_{t-1}$					
Rule I(2); D($\bar{\pi}_{t-1}, y_{t-1}$)					
$g_\pi = 3.00$, $g_y = 0.80$, $h = 1.00$		Dynamically unstable			
Rule II(2); D($\bar{\pi}_{t-1}, y_{t-1}$)					
$g_\pi = 1.20$, $g_y = 1.00$, $h = 1.00$		Dynamically unstable			
Rule III(2); L($\bar{\pi}_{t-1}, y_{t-1}$)					
$g_\pi = 1.50$, $g_y = 0.50$, $h = 0.00$	3.62	2.40	0.72	5.20	19.07
Rule IV(2); L($\bar{\pi}_{t-1}, y_{t-1}$)					
$g_\pi = 1.50$, $g_y = 1.00$, $h = 0.00$	3.63	2.14	1.04	5.19	18.29
Rule V(2); S($\bar{\pi}_{t-1}, y_{t-1}$)					
$g_\pi = 1.20$, $g_y = 0.06$, $h = 1.30$		Dynamically unstable			
Optimal L($\bar{\pi}_{t-1}, y_{t-1}$)					
$g_\pi = 2.50$, $g_y = 1.50$, $h = 0.00$	2.38	2.44	1.69	5.42	13.03
Optimal D($\bar{\pi}_{t-1}, y_{t-1}$)					
$g_\pi = 0.04$, $g_y = 0.21$, $h = 1.00$	4.96	4.21	0.87	8.58	42.75

difference rule D($\bar{\pi}_t, y_t$) that is shown in table 5.8 requires very low coefficients in order to ensure stability. Even so its performance is quite poor.[34]

5.4.3   A Nonnegative Nominal Interest Rate Constraint

In this subsection, we consider the occurrence of negative nominal interest rates. Negative nominal interest rates, although highly implausible in practice, are almost never excluded in policy rule analyses and our study is no exception. As noted in section 5.2, our model has many much-debated simplifications; however, one of its least debated approximations is its completely linear nature with its symmetry with respect to zero for all quantities including nominal

---

34. In rational expectations models, difference rules appear to perform much better, e.g., Fuhrer and Moore (1995) and Williams (1997).

interest rates. Indeed, it is straightforward to calculate the unconditional probability of obtaining a negative nominal funds rate for any given rule. For example, assuming an inflation target of 2 percent and an equilibrium real funds rate of 2.5 percent (which is obtained from the estimated constant term in the IS curve regression without de-meaned data), most of the optimized rules in table 5.3 give about a 20 percent probability of a negative interest rate. Clearly, these rules assume that nominal interest rates would be negative a nonnegligible proportion of the time.

Still, for policy rule analysis, we view the simple imposition of an interest rate nonnegativity constraint as unsatisfactory in several respects. Technically, such a nonlinear constraint renders our analytical methods difficult if not infeasible, though simulation methods are available; see Fuhrer and Madigan (1997) and Fair and Howrey (1996). More important, however, such a constraint, by limiting the degree to which the central bank can conduct expansionary monetary policy at low inflation rates, almost ensures dynamic instability in an otherwise linear model.[35] We do not view such instability as plausible. We think that there are always mechanisms by which the central bank can stimulate the economy even if short-term rates are near zero. Expansionary monetary policy could always be conducted by the injection of reserves through purchases of Treasury securities at all maturities (flattening the *entire* yield curve), or purchases of foreign exchange (unsterilized intervention), or even purchases (or financing) of corporate debentures and equity.[36] That is, our model, although not strictly true, may give a fairly accurate picture of the potential power of central banks. However, it must be admitted that there is little empirical basis for judging the performance of very low inflation economies in our sample.

5.5 Conclusions

An early working title of this paper was "Practical Inflation Targeting," by which we meant an exploration of plausible policy rules using a model of a form common at central banks. In this spirit, our examination of policy rules has been in part descriptive, and closely linked to what inflation-targeting central banks actually seem to be doing, as well as partly prescriptive, involving sifting and judging among various rules. From the latter perspective, our results suggest that certain simple forward-looking rules are able to perform quite well.

Of course, our prescriptive results about particular simple rules are conditional on our particular model, and there is much room for extensions and improvements. Questions regarding parameter uncertainty and structural stability are crucial before the results can be taken too seriously; however, judging

---

35. Intuitively, with an estimated equilibrium real funds rate of 2.5 percent, if inflation ever falls to, say, -3 percent, then with a zero nominal funds rate, the real funds rate is still restrictive, so the output gap decreases and inflation falls even more.

36. See the related discussion in Lebow (1993).

from the results of this conference (and the analysis of Rudebusch 1998b), questions about model uncertainty are likely an order of magnitude larger. Plausible model variation may strengthen our conclusions. For example, our model is backward looking and has no explicit role for expectations and no "credibility effect" in the Phillips curve. An expectations channel for monetary policy through the Phillips curve would most likely make inflation easier to control and more self-stabilizing under inflation targeting.[37] In this sense, relative to some of the other papers at this conference, we are stacking the cards against inflation targeting. Nonetheless, there can be no substitute to actually investigating the robustness of our results across model specifications.

However, we would like to emphasize that a forward-looking decision framework for inflation targeting can exhibit robustness to model variation. For example, as mentioned above, one implementation of inflation-forecast targeting is to choose from the set of conditional inflation forecasts (each based on a particular path for the instrument) the one that is most consistent with the inflation target—that is, approaches the inflation target at an appropriate rate, hits the inflation target at an appropriate horizon, and, more generally, minimizes the loss function—and then follow the corresponding instrument path. The construction of conditional forecasts of course depends on the model used, but the procedure itself is robust to known model variation.[38] Put differently, targeting rules allow the coefficients of the implied instrument rules to change with structural shifts in the model. It is this decision framework that we have tried to capture in the optimal targeting rule and in the simple inflation-forecast-targeting rules in subsection 5.3.8. In contrast, any given optimal explicit instrument rule depends on the precise model assumed and may be rather imperfect for a different model; any given reasonably robust explicit instrument rule may still be rather imperfect for a specific model.

Appendix

Unconditional Variances

The covariance matrix Σ_{YY} for the goal variables is given by

(A1) $$\Sigma_{YY} \equiv \mathrm{E}[Y_t Y_t'] = C\Sigma_{XX}C',$$

where Σ_{XX} is the unconditional covariance matrix of the state variables. The latter fulfills the matrix equation

---

37. The analysis in Svensson (forthcoming c) of inflation targeting in an open economy with forward-looking aggregate demand and supply confirms this.

38. In a forward-looking model, constructing conditional inflation forecasts for arbitrary instrument paths implies some problems that are not present in a backward-looking model. Svensson (forthcoming a) provides a solution.

(A2) $$\Sigma_{XX} \equiv \mathrm{E}[X_t X_t'] = M\Sigma_{XX}M' + \Sigma_{vv}.$$

We can use the relations $\mathrm{vec}(A + B) = \mathrm{vec}(A) + \mathrm{vec}(B)$ and $\mathrm{vec}(ABC) = (C' \otimes A)\,\mathrm{vec}(B)$ on equation (A2) (where $\mathrm{vec}(A)$ denotes the vector of stacked column vectors of the matrix A and $\otimes$ denotes the Kronecker product), which results in

$$\mathrm{vec}(\Sigma_{XX}) = \mathrm{vec}(M\Sigma_{XX}M') + \mathrm{vec}(\Sigma_{vv})$$

$$= (M \otimes M)\,\mathrm{vec}(\Sigma_{XX}) + \mathrm{vec}(\Sigma_{vv}).$$

Solving for $\mathrm{vec}(\Sigma_{XX})$ we get

(A3) $$\mathrm{vec}(\Sigma_{XX}) = [I - (M \otimes M)]^{-1}\mathrm{vec}(\Sigma_{vv}).$$

The Optimal Instrument Rule

The optimal instrument rule is the vector f in equation (9) that fulfills

$$f = -(R + \delta B'VB)^{-1}(U' + \beta B'VA),$$

where the 9×9 matrix V fulfills the Riccati equation

$$V = Q + Uf + f'U' + f'Rf + \delta M'VM,$$

where M is the transition matrix given by equation (10) and Q, U, and R are given by

$$Q = C_X'KC_X, \qquad U = C_X'KC_i, \qquad R = C_i'KC_i.$$

Furthermore, the optimal value of expression (3) is

(A4) $$X_t'VX_t + \frac{\delta}{1 - \delta}\mathrm{trace}(V\Sigma_{vv}),$$

where $\Sigma_{vv} = \mathrm{E}[v_t v_t']$ is the covariance matrix of the disturbance vector.

For $\delta = 1$ the optimal value of equation (5) is

(A5) $$\mathrm{E}[L_t] = \mathrm{trace}(V\Sigma_{vv}).$$

An Information Lag

With our state-space setup, the information lag in equation (18) requires inserting π_{t-4} as a tenth state variable and forming the extended 1×10 state-variable vector

$$\tilde{X}_t = \begin{bmatrix} X_t \\ \pi_{t-4} \end{bmatrix}.$$

Then the restriction can be written

$$\tilde{g}\tilde{X}_t = g_\pi \bar{\pi}_{t-1} + g_y y_{t-1},$$

$$\tilde{g} = g_\pi(\tilde{e}_{2:4} + \frac{1}{4}\tilde{e}_{10}) + g_y \tilde{e}_6,$$

$$\tilde{f} = h\tilde{e}_7 + \tilde{g},$$

$$i_t = \tilde{f}\tilde{X}_t,$$

where $\tilde{g}$ and $\tilde{f}$ are 1×10 row vectors and $\tilde{e}_j$ and $\tilde{e}_{j:k}$ are defined as e_j and $e_{j:k}$, except that they are 10×1 vectors.

An Instrument Rule That Responds to a Rule-Consistent Inflation Forecast

Suppose $T \geqslant 3$ (we deal with $T = 2$ below.) Then we have to write the model in state-space form with forward-looking variables. We first note that, since in our model the first element in B is zero, the first equation in (6) is

(A6) $$\pi_{t+1} = A_1.X_t + v_{1,t+1},$$

where $A_1.$ is the row vector $(a_{1k})_{k=1}^n$. Then π_{t+1} and $\pi_{t+1|t} = A_1.X_t$ are predetermined. In order to write the system in state-space form, we now define the $(T - 2) \times 1$ column vector of forward-looking variables, $x_t = (x_{lt})_{l=1}^{T-2}$, where

(A7) $$x_{lt} \equiv \pi_{t+l+1|t}$$

for $l = 1, \ldots, T - 2$. Observe that for $l = 1, \ldots, T - 3$, by the law of iterated expectations,

(A8) $$x_{l,t+1|t} = x_{l+1,t},$$

whereas for $l = T - 2$ we have

(A9) $$x_{T-2,t+1|t} = \pi_{t+T|t}.$$

Equation (A8) gives us $T - 3$ equations for the first $T - 3$ forward-looking variables x_{lt}, $l = 1, \ldots, T - 3$. We also need an equation for $x_{T-2,t}$. Lead equation (A6) by one period, and take expectations in period t,

(A10) $$x_{1t} \equiv \pi_{t+2|t} = A_1.X_{t+1|t} = A_1.[AX_t + B(hi_{t-1} - \phi\pi_{t+T|t})]$$
$$= A_1.(\tilde{A}X_t + \phi Bx_{T-2,t+1|t}),$$

where

(A11) $$\tilde{A} = A + hBe_7,$$

where we have used equations (6), (19), and (A9). Solve for $x_{T-2,t+1|t}$,

(A12) $$ x_{T-2,t+1|t} = -\frac{1}{\phi A_1.B} A_1.\tilde{A}X_t + \frac{1}{\phi A_1.B} x_{1t}, $$

which gives us the remaining equation (note that $A_1.B$ is a scalar).

Thus equations (A8) and (A12) give us $T - 2$ equations for the $T - 2$ forward-looking variables. With regard to the predetermined variables, we use equations (6), (19), (A9), (A11), and (A12) to write,

$$ X_{t+1} = \tilde{A}X_t + \phi B x_{T-2,t+1|t} $$

(A13)
$$ = \tilde{A}X_t + \phi B\left(-\frac{1}{\phi A_1.B} A_1.\tilde{A}X_t + \frac{1}{\phi A_1.B} x_{1t}\right) $$

$$ = \left(I - \frac{1}{A_1.B} BA_1.\right)\tilde{A}X_t + \frac{1}{A_1.B} B x_{1t}. $$

By combining equations (A13), (A8), and (A12), we can now write the system in state-space form,

(A14)
$$ \begin{bmatrix} X_{t+1} \\ x_{t+1|t} \end{bmatrix} = D \begin{bmatrix} X_t \\ x_t \end{bmatrix} + \begin{bmatrix} v_{t+1} \\ 0 \end{bmatrix}, $$

where the $(n + T - 2) \times (n + T - 2)$ matrix D is given by

$$ D = \begin{bmatrix} \left(I - \frac{1}{A_1.B} BA_1.\right)\tilde{A} & \frac{1}{A_1.B} Bu_{n+1} \\ D_{21} & D_{22} \end{bmatrix}, $$

where u_k, $k = 1, \ldots, n + T - 2$, is an $1 \times (n + T - 2)$ row vector with element k equal to unity and all other elements equal to zero and where the $(T - 2) \times n$ matrix D_{21} and the $(T - 2) \times (T - 2)$ matrix D_{22} are given by

$$ D_{21} = \begin{bmatrix} 0_{(T-3)\times n} \\ -\frac{1}{\phi A_1.B} A_1.\tilde{A} \end{bmatrix}, \quad D_{22} = \begin{bmatrix} 0_{(T-3)\times 1} & I_{T-3} \\ \frac{1}{\phi A_1.B} u_{n+1} \end{bmatrix}, $$

where $0_{k\times m}$ is a $k \times m$ matrix of zeros and I_m is an $m \times m$ identity matrix.

The system (A14) can then be solved with the help of known algorithms, for instance the one in Klein (1997). The solution results in a $(T - 2) \times n$ matrix H, expressing the forward-looking variables as a linear function of the state-variables,

(A15) $$ x_t = HX_t. $$

The dynamics of the predetermined variable are then given by

(A16) $$X_{t+1} = (D_{11} + D_{12}H)X_t + v_{t+1},$$

where D_{11} and D_{12} are the obvious submatrices of D. It furthermore follows that

$$x_{t+1|t} = D_{21}X_t + D_{22}x_t = (D_{21} + D_{22}H)X_t.$$

From equations (19) and (A9) follows that the equilibrium instrument rule can be written

$$i_t = fX_t,$$

$$f = he_7 + \phi u_{n+T-2}(D_{21} + D_{22}H).$$

Then we can use f in equations (10) and (11) and proceed as in the other cases. The matrix M in equation (10) will of course equal the matrix $D_{11} + D_{12}H$ in equation (A16).

For $T = 2$, by equations (19) and (A10), we directly get

$$\pi_{t+2|t} = A_1.(\tilde{A}X_t + \phi B\pi_{t+2|t})$$

$$= \frac{1}{1 - \phi A_1.B} A_1.\tilde{A}X_t;$$

hence,

$$i_t = hi_{t-1} + \frac{\phi}{1 - \phi A_1.B} A_1.\tilde{A}X_t,$$

$$f = he_7 + \frac{\phi}{1 - \phi A_1.B} A_1.\tilde{A}.$$

References

Andrews, Donald W. K. 1993. Tests for parameter instability and structural change with unknown change point. *Econometrica* 61 (4): 821–56.
Ball, Laurence. 1994. What determines the sacrifice ratio? In *Monetary policy,* ed. N. Gregory Mankiw, 155–82. Chicago: University of Chicago Press.
———. 1997. Efficient rules for monetary policy. NBER Working Paper no. 5952. Cambridge, Mass.: National Bureau of Economic Research.
Bank for International Settlements. 1995. *Financial structure and the monetary policy transmission mechanism.* Basel: Bank for International Settlements.
Bernanke, Ben S., and Frederic S. Mishkin. 1997. Inflation targeting: A new framework for monetary policy? *Journal of Economic Perspectives* 11:97–116.
Bernanke, Ben S., and Michael Woodford. 1997. Inflation forecasts and monetary policy. *Journal of Money, Credit and Banking* 29:653–84.
Black, Richard, Vincenzo Cassino, Aaron Drew, Eric Hansen, Benjamin Hunt, David

Rose, and Alasdair Scott. 1997. The forecasting and policy system: The core model. Research Paper no. 43. Wellington: Reserve Bank of New Zealand.

Black, Richard, Tiff Macklem, and David Rose. 1997. On policy rules for price stability. In *Price stability, inflation targets and monetary policy,* ed. Bank of Canada. Ottawa: Bank of Canada.

Blake, Andrew P., and Peter F. Westaway. 1996. Credibility and the effectiveness of inflation targeting regimes. *Manchester School* 64:20–50.

Blinder, Alan S. 1998. *Central banking in theory and practice.* Cambridge, Mass.: MIT Press.

Bomfim, Antulio N., and Glenn D. Rudebusch. 1997. Opportunistic and deliberate disinflation under imperfect credibility. San Francisco: Federal Reserve Bank of San Francisco. Manuscript.

Braun, Steven. 1990. Estimation of current quarter gross national product by pooling preliminary labor market data. *Journal of Business and Economic Statistics* 8: 293–304.

Brayton, Flint, and Eileen Mauskopf. 1987. Structure and uses of the MPS quarterly econometric model of the United States. *Federal Reserve Bulletin* 74:93–109.

Brayton, Flint, and Peter Tinsley. 1996. Guide to FRB/US: A macroeconometric model of the United States. Finance and Economics Discussion Paper no. 96-42. Washington, D.C.: Board of Governors of the Federal Reserve System.

Britton, Erik, Paul Fisher, and John Whitley. 1998. The inflation report projections: Understanding the fan chart. *Bank of England Quarterly Bulletin* 38 (1): 30–37.

Bryant, Ralph C., Peter Hooper, and Catherine L. Mann. 1993. Evaluating policy regimes and analytical models: Background and project summary. In *Evaluating policy regimes: New research in empirical macroeconomics,* ed. Ralph C. Bryant, Peter Hooper, and Catherine L. Mann. Washington, D.C.: Brookings Institution.

Cecchetti, Stephen G. 1995. Inflation indicators and inflation policy. In *NBER macroeconomics annual 1995,* ed. Ben S. Bernanke and Julio J. Rotemberg, 189–219. Cambridge, Mass.: MIT Press.

Chow, G. C. 1970. *Analysis and control of dynamic economic systems.* New York: Wiley.

Clarida, Richard, Jordi Galí, and Mark Gertler. 1997. Monetary policy rules in practice: Some international evidence. NBER Working Paper no. 6254. Cambridge, Mass.: National Bureau of Economic Research, November.

———. 1998. Monetary policy rules and macroeconomic stability: Evidence and some theory. NBER Working Paper no. 6442. Cambridge, Mass.: National Bureau of Economic Research.

Clark, Peter, Douglas Laxton, and David Rose. 1996. Asymmetry in the U.S. output-inflation nexus. *IMF Staff Papers* 43:216–51.

Coletti, Donald, Benjamin Hunt, David Rose, and Robert Tetlow. 1996. Bank of Canada's new Quarterly Projection Model. Part 3, The dynamic model: QPM. Technical Report no. 75. Ottawa: Bank of Canada.

Congressional Budget Office. 1995. CBO's method for estimating potential output. CBO memorandum, October. Available at http://www.cbo.gov.

Currie, David, and Paul Levine. 1984. Simple macropolicy rules for the open economy. *Economic Journal* 95 (suppl.): 60–70.

Diebold, Francis X., and Glenn D. Rudebusch. 1991. Forecasting output with the composite leading index: A real-time analysis. *Journal of the American Statistical Association* 86:603–10.

Fair, Ray C., and E. Philip Howrey. 1996. Evaluating alternative monetary policy rules. *Journal of Monetary Economics* 38:173–93.

Federal Reserve Bank of Kansas City. 1996. *Achieving price stability.* Kansas City: Federal Reserve Bank of Kansas City.

Feldstein, Martin, and James H. Stock. 1994. The use of a monetary aggregate to target nominal GDP. In *Monetary policy,* ed. N. Gregory Mankiw, 7–62. Chicago: University of Chicago Press.

Fischer, Stanley. 1996. Why are central banks pursuing long-run price stability? In *Achieving price stability.* Kansas City: Federal Reserve Bank of Kansas City.

Fuhrer, Jeffrey C. 1997. The (un)importance of forward-looking behavior in price specifications. *Journal of Money, Credit and Banking* 29 (August): 338–50.

Fuhrer, Jeffrey C., and Brian F. Madigan. 1997. Monetary policy when interest rates are bounded at zero. *Review of Economics and Statistics* 79:573–85.

Fuhrer, Jeffrey C., and George R. Moore. 1995. Monetary policy trade-offs and the correlation between nominal interest rates and real output. *American Economic Review* 85:219–39.

Haldane, Andrew G., ed. 1995. *Targeting inflation.* London: Bank of England.

———. 1997. Designing inflation targets. In *Monetary policy and inflation targeting,* ed. Philip Lowe, 74–112. Sydney: Reserve Bank of Australia.

———. 1998. On inflation-targeting in the United Kingdom. *Scottish Journal of Political Economy* 45 (1): 1–32.

Hallman, Jeffrey J., Richard D. Porter, and David H. Small. 1991. Is the price level tied to the M2 monetary aggregate in the long run? *American Economic Review* 81: 841–58.

Henderson, Dale W., and Warwick J. McKibbin. 1993. A comparison of some basic monetary policy regimes for open economies: Implications of different degrees of instrument adjustment and wage persistence. *Carnegie-Rochester Conference Series on Public Policy* 39:221–317.

Judd, John P., and Brian Motley. 1992. Controlling inflation with an interest rate instrument. *Federal Reserve Bank of San Francisco Economic Review,* no. 3:3–22.

Judd, John P., and Glenn D. Rudebusch. 1998. Taylor's rule and the Fed: 1970–1997. *Federal Reserve Bank of San Francisco Economic Review,* no. 3:3–16.

King, Mervyn A. 1994. Monetary policy in the U.K. *Fiscal Studies* 15 (3): 109–28.

———. 1996. How should central banks reduce inflation?—Conceptual issues. In *Achieving price stability.* Kansas City: Federal Reserve Bank of Kansas City.

Klein, Paul. 1997. Using the generalized Schur form to solve a system of linear expectational difference equations. Stockholm: Institute for International Economic Studies. Working paper.

Lebow, David E. 1993. Monetary policy at near zero interest rates. Division of Research and Statistics Working Paper no. 136. Washington, D.C.: Board of Governors of the Federal Reserve System.

Leiderman, Leonardo, and Lars E. O. Svensson, eds. 1995. *Inflation targets.* London: Centre for Economic Policy Research.

Lowe, Philip, ed. 1997. *Monetary policy and inflation targeting.* Sydney: Reserve Bank of Australia.

Lucas, Robert E. 1976. Econometric policy evaluation: A critique. *Carnegie-Rochester Conference Series on Public Policy* 1:19–46.

Mauskopf, Eileen. 1995. The monetary transmission mechanism in the United States: Simulations using the Federal Reserve Board's MPS model. In *Financial structure and the monetary policy transmission mechanism,* 563–80. Basel: Bank for International Settlements.

Mayes, David G., and Brendon Riches. 1996. The effectiveness of monetary policy in New Zealand. *Reserve Bank Bulletin* 59 (1): 5–20.

McCallum, Bennett T. 1988. Robustness properties of a rule for monetary policy. *Carnegie-Rochester Conference Series on Public Policy* 29:173–204.

———. 1997. Issues in the design of monetary policy rules. NBER Working Paper no.

6016. Cambridge, Mass.: National Bureau of Economic Research. (In *Handbook of macroeconomics*, ed. John B. Taylor. Amsterdam: North Holland, forthcoming.)

Meyer, Laurence H. 1997. The economic outlook and challenges for monetary policy. Remarks at the Charlotte Economics Club, Charlotte, N.C., 16 January.

Oliner, Stephen D., Glenn D. Rudebusch, and Daniel Sichel. 1996. The Lucas critique revisited: Assessing the stability of empirical Euler equations for investment. *Journal of Econometrics* 70:291–316.

Reserve Bank of New Zealand. 1997. *Monetary policy statement, June 1997.* Wellington: Reserve Bank of New Zealand.

Rogoff, Kenneth. 1985. The optimal degree of commitment to an intermediate monetary target. *Quarterly Journal of Economics* 100:1169–90.

Rudebusch, Glenn D. 1992. Trends and random walks in macroeconomic time series: A re-examination. *International Economic Review* 33:661–80.

———. 1995. Federal Reserve interest rate targeting, rational expectations, and the term structure. *Journal of Monetary Economics* 35:245–74.

———. 1998a. Do measures of monetary policy in a VAR make sense? *International Economic Review* 39:907–31.

———. 1998b. Is the Fed too timid? Monetary policy in an uncertain world. San Francisco: Federal Reserve Bank of San Francisco. Manuscript.

Sargent, Thomas L. 1987. *Dynamic macroeconomic theory.* Cambridge, Mass.: Harvard University Press.

Sims, Christopher A. 1982. Policy analysis with econometric models. *Brookings Papers on Economic Activity,* no. 1:107–52.

Smets, Frank. 1995. Central bank macroeconometric models and the monetary policy transmission mechanism. In *Financial structure and the monetary policy transmission mechanism,* 225–66. Basel: Bank for International Settlements.

Svensson, Lars E. O. 1996. Commentary: How should monetary policy respond to shocks while maintaining long-run price stability?—Conceptual issues. In *Achieving price stability.* Kansas City: Federal Reserve Bank of Kansas City.

———. 1997a. Inflation forecast targeting: Implementing and monitoring inflation targets. *European Economic Review* 41:1111–46.

———. 1997b. Inflation targeting in an open economy: Strict vs. inflation targeting. Public lecture at Victoria University of Wellington. (Reserve Bank of New Zealand Discussion Paper, forthcoming.)

———. Forthcoming a. Inflation targeting as a monetary policy rule. *Journal of Monetary Economics.*

———. Forthcoming b. Inflation targeting: Some extensions. *Scandinavian Journal of Economics.*

———. Forthcoming c. Open-economy inflation targeting. *Journal of International Economics.*

Taylor, John B. 1979. Estimation and control of a macroeconomic model with rational expectations. *Econometrica* 47:1267–86.

———. 1993. Discretion versus policy rules in practice. *Carnegie-Rochester Conference Series on Public Policy* 39:195–214.

———. 1996. How should monetary policy respond to shocks while maintaining long-run price stability—Conceptual issues. In *Achieving price stability.* Kansas City: Federal Reserve Bank of Kansas City.

Walsh, Carl E. 1997. Accountability, relative performance measures, and inflation targeting. Santa Cruz: University of California. Working paper.

———. 1998. *Monetary theory and policy.* Cambridge, Mass.: MIT Press.

Williams, John C. 1997. Simple rules for monetary policy. Washington, D.C.: Board of Governors of the Federal Reserve System. Working paper.

Comment   Frederic S. Mishkin

It is a pleasure to comment on this excellent paper by Glenn Rudebusch and Lars Svensson. In doing so, I first want to clarify what the paper is really about because its title might limit its audience, particularly among central bankers. Second, I will highlight some nice features of the analysis. Finally, I will discuss some of the major results in the paper and suggest why they are so important to practicing policymakers and then will make some concluding remarks.

What the Paper Is Really About

The paper is clearly targeted at central bankers, who, as Rudebusch and Svensson put it, "are among the most important ultimate consumers of this research." However, the paper's title, "Policy Rules for Inflation Targeting," suggests that the paper might only be of interest to central banks that are engaged in, or are contemplating engaging in, inflation targeting. This characterization of the paper would be incorrect because it is just as useful to central banks that have no intentions of engaging in inflation targeting as to those that do.

The authors state that they interpret inflation targeting as "implying a conventional quadratic loss function, where in addition to the variability of inflation around the inflation target there is some weight on the variability of the output gap." Although I agree with them that inflation targeting as practiced by central banks does display a concern for output variability as well as inflation variability in the loss function (e.g., see the case studies in Mishkin and Posen 1997 and Bernanke et al. 1999), I believe that this is also true for almost any central banker whom I encountered when I was among their ranks.

Inflation targeting involves (1) an institutional commitment to inflation control as the primary goal of monetary policy, (2) a publicly announced explicit inflation goal, with a focus on inflation forecasts using all available information to guide policy rather than one specific intermediate target such as a monetary aggregate, (3) a stress on transparency and communication with the public about the strategy of monetary policy, and (4) accountability of the central bank for achieving its stated inflation goals (see, e.g., King 1994; Leiderman and Svensson 1995; Bernanke and Mishkin 1997; Bernanke et al. 1999). Although many countries have adopted inflation targeting, such as New Zealand, Canada, the United Kingdom, Sweden, Spain, and Australia, other countries such as the United States have not. Nevertheless, because non–inflation targeters also care about inflation variability in their loss functions (as well as the other elements in the loss function used in this paper), the results in the paper are highly relevant to how they should conduct monetary policy. The title of

Frederic S. Mishkin is the A. Barton Hepburn Professor of Economics at the Graduate School of Business, Columbia University, and a research associate of the National Bureau of Economic Research.

the paper should not deter those who are not advocates of inflation targeting from reading this paper with great interest.

The second semantic problem with the title of this paper is that it refers to rules. In the dichotomy between rules and discretion that comes out of the rules-versus-discretion debate, a rule is seen as a precise, written description of how policy is to be conducted that helps to reduce the time-inconsistency problem. The classic example is Milton Friedman's constant money growth rate rule, in which a specific monetary aggregate is stipulated to grow at the same rate every year. Central bankers, in general, are very hostile to these types of rules because they stress the inability of written rules to deal with unforeseen shocks or changes in the structure of the economy and thus see the need for some discretion. Thus central bankers may be inclined to ignore this paper because of their hostility to rules. This would also be a mistake.

The authors clearly do not advocate that the rules they study in this paper be written down and followed slavishly by central banks. They emphasize that the optimal rules they derive are optimal only in the context of the specific model they study, and they acknowledge that there is substantial uncertainty about what is the appropriate model of the economy. They also acknowledge the possibility of a Lucas critique of their analysis in which adherence to their rules might affect expectations and hence the estimated parameters of their model, thus making the simulation results with their rules somewhat suspect. Thus the paper does not intend to suggest that central bankers should announce a rule of the type they study and then be obliged to follow it. Rather they see the analysis in the paper as providing guidance to central banks as to how they should conduct monetary policy and react to new information if they have sensible objectives. For example, one strong implication of the analysis is that good monetary policy should always react to increases in either the output gap or the deviation of inflation from the target level by increasing short-term real interest rates. This is an important prescription for monetary policy and one that has not always been followed in the past (Clarida, Galí, and Gertler 1998). It applies even if a central bank is exercising some discretion and is unwilling to commit to an explicit rule.

The basic point I am making here applies to all the papers in this conference volume. They focus on explicit rules because this is the only way we can scientifically analyze different approaches to the conduct of monetary policy. However, even if the monetary authorities are exercising some discretion, which is the case not only for non–inflation targeters but also for those engaging in inflation targeting,[1] they still need the guidance supplied by the analysis in these papers as to how the setting of policy instruments should respond to information as it comes in to the central bank.

---

1. As is made clear in Bernanke and Mishkin (1997), Mishkin and Posen (1997), and Bernanke et al. (1999), inflation targeting is a framework, not a rule, in which there is discretion, but the discretion is constrained by the transparency and accountability of the inflation-targeting framework.

Nice Features of the Analysis

The paper conducts its analysis of policy rules in the context of a small, simple macromodel. The use of such a simple model is necessary for tractability in the analysis, and I find the model to be very sensible. (I am clearly somewhat biased here because the model used in this paper is very similar to the one Arturo Estrella and I use in chap. 9 of this volume.) Some might criticize the model because of both its simplicity and the fact that implicitly it assumes that expectations formation is backward looking. One very nice feature of the paper is subsection 5.2.3, which spends some time justifying the use of this model by showing that it fits the data well, has sensible implications for sacrifice ratios, and has reasonable dynamics. In addition, this subsection shows that the authors' small model captures the key essentials of more complex models that monetary policymakers actually use, particularly those at the Board of Governors of the Federal Reserve System. Although not everyone would agree with their model, Rudebusch and Svensson's careful discussion of its key features shows that the analysis in their paper is highly relevant to policymakers who may have a more complicated view of the world.

Another nice feature of this paper and many others in the volume is that they allow for an interest-rate-smoothing objective of the monetary authorities in discussing policy rules by including interest rate variability in the loss function, something that has rarely been done in previous literature. From my experience, I can tell you that central bankers are indeed very concerned about interest rate smoothing, and by focusing on it, the papers in this volume will be more relevant to these monetary policymakers.

Why is it that interest rate stability and smoothing is of such concern to central bankers? I see two reasons. First is that central bankers are very averse to reversing course frequently on interest rates because they are concerned that it may reduce public confidence in central bank competence. When central banks that have recently been raising interest rates suddenly lower them (or vice versa), it may look like an admission of a previous policy mistake. Because central bankers, like most of us, do not like to admit publicly that they have been wrong, it is natural that they should want to avoid quick interest rate reversals. They can avoid this by moving interest rates in short steps in the same direction over a period of time, rather than moving interest rates by a large amount. The resulting interest rate smoothing is exactly what you would get if interest rate variability is penalized in the policymakers' objective function, and this is why it is so sensible to include interest rate variability in the loss function.

The second reason for worrying about interest rate variability in the loss function is that central bankers are concerned not only about inflation and output variability but also about financial stability. Indeed, on a day-to-day basis central bankers probably spend more time concerning themselves with financial stability objectives than with price stability, although you wouldn't always know this from their speeches. Interest rate instability can be a source of financial fragility because rises in interest rates can directly hurt the balance sheets of banks that engage in the asset transformation activity of borrowing short and lending long. Also, high interest rates can directly hurt business firms' cash flows, which also causes a deterioration in their balance sheets. The deterioration in both banks' and nonbank firms balance sheets can decrease financial stability and make moral hazard and adverse selection problems more severe in credit markets, thereby making it harder for financial markets to achieve their intended purpose of getting funds to people and firms with productive investment opportunities (e.g., see Mishkin 1997).[2] Thus interest rate variability can also harm the economy and rightfully belongs in the policymakers' loss function.

Because there are good reasons to include interest rate variability in the policymakers' loss function and because central bankers clearly worry about interest rate smoothing, analyzing the effects on optimal policy of interest-rate-smoothing objectives makes the results in this and the other papers in the conference that much more relevant and interesting to their targeted audience in the central banking community.

Major Results and Their Importance to Policymakers

One important finding of the paper is that rules that respond solely to inflation, particularly current inflation rather than forecasts of future inflation, do very badly, even if the objective of the central bank focuses solely on inflation stabilization and is not concerned with output stabilization. Rules that include a response to output gaps, such as Taylor-type rules do far better. In the context of the authors' macromodel, the output gap contains information about future inflation, and so this conclusion can be restated as saying that monetary policy should be very preemptive.

Some economists have argued that as long as the Federal Reserve strongly tightens monetary policy when inflation actually rises in order to squash it, inflation will be unlikely to appear because of the Fed's credibility and monetary policy will be successful at stabilizing both output and inflation. In other words, monetary policy can take a Bunker Hill stance and wait until it sees the whites of inflation's eyes before reacting. The Rudebusch-Svensson results suggest that a nonpreemptive monetary policy of this type will not be successful and will lead to much poorer monetary policy outcomes.

Rudebusch and Svensson's results on the need for preemptive monetary policy rely heavily on the feature of their Phillips-curve-type equation that inflation expectations are backward looking. In macromodels in which inflation expectations are forward looking, for example in several of the papers in this volume, "whites of their eyes" monetary policy, in which monetary policy re-

---

2. Mishkin (1997) also suggests that there are direct effects of interest rate increases on adverse selection because higher interest rates lead to more adverse selection in credit markets.

acts almost entirely to current inflation and hardly at all to output gaps, works quite well. The intuition is straightforward. Because expectations are forward looking, a strong reaction to inflation only when it appears is nevertheless taken into account in price-setting behavior and so inflation is far less likely rear its ugly head. With backward-looking expectations, monetary policy must be preemptive in order to head off inflation ahead of time because inflation expectations are slow to change. This and other papers in this volume therefore suggest a very important conclusion that at first sounds counterintuitive but is actually quite intuitive once you think about it: the more backward looking are inflation expectations, the more preemptive monetary policy needs to be.

Although I believe that inflation expectations reflect some element of forward-looking behavior, credibility for central banks is hard to come by and takes a long time to develop. Thus inflation expectations are likely to be more backward looking than forward looking. Indeed, this is what the evidence in papers such as Fuhrer (1997) suggests—backward-looking models seem to fit the data better—and this is one reason why a model like that used by Rudebusch and Svensson is taken more seriously by policymakers than models that rely on forward-looking expectations. Thus I lean toward Rudebusch and Svensson's view that their macromodel is more realistic than ones relying on forward-looking expectations, and so successful monetary policy must have a strong preemptive component.

Another striking result in this paper is that simple rules of the Taylor type perform quite well and are not far off in their performance from the optimal rule. Part of the reason might stem from the simplicity of the authors' macromodel, but I suspect that another factor is at work. If the monetary authority has the right basic approach to monetary policy—that is, it raises nominal interest rates by more than any increase in actual or expected inflation, so that inflation never spins out of control—then monetary policy will do pretty well. (Symmetrically, policy must lower nominal interest rates by more than any decline in inflation when it occurs.) This is also the implication of John Taylor's paper (chap. 7 of this volume), which suggests that the episodes in which monetary policy made its biggest mistakes occurred when it did not follow the basic prescription outlined above.

The conclusions from the Rudebusch-Svensson and Taylor papers are thus encouraging. Even if monetary policymakers don't get things perfect, they can still do pretty well by making sure that they do not make the mistakes of the past (see Clarida et al. 1998) by thinking that they have tightened monetary policy enough when they raise interest rates in the face of inflation increases, but by an amount less than the inflation increase.

Another important conclusion from this paper is that central banks and particularly inflation targeters should not be what Mervyn King calls "inflation nutters," that is, fanatics on controlling inflation at any cost. Central bank rhetoric about monetary policy often focuses almost solely on price stability, but as Taylor (1993) has emphasized there is a trade-off between inflation variability and output variability. Taking account of this trade-off does have important implications for monetary policy and indicates that inflation fanaticism is unwise. Two basic results in Rudebusch and Svensson's paper support this position. First, putting some weight on output gaps as well as on deviations from inflation in formulating monetary policy leads to a substantially lower value of the loss function. Second, policy settings that lead to a more gradual approach to the target level of inflation also produce lower values of the loss function. These results imply that even if the primary goal of monetary policy is price (inflation) stability, it is important for central banks to be flexible.

The need for flexibility is recognized by central banks, even those that have explicitly committed to inflation targeting. As discussed in Mishkin and Posen (1997) and in our book Bernanke et al. (1999), both the Bundesbank and inflation-targeting central banks in their disinflationary phases have lowered their inflation targets gradually toward their long-run goals. Furthermore, these central banks have expressed their concerns about the trade-off between inflation variability and output variability. Thus central banks with a strong commitment to fighting inflation cannot be characterized as "inflation nutters," and the findings in this paper provide a further rationale for the degree of flexibility that they have been exercising.

Concluding Remarks

Despite the title of the paper, which might limit its audience, this paper should be required reading for central bankers. Although it makes use of a simple macromodel, which not everyone would accept, it provides some basic insights that I believe would continue to hold up in more complex frameworks. Most important, this paper suggests that if central banks focus on the right basic strategy, they do not have to be perfect to do quite well.

References

Bernanke, Ben S., Thomas Laubach, Frederic S. Mishkin, and Adam S. Posen. 1999. *Inflation targeting: Lessons from the international experience.* Princeton, N.J.: Princeton University Press.

Bernanke, Ben S., and Frederic S. Mishkin. 1997. Inflation targeting: A new framework for monetary policy? *Journal of Economic Perspectives* 11:97–116.

Clarida, Richard, Jordi Galí, and Mark Gertler. 1998. Monetary policy rules and macroeconomic stability: Evidence and some theory. NBER Working Paper no. 6442. Cambridge, Mass.: National Bureau of Economic Research.

Fuhrer, Jeffrey C. 1997. The (un)importance of forward-looking behavior in price specifications. *Journal of Money, Credit and Banking* 29 (August): 338–50.

King, Mervyn A. 1994. Monetary policy in the U.K. *Fiscal Studies* 15 (3): 109–28.

Leiderman, Leonardo, and Lars E. O. Svensson, eds. 1995. *Inflation targets.* London: Centre for Economic Policy Research.

Mishkin, Frederic S. 1997. The causes and propagation of financial instability: Lessons for policymakers. In *Maintaining financial stability in a global economy.* Kansas City: Federal Reserve Bank of Kansas City.

Mishkin, Frederic S., and Adam S. Posen. 1997. Inflation targeting: Lessons from four countries. *Federal Reserve Bank of New York Economic Policy Review* 3, no. 3 (August): 9–110.
Taylor, John B. 1993. Discretion versus policy rules in practice. *Carnegie-Rochester Conference Series on Public Policy* 39:195–214.

Comment   James H. Stock

Glenn Rudebusch and Lars Svensson have provided a clear and interesting treatment of a large number of policy rules within a bivariate vector autoregression (VAR). They model the interest rate (the federal funds rate) as an exogenous variable under the perfect control of the Fed. Changes in the interest rate affect the deviation of real output from potential, which in turn affects inflation through an output-based Phillips curve. Control rules are evaluated in terms of their expected loss, which is a function of the variances of inflation, potential GDP, and the interest rate.

Their paper is clearly and precisely written and the results are well presented. Their discussion of loss functions and targets is lucid and compelling. The modeling decisions they made are sensible and permit the evaluation of a large number of rules. In future work along these lines, it would be of interest to consider a larger VAR that includes an additional interest rate (so that the Fed is not implicitly given control over the entire term structure in the simulations). Similarly, most methods for constructing potential GDP are questionable, and theirs is no exception. The pitfalls of estimating potential GDP could be sidestepped by specifying the Phillips curve in terms of unemployment rather than potential GDP. It would be useful to see whether their findings, particularly the importance of large coefficients in Taylor-type rules, hold up under these extensions. These comments are relatively minor, however, and in general their paper constitutes an excellent contribution to the literature on monetary policy rules.

Because Rudebusch and Svensson's paper is so clean and self-contained, in the remainder of these comments I will turn to the broader question that is one of the motivations for this conference, the construction and evaluation of control rules in the presence of model uncertainty. A policy rule that performs well under reasonable perturbations of a model, or under different plausible models, is robust to that model uncertainty. Although policy robustness is an underlying theme of this conference, it is important to emphasize two limitations of the robustness results reported in this volume.

James H. Stock is professor of political economy at the Kennedy School of Government, Harvard University, and a research associate of the National Bureau of Economic Research.
    The author is grateful to Glenn Rudebusch, Tom Sargent, and Lars Svensson for helpful discussions. This research was supported in part by National Science Foundation grant SBR-9409629.

First, the "conference rules" have been evaluated by various authors using their estimated models, but each of the estimated models contains considerable model uncertainty arising from the estimation of the model parameters. It is possible that a rule is robust across point estimates of models, which might be similar in important dynamic respects (after all, the models are estimated using the same data), but that the rule is not robust to 1 standard error changes in the parameters of the models. Robustness to sampling uncertainty needs to be investigated more carefully before any conclusions can be drawn about the robustness of the policy rules considered in this volume (I return to this point below).

Second, a theme of several papers is that inflation-forecast-targeting rules (in which the monetary authority adjusts the interest rate to move an inflation forecast toward a target) perform well in many of the models considered here. However, this conclusion is drawn by evaluating the performance of the inflation-targeting rule using the same model that is used to compute the inflation forecast. In contrast, the essence of policy robustness is whether a specific quantitative rule performs well under a model *other than that used to develop the policy*. Rudebusch and Svensson find that inflation-forecast-targeting rules, based on conditional inflation forecasts produced by their models, work well when evaluated using their model. The proper check of robustness, however, is whether inflation-forecast-targeting rules based on, say, the Rudebusch-Svensson model forecasts work well when the true model is something else.

To illustrate this point, suppose the Fed hires Rudebusch and Svensson to make their conditional forecasts: the Fed provides them a trial value of the interest rate, Rudebusch and Svensson compute inflation forecasts, and they iterate until the inflation forecasts from their model satisfy the Fed policymakers. Now suppose, however, that Rudebusch and Svensson's research assistant mistakenly feeds the conditional U.S. interest rate into a model of the Swedish economy rather than their U.S. model, so that Rudebusch and Svensson report back Swedish rather than U.S. inflation. One would expect this inflation-forecast-targeting rule, thus implemented, to produce outcomes for the U.S. that are badly wrong: the model used to generate the inflation forecasts differs sharply from the true model. While one would hope that such a gross mistake would not happen in practice, the essential point is that evaluating the robustness of inflation-targeting rules requires the evaluation of the model's conditional forecasts when that model is false. I know of no research on monetary policy rules that undertakes that evaluation.

The remainder of these comments take up this problem in the form of parametric model uncertainty, by which I mean uncertainty that can be summarized as uncertainty about the value of a finite-dimensional parameter. This complements Sargent's comments on Ball's paper (chap. 3 of this volume), in which Sargent considers the case of uncertainty that is nonparametric in the sense that the uncertainty can be formalized as over elements of an infinite-dimensional space. In particular, I will consider two approaches to parametric uncertainty. The first is a Bayesian approach that grows out of Brainard's (1967) early work on parameter uncertainty. I will argue that while this approach is appealing from the perspective of decision theory, and while it can yield intuitive results, in practice it places informational demands on policy-makers that are wholly unrealistic and therefore fails to provide a useful framework for constructing practical policies. In its place, I propose using minimax methods to construct optimal robust policies and implement these methods quantitatively in the Rudebusch-Svensson model.

Bayesian Approaches to Model Uncertainty

The Bayesian decision analytic approach to control under parametric uncertainty posits a loss function that is a function of future macroeconomic variables. The decision maker is assumed to have priors over all parameters in the model. Optimal policy is then solved by finding the policy that minimizes the expected loss, integrating over the parameters with respect to the prior density. This is conventionally done in the context of a single model. However, in this volume several distinct models are presented, so it is of interest to consider the result of this procedure when there is uncertainty over the class of models as well. In particular, consider two stylized single-equation models of inflation:

$$(1) \qquad \pi_t = \beta x_{t-1} + \varepsilon_t,$$

$$(2) \qquad \pi_t = \alpha \pi_{t-1} + \gamma x_{t-1} + \eta_t,$$

where π_t is inflation and x_t is the control variable. Evidently, the two models differ only in whether lagged inflation has an effect on future inflation. Suppose that the decision maker has Gaussian priors over β in the first model, so that $\beta \sim N(\overline{\beta}, \sigma_\beta^2)$. For the second model, the decision maker has the priors $\gamma \sim N(\overline{\gamma}, \sigma_\gamma^2)$.

Suppose the decision maker has quadratic loss, $(\pi_t - \pi^*)^2$, where π^* is the target rate of inflation. If the decision maker were sure that model (1) is correct, then the optimal policy would be

$$(3) \qquad x_{t-1}^{*,1} = [\overline{\beta}/(\overline{\beta}^2 + \sigma_\beta^2)]\pi^*.$$

On the other hand, if the decision maker were sure that model (2) is correct, the optimal policy would be

$$(4) \qquad x_{t-1}^{*,2} = [\overline{\gamma}/(\overline{\gamma}^2 + \sigma_\gamma^2)](\pi^* - \alpha\pi_{t-1}).$$

Now suppose that the decision maker does not know which model is correct but is sure that one of them is; he or she assigns prior probability λ to the event that model (1) is the true model. In this case, the optimal policy is

$$(5) \qquad x_{t-1}^* = \lambda x_{t-1}^{*,1} + (1 - \lambda)x_{t-1}^{*,2}.$$

The noteworthy feature of this result here is that when there is uncertainty over classes of models rather than just (smooth) uncertainty over the parameters in a model, the optimal policy is a linear combination of the two optimal policies in the individual models. At least in this simple example, then, one could imagine giving a board of policymakers the optimal policies resulting from the individual models and letting each policymaker compute his or her individual weighted average of these model-based policies, based on each individual's views of how likely a particular model is to be correct.

Although this result has intuitive appeal, there are reasons to doubt that its simple lessons can be made general enough to be useful for practical policy making. First, on a technical level, dynamic models with learning imply very different rules, in which there can be experimentation to learn about the parameters of the model (cf. Wieland 1996, 1998). It is not clear how this would generalize to the multimodel setting.

Second and more fundamentally, the calculations here require an unrealistic amount of information. Key to these calculations are the existence of prior distributions, which for nonlinear models need to be joint priors over all the parameters. While it is plausible that policymakers might have opinions about the value of the NAIRU or the slope of the Phillips curve, it is not plausible that they would have opinions about, say, the covariance between $\alpha_{\pi3}$ and β_{y2} in equations (1) and (2) in Rudebusch and Svensson's paper. Indeed, there has been great debate about how to construct priors for large autoregressive roots in univariate autoregressive models (see, e.g., the special issue of *Econometric Theory,* August/October 1994); I believe that a fair summary of this debate is that various Bayesians have agreed to disagree over how to construct their priors. If experts cannot construct priors for univariate autoregressions, it is entirely unrealistic for noneconometrician policymakers to construct priors for multiequation nonlinear dynamic models. Unfortunately, such priors are a necessity for the foregoing calculations, so the conventional decision analytic approach does not seem to be a promising direction for developing practical policy rules that address model uncertainty. It is therefore useful to explore an alternative approach based on minimax approaches to model uncertainty.

Minimax Approaches to Model Uncertainty

An alternative approach is to evaluate policies by their worst-case performance across the various models under consideration. The best policy from this perspective is the minimax policy that has the lowest maximum risk. Because Rudebusch and Svensson do not consider parameter uncertainty, as an illustration I will consider the effect of parameter uncertainty on policy choice using the Rudebusch-Svensson model.

Specifically, I consider their model (1)–(2), with their point estimates, and focus on the effects of uncertainty in two of the parameters, α_y and β_r. These are the two most interesting parameters of their model from an economic perspective: α_y is the slope of the (potential GDP) Phillips curve, and β_r is the impact effect on the GDP gap of a change in the interest rate.

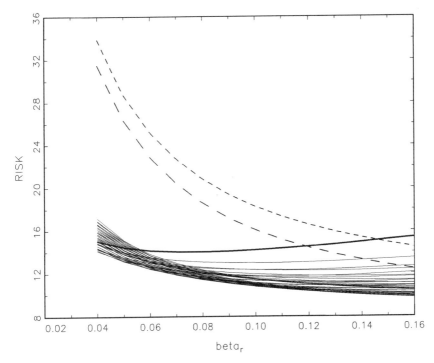

Fig. 5C.1   Risk functions for various policy rules, evaluated in the Rudebusch-Svensson model for $0.04 \leq \beta_r \leq 0.16$ and $\alpha_y = 0.20$

The loss function considered here is the one of the Rudebusch-Svensson loss functions,

$$(6) \qquad \text{Loss} = \text{var}(\pi_t) + \text{var}(y_t) + \tfrac{1}{2}\text{var}(\Delta i_t)$$

in their notation. To capture model uncertainty, values of parameters α_y and β_r within 2 standard errors of their point estimates were considered; that is, the parameters were varied in the ranges $0.08 \leq \alpha_y \leq 0.20$ and $0.04 \leq \beta_r \leq 0.16$.
The policy rules considered here are two-parameter modified Taylor rules of the type considered by Rudebusch and Svensson, specifically,

$$(7) \qquad i_t = g_\pi \overline{\pi}_t + g_y y_t.$$

Three types of policy rules were considered: the Taylor rule ($g_\pi = 1.5$, $g_y = 0.5$) and a modified Taylor rule with somewhat more response to output fluctuations ($g_\pi = 1.5$, $g_y = 1.0$); model-specific optimal rules of the type (7), in which the parameters are optimal for particular values of α_y and β_r; and the minimax rule that minimizes expected loss over all parameter values.
Slices of the risk function surface are presented in figure 5C.1 for these various policy rules; the slices present risk as a function of β_r for $\alpha_y = 0.20$. The upper lines are the risks of the two conference rules, the Taylor rule (*short*

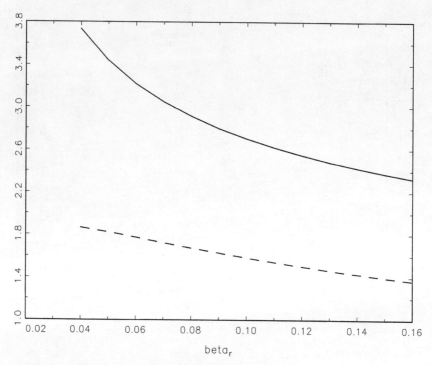

beta$_r$

Fig. 5C.2   Optimal parameter values for Taylor-type rules in the Rudebusch-Svensson model for $0.04 \leq \beta_r \leq 0.16$ and $\alpha_y = 0.14$

dashes) and the rule with $g_\pi = 1.5$ and $g_y = 1.0$ (*long dashes*). Each of the light solid lines is the risk function for a policy that is optimal for a particular value of (α_y, β_r); the lower envelope of these dotted lines constitutes an envelope of the lowest possible risk, across these parameter values. The heavy solid line is the risk of the policy that is minimax over $0.08 \leq \alpha_y \leq 0.20$ and $0.04 \leq \beta_r \leq 0.16$. (The model-optimal and minimax policies were computed by a simulated annealing algorithm with 1,000 random trials.)

Several observations are apparent. First, the Taylor rule has very large maximum risk. The risk is greatest when β_r is lowest. When monetary policy has little effect (β_r is small), the Taylor rule produces movements in interest rates that are too small to stabilize output and inflation as quantified by the loss function (6). It turns out that the minimax rule has a risk function that is tangent to the risk envelope, with the point of tangency corresponding to the model in which monetary policy has the smallest direct impact on the GDP gap and the Phillips curve is flattest ($\beta_r = 0.04$ and $\alpha_y = 0.08$). In the Rudebusch-Svensson model, this corresponds to the case in which monetary policy is least effective. Here the minimax policy is obtained by producing the optimal rule in the least favorable case for monetary control of inflation and output.

The model-specific optimal parameter values are plotted in figure 5C.2 for

$\alpha_y = 0.14$. Evidently, when the impact effect of monetary policy is small, the optimal response of monetary policy to inflation (*solid line*) and the output gap (*dashed line*) is large. This is the case for the minimax policy, in which $g_\pi = 3.86$ and $g_y = 1.48$. The minimax risk across all models for this policy is 15.61. For the Rudebusch-Svensson model with this parametric uncertainty, the minimax-optimal Taylor-type rule exhibits very strong reactions to inflation and the output gap to guard against the possibility that the true response of the economy to monetary policy is weak.

These results are only illustrative, but they indicate that quite different conclusions can be reached once we admit that there is parameter uncertainty in our models. In the Rudebusch-Svensson model, recognizing parameter uncertainty leads to "conservative" policies that exhibit more aggressive responses than are optimal for the point estimates of the model. It would be interesting to see this sort of analysis undertaken for some of the other models presented in this volume.

References

Brainard, W. 1967. Uncertainty and the effectiveness of policy. *American Economic Review* 57:411–25.

Wieland, V. 1996. Monetary policy, parameter uncertainty and optimal learning. Washington, D.C.: Board of Governors of the Federal Reserve System. Manuscript.

————. 1998. Monetary policy and uncertainty about the natural unemployment rate. Finance and Economics Discussion Paper no. 98-22. Washington, D.C.: Board of Governors of the Federal Reserve System.

Discussion Summary

Arturo Estrella asked whether the good performance of smoothing rules in the paper is related to the fact that the IS curve depends on the difference between the short-term nominal interest rate and recent inflation. Changes in the nominal rate reflected in the smoothing rules could be proxying for the difference between the nominal rate and recent inflation. *Svensson* replied that the reason for the bad performance of difference rules was not clear. There is a tendency to get an eigenvalue equal to one or above because the coefficients sum to one in the Phillips curve.

Andrew Haldane noted that most inflation-targeting countries seem to be small open economies. It would therefore be interesting to see how the results of the paper change in an open economy setting. Svensson's work and the Batini and Haldane paper presented at the conference suggest that the change in results would be substantial. Consider the example of simple rules. The two simple rules that perform well in the paper are the Taylor rule and a constant-interest-rate inflation forecast rule. In a model with only two equations, aggregate demand and aggregate supply, these rules, which condition on just two variables, come not surprisingly close to being fully optimal. In a setting with an important role for exchange rates, Svensson's work on inflation targeting in small open economies indicates that the Taylor rule might not do very well. The second rule holds interest rates constant, which is not admissible with a no-arbitrage condition in a forward-looking open economy setting. Regarding the latter point, *Rudebusch* replied that one of the reasons for the paper to look at constant-interest-rate inflation forecast rules is that inflation-targeting central banks, such as the Bank of England, produce these forecasts in their inflation reports. Therefore, these forecasts seem to be of interest for policy. *Svensson* agreed that simple rules work well because the model is simple enough for inflation and output to be sufficient statistics. With more variables, for example, fiscal policy, simple rules would work less well.

Volker Wieland noted that in the presence of uncertainty about multiplicative parameters, such as the effectiveness of monetary policy, in a linear model, the optimal rule exhibits a more cautious policy response. However, additive uncertainty, such as uncertainty about the natural rate, does not matter in a linear-quadratic framework. In a nonlinear model, additive uncertainty begins to matter. Nonlinearities could, for example, be in the preferences or in the constraints, such as zero-bound constraints on nominal interest rates or nonlinear Phillips curves. *John Williams* mentioned that in his own work on parameter uncertainty using the U.S. model (Williams 1997), the value of the loss function and the implicit optimal rule vary greatly with the parameter governing the slope of the Phillips curve. While this parameter is thus a key parameter for monetary policy, it is unfortunately also the least precisely estimated parameter of the model.

Frederic Mishkin made two points justifying rules based on constant-interest-rate inflation forecasts in the context of a closed economy. First, these rules help central banks communicate with the public. Second, these rules help guide discussions about monetary policy in central bank meetings. *Svensson* illustrated these points by noting that in the case of a strict inflation-forecast-targeting rule, the warranted change in interest rates can be expressed as the difference between the unchanged-interest-rate inflation forecast and the inflation target, divided by the policy multiplier, which is easy to communicate. In practice, inflation reports show such constant-interest-rate inflation forecasts.

William Poole stressed that to understand rules for the federal funds rate, it is essential to have two interest rates in the model because of the following reasoning. One of the attractive features of money growth rules is that the economy has a built-in stabilizing mechanism: with constant money growth, shocks to aggregate demand change interest rates, thus keeping the economy from "running off." Something similar happened in recent years with the Federal Reserve's federal funds rate targeting: long interest rates have changed in response to anticipated future federal funds rate moves, even when the Federal Reserve did not change the federal funds rate much. So the fact that bond markets are forward looking is a built-in stabilizing mechanism.

Ben McCallum approved of the emphasis on terminology in the paper. The distinction between targeting a variable and responding to a variable warrants consideration. However, the notion of inflation targeting is odd in the context of high λ-values, that is, when the weight on output variability is much higher than the weight on inflation. *Svensson* agreed with McCallum that to use the term "inflation targeting," the weight on inflation should be significant.

Robert King remarked that the term "interest rate smoothing" is usually used to denote inertia in the level of interest rates, represented by a large response coefficient on the lagged interest rate and small coefficients on contemporaneous output and inflation. From both the Rotemberg and Woodford and the Batini and Haldane papers it seems as if forward-looking models could rationalize that pattern of response. How does such a rule perform in the Rudebusch-Svensson model? *Rudebusch* replied that these rules are not desirable in their model. Moreover, Rudebusch disagreed with King's characterization of interest rate smoothing. Whether a rule smooths the interest rate depends on how persistent the arguments of the rule are. John Taylor's original rule has small response coefficients with no lagged term, and yet, it produces a path for the funds rate that is as smooth as the historical series. In a model with persistence in the output gap and inflation, it is not clear whether a large coefficient on the lagged interest rate is needed to smooth the funds rate.

Ben Friedman noted that the point about Brainard-type uncertainty rules driving the policymaker toward more conservatism depends not only on the model but also on the policy rule and the policy instrument. In the context of this discussion, the policy instrument is the interest rate, and therefore conservatism presumably means less variation in interest rates. In a world with money demand shocks, conservative policy thus leads to higher variability in monetary quantities. However, with a policy rule based on the monetary base, conservatism means that the money base grows more closely along a fixed growth path, which, for the same reasons but now played in reverse, means more interest rate volatility. Friedman asked whether this tension is handled conceptually in the approach presented in Stock's comment. *Stock* replied that in the example used in his discussion, the policy rule was based on interest rates. In a comparison of different instruments, it is not obvious that the optimal combination rule is going to be spanned by the submodels. Stock also remarked that conservatism does not necessarily mean gradualism. In his simulations, the Taylor rule was the most conservative rule in the sense that the response coefficients were smallest. However, the Taylor rule generated large losses and was far away from a minimax or optimal solution. *Bob Hall* remarked that the same question arises in prison sentences because of the unknown deterrent effect. Is it conservative to give felons short sentences?

Tom Sargent questioned the conclusion drawn in Stock's comment regarding the averaging of rules. If the analysis suggested by Stock is pursued with the model at hand, a dynamic model, the posterior over models becomes part of the state of the control problem, such as in Volker Wieland's thesis, implying that decision rules in this problem become functions of this distribution. Furthermore, the control problem is going to unleash an experimentation motive. If a decision maker is confronted with more than one possible model and a prior over those models, he wants to manipulate the data to learn more. The minimax caution characterization is a static problem, which will not survive the dynamics.

Reference

Williams, John C. 1997. Simple rules for monetary policy. Washington, D.C.: Board of Governors of the Federal Reserve System. Manuscript.

6 Robustness of Simple Monetary Policy Rules under Model Uncertainty

Andrew Levin, Volker Wieland, and John C. Williams

6.1 Introduction

In the face of uncertainty about the true structure of the economy, policy-makers may disagree about the macroeconomic effects of monetary policy and thus about the appropriate policy setting. One approach to resolving this problem is to search for monetary policy rules that work well across a wide range of structural models, that is, rules that are robust to model uncertainty.[1] In this paper, we investigate the characteristics of policy rules that yield low output and inflation volatility across four different structural macroeconometric models of the U.S. economy: the Federal Reserve Board staff model (cf. Brayton, Levin, et al. 1997), the Monetary Studies Research model of Orphanides and Wieland (1998),[2] the Fuhrer-Moore (1995) model, and Taylor's (1993b) multi-country model—henceforth referred to as the FRB, MSR, and FM models and

Andrew Levin, Volker Wieland, and John C. Williams are economists at the Board of Governors of the Federal Reserve System.

The authors appreciate the excellent research assistance of Steven Summer, as well as helpful comments from Flint Brayton, Larry Christiano, David Lindsey, Athanasios Orphanides, David Reifschneider, John Taylor, Robert Tetlow, and conference participants. The views expressed here are solely the responsibility of the authors and should not be interpreted as reflecting the views of the Board of Governors of the Federal Reserve System or the views of any other members of its staff.

1. We use the term "model uncertainty" to refer to lack of knowledge about which model among a given set of alternatives provides the best description of the economy. For a particular model, we treat the estimated parameters as known with certainty. A small literature exists on the problem of conducting monetary policy under model uncertainty (Karakitsos and Rustem 1984; Becker et al. 1986; Frankel and Rockett 1988; Holtham and Hughes-Hallett 1992; Christodoulakis, Kemball-Cook, and Levine 1993). Optimal policy under parameter uncertainty was investigated in the seminal paper of Brainard (1967) and was extended by the work of Kendrick (1982) and others; the more recent literature includes Balvers and Cosimano (1994) and Wieland (1996a, 1998).

2. MSR is a small macroeconometric model of the U.S. economy from 1980 to 1996, developed and used for research on monetary policy rules in the Monetary Studies Section at the Federal Reserve Board (e.g., Orphanides et al. 1997).

TMCM, respectively. All four models incorporate the assumptions of rational expectations, short-run nominal inertia, and long-run monetary neutrality but differ in many other respects (e.g., the dynamics of prices and real expenditures). We compute the inflation-output volatility frontier of each model for alternative specifications of the interest rate rule, subject to an upper bound on nominal interest rate volatility. We then evaluate robustness to model uncertainty by taking the rules that perform well in one model and measuring their performance in each of the other three models.

Our analysis provides strong support for rules in which the first difference of the federal funds rate responds to the current output gap and the deviation of the one-year average inflation rate from a specified target. First, in all four models, first-difference rules perform much better than rules of the type considered by Taylor (1993a) and Henderson and McKibbin (1993), in which the level of the federal funds rate responds to the output gap and inflation deviation from target. Second, more complicated rules (i.e., rules that respond to a larger number of variables, or additional lags of the output gap and inflation, or both) typically generate very small gains in stabilizing output and inflation compared with optimal first-difference rules. A closely related result is that rules involving model-based forecasts generally do not outperform first-difference rules based on the current output gap and inflation rate and quite often generate higher variability of output and inflation. Finally, the class of first-difference rules is robust to model uncertainty in the sense that a first-difference rule taken from the policy frontier of one model is very close to the policy frontier of each of the other three models. In contrast, we find that more complicated rules are somewhat less robust to model uncertainty: rules with a larger number of free parameters can be fine-tuned to the dynamics of a specific model but often perform poorly in other models compared with the best simple rules.

The approach of evaluating policy rules used in this paper follows the long and distinguished tradition dating to Phillips (1954).[3] As is standard in this literature, we assume the objective of policy is to minimize the weighted sum of the unconditional variances of the inflation rate and the output gap (the percentage deviation of GDP from its potential level). In addition, we allow interest rate volatility to enter into the policymakers' optimization problem. The funds rate is set according to a time-invariant policy rule. For a given class of policy rules, the policy frontier traces out the best obtainable outcomes in terms of inflation, output, and funds rate volatility. We refer to the policy rules underlying such a frontier as "optimal" in the sense that these rules represent solutions to the specified constrained optimization problem.

---

3. The literature on policy evaluation using traditional structural models is large and includes important contributions by Cooper and Fischer (1974) and Poole (1970). In recent papers, Fair and Howrey (1996), Ball (1997), and Rudebusch and Svensson (chap. 5 of this volume) derive optimal policies from traditional structural macroeconomic models. For a general survey of the recent literature on monetary policy and analysis of some key issues in a unified framework, see Clarida, Galí, and Gertler (forthcoming).

One major difference between our analysis and much of that in the previous literature is that we compute optimal policy frontiers using large rational expectations macroeconomic models—including models with more than 100 equations—as opposed to traditional structural models or small rational expectations models.[4] Policy rule analysis using traditional models is particularly prone to the Lucas critique (Lucas 1976). Fischer (1977) and Phelps and Taylor (1977) made strides in overcoming the inconsistency between policy and expectations inherent in traditional models by using small rational expectations structural models for policy analysis.[5] In the past, policy rule analysis using rational expectations models was hampered by the computational cost of solving and computing moments of models with more than a small number of equations. Analysis was generally limited to the comparison of a small set of policy regimes as in Bryant et al. (1989, 1993) and Taylor (1993b). Increases in computer speed and the development of efficient solution algorithms have made the computation of optimal frontiers of large linear rational expectations models feasible.

We present the policy frontiers in inflation-output volatility space, with each curve corresponding to a particular constraint on the volatility of the first difference of the funds rate. Interest rate volatility plays a key role in our analysis. All four models share the feature of a trade-off between interest rate volatility and inflation-output volatility, even at levels of interest rate volatility significantly above those implied by estimated policy rules or observed in the data. That is, the variability of output and inflation can be reduced by using highly aggressive rules, but such rules also induce wild fluctuations in interest rates. In this paper, we focus our attention on rules that feature relatively moderate levels of interest rate volatility.

One argument for doing so is that the relatively low level of funds rate volatility seen in the data may be a consequence of a preference on the part of policymakers for low interest rate volatility. Even if no fundamental preference for low interest rate volatility exists, two reasons remain to focus on rules that generate moderate levels of interest rate volatility. First, linear policy rules that generate highly volatile interest rates prescribe frequent and large violations of the nonnegativity constraint on the federal funds rate. In principle, one could analyze nonlinear rules that incorporate this lower bound on interest rates, but doing so would substantially raise the computational costs of our analysis.[6]

4. Williams (1999) compares the characteristics of optimal policies under rational expectations and alternative assumptions regarding expectations formation using the FRB staff model.
5. Taylor (1979) and, more recently, Fuhrer (1997a), Svensson (1997; forthcoming), and Tetlow and Muehlen (1996) derive optimal policies in small rational expectations structural macroeconomic models.
6. This nonlinearity has been investigated in the FM, MSR, and FRB models. Fuhrer and Madigan (1997) conducted deterministic simulations of the FM model to assess the extent to which the zero bound prevents real rates from falling and thus cushioning aggregate output in response to negative spending shocks. Orphanides and Wieland (1998) perform stochastic simulations of the MSR model and find that (1) the effectiveness of monetary policy is significantly reduced at infla-

Second, the hypothesized invariance of the estimated model parameters to changes in policy rules is unlikely to hold true under policies that are so dramatically different (in terms of funds rate volatility) from those seen during the sample periods over which the models were estimated.

The outline of the paper is as follows. Section 6.2 provides a brief description of the four models. Section 6.3 outlines the objective function and constraints used in determining the policy frontiers of each model and describes the computational methods used to obtain these frontiers. Section 6.4 analyzes the inflation-output volatility frontier of each model for the following classes of policy rules: three-parameter rules in which the funds rate responds to the current output gap, the four-quarter average inflation rate, and the lagged funds rate; more complicated rules that incorporate a larger number of observed state variables; and rules that incorporate model-based forecasts of the output gap and inflation rate. This section also considers the extent to which these results are sensitive to the information lags that policymakers typically face. Section 6.5 analyzes the performance of other simple rules and investigates several potential explanations for the superior performance of rules with a coefficient near unity on the lagged interest rate. Section 6.6 compares the extent to which simple and complicated rules are robust to model uncertainty. Conclusions then follow.

6.2   Comparison of Basic Model Properties

This section provides a brief overview of the structure and basic properties of the four models. Table 6.1 summarizes the basic features of each model, including (1) the level of aggregation for expenditures, prices, employment, and the external sector; (2) the specification of wage and price dynamics; (3) the forward-looking elements of the expenditure block, including the long-term bond maturity and the discount rate used in computing permanent income; and (4) the sample period used in estimating each model. The behavioral equations of the FM model were estimated using full-information maximum likelihood, while a combination of ordinary least squares, two-stage least squares, and generalized method of moments were used in estimating the parameters of the other three models.

6.2.1   Aggregate Demand

The FM model represents aggregate spending by a single reduced-form equation corresponding to an IS curve. The current output gap depends on its

tion targets below 1 percent and (2) distortions due to the zero bound generate a nonvertical long-run Phillips curve and result in higher inflation and output variability. Reifschneider and Williams (1998) find that under standard linear policy rules, the zero bound begins to reduce stabilization performance in the FRB model for inflation targets below 2 percent; however, by modifying these rules to account for the nonnegativity constraint on the federal funds rate, the performance deterioration due to the zero bound can be nearly eliminated, even for a zero inflation target.

Table 6.1   **Comparison of Model Specifications**

	FM	MSR	FRB	TMCM
IS components	1	5	17	10
Price variables	2	2	7	5
Labor variables	0	0	4	0
Asset prices	1	2	7	2
Foreign variables	0	0	3[a]	95
Wage and price dynamics	Staggered real wage contracts	Staggered real wage contracts	Generalized adjustment costs	Staggered nominal wage contracts
Maturity of bond	10 years	2 years	5–30 years[b]	2 years
Permanent income discount rate	n.a.	10% per quarter	7% per quarter	10% per quarter
Estimation period	1982–94[c]	1980–96	1966–95	1971–86

[a]The full FRB model contains over 400 foreign variables; in the version of the FRB model used in this paper, these have been replaced by three equations for foreign output, foreign prices, and the price of imported oil.
[b]The FRB model includes bonds with maturities of 5, 10, and 30 years, as well as equity prices. The 5-year bond is used in computing the cost of capital for business equipment and consumer purchases of durables.
[c]The parameters of the FM model were estimated using the sample period 1966:1–94:1. However, in constructing the innovation covariance matrix, we only use residuals for the period 1982:4–94:1.

lagged values over the past two quarters and the lagged value of the long-term real interest rate, which is defined as a weighted average of ex ante short-term real interest rates with maturity equivalent to a 10-year coupon bond. The parameter estimates are taken from Fuhrer (1997a). The FM model does not explicitly include trade variables or exchange rates; instead, net exports (and the relationship between real interest rates and real exchange rates) are implicitly incorporated in the IS curve equation.

The MSR model disaggregates real spending into five components: private consumption, fixed investment, inventory investment, net exports, and government purchases.[7] The aggregate demand components exhibit partial adjustment to their respective equilibrium levels, measured as shares of potential GDP. Equilibrium consumption is a function of permanent income (discounted 10 percent per quarter) and the real two-year bond rate, equilibrium fixed investment is a function of output growth and the real bond rate, and equilibrium inventory investment depends only on output growth. Equilibrium government purchases are a constant share of GDP. Net exports are assumed to be fixed in the simulations reported here.

TMCM disaggregates IS components further; for example, spending on

---

7. The demand side of this model is similar to Taylor (1993a) and Taylor and Williams (1993), while the wage-price sector is taken from Fuhrer (1997b).

fixed investment is separated into three components: equipment, nonresidential structures, and residential construction. The specification of these equations is very similar to that of the more aggregated equations in the MSR model. In TMCM, imports follow partial adjustment to an equilibrium level that depends on U.S. income and the relative price of imports, while exports display partial adjustment to an equilibrium level that depends on foreign output and the relative price of exports. Uncovered interest rate parity determines each bilateral exchange rate (up to a time-varying risk premium); for example, the expected one-period-ahead percentage change in the deutsche mark–dollar exchange rate equals the current difference between U.S. and German short-term interest rates.

The FRB model features about the same level of aggregation as TMCM for private spending but divides government spending into six components, each of which follows a simple reduced-form equation. The specification of most nontrade private spending equations follows Tinsley's (1993) generalized adjustment cost model. Each component has a specific flow or stock equilibrium condition; for example, equilibrium aggregate consumption is proportional to permanent income.[8] Households and businesses adjust their spending in each category according to the solution of a quadratic adjustment cost problem. The resulting spending decision rules are specified as forward-looking error correction equations: the current growth of each spending variable depends on up to three of its own lagged values and on expected future growth in equilibrium spending and responds negatively to the lagged percentage deviation between actual and equilibrium spending levels. Exports and nonoil imports are specified as error correction processes with long-run income and price elasticities set equal to unity. Uncovered interest rate parity determines the multilateral exchange rate, subject to a sovereign risk premium that moves with the U.S. net external asset position.

6.2.2 Aggregate Supply

In FM, MSR, and TMCM, the aggregate wage rate is determined by overlapping wage contracts. In particular, the aggregate wage is defined to be the weighted average of current and three lagged values of the contract wage rate. TMCM follows the specification in Taylor (1980), where the current nominal contract wage is determined as a weighted average of expected nominal contract wages, adjusted for the expected state of the economy over the life of the contract. FM and MSR use the overlapping real contract wage specification proposed by Buiter and Jewitt (1981) and implemented by Fuhrer and Moore (1995), in which the real contract wage—the contract wage deflated by the aggregate wage—is determined as a weighted average of expected real con-

---

8. The consumption equations are based on the life cycle theory and include different marginal propensities to consume out of different categories of wealth (labor income, property income, stock market) reflecting the differing characteristics of the owners of these assets. See Brayton, Mauskopf, et al. (1997) for a discussion.

tract wages, adjusted for the expected average output gap over the life of the contract.[9]

In FM and MSR, the aggregate price level is a constant markup over the aggregate wage rate. In contrast, the output price in TMCM follows a backward-looking error correction specification: current output price inflation depends positively on its own lagged value, on current wage inflation, and on lagged import price inflation and responds negatively (with a coefficient of -0.2) to the lagged percentage deviation of the actual price level from equilibrium. Import prices error-correct slowly to an equilibrium level equal to a constant markup over a weighted average of foreign prices converted to dollars. This partial adjustment of import and output prices imparts somewhat more persistence to output price inflation than would result from staggered nominal wages alone.

The FRB model explicitly models potential output as a function of the labor force, crude energy use, and a composite capital stock, using a three-factor Cobb-Douglas production technology. The equilibrium output price is a markup over a weighted average of the productivity-adjusted wage rate and the domestic energy price. The specification of wage and price dynamics follows the generalized adjustment cost framework used in the FRB IS block. Wage inflation depends on lagged wage inflation over the previous three quarters, as well as expected future growth in prices and productivity, and a weighted average of expected future unemployment rates. Price inflation depends on its own lagged values over the past two quarters, as well as expected future changes in equilibrium prices and expected future unemployment rates. In addition, both wages and prices error-correct to their respective equilibrium levels. As in the other models, a vertical long-run Phillips curve is imposed in estimation.

Unlike the other three models, the FRB model contains a detailed accounting of various categories of income, taxes, and stocks, an explicit treatment of labor markets, and endogenous determination of potential output. Long-run equilibrium in the FRB model is of the stock-flow type; the income tax rate and real exchange rate risk premium adjust over time to bring government and foreign debt-GDP ratios back to specified (constant) values.

6.2.3 Foreign Sector

Neither the FM nor the MSR model explicitly includes foreign variables; in contrast, both TMCM and the full FRB staff model include detailed treatments of foreign variables. TMCM features estimated equations for demand components and wages and prices for the other G-7 countries at about the level of aggregation of the U.S. sector. The full FRB staff model includes a total of 12 sectors (countries or regions) that encompass the entire global economy. Be-

---

9. For the FM model, we use the estimated parameters from Fuhrer (1997a). The MSR model uses the parameter estimates of Fuhrer (1997b), for which the implied response of inflation to output gaps is smaller than that obtained by Fuhrer and Moore (1995) and substantially larger than that of Fuhrer (1997a).

cause of the size of the model, the cost of solving and computing the moments of the full FRB model is prohibitive. Preliminary investigations using TMCM suggest that the characteristics of optimal U.S. monetary policies are not greatly affected by the precise specification of the foreign sector; the details of these results are described in the appendix.[10] Based on these results and the benefits of reduced computational cost, we replaced the full set of equations describing foreign countries in the FRB staff model with two simple reduced-form equations for foreign output and prices. For the remainder of the paper, we refer to this simplified version of the model as the FRB model.[11]

6.2.4 Dynamic Properties

We now turn to the basic dynamic properties of output and inflation—as measured by the unconditional autocorrelations—in the four models. Because output and inflation dynamics are sensitive to the specification of monetary policy, we begin by specifying a baseline monetary policy rule. For this purpose, we use the following interest rate reaction function, which was estimated using quarterly U.S. data over the sample period 1980:1–96:4:

$$r_t = -0.0042 + 0.795r_{t-1} + 0.625\pi_t + 1.171y_t - 0.967y_{t-1} + u_t,$$
$$(0.0036) \quad (0.07) \quad\quad (0.13) \quad\quad (0.26) \quad\quad (0.23)$$
(1)

$$\bar{R}^2 = 0.925, \quad SER = 0.010, \quad DW = 2.50,$$

where r_t is the federal funds rate, π_t is the four-quarter moving average of the inflation rate, and y_t is the current output gap.[12] Clarida, Galí, and Gertler (1998) and others argue that this period was characterized by a fairly stable policy regime that differed substantially from that of the 1960s and 1970s. This estimated policy rule features a relatively large coefficient on the lagged funds rate and a fairly aggressive response to increases in inflation and output gaps. Furthermore, the pattern of coefficients on the output gap and its lag suggest that policy not only responded to the level of output but also its recent growth.

Given this interest rate reaction function, we compute the dynamic properties of each model using the solution methods described in section 6.3 below. The inflation autocorrelogram of each model under the estimated policy rule

---

10. E.g., using TMCM, we computed optimal policies under two alternative assumptions regarding foreign monetary policies. In the baseline case, each foreign country is assumed to follow an independent constant growth rule for money; in the alternative case, the EU countries are assumed to follow a single currency policy described by a Taylor (1993a) rule, and Canada and Japan follow independent policies using the same Taylor rule specification. The optimal U.S. policy rules were almost identical across the two cases.

11. This version of the model is typically referred to as FRB/US, while the full model is referred to as FRB/GLOBAL.

12. Inflation is measured using the chain-weighted GDP deflator, and the output gap is based on estimates of potential output supplied by the Congressional Budget Office. This rule forms part of the MSR model and is taken from Orphanides and Wieland (1998).

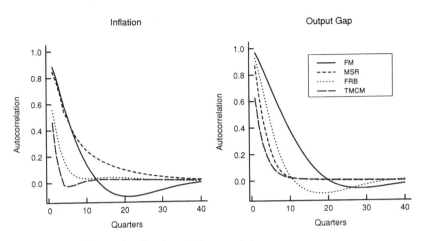

Inflation   Output Gap

Fig. 6.1   Persistence implications of four models

is depicted in the left-hand panel of figure 6.1.[13] Inflation is highly persistent in the FM and MSR models, a feature of the overlapping real wage contract that Fuhrer and Moore (1995) have emphasized. The FRB model exhibits somewhat less inflation persistence, but by far the least degree of inflation persistence is found in TMCM, for which the inflation autocorrelogram falls below zero after only four quarters. Even when combined with some inertia in price markups, the staggered nominal wage contract specification in TMCM delivers relatively low inflation persistence.

The right-hand panel of figure 6.1 depicts the output gap autocorrelogram of each model. In the FM model, the output gap is extremely persistent and displays some "overshooting" in that the autocorrelation turns negative after five years. The FRB model output gap displays considerably less persistence and slightly more overshooting than the FM model. The MSR and TMCM models—based on similar aggregate demand specifications—share the feature of a relatively low degree of output gap persistence, although it is slightly higher in the MSR model because the monetary policy response to inflation causes some of the persistence in inflation to spill over to output.

To provide a more detailed comparison of the dynamic properties of aggregate demand across models, it is useful to consider the following regression equation:

$$(2) \qquad \Delta y_t = -\delta y_{t-1} + \theta \Delta y_{t-1} - \phi(r_{t-1} - E_{t-1}\pi_t) + \varepsilon_t,$$

where $r_{t-1} - E_{t-1}\pi_t$ is the lagged value of the ex ante real federal funds rate. The parameter δ indicates the degree of persistence (speed of error correction)

13. Throughout the paper, inflation refers to the growth in the GDP price level for FM, MSR, and TMCM, and that of the personal consumption price index for FRB.

Table 6.2   Comparison of Output Dynamics

| | Models | | | | U.S. Data |
Coefficient	FM	MSR	TMCM	FRB	1966:1–95:4
δ	0.04	0.17	0.31	0.05	0.10 (0.03)
θ	0.49	0.45	−0.04	0.26	0.29 (0.08)
ϕ	0.03	0.05	0.06	0.04	0.08 (0.03)

Note: This table considers regression equation (2). The first four columns report asymptotic values of δ, θ, and ϕ for each of the four models, while the final column reports the coefficient estimates and ordinary least squares standard errors of this regression equation using U.S. data for the sample period 1966:1–95:4. For the data regression, expected inflation is proxied by the lagged inflation rate.

of the output gap, the parameter θ indicates the extent to which the output gap exhibits a short-run accelerator effect, and the parameter ϕ indicates the sensitivity of aggregate demand to a change in the short-term real interest rate. We use this simple specification to compare the basic properties of output dynamics between the models and to the data.

Table 6.2 indicates the asymptotic values of δ, θ, and ϕ for each model computed using the unconditional moments of each model, and the estimated coefficients and standard errors obtained from fitting equation (2) using U.S. data over the sample period 1966:1–95:4. Although the MSR model and TMCM have roughly similar output autocorrelograms, the table shows that these models actually imply very different behavior for the output gap. In particular, the output gap in TMCM error-corrects to zero rapidly and displays essentially no accelerator effect, whereas the output gap in the MSR model error-corrects more gradually and displays a strong accelerator effect. The FM and FRB models both imply a relatively high degree of persistence, while the accelerator effect in FM is nearly twice as strong as in the FRB model. Finally, the coefficients on the real short-term interest rate are similar across the four models, with FM displaying the least real interest rate sensitivity of output.

6.3 Computing Policy Frontiers

In this section, we indicate the methods used to solve each model and obtain its unconditional moments for a specific interest rate rule. Then we specify the objective function and constraints faced by the monetary policymaker, and we describe the methods used to obtain the optimal parameter values in each model for a given functional form of the interest rate rule.

6.3.1 Analyzing a Specific Rule

Our analysis incorporates a wide variety of interest rate rules, in which the federal funds rate may depend on its own lagged values as well as the current, lagged, and expected future values of other model variables. In general, the interest rate rule can be expressed as follows:

$$(3) \qquad r_t = \sum_{j=1}^{l} H_j^1 r_{t-j} + \sum_{j=1}^{m} H_j^2 E_t z_{t+j} + \sum_{j=0}^{n} H_j^3 z_{t-j},$$

where r_t is the federal funds rate and the column vector z is a set of model variables that enter the interest rate reaction function. The lagged funds rate coefficients are given by the row vector H_j^1 ($j = 1$ to l), while the coefficients on other model variables are given by the row vectors H_j^2 ($j = 1$ to m) and H_j^3 ($j = 0$ to n). Henceforth we will refer to the combined set of coefficients by the vector $H = \{H^1; H^2; H^3\}$. After discussing how to compute the moments of each model for a specific value of H, we will consider the problem of determining the optimal value of H for a given choice of the elements of z and the lead and lag orders l, m, and n.

As in Fuhrer (1997a), we analyze the performance of a specified policy rule in each model by computing the reduced-form representation of the saddle-point solution and then evaluating an analytic expression for the unconditional second moments of the model variables. For linear models, this approach yields accurate results far more efficiently than simulation-based methods. To take advantage of these methods, we have constructed a linearized version of TMCM and a log-linear version of the FRB model; however, these approximations have negligible effects on the relevant dynamic properties of the two models.

Thus each of the four models can be written in the following form:

$$(4) \qquad \sum_{j=1}^{M} A_j E_t x_{t+j} + \sum_{j=0}^{N} B_j x_{t-j} + C e_t = 0,$$

where x is the vector of all model variables and e is a vector of serially uncorrelated disturbances with mean zero and finite covariance matrix Ω. The interest rate reaction function comprises a single row of equation (4), while the remaining rows contain the structural equations of the model. Thus the parameters of the interest rate rule are contained in one row of the coefficient matrices A_j ($j = 1$ to M) and B_j ($j = 0$ to N), while this row of C is identically equal to zero.

We compute the unique stationary rational expectations solution to equation (4) using the Anderson and Moore (1985) implementation of the Blanchard and Kahn (1980) method, modified to take advantage of sparse matrix functions.[14] The reduced form of this solution can be expressed as follows:

$$(5) \qquad x_t = \sum_{j=1}^{N} D_j(H) x_{t-j} + F(H) e_t,$$

---

14. The algorithm is discussed in more detail in Anderson (1997). Sumner and Williams (1998) discuss methods to improve the computational efficiency of algorithms to solve linear rational expectations models.

where the reduced-form coefficient matrices D_j ($j = 1$ to K) and F depend on the monetary policy parameters H as well as the structural parameters of the model. By defining the vector $\tilde{X}_t = (x_{t-1}, \ldots, x_{t-K})'$, we can express this solution in companion form:

$$(6) \qquad \tilde{x}_t = P(H)\tilde{x}_{t-1} + Q(H)e_t.$$

Then the unconditional contemporaneous covariance matrix for $\tilde{x}_t$, denoted by V_0, is given by

$$(7) \qquad V_0 = \sum_{j=0}^{\infty} P^j Q \Omega Q' P'^j.$$

Using the implicit expression $V_0 = PV_0P' + Q\Omega Q'$, we compute V_0 iteratively using the doubling algorithm described in Hansen and Sargent (1997), modified to take advantage of sparse matrix functions. Given V_0, the autocovariance matrices of $\tilde{x}_t$ are readily computed using the relationship $V_j = P^j V_0$.

6.3.2 The Optimization Problem

For a given functional form of the interest rate rule, we assume that the interest rate rule is chosen to solve the following optimization problem:

$$(8) \qquad \min_{H} \lambda \operatorname{var}(y_t) + (1 - \lambda)\operatorname{var}(\pi_t^1)$$

$$\text{such that } \tilde{x}_t = P(H)\tilde{x}_{t-1} + Q(H)e_t, \qquad \operatorname{var}(\Delta r_t) \leq k^2,$$

where y_t indicates the output gap, π_t^1 indicates the one-quarter inflation rate, and var(s) indicates the unconditional variance of variable s. The weight $\lambda \in [0,1]$ reflects the policymaker's preference for minimizing output volatility relative to inflation volatility. We constrain the level of interest rate volatility by imposing the upper bound k on the standard deviation of the first difference of the federal funds rate; as discussed below, the benchmark value of k is set equal to the funds rate volatility under the estimated policy rule given in equation (1). Finally, throughout our analysis, we only consider policy rules that generate a unique stationary rational expectations solution.

To compute the policy frontier of each model for a particular functional form of the interest rate rule, we determine the parameters of this rule that maximize the objective function for each value of λ over the range zero to unity. Thus, for a given form of the interest rate rule, the policy frontier of each model traces out the best obtainable combinations of output and inflation volatility, subject to the upper bound on funds rate volatility. This approach differs slightly from that commonly found in the literature, in which interest rate volatility is incorporated into the objective function and each policy frontier is drawn using a different weight on interest rate volatility. The standard approach combines information about model-imposed constraints on policy with policymakers' preferences regarding funds rate volatility, whereas we prefer to maintain a strict distinction between the policymaker's preferences and the constraints implied by the model.

To obtain a benchmark value of k for each model, we obtain the rational expectations solution generated by the estimated policy rule in equation (1), and then we compute the standard deviation of the one-quarter change in the funds rate associated with this rule. It should be noted that this benchmark value of k differs across the four models, in part because each model has been estimated over a different sample period and as a result generates a different amount of funds rate volatility for the same policy rule. For example, the moments for the FRB model and TMCM depend in part on shocks from the 1970s—a period of substantial economic turbulence—while the shocks for the FM and MSR models are from the relatively tranquil 1980s and early 1990s. Henceforth, when we construct a policy frontier subject to the benchmark constraint that funds rate volatility does not exceed that of the estimated rule, we refer to the resulting policy frontier as an E-frontier.

For a particular functional form of the interest rate rule, we determine the policy frontier by solving the optimization problem in equation (8) for a range of values of the objective function weight λ. For a given value of λ, we start with an initial guess for the rule parameters, obtain the reduced-form solution matrices G and H, compute the unconditional moments, and calculate the value of the objective function; then a hill-climbing algorithm is applied that iteratively updates the parameter vector until an optimum is obtained.

Thus, to determine a single policy frontier, it is necessary to compute hundreds or even thousands of rational expectations solutions at alternative values of the policy rule parameters. Given our objective of performing a systematic analysis of policy frontiers for a wide range of functional forms of the interest rate rule, it is essential to make use of the highly efficient solution algorithms outlined above. On a Sun Ultra Enterprise 3000 computer—about as fast as an Intel Pentium II 300 MHz computer—only a few CPU seconds are needed to solve and compute the moments of a small-scale model like FM or MSR, while solving a large-scale macroeconometric model like TMCM or the FRB model requires about five CPU minutes.

6.4 Policy Frontiers for Simple and Complicated Rules

In this section, we analyze the properties of policy frontiers for several alternative specifications: rules in which the federal funds rate responds to only three variables (the current output gap, the four-quarter average inflation rate, and the lagged funds rate), more complicated rules that incorporate a larger number of observed state variables, and rules that incorporate model-based forecasts of the output gap and inflation rate. Finally, we consider the extent to which these results are sensitive to a one-quarter information delay.

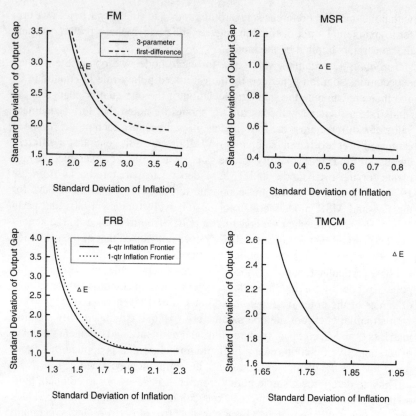

Fig. 6.2   **Policy frontiers for three-parameter rules**

6.4.1   Simple Policy Rules

We start by considering three-parameter rules in which the federal funds rate r_t is determined as a linear function of the current output gap, y_t, the four-quarter average inflation rate, π_t, and the lagged funds rate, r_{t-1}:

$$(9) \qquad r_t = \rho r_{t-1} + (1 - \rho)(r^* + \pi_t) + \alpha(\pi_t - \pi^*) + \beta y_t,$$

where r^* is the unconditional mean of the equilibrium real interest rate and π^* is the inflation target (both assumed to be constant throughout this paper).[15]

The solid lines in figure 6.2 depict the three-parameter E-frontier of each model. As expected, the frontier is convex to the origin, with truncated vertical and horizontal asymptotes as the objective function in equation (8) switches from exclusive concern about stabilizing inflation ($\lambda = 0$) toward exclusive concern about stabilizing output ($\lambda = 1$). Because we restrict attention to pol-

15. Because we ignore the nonnegativity constraint on nominal interest rates, we implicitly assume that the inflation target is sufficiently high so that its effects are negligible (cf. n. 6).

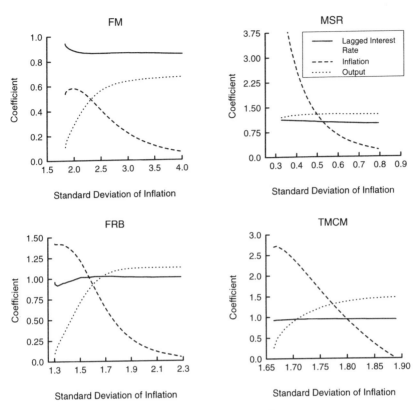

Fig. 6.3   Coefficients of optimal three-parameter rules

icy rules that generate a unique stationary rational expectations equilibrium, the unconditional variance of inflation is finite even in the case where $\lambda = 1$.

Each panel of figure 6.2 also indicates the relative performance of the estimated rule, denoted by the letter E. Because the estimated rule generates the same amount of funds rate volatility as the three-parameter E-frontier of each model, comparison of the estimated rule to the policy frontier is straightforward. The estimated rule performs appreciably worse than the optimal three-parameter rules for MSR, FRB, and TMCM, despite the fact that the estimated rule incorporates an additional variable (the lagged output gap). As discussed below, the optimal value of ρ for these three models is substantially higher than the estimated value of about 0.8 shown in equation (1).

The coefficient values for optimal three-parameter rules are shown in figure 6.3. In each model, a lower inflation coefficient generates a higher standard deviation of inflation, as one would expect. The output gap coefficients vary somewhat less along each policy frontier. The output gap coefficients for MSR are close to unity along the whole policy frontier. In the FRB model, the output gap coefficient is smaller for rules corresponding to low values of λ but is otherwise quite close to unity. The output gap coefficient in TMCM ranges between 0.6 and 1.5 along the policy frontier. Finally, the optimal output gap and inflation coefficients for the FM model are much smaller than for the other three models.

The key result to be noted from figure 6.3 is that the three-parameter policy frontiers of all four models are associated with rules in which the coefficient ρ on the lagged funds rate is very close to unity. In particular, the parameter ρ takes values in the range [0.84, 0.95] for the FM model, [1.0, 1.1] for the MSR model, [0.92, 1.03] for the FRB model, and [0.94, 0.98] for TMCM. Thus, as noted above, the relatively poor performance of the estimated reaction function in the latter three models can be attributed mainly to the fact that the estimated value of $\rho = 0.8$ in equation (1) is substantially smaller than the optimal value of ρ for these models.

To examine this feature more closely, we consider the class of first-difference rules, which are a special case of the three-parameter rules described by the previous equation:

$$(10) \qquad r_t = r_{t-1} + \alpha(\pi_t - \pi^*) + \beta y_t .$$

For three of the four models (MSR, FRB, and TMCM), the E-frontier for first-difference rules is virtually identical to the three-parameter E-frontier; that is, imposing the constraint $\rho = 1$ is essentially costless in these models. For the FM model, first-difference rules are associated with slightly higher output and inflation volatility compared with three-parameter rules, as seen by comparing the dashed and solid lines in the upper left-hand panel of figure 6.2.

Finally, the lower left-hand panel of figure 6.2 shows that stabilization performance deteriorates substantially in the FRB model if the simple policy rule is expressed in terms of the one-quarter inflation rate rather than the four-quarter average inflation rate. In all four models, policy rules that incorporate the four-quarter average inflation rate are strictly preferred to alternative rules that utilize a higher-frequency measure of the inflation rate.[16] The one-quarter inflation rate contains a substantial amount of high-frequency noise that is essentially unforecastable and immune to stabilization efforts; the four-quarter average inflation rate filters out some of this noise.

6.4.2   Complicated Policy Rules

In the simple rules described by equations (9) and (10), the funds rate is adjusted in response to only three variables: the current output gap, the four-

---

16. In this paper, we focus on rules in which the inflation variable is defined as the four-quarter average inflation rate. In fact, for the FM, MSR, and FRB models, using an even lower frequency measure of the inflation rate (e.g., the eight-quarter or twelve-quarter average inflation rate) provides small improvement in terms of the best obtainable outcomes for output and inflation volatility, while the four-quarter average inflation rate works best in TMCM. However, it should be emphasized that the results of this paper are not sensitive to the choice between a four-quarter, eight-quarter, or twelve-quarter inflation rate in the policy rule.

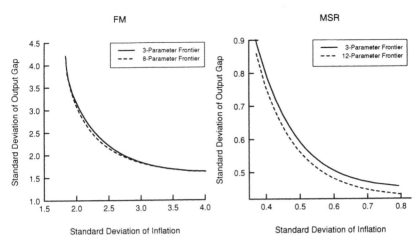

Fig. 6.4   Policy frontiers for complicated rules

quarter average inflation rate, and the lagged interest rate. In practice, central banks have access to far more information about the state of the economy. Optimal control theory indicates that the policy rule should incorporate all relevant information; that is, the rule should involve all of the state variables of the specific economic model under consideration. Thus, we investigate the extent to which complicated rules that respond to expanded subsets of the state variables can generate substantially lower output and inflation volatility.

Due to computational costs, our analysis of this issue focuses on the two smaller models, FM and MSR, for which we can obtain policy frontiers for rules that include all observed state variables. The FM model contains eight such variables (the lagged interest rate, the current values of the output gap and one-quarter inflation rate, two lags of the output gap, and three lags of the one-quarter inflation rate), while the MSR model contains twenty observed state variables. We have also investigated rules with up to six parameters in the FRB model and TMCM; the results of those experiments confirm the findings reported here for the two smaller models.

For the FM model, we find that the optimal eight-parameter rules put substantial weight on one or both of the lagged output terms that are excluded from the three-parameter policy rules. Furthermore, the optimal eight-parameter rules typically exhibit complicated patterns of weights on the current and lagged one-quarter inflation rates, whereas these weights are constrained to be equal in the three-parameter policy rules (which only respond to the four-quarter average inflation rate). Evidently, the optimal eight-parameter rules are fine-tuned to the model, in the sense that the pattern of coefficients on lagged output and inflation reflects the dynamic properties of the FM model. Nevertheless, as seen in the left-hand panel of figure 6.4, the eight-parameter policy frontier is nearly indistinguishable from the three-parameter policy frontier;

that is, more complicated rules provide only negligible improvements in output and inflation stability beyond that achieved by optimal simple rules.

Because demand is disaggregated into four components in the MSR model, additional gains in performance might be expected by augmenting the three-parameter rule in equation (9) to allow policy to respond differently to consumption, fixed investment, inventory investment, and government spending. Thus we consider twelve-parameter rules that include current values of these four components of aggregate demand as well as the variables in the eight-parameter rules described above. Unsurprisingly, the optimal twelve-parameter rules exhibit complicated coefficient patterns that are fine-tuned to the dynamics of the model. The right-hand panel of figure 6.4 shows that these complicated twelve-parameter rules yield visible but not striking improvements in output and inflation stability compared with simple three-parameter rules. Augmenting the twelve-parameter rule with other observed state variables (i.e., the lagged values of the individual components of aggregate demand) yields trivial improvements in the policy frontier.

We conclude from this analysis that small improvements in output and inflation stability may be possible by including more variables (i.e., more information about the state of the economy) in the interest rate rule. Of course, such benefits may be offset by the lower degree of transparency associated with complicated policy rules. Furthermore, section 6.6 considers the implications of model uncertainty and provides evidence that complicated policy rules are somewhat less robust than optimal simple rules.

6.4.3 Rules with Model-Based Forecasts

Simple policy rules that incorporate model-based forecasts of the output gap and inflation rate implicitly respond to all the observed states in the model (albeit in a highly restricted fashion) but are relatively parsimonious in terms of the number of free parameters in the rule. We have already noted that small reductions in output and inflation volatility can be obtained using complicated rules that respond to a large number of observed state variables. We now analyze the extent to which these performance gains can be achieved by simple rules that incorporate forecasts of the output gap and inflation rate. In this analysis, we assume the forecasts are consistent with the model and are known to the public.

Using three different approaches to incorporating model-based forecasts of the output gap and inflation rate, we find negligible benefits from using model-based forecasts rather than realized values of these variables. First, when we augment the class of three-parameter rules to allow policy to respond additionally to one-quarter and two-quarter forecasts of the output gap or the inflation rate, or both, we find very little improvement in performance relative to optimal three-parameter rules based only on current and lagged variables. Second, we consider three-parameter rules in which the current output gap is replaced by model-based forecasts of the future output gap at various horizons. In all four models, rules that respond to forecasts of the output gap yield at best very small improvements over rules that respond to the current output gap. Finally, we consider three-parameter rules that replace the current four-quarter average inflation rate with a model-based forecast of this inflation rate, at a forecast horizon of one to four quarters. For the FM and MSR models, using a model-based inflation forecast always results in worse performance than using the current inflation rate. For TMCM and the FRB model, using the two-quarter-ahead model-based inflation forecast generates a very small improvement in performance compared with using the current inflation rate.

6.4.4 Information Lags

In the preceding analysis, we have sidestepped one potentially important issue: policymakers may not have full knowledge of the current state of the economy but instead must act on data that comes in with a lag of weeks, months, or even longer. As McCallum (1994, 1997) has emphasized, policy rules must be *operational* in the sense that they can be implemented in real time. In this paper, we do not examine the implications of using mismeasured data but instead focus on the impact of information lags.[17]

A one-quarter information lag probably provides an accurate representation of the time delay with which information becomes available to policymakers. The first "advance" release of quarterly National Income and Product Accounts data occurs within one month of the end of the quarter, and monthly labor market and consumer price index data are available by the middle of the following month. Other weekly and monthly data become available with short lags. To make the contrast to the results based on complete current information as stark as possible, we restrict ourselves to policies that depend only on lagged inflation, output gaps, and interest rates. We do not consider rules that incorporate current-quarter forecasts based on lagged information; if anything, our approach introduces an additional upward bias in assessing the true costs associated with information lags.

Figure 6.5 compares the three-parameter policy frontiers using current and lagged variables. The imposition of lagged variables in the rule imposes miniscule costs in terms of stabilization in the FM and FRB models, and relatively small costs in the MSR model and TMCM. The characteristics of well-performing rules are also essentially unchanged. Evidently, a one-quarter information lag does not inhibit effective inflation and output stabilization in the models we consider here.

The reason for these small costs is that inflation and output are highly persistent in all four models, and thus the lagged inflation rate and lagged output gap are good proxies for the current values of these variables. Nevertheless, the degree of output persistence does vary across the four models and largely ac-

17. Sources of mismeasurement relevant for policy rules include the noise in the data due to sampling and data imputation methods and imprecise estimation of potential output and the natural rate of unemployment. Orphanides (1998) studies the relevance of measurement problems for policy rules. Wieland (1998) examines optimal policy when the natural rate is unknown.

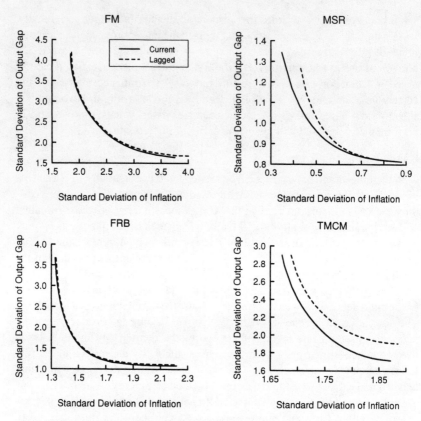

Fig. 6.5   **Implications of using lagged information**

counts for the differences in the costs of information lags. For the MSR model and TMCM, which display relatively low output persistence (first-order autocorrelation under first-difference rules of about .75 and .5, respectively), the cost of using lagged output gaps is larger than for the FM and FRB models with relatively high output persistence (.95 and .85 first-order autocorrelations under first-difference rules, respectively). In the case of inflation, any effects on performance due to the use of lagged variables is further dampened by the fact that rules on the three-parameter policy frontier involve the four-quarter average inflation rate. The marginal impact of the current inflation rate is thus relatively small, so the shift in timing has little effect on the stabilization properties of rules on the policy frontier.

6.5   Comparison of Alternative Simple Rules

In this section, we focus in greater detail on the properties of three-parameter rules of the form given in equation (9). This class of policy rules nests "level" rules such as those considered by Henderson and McKibbin

Table 6.3   **Parameter Values of Alternative Simple Rules**

Policy Rule	Parameters		
	α	β	ρ
A	1.3	0.6	1
B	0.8	1.0	1
C	3.0	0.8	1
D	1.2	1.0	1
T	0.5	0.5	0
T2	0.5	1.0	0
V	1.5	0.06	1.3
W	1.6	0.08	1.3

(1993) and Taylor (1993a), in which the lagged funds rate coefficient $\rho = 0$. We shall use the term "interest rate smoothing" to refer to rules in which this coefficient is substantially larger than zero, as in partial adjustment rules ($0 < \rho < 1$) and first-difference rules ($\rho = 1$).[18] As shown previously in figure 6.3, the optimal value of ρ even exceeds unity in certain cases but is never quite as large as the optimal values obtained by Rotemberg and Woodford (1997). Of course, level rules are also associated with persistence in the funds rate because output and inflation exhibit substantial persistence in all four models.

Table 6.3 indicates the values of α, β, and ρ for eight different rules in this class. Rules A and B are taken from the *E*-frontier of the FRB model, with the value of ρ constrained to unity. These rules correspond to values of $\lambda = 0.25$ and $\lambda = 0.75$, respectively (i.e., the weight on output volatility relative to inflation volatility), in the objective function given in equation (8). The two rules labeled C and D are more aggressive rules that stabilize output and inflation more effectively than rules A and B but induce substantially higher interest rate volatility.[19] Rule T is the rule proposed by Taylor (1993a). Rule T2 is a modified version of Taylor's rule in which the coefficient on the output gap has been doubled. Rules V and W are optimal policy rules for the dynamic general equilibrium model analyzed by Rotemberg and Woodford (1997).

Table 6.4 clearly shows that rules T and T2, in which the *level* of the funds

18. In the existing literature (e.g., Lowe and Ellis 1997; Goodhart 1998), the phrase "interest rate smoothing" has been used to refer to two different (albeit related) characteristics of interest rate behavior: (1) the degree of persistence in interest rates that results from partial adjustment or error correction specifications of the interest rate reaction function and (2) a policy preference for reducing the variance of short-term interest rates. Throughout this paper, we use the phrase "interest rate smoothing" to refer to policy rules in which the partial adjustment parameter ρ is significantly greater than zero and avoid using the phrase to refer to rules that generate relatively low interest rate volatility.

19. Rules C and D are included here to maintain consistency with the specifications used by other authors in this volume; these are the rules labeled I and II, respectively, in table 1 of the editor's introduction by John Taylor. The parameters of rules C and D were originally chosen based on a specification of the three-parameter rule that incorporated the twelve-quarter average inflation rate instead of the four-quarter average inflation rate.

Table 6.4 **Rule Comparison Table**

	Standard Deviations			
Model and Rule	SD(y)	SD(π)	SD(r)	SD(Δr)
FM				
A	3.78	1.85	8.89	1.97
B	2.37	2.45	7.71	1.83
C	5.15	1.60	15.39	3.92
D	2.85	2.17	8.61	2.07
T	2.68	2.63	3.57	0.75
T2	2.32	2.84	3.83	0.90
V	21.2	7.13	27.2	4.38
W	20.5	6.57	27.9	4.59
MSR				
A	0.84	0.40	1.17	0.34
B	0.58	0.53	1.33	0.48
C	1.07	0.29	1.40	0.43
D	0.64	0.44	1.35	0.48
T	0.99	0.70	1.01	0.30
T2	0.87	0.73	1.19	0.50
V	1.95	0.41	1.31	0.19
W	1.88	0.38	1.30	0.19
FRB				
A	2.12	1.46	4.34	1.22
B	1.41	1.65	4.50	1.22
C	2.77	1.37	7.11	2.34
D	1.62	1.56	4.84	1.39
T	2.92	1.86	2.51	0.90
T2	2.21	2.02	3.16	1.20
V	6.32	1.55	4.67	1.11
W	6.06	1.53	4.88	1.19
TMCM				
A	2.33	1.73	4.78	1.71
B	1.95	1.79	5.03	2.01
C	2.70	1.68	6.72	2.80
D	1.95	1.79	5.03	2.01
T	2.89	2.58	4.00	1.58
T2	2.55	2.36	4.35	2.41
V	4.31	2.06	4.24	1.24
W	4.26	2.02	4.47	1.33
U.S. data				
(1980:1–95:2)	2.4	2.1	3.7	1.3

Note: The U.S. data use a measure of potential output provided by the Congressional Budget Office. Caution should be used in comparing the sample moments with those of each model, because the sample period involves an exceptionally high initial inflation rate, whereas the model-based moments are unconditional deviations from steady state.

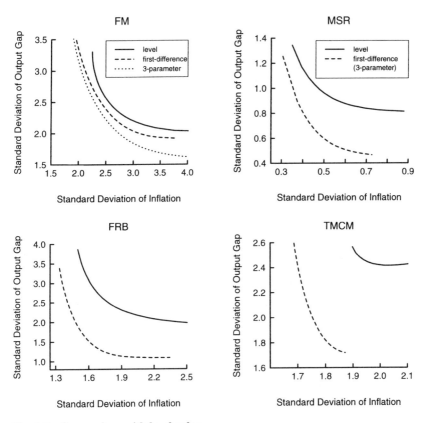

Fig. 6.6 Comparison with level rules

rate responds to the output gap and inflation rate, are dominated by rules like A and B, where the *first difference* of the funds rate responds to the output gap and inflation rate. Rules V and W perform relatively poorly in stabilizing output and inflation in all four models. One reason for these poor results is that rules V and W set ρ to about 1.3, which is much larger than the optimal range of about 0.9 to 1.1 for the four models considered here. Furthermore, even if policymakers only care about stabilizing inflation (i.e., λ = 0), the output gap coefficient should generally be larger than the values of 0.06 and 0.08 used in rules V and W, respectively, because the current output gap is an important leading indicator for the inflation rate.

Figure 6.6 provides further information on the benefits of a large coefficient on the lagged funds rate in comparison with level rules. The solid line indicates the E-frontier associated with level rules—that is, the inflation-output volatility frontier for rules having the form of equation (9) with ρ = 0, under the constraint that the standard deviation of Δr does not exceed that generated by the estimated rule in equation (1). The dotted and dashed lines show the

E-frontiers for three-parameter and first-difference rules, as previously depicted in figure 6.2. As previously noted, the E-frontiers for three-parameter and first-difference rules are virtually identical for three of the models, while the optimal three-parameter rules associated with the FM model incorporate values of ρ that are large but noticeably smaller than unity.

Figure 6.6 reveals very substantial gains from setting ρ near unity in all four models. In fact, these are the largest gains we have found among all the permutations of simple policy rules that we have investigated.[20] In the FRB model, for example, using a first-difference rule instead of a level rule can reduce the standard deviation of output by a full percentage point.

Although empirical evidence reveals a pattern of interest rate smoothing in many industrial countries and is a property of the estimated U.S. interest rate rule in equation (1), the normative case for interest rate smoothing has remained much less clear.[21] Lowe and Ellis (1997) have recently surveyed the literature and summarized several considerations that tend to favor interest rate smoothing.[22] One argument, advanced by Goodfriend (1991) and others, is particularly relevant to our analysis. For a given movement in the short-term interest rate, the impact on long-term interest rates is greater if the movement is expected to be sustained rather than short-lived. Thus interest rate smoothing offers the potential for greater control over long-term bond rates and hence over aggregate demand and inflation.

This rationale for interest rate smoothing is explicitly captured in the four rational expectations models considered here: in each model, monetary policy stabilizes output and inflation mainly through its influence on the long-term real interest rate, which is determined as a weighted average of current and expected future short-term rates.[23] For a given set of economic conditions, movements in the federal funds rate are expected to persist longer under the first-difference rule compared to the level rule; thus a given initial adjustment of the federal funds rate induces a larger movement in the long-term bond rate and thereby achieves more rapid stabilization of output and inflation.

---

20. The beneficial impact of interest rate smoothing extends to models that fall outside the class of models we consider here, such as the models in Rotemberg and Woodford (1997) and Rebelo and Xie (1997), that explicitly incorporate optimizing behavior of representative agents.

21. Clarida et al. (1998) also document the practice of interest rate smoothing for U.S. monetary policy.

22. E.g., policymakers may dislike frequent reversals in interest rates, either because such changes make the policymaker look poorly informed and undermine confidence in the central bank as argued by Caplin and Leahy (1996) or because it is difficult to obtain broad-based political support for such changes in direction as suggested by Goodhart (1996). Furthermore, by avoiding large movements in interest rates the central bank can reduce financial market volatility and in doing so reduces the likelihood of instability when particular institutions incur large losses. Finally, the nature of the decision-making process may lead to caution. E.g., Alan Blinder (1995), when vice-chairman of the Board of Governors, argued that uncertainty that policymakers have about the parameters of the underlying model justifies "stodginess" in monetary policy; see also the discussion in Blinder (1998).

23. TMCM and FRB also include an explicit exchange rate channel of monetary policy, while FRB includes a channel for wealth, which is negatively related to long-term real interest rates.

To evaluate the role of this mechanism in explaining the superior performance of rules with a large coefficient on the lagged funds rate, we conduct counterfactual experiments in each of the two smaller models, FM and MSR. In particular, we shorten the maturity of the term structure equation and compute new constrained inflation-output volatility frontiers based on rules with three parameters. In the FM model, we replace the 30-year bond rate with the current short-term rate in the IS curve.[24] We find that the range of values of ρ along the frontier declines from [0.85, 0.95] to [0.56, .08]. In the MSR model, we replace the eight-quarter maturity bond with the current funds rate in the consumption and investment equations and find that the range of coefficients on the lagged federal funds rate along the frontier declines from [1.0, 1.1] to [0.75, 1.0]. Thus, in both models, the optimal coefficient on the lagged funds rate is significantly reduced when the maturity of the relevant long rate is shortened.

In addition to the forward-looking characteristics of long-term bond rates, it is useful to consider several other factors that may contribute to the superior performance of rules with a large coefficient on the lagged funds rate. First, control theory suggests that the optimal policy rule should take into account all available information, including lagged values of the output gap and inflation rate. A rule with a high value of ρ implicitly makes the current interest rate depend on the complete history of output and inflation, albeit in a very restricted way. Thus the lagged funds rate may be serving as a simple proxy that permits additional information to be included in a suboptimal level rule.

We test this explanation by computing frontiers for rules that include all observable state variables and then checking whether these complicated rules are characterized by smaller lagged funds rate coefficients. Because of the high computational cost of conducting this experiment, we focus on the small models, FM and MSR. The policy frontiers associated with complicated rules for these models have already been shown in figure 6.4. Here we simply note that rules that include all observed state variables call for somewhat smaller coefficients on the lagged funds rate. In the FM model, the range of values of ρ along the frontier is almost identical for the case of three-parameter rules as for rules that respond to all observable state variables, while in the MSR model, the range of values of ρ decline from [1.0, 1.1] to [0.9, 1.0] for rules that respond to all observed state variables.

Next, we consider the relationship between the optimal value of ρ and the preference for funds rate volatility implicitly imposed in drawing the frontiers. For each model, figure 6.7 shows three frontiers with different restrictions on funds rate volatility. In each case the baseline E-frontier is shown as a solid line. Using frontier rules as a guide, the stabilization gains from increased funds rate volatility are evidently rather small. Table 6.5 shows typical values

24. We reduced the coefficient on the real rate to avoid increasing the interest sensitivity of aggregate demand.

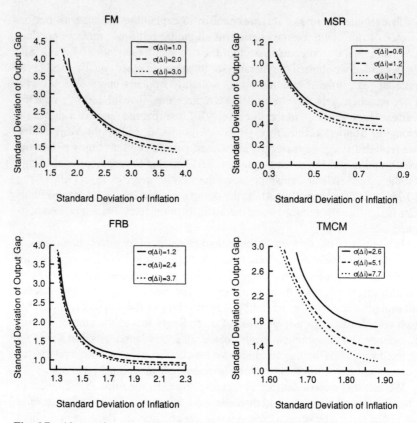

Fig. 6.7 **Alternative constraints on funds rate volatility**

of the standard deviation of the *level* of the funds rate generated by the policies that underlie the frontiers shown in the figure. In each case, outcomes corresponding to the baseline *E*-frontier are given in the first two columns. Except for the MSR model, relaxing the constraint on funds rate volatility much beyond that implied by the *E*-frontier entails so much volatility of the level of the funds rate that the optimal policy rule would regularly dictate negative nominal interest rates when the steady state nominal interest rate—that is, the sum of the steady state real interest rate and the target inflation rate—is reasonably low.

In all four models, relaxing the constraint on interest rate volatility results in smaller values of ρ for the three-parameter rules on the policy frontier. However, the quantitative results differ somewhat across models. In the FM model, the reduction in ρ is particularly pronounced: doubling the upper bound on SD(Δr) causes the range of values for ρ to drop from [0.85, 0.95] to [0.75, 0.92]. In the other three models, relaxing the funds rate volatility constraint leads to somewhat smaller reductions in the optimal value of ρ. In the

Table 6.5   **Volatility of Funds Rate Levels and Changes**

Model	*E*-Frontier		Alternative Frontier with Doubled Volatility		Alternative Frontier with Tripled Volatility	
	SD(Δr)	SD(r)	SD(Δr)	SD(r)	SD(Δr)	SD(r)
FM	1	5	2	7	3	9
MSR	0.6	1.5	1.2	2.3	1.7	2.9
FRB	1.2	4.5	2.4	6	3.7	9
TMCM	2.6	6	5.1	9	7.7	11

FRB model, doubling SD(Δr) reduces the optimal value of ρ by about 0.07 on average, from a range of [0.96, 1.02] to [0.93 0.96]. In TMCM and in MSR, doubling SD(Δr) only reduces the optimal value of ρ by about 0.03. Evidently, even with relatively high interest rate volatility, a relatively large coefficient on the lagged funds rate is preferred in these models.

Finally, we consider the extent to which interest rate rules with a large coefficient on the lagged funds rate stabilize the economy by generating secondary cycles, for example, overshooting of output. To highlight this feature, we analyze the dynamic response of output to an exogenous increase in aggregate demand under a level rule versus a three-parameter rule with a high coefficient on the lagged funds rate. Each rule corresponds to the policy frontier associated with the same level of interest volatility as that resulting from the estimated rule in equation (1). In the FM model, we consider a 1 standard deviation shock to the IS curve. In the MSR model, autonomous demand increases due to 1 standard deviation shocks to consumption, fixed investment, inventory investment, and government spending.

Figure 6.8 shows the stark contrast in the dynamic response of output under the two rules. In each model, the optimal three-parameter rule substantially dampens the response of output in the first few quarters compared to the optimal level rule and subsequently pushes output below potential for some time. Because the spending equations in both FM and MSR are forward looking, these expected future movements in output, prices, and short-term interest rates play a role in dampening the initial impact of the aggregate demand shock. Given the objective of minimizing the variance of output and inflation, there is a potential gain from reducing the peak response at the cost of increasing the extent of overshooting. In both models, moderate overshooting resulting from policy with large values of ρ is preferred to a monotone reversion to equilibrium values; for example, the optimal three-parameter rule reduces the standard deviation of output by 15 percent in FM and by nearly 40 percent in MSR, compared with the level rule.

In summary, our results suggest that the forward-looking feature of long-term bond rates is the principal explanation for the superior performance of rules in which the lagged funds rate coefficient ρ is near unity. In response to

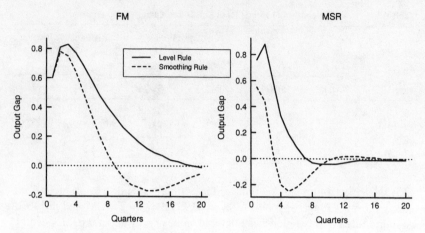

Fig. 6.8   Aggregate demand shocks under alternative rules

a shock, such an "interest rate smoothing" rule typically generates a small but persistent movement in the short rate, which induces a large movement in the current long-term bond rate and thereby facilitates the stabilization of output and inflation. If we relax the interest rate volatility constraint or expand the set of observed state variables in the policy rule, we observe small reductions in the optimal value of ρ, but our conclusions about the advantages of interest rate smoothing are not substantially affected. Finally, we find that interest rate smoothing reduces the variance of output by inducing secondary cycles, which reduce the initial impact of shocks due to the forward-looking nature of aggregate demand.

6.6   Robustness to Model Uncertainty

To evaluate the extent to which simple policy rules are robust to model uncertainty, we take first-difference rules from the policy frontier of one model and evaluate the performance of these rules in each of the other three models. In particular, we consider the first-difference rules A and B from the corresponding policy frontier of the FRB model; the parameter values for these rules are given in table 6.3. In the FRB model, both rules generate the same standard deviation of the first difference of the funds rate as that generated by the estimated rule given in equation (1). For each of the other models, we calculate the funds rate volatility associated with each of the two rules, and then we compute a separate policy frontier for each upper bound on funds rate volatility, using the class of three-parameter rules given by equation (9). For example, the "rule A" policy frontier for the MSR model is the three-parameter policy frontier for rules with the same funds rate volatility that rule A generates in this model. For the FM model, rules A and B produce virtually identical amounts of funds rate volatility.

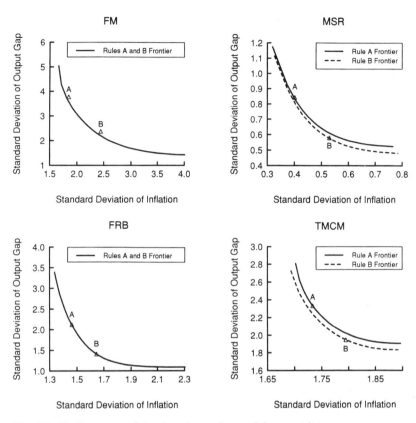

Fig. 6.9   Performance of simple rules under model uncertainty

The results of this analysis are depicted in figure 6.9, which shows that rules A and B provide reasonably efficient performance in stabilizing output and inflation in all four models. Conditional on the level of interest rate volatility implied by these rules, the coefficients of the rules are such that inflation and output volatility lie very near the three-parameter policy frontiers of all models. Evidently, in terms of efficiently reducing the volatility of output and inflation, well-chosen simple rules are very robust to the type of model uncertainty encompassed by these four models. Note that this comparison is constructed holding interest rate volatility fixed at the level generated by rule A or B. Nevertheless, while these results show that rules A and B are reasonably efficient, this figure does not indicate how well the rules perform in terms of specific values of λ.

Table 6.6 reports several summary statistics about the extent to which rules A and B are robust to model uncertainty. The fourth column reports the value of the objective function using the "true" value of λ (assumed to be 0.25 for rule A and 0.75 for rule B, which are the values used to determine these rules

Table 6.6   **Performance of Simple Rules under Model Uncertainty**

Model and Rule	Standard Deviations			Objective Function		
	y	π	Δr	Value	Loss	Implicit λ
FM						
A	3.78	1.85	1.97	6.15	0.86	0.1
B	2.37	2.45	1.83	5.72	1.28	0.4
MSR						
A	0.84	0.4	0.33	0.3	0.01	0.15
B	0.58	0.53	0.48	0.33	0	0.45
TMCM						
A	2.33	1.73	1.71	3.61	0.17	0.1
B	1.94	1.79	2	3.64	0.03	0.4

in the FRB model).[25] The fifth column reports the absolute loss in terms of the objective function implied by following the specified rule (A or B) instead of the three-parameter optimal rule (with the same amount of interest rate volatility) for the specified value of λ. The last column reports the value of λ that would be consistent with the choice of rule A or B for the particular model; for example, in the first row, the implicit value of $\lambda = 0.1$ means that policymakers with preferences described by $\lambda = 0.1$ would choose rule A in the FM model.

These results indicate that if a policymaker were to use the FRB model to choose a policy rule but the real world were actually described by one of the other three models, the policy rule would generate slightly greater output volatility and slightly less inflation volatility compared with the preferences of the policymaker. In particular, the implicit values of λ associated with rules A and B are all smaller in the non-FRB models than the "true" values used in choosing rules A and B in the FRB model. However, while rules A and B are suboptimal, the loss in terms of the objective function, measured either in absolute or percentage terms, is quite small in the MSR model and in TMCM. The somewhat larger loss in the FM model occurs because the optimal three-parameter rule for that model uses a coefficient below unity on the lagged funds rate.

Now we consider the extent to which complicated rules are robust to model uncertainty. In particular, we take two complicated rules (denoted by P and Q) from the twelve-parameter E-frontier of the MSR model and determine the performance of these rules in the FRB model and in TMCM. Because rules P and Q cannot be implemented directly in the FM model (which does not explicitly treat the components of aggregate demand), we also take two rules (denoted by R and S) from the eight-parameter E-frontier of the MSR model and evaluate the performance of these rules in the FM model. As above, the output and inflation variability of the complicated rules should be compared

25. To normalize the comparison of policy rules, these calculations assume that the value of k (the upper bound on funds rate volatility) for each model is given by the standard deviation of the funds rate resulting from rule A or B.

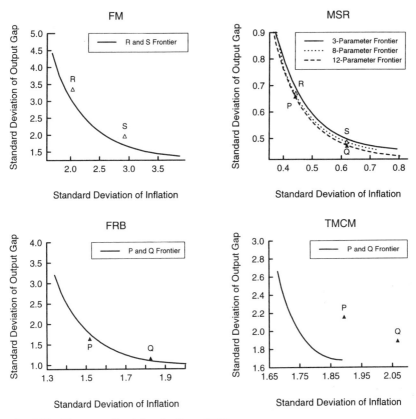

Fig. 6.10   Two complicated rules from MSR

with simple rules that generate the same level of interest rate volatility. Thus, for each model, we calculate the funds rate volatility associated with each of the two complicated rules, and then we compute a separate policy frontier for each upper bound on funds rate volatility, using the class of three-parameter rules given by equation (9).

As shown in the left-hand panels of figure 6.10, the more complicated rules lie fairly close to the three-parameter policy frontiers of the FM and FRB models. In TMCM, however, the two twelve-parameter rules are much less effective in stabilizing output and inflation than the optimal three-parameter rules. Thus, while small improvements in output and inflation variability may be obtained by using complicated policy rules, these rules are somewhat less robust to model uncertainty compared with simple rules. As discussed in section 6.2, the dynamic properties of output and inflation differ substantially across the four models. Thus it is not very surprising that fine-tuning a complicated rule to one particular model may not be appropriate when policymakers are concerned about model uncertainty.

6.7   Conclusions

This paper has investigated the performance of policy rules across four structural macroeconomic models with rational expectations. Although the four models differ in many important respects (e.g., the level of aggregation, the specification of output and price dynamics, and the treatment of the foreign sector), the characteristics of effective policy rules are essentially the same. To stabilize inflation and output at reasonably low levels of interest rate volatility, the policy rule should respond to the current output gap and to a smoothed measure of inflation and should incorporate a high degree of interest rate smoothing, that is, a coefficient near unity on the lagged funds rate. These results are essentially unchanged even if the policy rule is restricted to react to output and inflation data from the previous rather than the current quarter.

Interest rate smoothing provides the largest gains from any of the permutations of simple policy rules that we have investigated. Several factors contribute to this result: (1) Smooth changes in the short-term interest rate provide control over long-term interest rates and thereby over aggregate demand and inflation at low cost in terms of funds rate volatility. (2) Constraining interest rate volatility as we do in constructing the frontiers favors interest rate smoothing. (3) The lagged interest rate provides a measure of the existing state of the economy in models with output and inflation persistence. And (4) with a very high degree of smoothing, such as that associated with first-difference rules, output tends to exhibit "overshooting," which is preferable to returning monotonically to potential under the variance criterion employed here.

Simple rules derived from one model perform very well in the other three models; that is, these rules are robust to model uncertainty within this class of models. For a given model, complicated rules perform only slightly better than simple ones, even when all observed state variables are incorporated in the rule. Furthermore, these rules are somewhat less robust to model uncertainty compared with well-chosen simple rules. Thus fine-tuning a complicated policy rule to one specific model may not be advisable, because policymakers are faced with substantial uncertainty about the true structure of the economy as well as with competing views about the quantitative effects of alternative policy actions.

Finally, rules that incorporate forecasts of the output gap and inflation rate yield at most small improvements in performance over optimal rules based on current and lagged variables. This result is related to that regarding complicated rules: even in large models with hundreds of state variables, three variables (the current output gap, the current four-quarter average inflation rate, and the lagged funds rate) summarize nearly all the information relevant to setting the federal funds rate efficiently.

Table 6A.1   **Comparison of Foreign Monetary Policy Regimes in TMCM**

	$\lambda = 0.1$		$\lambda = 0.25$		$\lambda = 0.5$	
	Fixed μ	EMU	Fixed μ	EMU	Fixed μ	EMU
SD(y_t)	2.12	2.13	1.83	1.83	1.75	1.75
SD(π_t)	1.73	1.73	1.8	1.8	1.84	1.84
α	1.17	1.16	1.4	1.4	1.46	1.46
β	1.92	1.92	0.96	0.96	0.48	0.48

Note: This table provides information on the U.S. inflation-output volatility frontier for interest rate rules of the form $\Delta r_t = \alpha y_t + \beta(\pi_t - \pi^*)$, where r_t is the federal funds rate, y_t is the U.S. output gap, and $\pi_t - \pi^*$ indicates the deviation of U.S. inflation from the target rate. For $0 < \lambda < 1$, the policy frontier minimizes the objective function $\lambda \text{ var}(y_t) + (1 - \lambda) \text{ var}(\pi_t^1 - \pi^*)$ subject to the constraint that SD(Δr_t) ≤ 2.57, where SD(z) indicates the unconditional standard deviation of z. Fixed μ and EMU are the two alternative foreign monetary policy regimes described in the appendix.

Appendix
U.S. Monetary Policy under Alternative Foreign Policy Regimes

Our initial results indicate that within a fairly wide range of alternative foreign monetary policy assumptions (e.g., fixed money growth, interest rate rules), the specific foreign monetary policy regime appears to have only minor implications for the properties of a U.S. monetary policy rule. For example, consider the class of rules in which the first difference of the federal funds rate responds to the current output gap and inflation deviation from target.

Table 6A.1 provides information about the U.S. inflation-output volatility frontier under two alternative assumptions about foreign monetary policy: (1) each foreign G-7 country follows a fixed money growth rule or (2) France, Germany, Italy, and the United Kingdom belong to a monetary union in which the European Central Bank adjusts interest rates in response to the European average output gap and average inflation deviation from target, while Canada and Japan independently follow similar rules.[26] Table 6A.1 shows that in TMCM, neither the position of the U.S. inflation-output volatility frontier nor the coefficients of rules on the policy frontier are sensitive to this choice of foreign monetary policy assumptions. Impulse response functions generated using the full FRB staff model (cf. Levin, Rogers, and Tryon 1997) yield similar conclusions.[27]

Based on these results, the results in this paper are based on a smaller ver-

26. Wieland (1996b) analyzes macroeconomic performance of European countries under such a policy regime using TMCM.
27. Levin (1996) uses the full FRB/GLOBAL model to analyze the properties of interest rate rules under rational expectations as well as under alternative assumptions concerning expectations formation.

sion of the FRB staff model, referred to as the FRB model. In this model, foreign output, prices, and the oil import price deflator are generated by simple reduced-form equations. The trade-weighted real exchange rate is determined by the differential between U.S. and foreign ex ante long-term real interest rates, with an endogenous risk premium that ensures a stable ratio of net external debt to nominal GDP.

References

Anderson, Gary S. 1997. A reliable and computationally efficient algorithm for imposing the saddle point property in dynamic models. Washington, D.C.: Board of Governors of the Federal Reserve System. Manuscript.

Anderson, Gary S., and George R. Moore. 1985. A linear algebraic procedure for solving linear perfect foresight models. *Economics Letters* 17:247–52.

Ball, Laurence. 1997. Efficient rules for monetary policy. NBER Working Paper no. 5952. Cambridge, Mass.: National Bureau of Economic Research.

Balvers, Ronald, and Thomas Cosimano. 1994. Inflation variability and gradualist monetary policy. *Review of Economic Studies* 61:721–38.

Becker, R. G., B. Dwolatzky, E. Karakitsos, and B. Rustem. 1986. The simultaneous use of rival models in policy optimisation. *Economic Journal* 96:425–48.

Blanchard, O., and C. M. Kahn. 1980. The solution of linear difference models under rational expectations. *Econometrica* 48:1305–11.

Blinder, Allan. 1995. Central banking in theory and practice. Lecture 1: Targets, instruments and stabilisation. Marshall lecture presented at the University of Cambridge. Washington, D.C.: Board of Governors of the Federal Reserve System. Manuscript.

———. 1998. *Central banking in theory and practice.* Cambridge, Mass.: MIT Press.

Brainard, William. 1967. Uncertainty and the effectiveness of policy. *American Economic Review* 57:411–25.

Brayton, Flint, Andrew Levin, Ralph W. Tryon, and John C. Williams. 1997. The evolution of macro models at the Federal Reserve Board. *Carnegie-Rochester Conference Series on Public Policy* 42:115–67.

Brayton, Flint, Eileen Mauskopf, David Reifschneider, Peter Tinsley, and John Williams. 1997. The role of expectations in the FRB/US macroeconomic model. *Federal Reserve Bulletin* 83:227–45.

Bryant, Ralph C., David A. Currie, Jacob A. Frenkel, Paul R. Masson, and Richard Portes. 1989. *Macroeconomic policies in an interdependent world.* Washington, D.C.: International Monetary Fund.

Bryant, Ralph C., Peter Hooper, and Catherine L. Mann. 1993. *Evaluating policy regimes: New research in empirical macroeconomics.* Washington, D.C.: Brookings Institution.

Buiter, Willem H., and Ian Jewitt. 1981. Staggered wage setting with real wage relativities: Variations on a theme of Taylor. *Manchester School* 49:211–28. (In *Macroeconomic theory and stabilization policy,* ed. Willem H. Buiter. Manchester: Manchester University Press, 1989.)

Caplin, Andrew, and John Leahy. 1996. Monetary policy as a process of search. *American Economic Review* 86:689–702.

Christiano, Lawrence, Martin Eichenbaum, and Christopher Gust. 1997. Interest rate smoothing in an equilibrium business cycle model. Evanston, Ill.: Northwestern University. Manuscript.

Christodoulakis, Nico, David Kemball-Cook, and Paul Levine. 1993. The design of economic policy under model uncertainty. *Computational Economics* 6:219–40.

Clarida, Richard, Jordi Galí, and Mark Gertler. 1998. Monetary policy rules and macroeconomic stability: Evidence and some theory. NBER Working Paper no. 6442. Cambridge, Mass.: National Bureau of Economic Research.

———. Forthcoming. The science of monetary policy. *Journal of Economic Literature.*

Cooper, J. P., and Stanley Fischer. 1974. Monetary and fiscal policy in a fully stochastic St. Louis econometric model. *Journal of Money, Credit and Banking* 6:1–22.

Fair, Ray C., and E. Philip Howrey. 1996. Evaluating alternative monetary policy rules. *Journal of Monetary Economics* 38:173–93.

Fischer, Stanley. 1977. Long-term contracts, rational expectations, and the optimal money supply rule. *Journal of Political Economy* 85:191–206.

Frankel, Jeffrey A., and Katharine E. Rockett. 1988. International macroeconomic policy coordination when policymakers do not agree on the true model. *American Economic Review* 78:318–40.

Fuhrer, Jeffrey. 1997a. Inflation/output variance trade-offs and optimal monetary policy. *Journal of Money, Credit and Banking* 29:214–34.

———. 1997b. Towards a compact, empirically-verified rational expectations model for monetary policy analysis. *Carnegie-Rochester Conference Series on Public Policy* 47:197–230.

Fuhrer, Jeffrey, and Brian Madigan. 1997. Monetary policy when interest rates are bounded at zero. *Review of Economics and Statistics* 79:573–85.

Fuhrer, Jeffrey, and George R. Moore. 1995. Inflation persistence. *Quarterly Journal of Economics* 110:127–59.

Goodfriend, Marvin. 1991. Interest rates and the conduct of monetary policy. *Carnegie-Rochester Conference Series on Public Policy* 34:7–30.

Goodhart, Charles. 1996. Why do the monetary authorities smooth interest rates? London School of Economics Financial Markets Group Special Paper no. 81. London: London School of Economics.

———. 1998. Central bankers and uncertainty. Keynes lecture to the British Academy. London: London School of Economics. Manuscript.

Hansen, Lars P., and Thomas J. Sargent. 1997. Recursive linear models of dynamic economies. Chicago: University of Chicago. Manuscript.

Henderson, Dale, and Warwick J. McKibbin. 1993. A comparison of some basic monetary policy regimes for open economies: Implications of different degrees of instrument adjustment and wage persistence. *Carnegie-Rochester Conference Series on Public Policy* 39:221–318.

Holtham, Gerald, and Andrew Hughes-Hallett. 1992. International macroeconomic policy coordination when policymakers do not agree on the true model: Comment. *American Economic Review* 82:1043–56.

Karakitsos, E., and B. Rustem. 1984. Optimally derived fixed rules and indicators. *Journal of Economic Dynamics and Control* 8:33–64.

Kendrick, David. 1982. Caution and probing in a macroeconomic model. *Journal of Economic Dynamics and Control* 4:149–70.

Levin, Andrew. 1996. A comparison of alternative monetary policy rules in the Federal Reserve Board's multi-country model. *Bank for International Settlements Conference Papers* 2:340–66.

Levin, Andrew, John H. Rogers, and Ralph W. Tryon. 1997. Evaluating international economic policy with the Federal Reserve's global model. *Federal Reserve Bulletin* 10:797–817.

Lowe, Philip, and Luci Ellis. 1997. The smoothing of official interest rates. In *Monetary policy and inflation targeting: Proceedings of a conference,* ed. Philip Lowe. Sydney: Reserve Bank of Australia.

Lucas, Robert E., Jr. 1976. Econometric policy evaluation: A critique. *Carnegie-Rochester Conference Series on Public Policy* 1:19–46.

McCallum, Bennett. 1994. Specification of policy rules and performance measures in multi-country simulations studies. *Journal of International Money and Finance* 13:259–75.

————. 1997. Issues in the design of monetary policy rules. NBER Working Paper no. 6016. Cambridge, Mass.: National Bureau of Economic Research.

Orphanides, Athanasios. 1998. Monetary policy rules based on real-time data. Finance and Economics Discussion Paper no. 98-3. Washington, D.C.: Board of Governors of the Federal Reserve System.

Orphanides, Athanasios, David Small, Volker Wieland, and David W. Wilcox. 1997. A quantitative exploration of the opportunistic approach to disinflation. Finance and Economics Discussion Paper no. 97-36. Washington, D.C.: Board of Governors of the Federal Reserve System.

Orphanides, Athanasios, and Volker Wieland. 1998. Price stability and monetary policy effectiveness when nominal interest rates are bounded at zero. Finance and Economics Discussion Paper no. 98-35. Washington, D.C.: Board of Governors of the Federal Reserve System.

Phelps, Edmund S., and John B. Taylor. 1977. Stabilizing powers of monetary policy under rational expectations. *Journal of Political Economy* 85:163–90.

Phillips, A. W. 1954. Stabilization policies in a closed economy. *Economic Journal* 64:290–323.

Poole, William. 1970. The optimal choice of instruments in a simple stochastic macro model. *Quarterly Journal of Economics* 84:197–216.

Rebelo, Sergio, and Danyang Xie. 1997. On the optimality of interest rate smoothing. NBER Working Paper no. 5947. Cambridge, Mass.: National Bureau of Economic Research.

Reifschneider, David, and John C. Williams. 1998. Three lessons for monetary policy in a low inflation era. Washington, D.C.: Board of Governors of the Federal Reserve System. Manuscript.

Rotemberg, Julio, and Michael Woodford. 1997. An optimization-based econometric framework for the evaluation of monetary policy. In *NBER macroeconomics annual 1997,* ed. Ben S. Bernanke and Julio J. Rotemberg. Cambridge, Mass.: MIT Press.

Sumner, Steven, and John C. Williams. 1998. Evaluating solution methods for linear rational expectations models. Washington, D.C.: Board of Governors of the Federal Reserve System. Manuscript.

Svensson, Lars E. O. 1997. Inflation-forecast-targeting: Implementing and monitoring inflation targets. *European Economic Review* 41:1111–46.

————. Forthcoming. Open-economy inflation targeting. *Journal of International Economics.*

Taylor, John B. 1979. Estimation and control of a macroeconomic model with rational expectations. *Econometrica* 47:1267–86.

————. 1980. Aggregate dynamics and staggered contracts. *Journal of Political Economy* 88:1–23.

————. 1993a. Discretion versus policy rules in practice. *Carnegie-Rochester Conference Series on Public Policy* 39:195–214.

————. 1993b. *Macroeconomic policy in the world economy: From econometric design to practical operation.* New York: Norton.

————. 1995. Monetary policy implications of greater fiscal discipline. In *Budget deficits and debt: Issues and options.* Kansas City: Federal Reserve Bank of Kansas City.

Taylor, John B., and John C. Williams. 1993. Forecasting with rational expectations models. Washington, D.C.: Board of Governors of the Federal Reserve System. Manuscript.

Tetlow, Robert, and Peter von zur Muehlen. 1996. Monetary policy rules (I): How good is simple? Washington, D.C.: Board of Governors of the Federal Reserve System. Manuscript.

Tinsley, Peter. 1993. Fitting both data and theories: Polynomial adjustment costs and error-correction rules. Finance and Economics Discussion Paper no. 93-21. Washington, D.C.: Board of Governors of the Federal Reserve System.

Wieland, Volker. 1996a. Monetary policy, parameter uncertainty and optimal learning. Washington, D.C.: Board of Governors of the Federal Reserve System. Manuscript.

———. 1996b. Monetary policy targets and the stabilization objective: A source of tension in the EMS. *Journal of International Money and Finance* 15:95–116.

———. 1998. Monetary policy and uncertainty about the natural unemployment rate. Finance and Economics Discussion Paper no. 98-22. Washington, D.C.: Board of Governors of the Federal Reserve System.

Williams, John C. 1999. Simple rules for monetary policy. Finance and Economics Discussion Paper no. 99-12. Washington, D.C.: Board of Governors of the Federal Reserve System.

Comment   Lawrence J. Christiano and Christopher J. Gust

General Remarks

A key research objective in monetary economics is the identification of monetary policy rules with good operating characteristics. The primary strategy for achieving this objective is to construct quantitative monetary models and use them as laboratories for discriminating between alternative candidate rules.[1] A difficulty with this strategy is that economists have not yet converged on a single model. As a result, to build a case for a particular policy rule, it is not enough to show that it works well in just one model. After all, if the world is better described by some other model, it could still be that the policy rule might not perform well in practice. This is why robustness is an important characteristic for a policy rule to satisfy. That is, it must perform well across a variety of empirically plausible models.

The paper by Levin, Wieland, and Williams is an outstanding contribution to this research program. It examines the performance of a class of monetary policy rules in four large-scale models. The performance criteria they focus on

Lawrence J. Christiano is professor of economics at Northwestern University and a research associate of the National Bureau of Economic Research. Christopher J. Gust is an economist in the International Finance Division of the Board of Governors of the Federal Reserve System.

The authors are grateful to Marty Eichenbaum for numerous conversations. The first author is grateful to the National Science Foundation for a grant to the National Bureau of Economic Research.

1. An alternative, complementary strategy is implemented by John Taylor in chap. 7 of this volume. It is based on examining the historical record to see how well different policy rules have worked in practice.

include the variance of output and inflation. The class of rules considered have the following representation:

(1) $$r_t = c + \rho r_{t-1} + \alpha \pi_t + \beta y_t,$$

where π_t is the annualized rate of inflation, r_t is the annualized federal funds rate, and y_t is the log deviation of output from trend. This policy rule is often referred to as a Taylor rule. The key conclusions are as follows: (1) There is reason to be optimistic that a suitably parameterized Taylor rule can be found that can serve as a useful guide to the conduct of monetary policy. (2) Complicated rules are less robust across models than simple rules. (3) There are gains to increasing ρ. (4) Adding lags and other variables does not help much. (5) Whether one includes π_t, y_t or π_{t-1}, y_{t-1} in the policy rule makes little difference.

Of these, the first is the most important. This finding is consistent with the outcome of other simulation experiments reported in this volume. Moreover, the conclusion also appears to be consistent with informal observations. For example, in chapter 7 of this volume John Taylor makes a compelling case that the relatively good U.S. inflation experience of the past two decades reflects the Fed's adoption of a version of equation (1) with large values of α and β.

The second result is also of interest. The hunch that a result like conclusion 2 is true is an important motivation behind the current widespread interest in simple rules. However, we are not aware that anyone has attempted to check out this hunch formally before. The idea is the more complicated a rule, the more its parameters need to be "tuned" to the idiosyncrasies of a given model to make it perform well in that model. But this very tuning process may render the rule incompatible with the fine details of other models, giving rise to poor performance in those models. Presumably, the notion that complexity is the enemy of robustness cannot be established as a theorem, so it is interesting to see how it fares in quantitative models with solid empirical foundations. The remaining results are interesting at a practical level. Significantly, result 3 is also a finding of other papers. Result 4 is consistent with the authors' finding that replacing π_t by $E_t\pi_{t+1}$ does not help much, since including $E_t\pi_{t+1}$ is implicitly a way of adding lags and other variables. Result 5 is also of importance in view of lags in data collection that pose practical problems for implementing equation (1) in real time.

The Taylor Rule in a Limited Participation Model

The Levin, Wieland, and Williams paper is sure to be an important reference for some time to come. The authors have put in an enormous amount of painstaking, scholarly effort, with instructive results. They are to be applauded. In our discussion, we will assess the robustness of the authors' findings to a fifth model, the one developed in Christiano, Eichenbaum, and Evans (1998, hereafter CEE).

Looking at the CEE model may serve as a useful robustness check because it is in some respects very different from the four models considered by Levin, Wieland, and Williams and, indeed, from all the other models analyzed in this volume. For example, the CEE model does not assume that prices are sticky. Of course, to get monetary policy to matter at all, some kind of rigidity is needed. The rigidity we adopt is a version of the financial market friction suggested by Lucas in his article on limited participation models. Although prices are not sticky by assumption in our model, they do nevertheless turn out to be sticky as an equilibrium phenomenon.[2]

We reassess the authors' conclusions, primarily result 1, through the lens of the CEE model. We find it useful in our analysis to posit another rule as a benchmark for comparison. The rule that we use for this purpose is the "k percent rule." This rule specifies that money growth proceeds at a constant pace, independent of developments in the economy.

What sorts of pitfalls can interfere with the good performance of a monetary policy rule? There are at least two:

1. The rule could itself be a source of economic instability. There are two possibilities:
   a) The nonstochastic steady state equilibrium may be indeterminate. This can give rise to instability of two types:
      i) Real quantities may fluctuate in response to extraneous, sunspot shocks.
      ii) Real quantities may overreact to fundamental shocks.
   b) The nonstochastic steady state may be unstable. This happens when there exist no equilibrium paths converging to a nonstochastic steady state for initial conditions arbitrarily close to steady state.
2. The central bank may not have the commitment technology to actually implement the policy rule in practice.

We show that these two pitfalls are very real possibilities in our model economy. Regarding the first one, we show that there are large regions of the parameter space in which a monetary policy regime characterized by rule (1) makes the economy vulnerable to suboptimal fluctuations in real and nominal variables. After exploring several variants of rule (1), we find that there is none that completely eliminates this risk. Still, we find that the chances are smallest when ρ and α are large and β is small.

Others, including Rotemberg and Woodford in chapter 2 of this volume and Clarida, Galí, and Gertler (1998), have also encountered indeterminacy and explosiveness working with policy rules like (1).[3] However, our results differ from theirs in at least two ways. First, in our model, the region of the parameter

2. This is a theme emphasized in Christiano, Eichenbaum, and Evans (1997, 1998).
3. Benhabib, Schmitt-Grohe, and Uribe (1998) have also encountered indeterminacy when working with a policy rule like rule (1). They show that it is a real possibility for the likelihood of indeterminacy to increase as α rises.

space in which indeterminacy or explosiveness occurs when the monetary authority pursues an interest rate rule like (1) appears to be larger. Second, the likelihood of indeterminacy or explosiveness is increased, the more aggressively monetary policy reacts to output, that is, the larger is β. By contrast, Levin, Wieland, and Williams report that they never encounter indeterminacy or explosiveness. Others such as Rotemberg and Woodford in this volume and Clarida et al. (1998) do encounter these problems, but over a smaller region of the parameter space. Significantly, the likelihood of indeterminacy and explosiveness problems in these models is typically reduced the *larger* the value of β. Moreover, researchers increasingly are reporting the recommendation that β be set rather large. It is of interest to understand what are the key model features that account for these differences in results.

We conjecture that the key features that differentiate our model from the others lie in the mechanisms by which higher expected inflation affects the economy. Other models, following the IS-LM tradition, emphasize that higher anticipated inflation leads to a reduction in the real rate of interest, which in turn results in a rise in output and actual inflation by stimulating the investment component of aggregate demand. It is not surprising that in these models, aggressive increases in interest rates when inflation or output rises can prevent higher expected inflation from being self-fulfilling.

In our model, higher anticipated inflation induces households to substitute out of cash deposits in the financial sector and toward the purchase of goods. The resulting shortfall of cash in the financial sector puts upward pressure on the nominal rate of interest. If α in the Fed's policy rule were small, it would have to inject liquidity into financial markets in order to resist the rise in the interest rate. This expansion of liquidity would produce the increase in inflation that people anticipated. It is therefore not surprising that we obtain a result similar to one found for existing models: a large value of α reduces the likelihood that expectations of inflation can be self-fulfilling. However, unlike the existing literature, our model also suggests that a large value of β can actually *increase* the likelihood of indeterminacy. That is because the rise in the interest rate that occurs with a rise in inflation under the Fed's policy rule also produces a reduction in output. With a large β, that fall in output operates to offset the Fed's policy of raising the interest rate when $\alpha > 0$. In effect, raising β cancels out the indeterminacy-fighting properties of a high value of α. Finally, a large value of ρ can be helpful in reducing the likelihood of indeterminacy by amplifying increases in the interest rate.

The second pitfall refers to the fact there may be states of the world in which it is politically infeasible to implement the policy action dictated by equation (1). For example, an interest rate rule that reacts aggressively to inflation could require raising the interest rate after a supply shock that drives up prices and reduces output. Raising rates at a time when output is already low might be viewed as producing unacceptably large social costs. That this possibility may be of more than academic interest is suggested by the U.S. experience in the

1970s, when there was an acceleration in inflation. Statements by Arthur Burns, the Federal Reserve chairman at the time, indicate that it was not out of ignorance about the connection between money and inflation that he failed to raise interest rates in the 1970s. He claimed that, instead, it was his fear of the social consequences of such an action that prevented him from implementing a high-interest-rate policy.[4] We display a version of our model economy, in which there would be substantial pressure to deviate from a policy rule like (1) during a supply-shock-induced recession. The increased welfare gains from deviating to a *k* percent rule at that time are the equivalent of about 0.3 percent of consumption, forever. To get a sense of the magnitude of this, it corresponds roughly to the amount the federal government spends on the administration of justice, or on general science, space, and technology.[5] This is a substantial amount. These considerations make one wonder whether the Fed would have been able to resist the pressure to deviate from a rule like (1) and be accommodative if, instead of dropping in 1986, oil prices had risen.

In sum, our analysis provides somewhat less cause for optimism about the authors' conclusion 1. Our less optimistic view reflects differences in the models analyzed. The authors report that in their model, they did not encounter the possibility of indeterminacy or explosiveness. So a final assessment of conclusion 1 hinges on which of these models is a better approximation to the data. We do not have an answer to that question yet.

The next two sections present the quantitative exercises that are the basis for the conclusions just summarized.

Model

In this section, we describe the model used in our analysis and we present some empirical evidence in its favor. We examine the operating characteristics in our model of the following three variants on rule (1):

4. An excerpt from a speech by Arthur Burns in 1977 summarizes views that he repeated often during his tenure as chairman of the Federal Reserve:

> We well know—as do many others—that if the Federal Reserve stopped creating new money, or if this activity were slowed drastically, inflation would soon either come to an end or be substantially checked. Unfortunately, knowing that truth is not as helpful as one might suppose. The catch is that nowadays there are tremendous nonmonetary pressures in our economy that are tending to drive costs and prices higher. . . . If the Federal Reserve then sought to create a monetary environment that seriously fell short of accommodating the nonmonetary pressures that have become characteristic of our times, severe stresses could be quickly produced in our economy. The inflation rate would probably fall in the process but so, too, would production, jobs, and profits. The tactics and strategy of the Federal Reserve System—as of any central bank—must be attuned to these realities.

For additional discussion of Burns's (1978) speeches, see Chari, Christiano, and Eichenbaum (1998).

5. The preliminary estimate for 1997 of consumption of nondurable goods and services in the 1998 *Economic Report of the President* is $4.8 trillion, so that 0.3 percent of this is $16 billion. The federal expenditures in fiscal year 1997 on general science, space, and technology was $17 billion; on the administration of justice it was $20 billion.

$$r_t = c + \rho r_{t-1} + (1 - \rho)(\alpha E_t \pi_{t+1} + \beta y_t) \qquad \text{Clarida-Galí-Gertler,}$$

$$r_t = c + \rho r_{t-1} + \alpha \pi_t + \beta y_t \qquad \text{generalized Taylor,}$$

$$r_t = c + \rho r_{t-1} + \alpha \tilde{\pi}_{t-1} + \beta y_{t-1} \qquad \text{lagged Taylor.}$$

As before, r_t is the (annualized) nominal rate of interest that extends from the beginning of quarter t to the end of quarter t. Also, $\pi_t = \log P_t - \log P_{t-1}$, $\tilde{\pi}_t = \log P_t - \log P_{t-4}$, and $y_t = \log Y_t$, after a trend has been removed. We hereafter refer to the above as the CGG, GT, and LT policy rules, respectively.

We study the performance of these three rules in the CEE model. A detailed discussion of the model appears in CEE, and so we describe it only very briefly here. Apart from two modifications, it is basically a standard limited participation model. One modification is that in addition to having a technology shock, it also has a money demand shock. Traditionally, an important rationale for adopting an interest-rate-targeting rule was to eliminate the effects of money demand shocks from the real economy (see, e.g., Poole 1970). So, if anything, including them should bias things in favor of the interest-rate-targeting rule. A second difference is that although there is still a monetary authority on the sidelines transferring cash into and out of the financial system in our model economy, those transfers are endogenous when the monetary authority conducts its operations with the objective of supporting an interest-rate-targeting rule.

The representative household begins period t with the economy's stock of money, M_t, and then proceeds to divide it between Q_t dollars allocated to the purchase of goods and $M_t - Q_t$ dollars allocated to the financial intermediary. It faces the following cash constraint in the goods market:

$$Q_t + W_t L_t \geq P_t(C_t + I_t),$$

where I_t denotes investment, C_t denotes consumption, L_t denotes hours worked, and W_t and P_t denote the wage rate and price level. The household owns the stock of capital, and it has the standard capital accumulation technology:

$$K_{t+1} = I_t + (1 - 0.02)K_t.$$

The household's assets accumulate according to the following expression:

$$M_{t+1} = Q_t + W_t L_t - P_t(C_t + I_t) + R_t(M_t - Q_t + X_t) + D_t + r_t K_t,$$

where X_t is a date t monetary injection by the central bank and R_t denotes the gross rate of return on household deposits with the financial intermediary. Also, D_t denotes household profits, treated as lump-sum transfers, and r_t is the rental rate on capital. An implication of this setup is that the household's date t earnings of rent on capital cannot be spent until the following period, while its date t wage earnings can be spent in the same period. As a result, inflation acts like a tax on investment. The household's date t decision about Q_t must be made before the date t realization of the shocks, while all other decisions are made afterward. This assumption is what guarantees that when a surprise monetary injection occurs, the equilibrium rate of interest falls and output and employment rise. To assure that these effects are persistent, we introduce an adjustment cost in changing Q_t, $H_t = H(Q_t/Q_{t-1})$, where H_t is in units of time and H is an increasing function.[6] The household's problem at time zero is to choose contingency plans for C_t, I_t, Q_t, M_{t+1}, L_t, K_{t+1}, $t = 0, \ldots, \infty$, to maximize

$$E_0 \sum_{t=0}^{\infty} \beta^t U(C_t, L_t, H_t), \qquad U(C, L, H) = \log\left(C - \psi_0 \frac{(L + H)^{1+\psi}}{1 + \psi}\right),$$

subject to the information, cash, asset accumulation, and other constraints. Here, $\psi = 1/2.5$, $\beta = 1.03^{-0.25}$, and ψ_0 is selected so that $L_t = 1$ in nonstochastic steady state.

Firms must finance J_t of the wage bill by borrowing cash in advance from the financial intermediary, and $1 - J_t$ can be financed out of current receipts. The random variable, J_t is our money demand shock, and it is assumed to have the following distribution:

$$\log J_t = 0.95 \log J_{t-1} + \varepsilon_{J,t},$$

where $\varepsilon_{J,t}$ has mean zero and standard deviation 0.01. All of the rental payments on capital can be financed out of current receipts. This leads to the following first-order conditions for labor and capital:

$$\frac{W_t(R_t J_t + 1 - J_t)}{P_t} = \frac{f_{L,t}}{\mu}, \qquad \frac{r_t}{P_t} = \frac{f_{K,t}}{\mu},$$

where $\mu = 1.4$ is the markup of price over marginal cost, reflecting the existence of market power. Also, $f_{i,t}$ represents the marginal product of factor i, $i = L, K$, and

$$f(K_t, L_t, v_t) = \exp(v_t) K_t^{0.36} L_t^{0.64},$$

where

$$v_t = 0.95 v_{t-1} + \varepsilon_{v,t},$$

and $\varepsilon_{v,t}$ has mean zero and standard deviation 0.01.

Finally, we specify monetary policy in four ways. In the first, money growth is purely exogenous and has the following second-order moving average form:

---

6. To assure that the interest rate effect is persistent, we introduce a cost of adjusting Q_t:

$$H(Q_t/Q_{t-1}) = d\{\exp[c(Q_t/Q_{t-1} - 1 - x)]$$
$$+ \exp[-c(Q_t/Q_{t-1} - 1 - x)] - 2\},$$

where x denotes the average rate of money growth. We set $d = c = 2$ and $x = 0.01$.

$$x_t = x + 0.08\varepsilon_t + 0.26\varepsilon_{t-1} + 0.11\varepsilon_{t-2},$$

where ε_t is a mean-zero, serially uncorrelated shock to monetary policy and $x = 0.01$. This representation is CEE's estimate of the dynamic response of M1 growth to a monetary policy shock, after abstracting from the effects of all other shocks on monetary policy. Other representations of monetary policy analyzed here include the CGG, the GT, and the LT rules presented above. In these cases, the response of x_t to nonmonetary shocks is endogenous, although we preserve the assumption throughout that $Ex_t = x$.

Figure 6C.1 presents the dynamic response of the model's variables to an ε_t shock in period 2. The percentage deviation of the stock of money from its unshocked growth path is displayed in panel 6C.1c. The magnitude of the shock was chosen so that the money stock is eventually up by 1 percent. Panels 6C.1a, 6C.1b, and 6C.1f indicate that the impact effect on output of the monetary policy shock is so great that the price response is nil. Afterward, the price level rises slowly and does not reach its steady state position until around one year later. This sluggish response of the price level is what we had in mind in the introduction when we reported that even though we do not assume sticky prices, they nevertheless exhibit stickiness as an equilibrium phenomenon. Next, note the hump-shaped responses of employment, output, consumption, and investment. Finally, there is a persistent fall in the interest rate. As emphasized in CEE, these patterns are all qualitatively consistent with the data. They support the notion that our model represents a useful laboratory for evaluating the operating characteristics of alternative monetary policy rules.

Results

This section presents our quantitative results. We first display the regions of the policy parameter space in which indeterminacy, determinacy (i.e., local uniqueness of equilibrium), and explosiveness occur. We report that the region of indeterminacy and explosiveness is disconcertingly large. In the subsequent two sections we report some calculations to illustrate the economic meaning of the indeterminacy and explosiveness findings.

Indeterminacy, Determinacy, and Explosiveness

Figures 6C.2, 6C.3, and 6C.4 report regions of α and β where equilibrium is determinate (*white*), indeterminate (*gray*), and explosive (*black*), for $\rho = 0.0$, 0.5, and 1.5. The results are for the CGG, GT and LT rules, respectively.

Consider first the results for the CGG rule in figure 6C.2. When $\beta = 0$, determinacy requires $\alpha \geq 1$, a result also reported in CGG. Our results resemble those of CGG in supporting the notion that an aggressive response to expected inflation reduces the likelihood of indeterminacy. In contrast with CGG, however, we find that the likelihood of indeterminacy and explosiveness increase with β. The intuition for this was discussed in the second section of this comment.

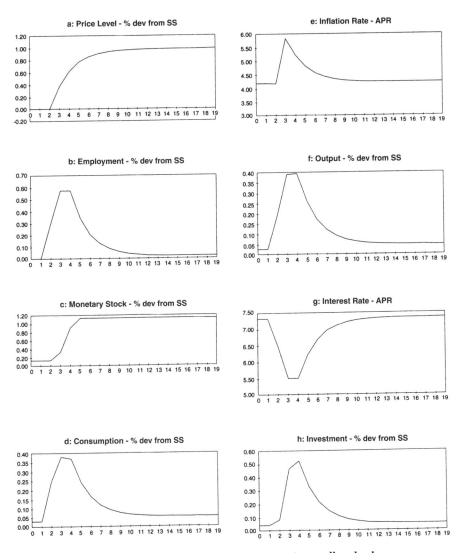

Fig. 6C.1   Response of model to an exogenous monetary policy shock
Note: % dev from SS: deviation from unshocked nonstochastic steady state growth path (percent).
APR: annualized percentage rate.

Now consider the results reported in figure 6C.3 for the GT rule. Chapter 7 of this volume, by Taylor, suggests that a good parameterization for equation (1) is $\rho = 0$, $\alpha = 1.5$, and $\beta = 1$. Interestingly, figure 6C.3 indicates that for our model, this parameterization lies in the explosiveness region. Thus our model indicates that the economy would perform very poorly with this policy rule. According to the results in chapter 2, by Rotemberg and Woodford, when $\rho = 0$ and $\alpha > 0$, increasing β raises the likelihood of equilibrium determinacy.

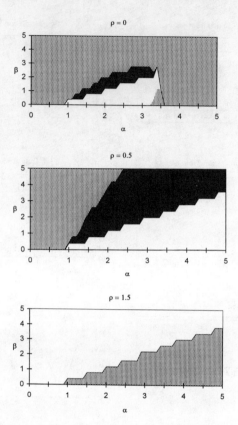

Fig. 6C.2   Regions of uniqueness, explosiveness, and indeterminacy: Clarida-Galí-Gertler rule

Note: White, uniqueness; *gray,* indeterminacy; *black,* explosiveness.

In our model, this is not the case. Either we enter the explosiveness region for large β, or we enter the region of indeterminacy. Interestingly, as ρ increases, the region of determinacy expands.

The results in figure 6C.4 for the LT policy rule resemble those in figure 6C.3. The preferred parameterization of Rotemberg and Woodford, $\alpha = 1.27$, $\beta = 0.08$, and $\rho = 1.13$, lies in the determinacy region for our model if we interpolate between the $\rho = 0.5$ and $\rho = 1.5$ graphs in figure 6C.4. A notable feature of the LT policy rule is that with ρ large, the determinacy region is reasonably large and resembles the determinacy region for the GT rule.

To summarize, an aggressive response to inflation (or expected inflation) increases the likelihood of determinacy. However, a more aggressive response to output has the opposite effect in our model. In addition, our results support the notion that choosing a high value of ρ increases the likelihood of determinacy. Finally, the CGG rule appears to have the smallest region of determinacy.

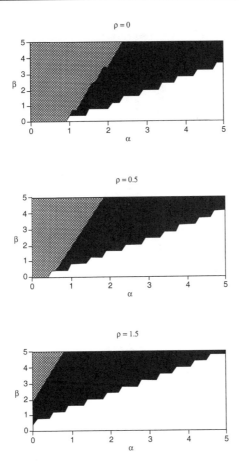

Fig. 6C.3   Regions of uniqueness, explosiveness, and indeterminacy: generalized Taylor rule
Note: White, uniqueness; *gray,* indeterminacy; *black,* explosiveness.

Illustrating Indeterminacy

We report some calculations to illustrate what can happen when there is indeterminacy. To this end, we worked with two versions of the CGG rule. The first is useful for establishing a benchmark and uses a version of the CGG rule for which there is a locally unique equilibrium ($\rho = 0.66$, $\beta = 0.48$, $\alpha = 1.8$). The second uses a version of the CGG rule for which there is equilibrium indeterminacy ($\rho = 0.66$, $\beta = 0.48$, $\alpha = 0.95$). We refer to the first rule as the stable CGG rule and to the second as the unstable CGG rule. We consider the dynamic response of the variables in our model economy to a 1 standard deviation innovation in J_t in period 2.

Figure 6C.5 displays the results for an economy operating under a k percent money growth rule (*dashed line*) and under the stable CGG rule (*solid line*).

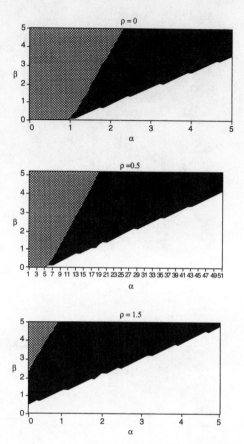

Fig. 6C.4   Regions of uniqueness, explosiveness, and indeterminacy: lagged Taylor rule

Note: White, uniqueness; *gray,* indeterminacy; *black,* explosiveness.

Note that under the k percent rule, the results are what one might expect from a positive shock to money demand: interest rates rise for a while and inflation, output, employment, consumption, and investment drop. Now consider the economy's response to the money demand shock under the stable CGG rule. As one might expect, this monetary policy fully insulates the economy from the effects of the money demand shock. Panel 6C.5c indicates that this result is brought about by increasing the money stock. Not surprisingly, the present discounted utility of agents in the economy operating under the stable CGG rule, 74.092, is higher than it is in the economy operating under the k percent rule, 74.036. These present discounted values are computed under the assumption that the money demand shock takes on its mean value in the initial period, and the capital stock is at its nonstochastic steady state level.

Now consider the results in figure 6C.6, which displays the response of the model variables to a money demand shock in two equilibria associated with

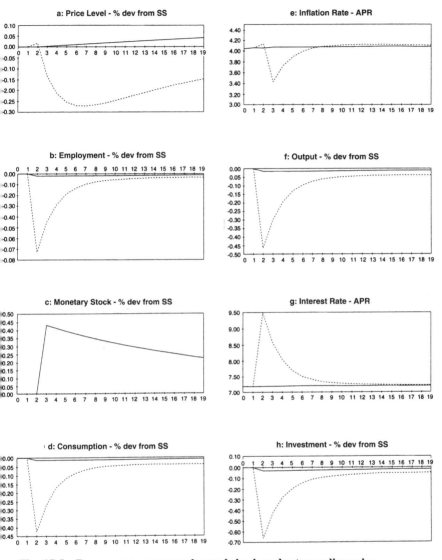

Fig. 6C.5   Responses to a money demand shock under two policy rules

Note: Solid line, stable CGG rule; *dashed line, k* percent rule. See also note to fig. 6C.1.

the unstable CGG policy rule. In equilibrium 2 (*dashed line*), the economy responds in essentially the same way that it does under the stable CGG rule. Now consider equilibrium 1 (*solid line*). The money demand shock triggers an expectation of higher inflation.[7] Seeing the inflation coming, the central bank

7. This illustrates the possibility mentioned in the second section of this comment that when there is equilibrium indeterminacy, an economy might "overreact to fundamental shocks."

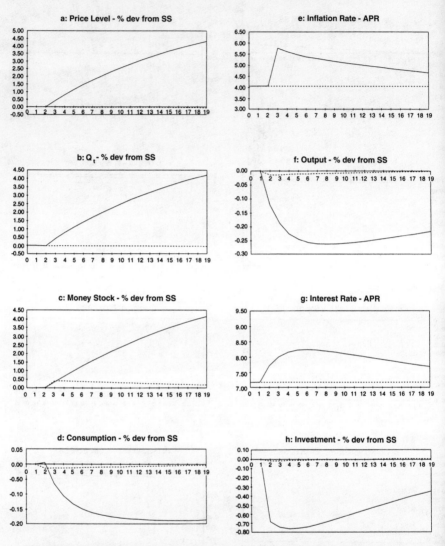

Fig. 6C.6   Response to a money demand shock under unstable CGG rule
Note: Solid line, equilibrium 1; *dashed line,* equilibrium 2. See also note to fig. 6C.1.

raises interest rates immediately by only partially accommodating the increased money demand.[8] In the following period households, anticipating higher inflation, shift funds out of the financial sector and toward consumption (panel 6C.6b shows that Q_t rises, relative to its steady state path, in period 3).

8. This is difficult to see in panel 6C.6c because of scale. Money growth in period 2 is nearly 6 percent, at an annual rate, in equilibrium 2. According to panel 6C.6g, this is enough to prevent a rise in the interest rate in that equilibrium. Money growth in period 2 of equilibrium 1 is less, namely, 5.5 percent, at an annual rate.

The central bank responds by only partially making up for this shortfall of funds available to the financial sector. This leads to a further rise in the interest rate and in the money supply. In this way, the money stock grows, and actual inflation occurs. Employment and output are reduced because of the high rate of interest. Investment falls a lot because the higher anticipated inflation acts as a tax on the return to investment. In addition, the rental rate on capital drops with the fall in employment.

The utility level associated with equilibrium 1 is 73.825, and the utility level in equilibrium 2 is 74.110. The utility numbers convey an interesting message. On the one hand, if the stable CGG rule is implemented, agents enjoy higher utility than under the k percent rule. On the other hand, if the unstable CGG policy rule is used, it is possible that utility might be less than what it would be under the k percent rule. In this sense, if there were any uncertainty over whether a given interest rate rule might produce indeterminacy, it might be viewed as less risky to simply adopt the k percent rule. In a way, this is a dramatic finding, since the assumption that money demand shocks are the only disturbances affecting the economy would normally guarantee the desirability of an interest rate rule like (1).

Illustrating Explosiveness and Implementation Problems

We now consider a version of our model driven only by technology shocks. We consider two versions of the LT policy rule. One adopts the preferred parameterization of Rotemberg and Woodford: $\alpha = 1.27$, $\beta = 0.08$, and $\rho = 1.13$. The other adopts a version of this parameterization that is very close to the explosive region in which β is assigned a value of unity. Figure 6C.7 reports the response of the economy to a 1 standard deviation negative shock to technology under two specifications of monetary policy. In one, monetary policy is governed by a k percent rule (*dashed line*), and in the other, it is governed by the LT rule just described (*solid line*).

Consider first the k percent rule. The technology shock drives up the price level, which remains high for a long period of time. Employment, investment, consumption, and output drop. There is essentially no impact on the rate of interest. The present discounted value of utility in this equilibrium is 74.095. Consider by contrast the LT rule. The rise in inflation in the first period leads the central bank to cut back the money supply in the following period (recall, this policy rule looks back one period). This triggers a substantial rise in the interest rate, which in turn leads to an even greater fall in employment, output, consumption, and investment than occurs under the k percent rule. The present discounted value of utility in this equilibrium is 74.036. It is not surprising that in this case, the k percent rule dominates the monetary policy rule in welfare terms, and in terms of the variability of output and inflation.

Now consider the operation of the nearly explosive policy rule, in figure 6C.8. With this rule, responses are much more persistent than under the previous rule. The response looks very much like a regime switch, with money growth and the interest rate shifting to a higher level for a long period of time.

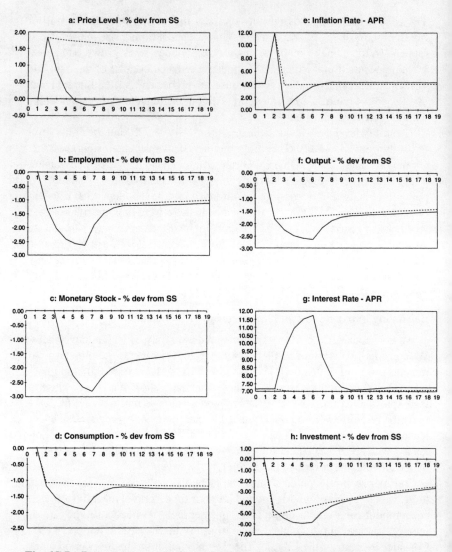

Fig. 6C.7   Response to a negative technology shock under two policy rules
Note: Solid line, Rotemberg-Woodford lagged response rule; *dashed line, k* percent rule. See also note to fig. 6C.1.

Given all the volatility in this equilibrium, it is not surprising that welfare is lower at 73.549.

These examples illustrate the practical difficulties that can arise in implementing an interest-smoothing rule like (1). In a recession, when output and employment are already low, the rule may require tightening even further. The social cost of doing that may be such that the pressures to deviate may be irresistible.

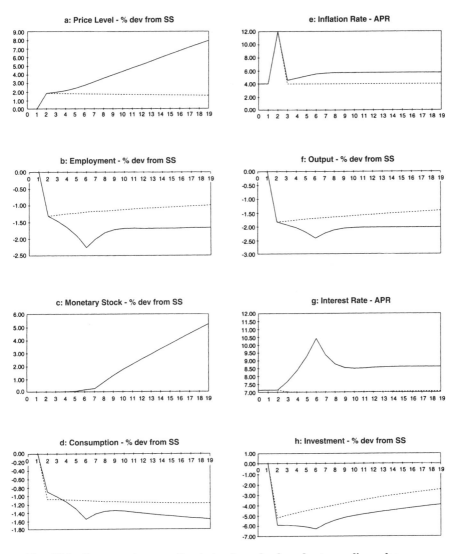

Fig. 6C.8   Response to a negative technology shock under two policy rules

Note: Solid line, perturbed Rotemberg-Woodford lagged response rule; *dashed line, k* percent rule.
See also note to fig. 6C.1.

Conclusion

In this comment we reassessed Levin, Wieland, and Williams's findings concerning the desirability of adopting an interest rate rule of the form (1). We did this using a model that is in several respects quite different from theirs. That model replaces the sticky price assumption used in their paper and in many of the papers at this conference with a particular credit market friction. Our analysis provides several reasons to be cautious in designing an interest rate rule. In this conclusion, we would like to stress two.

First, which parameterized version of rule (1) will work well is sensitive to the nature of the fundamental shocks driving the economy. At the same time, there is little consensus on what the nature of those shocks might be. To illustrate the problem, we showed that when Rotemberg and Woodford's preferred rule is applied in our model and the disturbances are shocks to technology, a simple k percent monetary policy rule dominates their policy rule. Second, in our model there are large portions of the parameter space in which application of an interest rate rule implies equilibrium indeterminacy or explosiveness. This suggests an element of risk associated with the adoption of this type of rule. The uncertainty we have in mind here stems from two sources. First, in advocating the use of a particular rule of the form (1), one cannot be sure precisely what parameter values policymakers will use in practice. Even if one were confident that the rule being advocated had attractive properties, a policymaker may implement a version with different parameter values, and which gives rise to indeterminacy. We showed how, under these circumstances, a k percent rule might dominate an interest-rate-smoothing rule, even in the supposedly ideal case where the only shocks driving the economy are disturbances to money demand. Second, the region of indeterminacy for the parameters of a policy rule no doubt is partly a function of the underlying model parameters. These parameter values are not known with certainty. So, in principle, one might construct a set of policy rule parameter values that exhibit determinacy under the estimated model parameter values. But if the actual parameter values were different, say for sampling reasons, it could be that the constructed policy rule might produce indeterminacy. The analysis in this comment suggests to us that these sources of concern deserve further investigation.

References

Benhabib, Jess, Stephanie Schmitt-Grohe, and Martin Uribe. 1998. Monetary policy and multiple equilibria. New York: New York University. Manuscript.

Burns, Arthur. 1978. *Reflections of an economic policy maker: Speeches and congressional statements: 1969–1978.* Washington, D.C.: American Enterprise Institute for Public Policy Research.

Chari, V. V., Lawrence J. Christiano, and Martin Eichenbaum. 1998. Expectation traps and discretion. *Journal of Economic Theory* 81 (2): 462–98.

Christiano, Lawrence J., Martin Eichenbaum, and Charles Evans. 1997. Sticky price and limited participation models: A comparison. *European Economic Review* 41 (6): 1201–49.

———. 1998. Modeling money. NBER Working Paper no. 6371. Cambridge, Mass.: National Bureau of Economic Research.

Clarida, Richard, Jordi Galí, and Mark Gertler. 1998. Monetary policy rules and macroeconomic stability: Evidence and some theory. NBER Working Paper no. 6442. Cambridge, Mass.: National Bureau of Economic Research.

Poole, William. 1970. Optimal choice of monetary policy instruments in a simple stochastic macro model. *Quarterly Journal of Economics* 84 (May): 197–216.

Discussion Summary

Ben McCallum found the paper "just superb."

Mark Gertler noted an advantage of a certain type of interest rate smoothing, beyond the advantages mentioned in the paper. In particular, a rule that calls for the adjustment of the difference in the interest rate, as opposed to the level, does not require that the policymaker know the long-run equilibrium real rate of interest. With a level rule, on the other hand, stability and convergence problems may arise if the policymaker is uncertain about the long-run equilibrium real rate.

Glenn Rudebusch remarked that the point made by William Poole during the discussion of the Rudebusch and Svensson paper was addressed in this paper. All the models in this paper had two interest rates, a short rate and a long rate linked by a term structure. This paper does the exercise of taking out the long rate, which results in a lower coefficient on the lagged interest rate.

Richard Clarida stressed that the forward-looking Taylor rule advocated in Clarida, Galí, and Gertler (1998) is really a simple rule. It has the same number of parameters as the original Taylor rule. The inflation forecast comes from a projection on lagged data that, with a large number of state variables, may result in a good approximation of the optimal rule.

Donald Kohn was struck by the fact that what used to be a vice of monetary policy, moving too slowly, has turned into a virtue. The smoothness of interest rates reflects gradual learning about the size of the shocks hitting the economy by the monetary policy authority. This was a vice when it gave rise to the "too little, too late" syndrome that got built into business cycles and monetary policy reactions. Kohn wondered if a sluggish reaction is working better here, in a forward-looking model, because the private sector knows what is going on and therefore stabilizes the economy. In the real world, this is not what happens. Both the private sector and the policymaker learn gradually about the size of a shock, which could perhaps lead to instability with a slow policy reaction.

Robert King applauded the narrowing of the gap between the way models are built by academic researchers and by the staff of the Federal Reserve Board. King then asked if the MSR model could be put into the public domain. *John Taylor* added that one of his goals as editor of the conference volume was to ensure the replicability of the results.

Ben McCallum questioned whether rules with a response coefficient on the lagged interest rate equal to one always involve slower adjustment by the Federal Reserve than what was done historically and less fluctuations in nominal interest rates, in particular on the weekly or monthly level. *Bob Hall* mentioned that the appropriate definition of smoothness, going back to Christopher Sims's thesis, is that the variances of interest rate changes be small. This requires both the random walk character and small innovations. The term "smoothness" has been misused somewhat at the conference. There is nothing in the Taylor rule that says it is not smooth. *John Taylor* suggested that more analysis should be done in the frequency domain, since some of the gains of interest rate smoothing could arise from volatilities at unimportant frequencies. *Lars Svensson* mentioned a few experiments performed in the context of his work with Rudebusch, not reported in the paper, on putting the variance of interest rate differences in the loss function. The weights in the loss function on the variance of the interest rate and the variance of the first difference of interest rates have very different effects on the optimal rule. Increasing the weight on the former reduces the response coefficients, while increasing the weight on the latter introduces the lagged interest rate into the reaction function and increases its response coefficient.

Reference

Clarida, R., J. Galí, and M. Gertler. 1998. Monetary policy rules and macroeconomic stability: Evidence and some theory. NBER Working Paper no. 6442. Cambridge, Mass.: National Bureau of Economic Research.

7   A Historical Analysis of
Monetary Policy Rules

John B. Taylor

This paper examines several eras and episodes of U.S. monetary history from the perspective of recent research on monetary policy rules.[1] It explores the timing and the political economic reasons for changes in monetary policy from one policy rule to another, and it examines the effects of different monetary policy rules on the economy. The paper also defines—using current information and the vantage point of history—a quantitative measure of the size of past mistakes in monetary policy. And it examines the effects that these mistakes may have had on the economy. The history of these changes and mistakes is relevant for monetary policy today because it provides evidence about the effectiveness of different monetary policy rules.

The Rationale for a Historical Approach

Studying monetary history is, of course, not the only way to evaluate monetary policy. Another approach is to build structural models of the economy and then simulate the models stochastically with different monetary policy rules.

John B. Taylor is the Mary and Robert Raymond Professor of Economics at Stanford University and a research associate of the National Bureau of Economic Research.

The author thanks Lawrence Christiano, Richard Clarida, Milton Friedman, conference participants, and participants in seminars at the Federal Reserve Bank of Minneapolis, Lehigh University, and Wayne State University for very helpful comments.

1. In this paper a monetary policy *rule* is defined as a description—expressed algebraically, numerically, graphically—of how the *instruments* of policy, such as the monetary base or the federal funds rate, change in response to economic variables. Thus a constant growth rate rule for the *monetary base* is an example of a policy rule, as is a contingency plan for the monetary base. A description of how the *federal funds rate* is adjusted in response to inflation or real GDP is another example of a policy rule. A policy rule can be normative or descriptive. According to this definition, a policy rule can be the outcome of many different institutional arrangements for monetary policy, including gold standard arrangements in which there is no central bank. The term *regime* is usually used more broadly than the specific definition of a policy rule used in this paper. E.g., the term "policy regime" is used by Bordo and Schwartz (1999) to mean people's expectations as well as the institutional arrangements.

A model economy provides information about how the actual economy would operate with different policies. One monetary policy rule is better than another monetary policy rule if it results in better economic performance according to some criterion such as inflation or the variability of inflation and output.[2] This model-based approach has led to practical proposals for monetary policy rules (see Taylor 1993a), and the same approach is now leading to new or refined proposals. The model-based approach has benefited greatly from advances in computers, solution algorithms, and economic theories of how people forecast the future and how market prices and wages adjust to changing circumstances over time.

Despite these advances, the model-based approach cannot be the sole grounds for making policy decisions. No monetary theory is a completely reliable guide to the future, and certain aspects of the current models are novel, especially the incorporation of rational expectations with wage and price rigidities. Hence, the historical approach to monetary policy evaluation is a necessary complement to the model-based approach. By focusing on particular episodes or case studies one may get a better sense about how a policy rule might work in practice. Big historical changes in policy rules—even if they evolve slowly—allow one to separate policy effects from other influences on the economy. Because models, even simple ones, are viewed as black boxes, the historical approach may be more convincing to policymakers.[3] Moreover, case studies are useful for judging how much discretion is appropriate when a policy rule is being used as a guideline for central bank decisions.

Overview

I begin the analysis with a description of the framework I use to examine the history of monetary policy rules. I focus entirely on interest rate rules in which the short-term interest rate instrument of the central bank is adjusted in response to the state of the economy. When analyzing monetary policy using the concept of a policy rule, one must be careful to distinguish between instrument changes due to "shifts" in the policy rule and instrument changes due to "movements along" the policy rule. To make this distinction, I assume a particular functional form for the policy rule. The functional form is the one I suggested several years ago as a normative recommendation for the Federal Reserve (Taylor 1993a). According to this policy rule, the federal funds rate is adjusted by specific numerical amounts in response to changes in inflation and

2. Examples of this approach include the econometric policy evaluation research in Taylor (1979, 1993b), McCallum (1988), Bryant, Hooper, and Mann (1993), Sims and Zha (1995), Bernanke, Gertler, and Watson (1997), Brayton et al. (1997), and many of the papers in this conference volume.

3. In fact, the historical approach is frequently used in practice by policymakers, although the time periods are so short that it may seem like real-time learning. If policymakers were using a particular type of policy and found that it led to an increase in inflation, or a recession, or a slowdown in growth, then they probably would, at the next opportunity, change the policy, learning from the unfavorable experience.

real GDP. This functional form with these numerical responses describes the actual policy actions of the Federal Reserve fairly accurately in recent years, but in this paper I look at earlier periods when the numerical responses were different and examine whether economic performance of the economy was any different.

I examine several long time periods in U.S. monetary history, one around the end of the nineteenth century and the others closer to the end of the twentieth century. The earlier period from 1879 to 1914 is the classical international gold standard era; it includes 11 business cycles, a long deflation, and a long inflation. The later period from 1955 to 1997 encompasses the fixed exchange rate era of Bretton Woods and the modern flexible exchange rate era, including 7 business cycles, an inflation, a sharp disinflation, and the recent 15-year stretch of relatively low inflation and macroeconomic stability. The change in the policy rule over these periods has been dramatic. The type of policy rule that describes Federal Reserve policy actions in the past 10 or 15 years is far different from the ones implied by the gold standard, by Bretton Woods, or by the early part of the flexible exchange rate era.

It turns out that macroeconomic performance—in particular, the volatility of inflation and real output—was also quite different with the different policy rules. Moreover, the historical comparison gives a clear ranking of the policy rules in terms of economic performance. To ensure that this ranking is not spurious—reflecting reverse causation, for example—I try to examine the reasons for the policy changes. I think these changes are best understood as the result of an evolutionary learning process in which the Federal Reserve—from the day it began operations in 1914 to today—has searched for policy rules to guide monetary policy decisions and has changed policy rules as it has learned.

I then consider three specific episodes when "policy mistakes" were made. I define policy mistakes as big departures from two *baseline* monetary policy rules that both this historical analysis and earlier models-based analysis suggest would have been good policy rules. According to this definition, policy mistakes include (1) excessive monetary tightness in the early 1960s, (2) excessive monetary ease and the resulting inflation of the late 1960s and 1970s, and (3) excessive monetary tightness of the early 1980s. I contrast these three episodes with the more recent period of low inflation and macroeconomic stability during which monetary policy has followed the baseline policy rule more closely. I think the analysis of these three episodes and the study of the gradual evolution of the parameters of monetary policy rules from one monetary era to the next gives evidence in favor of the view that a monetary policy that stays close to the baseline policy rules would be a good policy.[4]

---

4. Judd and Trehan (1995) first brought attention to the difference between the interest rates implied by the policy rule I suggested in Taylor (1993a) and actual interest rates in the late 1960s and 1970s during the Great Inflation.

7.1 From the Quantity Equation of Money to a Monetary Policy Rule

The quantity equation of money ($MV = PY$) provided the analytical framework with which Friedman and Schwartz (1963) studied monetary history in their comprehensive study of the United States from the Civil War to 1960. As they state in the first sentence of their study, "This book is about the stock of money in the United States." A higher stock of money (M) would lead to a higher price level (P) other things—namely, real output (Y) and velocity (V)—equal, as they showed by careful study of episode after episode. In each episode they demonstrated why the money stock increased (gold discoveries in the nineteenth century, for example) or decreased (policy mistakes by the Federal Reserve in the twentieth century, for example), and they focused on the roles of particular individuals such as William Jennings Bryan and Benjamin Strong. But the quantity equation of money transcended any individual or institution: with the right interpretation it was useful both for the gold standard and the greenback period and whether a central bank existed or not.

The idea in this paper is to try to step back from the debates about current policy, as Friedman and Schwartz (1963) did, and examine the history of monetary policy via an analytical framework. However, I want to focus on the short-term interest rate side of monetary policy rather than on the money stock side. Hence, I need a different equation. Instead of the quantity equation I use an equation—called a monetary policy rule—in which the short-term interest rate is a function of the inflation rate and real GDP.[5] The policy rule is, of course, quite different from the quantity equation of money, but it is closely connected to the quantity equation. In fact, it can be easily derived from the quantity equation. To a person thinking about current policy, the quantity equation might seem like an indirect route to a interest rate rule for monetary policy, but it is a useful route for the study of monetary history.

7.1.1 Deriving a Monetary Policy Rule from the Quantity Equation

First imagine that the money supply is either fixed or growing at a constant rate. We know that velocity depends on the interest rate (r) and on real output or income (Y). Substituting for V in the quantity equation one thus gets a relationship between the interest rate (r), the price level (P), and real output (Y). If we isolate the interest rate (r) on the left-hand side of this relationship, we see a function of two variables: the interest rate as a function of the price level

---

5. Two useful recent studies have looked at monetary history from the vantage point of a monetary policy rule stated in terms of the interest rate instrument rather than a money instrument. These are Clarida, Galí, and Gertler (1998), who look at several other countries in addition to the United States, and Judd and Rudebusch (1998), who contrast U.S. monetary policies under Greenspan, Volker, and Burns. Clarida et al. (1998) show that British participation in the European Monetary System while Germany was tightening monetary policy led to a suboptimal shift of the baseline policy rule for the United Kingdom. Two earlier influential studies using the Friedman and Schwartz (1963) approach to monetary history and policy evaluation are Sargent (1986) and Romer and Romer (1989).

and real output. Shifts in this function would occur when either velocity growth or money growth shifts. Note also that such a function relating the interest rate to the price level and real output will still emerge if the money stock is not growing at a fixed rate, but rather responds in a systematic way to the interest rate or to real output; the response of money will simply change the parameters of the relationship.

The functional form of the relationship depends on many factors including the functional form of the relationship between velocity and the interest rate and the adjustment time between changes in the interest rate and changes in velocity. The functional form I use is linear in the interest rate and in the logarithms of the price level and real output. I make the latter two variables stationary by considering the deviation of real output from a possibly stochastic trend and by considering the first difference of the log of the price level—or the inflation rate. I also abstract from lags in the response of velocity to interest rates or income. These assumptions result in the following linear equation:

$$(1) \qquad r = \pi + gy + h(\pi - \pi^*) + r^f,$$

where the variables are r = the short-term interest rate, π = the inflation rate (percentage change in P), and y = the percentage deviation of real output (Y) from trend and the constants are g, h, π^*, and r^f. Note that the slope coefficient on inflation in equation (1) is $1 + h$; thus the two key response coefficients are g and $1 + h$. Note also that the intercept term is $r^f - h\pi^*$. An interpretation of the parameters and a rationale for this notation is given below.

7.1.2   Interpreting the Monetary Policy Rule

Focusing now on the functional form for the policy rule in equation (1), our objective is to determine whether the parameters in the policy rule vary across time periods and to look for differences in economic performance that might be related to any such variations across time periods. Note how this historical policy evaluation method is analogous to model-based policy evaluation research in which policy rules (like eq. [1]) with various parameter values are placed in a model and simulations of the model are examined to see if the variations in the parameter values make any difference for economic performance. Equation (1) is useful for this historical analogue of the model-based approach because it can describe monetary policy in different historical time periods when there were many different policy regimes. In each regime the response parameters g and $1 + h$ would be expected to differ, though in most regimes they would be positive. To see this, consider several types of regimes.

Constant Money Growth. We have already seen that the quantity equation with fixed money growth implies a relationship like equation (1). To see that the parameters g and $1 + h$ are positive with fixed money growth consider the demand for money in which real balances depend negatively on the interest rate and positively on real output. Then, in the case of fixed money growth, an increase in inflation would lower *real* money balances and cause the interest rate to rise: thus higher inflation leads to a higher interest rate.[6] Or suppose that real income rises thus increasing the demand for money; then, with no adjustment in the supply of money, the interest rate must rise. In other words, the monetary policy rule with positive values for g and $1 + h$ provides a good description of monetary policy in a fixed money growth regime. However, the monetary policy rule also provides a useful framework in many other situations.

International Gold Standard. Important for our historical purposes is that such a relationship also exists in the case of an international gold standard. The short-run response $(1 + h)$ of the interest rate to the inflation rate in the case of a gold standard is most easily explained by the specie flow mechanism of David Hume. If inflation began to rise in the United States compared with other countries, then a balance-of-payments deficit would occur because U.S. goods would become less competitive. Gold would flow out of the United States to finance the trade deficit; high-powered money growth would decline and the reduction in the supply of money compared with the demand for money would put upward pressure on U.S. interest rates. The higher interest rates and the reduction in demand for U.S. exports would put downward pressure on inflation in the United States.[7] Similarly, a reduction in inflation in the United States would lead to a trade surplus, a gold inflow, an increase in the money supply, and downward pressure on U.S. interest rates.

Fluctuations in real output would also cause interest rates to adjust. Suppose that there were an increase in real output. The increased demand for money would put upward pressure on interest rates if the money supply were unchanged. Amplifying this effect under a gold standard would be an increase in the trade deficit, which would lead to a gold outflow and a decline in the money supply.

These interest rate responses would occur with or without a central bank. If there were a central bank, it could increase the size of the response coefficients if it played by the gold standard's "rules of the game." Interest rates would be even more responsive, because a higher price level at home would then bring about an increase in the "bank rate" as the central bank acted to help alleviate the price discrepancies. The U.S. Treasury did perform some of the functions of a central bank during the gold standard period; it even provided liquidity during some periods of financial panic, though not with much regularity or predictability. However, there is little evidence that the U.S. Treasury per-

6. Note that this effect of inflation on the interest rate is a short-term "liquidity effect" rather than a longer term "Fisherian" or "expected inflation" effect. The expected inflation effect would occur if the growth rate of the money supply increased or if π^* (the target inflation rate in the policy rule) increased.

7. Short-term capital flows would of course limit the size of such interest rate changes. One reason why U.S. short-term interest rates did not move by very much in response to U.S. inflation fluctuations (as shown below) may have been the mobility of capital.

formed "rules of the game" functions as the Bank of England did during the gold standard era.

Leaning against the Wind. The most straightforward application of equation (1) is to situations where the Fed sets short-term interest rates in response to events in the economy. Then equation (1) is a central bank interest rate reaction function describing how the Federal Reserve takes actions in the money market that cause the interest rate to change in response to changes in inflation and real GDP. For example, if the Fed "leaned against the wind," easing money market conditions in response to lower inflation or declines in production and tightening money market conditions in response to higher inflation or increases in production, then one would expect g and $1 + h$ in equation (1) to be positive. However, "leaning against the wind" policies have not usually been stated quantitatively; thus the size of the parameters could be very small or very large and would not necessarily lead to good economic performance.

Monetary Policy Rule as a Guideline or Explicit Formula. Finally, equation (1) could represent a guideline, or even a strict formula, for the central bank to follow when making monetary policy decisions. As in the previous paragraph, decisions would be cast in terms of whether the Fed would raise or lower the short-term interest rate. But equation (1) would serve as a normative guide to these decisions, not simply a description of them after the fact. If the policy rule called for increasing the interest rate, for example, then the Federal Open Market Committee (FOMC) would instruct the trading desk to make open market sales and thereby adjust the money supply appropriately to bring about this increase. In this case, the parameters of equation (1) have a natural interpretation: π^* is the central bank's target inflation rate, r^f is the central bank's estimate of the equilibrium real rate of interest, and h is the amount by which the Fed raises the ex post real interest rate $(r - \pi)$ in response to an increase in inflation. In the case that $g = 0.5$, $h = 0.5$, $\pi^* = 2$, and $r^f = 2$, equation (1) is precisely the form of the policy rule I suggested in Taylor (1993a). Others have suggested that g should be larger, perhaps closer to one (see Brayton et al. 1997). Thus an alternative baseline rule considered below sets $g = 1$. These are the parameter values that define the baseline policy rules for historical comparisons in this paper.

7.1.3 The Importance of the Size of the Coefficients

To summarize, a constant growth rate of the money stock, an international gold standard, an informal policy of leaning against the wind, and an explicit quantitative policy of interest rate setting all will tend to generate positive responses of the interest rate to changes in inflation or real output, as described by equation (1). And we expect that g and $1 + h$ in equation (1) would be greater than zero in all these situations. However, the magnitude of these coefficients will differ depending on how monetary policy is run.

In the case of the gold standard or a fixed money growth policy, the size of the coefficients depends on many features of the economy. Under a gold standard, the size of the response of the interest rate to an increase in inflation will depend on the sensitivity of trade flows to international price differences. It will also depend on the size of the money multiplier, which translates a change in high-powered money due to a gold outflow into a change in the money supply. The interest rate elasticity of the demand for money is also a factor.

With a policy that keeps the growth rate of the money stock constant, the response of the interest rate to an increase in real output will depend on both the income elasticity of money demand and the interest rate elasticity of money demand. The higher the interest rate elasticity of money demand (or velocity), the smaller would be the response of interest rates to an increase in output or inflation.

The size of these coefficients makes a big difference for the effects of policy. Simulations of economic models indicate, for example, that the coefficient h should not be negative; otherwise $1 + h$ will be less than one and the real interest rate would fall rather than rise when inflation rose. As a result inflation could be highly volatile. As I show below there is evidence that h was negative during the late 1960s and 1970s when inflation rose in the United States. Hence, policymakers need to be concerned about the size of these coefficients.

A recent example of this concern demonstrates the usefulness of thinking about monetary history from the perspective of equation (1). Consider Alan Greenspan's (1997) recent analysis of the size of the interest rate response to real output with a constant money growth rate. In commenting on a money growth strategy, Greenspan reasoned: "Because the velocity of such an aggregate [M1] varies substantially in response to small changes in interest rates, target ranges for M1 growth in [the FOMC's] judgement no longer were reliable guides for outcomes in nominal spending and inflation. In response to an unanticipated movement in spending and hence the quantity of money demanded, a small variation in interest rates would be sufficient to bring money back to path but not to correct the deviation in spending" (1997, 4–5). In other words, in Greenspan's view the interest rate elasticity of velocity is so large that the interest rate would respond by too small an amount to an increase in output. In terms of equation (1) the parameter g is too small, according to Greenspan's analysis, under a policy that targets the growth rate of M1.

7.2 The Evolution of Monetary Policy Rules in the United States: From the International Gold Standard to the 1990s

Figures 7.1 and 7.2 illustrate the historical relation between the variables in equation (1). They show the interest rate (r), the inflation rate (π), and real GDP deviations (y) during two different time periods: 1880–1914 versus 1955–97. The upper part of each figure shows real output, an estimate of the trend in real output, and the percentage deviation of real output from this trend. Our focus is on the deviations of real output from trend rather than on the

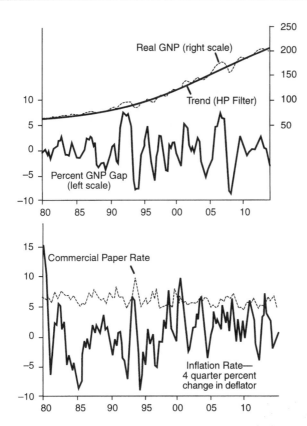

Fig. 7.1   The 1880–1914 period: short-term interest rate, inflation, and real output
Source: Quarterly data on real GNP, the GNP deflator, and the commercial paper rate are from Balke and Gordon (1986). Real output data are measured in billions of 1972 dollars and the trend is created with the Hodrick-Prescott filter.

average output growth rate in the two periods. The lower part of each figure shows a short-term interest rate (the commercial paper rate in the earlier period and the federal funds rate in the later period) and the inflation rate (a four-quarter average of the percentage change in the GDP deflator). Recall that the earlier period coincides with the classical international gold standard, starting with the end of the greenback era when the United States restored gold convertibility and ending with the suspension of convertibility by many countries at the start of World War I.

7.2.1   Changes in Cyclical Stability

The contrast between the display of the data in figure 7.1 and figure 7.2 is striking. First, note that business cycles occur much more frequently in the earlier period (fig. 7.1) than in the later period (fig. 7.2), and the size of the

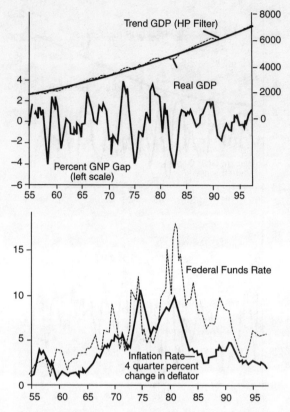

Fig. 7.2   The 1955–97 period: short-term interest rate, inflation, and real output
Source: Quarterly data are from the DRI data bank. Real output is measured in billions of 1992 dollars and the trend is created with the Hodrick-Prescott filter.

fluctuations of inflation and real output is much greater. From 1880 to 1897 there was deflation on average. From 1897 to 1914 prices rose on average. But throughout the whole period there were large fluctuations around these averages. The later period is not of course uniform in its macroeconomic performance. The late 1960s and 1970s saw a large and persistent swing in inflation, while the years since the mid-1980s have seen much greater macroeconomic stability.

One way to highlight the greater macroeconomic turbulence in the earlier years is to consider the period from 1890 to 1897, which saw three recessions. These years were so bad that they were called the "Disturbed Years" by Friedman and Schwartz (1963). One cannot avoid the temptation to contrast 1890–97 with 1990–97. If we had the same business cycle experience in the later years, we would have had a recession in 1990–91 slightly longer than the one we actually had. But we would have also had another recession starting in January 1993 just as President Clinton started in office and yet another recession starting in 1995. The trough of that third recession of the 1990s would have occured in June of 1997. Even allowing for measurement error due to overemphasis of goods versus services in the earlier period, it appears that the earlier period was less stable.[8] To be sure, if one ignores the long swing of average deflation and then inflation, the fluctuations in inflation were much less persistent during the gold standard period, as emphasized in a comparison by McKinnon and Ohno (1997, 164–71). But this long-term deflation and inflation should count as part of the sub-par inflation performance during this period.

7.2.2 Changes in Interest Rate Responses

A second, and even more striking, contrast between the two periods is the response of the short-term interest rate to inflation and output. While the short-term interest rate is procyclical during both the earlier period and the later period, the elasticity of its response to output is clearly much less in the earlier period than in the later period. Cagan (1971) first pointed out the increased cyclical sensitivity of the interest rate to real output fluctuations, and it is more evident now than ever. The short-term interest rate is also much less responsive to fluctuations in the inflation rate in the earlier period. It appears that the gold standard did lead to a positive response of interest rates to real output and inflation, but this response is much less than for the monetary policy in the post–World War II period.

The huge size of these differences is readily visible in figures 7.1 and 7.2. But to see how the responses changed during the post–World War II period it is necessary to go beyond these time-series charts. Some numerical information about the size of these differences is provided in table 7.1. The table shows least squares estimates of the coefficients on real output (the parameter g in eq. [1]) and the inflation rate (the parameter $1 + h$ in eq. [1]) for different time periods.[9]

The far right-hand column shows the results for each of the two full periods. Observe that the estimated values of g and $1 + h$ are about 10 times larger in the Bretton Woods and post–Bretton Woods eras than in the international gold standard era. It is clear that the gold standard implied much smaller response coefficients for the interest rate than Federal Reserve policy has implied in later periods.

---

8. Romer (1986) demonstrated that biases in the pre–World War I data tend to overestimate the volatility in comparison with later periods.

9. As explained above this equation is actually a reduced form of several structural equations, especially in the gold standard and Bretton Woods periods. I have purposely tried to keep the statistical equations as simple as the theoretical policy rule in eq. (1). No attempt has been made to correct the estimates for serial correlation of the errors in the equation. I want to allow for the possibility that monetary policy mistakes are serially correlated in ways not necessarily described by simple time-series models. In fact, this serial correlation is very large, especially in the gold standard period when the equations fit very poorly. Hence, the "t-statistics" in parentheses are not useful for hypothesis testing. See Christiano, Eichenbaum, and Evans (1997) for a comprehensive analysis of estimation and identification issues in the case of reaction functions.

Table 7.1   Monetary Policy Rules: Descriptive Statistics

	International Gold Standard Era		
Variable	1879:1–91:4 Coefficient	1897:1–1914:4 Coefficient	1879:1–1914:4 Coefficient
Constant	6.458 (70.5)	5.519 (47.3)	5.984 (75.0)
π	0.019 (1.01)	0.034 (1.03)	0.006 (0.32)
y	0.059 (2.28)	0.038 (1.89)	0.034 (1.52)
R^2	0.15	0.07	0.02

	Bretton Woods and Post–Bretton Woods Eras		
	1960:1–79:4 Coefficient	1987:1–97:3 Coefficient	1954:1–97:3 Coefficient
Constant	2.045 (6.34)	1.174 (2.35)	1.721 (5.15)
π	0.813 (12.9)	1.533 (9.71)	1.101 (15.1)
y	0.252 (4.93)	0.765 (8.22)	0.329 (3.16)
R^2	0.70	0.83	0.58

Note: These are ordinary least squares estimates of the coefficients of the variables in eq. (1). The left-hand-side variable (r) is measured by the commercial paper rate for the years 1879–1914 and by the federal funds rate for the years 1954–97. The variable π is measured by the average inflation rate over four quarters, and the variable y is measured by the percentage deviation of real output from a trend. Numbers in parentheses are ratios of coefficients to standard errors. See figs. 7.1 and 7.2 for data sources.

Note also that the size of these coefficients has increased gradually over time. Compared with the 1960s and 1970s the coefficients on real output tripled in size by the 1987–97 period while the coefficient on inflation doubled in size. They are now close to the values of the rule I suggested in Taylor (1993a). Hence, when viewed over the past century we have seen an evolution of the monetary policy rule as I have defined and characterized it empirically here. The monetary policy rule had very low interest rate responses during the gold standard era. It had higher responses during the 1960s and the 1970s, and it had still higher responses in the late 1980s and 1990s.

7.2.3   A Graphical Illustration of the Importance of the Size of the Inflation Response

Figure 7.3 shows how dramatically the monetary policy rule has changed from the 1960–70s to the 1980–90s. The two solid lines show two monetary policy rules corresponding to the two periods. The slopes of the solid lines measure the size of the interest rate responses to inflation in the policy rule. I abstract from output fluctuations in figure 7.3, by assuming that the economy is operating at full employment with real GDP equal to potential GDP ($y = 0$). The dashed line in figure 7.3 has a slope of one and shows a constant real interest rate of 2 percent. If the actual long-run real interest rate is 2 percent,

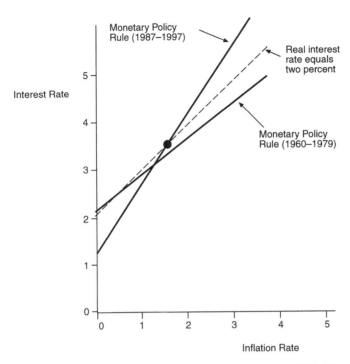

Fig. 7.3   Two estimated monetary policy rules: 1960–79 versus 1987–97

then the intersection of the dashed line and the policy rule line gives the long-run average inflation rate.

Observe that the slope of the policy rule has gone from below one to above one. A slope below one would lead to poor economic performance according to variety of models. With the slope less than one, an increase in inflation would bring about a *decrease* in the real interest rate. This would increase demand and add to upward pressures on inflation. This is exactly the wrong policy response to an increase in inflation because it would lead to ever increasing inflation. In contrast, if the slope of the policy rule were greater than one, an increase in inflation would bring about an *increase* in the real interest rate, which would be stabilizing.

These theoretical arguments are illustrated in figure 7.3. For a long-run equilibrium, we must be at the intersection of the policy rule line and the dashed line representing the long-run equilibrium real interest rate. If the slope of the policy rule line is greater than one, higher inflation leads to higher real interest rates and the inflation rate converges to an equilibrium at the intersection of the policy rule line and the dashed real interest rate line. For example, if the equilibrium real interest rate is 2 percent as in figure 7.3, the equilibrium inflation rate is about 1.5 percent for the recent, more steeply sloped, monetary policy rule in figure 7.3. However, if the slope of the policy rule line is less than one, higher inflation leads to a lower real interest rate, which leads to even higher inflation; the inflation rate is unstable and would not converge to an equilibrium. In sum, figure 7.3 shows why the inflation rate would be more stable in the 1987–97 period than in the 1960–79 period.

7.3   Effects of the Different Policy Rules on Macroeconomic Stability

Can one draw a connection between the different policy rules and the economic performance with those policy rules? In particular, within the range of policy rules we have seen, is it true that more responsive policy rules lead to greater economic stability? Making such a connection is complicated by other factors, such as oil shocks and fiscal shocks, but it is at least instructive to try.

7.3.1   Three Monetary Eras

As the analysis summarized in table 7.1 indicates, three eras of U.S. monetary history can be clearly distinguished by big differences in the degree of responsiveness of short-term interest rates in the monetary policy rule.

First, during the period from about 1879 to about 1914 short-term interest rates were very unresponsive to fluctuations in inflation and real output. Second, during the period from about 1960 to 1979 short-term interest rates were more responsive, but still small in the sense that the response of the nominal interest rate to changes in inflation was less than one. Third, during the period from about 1986 to 1997 the nominal interest rate was much more responsive to both inflation and real output fluctuations.

These three eras can also be distinguished in terms of overall economic stability. Of the three, there is no question that the third had the greatest degree of economic stability. Figure 7.1 shows that both inflation and real output had smaller fluctuations during this period. The period contains both the first and second longest peacetime expansions in U.S. history. Moreover, inflation was low and stable. And, of course, this is the period in which the monetary policy rule had the largest reaction coefficients, giving support to model-based research that this was a better policy rule than those implied by the two earlier periods.

The relative ranking of the first and second periods is more ambiguous. Real output and inflation fluctuations were larger in the earlier period. But while inflation was more variable, there was much less persistence of inflation during the gold standard than in the late 1960s and 1970s. However, the different exchange rate regimes are another monetary factor that must be taken into account. It was the gold standard that kept the long-run inflation rate so stable in the earlier period. Bretton Woods may have provided a similar constraint on inflation during the early 1960s, but as U.S. monetary policy mistakenly became too easy, it was not inflation that collapsed, it was the Bretton Woods system. And after the end of Bretton Woods this external constraint on inflation was removed. With the double whammy of the loss of an external constraint and an inadequately responsive monetary policy rule in place, the inevitable result was the Great Inflation.

If one properly controls for the beneficial external influences of the gold standard on long-run inflation during the 1879–1914 period, one obtains an unambiguous correlation between monetary policy rule and macroeconomic stability. The most economically stable period was the one with the most responsive policy rule. The least economically stable (again adjusting for the gold standard effects) was the one with the least responsive policy rule. The late 1960s and 1970s also rank lower than the most recent period in terms of economic stability and had a less responsive monetary policy rule.

7.3.2   Explaining the Changes in the Policy Rules

In any correlation analysis between economic policy and economic outcomes there is the possibility of reverse causation. Could the lower responsiveness of interest rates in the two earlier periods compared with the later period have been caused by the greater volatility of inflation and real output? If one examines the history of changes in the monetary policy rule I think it becomes clear that the answer is no. The evolution of the monetary policy rule is best understood as a gradual process of the Federal Reserve learning how to conduct monetary policy. This learning occurred through research by the staff at the Fed, through the criticism of monetary economists outside the Fed, through observation of central bank behavior in other countries, and through direct personal experience of members of the FOMC. And, of course, there were steps backward as well as forward.[10]

This learning process occurred as the United States moved further and further away from the classical international gold standard. Under the gold standard, increases and decreases in short-term interest rates were explained by the interaction of the quantity of money supplied (determined by high-powered money through the inflow and outflow of gold) and the quantity of money demanded (which rose and fell as inflation and output rose and fell). A greater response of the short-term interest rate to rising or falling price levels and to rising or falling output would probably have reduced the shorter run variability of inflation and output. For example, lower interest rates during the start of the deflation period may have prevented the deflation. But because of the fixed exchange rate feature of the gold standard, the U.S. inflation rate was constrained to be close to the inflation rates of other gold standard countries; the degree of closeness depended on the size and the duration of deviations from purchasing power parity.

The Federal Reserve started operations at the same time as the classical gold standard ended: 1914. From the start there was therefore uncertainty and dis-

---

10. If economists' research on the existence of a long-run trade-off between inflation and unemployment helped lead to the Great Inflation in the 1970s, then this research should be counted as a step backward. The effect of economic research and other factors that may have led to the Great Inflation are discussed in De Long (1997) and in my comment on De Long's paper.

agreement about how monetary policy should be conducted without the constraints of the gold standard and fixed exchange rates. The Federal Reserve Act indicated that currency—best interpreted now as the monetary base or high-powered money—was to be elastically provided. But how was the Fed to determine the degree of this elasticity?

The original idea was that two factors—each pulling in an opposite direction—were to be balanced out. One was the gold standard itself; with a gold reserve requirement limiting the amount of Federal Reserve liabilities, the supply of money was limited. This was a long-run constraint on the supply of money; it worked through gold inflows and gold outflows and the gradual adjustment of the U.S. price level compared with foreign price levels. The other factor, which worked more quickly, was "real bills" or "needs of trade" doctrine under which the supply of money was to be created in sufficient amounts to meet the demand for money. Clearly, the needs-of-trade criterion was not effective on its own because it did not put a limit on the amount of money creation. Therefore, with the suspension of the gold standard and with the real bills criterion ineffective in determining the supply of money, the Federal Reserve began operations with no criteria for determining the appropriate amount of money to supply. Hence, ever since this uncertain beginning, the Fed has been searching for such criteria. From the perspective of this paper, we can think of the Fed as searching for a good monetary policy rule.

This search is evident in many Federal Reserve reports. Early on, the idea of "leaning against the wind" was discussed as a counterbalance to the needs-of-trade criterion. For example, the Fed's annual report for 1923 stated that "it is the business of the [Federal] Reserve system to work against extremes either of deflation or inflation and not merely to adapt itself passively to the ups and downs of business" (quoted in Friedman and Schwartz 1963, 253). But there was no agreement about how much leaning against the wind there should be. As discussed above, leaning against the wind would result in a policy rule of the type in equation (1), but the parameters of the policy rule could be far from optimal. That the Fed was unable throughout the interwar period to find an effective policy rule for conducting monetary policy is evidenced by the disastrous economic performance during the Great Depression when money growth fell dramatically.

The search for a monetary policy rule was postponed during World War II and in the postwar period by the overriding objective of keeping Treasury borrowing costs down. (Effectively the Fed set $g = 0$ and $h = -1$ so that r was a constant stipulated by the U.S. Treasury.) However, after the 1951 Treasury–Federal Reserve Accord, the Fed once again needed a policy rule for conducting monetary policy. Leaning against the wind—now articulated by William McChesney Martin—again became a guideline for short-run decisions about changes in the money stock. But the idea was still very vague. As stated by Friedman and Schwartz (1963) in discussing the mid-1950s when William McChesney Martin was chairman, "There was essentially no discussion of how to determine which way the relevant wind was blowing. . . . Neither was there any discussion of when to start leaning against the wind. . . . There was more comment, but hardly any of it specific about how hard to lean against the wind" (631–32).

The experience of new board member Sherman Maisel indicates that the search was still going on 10 years later in the mid-1960s. According to Maisel in his candid memoirs, "After being on the Board for eight months and attending twelve open market meetings, I began to realize how far I was from understanding the theory the Fed used to make monetary policy. . . . Nowhere did I find an account of how monetary policy was made or how it operated" (1973, 77). Maisel was particularly concerned about various money market conditions indexes such as free reserves that came up in Fed deliberations, because of the difficulty of measuring the impact of these changes on the economy. He states, "Money market conditions cannot measure the degree to which markets should be tightened or for how long restraint should be retained" (82). And when referring to a decision to raise the short-term interest rate in 1965, he states, "It became increasingly clear that an inflationary boom was getting underway and that monetary policy should have been working to curb it" (81). However, he argued that the actions taken to raise interest rates were insufficient to curb the inflation. In retrospect he was correct. Interest rates did not go high enough. With no quantitative measure of how high interest rates should go, the chance of not raising them high enough was great.

The increased emphasis on money growth in the 1970s played a very useful role in clarifying the serious problems of interest rate setting without any quantitative guidelines. And money growth targets had a very useful role in the disinflation of the 1979–81 period because it was clear that interest rates would have to rise by large amounts as the Fed lowered the growth rate of the money supply. But after the disinflation was over, money growth targets again receded to being a longer run consideration in Federal Reserve operations as the demand for money appeared to be less stable. Moreover, as noted earlier, according to Greenspan's (1997) analysis, keeping money growth constant does not give sufficient response of interest rates to inflation or real output when the aim is to keep inflation low and steady.

The importance of having a policy rule to guide policy became even more important when the Bretton Woods system fell apart in the early 1970s. Until then the long-run constraints on monetary policy were similar to those of the international gold standard. If the Fed did not lean hard enough against the wind, the higher inflation rate would start to put pressure on the exchange rate and the Fed would have to raise interest rates to defend the dollar. But without the dollar to defend, this constraint on monetary policy was lost. After Bretton Woods ended there was an even greater need for the Fed to develop a monetary policy rule that was sufficient to contain inflation without the external constraint. This need was one of the catalysts for the rational expectations econometric policy evaluation research in the 1970s and 1980s.

This brief review of the evolution of policy indicates that macroeconomic events, economic research, and policymakers at the Fed have gradually brought forth changes in the monetary policy rule in the United States. I think this gradual evolution makes it clear that the causation underlying the negative correlation between the size of the policy response of interest rates to output or inflation and the volatility of output or inflation goes from policy to outcome, not the other way around.

If we apply this learning hypothesis to the changes in the estimated policy rule described above, it suggests that the Federal Reserve learned over time to have higher response coefficients in a policy rule like equation (1). What led the Fed to change its policy in such a way that the parameter h changed from a negative number to a positive number? Experience with the Great Inflation of the 1970s that resulted from a negative value for h may be one explanation. Academic research on the Phillips curve trade-off and the effects of different policy rules resulting from the rational expectations revolution may be another.[11]

7.4   "Policy Mistakes": Big Deviations from Baseline Policy Rules

The historical analysis thus far in this paper has not assumed that any particular policy rule was better than the others. However, that was the conclusion of the analysis: a comparison of policy rules and economic outcomes points to the rule the Fed has been using in recent years as a better way to run monetary policy than the way it was run in earlier years. That conclusion of the historical analysis bolsters the very similar conclusion of the model-based research summarized in the introduction to this paper.

Once one has focused on a particular policy rule, however, there is another way to use history to check whether the policy rule would work well. With a preferred policy rule in hand, one can look at episodes in the past when the instrument of policy—the federal funds rate in this case—deviated from the settings given by the preferred policy rule. We can characterize such deviations as "policy mistakes" and see if the economy was adversely affected as a result of these mistakes.[12]

Figures 7.4, 7.5, and 7.6 summarize the results of this historical "policy mistake" analysis. They show the actual federal funds rate and the value of the federal funds rate implied by two policy rules. The gap between the actual

---

11. Chari, Christiano, and Eichenbaum (1998) argue that the Fed was too accommodative to inflation (h was too low) in the 1970s because high expectations of inflation raised the costs of disinflation, rather than because the Fed still had something to learn about the Phillips curve trade-off or about the effects of different policy rules. I find the learning argument more plausible in part because it explains the end of the inflation and the change in the policy rule.

12. We are, of course, looking at these past episodes with the benefit of later research and experience. The term "mistake" does not necessarily mean that policymakers of the past had the information to do things differently.

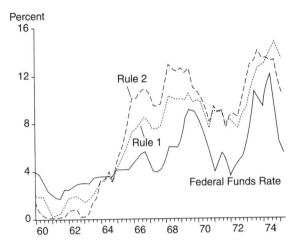

Fig. 7.4   Federal funds rate: too high in the early 1960s; too low in the late 1960s
Note: Rules 1 and 2 are given by the monetary policy rule in eq. (1) with $g = 0.5$ and 1.0, respectively.

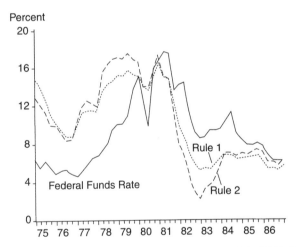

Fig. 7.5   Federal funds rate: too low in the 1970s; on track in 1979–81; too high in 1982–84
Note: See note to fig. 7.4.

federal funds rate and the policy rules is a measure of the policy mistake. One of the monetary policy rules I use is the one I suggested in Taylor (1993a), which is equation (1) with the parameters g and h equal to 0.5. This is rule 1 in figures 7.4, 7.5, and 7.6. As mentioned above, more recent research has suggested that g should be closer to 1.0, giving a more procyclical interest rate. This variant is rule 2 in the figures.

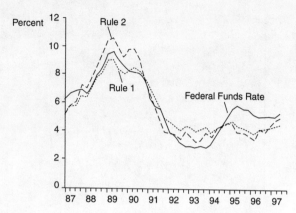

Fig. 7.6   Federal funds rate: on track in the late 1980s and 1990s
Note: See note to fig. 7.4.

The gap between the actual federal funds rate and the policy rule is particularly large in three episodes shown in figures 7.4 and 7.5, especially in comparison with the relatively small gap in the late 1980s and 1990s shown in figure 7.6.

The first episode occurred in the early 1960s when the mistake was making monetary policy too tight. Regardless of whether g is 0.5 or 1.0 the actual federal funds rate is well above the policy rule. The gap between the funds rate and the baseline policy was between 2 and 3 percentage points and this gap lasted for about three and a half years.[13]

It is interesting to note that Friedman and Schwartz (1963, 617) also concluded that monetary policy was overly restrictive during this period. They cite several reasons why policy may have been too tight. First, the Fed was concerned about the balance of payments and an outflow of gold. Second, in looking back at the previous recovery, it appeared to the Fed that policy had eased too soon after the recession. What was the result of this policy mistake? The recovery from the 1960–61 recession was weak and the eventual expansion was slow for several years from about 1962 to 1965. In fact, the economy did not appear to catch up to its potential until 1965. The New Economics introduced by President Kennedy and his economic advisers was addressed at this prolonged period with real output below potential.

The second episode started in the late 1960s and continued throughout the 1970s—a mistake with so much serial correlation it would pass a unit root test! In this case the monetary policy mistake was being way too easy. As shown in figures 7.4 and 7.5, the gap between the funds rate and the baseline policy

13. With its high output response, rule 2 brings the interest rate below zero for several quarters, so the interest rate is set to a small positive number in the chart.

started growing in the late 1960s. It grew as large as 6 percentage points and persisted in the 4 to 6 percentage point range until the late 1970s when Paul Volcker took over as Fed chairman. The excessive ease in policy began well before the oil price shocks of the 1970s, thus raising doubts that these shocks were the cause of the 1970s Great Inflation.

What caused this monetary policy mistake? Economic research of the 1960s suggested that there was a long-run trade-off between inflation and unemployment; this research probably reduced some of the aversion to inflation by the Federal Reserve. At the least the belief by some in a long-run Phillips curve made defending low inflation more difficult at the Fed. Note that the mistake began well before the Friedman-Phelps hypothesis was put forward. Moreover, as the quotes from Maisel's memoirs above make clear, the Fed's use of money market conditions caused them to understate the degree of tightness. De Long (1997) argues that the overly expansionary policy was due to a great fear of unemployment carried over from the Great Depression, though he does not attempt to explain why this mistake occurred when it did. While the causes of this mistake may be uncertain, there is little doubt that it was responsible for bringing on the Great Inflation of the 1970s. In my view this mistake is the second most serious monetary policy mistake in twentieth-century U.S. history, the most serious being the Great Depression. If a policy closer to the baseline were followed, the rise in inflation may have been avoided.

The third episode occurred after the disinflation of the early 1980s. The increase in interest rates in 1979 and 1980 was about the right magnitude according to either of the policy rules. But both rule 1 and rule 2 indicate that the funds rate should have been lowered more than it was in the 1982–84 period. During this period the interest rate was well above the value implied by the two policy rules. However, it should be emphasized that this period occurred right after the end of the 1970s inflation, and interest rates higher than recommended by the policy rules may have been necessary to keep expectations of inflation from rising and to help establish the credibility of the Fed. In effect the Fed was in a transition between policy rules. In my view this period has less claim to being a "policy mistake" than the other two periods.

7.5 Conclusions

The main conclusions of this paper can be summarized as follows. First, a monetary policy rule for the interest rate provides a useful framework with which to examine U.S. monetary history. It complements the framework provided by the quantity equation of money so usefully employed by Friedman and Schwartz (1963). Second, a monetary policy rule in which the interest rate responds to inflation and real output is an implication of many different monetary systems. Third, the monetary policy rule has changed dramatically over time in the United States, and these changes are associated with equally dramatic changes in economic stability. Fourth, an examination of the underlying reasons for the monetary policy changes indicates that they have caused the changes in economic outcomes, rather than the reverse. Fifth, a monetary policy rule in which the interest rate responds to inflation and real output more aggressively than during the 1960s and 1970s or than during the international gold standard—and more like the late 1980s and 1990s—is a good policy rule. Sixth, if one defines policy mistakes as deviations from such a good policy rule, then such mistakes have been associated with either high and prolonged inflation or drawn-out periods of low capacity utilization, much as simple monetary theory would predict.

Overall the results of the historical approach in this paper are quite consistent with the results of the model-based approach to monetary policy evaluation. But in an important sense this paper has only touched the surface; many other issues could be explored with a historical approach. For example, two difficult problems with monetary policy rules such as equation (1) have been mentioned by Alan Greenspan (1997): both potential GDP and the real rate of interest are uncertain. Uncertainty about the level of potential GDP (and the natural rate of unemployment) is a problem faced by monetary policymakers today regardless of whether they use a policy rule for guidance. Looking back at previous episodes and seeing the results of mismeasuring either potential GDP or the real rate of interest might help reduce the probability of making the next monetary policy mistake.

References

Balke, Nathan S., and Robert J. Gordon. 1986. Appendix B: Historical data. In *The American business cycle: Continuity and change,* ed. Robert J. Gordon. Chicago: University of Chicago Press.

Bernanke, Ben, Mark Gertler, and Mark Watson. 1997. Systematic monetary policy and the effects of oil price shocks. *Brookings Papers on Economic Activity,* no. 1:91–157.

Bordo, Michael D., and Anna J. Schwartz. 1999. Monetary policy regimes and economic performance: The historical record. In *Handbook of macroeconomics,* ed. John B. Taylor and Michael Woodford. Amsterdam: North Holland.

Brayton, Flint, Andrew Levin, Ralph Tryon, and John Williams. 1997. The evolution of macro models at the Federal Reserve Board. *Carnegie-Rochester Conference Series on Public Policy* 47:43–81.

Bryant, Ralph, Peter Hooper, and Catherine Mann. 1993. *Evaluating policy regimes: New empirical research in empirical macroeconomics.* Washington, D.C.: Brookings Institution.

Cagan, Phillip. 1971. Changes in the cyclical behavior of interest rates. In *Essays on interest rates,* ed. Jack M. Guttentag. New York: Columbia University Press.

Chari, V. V., Lawrence Christiano, and Martin Eichenbaum. 1998. Expectation traps and discretion. *Journal of Economic Theory* 81 (2): 462–98.

Christiano, Lawrence J., Martin Eichenbaum, and Charles L. Evans. 1997. Monetary policy shocks: What have we learned and to what end? In *Handbook of macroeconomics,* ed. John B. Taylor and Michael Woodford. Amsterdam: North Holland.

Clarida, Richard, Jordi Galí, and Mark Gertler. 1998. Monetary policy rules in practice: Some international evidence. *European Economic Review* 42:1033–67.

De Long, J. Bradford. 1997. America's peacetime inflation: The 1970s. In *Reducing inflation: Motivation and strategy,* ed. Christina D. Romer and David H. Romer. Chicago: University of Chicago Press.

Friedman, Milton, and Anna Schwartz. 1963. *A monetary history of the United States, 1867–1960.* Princeton, N.J.: Princeton University Press.

Greenspan, Alan. 1997. Remarks at the 15th anniversary conference of the Center for Economic Policy Research. Stanford University, 5 September.

Judd, John F., and Glenn D. Rudebusch. 1998. Taylor's rule and the Fed: 1970–1997. *Federal Reserve Bank of San Francisco Economic Review,* no. 3:3–16.

Judd, John F., and Bharat Trehan. 1995. Has the Fed gotten tougher on inflation? *Federal Reserve Bank of San Francisco Weekly Letter,* no. 95–13.

Maisel, Sherman J. 1973. *Managing the dollar.* New York: Norton.

McCallum, Bennett. 1988. Robustness properties of a rule for monetary policy. *Carnegie-Rochester Conference Series on Public Policy* 29:173–203.

McKinnon, Ronald I., and Kenichi Ohno. 1997. *Dollar and yen.* Cambridge, Mass.: MIT Press.

Romer, Christina D. 1986. Is the stabilization of the postwar economy a figment of the data? *American Economic Review* 76:314–34.

Romer, Christina D., and David Romer. 1989. Does monetary policy matter? A new test in the spirit of Friedman and Schwartz. In *NBER macroeconomics annual 1989,* ed. O. J. Blanchard and S. Fischer. Cambridge, Mass.: MIT Press.

Sargent, Thomas. 1986. The end of four big inflations. In *Rational expectations and inflation,* ed. Thomas Sargent, 40–109. New York: Harper and Row.

Sims, Christopher, and Tao Zha. 1995. Does monetary policy generate recessions? Atlanta: Federal Reserve Bank of Atlanta. Working paper.

Taylor, John B. 1979. Estimation and control of a macroeconomic model with rational expectations. *Econometrica* 47 (5): 1267–86.

———. 1993a. Discretion versus policy rules in practice. *Carnegie-Rochester Conference Series on Public Policy* 39:195–214.

———. 1993b. *Macroeconomic policy in a world economy: From econometric design to practical application.* New York: Norton.

Comment   Richard H. Clarida

It is a pleasure to discuss this paper by John Taylor. In it, he proposes to use the Taylor rule as an analytical framework for the interpretation of monetary history, much as Friedman and Schwartz employed the quantity equation. I agree with the approach that he is trying to promote, I concur in general with the inferences he draws from it, and I believe that this way of interpreting monetary history can be, and in my work with Jordi Galí and Mark Gertler (1998a, 1998b) has already been, applied in fruitful ways that complement the application emphasized in this paper.

Richard H. Clarida is professor of economics and international affairs and chairman of the Department of Economics, Columbia University.

The basic idea is straightforward, and much of the paper is devoted to justifying its application. A baseline, or reference, time path of the short-term (federal funds) interest rate is constructed using a Taylor (1993) rule of the form

$$r_t = r^f + \pi^* + h(\pi_t - \pi^*) + gy_t,$$

where r^f is the long-run equilibrium real interest rate, π^* is the long-run equilibrium rate of inflation, and y_t is the output gap. After the baseline is constructed, the actual time path of the short-term interest rate is compared to the baseline path. Episodes (i.e., sequences of observations) in which the funds rate is persistently higher than the baseline path are interpreted as episodes of excessively "tight" monetary policy, while episodes in which the funds rate is consistently below the baseline are interpreted as episodes in which monetary policy is too "easy." Although Taylor provides some qualification in footnote 12, he is explicit in his interpretation of these episodes of "easy" and "tight" policy as representing policy mistakes.

Now if, as we have learned from the central bankers present at this conference, the Taylor rule can be and is used as a benchmark for assessing the current stance of actual monetary policies, then certainly it can also be used as part of a framework to interpret monetary history. But certainly the caveats that apply to its use as a benchmark for current policy also apply, and perhaps with even greater force, to its use as a framework for interpreting monetary history. Unobservable but essential inputs to the Taylor rule such as the equilibrium real interest rate and the NAIRU fluctuate over time. Data get revised, and with these revisions the amplitudes—and sometimes the signs—of business cycle indicators appear much different with hindsight than they did to contemporaries. Taylor's paper exhibits the appreciation and awareness of these issues that I would expect of him, and subsequent authors that pursue this approach would do well to emulate him.

As applied to U.S. monetary policy since 1960, I believe Taylor's interpretations are largely correct. In fact, my paper with Jordi Galí and Mark Gertler (1998a) makes very similar points using an estimated version of what we call a "forward-looking" Taylor rule. A forward-looking Taylor rule estimated over the post-1979 period—with $h = 1.96$ and $g = 0.07$—captures all the major swings in the funds rate. When we backcast the post-1979 rule on the pre-1979 data, we also infer—as does Taylor—that policy was "too easy" between 1965 and 1979. Indeed, our parameter estimates for the 1960–79 period ($h = 0.80$ and $g = 0.52$) confirm Taylor's interpretation that the source of the 1965–79 policy mistake was that the Fed, when faced with an increase in inflation, raised the funds rate, *but by less than the rise in inflation so that a rise in inflation was countered by a fall in the real interest rate.* This finding is perfectly consistent with, indeed it can be viewed as the explanation for, Mishkin's (1981) famous empirical result that during the 1970s the ex ante real interest rate varied inversely with inflation.

Why is it that before 1979, the Fed appears to have followed a policy that, with hindsight, was clearly inferior to the policy it has followed since? According to Clarida et al.:

Another way to look at the issue is to ask why it is that the Fed maintained persistently low short term real rates in the face of high or rising inflation. One possibility, emphasized by DeLong (1997), is that the Fed thought the natural rate of unemployment at this time was much lower [and potential output higher] than it really was. . . . Another . . . possibility is that, at the time, neither the Fed nor the economics profession understood the dynamics of inflation very well. Indeed, it was not until the mid-to-late 1970s that . . . textbooks began emphasizing the absence of a long run trade-off between inflation and output. The idea that expectations may matter in generating inflation and that credibility is important in policy-making were simply not well established during that era. What all this suggests is that in understanding historical economic behavior, it is important to take into account the state of policy-maker's knowledge of the economy and how it may have evolved over time. Analyzing policy-making from this perspective, we think, would be a highly useful undertaking. (1998a, 24)

To this, I might add that I believe policymakers and the profession only began, in the late 1960s, to appreciate the distinction between movements in nominal and real interest rates.

As Taylor suggests in his paper, a systematic policy of raising the funds rate by less than inflation "would ultimately imply an unstable inflation rate." In Clarida et al. (1998a), we embed a forward-looking Taylor rule with $h < 1$ in a version of the sticky price models found in King and Wolman (1996), Woodford (1996), and McCallum and Nelson (chap. 1 of this volume). We find that for $h < 1$, there can be bursts of inflation and output fluctuations that result from self-fulfilling changes in expectations. These sunspot fluctuations may arise because under this rule individuals correctly anticipate that the Fed will accommodate a rise in expected inflation by letting real interest rates decline. These sunspot fluctuations do not arise when $h > 1$.

As Taylor mentions in his paper, in Clarida et al. (1998b), we introduce another way to use the Taylor rule baseline to interpret recent monetary history. Specifically, we interpret the collapse in September 1992 of the European Monetary System (EMS) by calculating for France, Italy, and Britain during the several years leading up to and several years following the collapse a stress indicator defined as

$$\text{stress}_{j,t} = r_{j,t} - r_{j,t}^{\text{fltr}}.$$

When $stress_{j,t}$ is positive, short-term interest rates in country j are higher than they would be if they were set according to a Taylor rule based on inflation and output in country j. Does this mean that monetary policy in country j is "too tight"? In this instance no, because with the dismantling of capital controls in the 1990s, these countries' decisions to fix their exchange rates meant they gave up autonomy over their national monetary policies. The EMS evolved into a system in which Germany set the level of interest rates for all member countries; any remaining fluctuations in country-specific interest differentials with Germany reflected the changing sentiments of speculators regarding the commitment of that country to the fixed exchange rate. How then do we interpret a positive reading of stress? It is a measure, in basis points, of the cost to country j of belonging to a fixed exchange rate system when monetary policy is not being set based on the macroeconomic conditions in country j.

References

Clarida, R., J. Galí, and M. Gertler. 1998a. Monetary policy rules and macroeconomic stability: Evidence and some theory. NBER Working Paper no. 6442. Cambridge, Mass.: National Bureau of Economic Research.
———. 1998b. Monetary policy rules in practice: Some international evidence. *European Economic Review* 42:1033–67.
King, R., and A. Wolman. 1996. Inflation targeting in a St. Louis model of the 21st century. NBER Working Paper no. 5507. Cambridge, Mass.: National Bureau of Economic Research.
Mishkin, F. 1981. The real interest rate: An empirical investigation. *Carnegie-Rochester Conference Series on Public Policy* 15:151–200.
Taylor, J. 1993. Discretion versus policy rules in practice. *Carnegie-Rochester Conference Series on Public Policy* 39:195–214.
Woodford, M. 1996. Control of the public debt: A requirement for price stability? NBER Working Paper no. 5684. Cambridge, Mass.: National Bureau of Economic Research.

Discussion Summary

Laurence Ball asked Taylor for his conjecture on how much of the economy's better performance under Alan Greenspan than under Arthur Burns was attributable to optimal policy and how much to better luck in the sense of not experiencing the Vietnam War and two oil shocks. This could be addressed formally by decomposing output variance into the variance of shocks and variance caused by deviations from the optimal rule. *Taylor* replied that his view on this issue was influenced by De Long (1997), who indicates that the policy mistake, under this definition, began well before the oil shocks. A more responsive policy rule could have led to a bigger decline in output during the first oil shock, but it is quite likely that inflation would not have risen so much. Thus the economy would have gotten away with a much smaller disinflation in the early 1980s.

Ball then questioned the result that policy was too tight in 1983, whereas there was a rapid recovery going on during that time. *Taylor* responded that the policy mistake had already occurred at the beginning of 1982. While the general raising of interest rates by Volcker during 1979–81 was about right, the funds rate should have been lowered by a greater amount when the economy really sank. *Glenn Rudebusch* expressed doubts as to whether another measure of output gap rather than the one used in the paper would have shown such a deep recession for 1982. *Taylor* replied that the gap obtained with the Hodrick-Prescott filter looked similar to the one in Judd and Trehan (1995). *Martin Feldstein* mentioned that part of the reason for overtight interest rates at that point was that Volcker felt keeping up with the disinflation for much longer was politically unsustainable; hence, the disinflation had to occur in a shorter than optimal length of time. *Edward Gramlich* mentioned that Volcker shifted from the money to the funds standard during that period. This happened at least in part because there was a shift in money demand due to, for example, interest payments on demand deposits. *Donald Kohn* added that money growth was accelerating toward the end of 1982 and inflation expectations were persistently high, much higher than ex post realized inflation. *Frederic Mishkin* added that after a history of bad policy, Volcker wanted to be tough in order to gain credibility. *Ben McCallum* mentioned that the Federal Reserve was below its M1 target in 1981. *William Poole* stressed that the economy sank much more quickly than anybody anticipated in 1982. There was an enormous inventory runoff, and the unemployment rate shot up in literally two months.

Bob Hall noted that during the national bank era, prior to the creation of the Federal Reserve, the control of the price level was through the commodity definition of the dollar. Federal involvement in the portfolio sense of controlling the quantity of money was only indirect, through the national bank notes. Hall expressed concern about the fact that the paper repeats what he sees as the mistake of Friedman and Schwartz in trying to understand the commodity standard as if it were a portfolio-based monetary standard. *Taylor* replied that the gold standard kept the price level stable during that period through the pressure of purchasing power parity, similar to the early time in Bretton Woods.

Michael Woodford remarked that the coefficient on inflation for the nineteenth-century period was even lower than in the 1970s. The Gibson paradox suggests that under the gold standard, interest rates seem to be related to the price level rather than the inflation rate. Even if interest rates rise with the price level but are not associated with the inflation rate, the real rate does not need to fall since the inflation rate and even the price level were mean reverting during that period.

Robert King wondered about the determination of the trend in inflation with an interest rate rule. Under the monetarist, Friedman and Schwartz interpretation the trend in money growth determines the trend in inflation. *Taylor* suggested thinking about the policy rule as an inverted money demand equation. An inflation coefficient greater than one will generate a stable inflation rate. If inflation rises, real interest rates rise in the same way as with a money-based rule. Therefore, this is not inconsistent with the money-based view on the determination of the inflation rate.

King then noted that an output gap measured by the Hodrick-Prescott filter implied that the Federal Reserve had to react to output in the future. *Taylor* agreed but reminded him that already with revised data, as mentioned by Donald Kohn before, policy rules look very different than with actual data.

Martin Feldstein remarked that Taylor rightly stresses, and the diagrams in the paper nicely show, that the response coefficient on inflation has to be greater than one, so that when inflation increases, real rates rise. In the 1960s and 1970s, for the reasons given by De Long (1997), the focus was too much on nominal rates. Even though nominal rates were tightened, real rates were going down. However, what really matters are the real net rates as shown in the following equation:

$$R_N = (1 - \theta)i - \pi.$$

If the nominal rate, i, is raised one to one with inflation, π, the real net rate, R_N, falls by the marginal tax rate coefficient θ. If the real net rate should rise when inflation goes up, the derivative of i with respect to π has to be at least equal to $1/(1 - \theta)$. The coefficient θ is equal to 1/3, which means that in the policy rule, the coefficient on inflation should be greater than one. Of course, there are a lot of markets in which taxes do not matter or for some players the marginal tax rate is higher than that, so this makes not too much of a point about a value of exactly 1/3 for θ, but it makes a point that the coefficient on inflation should be greater than one and that 1.5 might not be a bad number at all.

Poole recalled that in the early 1970s, Friedman's natural rate hypothesis did not sweep the profession instantaneously. Year after year, prominent members of the profession came to the academic consultants' meetings reporting that this was a nice theoretical idea, but that in practice there was a long-run trade-off between unemployment and inflation. The real rate of interest was not yet a variable in the Federal Reserve's macromodel, built in the mid-1960s, until its revision in 1968. The influence of fiscal policy on aggregate demand was vastly overestimated. The potential impact of tight money on housing and fiscal policy—all sorts of excuses were made to delay actions. It was not until 1975, the end of the Burns era, that the Federal Reserve finally decided that the long-run Phillips curve was indeed vertical. *Ben McCallum* noted that Taylor (1996) supports the point just made. A small piece of documentation is a long speech about inflation written by Arthur Burns and published by the Federal Reserve Bank of Richmond during the late 1970s. In that 20-page document, monetary policy is not mentioned in any shape or form.

McCallum liked Taylor's approach of running a policy rule through history and encouraged further research in this direction.

John Lipsky pointed out that market participants have paid increasing attention to the Taylor rule formulation as an indicator of the appropriateness of Fed policy. Its predictive power has been extremely impressive over the past few years. Lipsky conjectured that the deregulation of financial markets and pervasive securitization is enhancing the linkage between the real economy, policy, and financial markets. Thus the impact of monetary policy has been boosted, underscoring the importance of research on potential policy rules like the Taylor rule.

References

De Long, J. Bradford. 1997. America's peacetime inflation: The 1970s. In *Reducing inflation: Motivation and strategy,* ed. Christina Romer and David Romer. Chicago: University of Chicago Press.
Judd, John F., and Bharat Trehan. 1995. Has the Fed gotten tougher on inflation? *Federal Reserve Bank of San Francisco Weekly Letter,* no. 95–13.
Taylor, John. 1996. How should monetary policy respond to shocks while maintaining long-run price stability?—Conceptual issues. In *Achieving price stability.* Kansas City: Federal Reserve Bank of Kansas City.

8   What Should the Monetary Authority Do When Prices Are Sticky?

Robert G. King and Alexander L. Wolman

8.1   Introduction

Practical macroeconomics gives a simple and direct answer to the question in the title of this chapter: monetary policy should regulate aggregate demand to stabilize output and inflation. Stabilizing output is presumed to eliminate the "Okun gaps" that arise from changes in aggregate demand when prices are sticky. Low and stable inflation is widely viewed as an important policy goal: high and variable inflation is taken to increase relative price variability as well as increasing other costs of production and exchange. To determine how to balance Okun gaps against costs of inflation—either in level or variability—it is necessary to assume a loss function for the monetary policy authority. While the specific form of the loss function plays a key role in determining the details of optimal monetary policy, a general presumption is that optimal policy involves variability in both inflation and real economic activity. From this standard perspective, a monetary policy that is directed principally toward stabilizing the price level—as proposed in the Mack bill—appears obviously inefficient.[1]

Robert G. King is the Carter Glass Professor of Economics and the Robert P. Black Research Professor of Economics at the University of Virginia. He is also a consultant to the Federal Reserve Bank of Richmond and a research associate of the National Bureau of Economic Research. Alexander L. Wolman is an economist at the Federal Reserve Bank of Richmond.

The views expressed here are the authors' and not necessarily those of the Federal Reserve Bank of Richmond or the Federal Reserve System. The authors would like to thank Mike Dotsey and Andreas Hornstein for helpful and detailed discussions. They have also received useful questions and suggestions from many people, including Charles Evans, Aubhik Khan, Ellen McGrattan, Lars Svensson, John Taylor, and Michael Woodford as well as many participants in a seminar at the Federal Reserve Board and in the NBER conference. King's participation in this research was supported by the National Science Foundation and the Bankard Public Policy Fund of the University of Virginia.

1. The Mack bill refers to S.611, a bill introduced before the 105th Congress on 17 April 1997, which would "require the Board of Governors of the Federal Reserve System to focus on price stability in establishing monetary policy."

In this chapter, we provide a simple yet fully articulated macroeconomic model where this intuition is incorrect. In our model economy, macroeconomic equilibrium is inefficient because producers have market power and Okun gaps can arise as a result of price stickiness. However, the monetary authority should nevertheless make the price level the sole objective of monetary policy. Further, the price level stabilization policy is optimal in a very specific sense: it maximizes the utility of the representative individual in the economy. To derive this result, we draw on two broad areas of recent literature.

First, we use the standard public finance approach to policy analysis. While this approach is little used in practical macroeconomics, it is being increasingly applied in dynamic macroeconomic theory.[2] In general, the public finance approach focuses on identifying distortions and measuring the resulting costs to individuals, which are sometimes called "Harberger triangles." Optimal policy then involves trading off various distortions—minimizing the sum of the Harberger triangles—given the available policy instruments. Practical macroeconomics has tended to deviate from the public finance approach because the conventional wisdom—famously articulated by James Tobin (1977)—is that "it takes a heap of Harberger triangles to fill an Okun gap." Okun gaps were seen by Tobin and many others as fundamentally different phenomena, not amenable to being studied with public finance tools because they did not involve microeconomic distortions.

Second, we draw on recent developments in "New Keynesian" macroeconomics that provide a microstructure for sticky prices and thus facilitate the unified approach to policy analysis. Our model economy contains two central New Keynesian features: an explicit modeling of imperfect competition in product markets and an optimizing approach to sticky prices.[3] We then embed these price-setting mechanisms in a dynamic general equilibrium model, of the form studied in real business cycle research. This "new neoclassical synthesis" framework is more and more widely used for the positive analysis of the business cycle but is just beginning to be employed for the study of optimal monetary policy.[4] Models using the framework have a well-defined Okun gap that can fluctuate through time with aggregate demand, but Harberger-type analysis is nonetheless the appropriate way to identify distortions and characterize optimal policy. This is because Okun gaps can be interpreted as arising from microeconomic distortions. Specifically, with some prices fixed, nominal distur-

---

2. Notable contributions include Lucas and Stokey (1983), Judd (1985), Chamley (1986), and Chari, Christiano, and Kehoe (1991).

3. The imperfect competition approach to product markets has been developed by a number of authors, notably Blanchard and Kiyotaki (1987) and Rotemberg (1987). The optimizing approach to sticky prices has also been an area of extensive research, with some important contributions being Calvo (1983), Rotemberg (1982), and Yun (1996).

4. See Goodfriend and King (1997) for a summary of these ongoing developments in business cycle modeling. There is a much smaller literature on optimal monetary policy in this class of models, which includes Ireland (1995, 1996, 1997), Rotemberg and Woodford (1997; chap. 2 of this volume), Yun (1994, chap. 4), and Aiyagari and Braun (1997).

bances affect the markup of price over marginal cost. The markup is the economy's terms of trade between output and inputs and is a key distortion that can be influenced by real and nominal shocks.[5] In particular, changes in output that result from nominal disturbances are always accompanied by changes in the markup.

The approach that we take differs from those taken in other chapters in this volume. While we are making progress on building a small-scale, fully articulated macroeconomic model that can be used for the twin purposes of explaining postwar U.S. data and conducting simulations of alternative policy rules, we do not yet have a specific quantitative model that we use to identify the main sources of economic fluctuations. For this reason, we cannot ask the questions that are posed in many other chapters, such as "What is the trade-off between inflation variability and output variability, under alternative specifications of the interest rate rule?" However, we can study optimal policy within a basic macroeconomic model that captures central features of a broad class of models. Our analysis of optimal policy is centered on questions that are related to those in other chapters:

What is the optimal monetary policy response to a particular structural shock, such as a productivity shock?

What are the implications of this optimal policy response for output, inflation, and interest rates?

As a by-product of answering these questions, we also learn about the optimal long-run rate of inflation. Our findings can be summed up in remarkably simple terms: both in the long run and in response to higher frequency shocks, optimal monetary policy involves stabilizing the price level. Intuitively, it is perhaps not surprising that sticky prices make it optimal for the price level not to vary. After all, if the price level never changes, then in a sense it does not matter whether prices are sticky. By studying a simple model in detail in this chapter, we work toward understanding the broader circumstances in which this intuition is correct. While we focus on productivity shocks in our discussion, we have applied our approach to aggregate demand shocks (government purchase shocks and preference shocks) and to money demand shocks: all of these shocks lead to the same simple message about the importance of stabilizing the price level.

Our model does imply that there is an optimal interest rate rule, which takes a simple form. Since the price level never changes under optimal policy, the nominal rate set by the monetary authority must track the underlying real rate that would prevail under price flexibility. We show how to make this interest rate rule consistent with price level determinacy by incorporating a simple

5. This theme is developed in more detail in Goodfriend and King (1997). The idea that *all* effects of monetary policy in "new synthesis" models can be interpreted as relative price distortions appears initially in Woodford's (1995) comments on Kimball (1995).

specification of how the monetary authority would respond to deviations of the price level from its path under optimal policy.

Relative to other chapters in this volume, the approach we take is most similar to that of Rotemberg and Woodford in chapter 2. Both chapters use as their analytical framework an optimizing sticky price model; both also use the representative agent's expected utility as the welfare criterion. Where we differ from our compatriots is in the treatment of steady state distortions. Rotemberg and Woodford assume that fiscal or other mechanisms eliminate the monopolistic competition distortion in steady state, so that distortions only arise out of steady state. We assume that monetary policy is the only tool available for combating distortions, in or out of steady state. Further, we find that the policy of stabilizing the price level is optimal even when there are large steady state distortions.

The chapter proceeds as follows. In section 8.2 we lay out the basic model, which features staggered price setting. In section 8.3, we illustrate the nonneutralities that occur in our model, including the effects of sustained (steady state) inflation and the effects of various monetary shocks. Section 8.4 discusses the nature of constraints on the monetary authority, which we interpret as constraints on allocations that a social planner can choose. In section 8.5, we lay out the nature of the (real) optimum problem for that social planner. In section 8.6, we determine that the steady state solution to this problem involves real allocations that would be achieved in a market economy only under a zero inflation rate, a result that we call a modified golden rule for monetary policy. In section 8.7, we discuss the nature of optimal allocations in an economy with productivity shocks, under the assumption that the monetary authority can credibly commit to future actions; optimal allocations again involve price level stability. However, imperfect competition means that there are temptations for the monetary authority to abandon the price level policy, and we explore this issue quantitatively in section 8.8. Section 8.9 discusses the nature of an interest rate rule that would achieve the optimal outcomes. Section 8.10 concludes.

8.2 A Macromodel with Staggered Price Setting

The macroeconomic model assumes that final product prices are set optimally by monopolistically competitive firms, which satisfy all demand at posted prices. The model is in the tradition of Taylor (1980), in that price setting is staggered: each firm sets its price for J periods with $1/J$ of the firms adjusting each period. In common with Taylor's model, monetary policy matters because stickiness in individual prices gives rise to stickiness in the price level, and hence to nonneutrality.[6] In our exposition of this model, we focus on the case in which there is two-period pricing setting, but we discuss extensions

---

6. Taylor (1980) focused on nominal rigidity in wages rather than prices. The methods that are used in this paper could also be applied to such environments.

for larger *J* and richer time-dependent price-setting schemes at various places below.

The model is designed to be representative of recent work on the new neoclassical synthesis, in that New Keynesian–style price stickiness is introduced into an economy with otherwise neoclassical features including intertemporal optimization on the part of households and firms. However, five features deserve special attention. First, we abstract from capital accumulation to simplify the analysis as much as possible.[7] Second, we assume that the production function for all final products is constant returns in the single variable factor, labor, to approximate the relationship between output and input in a more realistic model in which firms can simultaneously vary labor and capacity utilization (see Dotsey, King, and Wolman 1997). Third, we use a form of preferences for the representative agent that allows for an arbitrarily high labor supply elasticity in response to monetary disturbances, while retaining a zero response of labor input to productivity disturbances if prices are flexible. This permits our model to generate large and persistent effects of money on output.[8] Fourth, we abstract from money demand distortions associated with positive nominal interest rates (triangles under the money demand curve). There are two motivations for this assumption. Empirically, transactions balances increasingly bear interest, so that this abstraction is increasingly more realistic. Theoretically, this assumption allows us to focus completely on the effects of monetary policy that operate through sticky prices. Fifth, we abstract from fiscal policy, by assuming that lump-sum taxes and transfers are available to offset changes in the money supply. The joint determination of optimal monetary and fiscal policy with sticky prices is an interesting issue, and one on which considerable progress has been made by Yun (1994). We focus on monetary policy in order to clearly exposit the basic implications of price stickiness and also because we think that current policy structures assign the task of stabilization policy to the monetary authority in most countries.

As exposited in this section, the model is one in which monopolistically competitive firms set their prices every two periods, but the conclusions we reach apply to arbitrary patterns of staggered price setting. There is a continuum of these firms, and they produce differentiated consumption goods using as the sole input labor provided by consumers at a competitive wage. Consum-

---

7. In the case of two-period price setting, this simplification should allow us to derive analytical results for our model, but we have not yet worked these out.

8. Models with sticky prices have the generic feature that persistence of the real effect of a monetary shock is almost completely determined by the change in the incentive to adjust price induced by the shock. Typical preference specifications generate large changes in this incentive, and hence real effects that do not persist. In contrast, the preferences used here create only small incentives to adjust, and hence persistent effects of the shock. We use this preference specification because we believe that monetary shocks do have persistent real effects empirically, arising from economic mechanisms that enhance the supply responsiveness of the economy to nominal disturbances. Some New Keynesian economists—such as Ball and Romer (1990) and Jeanne (1998)—would argue that this preference specification is proxying for institutional features of the labor market, such as efficiency wages, that are ultimately responsible for enhancing nonneutrality and persistence.

ers are infinitely lived and purchase consumption goods using income from their labor and income from firms' profits. Consumers also must hold money in order to consume, although we assume that money bears a near competitive rate of interest, so that there are no distortions associated with money demand.

8.2.1 Consumers

Consumers have preferences over a consumption aggregate (c_t) and leisure $(1 - n_t)$ given by

$$(1) \qquad \sum_{t=0}^{\infty} \beta^t u(c_t, n_t; a_t),$$

where the flow utility is

$$(2) \qquad u(c_t, n_t; a_t) = \ln\left(c_t - \frac{a_t \theta}{1 + \gamma} n_t^{1+\gamma}\right).$$

In this specification and below, a_t is a random preference shifter that also acts as a productivity shock.[9]

Microstructure of Consumption

As in Blanchard and Kiyotaki (1987) and Rotemberg (1987), we assume that every producer faces a downward-sloping demand curve with elasticity ε. With a continuum of firms, the consumption aggregate is an integral of differentiated products

$$c_t = \left(\int c(\omega)^{(\varepsilon-1)/\varepsilon} d\omega\right)^{\varepsilon/(\varepsilon-1)}$$

as in Dixit and Stiglitz (1977).

Focusing on the case in which prices are fixed for just two periods, and noting that all producers that adjust their prices in a given period choose the same price, we can write the consumption aggregate as

$$(3) \qquad c_t = c(c_{0,t}, c_{1,t}) = \left(\frac{1}{2} c_{0,t}^{(\varepsilon-1)/\varepsilon} + \frac{1}{2} c_{1,t}^{(\varepsilon-1)/\varepsilon}\right)^{\varepsilon/(\varepsilon-1)},$$

where $c_{j,t}$ is the quantity consumed in period t of a good whose price was set in period $t - j$. The constant elasticity demands for each of the goods take the form

$$(4) \qquad c_{j,t} = \left(\frac{P_{j,t}}{P_t}\right)^{-\varepsilon} c_t,$$

---

9. It may seem unusual to have the same random variable shifting both preferences and technology. In order for eq. (2) to be consistent with balanced growth occurring through growth in technology, it must be that the preference and productivity shifters grow at the same rate. We also assume that they vary together over the business cycle.

where $P_{j,t}$ is the nominal price at time t of any good whose price was set j periods ago and P_t is the price index at time t, which is given by

$$(5) \qquad P_t = \left(\frac{1}{2} P_{0,t}^{1-\varepsilon} + \frac{1}{2} P_{1,t}^{1-\varepsilon} \right)^{1/(1-\varepsilon)}.$$

Intertemporal Optimization

Consumers choose contingency plans for consumption demand and labor supply to maximize expected utility (1), subject to an intertemporal budget constraint,

$$(6) \qquad c_t + \frac{M_t}{P_t} + v_t s_t + \frac{B_t}{P_t} = z_t s_{t-1} + v_t s_{t-1} + w_t n_t + (1 + R_{t-1}^M) \frac{M_{t-1}}{P_t}$$

$$+ (1 + R_{t-1}) \frac{B_{t-1}}{P_t}.$$

In this expression, the uses of the individual's date t wealth are consumption (c_t), acquisition of money balances (M_t/P_t) and nominal one-period bonds (B_t/P_t), and purchases of shares s_t in the representative firm at price v_t. The sources of wealth are current labor income $w_t n_t$, the value of previous-period money balances $(1 + R_{t-1}^M)(M_{t-1}/P_t)$ and maturing bonds $(1 + R_{t-1})(B_{t-1}/P_t)$, and the value of previous-period asset holdings, including current profits (z_t). The interest rate on bonds is endogenous, while the monetary authority pays interest on money at a rate R_t^M marginally below R_t. In terms of this asset structure, there are two additional points to be made. First, the representative firm is an average (portfolio) of firms that set prices at different prior periods. Second, in equilibrium, asset prices must adjust so that $s_t = 1$.

The first-order conditions for the household's optimal choice problem for the allocation of consumption and leisure over time are[10]

$$(7) \qquad 0 = \beta^t E_0 \left(\frac{\partial u(c_t, n_t, a_t)}{\partial c_t} - \lambda_t \right),$$

$$(8) \qquad 0 = \beta^t E_0 \left(\frac{\partial u(c_t, n_t, a_t)}{\partial n_t} + \lambda_t w_t \right).$$

In these expressions, λ_t measures the utility value of a unit of real income at date t (the multiplier on the asset accumulation constraint), and the marginal utility of consumption is equated to it. The marginal disutility of work is equated to $w_t \lambda_t$, where w_t is the real wage rate.

---

10. In appendix A of this paper, we describe the representative agent's choice problem in detail, with money demand motivated by a transactions time requirement. In this extended setting, conditions (7) and (8) are limiting versions when there is a small marginal cost of transacting, as we assume in the body of the paper.

Although there is intertemporal choice of consumption and leisure, the assumed form of preferences means that there is a simple labor supply function, which is related solely to the real wage rate at date t. To derive this labor supply function, note that the utility function implies that

$$\frac{\partial u(c_t, n_t, a_t)}{\partial c_t} = \left(c_t - \frac{a_t \theta}{1 + \gamma} n_t^{1+\gamma} \right)^{-1},$$

$$\frac{\partial u(c_t, n_t, a_t)}{\partial n_t} = -a_t \theta n_t^{\gamma} \left(c_t - \frac{a_t \theta}{1 + \gamma} n_t^{1+\gamma} \right)^{-1}.$$

Equating the marginal rate of substitution between leisure and consumption to the real wage yields a labor supply function with a constant wage elasticity (equal to $1/\gamma$):

$$(9) \qquad\qquad n_t = \left(\frac{w_t}{a_t \theta} \right)^{1/\gamma}.$$

Labor supply is raised by the real wage and lowered by the productivity shifter, so there is no trend growth in hours worked when the real wage and productivity have a common trend.

Money Demand

The representative consumer must hold enough money to cover the quantity of his purchases:

$$(10) \qquad\qquad M_t = k P_t c_t.$$

We think of this money demand function as a limiting case that applies when money is interest bearing, when there is a satiation level of cash balances (k) per unit of consumption, and the interest rate on money is close to the market rate. In such a setting, we should be able to ignore the "triangles under the demand curve for money" in order to focus on other costs of inflation.[11]

Other Financial Assets

Consumers also hold a diversified portfolio of shares in the monopolistically competitive firms, which pays dividends equal to the firms' monopoly profits. The real and nominal interest rates in this economy are governed by Fisherian principles. The real interest rate, r_t, must satisfy

---

11. Wolman's (1997) estimates of a "transactions technology"–based money demand function indicate the presence of a satiation level of cash balances per unit of consumption. They also indicate that most of the welfare gains from reducing average inflation from 5 percent to the Friedman rule are gained by making inflation zero.

(11)
$$E_t\left(\beta\frac{\lambda_{t+1}}{\lambda_t}(1 + r_t)\right) = 1,$$

and the nominal interest rate, R_t, must satisfy

(12)
$$E_t\left(\beta\frac{\lambda_{t+1}}{\lambda_t}\cdot\frac{P_t}{P_{t+1}}(1 + R_t)\right) = 1.$$

8.2.2 Firms

Each firm produces with an identical technology that is linear in labor and subject to random variation in productivity:

(13)
$$c_{j,t} = a_t n_{j,t},$$

where $n_{j,t}$ is the labor input employed in period t by a firm whose price was set in period $t - j$. Given the price that a firm is charging, it hires enough labor to meet the demand for its product at that price. Firms that do not adjust their prices in a given period can thus be thought of as passive, whereas firms that adjust their prices do so optimally.

Firms set their prices to maximize the present discounted value of their profits. Given that it has a relative price $p_{j,t} = P_{j,t}/P_t$, real profit $z_{j,t}$ for a firm of type j is

(14)
$$z_{j,t} = p_{j,t}a_t n_{j,t} - w_t n_{j,t},$$

that is, revenue less cost. To derive later results, it is useful to define real marginal cost ψ_t, which is equal to w_t/a_t in our setting. Then profit for a firm of type j is

(15)
$$z_{j,t} = p_{j,t}^{-\varepsilon}c_t(p_{j,t} - \psi_t),$$

using the requirement that demand equal output ($c_{j,t} = p_{j,t}^{-\varepsilon} c_t = a_t n_{j,t}$).

Optimal Pricing without Price Stickiness

If prices were fully flexible, then a familiar set of expressions would govern optimal pricing in this constant elasticity, constant marginal cost world. Optimal monopoly pricing is illustrated in figure 8.1. Panel 8.1a shows the demand curve for the firm, $p_{j,t}^{-\varepsilon}c_t$, under the assumption that the level of aggregate demand is unity ($c_t = 1$) and the demand elasticity is four ($\varepsilon = 4$). Panel 8.1b shows profit as a function of the relative price. The relative price that maximizes profit is given by

$$p_t^* = \frac{\varepsilon}{\varepsilon - 1}\psi_t.$$

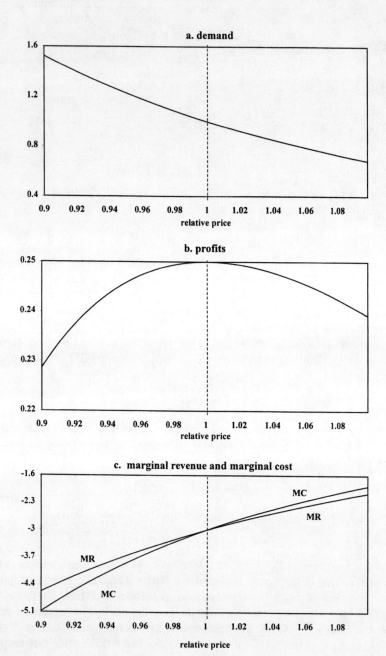

Fig. 8.1   Optimal pricing

In drawing the diagram, we have assumed real marginal cost is $(\varepsilon - 1)/\varepsilon$ so that the optimal relative price is unity.

Panel 8.1c shows the marginal revenue and marginal cost schedules that are relevant when the monopoly problem is written with price as the decision variable, rather than quantity as in the standard textbook presentation. Marginal revenue is negative, as the elasticity of demand must exceed one for the profit maximization problem to make sense (marginal revenue is $(1 - \varepsilon)p_{j,t}^{-\varepsilon}c_t$). For low levels of the relative price, marginal revenue exceeds marginal cost $(-\varepsilon p_{j,t}^{-\varepsilon-1}c_t\psi_t)$ and it is desirable to raise the price. Correspondingly, for high levels of the relative price, marginal revenue is less than marginal cost and profits could be increased by lowering the relative price.

Our model economy is one in which there are substantial real consequences of the market power shown in figure 8.1. In constructing this figure and in conducting simulations, the assumption that the demand elasticity is 4 implies a steady state markup of 1.33 when there is no price stickiness (or zero inflation). Combined with a highly elastic supply of labor ($\gamma = 0.10$), this implies that output is about 6 percent of its efficient level.[12] While this level of distortion is certainly too high, the extreme assumption does serve to stress that our results on optimal policy are valid for economies in which there are substantial departures of output from its efficient level and large effects of money on output.

Optimal Price Setting When Prices Are Sticky

Maximization of present value implies that a firm chooses its current relative price taking into account the effect on current and expected future profits. When it sets its nominal price at t, the firm knows that its relative price will move through time according to

$$(16) \qquad p_{1,t+1} = \frac{p_{0,t}}{\Pi_{t+1}},$$

where Π_{t+1} is the gross inflation rate between t and $t + 1$ ($\Pi_{t+1} = P_{t+1}/P_t$). That is: if there is positive inflation, the firm expects that its relative price will fall as a result of the fact that it has a nominal price that is fixed for two periods.[13]

The optimal relative price must balance effects on profits today and tomorrow, given that inflation erodes the relative price. Formally, an optimal relative price satisfies

---

12. The marginal rate of substitution, $-D_2u\,(c_t, n_t, a_t)/D_1u(c_t, n_t, a_t)$ is equal to $a_t\theta n_t^\gamma$ and the real wage rate is equal to a_t/μ, where μ is the average markup of price over marginal cost. Accordingly, the ratio of labor to its efficient level is given by $n_t/n^* = \mu^{-1/\gamma}$. The calculation in the text assumes that $\gamma = 0.10$ and $\mu = 1.33$.

13. If the nominal price that the firm charges is $P_{0,t} = P_{1,t+1}$, then $p_{0,t} = P_{0,t}/P_t$ and $p_{1,t+1} = P_{1,t+1}/P_{t+1} = (P_{0,t}/P_t)(P_t/P_{t+1})$.

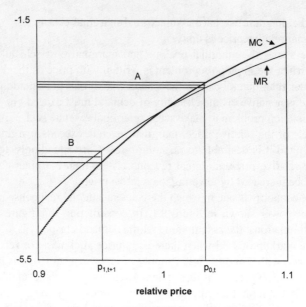

Fig. 8.2   Optimal pricing with stickiness

$$(17) \quad 0 = \lambda_t \frac{\partial z(p_{0,t}, c_t, \psi_t)}{\partial p_{0,t}} + \beta E_t \left(\lambda_{t+1} \frac{\partial z(p_{1,t+1}, c_{t+1}, \psi_{t+1})}{\partial p_{1,t+1}} \cdot \frac{1}{\Pi_{t+1}} \right).$$

Multiplying equation (17) by $p_{0,t}$ yields a more symmetric form of the efficiency condition that will be convenient for deriving optimal policy:

$$(18) \quad 0 = \lambda_t p_{0,t} \frac{\partial z(p_{0,t}, c_t, \psi_t)}{\partial p_{0,t}} + \beta E_t \left(\lambda_{t+1} p_{1,t+1} \frac{\partial z(p_{1,t+1}, c_{t+1}, \psi_{t+1})}{\partial p_{1,t+1}} \right).$$

Figure 8.2 shows two central aspects of this efficiency condition (this figure repeats panel c of figure 8.1 but adds some additional information). First, the marginal profit terms in equation (18) are gaps between marginal revenue and marginal cost at t and $t + 1$: with price stickiness, the firm can no longer make these both zero, but it can choose its price to balance the gaps through time. Second, figure 8.2 shows a firm setting a relative price p_0 that is too high relative to the static optimum—in the sense that marginal revenue is less than marginal cost—and a related price p_1 that is too low. This would be an optimal policy, for example, in a steady state situation of sustained inflation. Efficient price setting equates the boxes marked A and B, which correspond to the consumption value of profits lost at t, which is $p_{0,t} \cdot \partial z(p_{0,t}, c_t, \psi_t/\partial p_{0,t}$ in equation (18), and the profits lost at $t + 1$, which is $p_{1,t+1} \cdot \partial z(p_{1,t+1}, c_{t+1}, \psi_{t+1})/\partial p_{1,t+1}$.[14]

---

14. Technically, we must have $\lambda_t = \lambda_{t+1}$ and $\beta = 1$, as well as $\Pi > 1$ to use our diagram exactly.

As in Taylor's (1980) model, there is a forward-looking form of the price equation that can be developed. Using the expressions for marginal revenue and marginal cost, we can show that the optimal price is

$$
(19) \qquad p_{0,t} = \frac{\varepsilon}{\varepsilon - 1} \frac{\sum_{j=0}^{1} \beta^j E_t[\lambda_{t+j}\, \psi_{t+j}\, (P_{t+j}/P_t)^\varepsilon c_{t+j}]}{\sum_{j=0}^{1} \beta^j E_t[\lambda_{t+j}\, (P_{t+j}/P_t)^{\varepsilon-1} c_{t+j}]}.
$$

Thus equation (18) implicitly links the current relative price chosen by a price-setting firm to current and future marginal cost, as well as expected inflation and interest rates. Further, near zero inflation, this expression is well approximated by

$$
\log p_{0,t} = \log\left(\frac{\varepsilon}{\varepsilon - 1}\right) + \frac{1}{1 + \beta}\log \psi_t
$$

$$
+ \frac{\beta}{1 + \beta}(E_t \log \psi_{t+1} + E_t \log P_{t+1} - \log P_t),
$$

which is even more like Taylor's forward-looking specification. Approximately, therefore, an adjusting firm sets a relative price that is a weighted average of the real marginal cost it expects over the next two periods, with a correction for the effect of expected inflation.

8.3   Influences of Money on Economic Activity

In this section, we discuss how monetary policy affects economic activity in our model. Before getting into the details, however, it is useful to think about why a monetary authority might seek to influence economic activity in this type of model. The rationale is as follows. Since there is monopolistic competition, there is a positive markup of price over marginal cost even without sticky prices. The markup is an inefficiency, as it implies that the resource cost of producing the marginal good is below the utility benefit of consuming the marginal good.[15] As stressed by Mankiw (1990) and Romer (1993), it is consequently desirable to have policies that expand aggregate economic activity, if such policies are feasible. Sticky prices give the monetary authority some ability to alter the markup and to thus expand or contract economic activity, although we will see below that there are severe limitations on that ability in the long run. Sticky prices also introduce the possibility of a second distortion, namely, variation in the relative prices of the differentiated products. Because the differentiated products are produced using a common production technology, efficiency dictates that their relative prices should be identical. However,

---

15. An alternative, equally valid interpretation is that the marginal product of labor exceeds the marginal payment to labor, as measured by the real wage.

since some nominal prices are prohibited from adjusting in a given period, relative prices will not be identical for all goods if firms that are able to adjust their nominal prices choose to do so. This situation will occur, for example, if there is a nonzero inflation rate.

8.3.1 Effects of Steady Inflation

The effect of steady inflation on the two distortions—the relative price distortion and the markup distortion—can be seen by referring to the equations for the price index and the optimal price of an adjusting firm. The relative price distortion is minimized (eliminated, in fact) at a zero inflation rate, and the markup distortion is minimized at a slightly positive inflation rate. The fact that these distortions are not invariant to steady state inflation means that the model exhibits nonsuperneutrality, or, in the lingo of sticky price models, a nonvertical long-run Phillips curve. As will be shown below, however, the long-run Phillips curve is nearly vertical. Furthermore, there is a negative relationship between inflation and output over most positive inflation rates. We analyze the effect of steady inflation on relative price distortions first and then turn to its effect on the markup distortion.

Relative Price Distortions

To begin, if the gross inflation rate is $\Pi \equiv P_t/P_{t-1}$, then the ratio of relative prices of adjusting and nonadjusting firms is $\Pi = P_{0,t}/P_{0,t-1}$. That is, with positive and steady inflation an adjusting firm in the current period sets its nominal price at a level Π times greater than a firm that adjusted in the previous period. Further, from equation (5), the price index in steady state is

$$(20) \qquad P_t = \left(\frac{1}{2} P_{0,t}^{1-\varepsilon} + \frac{1}{2} \Pi^{\varepsilon-1} P_{0,t}^{1-\varepsilon} \right)^{1/(1-\varepsilon)},$$

so the ratio P_0/P—which can be thought of as a measure of the variation in relative prices—is increasing in inflation (since $P_0/P = [(1 + \Pi^{\varepsilon-1})/2]^{1/(\varepsilon-1)}$).

Variation in relative prices implies that there is a gap between potential and actual consumption, where potential consumption is the maximum quantity of the consumption aggregate that can be obtained from a given level of technology and labor input. Since the aggregator, $c(c_{0,t}, c_{1,t})$, is concave and symmetric, potential consumption corresponds to equal quantities of each of the different goods. However, equal quantities will be *chosen* by individuals only if there is no variation in relative prices, and since zero inflation equates relative prices, it achieves potential consumption. Mathematically, equations (3) and (4) can be manipulated to show that in steady state, the ratio of actual to potential consumption is given by

$$(21) \qquad \frac{c}{c^p} = \left(\frac{1}{2} \right)^{1/(\varepsilon-1)} \frac{(1 + \Pi^{\varepsilon-1})^{\varepsilon/(\varepsilon-1)}}{1 + \Pi^\varepsilon},$$

which uses the fact that potential consumption is simply the linear index of consumption, $c^p = c_0/2 + c_1/2$. Expression (21) confirms that with price stability ($\Pi = 1$), actual and potential consumption are equal, whereas the relative price variation induced by inflation makes actual consumption less than potential. The relative price distortion is quite small at low inflation rates.

Average Markup Distortion

The effect of inflation on the average markup can be seen by combining the price index with the steady state version of the optimal price equation (19). In our economy, as in others with marginal cost that is common across firms, the average markup (μ) is simply the inverse of real marginal cost. Using this fact, the optimal price equation becomes

$$(22) \qquad P_0 = P\frac{\varepsilon}{\varepsilon - 1}\left(\frac{1}{\mu}\right)\left(\frac{1 + \beta\Pi^\varepsilon}{1 + \beta\Pi^{\varepsilon-1}}\right).$$

When we combine this expression with the price index, $P = P_0[(1 + \Pi^{\varepsilon-1})/2]^{1/1-\varepsilon}$, the average markup is

$$(23) \qquad \mu = \frac{\varepsilon}{\varepsilon - 1}\left(\frac{1 + \Pi^{\varepsilon-1}}{2}\right)^{1/(1-\varepsilon)}\left(\frac{1 + \beta\Pi^\varepsilon}{1 + \beta\Pi^{\varepsilon-1}}\right).$$

The inflation rate therefore affects the average markup, with the "static" markup $\varepsilon/(\varepsilon - 1)$ resulting from zero inflation ($\Pi = 1$).

There are two components in the inflation-markup link. Higher inflation makes adjusting firms choose a higher markup when they do adjust, but it also makes the markup of nonadjusting firms erode more severely. In general, for high enough inflation the effect on adjusting firms dominates, so that higher inflation is associated with a higher markup. While these counteracting effects are qualitatively interesting, figure 8.3a shows that they are small in the following sense. When $\varepsilon = 4$, the steady state markup is minimized at an extremely low inflation rate (approximately 1 percent annually), and this result carries over to any reasonable degree of market power (higher or lower than $\varepsilon = 4$); furthermore, for a given value of ε, the markup is essentially insensitive to inflation. That is: over the inflation rates shown in figure 8.3, which are between -1 and 2 percent at an annual rate, the markup changes only at the fifth digit (see the markup scale in fig. 8.3a).[16]

Since the relative price distortion is eliminated at zero inflation, it follows that steady state welfare is maximized at some inflation rate between zero and that which minimizes the markup. We define $\hat{\Pi}$ to be the inflation rate that

16. Goodfriend and King (1997) perform a similar calculation with a model of four-quarter price stickiness and a wider range of inflation rates. They find that the average markup rises more rapidly at higher rates of inflation.

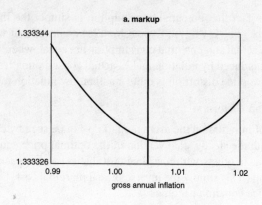

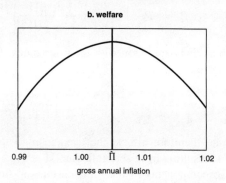

Fig. 8.3   Steady state

maximizes steady state welfare; it is illustrated in figure 8.3b, which plots steady state welfare as a function of inflation.

8.3.2   Dynamic Response to Monetary Disturbances

There are two central implications of New Keynesian macroeconomic models beginning with Taylor (1980). First, there can be large and persistent effects of changes in money. Second, it is crucial to specify the dynamic nature of the monetary change and the corresponding beliefs that agents hold. To display these crucial implications in our context, we close the model by adding a policy rule. For expository purposes, we begin by assuming an exogenous process for the money growth rate and examining responses to two types of shocks. First, we look at a persistent increase in the money growth rate, but one that ultimately dies away so that trend inflation is unaffected. Second, we look at a permanent decrease in the money growth rate, which results in a permanent reduction in the inflation rate. Then, because monetary policy in the industrialized countries is generally conducted with an interest rate instrument, we ex-

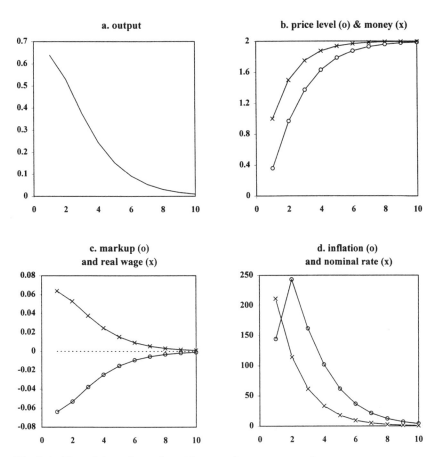

Fig. 8.4   Unanticipated, persistent increase in money growth

Note: x-Axes in quarters; y-axes in percentage deviations from steady state, except panel d, which is in basis points at an annual rate.

amine the effect of a temporary policy shock when policy is given by an interest rate feedback rule.

Effects of a Persistent Increase in Money Growth

As illustrated in figure 8.4, an unanticipated persistent increase in the money growth rate generates a persistent increase in output, as money growth exceeds inflation for several periods. (The policy shock corresponds to a 1 percent increase in money on impact and ultimately a 2 percent increase in the level of money).[17] There are two complementary ways of thinking about the output

17. Technically, the driving process for money is $\log M_t - \log M_{t-1} = \frac{1}{2} (\log M_{t-1} - \log M_{t-2}) + \xi_t$, with ξ_t being a sequence of random shocks.

expansion, which begins with an immediate increase in output of about two-thirds of a percent and then dies away through time. First, the monetary expansion produces an increase in aggregate demand, which is accommodated by firms that are holding prices fixed (the strength of this aggregate demand effect can be measured as the distance between the money and price responses). Second, the increase in output reflects the monetary authority's ability to change the extent of distortions in the economy and relative prices. In particular, the average markup falls in the face of a monetary expansion. Since the average markup is the reciprocal of real marginal cost ($\mu = P/(P\psi) = 1/\psi$) and since marginal cost is the real wage divided by labor productivity ($\psi_t = w_t/a_t$), there is a corresponding rise in the real wage that stimulates aggregate supply. Given an assumed high-amplitude response of labor supply to wages, this decline in the markup results in a significant expansion of aggregate output. On net, the monetary authority has stimulated the economy by driving down the markup temporarily, taking advantage of preset prices.

One notable feature of this dynamic response, as in Taylor (1980), is that the persistence in real variables is much greater than the duration of fixed prices. Recent research by Chari, Kehoe, and McGrattan (1996) has stressed that this persistence in real output requires that increases in output carry with them only small increases in marginal cost. In our example economy in figure 8.4 the labor supply is highly elastic, which translates into low elasticity of marginal cost with respect to output. More specifically, the elasticity of real marginal cost with respect to output is γ, and figure 8.4 was generated with $\gamma = 0.1$.[18] We use this specification throughout the current analysis, as we think that a more complete macroeconomic model with variable capacity utilization and indivisible labor may generate a large and persistent effect of monetary shocks.[19]

Another notable feature of this response is the behavior of the nominal interest rate, which exhibits a persistent increase, reflecting mainly the behavior of expected inflation. It is a general feature of sticky price models that persistent increases in the money supply generate persistent increases in expected inflation, and usually the nominal interest rate. This result is troubling if one believes that monetary policy is appropriately modeled by an exogenous money growth rate, as it conflicts with the conventional wisdom that expansionary monetary policy involves a decrease in the nominal interest rate. We will see below that if policy is modeled as an interest rate feedback rule, then expansionary (contractionary) shocks do generate decreases (increases) in the nominal interest rate.

18. In contrast to the preference specification used here, the more standard form ($\ln c - \theta n^{1+\gamma}$) implies an elasticity of real marginal cost with respect to output that is at least unity, due to the income effect on labor supply.

19. See Dotsey et al. (1997) for an analysis along these lines.

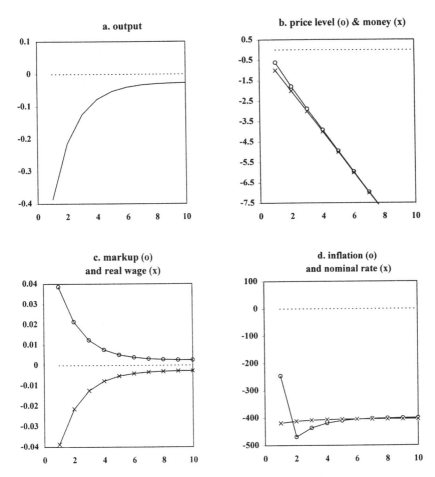

Fig. 8.5   Unanticipated, permanent decrease in money growth
Note: For axis units, see note to fig. 8.4.

Effects of a Permanent Decrease in Inflation

Figure 8.5 contains impulse response functions for an unanticipated permanent decrease in the money growth rate. Aside from the sign difference, these responses look similar to figure 8.4, confirming the standard notion that disinflation is costly with sticky prices. However, it is important to stress two features of this policy shock. First, the magnitude of the temporary aggregate contraction is smaller, about half as large as in figure 8.4. Second, the sustained deflation also has a long-run effect on relative prices and relative quantities as individuals substitute across goods. The initial steady state inflation rate in figure 8.5 is zero, so a permanent decrease in inflation raises the markup permanently (see eq. [23]).

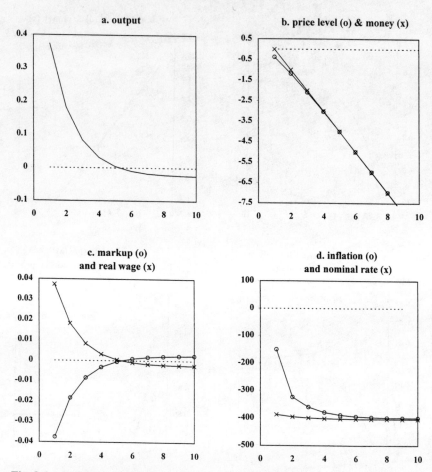

Fig. 8.6   Anticipated, permanent decrease in money growth
Note: For axis units, see note to fig. 8.4.

Ball (1995) has stressed that sticky price models generally imply that there is a very different effect of a credible anticipated disinflation: our model is no exception. As illustrated in figure 8.6, an anticipated deflation is expansionary: consumption actually rises for several periods. This expansion occurs because firms act in advance of the policy change, lowering their relative prices now because they know that future inflation will be lower. Since figure 8.6 assumes that the starting point is zero inflation, agents will be in a worse steady state in the long run (the markup will be slightly higher), with lower consumption and higher leisure. However, during the transition they benefit from a *lower* markup and corresponding higher level of output. As with figure 8.5, however, it is again the case that the effect of a sustained deflation is smaller than the effect of a temporary change in the money growth rate, even though both disturbances are normalized to have the same (1 percent) effect on money in the initial period. That is: the forward-looking price setting built into this model implies that the effects of anticipated and unanticipated changes in the trend inflation rate are smaller than the effects of shocks that are not permanent.

Effects of an Interest Rate Shock

It is straightforward to analyze how the model behaves in response to policy shocks when policy is given by an interest rate rule, which is the more relevant case empirically. Suppose that instead of an exogenous money growth rate, the monetary policy rule specifies that

$$(24) \qquad R_t = f \cdot (\ln P_t - \ln \overline{P}_t) + e_t,$$

where R_t is the nominal interest rate, $\overline{P}_t$ is a target price level that either is constant or grows at a constant rate, f is a positive coefficient that describes the feedback from price level deviations to nominal interest rate changes, and e_t is a random variable that follows a stochastic process known to agents in the economy. Figure 8.7 illustrates the response of key variables to an unanticipated decrease in e_t, assuming that e_t follows an AR(1) process with autoregressive coefficient 0.5. Such a decrease in R is an expansionary policy shock: while the nominal interest rate falls 100 basis points on impact and then climbs back to its steady state value, the money supply behaves almost as a mirror image, rising on impact by about 0.6 percent, and then falling back to its steady state level. Because the policy rule involves feedback from the price level instead of inflation, the money supply and the price level both return to their steady state levels.[20] It may seem puzzling at first that an expansionary policy shock generates an increase in the nominal interest rate with a money supply rule, but a decrease with an interest rate rule. The resolution lies in the behavior of the money supply in these two cases. With the money supply rule, an expansionary shock involves an initial increase in the money supply that is amplified over time, at a decreasing rate, until a steady state with a higher quantity of money has been reached. In contrast, with the interest rate feedback rule, an expansionary shock involves an initial increase in money that is *reversed* over time. The money rule thus leads to an increase in expected inflation following the initial unexpected rise in the price level, whereas the interest rate rule leads to a decrease in expected inflation.

8.4   Constraints on Monetary Policy

We now turn to the central topic of the paper, optimal monetary policy. That is, we turn to describing how the monetary authority should behave, having already described how the model economy behaves given specific monetary

---

20. A similar rule with feedback from inflation rather than the price level would generate base drift, permanent changes in the price level and money supply.

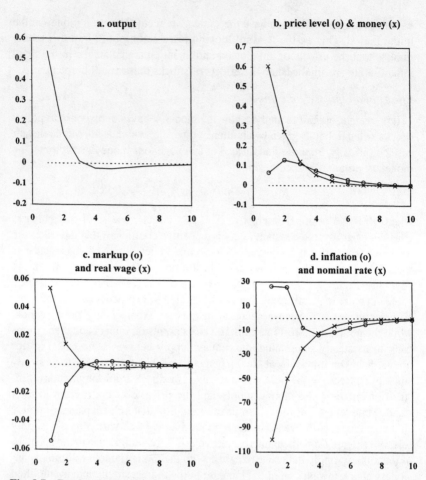

Fig. 8.7 Persistent shock to an interest rate rule
Note: For axis units, see note to fig. 8.4.

policy actions. To keep the analysis as simple as possible, we assume that there is a single shock to macroeconomic activity—an aggregate shock to productivity—in this section. Later we discuss generalizing the analysis to accommodate other types of shocks. The objective of optimal policy is to maximize welfare, that is, the representative agent's lifetime utility. Absent monopolistic competition and sticky prices, laissez faire would be an optimal policy, with any rate of inflation yielding the same welfare level.

In our model, however, monopolistic competition and sticky prices are key features. In principle, the policymaker would like to offset the effects of monopolistic competition and sticky prices; specifically, it would like to make relative prices behave as if these two frictions were absent. In pursuing this objective, the policymaker is constrained in two ways. First, the economy has exogenous technology and limited resources. Second, firms are monopolistically competitive with sticky prices, and in setting prices they take into account the demand curves and marginal costs they expect to face. Firms' expectations, in turn, depend on their beliefs about how policy is conducted.

We assume that policy is conducted with commitment; the monetary authority chooses a state-contingent plan and sticks with it, even though the plan is time inconsistent. The policymaker in our model does not have access to a full set of fiscal policy instruments. With such instruments it would be possible to achieve a first-best allocation; production subsidies financed by lump-sum taxation would succeed in offsetting the effects of imperfect competition. Alternatively, as in Yun (1994), the combined fiscal and monetary authorities could be constrained to raise revenue with distorting taxes, so that the first-best allocation might not be achievable, but a combined Ramsey taxation approach applied. Rotemberg and Woodford, in chapter 2 of this volume, assume that fiscal instruments are available to eliminate steady state distortions, leaving to monetary policy the job of business cycle stabilization. We assume that there are no fiscal interventions available, and we impose no fiscal constraints on the monetary authority's plans.[21] That is: our objective is to isolate principles of optimal monetary policy without a complicating discussion of fiscal issues.

Resource Constraints

The constraints involving technology and resources are given by the production functions

$$(25) \qquad c_{j,t} \leq a_t n_{j,t} \qquad \text{for } j = 0, 1,$$

the consumption aggregator

$$(26) \qquad c_t \leq \left(\frac{1}{2} c_{0,t}^{(\varepsilon-1)/\varepsilon} + \frac{1}{2} c_{1,t}^{(\varepsilon-1)/\varepsilon} \right)^{\varepsilon/(\varepsilon-1)},$$

and agents' limited time endowments

$$(27) \qquad 1 \geq n_t = \frac{1}{2} n_{0,t} + \frac{1}{2} n_{1,t}.$$

Implementation Constraint

The monetary authority must choose quantities that are consistent with monopolistic competition and sticky prices. In the current model with two-period price stickiness, the single constraint involving firms' price setting is as follows: quantities must be consistent with the fact that any firm adjusting its price will do so optimally. We call this constraint an "implementation constraint" because it describes how the monetary authority is constrained by the

---

21. As mentioned previously, the monetary authority does have lump-sum taxes available to finance monetary policy actions.

fact that it must induce sticky price, monopolistically competitive firms to implement its chosen quantities.

The most convenient formulation of the implementation constraint is based on the requirement that the present value of marginal profits from a price change is zero (as in eq. [18]):

$$\lambda_t p_{0,t} \frac{\partial z_{0,t}}{\partial p_{0,t}} + \beta E_t \lambda_{t+1} p_{1,t+1} \frac{\partial z_{1,t+1}}{\partial p_{1,t+1}} = 0.$$

It is then straightforward to rewrite the implementation constraint in terms of real quantities only, without any nominal magnitudes or relative prices:

$$(28) \qquad x(c_{0,t}, c_t, n_t, a_t) + \beta E_t x(c_{1,t+1}, c_{t+1}, n_{t+1}, a_{t+1}) = 0,$$

where x is a function that involves real quantities only, as we discuss next. To derive this version of the constraint on the monetary authority, we use the demand function ($c_{j,t} = p_{j,t}^{-\varepsilon} c_t$) to eliminate relative prices. We eliminate real marginal cost by using its definition as w_t/a_t and then use the equality between the real wage and the marginal rate of substitution between consumption and leisure to eliminate the real wage. In the current model, the x function reduces to[22]

$$(29) \qquad x(c_{j,t}, c_t, n_t, a_t) = \lambda_t c_t \left[(1 - \varepsilon) \left(\frac{c_{j,t}}{c_t} \right)^{1-1/\varepsilon} + \varepsilon \theta n_t^{\gamma} \left(\frac{c_{j,t}}{c_t} \right) \right].$$

In what sense is equation (28) a constraint on the policymaker? As a simple example, suppose the policymaker wanted to raise output through a monetary injection in period t. One rationale for the expansion might be that output is inefficiently low: since some firms cannot adjust their prices, an increase in aggregate demand is desirable because it will raise output toward the efficient level. However, firms that do adjust their prices—both in current and future periods—behave according to equation (19), raising their prices in the face of an increase in demand. In this way the behavior of price-setting firms constrains (but does not eliminate) the monetary authority's ability to manipulate real quantities.

8.5   The Real Policy Problem

To determine optimal monetary policy, we first determine choices for real activity that are optimal subject to the resource and implementation constraints. Subsequently, we determine the behavior of nominal variables and relative prices that are consistent with these real quantities. While unusual in macroeconomics, this two-step practice is common in public finance and other

22. As above, we use λ_t to denote the marginal utility of consumption in period t. As such, λ_t is a function of c_t, n_t, and a_t.

areas of applied general equilibrium analysis. To make this problem relatively easy to state formally, we also ignore expectations throughout this section; in related work using a complete contingent markets approach, we have found that similar efficiency conditions describe optimal policy under uncertainty.

Optimal policy under commitment can be found by writing a restricted social planner's problem that involves maximizing expression (2) with a choice of sequences for $c_{0,t}$, $c_{1,t}$, c_t, $n_{0,t}$, $n_{1,t}$, n_t, subject to conditions (25)–(28). The Lagrangian for this problem is

$$
\begin{aligned}
L = {} & \sum_{t=0}^{\infty} \beta^t u(c_t, n_t, a_t) \\
& + \sum_{t=0}^{\infty} \beta^t \phi_t [x(c_{0,t}, c_t, n_t, a_t) + \beta x(c_{1,t+1}, c_{t+1}, n_{t+1}, a_{t+1})] \\
& + \sum_{t=0}^{\infty} \beta^t \Lambda_t [c(c_{0,t}, c_{1,t}) - c_t] \\
& + \sum_{t=0}^{\infty} \beta^t \Omega_t \left(n_t - \frac{1}{2} n_{0,t} - \frac{1}{2} n_{1,t} \right) \\
& + \sum_{t=0}^{\infty} \beta^t [\rho_{0,t}(a_t n_{0,t} - c_{0,t}) + \rho_{1,t}(a_t n_{1,t} - c_{1,t})].
\end{aligned}
$$

(30)

We will discuss the various multipliers in this Lagrangian as they appear in the analysis below.

8.5.1 Background to the Policy Problem

The optimal policy problem described by equation (30) is a *restricted* planner's problem because any social planner worth his or her salt would not be constrained by staggered price setting. To see how our specific restriction plays a role, we can imagine a series of problems with weaker restrictions.

First, if we were to remove constraint (28), the problem would be that of a planner constrained only by tastes and technology, as typically defined. The optimal allocations would make consumption at both types of firms equal (since the aggregator is concave and symmetric in these quantities). Further, the unrestricted social planner would choose aggregate consumption and work effort so that the marginal rate of substitution

$$
- \frac{\partial u(c_t, n_t, a_t)}{\partial n_t} \bigg/ \frac{\partial u(c_t, n_t, a_t)}{\partial c_t}
$$

equaled the marginal rate of transformation a_t.

Second, consider an intermediate planner, who cannot overcome monopolistic competition but can force firms to change their prices each period. Instead of facing constraint (28), such a planner would face the constraint $x(c_t, c_t, n_t, a_t) = 0$. Symmetry and concavity of the aggregator c would again make it unambiguous that optimal policy would equate consumption across the differentiated products. However, the planner could no longer equate the marginal rate of substitution to a_t because this would not respect the implementation constraint; that is, it would be inconsistent with monopolistic competition. Considering this intermediate problem reveals that if monetary policy can cause consumption of all the goods to be equated, it will have "undone" the price stickiness. We saw above, however, that it is price stickiness—combined with imperfect competition—that gives the monetary authority some real leverage in the economy. The monetary authority's optimality conditions must then effectively involve balancing the distortions arising from price stickiness against the ability to affect real quantities.

8.5.2 Optimality Conditions

The first-order conditions for equation (30) can be written in the following time-invariant form if we define an artificial multiplier ϕ_{-1} to enter several of the constraints at date $t = 0$; we return later to a more detailed discussion of the role of this multiplier. Optimal choice of the labor input at each type of firm implies

$$(31) \qquad 0 = \frac{\partial L}{\partial n_{j,t}} = \beta^t \left(\rho_{j,t} a_t - \frac{1}{2} \Omega_t \right) \qquad \text{for } j = 0, 1,$$

and optimal choice of the consumption levels from each type of firm implies

$$(32) \qquad 0 = \frac{\partial L}{\partial c_{j,t}} = \beta^t \left(\Lambda_t \frac{\partial c(c_{0,t}, c_{1,t})}{\partial c_{j,t}} - \rho_{j,t} + \phi_{t-j} \frac{\partial x(c_{j,t}, c_t, n_t, a_t)}{\partial c_{j,t}} \right)$$
$$\text{for } j = 0, 1.$$

Optimal choice of aggregate consumption and labor requires

$$(33) \qquad 0 = \frac{\partial L}{\partial c_t} = \beta^t \left(\frac{\partial u(c_t, n_t, a_t)}{\partial c_t} - \Lambda_t + \sum_{j=0}^{1} \phi_{t-j} \frac{\partial x(c_{j,t}, c_t, n_t, a_t)}{\partial c_t} \right)$$

and

$$(34) \qquad 0 = \frac{\partial L}{\partial n_t} = \beta^t \left(\frac{\partial u(c_t, n_t, a_t)}{\partial n_t} + \Omega_t + \sum_{j=0}^{1} \phi_{t-j} \frac{\partial x(c_{j,t}, c_t, n_t, a_t)}{\partial n_t} \right).$$

In addition to these quantity efficiency conditions, the first-order conditions include the constraints themselves, (25)–(28), which all will hold with equality.

Note that for $t = 0$ we have introduced ϕ_{-1} in equations (32)–(34), whereas it is not present in equation (30). As in Kydland and Prescott (1980), the purpose of introducing this artificial multiplier is to have a convenient mathematical expression for the policymaker's problem in a world of commitment, as we discuss further below. With this multiplier in place, the efficiency conditions for a successor government at date $t + 1$ would take exactly the same form as those efficiency conditions for the current government that occur for $t + 1$, $t + 2$, and so forth.

8.5.3   General Implications

Some of the first-order conditions for our restricted social planning problem look just like those for an unrestricted social planner. For example, optimal labor allocations equate the utility-denominated price of a unit of each type of good ($\rho_{j,t}$) to a measure of unit cost, the utility-denominated value of labor (Ω_t) divided by productivity (a_t).

However, the other conditions reflect the implementation constraint's effect on the restricted social planner's behavior. Comparing these first-order conditions to the analogues from the decentralized formulation of the model provides some insight into the optimal policy problem. First, however, it is necessary to say a word about ϕ_t. The multiplier ϕ_t is the shadow value of decreasing a price-setting firm's marginal present discounted profits with respect to relative price. Because the planner would like firms to have positive marginal profits, the multiplier is negative.[23] For consumption and labor, the individual's first-order conditions were

(37)
$$0 = \beta^t \left(\frac{\partial u(c_t, n_t, a_t)}{\partial c_t} - \lambda_t \right),$$

$$0 = \beta^t \left(\frac{\partial u(c_t, n_t, a_t)}{\partial n_t} - \lambda_t w_t \right).$$

As in section 8.2 above, λ_t is the shadow value of a unit of consumption to the individual, whereas Λ_t is the value the *planner* attaches to a marginal unit of consumption. In a competitive economy these objects are identical. With monopolistic competition, the planner values the marginal unit of consumption more than an individual does because higher aggregate consumption alleviates the monopoly pricing constraint (28). A marginal unit of labor input has a similar

---

23. Note that the second set of terms in eq. (30), which is written there as

(35)
$$+\sum_{t=0}^{\infty} \beta^t \phi_t [x(c_{0,t}, c_t, n_t, a_t) + \beta x(c_{1,t+1}, c_{t+1}, n_{t+1}, a_{t+1})],$$

can alternatively be written as

(36)
$$-\sum_{t=0}^{\infty} \beta^t \phi_t [0 - x(c_{0,t}, c_t, n_t, a_t) - \beta x(c_{1,t+1}, c_{t+1}, n_{t+1}, a_{t+1})];$$

zero is the "bound" on marginal profits, and $-\phi$ is the value of relaxing that bound.

effect ($\Omega_t > -\partial u(c_t, n_t, a_t)/\partial n_t$) because labor supply dictates that higher labor input corresponds to a higher real wage and hence a lower markup.

The first-order conditions for c_j do not have as simple an analogue in the decentralized problem, but they can be easily understood as describing how the policymaker equates appropriately defined marginal rates of substitution and transformation between c_0 and c_1. Rewriting equation (32) as

$$(38) \quad \Lambda_t \frac{\partial c(c_{0,t}, c_{1,t})}{\partial c_{j,t}} + \phi_{t-j} \frac{\partial x(c_{j,t}, c_t, n_t, a_t)}{\partial c_{j,t}} = \rho_{j,t} \quad \text{for } j = 0, 1,$$

and dividing equation (38) for c_0 by (38) for c_1 yields

$$(39) \quad \frac{\Lambda_t \dfrac{\partial c(c_{0,t}, c_{1,t})}{\partial c_{0,t}} + \phi_t \dfrac{\partial x(c_{0,t}, c_t, n_t, a_t)}{\partial c_{0,t}}}{\Lambda_t \dfrac{\partial c(c_{0,t}, c_{1,t})}{\partial c_{1,t}} + \phi_{t-1} \dfrac{\partial x(c_{1,t}, c_t, n_t, a_t)}{\partial c_{1,t}}} = \frac{\rho_{0,t}}{\rho_{1,t}}.$$

The left-hand side is the policymaker's marginal rate of substitution between $c_{0,t}$ and $c_{1,t}$; it describes how much $c_{0,t}$ the policymaker would forgo to gain a marginal increase in $c_{1,t}$. The decrease in $c_{0,t}$ has two effects. First, it mechanically decreases the index of consumption, and marginal consumption is valued at Λ_t. Second, it affects marginal profits ($\partial x(c_{0,t}, c_t, n_t, a_t)/\partial c_{0,t}$), and *marginal marginal profits* are valued at ϕ_t. Increasing $c_{1,t}$ has similar effects, except that the change in marginal profits is valued with last period's multiplier, reflecting the importance of firms who set their prices in that period. Under commitment, the policymaker takes into account the effect current-period policy actions have on previous-period decisions. The right-hand side of equation (39) is the marginal rate of transformation between $c_{0,t}$ and $c_{1,t}$; it describes how much $c_{1,t}$ could be produced using the resources freed up by a marginal decrease in the production of $c_{0,t}$.

8.5.4   Time Invariance and Time Consistency

We are interested in optimal allocations that arise when the policy authority can fully commit to follow through on a plan that is optimal, that is, the solution to a maximization problem such as that discussed above. This focus raises a set of interrelated conceptual and technical issues.

Technically, an unusual aspect of the restricted social planning problem is that there is a forward-looking constraint (28), as in Aiyagari and Braun (1997). This is reflected in the form of the efficiency conditions (33) and (34) for choices at date t, which involve the lagged multiplier ϕ_{t-1}. Intuitively, the presence of this lagged multiplier originates from the fact that for any date $t > 0$, a change in c_t affects the pricing decision of firms in period $t - 1$. In fact, we can rewrite the implementation constraint terms in the Lagrangian as follows,

$$
\begin{aligned}
(40) \quad & \sum_{t=0}^{\infty} \beta^t \phi_t [x(c_{0,t}, c_t, n_t, a_t) + \beta x(c_{1,t+1}, c_{t+1}, n_{t+1}, a_{t+1})] \\
& = \phi_0 x(c_{0,0}, c_0, n_0, a_0) + \sum_{t=1}^{\infty} \beta^t [\phi_t x(c_{0,t}, c_t, n_t, a_t) + \phi_{t-1} x(c_{1,t}, c_t, n_t, a_t)].
\end{aligned}
$$

This rewriting stresses that there is an asymmetry attached to the initial start-up period. Above, we eliminated this asymmetry by including a lagged multiplier, so that the first term on the right-hand side of equation (40) is implicitly written as $\phi_t x(c_{0,t}, c_t, n_t, a_t) + \phi_{t-1} x(c_{1,t}, c_t, n_t, a_t)$ for $t = 0$. Including the lagged multiplier yields a time-invariant system. Time invariance is desirable from a computational point of view, since it allows us to employ standard fixed-coefficient linear rational expectations solution methods to calculate the solution to the restricted social planning problem.

Conceptually, if the policy authority is free to reformulate its optimal plan on a period-by-period basis, then there is a problem of time inconsistency of optimal plans as in Kydland and Prescott (1977) and Barro and Gordon (1983). It is then not sensible to formulate the optimal policy problem as we have, which is based on the assumption that the monetary authority can choose a sequence of binding actions for every period. Our implicit assumption is that the policy authority is required to commit to a state-contingent plan in period zero and follow it in all subsequent periods. Following Kydland and Prescott (1980), we view the introduction of the artificial multiplier as a device corresponding to the focus of our investigation: we want to consider the behavior of an economy after the effects of an initial "start-up" period have worn away. That is, we are looking at a stochastic steady state in which a monetary authority has long been following an optimal monetary policy. We can calculate the effect of an initial start-up period by setting the lagged multiplier ϕ_{-1} to zero and studying the resulting paths of economic activity from this initial condition. Computing the magnitude of welfare in this situation, relative to one that starts with ϕ_{-1} equal to its steady state value, provides a measure of the temptation for a policymaker to renege on a previously chosen plan.

We divide our discussion of optimal monetary policy into two questions. First, what pattern of real quantities should the monetary authority pick as its long-run objective and what does this imply about the optimal rate of inflation? Second, how should quantities vary in response to productivity shocks and what does this imply about the relationship of nominal variables to the business cycle?

8.6   A Monetary Modified Golden Rule

In section 8.3, we noted that relative price distortions are minimized at zero inflation, and the smallest average markup is achieved at a low but positive inflation rate. Not surprisingly, then, the highest steady state flow of momentary utility is achieved at a low but positive inflation rate, defined as $\hat{\Pi}$ in subsection 8.3.1. However, this low but positive inflation rate is not the optimal policy in steady state. Instead, the steady state of the solution to the optimal policy problem is zero inflation. The distinction between these two optimal policy problems is subtle but important: if the monetary authority is constrained to choosing a constant inflation rate, it would choose $\hat{\Pi}$, but if unconstrained, it would choose a path that ended in a steady state of *zero* inflation.

Henceforth, we will refer to this surprising result as a modified monetary golden rule. We now substantiate it by examining the constraints and first-order conditions, and showing that optimal policy mandates $c_{0,t} = c_{1,t} = c_t$, which is only consistent with equilibrium under zero inflation. It is straightforward to impose a steady state on equations (25)–(28) and thereby show that it is feasible for a steady state to have $c_{0,t} = c_{1,t} = c_t$ and $x_{j,t} = 0$ for all j. To show that this is also desirable for the social planner, we must examine the first-order conditions. The crucial condition is (39), repeated here in its steady state form:

(41)
$$\frac{\Lambda_t \dfrac{\partial c(c_0, c_1)}{\partial c_0} + \phi \dfrac{\partial x(c_0, c, n, a)}{\partial c_0}}{\Lambda_t \dfrac{\partial c(c_0, c_1)}{\partial c_1} + \phi \dfrac{\partial x(c_1, c, n, a)}{\partial c_1}} = \frac{\rho_0}{\rho_1}.$$

where variables without time subscripts denote steady state values.

To determine whether it is desirable for the steady state to have $c_0 = c_1 = c$, we need to know whether equation (41) is satisfied by these values. As discussed previously, the right-hand side of this expression is always unity since the utility cost of producing each good is identical: $\rho_0 = \rho_1 = \Omega/a$. The symmetry of the aggregator function implies that $\partial c(c_0, c_1)/\partial c_0 = \partial c(c_0, c_1)/\partial c_1 = 1/2$. Further, the effect of consumption associated with today's price setters on today's implementation constraint, $\partial x(c_0, c, n, a)/\partial c_0$, is just the same as the effect of consumption associated with yesterday's price setters on yesterday's implementation constraint, $\partial x(c_1, c, n, a)/\partial c_1$. Hence, the left-hand side is also equal to unity when $c_0 = c_1 = c$. Imposing $c_0 = c_1 = c$ on equations (31)–(34) in steady state then implies unique values for the key endogenous variables.

This result may seem very special, but it can be shown to generalize to many other related environments, including models with multiperiod price setting and with randomly timed adjustments by individual firms of a very rich form (as in Calvo 1983; Levin 1991). Rather than pursue these extensions, we concentrate on the intuition behind this general result in the simple case at hand.

As the title of this section suggests, there is an analogy between the suboptimality of $\hat{\Pi}$ and the suboptimality of the golden rule in growth models. It is suboptimal to maintain a capital stock corresponding to the highest sustainable constant consumption in the one-sector growth model because, in the transition to a lower capital stock, consumption and hence utility can be increased. Eventually, at the modified golden rule steady state, consumption will be lower into the infinite future. But the fact that future utility is discounted makes it optimal to move from the golden rule to the modified golden rule. In our model, it is suboptimal to maintain $\hat{\Pi}$, the constant inflation rate that yields highest welfare, because, in the transition to a lower inflation rate, consumption and hence utility can be increased. Eventually, and in particular in the new steady state, the markup will be higher and consumption and utility lower, but in the early stages of the transition, utility is higher. The fact that future utility is discounted makes it optimal to undertake this transition.

One perspective on the optimality of zero inflation comes from looking back at figure 8.6, which shows the expansionary effect of an anticipated disinflation. Given that the steady state solution has zero inflation and that solution is saddle-path stable, it must be that if a policymaker wakes up in a world with low but positive inflation, it is optimal to disinflate. Figure 8.6 shows exactly this pattern: a disinflation that is announced in advance generates increases in period utility for several periods, followed in the long run by a decrease. The benefit of the transition comes because it involves a lower markup; adjusting firms lower their relative prices in anticipation of the slowdown in money growth. With a lower markup, the real wage is higher and consumption and utility are higher, given that productivity is unchanged.[24]

The above argument is straightforward in implying that optimal policy has a steady state with lower inflation than $\hat{\Pi}$, but by itself it leaves unanswered the following interrelated questions. First, what is it about zero inflation that makes the argument for an announced disinflation invalid once zero is reached? Second, how can it be that the specific optimality of zero inflation does not depend on parameter values, in particular the discount factor? Zero inflation is special in that it involves elimination of the relative price distortion. By reducing inflation toward zero, the monetary authority earns a benefit from bringing relative prices into line. By further reducing inflation, the monetary authority incurs a cost in terms of relative price distortions.

As for the invariance of the zero inflation result under changes in the discount factor, the missing link in this puzzle is that $\hat{\Pi}$ itself depends on β. From equation (23), one can show that $\hat{\Pi}$ converges to unity from above as β converges to unity from below.[25] If β is high, there is little incentive to announce a disinflation because the long-run increase in the markup—and corresponding decrease in welfare—is not discounted very much. However, high β also implies that $\hat{\Pi}$ is close to unity, so the disinflation consistent with optimal policy

24. Of course the figure is generated using particular parameters. The result that zero inflation is the steady state of the solution to the optimal policy problem does not depend on parameters within the class of models we consider.

25. From eq. (23), the constant gross inflation rate that minimizes the markup converges to unity with the discount factor. Because unity is also the inflation rate that eliminates the relative price distortion, it follows that $\hat{\Pi}$ converges to unity with the discount factor ($\hat{\Pi}$ is always between unity and the inflation rate that minimizes the markup).

is very small. In contrast, if the discount factor is low, optimal policy involves a larger disinflation in the long run ($\hat{\Pi}$ is higher), but the long run is discounted more heavily.

Thus far our explanation of the zero-inflation result has been focused on why it would be optimal to disinflate to get to zero inflation. Earlier, however, we showed that positive monetary shocks were expansionary, which suggests that the monetary authority would actually choose to leave an initial steady state of price stability for positive inflation. This is incorrect because in steady state any inflation is expected. Accordingly, the planner who wants to have an expansion at t must pay for it at $t - 1$ in terms of effects on the implementation constraint, which is sufficiently costly that he chooses to forgo his leverage on the average markup.

8.7   Optimal Stabilization Policy

We now turn our attention to describing the behavior of real economic activity under optimal stabilization policy, specifically the response of economic activity to productivity disturbances. With a steady state that equates consumption across firms of different types (as would occur under price stability), we can analyze optimal stabilization policy by log-linearizing the system of equations (25)–(28) and (31)–(34) in the neighborhood of this steady state. The resulting linear system is described fully in appendix B. It is straightforward to use that linear system to analyze the optimal response of real quantities to a productivity shock. That optimal response turns out to involve equality of all relative prices, which translates into zero inflation just as in steady state. In what follows, we describe how to show this result and discuss the mechanics of how monetary policy can achieve it.

8.7.1   Real Dynamics under Optimal Policy

As one might expect, an important equation for understanding optimal policy is the optimal pricing equation or, equivalently, the implementation constraint (28). In its linearized form, that equation is

$$dx_{0,t} + \beta \cdot dx_{1,t+1} = 0,$$

and the linearized x functions are given by[26]

(42)
$$dx_{j,t} = \lambda c[(1 - \varepsilon)(1 - 1/\varepsilon) + \varepsilon\theta n^\gamma](dc_{j,t}/c - dc_t/c)$$
$$+ \gamma\varepsilon\theta\lambda cn^\gamma(dn_t/n), \quad \text{for } j = 0, 1.$$

---

26. Note that there are extra terms involving deviations in c and λ which vanish because they are multiplied by zero, the steady state value of x: at the steady state, adjusting and nonadjusting firms charge the same price, and it is the price that sets "marginal profits" equal to zero period by period.

If a productivity shock is not to optimally induce price variation, it must not cause marginal profits to deviate from zero for adjusters or nonadjusters. Referring to equation (42), this would mean holding x_j at zero (so $dx_j = 0$) and holding $c_j = c$. For these requirements to be mutually consistent, it must be that labor input does not respond to the shock. For the preferences in equation (2), it is in fact the case that labor input will not respond to productivity shocks as long as the markup does not respond (see eq. [9], and recall that the markup is a_t/w_t). And from equation (19), an unchanged constant markup ($= 1/\psi_t$) is consistent with adjusting firms not changing their relative prices if the price level is constant (under these conditions the numerator and denominator of eq. [19] cancel once real marginal cost is factored out of the numerator).

So far this line of reasoning does not prove that a constant price level is part of the optimal response to a productivity shock, but it does suggest a constructive method of proof. First, conjecture zero response of labor input, and responses of c_t and $c_{j,t}$ exactly equal to the change in productivity. Next refer to equation (39); if symmetry with respect to c_0 and c_1 is maintained, as it will be according to the conjecture, then it must be that $\phi_t = \phi_{t-1} = \phi$. Expand the conjecture, then, to include zero response of ϕ_t. Confirming that the conjecture is correct requires some tedious algebra that we will not reproduce, but conceptually it is straightforward. Simply impose the conjecture on the linearized equations in appendix B, and verify that those equations are satisfied. They are.

In response to a productivity shock, then, the monetary authority should accommodate so that the price level is unchanged and firms continue to maximize profits on a period-by-period basis. Figure 8.8 displays impulse response functions under optimal monetary policy for a serially correlated ($\rho = 0.9$), positive productivity shock. Those responses are identical to what would be found in a real business cycle model. With the price level constant, the nominal interest rate behaves identically to the real interest rate. Because it essentially tracks expected consumption growth, the real interest rate falls initially and then gradually rises back to its steady state level.

We have thus verified that the constant inflation, constant markup policy conjectured to be optimal by Goodfriend and King (1997) and King and Wolman (1996) is in fact optimal. However, the fact that there are no money demand distortions in the current framework implies that *zero* inflation is optimal. Our demonstration of the desirability of a constant price level proceeds differently from that of Rotemberg and Woodford (1997) in that we do not assume that a combined fiscal and monetary authority has overcome the underlying monopolistic competition distortions in the economy.

8.7.2 Optimal Monetary Policy

Because the real effects of monetary policy work through relative prices in this model, they can be interpreted as working through relative quantities. In fact, it is possible to fully describe the real outcomes under optimal monetary policy without any discussion of nominal variables, although we chose not to

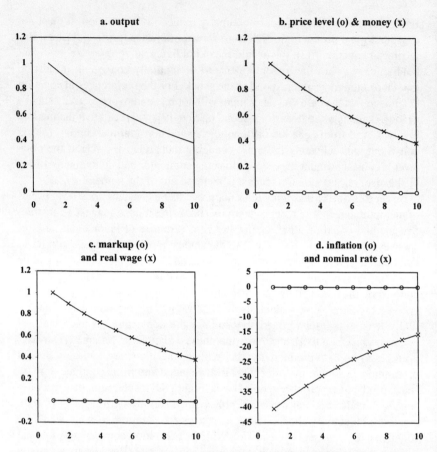

Fig. 8.8   Persistent productivity shock with optimal policy response
Note: For axis units, see note to fig. 8.4.

pursue this expository strategy in the previous subsection. In practice, however, monetary policy operates through nominal variables such as the nominal interest rate, the money stock, and the price level. This subsection details how to reinterpret optimal policy in terms of the nominal variables that would produce our optimal allocations in (monopolistically competitive) general equilibrium.

The state variables of the model include prices set by firms in previous periods, which are relevant since these firms are unable to change their prices. In the two-period case, the only relevant historical information is $P_{1,t} = P_{0,t-1}$. The real policy problem provides optimal quantities at date t, $c_{0,t}$ and $c_{1,t}$. "Decentralizing" this optimal policy requires that the relative nominal prices satisfy

(43) $$P_{0,t}/P_{1,t} = (c_{0,t}/c_{1,t})^{-1/\varepsilon}.$$

Since $P_{1,t}$ is predetermined, equation (43) implies a unique level of $P_{0,t}$, and thus the price level is uniquely determined under optimal policy by equation (5), as $P_t = (\frac{1}{2}P_{0,t}^{1-\varepsilon} + \frac{1}{2}P_{1,t}^{1-\varepsilon})^{1/(1-\varepsilon)}$. Given the price index and the level of real activity, equation (10) dictates that the quantity of money must be

$$M_t = kP_t c_t.$$

The real interest rate must satisfy the real Fisher equation (11), which links it to the marginal utility of consumption,

$$1 + r_t = \left(\beta E_t \frac{\lambda_{t+1}}{\lambda_t}\right)^{-1},$$

and the nominal interest rate must satisfy equation (12),

$$1 + R_t = \left[\beta E_t\left(\frac{\lambda_{t+1}}{\lambda_t}\frac{P_t}{P_{t+1}}\right)\right]^{-1},$$

so that we can also determine the relevant interest rates under optimal policy. Combining these equations with the result that $P_t = P_{t-1}$, we find that the real interest rate r_t is equal to the nominal interest rate R_t.

Since there is a predetermined price level from the previous period, P_{t-1}, and it is optimal to maintain that price level in the current period, there is a simpler way to provide a monetary interpretation of optimal policy. With all real variables determined by the solution to the real policy problem, the money supply is then given from equation (10) as

$$M_t = kP_{t-1}c_t.$$

In this setting, as in the more general case, the fact that yesterday's price level is an observable, predetermined variable provides the anchor needed to produce determinacy.

8.7.3   Extensions to Multiperiod Price Setting

Our analysis has focused on the two-period case of Taylor-style staggering for concreteness. However, it is easy to extend the analysis of optimal policy in two directions. First, one can determine an optimal policy for multiperiod price setting with two minor modifications of the approach that we developed above: it is necessary to (1) modify the implementation constraint to $0 = E_t \sum_{j=0}^{J-1}\beta^j x(c_{j,t+j}, c_{t+j}, n_{t+j}, a_{t+j})$ in the J-period case and (2) introduce additional constraints on real quantities at date t of the form $(c_{1,t}/c_{2,t})^{-1/\varepsilon} = (c_{0,t-1}/c_{1,t-1})^{-1/\varepsilon}$.[27] An important consequence of these modifications is that more lags of the multiplier ϕ are added to the dynamic system. Second, we can incorporate randomly timed adjustments by individual firms of a very rich form (as in Levin's 1991 extension of the Calvo 1983 framework). In this case the distribution of

---

27. We provide an example of this structure in section 8.8 below.

firms would no longer be uniform with respect to time since last price adjustment, and consequently the implementation constraint would have unequal (declining) weights on $x_{j,t+j}$, $j = 0, 1, \ldots, J - 1$.

8.8   Temptations for the Monetary Authority

While we have demonstrated that a policy of pegging the price level is optimal under commitment, there are temptations for the monetary authority to deviate from this plan. In this section, we provide two examples of how this temptation might arise and quantify its magnitude.

8.8.1   Starting Up

The most basic temptation is that associated with "starting up" the policy of pegging the price level. For example, if a rule like the Mack bill were adopted, one option would be for Congress to allow the Federal Reserve System two years to choose a price level that it would peg, perhaps so that it could get appropriate policy procedures in place.

In our model economy, this would correspond to an optimal monetary policy problem with the initial multiplier ϕ_0 set equal to zero; all lagged product prices and quantities would be given by history, but since optimal policy under commitment was not followed in the past, the lagged multiplier would not be given by history. (Technically, it would then be appropriate for the monetary authority to ignore the lagged multiplier, that is, set it to zero.) The results of simulating optimal policy in this setting are shown in figure 8.9 for a model with four-quarter price setting.[28]

In the initial period, the money stock more than doubles, and with a majority of prices fixed, this yields a huge increase in output (almost as large as the increase in the money stock). There is a jump in the price level, and the corresponding high inflation rate is maintained for the four quarters until all firms have had the opportunity to adjust their prices. In this transitional period the money supply is decreasing, however. Nominal interest rates are low during the transition; this is reconciled with the high expected inflation through anticipated decreases in consumption. In terms of the representative agent's preferences, the transition yields the equivalent of a 1.6 percent per year permanent increase in consumption. In other words, the temptation for the monetary authority to ignore ϕ_0 in *any* period would be large. The fact that the model is parameterized with a high labor supply elasticity and a high markup is directly responsible for the size of the temptation; the higher the labor supply elasticity, the greater the consequences of a given markup. With this parameterization, steady state output is far below what it would be with perfect competition, so

28. In the four-quarter price-setting case, there are three lagged multipliers that must be set to zero. As described in subsection 8.7.3, when prices may be fixed for more than two periods, lagged ratios of real quantities are also relevant state variables.

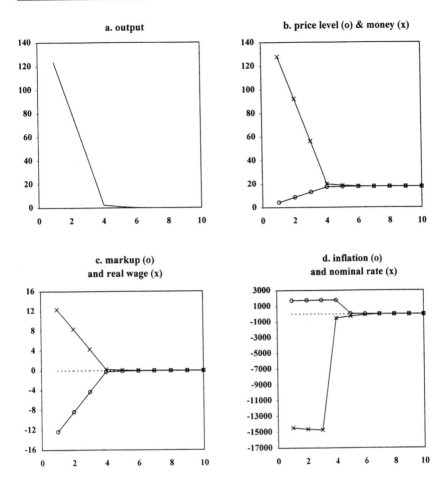

Fig. 8.9   Exploiting initial conditions with four-quarter staggering
Note: For axis units, see note to fig. 8.4.

the monetary authority can generate large movements in output on a temporary basis.

8.8.2   An Unusual Shock

In section 8.7, we assumed that the monetary authority had to determine
how it would respond to shocks before they occurred. This assumption was at
the heart of our analysis of how monetary policy should respond to a productivity shock: we were interested in how the monetary authority should respond as
part of a *policy.* An alternative is to determine how the monetary authority
should respond to a shock that is unusual, in the sense that it is unexpected and
viewed as never to recur. In this case, the monetary authority should exploit
initial conditions, setting lagged ϕs to zero.

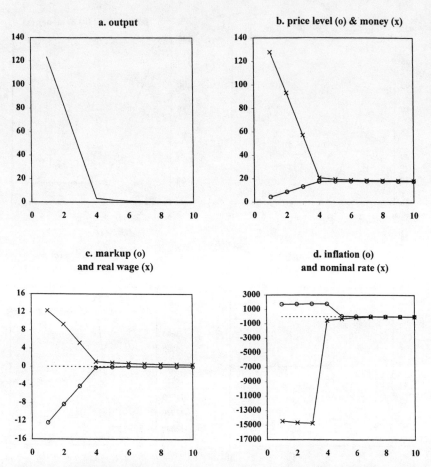

Fig. 8.10   Exploiting initial conditions in the face of a productivity shock
Note: For axis units, see note to fig. 8.4.

The results are shown in figure 8.10. A productivity shock is now accompanied by a burst of inflation, and in fact the inflationary response associated with $\phi_0 = 0$ dominates the response associated with the productivity shock. Another way of seeing this point is to look across some prior figures: the response to an unusual shock in figure 8.10 looks much more like the figure 8.9 case of starting up, where the only deviation from steady state initial conditions is in ϕ_0, than it looks like the optimal policy response in figure 8.7, where the only deviation from steady state initial conditions is in the productivity shock.

How are we to interpret these temptations to deviate from optimal policy under commitment? To begin, the fact that the temptations are so large hinges on the magnitude of the economy's existing distortions. To the extent that our parameterization of those distortions is proxying for other features of actual economies, one would want to better understand those other features before passing final judgment on the size of the temptations. Conditional on the large temptation being accurate, a natural interpretation is that it points to the need for some commitment device, with an act of Congress being a natural example. Without a commitment device, one is led to consider whether optimal policy under commitment can be sustained through reputation effects or trigger strategies. Ireland (1997) has investigated this issue in a sticky price model where optimal policy can be sustained through reputation; whether our model admits such equilibria is an open question.

8.9   Interest Rate Rules and Economic Activity

In contrast to other chapters in this volume, our work has concentrated on determining optimal monetary policy rather than on making comparisons across alternative monetary policy rules, with some specific emphasis on interest rate rules following Taylor (1993). In this section, we discuss two aspects of interest rate rules and macroeconomic activity, suggesting how our analysis could be extended to bring it more into line with the other research reported in this volume.

8.9.1   An Optimal Interest Rate Rule

Our characterization of optimal monetary policy implies that there should be zero inflation, so that nominal and real interest rates are identical. Optimal monetary policy therefore can be implemented through an interest rate rule of the form

$$(44) \qquad\qquad R_t = r_t^* + f \cdot (\ln P_t - \ln \overline{P}),$$

where r_t^* is the real interest rate determined by the real Fisher equation (11) and the optimal quantity response. As with the interest rate rule that we used to study the response of the economy to interest rate shocks (24), the optimal interest rate rule (44) also involves a positive response of the nominal rate to deviations of the price level from its target. This response assures that there is a determinate price level under optimal policy but otherwise is unimportant since with $R_t = r_t^*$ it follows that $f \cdot (\ln P_t - \ln \overline{P}) = 0$.

Implementing optimal policy, however, requires knowing how the underlying real interest rate—the real interest rate that would obtain if prices were flexible—responds to shocks. To illustrate that this is a nontrivial problem for a monetary authority, figure 8.11 shows the response of the real interest rate under three different assumptions about the productivity process. The first is the first-order scheme for which we described optimal policy in figure 8.8; the second makes productivity a second-order autoregression, $\ln a_t = 1.3 \ln a_{t-1} - 0.4 \ln a_{t-2} + e_t$; and the third assumes that productivity is difference stationary, $\ln a_t = 1.3 \ln a_{t-1} - 0.3 \ln a_{t-2} + e_t$. All of these specifications can be

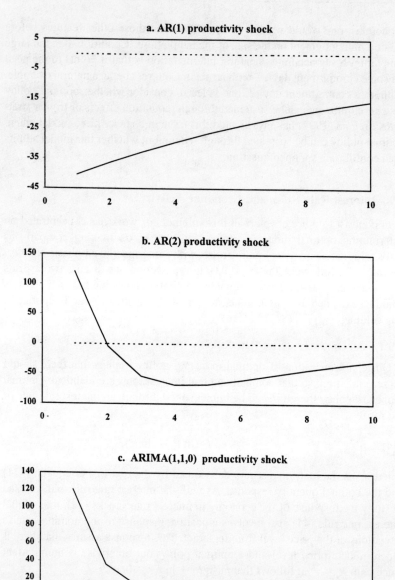

Fig. 8.11 Behavior of the real interest rate under optimal policy
Note: x-Axes in quarters; y-axes in basis points.

captured as special cases of the second-order stochastic difference equation $\ln a_t = \zeta_1 \ln a_{t-1} - \zeta_2 \ln a_{t-2} + e_t$.

Our model economy is very simple: there is no investment and labor does not respond to productivity shocks under the optimal allocation, so output and consumption track productivity perfectly. This simplicity also means that the real interest rate approximately tracks the expected growth rate of productivity,[29]

$$r_t^* = E_t(\ln a_{t+1} - \ln a_t) = [(\zeta_1 - 1)\ln a_t - \zeta_2 \ln a_{t-1}].$$

Under our basic specification, productivity (and hence output) is a stationary first-order autoregression, so the real interest rate depends negatively on the level of output ($\zeta_1 - 1 < 0$ and $\zeta_2 = 0$ imply that $r_t^* = (\zeta_1 - 1)\ln a_t$). By contrast, under our third specification, there is *no* connection between the level of the real interest rate and the *level* of output: productivity *growth* is a stationary first-order autoregression ($\zeta_1 = 1.3$ and $\zeta_2 = 0.3$) so that the real interest rate rises when output *growth* is unexpectedly strong, $r_t^* = 0.3(\ln a_t - \ln a_{t-1})$. Finally, the second specification combines an initial period of positive growth effects with a subsequent period of negative growth effects, and thus aspects of each of the other specifications.

From the standpoint of a central bank using an interest rate instrument, the difficulty is that optimal policy requires knowledge of the structure of the economy if there is a single type of productivity shock and of the type of shock that is currently occurring if there are multiple shocks.

8.9.2 Comparison of Alternative Rules

To compare alternative monetary policy rules with the optimal rule that we have discussed, it is necessary to take a stand on the details of the structure of the economy, including the internal mechanisms and forcing processes. Then one can calculate the stationary level of lifetime utility (1) under the optimal and alternative rules.[30] As the analysis of Rotemberg and Woodford in chapter 2 of this volume indicates, the results of policy analysis along these lines depend importantly on the particular structure of the economy; we do not pursue such analysis here because we are not yet willing to take a stand on the details of that structure.

---

29. This expression is exact under optimal monetary policy, since this makes employment constant and the marginal utility of consumption is then

$$D_1 u(c_t, n_t, a_t) = \left(c_t - a_t \frac{\theta}{1 + \gamma} n_t^{1+\gamma}\right)^{-1} = a_t^{-1}\left(n - \frac{\theta}{1 + \gamma} n_t^{1+\gamma}\right)^{-1}.$$

It would be exact under all policies if the preference specification were $u = \ln c - \theta n^{1+\gamma}$.

30. This approach is similar to that of Rotemberg and Woodford (chap. 2 of this volume), who look at policies in terms of their effect on the stationary level of momentary utility (1).

8.10   Conclusions

This chapter provides a basic example of the analysis of optimal monetary policy in an environment with imperfect competition and sticky prices. The general approach resembles that traditional in public finance rather than practical macroeconomics. That is: we derive optimal policy by maximizing the welfare of the economy's representative agent, subject to resource constraints and an additional condition that summarizes the implications of imperfect competition and sticky prices for what the monetary authority can feasibly select. We show that a policy of stabilizing the price level is optimal in two respects. First, the average rate of inflation should be zero. Second, the price level should not vary with the business cycle.

While this result was obtained in a very simple economy, the methods applied in this paper are capable of extending the analysis of monetary policy well beyond settings in which there is a single shock (to productivity), strong assumptions about preferences (implying constant demand elasticities and zero optimal labor response to productivity shocks), a single factor of production (labor), a single location of real distortions (imperfect competition in the commodity market), and complete information about underlying shocks. We thus outline some directions in which it is important for this research to be extended.

Multiple Shocks. Within the simple model without capital, there are two important directions of extensions. First, one would like to understand how the economy responds to "aggregate demand" shocks, such as changes in government demand for final output and exogenous changes in the timing of consumption decisions by households. We have undertaken these extensions and find that the policy of smoothing the price level continues to be optimal. Second, it is important to think about the effects of energy shocks. One direct interpretation is that these are productivity shocks, in which case we already have the answer. But an alternative approach would be to add energy as an input to final consumption that was in exogenous supply and was sold by flexible price firms. One would no longer expect that optimal monetary policy would smooth all measures of the price level (in particular, not the final consumption deflator) but rather an index corresponding to the prices of imperfectly competitive sticky price firms.

Alternative Preference Specifications. Our example economy incorporated strong—constant elasticity utility—assumptions about the preferences of individuals for differentiated products and for the trade-off between consumption and leisure. Public finance theory teaches us that the exact optimality of tax equalization (across products) or tax smoothing (over time) typically requires constant elasticities. Our general analytical approach does not require this set of assumptions, which we used because they are simple and conventional in the literature. It would be useful to explore how alternative preference specifications would alter our conclusions about the optimal rate of inflation and the optimal cyclical variation in the price level.

Richer Production Structure. In our view, a successful positive model of the business cycle requires the endogenous determination of investment and capacity utilization. Thus it is important to determine the nature of optimal monetary policy when the production structure is enriched along these lines.

Richer Pricing Structure. Our analysis has concentrated entirely on time-dependent pricing. It would be useful to extend the analysis to state-dependent pricing, and it seems feasible to use the framework of Dotsey, King, and Wolman (forthcoming) for this purpose.

Additional Sources of Distortions. Many economists believe that the labor market does not clear in the way that we have specified in this chapter, but that (1) there is market power on the part of firms and workers, or (2) there are incentive problems arising from incomplete information about worker characteristics or effort. For example, Romer (1993) argues that additional "real rigidities" along these lines are a necessary ingredient of a successful business cycle theory, with implications for the nature of optimal monetary policy. The general approach developed in our research appears capable of handling extensions to additional distortions, say along efficiency wage lines, which would introduce another implementation constraint into the real policy problem. Exploring the implications of these frictions for optimal monetary policy seems feasible and fascinating.

Incomplete Information. Our analysis is conducted under the assumption that the monetary authority has full current information about the shocks that are impinging on the economy. McCallum (1997) has stressed that monetary policy rules should be operational, in the sense of respecting the informational constraints on the monetary authority. It is important to extend our analysis to situations of incomplete information, and we believe that it is feasible to do so.

More General Specification of Policy. We have restricted the monetary authority to following deterministic rules. However, it may be optimal to employ a randomized rule because of the presence of distortions (technically, the form of the implementation constraint). For example, the monetary authority might choose a policy that randomly expanded the economy but was accompanied by a commitment to disinflate whenever expansions occurred.[31] Recent analy-

---

31. The possible desirability of this sort of policy was suggested to us by Athanasios Orphanides.

ses of optimal fiscal policies, such as that of Bassetto (1997), permit the policy authority to follow such randomized strategies and determine whether they are part of an optimal plan.

This is a lengthy list of open topics, but in principle each topic can be analyzed with the same basic approach used in the current paper. That approach uses standard tools of public finance to analyze optimal policy in what have now become standard models of monopolistic competition and sticky prices.

Appendix A
The Household's Choice Problem

This appendix provides more detail on the household's dynamic choice problem for aggregate consumption and labor supply that leads to equations (7) and (8). We also use this appendix to sketch out the incorporation of a "shopping time" approach to money demand along the lines of King and Wolman (1996), when there is interest-bearing money. The household's optimization problem can be written in dynamic programming form as

$$v(m_{t-1}, b_{t-1}, s_{t-1}, \sigma_t) = \max_{(c_t, n_t, s_t, m_t, b_t)} \{u(c_t, n_t, a_t) + \beta E v(m_t, b_t, s_t, \sigma_{t+1} | \sigma_t)\},$$

where the relevant aggregate state variables at date t are σ_t. (We write conditional expectations such as $E\{v(m_t, b_t, s_t, \sigma_{t+1}) | \sigma_t\}$ more compactly as $E_t v(m_t, b_t, s_t, \sigma_{t+1})$ below.) The maximization takes place subject to the budget constraint (6), which we write as

$$c_t + m_t + v_t s_t + b_t + w_t h(m_t / c_t) =$$

$$z_t s_{t-1} + v_t s_{t-1} + w_t n_t + (1 + R_{t-1}^M)(P_{t-1}/P_t) m_t + (1 + R_{t-1})(P_{t-1}/P_t) b_{t-1}.$$

In these expressions, $m_t = M_t/P_t$ is current real balances, $b_t = B_t/P_t$ is current real bonds, and $h(m_t/c_t)$ is the amount of time spent in transactions activity. Forming a Lagrangian

$$L_t = \{u(c_t, n_t, a_t) + \beta E_t v(m_t, b_t, s_t, \sigma_{t+1})\}$$

$$+ \lambda_t [z_t s_{t-1} + v_t s_{t-1} + w_t n_t + (1 + R_{t-1}^M)(P_{t-1}/P_t) m_{t-1}$$

$$+ (1 + R_{t-1})(P_{t-1}/P_t) b_{t-1} - c_t - m_t - v_t s_t - b_t - w_t c_t h(m_t / c_t)],$$

we find that the first-order conditions are

$$\frac{\partial u(c_t, n_t, a_t)}{\partial c_t} = \lambda_t \left[1 - w_t \frac{m_t}{c_t^2} h'\left(\frac{m_t}{c_t}\right) \right],$$

$$\frac{\partial u(c_t, n_t, a_t)}{\partial n_t} = -\lambda_t w_t,$$

$$\lambda_t \left[1 + \frac{w_t}{c_t} h'\left(\frac{m_t}{c_t}\right) \right] = \beta E_t \frac{\partial v(m_t, b_t, s_t, \sigma_{t+1})}{\partial m_t} = \beta E_t \left(\lambda_{t+1}(1 + R_t^M) \frac{P_t}{P_{t+1}} \right),$$

$$\lambda_t = \beta E_t \frac{\partial v(m_t, b_t, s_t, \sigma_{t+1})}{\partial b_t} = \beta E_t \left(\lambda_{t+1}(1 + R_t) \frac{P_t}{P_{t+1}} \right),$$

$$\lambda_t v_t = \beta E_t \frac{\partial v(m_t, b_t, s_t, \sigma_{t+1})}{\partial s_t} = \beta E_t [\lambda_{t+1}(z_{t+1} + v_{t+1})],$$

where the final equalities on the right-hand sides of the final three equations arise from standard "envelope theorem" arguments, such as those found in Stokey and Lucas (1989).

These five conditions have the following interpretations. The first two conditions are requirements for efficient consumption and labor supply. The third is the requirement for efficient holdings of real money balances, that is, the model's implicit money demand function. The fourth is the efficiency condition for holding of nominal bonds, that is, the nominal Fisher equation in the text. The fifth is the efficiency condition for holding risky assets, such as the equities in our model.

The nature of the real demand for money implicit in these equations can be highlighted by combining the third and fourth equations to yield

$$\lambda_t \left(\frac{w_t}{c_t} h'\left(\frac{m_t}{c_t}\right) \right) = \beta E_t \left(\lambda_{t+1}(R_t^M - R_t) \frac{P_t}{P_{t+1}} \right).$$

We now turn to thinking about the limiting form of these equations that obtains when R_t^M approaches R_t; that is, the real cost of holding money goes to zero. Then the demand for money approaches

$$m_t = kc_t,$$

where k is a constant such that $h'(k) = 0$, which represents the satiation level of real cash balances.

Appendix B
Linearized Equations for Optimal Policy

This appendix contains the linearized equations of the model with optimal policy. For convenience we first reproduce the optimal policy problem. Then we list the first-order conditions in their true and linearized forms. In the linearized equations, $\hat{s}_t$ denotes the percentage deviation of s from its steady state value, whereas ds_t denotes the level deviation from steady state. Unsubscripted endogenous variables denote steady state values.

The Lagrangian for the optimal policy problem is

$$L = \sum_{t=0}^{\infty} \beta^t u(c_t, n_t, a_t)$$

$$+ \sum_{t=0}^{\infty} \beta^t \phi_t [x(c_{0,t}, c_t, n_t, a_t) + \beta x(c_{1,t+1}, c_{t+1}, n_{t+1}, a_{t+1})]$$

(B1)
$$+ \sum_{t=0}^{\infty} \beta^t \Lambda_t [c(c_{0,t}, c_{1,t}) - c_t]$$

$$+ \sum_{t=0}^{\infty} \beta^t \Omega_t (n_t - 0.5 n_{0,t} - 0.5 n_{1,t})$$

$$+ \sum_{t=0}^{\infty} \beta^t [\rho_{0,t}(a_t n_{0,t} - c_{0,t}) + \rho_{1,t}(a_t n_{1,t} - c_{1,t})].$$

The first-order conditions are as follows: for labor input at firms with prices set in periods t and $t - 1$

(B2) $\qquad 0 = \dfrac{\partial L}{\partial n_{j,t}} = \beta^j (\rho_{j,t} a_t - 0.5 \Omega_t) \qquad$ for $j = 0, 1,$

(B3) $\qquad\qquad 0 = \hat{a}_t + \hat{\rho}_{j,t} - \hat{\Omega}_t \qquad$ for $j = 0, 1;$

for consumption of goods with prices set in periods t and $t - 1$

(B4)
$$0 = \frac{\partial L}{\partial c_{j,t}} = \beta^t \left(\Lambda_t \frac{\partial c(c_{0,t}, c_{1,t})}{\partial c_{j,t}} - \rho_{j,t} + \phi_{t-j} \frac{\partial x(c_{j,t}, c_t, n_t, a_t)}{\partial c_{j,t}} \right)$$

$$\text{for } j = 0, 1,$$

(B5)
$$0 = \Lambda \left(0.5 \hat{\Lambda}_t + c \sum_{i=0}^{1} \frac{\partial^2 c(\cdot)}{\partial c_i \partial c_j} \hat{c}_{j,t} \right) - \rho_j \hat{\rho}_{j,t} + \frac{\partial x(\cdot)}{\partial c_j} d\phi_{t-j}$$

$$+ \phi \left(\frac{\partial^2 x(\cdot)}{\partial c_j^2} c \hat{c}_{j,t} + \frac{\partial^2 x(\cdot)}{\partial c_j \partial c} c \hat{c}_t + \frac{\partial^2 x(\cdot)}{\partial c_j \partial n} n \hat{n}_t + \frac{\partial^2 x(\cdot)}{\partial c_j \partial a} a \hat{a}_t \right);$$

for the consumption index

(B6) $\quad 0 = \dfrac{\partial L}{\partial c_t} = \beta^t \left(\dfrac{\partial u(c_t, n_t, a_t)}{\partial c_t} - \Lambda_t + \displaystyle\sum_{i=0}^{1} \phi_{t-j} \dfrac{\partial x(c_{it}, c_t, n_t, a_t)}{\partial c_t} \right),$

(B7)
$$0 = cU_{cc}\hat{c}_t + nU_{cn}\hat{n}_t + aU_{ca}\hat{a}_t - \Lambda\hat{\Lambda}_t + \frac{\partial x(\cdot)}{\partial c}\sum_{i=0}^{1} d\hat{\phi}_{t-i}$$

$$+ \phi c\sum_{i=0}^{1} \frac{\partial^2 x(\cdot)}{\partial c_i\partial c}\hat{c}_{i,t} + 2\phi\left(\frac{\partial^2 x(\cdot)}{\partial c^2}c\hat{c}_t + \frac{\partial^2 x(\cdot)}{\partial c\partial n}n\hat{n}_t + \frac{\partial^2 x(\cdot)}{\partial c\partial a}a\hat{a}_t\right);$$

and for total labor input

(B8) $$0 = \frac{\partial L}{\partial n_t} = \beta^t\left(\frac{\partial u(c_t,n_t,a_t)}{\partial n_t} + \Omega_t + \sum_{j=0}^{1}\phi_{t-j}\frac{\partial x(c_{j,t},c_t,n_t,a_t)}{\partial n_t}\right),$$

(B9)
$$0 = cU_{cn}\hat{c}_t + nU_{nn}\hat{n}_t + aU_{an}\hat{a}_t + \Omega\hat{\Omega}_t + \frac{\partial x(\cdot)}{\partial n}\sum_{i=0}^{1} d\hat{\phi}_{t-i}$$

$$+ \phi c\sum_{i=0}^{1} \frac{\partial^2 x(\cdot)}{\partial n\partial c_i}\hat{c}_{i,t} + 2\phi\left(\frac{\partial^2 x(\cdot)}{\partial n\partial c}c\hat{c}_t + \frac{\partial^2 x(\cdot)}{\partial n^2}n\hat{n}_t + \frac{\partial^2 x(\cdot)}{\partial n\partial a}a\hat{a}_t\right).$$

The constraints involve technology,

(B10) $$c_{j,t} = a_t n_{j,t} \quad \text{for } j = 0, 1,$$

(B11) $$0 = \hat{c}_{j,t} - \hat{a}_t - \hat{n}_t;$$

the consumption aggregator,

(B12) $$c_t = \left(\frac{1}{2}c_{0,t}^{(\epsilon-1)/\epsilon} + \frac{1}{2}c_{1,t}^{(\epsilon-1)/\epsilon}\right)^{\epsilon/(\epsilon-1)},$$

(B13) $$0 = -\hat{c}_t + \frac{1}{2}\sum_{i=0}^{1}\hat{c}_{i,t};$$

time,

(B14) $$\hat{n}_t = \frac{1}{2}n_{0,t} + \frac{1}{2}n_{1,t},$$

(B15) $$0 = -\hat{n}_t + \frac{1}{2}\sum_{i=0}^{1}\hat{n}_{i,t};$$

and optimal price setting

(B16) $$x(c_{0,t},c_t,n_t,a_t) + \beta x(c_{1,t+1},c_{t+1},n_{t+1},a_{t+1}) = 0,$$

(B17) $$0 = dx_{0,t} + \beta \cdot dx_{1,t+1}.$$

In these equations, $x(c_{i,t}, c_t, n_t, a_t)$ is the change in period t profits associated with a marginal price change in period $t - i$, assuming that the nominal price chosen in period $t - i$ is in effect in period t:

(B18) $$x(c_{j,t},c_t,n_t,a_t) \equiv \lambda_t c_t \left[(1 - \varepsilon)\left(\frac{c_{j,t}}{c_t}\right)^{1-1/\varepsilon} + \varepsilon\theta n_t^\gamma \frac{c_{j,t}}{c_t} \right],$$

(B19) $$dx_{j,t} = \lambda c[(1 - \varepsilon)(1 - 1/\varepsilon) + \varepsilon\theta n^\gamma](\hat{c}_{j,t} - \hat{c}_t) + \lambda c\gamma\varepsilon\theta n^\gamma \hat{n}_t;$$

and λ_t is the marginal utility of consumption:

(B20) $$\lambda_t \equiv \frac{\partial u(c_t,n_t,a_t)}{\partial c_t} = \left(c_t - \frac{a_t\theta}{1 + \gamma}n_t^{1+\gamma} \right)^{-1},$$

(B21) $$\hat{\lambda}_t = -\lambda c\hat{c}_t + a\theta\lambda n^{1+\gamma}\hat{n}_t + \frac{a\theta\lambda n^{1+\gamma}}{1 + \gamma}\hat{a}_t.$$

The above linearizations make use of the facts that in steady state, $\partial x(\cdot)/\partial a = 0$ and $\partial c(\cdot)/\partial c_j = 0.5$.

References

Aiyagari, S. Rao, and R. Anton Braun. 1997. Some models to guide the Fed. *Carnegie-Rochester Conference Series on Public Policy* 48 (1): 1–42.

Ball, Laurence. 1994. Credible disinflation with staggered price setting. *American Economic Review* 84:282–89.

———. 1995. Disinflation with imperfect credibility. *Journal of Monetary Economics* 35:5–23.

Ball, Laurence, and David Romer. Real rigidities and the non-neutrality of money. *Review of Economic Studies* 57:183–203.

Barro, Robert J., and David B. Gordon. 1983. Rules, discretion and reputation in a model of monetary policy. *Journal of Monetary Economics* 12:101–21.

Bassetto, M. 1997. Optimal taxation with heterogeneous agents. Chicago: University of Chicago, November. Manuscript.

Blanchard, O. J., and N. Kiyotaki. 1987. Monopolistic competition and the effects of aggregate demand. *American Economic Review* 77 (September): 647–66.

Calvo, Guillermo A. 1983. Staggered prices in a utility-maximizing framework. *Journal of Monetary Economics* 12:383–98.

Chamley, Christophe. 1986. Optimal taxation of capital income in general equilibrium with infinite lives. *Econometrica* 54:607–22.

Chari, V. V., Lawrence J. Christiano, and Patrick Kehoe. 1991. Optimal fiscal and monetary policy, some recent results. *Journal of Money, Credit and Banking* 23:519–40.

Chari, V. V., Patrick J. Kehoe, and Ellen R. McGrattan. 1996. Sticky price models of the business cycle: Can the contract multiplier solve the persistence problem? Research Department Staff Report no. 217. Minneapolis: Federal Reserve Bank of Minneapolis.

Dixit, Avinash, and Joseph Stiglitz. 1977. Monopolistic competition and optimum product diversity. *American Economic Review* 67:297–308.

Dotsey, Michael, Robert G. King, and Alexander L. Wolman. 1997. Staggered price-setting and elastic factor supply. Manuscript.

―――. Forthcoming. State dependent pricing and the general equilibrium dynamics of money and output. *Quarterly Journal of Economics.*

Goodfriend, Marvin S., and Robert G. King. 1997. The new neoclassical synthesis and the role of monetary policy. In *NBER macroeconomics annual 1997*, Ben Bernanke and Julio Rotemberg, 231–82. Cambridge, Mass.: MIT Press.

Ireland, Peter N. 1995. Optimal disinflationary paths. *Journal of Economic Dynamics and Control* 19:1429–48.

―――. 1996. The role of countercyclical monetary policy. *Journal of Political Economy* 104:704–23.

―――. 1997. Sustainable monetary policies. *Journal of Economic Dynamics and Control* 22:87–108.

Jeanne, Olivier. 1998. Generating real persistent effects of monetary shocks: How much nominal rigidity do we really need? *European Economic Review* 42 (6): 1009–32.

Judd, Kenneth. 1985. Redistributive taxation in a simple perfect foresight model. *Journal of Public Economics* 28:59–83.

Kimball, Miles S. 1995. The quantitative analytics of the basic neomonetarist model. *Journal of Money, Credit and Banking* 27:1241–77.

King, Robert G., and Alexander L. Wolman. 1996. Inflation targeting in a St. Louis model of the 21st century. *Federal Reserve Bank of St. Louis Review* 78:83–107.

Kydland, Finn, and Edward C. Prescott. 1977. Rules rather than discretion: The inconsistency of optimal plans. *Journal of Political Economy* 85:473–91.

―――. 1980. Dynamic optimal taxation, rational expectations and optimal control. *Journal of Economic Dynamics and Control* 2:79–91.

Levin, Andrew. 1991. The macroeconomic significance of nominal wage contract duration. Discussion Paper no. 91–08. San Diego: University of California.

Lucas, Robert E., Jr., and Nancy L. Stokey. 1983. Optimal fiscal and monetary policy in an economy without capital. *Journal of Monetary Economics* 12:55–93.

Mankiw, N. Gregory. 1990. A quick refresher course in macroeconomics. *Journal of Economic Literature* 38:1645–60.

McCallum, Bennett T. 1997. Issues in the design of monetary policy rules. NBER Working Paper no. 6016. Cambridge, Mass.: National Bureau of Economic Research. (In *Handbook of macroeconomics*, ed. John B. Taylor and Michael Woodford. Amsterdam: North Holland, forthcoming.)

Romer, David. 1993. The New Keynesian synthesis. *Journal of Economic Perspectives* 7:5–22.

Rotemberg, Julio J. 1982. Sticky prices in the United States. *Journal of Political Economy* 90:1187–1211.

―――. 1987. The new Keynesian microfoundations. In *NBER macroeconomics annual 1987*, ed. Olivier Blanchard and Stanley Fischer, 63–129. Cambridge, Mass.: MIT Press.

Rotemberg, Julio J., and Michael Woodford. 1997. An optimization-based econometric framework for the evaluation of monetary policy. In *NBER macroeconomics annual 1997*, ed. Ben Bernanke and Julio Rotemberg, 297–345. Cambridge, Mass.: MIT Press.

Stokey, Nancy L., and Robert E. Lucas Jr., with Edward C. Prescott. 1989. *Recursive methods in economic dynamics.* Cambridge, Mass.: Harvard University Press.

Taylor, John B. 1980. Aggregate dynamics and staggered contracts. *Journal of Political Economy* 88:1–24.

―――. 1993. Discretion versus policy rules in practice. *Carnegie-Rochester Conference Series on Public Policy* 39:195–214.

Tobin, James. 1977. How dead is Keynes? *Economic Inquiry* 15:459–68.

Wolman, Alexander L. 1997. Zero inflation and the Friedman rule: A welfare comparison. *Federal Reserve Bank of Richmond Economic Quarterly* 83:1–21.

Woodford, Michael. 1995. Comment on "The quantitative analytics of the basic neo-monetarist model." *Journal of Money, Credit and Banking* 27:1278–89.
Yun, Tack. 1994. Optimal fiscal and monetary policy in an economy with nominal price rigidity. Chapter in Ph.D. diss., University of Chicago.
————. 1996. Nominal price rigidity, money supply endogeneity, and business cycles. *Journal of Monetary Economics* 37:345–70.

Comment   Benjamin M. Friedman

Robert King and Alexander Wolman have written a highly appropriate paper for a conference on monetary policy rules. Their paper usefully anchors, both methodologically and substantively, one end of the intellectual spectrum under debate here. King and Wolman argue rigorously for a rigorous rule of price stability. Their paper is sharp and clear on both counts. The monetary policy rule that they find optimal in the model they present differs from many of the "rules" considered in other papers at this conference in that (1) it is a genuine *rule,* the effects of which center on credible commitment by the central bank, not merely an indicative guide or "rule of thumb," and (2) it focuses on stabilization of prices, to the exclusion of any direct concern for smoothing output, interest rates, or other variables.

Moreover, the paper is forthright—comprehensively so—about the limitations inherent in the framework of analysis it deploys. As a result, a perfectly accurate response to many of my remarks as discussant would be "We know that, and in fact on page such and such we talked about that issue ourselves." But while that response would be true, it would miss the point. Being forthright about a model's limitations does not render them without force. In my comments on the paper I shall first explain why I find the authors' case for a price stability rule unpersuasive, then discuss several features of the underlying model that merit attention even though they do not bear centrally on the paper's basic recommendation, and finally step aside from the paper as a whole to pose two somewhat more general questions about a price stability rule for monetary policy.

Why the Paper's Case for a Price Stability Rule Is Unpersuasive

The analysis that King and Wolman carry out in this paper is impressive and serious. The model that they construct embodies many useful properties—not least an explicit recognition that prices are sticky and a real attempt to represent, internally, the monopolistically competitive process that makes them so. (The model also renders the inflation rate persistent.) Nevertheless, I do not recognize in their model the key features of the actual monetary policy envi-

Benjamin M. Friedman is the William Joseph Maier Professor of Political Economy at Harvard University and a research associate of the National Bureau of Economic Research.

ronment that lead me to believe that a strict price stability rule would be a poor way to conduct monetary policy. There are three main reasons.

First, the central bank in the world of King and Wolman's paper anticipates and understands all shocks. (In fact, King and Wolman consider only one kind of shock, a simultaneous shock to preferences and productivity, but that is another matter.) Much of what makes monetary policy making hard, with or without a rule, is precisely that central bankers cannot know that a shock is coming in advance, and once it occurs they usually do not know just what kind of shock it is. In the specific context of price stability, the hard questions that therefore arise are whether, and if so, when and how, to return to a preestablished price path, once the economy is knocked off of it. Here that never happens. Because policymakers can anticipate each shock, and act as it occurs, the aggregate price level never gets knocked off of its stable trajectory in the first place.

Second, while prices in the King-Wolman model are sticky, nominal wages are not. As a result, when a productivity shock occurs, not only is there no impediment to reaching supply-equals-demand equilibrium in the labor market, but workers and firms can reach the market-clearing real wage with *any* price level that the central bank chooses to set. (In King and Wolman's model the productivity shock that shifts labor demand also shifts labor supply in an exactly offsetting way, and so the quantity of labor input remains unaffected, but the real wage does have to move.) This structure is exactly the opposite of the more familiar story in which *nominal wages* are sticky, and part of the job of monetary policy is to use *price level* adjustment to move the real wage toward its postshock market-clearing value. King and Wolman take pains to analyze carefully the real implications, in their monopolistic competition setting, of relative prices on different goods being out of line. By contrast, what seems to me an even more important relative price—the real wage—is, by assumption, never out of line.

Third, King and Wolman never explicitly show the value of commitment to the price stability rule they espouse. In a brief but much to the point section of the paper, they do show that "there are temptations for the monetary authority to deviate from this plan," and that if a shock arises that is "unexpected and viewed as never to recur," the optimal one-shot response is "a burst of inflation" that raises output. But what is the *cost* of this departure from price stability? Barro and Gordon (1983), in their paper that did much to stimulate interest in commitment to a monetary policy rule, used a simple model of reputation effects to address this question. King and Wolman show that the temptation is large but then leave the matter at that.

Further Peculiarities of the Model and Its Use

In addition to the flexibility of money wages, the odd (but here rather harmless) assumption that productivity shocks exactly mirror shocks to individuals' labor-leisure preferences, and the absence of any shocks at all to either money demand or real aggregate demand, two further aspects of King and Wolman's analysis merit specific comment. Neither is central to their principal argument, but in light of the focus of this conference each bears attention.

First, the argument made here for a stable price path with *zero* inflation, as opposed to a price path with a modest upward tilt, amounts to turning Feldstein's (1979) familiar argument on its head. In King and Wolman's model, the long-run average inflation rate matters in two ways. Relative price distortions, which are strictly welfare reducing because they lead to suboptimal allocations among different consumption goods, are eliminated by *zero* inflation. But the distortion due to firms' average markup of price over production cost, which is also welfare reducing in that it depresses aggregate output, is minimized not at zero inflation but at an inflation rate that is small but *positive*. Not surprisingly, King and Wolman find that for reasonable parameter values the relative price distortion is quantitatively unimportant. Why, then, doesn't the optimal price trajectory slope upward at the rate that minimizes the welfare loss due to the markup?

Their answer is a reverse Feldstein argument: Suppose that the economy is already at the markup-minimizing positive inflation rate. Because of the staggered price setting that underlies the stickiness of prices, a preannounced transition to lower inflation—say, zero—temporarily *raises* output. In the new state of zero inflation that prevails after the transition, the average markup is permanently higher, and therefore output and consumption are permanently lower. But, King and Wolman argue, the fact that this permanent reduction of output occurs only in the future, while the surge of output associated with the transition happens immediately, means that expected utility, appropriately discounted over the infinite future, is enhanced.

It is not clear how they can make this call without knowing the magnitudes of the temporary output increase and the permanent output reduction, the specific discount rate, and so on. Most obviously, in the limit as the discount rate goes to zero, *no* temporary increase in output, no matter how large, can offset the utility-reducing effect of even a small permanent reduction of output thereafter. Moreover, by analogy with what Feldstein has argued, taking into account that the larger permanent average markup and therefore the smaller permanent average output will occur in a growing economy would further bias the answer toward simply keeping inflation at the positive rate that minimizes the markup. But at the least, a reader familiar with Feldstein's (1979) paper will find the logic here familiar, albeit with the crucial signs reversed. Ironically, in King and Wolman's setting, applying Feldstein's logic with *Feldstein's* signs would mean that the King-Wolman model resembles the recent analysis by Akerlof, Dickens, and Perry (1996) in providing an argument that a low but positive long-run inflation rate is preferable to zero in that it minimizes output-depressing distortions.

One additional feature of King and Wolman's analysis merits specific comment. Although they never write down a money demand function, or provide much other detail about the nature of asset markets in their model, they do assume that people must hold money to buy consumption goods and that the nonmoney asset is an equity security. They choose to disregard the familiar welfare loss associated with "triangles under the money demand function," however, on the ground that nowadays most of what people use as money bears a "competitive return." I certainly sympathize with the view that, at least at the inflation rates that seem relevant in most western industrialized countries today, the money demand triangles that over the years have been such an obsession in much of welfare theoretic analysis of monetary policy are uninteresting.

But if the story here is not just that this matter is too small to bother with, but rather that money bears a "competitive return" in the sense that the return on money equals the return on the alternative asset, that leaves open the question of what determines how much money people hold. Because much of King and Wolman's analysis of monetary policy begins with the central bank's varying money supply, presumably a well-behaved money *demand,* however derived, must in the end be integral to their story.

Further Thoughts on a Stable Price Rule for Monetary Policy

I shall conclude with two somewhat broader questions about the rationale and the design of a stable price rule for monetary policy.

First, on the rationale: Does anybody still think time inconsistency is a problem that needs solving in the monetary policy of the world's major economies? Two decades ago, when high and rising inflation rates stood out as the chief economic problem in the majority of industrialized countries, it was at least plausible—though even then hardly a sure thing—to suggest that this inflation was a consequence of a policy-making framework based on discretionary actions by the central bank. If so, then the gain from restricting that discretion was potentially large. But by now most industrialized countries have succeeded in slowing their inflation to very low levels, indeed approximately zero for practical purposes in some countries. More to the point, many countries, including in particular the United States, have done so under formal policy-making institutions no different from what they had before. Even some of the countries that have introduced formal inflation targets (and that is not always the same as a genuine, committed policy rule) have done so only *after* achieving the crucial turnaround in their inflation problems.

This is not to say that the analysis of time inconsistency by Kydland and Prescott (1977), Barro and Gordon (1983), and others was logically wrong. But I believe it shows that it *was* wrong to conclude from that analysis that committing the central bank to a monetary policy rule was required to resolve the time-inconsistency problem. Maybe, as Barro and Gordon themselves suggested, the central bank's own awareness of reputation effects has provided the solution. Perhaps, following Rogoff (1985), the appointment of "conservative" central bankers has been the answer. There remains much room for research and debate about how different industrialized countries have solved their respective inflation problems. But the fact remains that most have done so. Before seriously considering committing monetary policy to a price stability rule, therefore—or, for that matter, any other rule—we ought at least to know what is the problem that commitment to a rule is supposed to solve. High inflation due to time inconsistency is no longer a satisfactory answer.

Last, a question about the design of a price stability rule if there were to be one: I conjecture that, especially in the United States, there is a trade-off between adhering to a genuine long-run price-targeting path, in the sense that bygones are *not* bygones and departures from the path *are* corrected (and in contrast to a strategy that accepts past mistakes and therefore under which the price level has infinite long-run variance), and aiming at a price path with zero slope. In other words, monetary policy can eliminate price level "base drift," or it can aim at zero inflation, but it cannot do both.

The reason is that, unlike in King and Wolman's model, actual central banks cannot anticipate all disturbances, and so from time to time the actual price level will depart from whatever is the targeted trajectory. Some of those departures will be on the low side, some on the high side. But whenever actual prices are above the targeted path, if that path is horizontal then returning to it requires that prices fall absolutely. By contrast, if the specified path is upward sloping—for example, at 2.5 percent per annum as in the case of the Bank of England's target—returning to it simply requires that for a while prices increase less rapidly than the path does, or perhaps even remain unchanged.

Would the Federal Reserve, as a part of its publicly announced policy strategy, deliberately seek falling prices? Should it do so? Unless the answers to these questions are yes—and I doubt that they are—then the most that monetary policy can do with respect to prices and inflation is either aim at a horizontal price path but let bygones be bygones (especially on the upside), or hold to a long-run price path without base drift but do so for a path with upward slope.

References

Akerlof, George, William T. Dickens, and George L. Perry. 1996. The macroeconomics of low inflation. *Brookings Papers on Economic Activity,* no. 1:1–59.
Barro, Robert J., and David B. Gordon. 1983. Discretion and reputation in a model of monetary policy. *Journal of Monetary Economics* 12 (July): 101–21.
Feldstein, Martin S. 1979. The welfare cost of permanent inflation and optimal short-run economic policy. *Journal of Political Economy* 87 (August): 749–68.
Kydland, Finn E., and Edward C. Prescott. 1977. Rules rather than discretion: The inconsistency of optimal plans. *Journal of Political Economy* 85 (June): 473–91.
Rogoff, Kenneth. 1985. The optimal degree of commitment to an intermediate monetary target. *Quarterly Journal of Economics* 100 (November): 1169–89.

Discussion Summary

Frederic Mishkin strongly disagreed with Friedman and made three points on why time consistency might not work in the future. First, the Federal Reserve has an excellent chairman at the moment and an Open Market Committee (FOMC) that does understand policy. Second, the administration has been very supportive of the Federal Reserve, even when it raises interest rates. Third, the economy has had very favorable shocks, which means that the political pressure on the Federal Reserve has not been as severe as it could have been with less favorable supply shocks. Part of what has happened is that central banks have dealt with time inconsistency by being more transparent, by making themselves more accountable, and by being more explicit about numerical inflation goals. *Friedman* replied that there was no disagreement since Mishkin just said that central banks are handling their problems on their own and do not need a rule to which to commit. *Tom Sargent* asked Friedman what he meant by "they are handling it on their own." The paper is sharp in its definition of the game that is being played. "Handling it on their own" sounds as if Friedman was predicting the same outcome from a different game, in which both sides choose sequentially. In this model, however, the outcome will not be the same and the appeal to reputation is not going to help for reasons isolated by Chari, Christiano, and Kehoe (1996). *Bob Hall* remarked that Kydland and Prescott (1977) and Barro and Gordon (1983) are must-reads for central bankers everywhere in the world. *Lars Svensson* also cautioned that these time-inconsistency issues should not be dismissed easily. Ten years ago, time-consistency issues were still very relevant in countries other than the United States. *William Poole* also noted that there was no inflation problem in 1963 and many members of the profession ridiculed the Eisenhower administration's 1950s campaign against "creeping inflation." Everything that Ben Friedman just said had already been said back in 1963.

Svensson wondered about the absence of any mechanism that would make it possible for the central bank to be committed to its rule. *Robert King* suggested that one answer to this question is that this might be a rule formulated outside the central bank, such as a law passed by U.S. Congress. *Ben McCallum* remarked that the discussion about the desirability of a monetary policy rule passed by Congress is tricky. McCallum's view on this issue is that a rule, mandating inflation to be the Federal Reserve's primary objective, passed by Congress, would make the Fed more independent.

Michael Woodford noted that in his paper with Rotemberg the first best solution also involves complete price stability. Achieving that first best may involve driving the nominal interest negative, which leads to a trade-off between price level and interest rate stabilization in order to have low average inflation consistent with the zero nominal interest rate bound. In this framework, some kinds of real shocks to aggregate demand can be easily added to the model without changing the results, such as government spending shocks, stochastic shocks to the rate of time preference, or changing preferences over consumption versus saving in the private sector. With these real shocks, the first-best equilibrium is still stable prices that undo the distortions associated with the reasons for price stickiness. Introducing nominal wage inflexibility does change the conclusion. If the relevant nominal inflexibility was in wages, complete nominal wage stability would probably be first best undoing that distortion, meaning that in response to a technology shock the price level would move. In particular, with a negative supply shock prices should be allowed to go up, but only by a certain amount once. So there will not be persistent inflation, which is quite different from the monetary policy responses to supply shocks in the 1970s.

Robert King broadly agreed with the comments made by Friedman about the sensitivity of the price-level-targeting result to the nature of nominal rigidities. But he argued that the methods of the paper should be applied to models with alternative nominal rigidities, such as sticky wages, to determine the extent of such policy sensitivity.

On the time-consistency issue, King made the observation that there was uncertainty about whether Alan Greenspan would continue as chairman of the Federal Reserve or would be replaced by a new chairman who was less concerned with low inflation. During the intense public discussion of this topic, the long rate of interest went up 100 basis points, indicating that the time-inconsistency issue was still unresolved.

References

Barro, Robert J., and David B. Gordon. 1983. Rules, discretion and reputation in a model of monetary policy. *Journal of Monetary Economics* 12 (1): 101–21.
Chari, V. V., Lawrence J. Christiano, and Patrick J. Kehoe. 1996. Optimality of the Friedman rule in economies with distorting taxes. *Journal of Monetary Economics* 37 (2): 203–23.
Kydland, Finn E., and Edward C. Prescott. 1977. Rules rather than discretion: The inconsistency of optimal plans. *Journal of Political Economy* 85 (3): 473–91.

9   Rethinking the Role of NAIRU in Monetary Policy: Implications of Model Formulation and Uncertainty

Arturo Estrella and Frederic S. Mishkin

9.1   Introduction

Because the effects of monetary policy on the aggregate economy have long lags, monetary policy must necessarily be preemptive; that is, it must act well before inflation starts to rise.[1] This, of course, is easier said than done. In order to act preemptively, monetary policymakers must have signals that help them forecast future changes in inflation. One such signal that has received substantial attention both in the academic literature and in the press is the gap between unemployment and NAIRU, the nonaccelerating inflation rate of unemployment.[2] In other words, NAIRU is the unemployment rate at which inflation is expected to neither increase or decrease.

The NAIRU concept has come under quite serious attack in recent years. In the early to mid-1990s, the common view in the economics profession was that NAIRU in the United States was around 6 percent. However, when the un-

Arturo Estrella is senior vice president of the Research and Market Analysis Group of the Federal Reserve Bank of New York and a member of the Research Task Force of the Basle Committee on Banking Supervision. Frederic S. Mishkin is the A. Barton Hepburn Professor of Economics at the Graduate School of Business, Columbia University, and a research associate of the National Bureau of Economic Research.

The authors thank participants at the conference and at seminars at the Federal Reserve Bank of New York and Columbia University for their helpful comments, and Elizabeth Reynolds for excellent research assistance. The views expressed in this paper are those of the authors and do not necessarily represent those of the Federal Reserve Bank of New York, the Federal Reserve System, Columbia University, or the National Bureau of Economic Research.

1. If price stability has already been achieved, then inflation falling below its target is every bit as damaging as a rise in inflation above the target. Thus, in this situation, monetary policy must also be just as preemptive against declines in inflation below target levels.

2. See, e.g., Stiglitz (1997), Gordon (1997), Staiger, Stock, and Watson (1997a, 1997b), and Council of Economic Advisers (1997, 45–54). For a history of NAIRU, see Espinosa-Vega and Russell (1997). The NAIRU acronym would better be expressed as NIIRU (the nonincreasing inflation rate of unemployment) because it is the unemployment rate at which inflation is expected to neither increase or decrease.

employment rate began to fall below 6 percent in 1995 and remained well below that level thereafter without any increase in inflation—indeed inflation actually fell—concern arose that the NAIRU concept might be seriously flawed. In addition, recent academic research has shown that there is great uncertainty in the estimates of NAIRU (e.g., Staiger et al. 1997a, 1997b), suggesting that looking at the unemployment rate relative to NAIRU might not be a very helpful guide for monetary policy.

In this paper, we rethink the NAIRU concept and examine whether NAIRU might have a useful role in monetary policy making. We argue that the answer is yes. However, the positive answer depends critically on redefining NAIRU very carefully and distinguishing it from a long-run concept like the natural rate of unemployment, something that is not typically done in the literature. Furthermore, as we will see, the view that the NAIRU concept implies that the monetary authorities should try to move the economy toward the NAIRU, thus to some extent treating it as a target, is both incorrect and misguided.

The first step in our analysis, in section 9.2, is to think about defining NAIRU in the context of setting monetary policy instruments. We adopt a definition that focuses on NAIRU as a reference point for monetary policy and show that our definition of NAIRU is a short-run concept and is not the same as the natural rate of unemployment. Understanding that short-run NAIRU and the natural rate of unemployment differ is important, not only for the theoretical analysis to follow, but also because it suggests that short-run NAIRU is likely to be highly variable, in contrast to the natural rate of unemployment. One immediate implication is that thinking of NAIRU as a level at which the unemployment rate should settle is not very useful for policy purposes.

Our approach to the construction of short-run NAIRU is fairly general. Although we define this concept in the context of a particular model of inflation that is adapted from the current literature, the same approach can be applied to any predictive model of inflation in which unemployment plays an important role.

Once we have defined short-run NAIRU, we then go on to examine how it might be used in policy making. We do this in several steps. First, we look in section 9.3 at the certainty-equivalent case, when only inflation enters the policymakers' objective function and then when unemployment (or equivalently, output) as well as inflation are part of policymakers' objectives. Although the certainty-equivalent case is useful as a starting point for the analysis, we cannot stop here because several sources of uncertainty have important implications for how monetary policy should be conducted. In addition to uncertainty about estimates of the actual value of NAIRU, there is uncertainty about the estimated parameters of the model, especially the parameters that measure the effect of the NAIRU gap on inflation and the impact of monetary policy instruments on the NAIRU gap. We examine in section 9.4 what effect these sources of uncertainty have on how short-run NAIRU might be used in monetary policy making, again under the pure price stability objective and then when unemployment as well as inflation enter the policymakers' objective function.

Our theoretical analysis shows that uncertainty about the level of short-run NAIRU does not necessarily imply that monetary policy should react less to the NAIRU gap. However, uncertainty about the effect of the NAIRU gap on inflation does require an adjustment to the reference point for monetary tightening in terms of the level of unemployment and to the weight applied to the gap between actual and target inflation. Furthermore, as in Brainard (1967), uncertainty about the effect of the monetary policy instrument on the NAIRU gap reduces the magnitude of the policy response.

There is another sense in which uncertainty about NAIRU may have an effect on policy. There may be uncertainty not just about the level of NAIRU or its effect but about the way it is modeled: the exact form of the model specification may be unknown. Errors in model selection may result in excess uncertainty regarding both inflation forecasts and the parameters of the model. Thus model selection has the potential to increase uncertainty about the effect of the NAIRU gap and to reduce the effectiveness of policy, and the magnitude of this problem may be more difficult to determine than that of simple parameter uncertainty. In section 9.5, we focus on the losses associated with leaving out key information from the model.

Although our theoretical framework shows the qualitative effects of uncertainty on how monetary policy should be conducted, it cannot tell us whether these effects are economically important. To examine this question, we estimate in section 9.6 a simple NAIRU gap model for the United States to obtain quantitative measures of uncertainty and to assess how these measures affect our view of the optimal reaction of monetary policy to movements in unemployment relative to short-run NAIRU. Using an analogous model based on monthly data, we then examine how in practice the short-run NAIRU concept could be used in the actual conduct of monetary policy. The estimated models provide us with measures of short-run NAIRU that indicate that it is highly variable, suggesting that trying to drive the unemployment rate toward NAIRU, whether it is a short-run or a long-run concept, would be an inappropriate way to think about how monetary policy should be conducted. In particular, we use our analysis to evaluate whether the setting of monetary policy instruments in the face of rapidly falling unemployment rates in recent years makes sense.

9.2   Defining Short-Run NAIRU: Why It Differs from the Natural Rate of Unemployment

The concept of the natural rate of unemployment was first developed by Friedman (1968) and Phelps (1968) to argue that there would be no long-run trade-off between unemployment and inflation. The natural rate of unemployment is defined as the level of unemployment to which the economy would converge in the long run in the absence of structural changes to the labor market. An implication of this definition is that expansionary monetary policy that leads to higher inflation would not be able to produce lower unemployment on average. Indeed, as mentioned in Friedman (1968), higher inflation might even have the opposite effect of raising unemployment in the long run because it would interfere with efficient functioning of labor markets. The concept of a natural rate of unemployment leads to the following characterization of an expectations-augmented Phillips curve:

$$\pi_t = \pi_t^e + \beta(L)(u_t - \bar{u}_t) + \delta' z_t + \varepsilon_t,$$

where

π_t = inflation rate from $t - 1$ to t
π_t^e = inflation rate expected at $t - 1$
u_t = unemployment rate at time t
$\bar{u}_t$ = natural rate of unemployment at time t, which could be a constant but could shift with structural changes in the economy
z_t = a vector of variables such as supply shocks, which have zero ex ante expectation
ε_t = an unspecified disturbance term

In order to estimate this expectations-augmented Phillips curve, researchers typically assume that the expected inflation can be measured as a distributed lag on past inflation and other variables, and that the inflation rate is integrated of order one, so that $\Delta\pi_t$ is stationary. The resulting Phillips curve is then

$$(1) \qquad \Delta\pi_t = \beta(L)(u_t - \bar{u}_t) + \gamma(L)\Delta\pi_{t-1} + \delta' z_t + \varepsilon_t.$$

The NAIRU concept was first developed in a paper by Modigliani and Papademos (1975) and is defined as the rate of unemployment at which there is no tendency for inflation to increase or decrease. In empirical work such as Staiger et al. (1997a, 1997b) and Gordon (1997), NAIRU is viewed as being equivalent to the natural rate of unemployment, $\bar{u}_t$, in equation (1) and is typically estimated by assuming that $\bar{u}_t$ is a constant, a random walk, or a linear transformation of some step function or spline.[3]

For policy purposes, equation (1) indicates that it is perfectly appropriate to think about the unemployment gap, $u_t - \bar{u}_t$, as one determinant of changes in the rate of inflation, recognizing that other factors, represented by the past history of inflation and the z_t variables, also affect the inflation process. However, current unemployment is frequently compared with the estimated value of NAIRU, and the resulting NAIRU gap is taken to be an indicator of inflationary pressure. Under a strong form of this view, if policymakers wish to drive inflation down, they need to raise the unemployment level above NAIRU,

3. See, e.g., Staiger et al. (1997a).

whereas if inflation is at its desired level, monetary policy needs to keep unemployment from falling below NAIRU.

Policy discussions, therefore, frequently focus on the difference between the current level of unemployment and NAIRU as estimated above, in other words, on the variable that enters the first term of equation (1) in a distributed lag. This implicit comparison has the advantage of simplicity: it focuses the discussion on a single indicator of inflationary pressure, the unemployment gap, that we know from the model should be zero in long-run equilibrium. However, this advantage is overwhelmed by a number of serious problems associated with this procedure.

First, monetary policy does not generally focus only on long-run equilibrium, so the gap as defined above may be of limited usefulness. Second, even if equation (1) is viewed as a short-run forecasting equation, the dependent variable is contemporaneous monthly or quarterly inflation, which is quite unlikely to be the policy target in practice. Third, the current unemployment gap is only one of many explanatory variables in the equation, including several lags of the gap itself. Focusing on only one variable gives an incomplete picture. Fourth, the equation may not even represent the optimal forecast of inflation, since other potentially important variables may be omitted.

Finally, focusing on the unemployment gap may create the impression that the goal of policy is to drive unemployment toward NAIRU as a target level. As equation (1) illustrates, the current unemployment gap, $u_t - \bar{u}_t$, is only one of many explanatory variables in the Phillips curve equation. The presence of lags of $\Delta \pi$ in the equation suggests that inflation may decelerate because expected inflation is falling, even if the unemployment rate is below the natural rate of unemployment. Similarly, if there have been favorable supply shocks, inflation in the future may decelerate even though the unemployment rate is well below the natural rate. The presence of lags of the unemployment gap suggests complicated dynamics in which a current negative unemployment rate could also be associated with decelerating inflation. The presence of many other variables besides the current unemployment gap in the expectations-augmented Phillips curve equation therefore implies that the unemployment rate at which there is no tendency for inflation to rise or fall over the policy horizon can be quite different from the natural rate of unemployment, $\bar{u}_t$. In other words, it can be quite misleading to focus on NAIRU, as an estimate in equation (1) of the natural rate of unemployment, because it is not clear that the introduction of policy shocks designed to drive unemployment toward this characterization of NAIRU will do anything to control inflation either in the short run or in the long run.

Therefore, we propose an alternative way of thinking about NAIRU as a reference point for unemployment that reflects inflationary pressures over the short- or intermediate-run policy horizon. The key idea is that the reference point for unemployment at which inflation will neither increase nor decrease over the relevant policy horizon, which can be thought of as a short-run

NAIRU, embodies not only $\bar{u}_t$, the natural rate of unemployment, but also the other variables that help predict inflation. In other words, we would like to express the change in inflation over the relevant policy horizon as a function of $u_t - n_t$, where n_t is an appropriately constructed short-run NAIRU.

Thus suppose that the policy horizon for inflation is from j to $j + k$ months ahead and define

$$\Delta\pi_t^{(j,k)} = (1200/k) \log(p_{t+j+k}/p_{t+j}) - 100 \log(p_t/p_{t-12})$$

as the difference between current annual inflation and inflation over the policy horizon, where p_t is the price level in month t. We then construct equation (2):

(2) $\Delta\pi_t^{(j,k)} = \alpha + \beta(L)u_t + \gamma(L)\Delta\pi_t + \delta'x_t + \varepsilon_t,$

which is similar to equation (1), save for the dependent variable and the inclusion of a vector x that contains any predetermined variables that help predict inflation at the targeted horizon.[4]

In order to express the change in inflation as a function of the difference between unemployment and a short-run NAIRU, equation (2) can always be rewritten as

(3) $\Delta\pi_t^{(j,k)} = \beta_0(u_t - n_t) + \varepsilon_t$

with

(4)
$$n_t = \text{short-run NAIRU}$$
$$= -[\alpha + (\beta(L) - \beta(0))u_t + \gamma(L)\Delta\pi_t + \delta'x_t]/\beta(0),$$

where all the predictive power of the equation has been subsumed in the short-run NAIRU n_t. This short-run NAIRU is not an estimate of the long-run equilibrium natural rate, but a reference rate that represents the level of current unemployment that would correspond to a forecast of no inflation change over the policy horizon.[5] Another important point that immediately falls out of this equation is that since short-run NAIRU is related to past lags of unemployment, inflation, and any other variables that help forecast changes in inflation, short-run NAIRU may undergo substantial fluctuations even if the natural rate of unemployment is a constant.

Equation (3) has several important advantages over equation (1). In contrast

---

4. The variable x differs from z in the Gordon (1997) and Staiger et al. (1997a, 1997b) equations in that z represents primarily supply shocks that are contemporaneous with the dependent variable, whereas x is more general in that it includes any predetermined variables other than unemployment and inflation (and their lags) that help predict future inflation.

5. Eq. (4) is a generalization of the model of short-run NAIRU in Estrella (1997). After writing this paper, we discovered that Layard and Bean (1988) also have a similar definition of short-run NAIRU in the context of a one-period change in inflation.

to the conventional equation, the dependent variable in equation (3) is the change in inflation over the target horizon. Second, the current NAIRU gap, $u_t - n_t$, is the only explanatory variable in the equation and it subsumes all the predictive power of the equation. Third, the equation provides an optimal forecast of targeted inflation, given current information.

We note, however, that our approach to short-run NAIRU is fairly general and is largely independent of the particular form of equation (3). The definition of short-run NAIRU in equation (4) simply collects all the systematic terms in equation (3), other that the current rate of unemployment. Hence, this technique is applicable to any forecasting equation for $\Delta\pi_t^{(j,k)}$, as long as the current unemployment rate u_t enters significantly in the equation.[6]

The analysis of this paper will focus on equations (2) and (3) and on our corresponding definition of short-run NAIRU. For the purposes of theoretical analysis, we use a simplified version of these equations with a limited lag structure. We return to the more general specification, however, when we consider empirical estimates using monthly data in section 9.6.

9.3   The Role of NAIRU in Policy Making: The Certainty-Equivalent Case

9.3.1   Objective Function with Inflation Only

For the theoretical analysis, we start with a simple joint model of unemployment and inflation that is isomorphic to the one employed by Svensson (1997) with an output gap. In addition to inflation π and an unemployment gap $\tilde{u}$, the model contains an exogenous variable x and a monetary policy control variable r. This model will be the basis for the next few sections of the paper. However, some specific assumptions will be adjusted in subsequent sections in order to address particular issues. Assume for the purposes of this section that the parameters of the model are known with certainty.

$$(5) \qquad \pi_t = \pi_{t-1} - a_1\tilde{u}_{t-1} + a_3 x_{t-1} + \varepsilon_t,$$

$$(6) \qquad \tilde{u}_t = b_1\tilde{u}_{t-1} + b_2 r_{t-1} + b_3 x_{t-1} + \eta_t,$$

$$(7) \qquad x_t = c_3 x_{t-1} + \nu_t,$$

where $\tilde{u}_t = u_t - \bar{u}$ and r_t is the monetary policy variable. Equation (5) is a dynamic Phillips curve in which both unemployment and x are predictors of inflation one period ahead, say a year. Equation (6) is an IS curve, and equation (7) defines the dynamics of the exogenous variable x. The equilibrium level of

---

6. In eq. (2), we think of π as an I(1) process, which is consistent with current econometric evidence and practice. See, e.g., Stock (1991) and King and Watson (1994, sec. 4). Alternatively, one could think of π as an I(0) process and include a level of π in the x-vector in eq. (2).

all the variables is zero. Note, therefore, that the policy variable r might be more similar to a change in the interest rate rather than the level.

The reduced-form expression for inflation two periods ahead based on current values of the variables is

$$
\begin{aligned}
(8) \qquad \pi_{t+2} = \; &\pi_t - a_1(1 + b_1)\tilde{u}_t - a_1 b_2 r_t \\
&+ [a_3(1 + c_3) - a_1 b_3]x_t + \xi_{t+2},
\end{aligned}
$$

where

$$
\xi_{t+2} = -a_1 \eta_{t+1} + a_3 v_{t+1} + \varepsilon_{t+1} + \varepsilon_{t+2}.
$$

Assume now that the policy objective is to minimize

$$
E_t(\pi_{t+2} - \pi^*)^2 = (E_t \pi_{t+2} - \pi^*)^2 + V_t \pi_{t+2}.
$$

Although this assumption seems simplistic, Svensson (1997) has shown that the solution obtained in this manner is equivalent to the dynamic solution of a model in which the target is a weighted sum of all future squared deviations of inflation from the target level. Note also that equation (8) is analogous to equation (2) above in that it corresponds to an optimal forecast of inflation acceleration over the policy horizon, which is given by

$$
E_t \pi_{t+2} = \pi_t - a_1(1 + b_1)\tilde{u}_t - a_1 b_2 r_t + [a_3(1 + c_3) - a_1 b_3]x_t.
$$

The conditional variance of inflation is

$$
V_t \pi_{t+2} = \sigma_\xi^2.
$$

Since the variance of inflation does not depend on the policy variable, the result is determined by certainty equivalence; that is, the optimal rule may be obtained by setting expected inflation equal to the target, π^*, and solving for the value of the policy variable. The optimal value of the policy variable is given by

$$
\begin{aligned}
(9) \qquad r_t^* = \; &-\frac{1 + b_1}{b_2}\tilde{u}_t + \frac{a_3(1 + c_3) - a_1 b_3}{a_1 b_2}x_t + \frac{1}{a_1 b_2}(\pi_t - \pi^*) \\
= \; &-\frac{1 + b_1}{b_2}(\tilde{u}_t - n_t) + \frac{1}{a_1 b_2}(\pi_t - \pi^*),
\end{aligned}
$$

where the short-run NAIRU (defined as a deviation from $\bar{u}$) is

$$
(10) \qquad n_t = \frac{a_3(1 + c_3) - a_1 b_3}{a_1(1 + b_1)}x_t.
$$

Equation (9) is a variant of the Taylor (1993) rule, which differs in that it is expressed in terms of unemployment rather than output. In addition, it allows for the reference point for monetary tightening in terms of the level of unemployment to be a short-run NAIRU rather than a fixed natural rate. In effect what this variation on the Taylor rules does is bring in additional information that helps forecast inflation in deriving an optimal setting of the policy instruments.

Even in this relatively simple setting, short-run NAIRU n_t is not a constant but is instead a function of the exogenous variable x. If lags of inflation, unemployment, and the policy variable appear in equations (5) and (6), their role in the policy rule—and therefore in the definition of short-run NAIRU—would be like that of x in the model. Of course, if the only variable that helps predict inflation over the policy horizon, other than the unemployment rate, is a constant, then NAIRU will be constant as in a more standard formulation. Note also that, like $\bar{u}$, the short-run NAIRU of our theoretical model is measured in relation to $\bar{u}$. In empirical applications, we would want to focus on the equivalent of $n_t + \bar{u}$ as a measure of short-run NAIRU.

Equation (9) also helps to clarify the proper use of NAIRU for policy purposes. The policy objective is not to drive unemployment to NAIRU, which is a temporary and variable reference point, but to use the NAIRU unemployment gap as one indicator of the direction to move the policy variable, by an amount dictated by the coefficients of the model. Also, the NAIRU gap indicator is not to be interpreted in isolation but must be weighed against the effect on the optimal setting of the policy variable suggested by the other indicator that is also included in the reaction function, the gap between actual and target inflation.

It is also important to recognize that our equation (9) variant of the Taylor rule is completely consistent with the result of Svensson (1997). Setting the policy instrument according to equation (9) is equivalent to setting expected inflation over the policy horizon equal to the inflation target π^*, which is the Svensson (1997) optimality condition if only inflation is in the objective function.

We can also draw some conclusions about the sign of the coefficient of x in the definition of NAIRU, based on whether x represents a supply or a demand effect. For example, if x is a supply effect such as an oil price shock, then a_3 and b_3 would have the same sign. Since the other parameters in equation (10) were chosen to have positive values, the two terms in the coefficient would be offsetting and the net effect of x on short-run NAIRU would be indeterminate. In contrast, if x represents a demand effect, then a_3 and b_3 would have opposite signs and the two terms would be reinforcing. The sign of the effect is positive if the demand variable x increases inflation and vice versa. In other words, a demand shock that raises inflation would lead to a higher value of short-run NAIRU, which implies more tightening given the same value of unemployment.

Supply and demand shocks also have differential effects on the overall implication about the optimal setting of the policy variable. The cumulation of supply effects would tend to drive both unemployment and inflation in the same direction, producing offsetting effects in equation (9). Cumulated demand effects, however, would drive inflation and unemployment in different directions, providing an unambiguous policy reaction. Therefore, demand effects that raise inflation should provoke a policy tightening.

9.3.2 Output as Well as Inflation in the Objective Function

Even when inflation is the only concern of policymakers, as in subsection 9.3.1, the optimal policy assigns a significant role to the level of unemployment or to the unemployment gap, as seen in equation (9). In this section, we explore how policy should be conducted when policymakers include both inflation and output in their objectives. We do this by including a second term in the objective function, which now becomes

$$E_t(\pi_{t+2} - \pi^*)^2 + \lambda E_t \tilde{u}_{t+1}^2.$$

The economic significance of this change is that the policy objective assigns some weight to reducing the variability of unemployment around zero, which is the equilibrium level.[7]

The optimal value of the policy variable in this case is

$$r_t^{(\lambda)} = \frac{1}{(a_1^2 + \lambda)b_2}\{-[(1 + b_1)(a_1^2 + \lambda) - \lambda]\tilde{u}_t$$

$$+ [a_1 a_3(1 + c_3) - (a_1^2 + \lambda)b_3]x_t + a_1(\pi_t - \pi^*)\}.$$

The modification of the objective function to reflect an unemployment target changes the weights on u, x, and $\pi_t - \pi^*$ in the optimal policy rule but does not affect its general form. Specifically, the weight on $\tilde{u}_t$ relative to the weight on $\pi_t - \pi^*$ rises with λ. In the extreme, if the weight on unemployment becomes infinitely large (λ approaches infinity), the optimal rule simplifies to

$$r_t^{(\infty)} = -\frac{b_1}{b_2}\tilde{u}_t - \frac{b_3}{b_2}x_t,$$

in which the inflation gap has disappeared and only an unemployment gap remains. This result may also be obtained by certainty equivalence, setting expected unemployment equal to its equilibrium level and solving for the value of the policy variable.

---

7. Once again, this is a relatively simple objective function designed to highlight the key points of this paper. A more complex dynamic solution of a similar model may be found in Svensson (1997), which exhibits properties that are qualitatively analogous to those of the simpler model of this paper.

9.4   NAIRU and Policy Making: Implications of Parameter Uncertainty

9.4.1   Objective Function with Inflation Only

Uncertainty about the Natural Rate of Unemployment

We begin to examine the consequences of uncertainty in the model of section 9.3 by looking at the effects of uncertainty regarding the natural rate of unemployment or, equivalently, long-run NAIRU. We start with this particular question for two reasons. First, it seems that in the policy discussion on the use of NAIRU, it is this question that is most frequently in the mind of the policymaker, although it is not always precisely formulated. Second, the examination of this narrower issue provides helpful intuition for the more general results that follow in the rest of this section.

Thus consider a more focused version of the model of section 9.3 in which traditional long-run NAIRU is the appropriate reference point for monetary policy in terms of the unemployment rate:

$$\pi_t = \pi_{t-1} - a_1(u_{t-1} - \bar{u}) + \varepsilon_t$$

(5a)

$$= \pi_{t-1} - a_1 u_{t-1} + a_0 + \varepsilon_t,$$

(6a) $$u_t - \bar{u} = b_1(u_{t-1} - \bar{u}) + b_2 r_{t-1} + \eta_t,$$

where $a_0 = a_1 \bar{u}$ and, as in section 9.3, $\bar{u}$ is the natural rate and r_t is the monetary policy variable. We write these equations explicitly in terms of $\bar{u}$ in order to focus on uncertainty with regard to this parameter. For the same reason, we assume that the parameters b_1 and b_2 in equation (6a) are known.

The second expression for equation (5a), under the natural stochastic assumptions, may be estimated using least squares. It is straightforward then to calculate the asymptotic distribution of the parameter estimates, which are consistent. In particular, we can derive that $T V(\hat{a}_1, \hat{a}_0)$, the asymptotic variance of the vector of estimates $(\hat{a}_1, \hat{a}_0)$ multiplied by the number of observations T, is

$$\left(\frac{\sigma_\varepsilon^2}{\sigma_u^2}\right)\begin{bmatrix} 1 & \bar{u} \\ \bar{u} & \bar{u}^2 + \sigma_u^2 \end{bmatrix},$$

where $\bar{u}$ and σ_u^2 are the unconditional asymptotic mean and variance of u_t and $\sigma^2\varepsilon$ is the variance of ε_t. Now, if J is the Jacobian of the transformation $(a_1, a_0) \mapsto (a_1, \bar{u}) = (a_1, a_0/a_1)$, then asymptotically $T V(\hat{a}_1, \hat{\bar{u}}) = T J V(\hat{a}_1, \hat{a}_0)J'$, which equals

$$\begin{bmatrix} \sigma_\varepsilon^2/\sigma_u^2 & 0 \\ 0 & \sigma_\varepsilon^2/a_1^2 \end{bmatrix},$$

where we have made use of the fact that the unconditional mean of equation (5a) is $\overline{\Delta\pi} = 0$.

The foregoing derivations may now be incorporated into the optimization problem of section 9.3, again with the objective function $E_t(\pi_{t+2} - \pi^*)^2$, but now

$$E_t \pi_{t+2} = \pi_t - a_1(1 + b_1)(u_t - \bar{u}) - a_1 b_2 r_t$$

and

$$V_t \pi_{t+2} = \sigma_{a_1}^2 [(1 + b_1)(-u_t + \bar{u}) - b_2 r_t]^2 + a_1^2(1 + b_1)^2 \sigma_u^2$$
$$+ \sigma_{a_1}^2 \sigma_u^2 (1 + b_1)^2 + \sigma_\xi^2.$$

In the expression for the variance, the terms that include σ_u^2 do not depend on the policy variable. Since the estimators of $\bar{u}$ and a_1 are orthogonal, the optimal rule will not depend on the uncertainty with regard to $\bar{u}$, as shown in the expression

$$r_t^* = -\frac{1 + b_1}{b_2}(u_t - \bar{u}) + \frac{1}{1 + \tau_1^{-2}} \cdot \frac{\pi_t - \pi^*}{a_1 b_2},$$

where $\tau_1 = a_1/\sigma_{a_1}$.

Thus uncertainty about the natural rate, in and of itself, does not affect the solution to the policymaker's optimization problem, as defined in this section and in section 9.3. However, the uncertainty about the natural rate does increase the cost function because, as seen above, it increases the conditional variance of π_{t+2}. The uncertainty about the parameter a_1, the effect on inflation acceleration of the gap between unemployment and the natural rate, does figure in the optimal policy through the term $(1 + \tau_1^{-2})^{-1}$, which is a essentially a function of the t-statistic on a_1. Its effect, however, is not on the term containing the unemployment gap, but rather on the term containing the gap between current and target inflation. The greater the uncertainty about a_1, the lower τ_1 and therefore $(1 + \tau_1^{-2})^{-1}$, so the less weight the policymaker should place on the current inflation gap. This result is very robust, as it obtains in the models of subsequent sections, in which we introduce more complex specifications with fairly general parameter uncertainty.

General Parameter Uncertainty

Consider again the model defined by equations (5), (6), and (7) of subsection 9.3.1, but assume now that there is uncertainty at time t about all the coefficients of the model $(a_1, a_3, b_1, b_2, b_3, c_3)$ and about the disturbance of the reduced form (ξ), but that the uncertainty in all of these variables is pairwise orthogonal. Although these uncertainty assumptions are not entirely general— on account of the assumed orthogonality—they are more extensive than those that the previous literature has examined.[8] The orthogonality assumptions are

---

8. Other papers that look at the effect of parameter uncertainty in a similar context are Svensson (1997), Clarida, Galí, and Gertler (forthcoming), and Wieland (1998).

easily relaxed for coefficients belonging to the same equation, but the inclusion of the corresponding covariances does not provide greater intuition and is therefore not pursued here. Thus, at time t, the expectation and variance of inflation at time $t + 2$ are given by

$$E_t \pi_{t+2} = \pi_t - a_1(1 + b_1)\tilde{u}_t - a_1 b_2 r_t + [a_3(1 + c_3) - a_1 b_3]x_t$$

and

$$V_t \pi_{t+2} = [a_1^2 \sigma_{b_1}^2 + \sigma_{a_1}^2 (1 + b_1)^2 + \sigma_{a_1}^2 \sigma_{b_1}^2]\tilde{u}_t^2 + (a_1^2 \sigma_{b_2}^2 + \sigma_{a_1}^2 b_2^2 + \sigma_{a_1}^2 \sigma_{b_2}^2)r_t^2$$

$$+ [a_3^2 \sigma_{c_3}^2 + \sigma_{a_3}^2 (1 + c_3)^2 + \sigma_{a_3}^2 \sigma_{c_3}^2 + a_1^2 \sigma_{b_3}^2 + \sigma_{a_1}^2 b_3^2 + \sigma_{a_1}^2 \sigma_{b_3}^2]x_t^2$$

$$+ 2\sigma_{a_1}^2 [(1 + b_1)b_2 \tilde{u}_t r_t + b_2 b_3 r_t x_t + (1 + b_1)b_3 \tilde{u}_t x_t] + \sigma_\xi^2,$$

where the values of the coefficients denote their expected values.[9]

As in subsection 9.3.1, the policy objective is to choose r_t so as to minimize the objective function

$$E_t(\pi_{t+2} - \pi^*)^2 = (E_t \pi_{t+2} - \pi^*)^2 + V_t \pi_{t+2}.$$

In this case, the optimal value of the policy variable is given by

$$r_t^* = \frac{1}{1 + \tau_2^{-2}}\left[-\frac{1 + b_1}{b_2}\tilde{u}_t - \frac{b_3}{b_2}x_t \right.$$

(11)

$$\left. + \frac{1}{1 + \tau_1^{-2}}\left(\frac{\pi_t - \pi^*}{a_1 b_2} + \frac{a_3(1 + c_3)}{a_1 b_2}x_t \right) \right],$$

where $\tau_1 = a_1/\sigma_{a_1}$ and $\tau_2 = b_2/\sigma_{b_2}$. Equation (11) can be rewritten as

$$r_t^* = \frac{1}{1 + \tau_2^{-2}}\left(-\frac{1 + b_1}{b_2}(\tilde{u}_t - (n_t + \phi_t)) \right.$$

(12)

$$\left. + \frac{1}{1 + \tau_1^{-2}} \cdot \frac{1}{a_1 b_2}(\pi_t - \pi^*) \right),$$

where

$$\phi_t = -\frac{1}{1 + \tau_1^2} \cdot \frac{a_3(1 + c_3)}{a_1(1 + b_1)}x_t.$$

9. This convention economizes on notation and is correct by definition if the coefficient estimates are unbiased.

Comparison of equations (9) and (12) indicates that the presence of uncertainty introduces two multiplicative terms of the form $(1 + \tau_i^{-2})^{-1}$. These terms are essentially functions of the t-statistics corresponding to the parameters a_1 and b_2, respectively, which correspond to the one-period-ahead effects of unemployment on inflation and of the policy variable on unemployment. All other variance-related terms in the objective function drop out of the calculation. When there is no uncertainty about a_1 and b_2, the two multiplicative terms become one, reverting to the certainty-equivalent case of subsection 9.3.1.

One of the two uncertainty effects—the one related to b_2, the coefficient on the policy variable in equation (6)—takes a form that is predictable from the analysis by Brainard (1967). Specifically, as σ_{b_2} rises, the term $(1 + \tau_2^{-2})^{-1}$ falls so that uncertainty about the magnitude of the effect of the policy variable leads to a partial policy reaction—a reaction that is less than that in the certainty-equivalent case.

In contrast, uncertainty about a_1, the effect of unemployment on the change in inflation in equation (5), has an effect not on the scale of the policy reaction, but rather on the weight applied to $\pi_t - \pi^*$ and on the reference point in terms of unemployment at which that reaction occurs. Specifically, as σ_{a_1} rises, the term $(1 + \tau_1^{-2})^{-1}$ falls so that the weight on $\pi_t - \pi^*$ falls. A rise in σ_{a_1} causes the term $(1 + \tau_1^2)^{-1}$ and the absolute value of the adjustment term ϕ_t to rise. If x has a positive impact on inflation (i.e., $a_3 x_t$ is positive), then ϕ_t is negative and so the reference point for monetary tightening in terms of unemployment, $n_t + \phi_t$, falls.

The effect of uncertainty about a_1 on how the reference point responds to change in x is somewhat more complex. The net effect on the reference point $n_t + \phi_t$ depends on whether x is a supply or demand variable, as discussed in subsection 9.3.1. Consider the combined expression

$$n_t + \phi_t = \left(\frac{1}{1 + \tau_1^{-2}} \cdot \frac{a_3(1 + c_3)}{a_1(1 + b_1)} - \frac{b_3}{1 + b_1} \right) x_t.$$

If x is a supply variable, the direction of the effect of uncertainty on the magnitude of the reference point is unclear. It is clear, however, that as uncertainty about a_1 approaches infinity, the sign of the coefficient is the same as the sign of $-b_3$. If x is a demand variable, uncertainty reduces the absolute magnitude of the reference point unambiguously.

9.4.2   Output as Well as Inflation in the Objective Function

We now modify the results of the previous subsection by assuming that the policy objective function includes both inflation and unemployment. As in subsection 9.3.2, the objective function becomes

$$E_t(\pi_{t+2} - \pi^*)^2 + \lambda E_t \tilde{u}_{t+1}^2.$$

The optimal value under parameter uncertainty is

$$r_t^{(\lambda)} = \frac{1}{1 + \tau_2^{-2}} \left[\left(-\frac{1 + b_1}{b_2} + \frac{\lambda}{a_1^2 + \sigma_{a_1}^2 + \lambda} \right) \tilde{u}_t \right.$$

$$\left. + \left(-\frac{b_3}{b_2} + \frac{a_1 a_3 (1 + c_3)}{a_1^2 + \sigma_{a_1}^2 + \lambda} \right) x_t + \frac{a_1 (\pi_t - \pi^*)}{a_1^2 + \sigma_{a_1}^2 + \lambda} \right].$$

The effect of including a target for unemployment, as represented by λ, is analogous to the effect of uncertainty about a_1. In the above equation, these two terms occur additively in the same expression in the terms corresponding to the exogenous variable and the inflation gap. Only in the unemployment term does λ appear separately. Intuitively, the reason for this is that uncertainty about a_1 makes the relationship expressed in equation (5) less reliable, so policy becomes more concerned with affecting the "intermediate target" of equilibrium unemployment.

If the weight on unemployment becomes infinitely large, the optimal rule simplifies to

$$r_t^{(\infty)} = \frac{1}{1 + \tau_2^{-2}} \left(-\frac{b_1}{b_2} \tilde{u}_t - \frac{b_3}{b_2} x_t \right)$$

in which, as in the certainty-equivalent case, the inflation gap has disappeared and only an unemployment gap remains. Here the only effect of uncertainty is of the rescaling type, as identified by Brainard (1967).

9.5 NAIRU and Policy Making: The Implications of Model Selection

In this section, we discuss another type of uncertainty that affects the definition of short-run NAIRU, its computation, and the policy rule that results from inflation targeting. Specifically, we focus on uncertainty regarding the correct form of the basic model and the associated problem of model selection. Whereas in section 9.4 we assumed that the form of the model was known but that the parameters were estimated with uncertainty, we now suppose that the policymaker ignores some key information variable in the optimization problem.[10]

In general, if inflation two periods ahead is the policy target, and if a variable helps predict inflation at that horizon, it is inefficient not to include the information in the model. For example, the models of sections 9.3 and 9.4 define the policy rule in terms of a short-run NAIRU, which in turn is a function of the exogenous variable x. What is the result of ignoring the predictive content

---

10. The complementary problem of including too many variables in the model is in principle less serious, since consistent parameter estimates should assign zero weight to the superfluous variables.

of x? Alternatively, what is the cost of relying on a long-run equilibrium NAIRU (zero in this case) when a short-run informative NAIRU is available?

Thus suppose that the policymaker ignores the presence of x in the basic model (5)–(7). The values of a_3 and b_3 are implicitly set to zero, while the third equation is dropped altogether. Under these conditions, the constrained optimal rule for inflation targeting becomes

$$\tilde{r}_t^* = \frac{1}{1 + \tau_2^{-2}}\left(-\frac{1 + b_1}{b_2}\tilde{u}_t + \frac{1}{1 + \tau_1^{-2}} \cdot \frac{\pi_t - \pi^*}{a_1 b_2}\right).$$

We know, of course, that the value of the objective function has to be higher (i.e., worse) when evaluated at this constrained optimum than when evaluated at the unconstrained optimum r_t^* as in subsection 9.4.1. In fact, we can calculate the difference between the constrained and unconstrained values as

$$\frac{1}{1 + \tau_2^{-2}} \cdot \frac{1}{a_1^2 + \sigma_{a_1}^2}[a_1 a_3(1 + c_3) - (a_1^2 + \sigma_{a_1}^2)b_3]^2 x_t^2.$$

Somewhat surprisingly, uncertainty about b_2 ameliorates the left-out-variable problem.[11] Uncertainty about a_1, in contrast, can make matters worse.

The left-out-variable problem can also increase uncertainty regarding the estimates of the included coefficients, with consequences for the size of the policy response or the reference point for monetary tightening in terms of unemployment. To see this, suppose the inflation equation (5) is estimated by ordinary least squares, leaving out the variable x, after rewriting it in the following form

(5′) $$\pi_t - \pi_{t-1} = -a_1\tilde{u}_{t-1} + \varepsilon_t.$$

One implication of leaving out x, well known from econometrics textbooks, is that the estimate of a_1 may be biased. This occurs unless x and u are contemporaneously uncorrelated.[12] However, even if the two regressors are indeed uncorrelated so that the estimate of a_1 is unbiased, uncertainty in the estimate is greater by the amount

$$\frac{\Sigma_t \pi_t^2}{\Sigma_t \tilde{u}_{t-1}^2} \cdot \frac{R_u^2 - R_c^2}{n},$$

where the numerator of the last term is the difference between the R^2s of the unconstrained and constrained models. Thus excluding the variable x from the model, in addition to producing a policy rule that improperly excludes x, in-

---

11. The intuition is that as uncertainty about b_2 grows, the optimal response of the policy variable r is reduced so that there is less loss from using the incorrect model.

12. See, e.g., Theil (1971, sec. 11.2). This problem may be bypassed formally by thinking of x as the component of the additional variable that is uncorrelated with u.

creases uncertainty about a_1. One possible consequence is that, for the reasons provided in section 9.4, the policymaker may react to the higher level of σ_{a_1} by adjusting the weight on $\pi_t - \pi^*$ downward and by increasing the absolute size of the NAIRU adjustment ϕ_t.

9.6   Empirical Estimates of Short-Run NAIRU

9.6.1   Empirical Evidence on the Importance of Uncertainty

Although our theoretical framework shows qualitatively the effects of uncertainty on how monetary policy should be conducted, it cannot tell us whether these effects are economically important. To examine this question, we estimate in this section a simple NAIRU gap model for the United States to obtain measures of uncertainty and to assess how these measures affect our view of the optimal reaction of monetary policy to movements in unemployment relative to short-run NAIRU. In order to have in the model a simple lag structure that mimics that of the theoretical model (5)–(7), we start by estimating a model with annual U.S. data over the period 1956–96. The model is

$$(13) \qquad \pi_t - \pi_{t-1} = \alpha_0 + -\alpha_1 u_{t-1} + \alpha_2 u_{t-2} + \varepsilon_t,$$

$$(14) \qquad u_t = \beta_0 + \beta_1 u_{t-1} + \beta_2 u_{t-2} + \beta_3 r_{t-1} + \beta_4 r_{t-2} + \eta_t,$$

where π is the log change in the CPI from December of year $t - 1$ to December of year t, u is the unemployment rate in December of year t, and r is the average monthly three-month Treasury bill rate during year t. Note that α_1 and β_3 correspond to a_1 and b_2 in the theoretical model, and that the key uncertainty ratios τ_1^{-2} and τ_2^{-2} will be based on the former. The results are presented in table 9.1.

These estimates provide some guidelines regarding the importance of uncertainty for monetary policy in this context. First, the adjustments to the unemployment reference point and to the policy reaction as a result of parameter

Table 9.1   Estimates of Annual U.S. Model, 1956–96

Coefficient	Estimate	t	$(1 + t^{-2})^{-1}$
α_0	1.67	1.49	
α_1	1.24	4.68	.956
α_2	.98	3.70	
R^2	.366		
β_0	.70	1.31	
β_1	1.00	7.06	
β_2	$-.23$	-2.18	
β_3	.48	6.30	.975
β_4	$-.36$	-3.84	
R^2	.833		

Table 9.2   Implicit Interest Rate Rules

Rule	Weight on Lagged Interest Rate	Inflation Gap	Unemployment or Output Gap
Unadjusted			
Annual	.77	1.70	-2.56
Quarterly	.94	.47	-.70
With output gap	.94	.47	.35
Uncertainty adjusted			
Annual	.77	1.59	-2.49
Quarterly	.94	.44	-.69
With output gap	.94	.44	.34

uncertainty are not large. The key parameters are estimated with some precision, and the implied multiplicative adjustment factors are both close to one. The Brainard-type adjustment—a 2.5 percent reduction—is particularly small, suggesting that the magnitude of the policy reaction should only be shaded down slightly to reflect parameter uncertainty. However, the unemployment effect adjustment is also less than 5 percent.

These results are confirmed by looking at the implicit optimal policy that corresponds to the two-year-ahead inflation target of the theoretical model in which only inflation is included in the objective function. The rule that results is very similar to the simple Taylor (1993) rule when adjustments are made for the fact that Taylor's rule was defined in terms of quarterly data and an output gap. The annual and quarterly results are presented in table 9.2. If δ is the weight on the lagged interest rate in the annual model, the corresponding quarterly lag is assigned a weight of $\delta^{1/4}$ and the weights on the inflation and unemployment gaps are divided by $1 + \delta^{1/4} + \delta^{2/4} + \delta^{3/4}$. A rule based on the output gap is obtained by applying a simple Okun's law adjustment, dividing the unemployment weight by 2.

The table confirms that the practical significance of parameter uncertainty is quite small. Furthermore, the quarterly results with the output gap are remarkably similar, even numerically, to the parameters suggested by Taylor (1993). The only key difference is that the interest rate is assumed to be much more persistent here, since Taylor did not include a lagged interest rate in the form of his rule.[13]

9.6.2 Empirical Estimates of Short-Run NAIRU

In this subsection, we present estimates of short-run NAIRU. For these purposes, we return to the more general model (2)–(4) and estimate the equations with monthly data from January 1954 to November 1997, using a 12-month-

---

13. Recent estimates of the Taylor rule by Rudebusch and Svensson (chap. 5 of this volume) and Rotemberg and Woodford (chap. 2), among others, suggest that the persistence parameter is close to one. Fuhrer and Moore (1995) assume that it equals one.

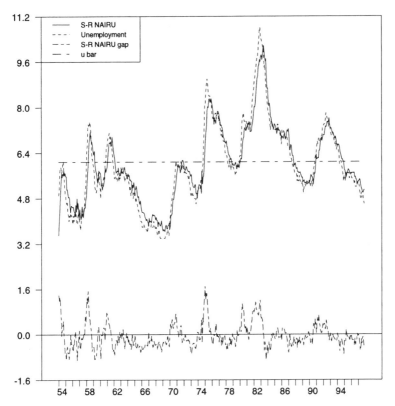

Fig. 9.1   Short-run NAIRU, unemployment, and short-run NAIRU gap, January 1954 to November 1997

ahead, 12-month horizon ($j = k = 12$) and 12 lags of both the change in inflation and unemployment.[14] Figure 9.1 shows estimated short-run NAIRU together with the contemporaneous unemployment rate, as well as the short-run NAIRU gap. This figure demonstrates the high variability of short-run NAIRU, in contrast with long-run measures designed to estimate a natural rate as in Gordon (1997) and Staiger et al. (1997a, 1997b). For example, consider a version of our equation (1), which may be used to estimate a constant $\bar{u}$ that is comparable to the long-run measure of those papers:

$$(1')\qquad \Delta\pi_t = \beta(L)(u_t - \bar{u}_t) + \gamma(L)\Delta\pi_{t-1} + \varepsilon_t.$$

When estimated over the same period as equations (2), (3), and (4), the estimate of $\bar{u}$ is 6.1 percent, as shown in figure 9.1.

---

14. Somewhat surprisingly, extending the horizon to $j + k = 60$ months or even longer does not materially affect the point estimates of short-run NAIRU. Of course, the fit of the equation deteriorates with longer horizons.

Staiger et al. (1997a) have pointed out that such estimates of a constant long-run NAIRU tend to be quite imprecise. Using the delta method in an equation similar to (1'), they obtain an estimate of $\bar{u} = 6.2$ percent, with a standard error of about 0.6. Our estimate of $\bar{u} = 6.1$ has a standard error of 0.43, which is somewhat smaller—perhaps partly because of our larger sample—but is of the same order of magnitude. Estimates of short-run NAIRU n_t are more precise. The standard error of n_t is a time-varying function of the values of the variables in expression (4). Over the sample period, the standard errors range from 0.11 to 0.42, with a mean of 0.20, less than half of the standard error of $\bar{u}$.[15]

Thus short-run NAIRU is estimated with more than twice the precision than standard long-run NAIRU. The practical significance of this result, however, is limited, since we have shown in the theoretical sections that this type of uncertainty plays no role in the determination of the policy rule. Nevertheless, a reduction in the uncertainty may produce a reduction in the value of the cost function, as shown in section 9.5, even if the policy rule remains unaltered.

9.6.3 A Case Study: Recent Signals from a Short-Run NAIRU

Using the estimates of the NAIRU gap from subsection 9.6.2, we now examine the hypothetical results of using the methodology of this paper in the conduct of monetary policy in the United States since June 1992, when the unemployment rate began a prolonged decline. The results will of course be somewhat simplistic, but they may provide some general support for the concepts developed in this paper.

If we refer to one of the policy rules in the theoretical part of the paper, say to equation (9), we note that the appropriate interest rate is determined essentially by two gaps: the difference between unemployment and short-run NAIRU and the difference between actual and target inflation. We present in figure 9.2a the gap between short-run NAIRU and unemployment (signed so that a positive value indicates that monetary policy should be tightened) and the level of inflation (12 previous months) since 1992.

From June 1992 to the end of 1993, declining unemployment brought the NAIRU gap from levels suggesting, if anything, the need for ease to relatively neutral levels. Meanwhile, inflation declined over the period and, in fact, continued to decline into the beginning of 1994. Beginning in 1994, however, the NAIRU gap became positive and remained so until early 1995, suggesting a need for tightening. In addition, inflation stopped declining, remaining around the 3 percent level. These two factors combined are consistent with the monetary tightening undertaken by the Federal Reserve throughout 1994 and into early 1995.

Since then, the NAIRU gap has indicated some pressure to tighten twice, in 1996 and 1997. In the first case, the pressure from the NAIRU gap was accom-

---

15. All our standard errors are estimated consistently using the Newey-West technique with a 24-lag window (Newey and West 1987).

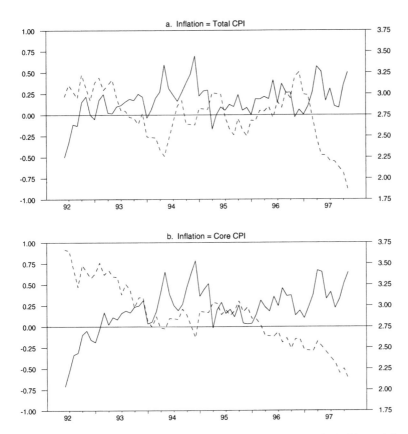

Fig. 9.2   NAIRU gap (*solid line, left-hand scale*) **and inflation** (*dashed line, right-hand scale*), **June 1992 to November 1997**

panied by a rise in inflation. Even though inflation subsided toward the end of the year, this episode may seem somewhat inconsistent with the absence of further tightening. Figure 9.2b suggests one reason for this result. Figure 9.2b presents the results of repeating the analysis of figure 9.2a, but using core inflation (excluding food and energy prices) instead of total inflation. Core inflation tends to be a better signal of persistent changes in inflation than total inflation.

Figure 9.2b shows both the level of core inflation as well as the gap between unemployment and short-run NAIRU computed using core inflation in equations (2), (3), and (4). Comparisons of the two panels of figure 9.2 suggests that the effect of using core inflation in the calculation of the NAIRU gap is very slight. But core inflation was falling in 1996, in contrast to the rising total inflation, and this fall may have offset the tightening signals from the NAIRU gap.

In 1997, the pressure arising from the unemployment gap seemed stronger than in the previous year. Inflation, however, both total and core, moved downward again, offsetting at least partially the signals from the NAIRU gap indicator. Arguably, only during 1994 and early 1995 were there consistent signals for tightening, and this is when the Federal Reserve engaged in most of its monetary tightening.

In order to evaluate the net effect of the unemployment and inflation indicators, it would be helpful to summarize the information in a single measure, as in the policy rules of table 9.2. We would like to do this, not to explain actual policy, but to suggest how the theoretical constructs of this paper could be used in practice. However, this is a problem for two reasons. First, we would have to construct a full optimization model in the context of the monthly equations, which is beyond the scope of the present paper.[16] Second, we would have to know or make an assumption about the target level of inflation. Thus we present only a limited version of a policy rule in which we deal with those problems as follows.

First, we take the weights for the NAIRU and inflation gaps from the annual results of table 9.2 allowing for uncertainty, making allowance also for the monthly frequency of our data. Since the coefficient of the lagged interest rate, $\delta^{1/12} = 0.98$, is very close to one, we further simplify by assuming that the weights are used to calculate a monthly change in the interest rate. We then divide the annual weights by $1 + \delta^{1/12} + \cdots + \delta^{11/12}$ to obtain weights of -0.23 for the NAIRU gap and 0.15 for the inflation gap with total inflation and -0.25 and 0.19, respectively, using core inflation.[17] To deal with the second problem, the fact that the inflation target is unknown, we scale the results so that the policy rule with total inflation is neutral, on average, over the period since June 1992. This assumption is equivalent to an inflation target of 3 percent.

The results are presented as the solid lines in the two panels of figure 9.3. Note that the weighted results are consistent with our earlier discussion of the individual components. In panel 9.3a, which contains the results using the total CPI, the strongest signal for tightening comes during 1994. Note also, however, that there were distinct signals for tightening in 1992–93 and 1996–97, and that there were fairly strong signals for easing at the beginning and toward the end of the sample period. In panel 9.3b, which contains results using the core CPI, there are also strong signals to tighten in 1994, but because the core inflation rate was higher than total CPI in late 1992 and early 1993, there are also strong signals to tighten in this period. In contrast to panel 9.3a, the results with the core CPI do not suggest any need to tighten in 1996.

16. A model along those lines has been developed for the United States in Clarida et al. (forthcoming). See also the references in that paper.

17. Adjusting fully for coefficient uncertainty would require, in addition to the adjusted weights, an adjustment to short-run NAIRU corresponding to the term ϕ_t defined in subsection 9.4.1. We do not make this adjustment here because our equation for monthly NAIRU is essentially a reduced form and the components are difficult to disentangle, and also because the coefficient of the adjustment factor $(1 + \tau_i^2)^{-1} \leq 0.065$ is empirically small.

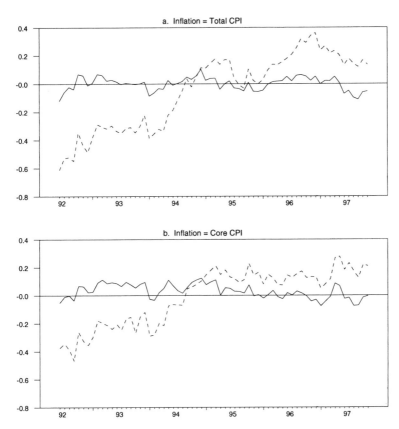

Fig. 9.3   Simple policy rules based on short-run NAIRU (*solid line*) and long-run NAIRU (*dashed line*), June 1992 to November 1997

We may contrast these results with a rule based on the standard unemployment gap—the gap between unemployment and a constant long-run NAIRU. The results are presented as the dashed lines in the two panels of figure 9.3. To obtain weights that are consistent with the assumption of a constant NAIRU, we estimated equations (13) and (14) without the second lag of unemployment, which produces an estimate of NAIRU that is constant. These new weights are -0.35 for the NAIRU gap and 0.34 for the inflation gap using total inflation and -0.36 and 0.37, respectively, using core inflation. Note, however, that if we use the same weights as before, the qualitative results are the same as with these weights.

The results for the long-run NAIRU gap, which are driven by the large steady decline in unemployment over this period, are fairly robust. The main feature of the alternative rule is that it argues for easing throughout the first part of the period, and then for tightening throughout the second part of the period. What this rule misses is that a long-run natural rate is not the best reference point for unemployment if the goal is to target inflation in the short run.

9.7 Summary and Conclusions

In this paper, we examine how a variant of the NAIRU concept can be usefully employed in the conduct of monetary policy. By thinking of NAIRU in this way, we obtain insights that might be quite useful to monetary policymakers. Because there are quite a few results sprinkled throughout the paper, we list the main ones here.

- The NAIRU concept that is useful for the conduct of monetary policy differs from the estimate of the natural rate of unemployment, the long-run concept used previously by many researchers. Instead, NAIRU can be viewed as a short-run construct, which is related to past levels of unemployment and inflation as well as other economic variables, that helps forecast future accelerations or decelerations of inflation.
- Short-run NAIRU should be viewed, not as a target for policy, but as an aid in defining the reference point that policymakers can compare to the current rate of unemployment to derive a signal for the appropriate stance of policy. Furthermore, as long as inflation is an element in the policymakers' objective function, the NAIRU gap is not the only signal that should affect the setting of policy instruments: the deviation of inflation from its target level also has an important role in the determination of the appropriate stance of policy.
- The policy rule that comes out of our analysis is a variant of a Taylor rule using an unemployment gap rather than an output gap, but it has one major difference from more standard formulations. The standard Taylor rule implicitly assumes that the reference point to which unemployment should be compared in the unemployment gap term is constant, while in our formulation, the reference point is related to short-run NAIRU, which can have substantial short-run fluctuations over time.
- Uncertainty about the level of NAIRU has no influence on the setting of policy instruments, although it does affect the value of the objective function. This type of uncertainty makes the economy worse off but does not alter policy behavior.
- Uncertainty about the effect of unemployment on inflation leads to an additive adjustment to short-run NAIRU to calculate the reference point for monetary tightening in terms of the level of unemployment. In addition, uncertainty about the unemployment effect on inflation changes the weight on the inflation gap in the policy rule.
- Uncertainty about the effect of the policy variable leads to a scaling down of the reaction of the policy variable, the well-known Brainard (1967) result.
- Uncertainty about model selection can have important effects on the form of the policy rule. In particular, if a constant NAIRU is used—as occurs if

NAIRU is viewed as a long-run concept—so that information about the state of the economy that could be used to forecast inflation is ignored, the performance of the policy rule can be substantially worse. In addition, leaving out relevant variables that help forecast inflation increases the uncertainty about the effect of unemployment on inflation, with the resulting implications described above.

• Although parameter uncertainty has potentially large effects on how policy should be conducted, our empirical results suggest that parameter uncertainty may not be all that important for the setting of policy. We find some evidence of changes in the policy rule resulting from the parameter uncertainty we explored in our theoretical model, but these effects are very modest. They affect the weights in the policy rule by less than 5 percent in both the case of uncertainty about the impact of unemployment and the case of uncertainty about the effect of the policy variable.

• Estimates of short-run NAIRU are highly variable over time. However, there is a fair degree of precision in these estimates.

• Substantial positive NAIRU gap estimates arose throughout 1994 and early 1995 and in parts of 1996 and 1997. However, core inflation was substantially lower in 1996 and 1997 than in 1994. Thus the one period since June 1992 during which there were consistent signals for tightening occurred during 1994 and early 1995, which is when the Fed engaged in most of its monetary tightening.

These results suggest that a short-run NAIRU is indeed a useful concept and that it can be used by policymakers, particularly in deciding how monetary policy should be conducted. However, there are some subtle issues in how the short-run NAIRU concept might be used correctly. First, because our view of NAIRU sees it as a short-run construct, it is dangerous to think of NAIRU as a potential target for unemployment that stays around a particular value, such as 6 percent, for any period of time. Second, deviation of inflation from its target is every bit as important a factor in thinking about setting policy as is the NAIRU gap. Third, uncertainty about parameter values and model selection does have effects on the optimal setting of policy instruments but does not appear to be a barrier to a useful role for the NAIRU concept in policy decisions.

We hope that this paper helps resurrect NAIRU as a useful concept, but only if it is used properly. As we have shown, a short-run NAIRU is a useful construct because it helps tell policymakers what might happen to inflation in the future. Furthermore, the model of this paper suggests that policymakers may want to avoid the impression that an objective of policy is to raise unemployment when it falls below NAIRU or to lower it when it is above NAIRU. To view policy in this way might lead the public to think that policymakers are against low unemployment, an outcome that can reduce support for central bank efforts to control inflation.

References

Brainard, William. 1967. Uncertainty and the effectiveness of policy. *American Economic Review Papers and Proceedings* 57:411–25.

Clarida, Richard, Jordi Galí, and Mark Gertler. Forthcoming. The science of monetary policy. *Journal of Economic Literature.*

Council of Economic Advisers. 1997. *Economic report of the president.* Washington, D.C.: Government Printing Office.

Espinosa-Vega, Marco A., and Steven Russell. 1997. History and theory of the NAIRU: A critical review. *Federal Reserve Bank of Atlanta Economic Review* 82:4–25.

Estrella, Arturo. 1997. Aggregate supply and demand shocks: A natural rate approach. Research Paper no. 9737. New York: Federal Reserve Bank of New York.

Friedman, Milton. 1968. The role of monetary policy. *American Economic Review* 58:1–21.

Fuhrer, Jeffrey C., and George R. Moore. 1995. Monetary policy trade-offs and the correlation between nominal interest rates and real output. *American Economic Review* 85:219–39.

Gordon, Robert J. 1997. The time-varying NAIRU and its implications for economic policy. *Journal of Economic Perspectives* 11:11–32.

King, Robert G., and Mark W. Watson. 1994. The post-war U.S. Phillips curve: A revisionist econometric history. *Carnegie-Rochester Conference Series on Public Policy* 41:157–219.

Layard, Richard, and Charles R. Bean. 1988. Why does unemployment persist? Discussion Paper no. 321. London: London School of Economics, Centre for Labour Economics, August.

Modigliani, Franco, and Lucas Papademos. 1975. Targets for monetary policy in the coming year. *Brookings Papers on Economic Activity,* no. 1:141–63.

Newey, Whitney K., and Kenneth D. West. 1987. A simple-positive semi-definite, heteroskedasticity and autocorrelation consistent covariance matrix. *Econometrica* 55:703–8.

Phelps, Edmund. 1968. Money-wage dynamics and labor-market equilibrium. *Journal of Political Economy* 76:678–711.

Staiger, Douglas, James H. Stock, and Mark W. Watson. 1997a. How precise are estimates of the natural rate of unemployment? In *Reducing inflation: Motivation and strategy,* ed. Christina D. Romer and David H. Romer. Chicago: University of Chicago Press.

———. 1997b. The NAIRU, unemployment and monetary policy. *Journal of Economic Perspectives* 11:33–49.

Stiglitz, Joseph. 1997. Reflections on the natural rate hypothesis. *Journal of Economic Perspectives* 11:3–10.

Stock, James H. 1991. Confidence intervals for the largest autoregressive root in U.S. macroeconomic time series. *Journal of Monetary Economics* 28:435–59.

Svensson, Lars E. O. 1997. Inflation forecast targeting: Implementing and monitoring inflation targets. *European Economic Review* 41:1111–46.

Taylor, John B. 1993. Discretion versus policy in practice. *Carnegie-Rochester Conference Series on Public Policy* 39:195–214.

Theil, Henri. 1971. *Principles of econometrics.* New York: Wiley.

Wieland, Volker. 1998. Monetary policy and uncertainty about the natural unemployment rate. Finance and Economics Discussion Paper no. 98-22. Washington, D.C.: Board of Governors of the Federal Reserve System.

Comment   Robert E. Hall

Reading Estrella and Mishkin's paper made me aware for the first time of the difference in the use of the term NAIRU between academics and practitioners. As an academic out of touch with the parlance of central bankers, I thought that the NAIRU was the unemployment rate such that there is no pressure on inflation from the labor market. In my mind, the NAIRU was effectively another name for the natural rate of unemployment. I learned from this paper that—in circles closer to the real world—the NAIRU is the unemployment rate such that pressure from the labor market is sufficient to offset supply shocks or other transitory sources of inflation. The NAIRU, in those circles, would be the target unemployment rate for a monetary policy that sought to stabilize the inflation rate period by period. Alternatively, as this paper shows, the NAIRU is an element in a monetary policy that rolls with the punches and permits some variation in inflation in the shorter run because there is value in stabilizing real activity as well as inflation.

I will start with some comments on equation (1'), the framework for estimating the natural rate. These comments also apply to the related work by Staiger, Stock, and Watson (1997). The idea of this research is expressed in the following equation:

$$\pi_t = \alpha - \beta u_t + \gamma(L)\pi_{t-1} + \varepsilon_t.$$

My notation is the same as the paper's. The natural rate $\bar{u}$ is defined as the value of u such that the inflation rate stays at the constant level π. It is

(1) $$\bar{u} = \frac{\alpha - [1 - \gamma(1)]\pi}{\beta}.$$

Here $\gamma(1)$ is the sum of the coefficients on lagged inflation in the Phillips curve.

To interpret this equation, we need to go back to the very dawn of the rational expectations era. Prior to Milton Friedman's (1968) American Economic Association presidential address, this equation was seen as describing a long-run trade-off between inflation and unemployment. If $\gamma(1) < 1$, the trade-off is positive. Friedman made a broad argument from first principles that there could not be a long-run trade-off; rather, the unemployment rate would tend to the natural rate, invariant under inflation in the longer run. There followed a brief period of research based on the mistaken belief that Friedman's hypothesis could be tested by estimating $\gamma(L)$ and testing the hypothesis $\gamma(1) = 1$. Then Sargent (1971) straightened the subject out by observing that the coefficients $\gamma(L)$ depend on the nature of monetary policy. If policy makes inflation return to a normal level by offsetting movements away from that level, then

Robert E. Hall is the McNeil Joint Professor of Economics and Senior Fellow of the Hoover Institution at Stanford University and a research associate of the National Bureau of Economic Research.

$\gamma(1) < 1$ even if Friedman is right—as we all now agree—that unemployment is invariant in the long run to the choice of inflation target.

Estrella and Mishkin are unwilling to face up to Sargent's point. Despite the emphasis I gave at the conference to this point, they have not altered this part of the paper and do not cite Sargent, who was present at the conference and agreed that this paper fell into the trap he identified in 1971.

From equation (1), it is apparent that $\bar{u}$ is not identified as a general matter by the equation. There are two possible identifying hypotheses. First, if the long-run rate of inflation, π, is known and is truly constant over time, then the other coefficients in equation (1) can be estimated by standard methods and the equation solved for $\bar{u}$. Second, one could assume that $\gamma(1) = 1$. The authors do the second. I do not believe that this assumption makes sense, especially for data starting after the rationalization of monetary policy in 1979.

We normally view the coefficients $\gamma(L)$ as a description of expectations about inflation. The Phillips curve relates unexpected inflation to the unemployment rate. Under that interpretation, the coefficients $\gamma(L)$ sum to one if inflation does not revert to some mean value but is an integrated process. But one feature of monetary policy agreed upon by every commentator is that policy should always induce mean reversion in inflation. The debates in monetary policy are over the speed of the mean reversion, and also over whether we should induce mean reversion in the price level. In the latter case, mean reversion in the inflation rate occurs automatically. And, at least since 1979, there seems little doubt that policy has tried and succeeded in making inflation mean reverting. Any hint of an upsurge in inflation results in the Fed's stepping on the brake to bring inflation back to target.

A second reason to expect mean reversion in the rate of inflation is that the main source of price disturbances—movements in the price of oil—are temporary. Even without good monetary policy, bursts of inflation are temporary.

Although simple tests of mean reversion of inflation support the hypothesis, I learned at the conference from the master of this craft—James Stock—that one cannot reject the hypothesis of no mean reversion. That gives Estrella and Mishkin some support. But my impression is that the test is not very powerful. Someone like myself, a Bayesian in such matters, can follow his prior and believe that $\gamma(1)$ is well below one. As a result, I do not find the empirical results in this paper, based on the fundamental identifying hypothesis $\gamma(1) = 1$, to be informative.

A second factor also inhibits this type of empirical research. Suppose that the Fed determines policy by minimizing the expected value of the squared deviation of inflation from target. To do so, it sets the current values of variables it controls, such as the unemployment rate, in such a way as to make them uncorrelated with the future inflation deviation. In such a world, a researcher running Phillips curve regressions would find a completely flat relation between unemployment and inflation. It is well known that optimization can completely conceal structural relationships. The fact that Estrella and Mishkin's Phillips curve slopes downward and is not completely flat shows that the Fed is not pursuing a policy that conceals the slope. But the problem still lurks in the background. To the extent that there is purposeful policy, the slope of the Phillips curve obtained by regression is biased, and the value of the natural rate is correspondingly biased. In general, I think the paper neglects identification issues in a pretty serious way.

There is a robust estimator of the natural rate available, but it is not discussed in the paper. As Friedman pointed, the unemployment rate fluctuates around the natural rate irrespective of the monetary regime. Hence, the average value of the unemployment rate is a good estimate of the natural rate. No further identifying hypotheses are needed. Two estimates based on this method are 6.08 (0.51) for 1960–96 and 6.05 (0.30) for 1983–96. The standard errors are based on an AR(2) error process. These results are quite similar to Estrella and Mishkin's, though the standard errors are larger. Of course, a finding that the natural rate is over 6 percent only deepens the mystery of low inflation in 1998, with an unemployment rate almost 2 percentage points lower than the natural rate.

To summarize in this area, I believe that Estrella and Mishkin neglect identification issues but nonetheless find reasonable values of the natural rate. But I think that they seriously understate the sampling variation in their estimates. I do not believe that we know the natural rate at any particular time with a precision of a few tenths of a percentage point, as they claim.

The paper pays a lot of attention to uncertainty. It uses the framework of quadratic preferences, which is a reasonable starting point. But decision makers with quadratic preferences do not behave in a precautionary way. There are no catastrophes in the way that a quadratic decision maker views alternative random outcomes. For example, a consumer with quadratic preferences does not have marginal utility rising to infinity as consumption approaches zero. Instead, marginal utility is finite at zero consumption. Consequently, quadratic decision makers do not take special precautions to avoid situations like zero consumption or 20 percent inflation. An early next step in the research should be the exploration of behavior under more realistic preferences, such as constant relative risk aversion.

In particular, Brainard's (1967) point that uncertainty about the slopes of structural relations makes decision makers more timid is firmly rooted in quadratic preferences. Decision makers who are anxious to avoid catastrophic outcomes may need to take aggressive action in the presence of slope uncertainties. I believe the special features of Brainard's analysis are inadequately appreciated.

The paper's findings, in table 9.2, of small adjustments for parameter uncertainty need to be accompanied by two warnings. First, as I just noted, they are special to quadratic preferences; precautionary decision making would be different. Second, I think the paper understates the actual amount of parameter uncertainty. Its lack of concern with identification and corresponding use of least squares almost automatically causes it to understate sampling variation.

References

Brainard, William C. 1967. Uncertainty and the effectiveness of policy. *American Economic Review Papers and Proceedings* 57, no. 2 (May): 411–25.
Friedman, Milton. 1968. The role of monetary policy. *American Economic Review* 58, no. 1 (March): 1–17.
Sargent, Thomas J. 1971. A note on the accelerationist controversy. *Journal of Money, Credit and Banking* 8:721–25.
Staiger, Douglas, James H. Stock, and Mark W. Watson. 1997. How precise are estimates of the natural rate of unemployment? In *Reducing inflation: Motivation and strategy*, ed. Christina D. Romer and David H. Romer. Chicago: University of Chicago Press.

Discussion Summary

Donald Kohn never heard NAIRU discussed as a target at a Federal Open Market Committee meeting, as implied in the paper, but rather as an input into an inflation forecast. Moreover, those inflation forecasts take account of a wider variety of factors affecting prices and therefore already embody the fact that the unemployment rate could differ from its long-run natural rate for quite some time and still be consistent with steady inflation.

Laurence Ball expressed confusion about the empirical results in the paper, especially about figure 9.1. NAIRU seems to be very close to actual unemployment. For example, the unemployment rate in 1982 consistent with stable inflation was about 10 percent. The actual unemployment rate in 1982 was about 10.5 percent, so for the difference between these two rates to matter, it must be multiplied by a huge multiplier. *Bob Hall* agreed that figure 9.1 was very confusing.

Laurence Meyer remarked that tightness in the labor market and supply shocks should not be put into a single variable. Since supply shocks are often transitory, the central bank should not be looking at short-run NAIRU in any case.

James Stock made two comments. First, the issue regarding the sum of the coefficients in the Phillips curve came from the outward drift in the Phillips curve in the 1970s. Emprically, a good specification of inflation is a unit root with a moving average (MA). The MA has with a root of about 0.4, which implies a first AR coefficient of 0.6. *Richard Clarida* objected that with post-1979 data, a standard Dickey-Fuller test does find mean reversion in inflation.

Mishkin noted that with a large MA coefficient, unit root tests are typically affected by a small-sample problem. In this case, a significant Dickey-Fuller test is on the order of 10 rather than 2.5.

Stock's second comment was that in terms of forecasting inflation, many variables have forecast better than unemployment over the last 30 years, such as the natural rate of new claims to unemployment insurance, capacity utilization, housing starts, and adjustments in any of these variables.

Edward Gramlich asked Hall whether the sample mean in his estimation of NAIRU is subject to regime changes. *Hall* replied that this depends on the length of the sample. He mentioned that Milton Friedman avoided taking a stand on the issue of how long it takes for the sample mean of unemployment to respond to a change in policy regime. Regarding the question whether the natural rate of unemployment has declined in the last few years, there is persuasive evidence that it has. Labor macroeconomists find that the duration of unemployment is extremely low. The labor market seems to deal better with routine unemployment, and computer matching starts mattering for the duration of unemployment.

David Longworth mentioned that none of the papers in the conference looks at the changes in the variances of the equations themselves. There are some rules, such as inflation targeting, that would be expected to lower the variance in the Phillips curve.

John Williams noted that the Phillips curve is estimated in the Federal Reserve Board's large-scale macroeconometric model by including expected inflation on the right-hand side and then imposing the condition that the sum of coefficients on all leads and lags of inflation be one.

Michael Woodford remarked that a policy rule based on the difference between NAIRU and current unemployment, as defined by these authors, is equivalent to a policy rule based on inflation and a forecast of future inflation. He asked in that case why a discussion of current economic conditions by policymakers should focus on beliefs about NAIRU rather than on inflation forecasts directly.

Contributors

Nicoletta Batini
Bank of England
Threadneedle Street
London EC2R 8AH, England

Laurence Ball
Department of Economics
Johns Hopkins University
Baltimore, MD 21218

Lawrence J. Christiano
Department of Economics
Northwestern University
2003 Sheridan Road
Evanston, IL 60208

Richard H. Clarida
Department of Economics
Columbia University
420 West 118th Street, Room 1014 IAB
New York, NY 10027

Arturo Estrella
Research Department
Federal Reserve Bank of New York
33 Liberty Street
New York, NY 10045

Martin Feldstein
National Bureau of Economic Research
1050 Massachusetts Avenue
Cambridge, MA 02138

Benjamin M. Friedman
Department of Economics
Littauer Center 127
Harvard University
Cambridge, MA 02138

Mark Gertler
Department of Economics
New York University
269 Mercer Street, 7th Floor
New York, NY 10003

Christopher J. Gust
International Finance Division
Federal Reserve Board
20th and Constitution Avenue NW
Washington, DC 20551

Andrew G. Haldane
Bank of England
Threadneedle Street
London EC2R 8AH, England

Robert E. Hall
Hoover Institution
Stanford University
Stanford, CA 94305

Robert G. King
Department of Economics
University of Virginia
Rouss Hall
Charlottesville, VA 22903

Donald L. Kohn
Federal Reserve Board
20th and Constitution Avenue NW
Washington, DC 20551

Andrew Levin
Federal Reserve Board
20th and Constitution Avenue NW
Washington, DC 20551

Bennett T. McCallum
Graduate School of Industrial
    Administration
Carnegie Mellon University
Pittsburgh, PA 15213

Frederic S. Mishkin
Graduate School of Business
Uris Hall 619
Columbia University
New York, NY 10027

Edward Nelson
Monetary Assessment and Strategy
    Division
Bank of England
Threadneedle Street
London EC2R 8AH, England

Julio J. Rotemberg
Graduate School of Business
Harvard University
Morgan Hall, Soldiers Field
Boston, MA 02163

Glenn D. Rudebusch
Federal Reserve Board of San Francisco
101 Market Street
P.O. Box 7702
San Francisco, CA 94120

Thomas J. Sargent
Hoover Institution
HHMB-Room 243
Stanford University
Stanford, CA 94305

James H. Stock
Kennedy School of Government
Harvard University
Cambridge, MA 02138

Lars E. O. Svensson
Institute for International Economic
    Studies
Stockholm University
S-10691 Stockholm, Sweden

John B. Taylor
Department of Economics
Landau Center
Stanford University
Stanford, CA 94305

Volker Wieland
Federal Reserve Board
20th and Constitution Avenue NW
Washington, DC 20551

John C. Williams
Federal Reserve Board
20th and Constitution Avenue NW
Washington, DC 20551

Alexander L. Wolman
Research Department
Federal Reserve Bank of Richmond
701 East Byrd Street
P.O. Box 27622
Richmond, VA 23261

Michael Woodford
Department of Economics
Princeton University
Princeton, NJ 08544

Author Index

Subject Index

Business cycles: 1880–1914 and 1955–97 periods, 327–29

Calvo-Rotemberg model: price adjustment, 48–51; in simulations of structural macroeconomic model, 32–39; test of inflation persistence in, 50–51

Central bank: alternative good rules for, 120; concern with financial stability, 249–50; concern with interest rate smoothing and stability, 249–50; inflation forecasts of, 217–22; inflation forecasts related to information availability, 217–23; policy models of, 206; recognized need for flexibility, 252

Christiano, Eichenbaum, and Evans model (CEE model): conclusions, 300–303; policy rule performance in, 303–6, 315–16; results, 306–15

Closed economy model: extension of Svensson-Ball closed economy model, 128–30; inflation targeting in, 135; Taylor rule as optimal policy, 131

Conference rules: assessment of robustness, 5–10; with contemporaneous and lagged information, 233, 235–37, 254; role of exchange rate and inflation forecasts, 11–12; simple and complex, 10–11

Control rules: in presence of model uncertainty, 253–54

Data: central bank use of lagged, 93–94; lagged data in structural macroeconomic model simulations, 34–43; rules devised from revised, 196

Data sources: in model of policy rule performance, 16

Economic activity: monetary policy influence on, 361–69; with optimal interest rate rule, 387–89; under optimal stabilization policy, 380–84; with structural disturbances, 69

Economic shocks: exchange rates as source of, 193; information to assess, 197; of price stickiness, 353n8; in rational expectations macromodel, 168–69; responses of output and inflation model to, 210–13

Exchange rate: channels to affect inflation, 192–94; effect of inflation targeting on, 127–28; under gold standard, 333; role in monetary policy rules, 11; smoothing of, 156; in Svensson-Ball model of open economy, 128–30, 135–36

Federal funds rate: deviations from baseline policy rules, 336–39; in estimated sticky price model, 57, 65; in macroeconomic models of U.S. economy, 264, 272–90; in monetary policy mistake analysis, 336–40, 342–43

Federal Open Market Committee (FOMC): forecasts of, 197–99; use of information from predictions of rules, 195–97

Federal Reserve Board: criteria for determining money supply, 334; monetary policy